NOVELL'S

Guide to
IntranetWare™ Networks

NOVELL'S

Guide to
IntranetWare™ Networks

Jeffrey F. Hughes and Blair W. Thomas

Novell Press, San Jose

Novell's Guide to IntranetWare™ Networks

Published by
Novell Press
2180 Fortune Drive
San Jose, CA 95131

Library of Congress Catalog Card No.: 96-078234

ISBN: 0-7645-4516-7

Printed in the United States of America

10 9 8 7 6 5 4 3 2

2B/SQ/RR/ZW/FC

Distributed in the United States by IDG Books Worldwide, Inc.

Distributed by Macmillan Canada for Canada; by Contemporanea de Ediciones for Venezuela; by Distribuidora Cuspide for Argentina; by CITEC for Brazil; by Ediciones ZETA S.C.R. Ltda. for Peru; by Editorial Limusa SA for Mexico; by Transworld Publishers Limited in the United Kingdom and Europe; by Academic Bookshop for Egypt; by Levant Distributors S.A.R.L. for Lebanon; by Al Jassim for Saudi Arabia; by Simron Pty. Ltd. for South Africa; by Pustak Mahal for India; by The Computer Bookshop for India; by Toppan Company Ltd. for Japan; by Addison Wesley Publishing Company for Korea; by Longman Singapore Publishers Ltd. for Singapore, Malaysia, Thailand, and Indonesia; by Unalis Corporation for Taiwan; by WS Computer Publishing Company, Inc. for the Philippines; by WoodsLane Pty. Ltd. for Australia; by WoodsLane Enterprises Ltd. for New Zealand. Authorized Sales Agent: Anthony Rudkin Associates for the Middle East and North Africa.

For general information on IDG Books Worldwide's books in the U.S., contact our Consumer Customer Service department at 800-762-2974. For reseller information, including discounts and premium sales, contact our Reseller Customer Service department at 800-434-3422. For information on where to purchase IDG Books Worldwide's books outside the U.S., contact our International Sales department at 415-655-3078 or fax 415-655-3281. For information on foreign language translations, contact our Foreign & Subsidiary Rights department at 415-655-3018 or fax 415-655-3281. For sales inquiries and special prices for bulk quantities, contact our Sales department at 415-655-3200. For information on using IDG Books Worldwide's books in the classroom or for ordering examination copies, contact our Educational Sales department at 800-434-2086 or fax 817-251-8174. For authorization to photocopy items for corporate, personal, or educational use, contact the Copyright Clearance Center, 222 Rosewood Drive, Danvers, MA 01923, or fax 508-750-4470. For general information on Novell Press books in the U.S., including information on discounts and premiums, contact IDG Books Worldwide at 800-434-3422 or 415-655-3200. For information on where to purchase Novell Press books outside the U.S., contact IDG Books Worldwide's International department at 415-655-3021 or fax 415-655-3295.

John Kilcullen, *President & CEO, IDG Books Worldwide, Inc.*

Brenda McLaughlin, *Senior Vice President & Group Publisher, IDG Books Worldwide, Inc.*

The IDG Books Worldwide logo is a trademark under exclusive license to IDG Books Worldwide, Inc., from International Data Group, Inc.

Rosalie Kearsley, *Publisher, Novell Press, Inc.*

Novell Press and the Novell Press logo are trademarks of Novell, Inc.

Welcome to Novell Press

Novell Press, the world's leading provider of networking books, is the premier source for the most timely and useful information in the networking industry. Novell Press books cover fundamental networking issues as they emerge — from today's Novell and third-party products to the concepts and strategies that will guide the industry's future. The result is a broad spectrum of titles for the benefit of those involved in networking at any level: end-user, department administrator, developer, systems manager, or network architect.

Novell Press books are written by experts with the full participation of Novell's technical, managerial, and marketing staff. The books are exhaustively reviewed by Novell's own technicians and are published only on the basis of final released software, never on prereleased versions. Novell Press at IDG Books Worldwide is an exciting partnership between two companies at the forefront of the knowledge and communications revolution. The Press is implementing an ambitious publishing program to develop new networking titles centered on the current IntranetWare version of NetWare and on Novell's GroupWise and other popular groupware products.

Novell Press books are translated into 12 languages and are available at bookstores around the world.

Rosalie Kearsley, Publisher, Novell, Inc.
David Kolodney, Associate Publisher, IDG Books Worldwide, Inc.

Novell Press

Publisher
Rosalie Kearsley

Associate Publishers
Colleen Bluhm
David Kolodney

Associate Acquisitions Editor
Anne Hamilton

Communications Project Specialist
Marcy Shanti

Executive Managing Editor
Terry Somerson

Development Editor
Jim Sumser

Copy Editor
Carolyn Welch

Editorial Assistant
Sharon Eames

Technical Editor
DeeAnne Higley

Media/Archive Coordination
Leslie Popplewell
Melissa Stauffer

Production Director
Andrew Walker

Production Associate
Christopher Pimentel

Supervisor of Page Layout
Craig A. Harrison

Project Coordination
Phyllis Beaty
Ben Schroeter

Graphics Specialist
Kurt Krames

Production Staff
Diann Abbott
Mario F. Amador
Stephen Noetzel
Elsie Yim

Quality Control
Mick Arellano

Proofreader
Christine Langin-Faris

Indexer
Elizabeth Cunningham

Cover Photographer
Dave Crosier

For Wendy, Laurin, and McKenna
JFH

To Pam and Jessa
BWT

Foreword

Today, when we look back to the days of crank-driven telephones and old-fashioned shared "party lines," we tend to chuckle at the quaintness of the fledging telephone technology. In the future, we will find ourselves laughing in much the same way at the thought of PC networks running on a single server.

Why is it that the modern global telephone system can allow callers to instantly locate and communicate with people world over whom they may have never previously encountered? It is possible because there exists a single logical directory that encompasses all of the phone numbers on the worldwide telephone net. Although it is physically split into parts (in the U.S. these are the area codes), this worldwide telephone network presents itself to us as one unified logical system. Access to phone numbers is through both the white pages and the yellow pages directories. The white pages assume knowledge of the exact name of the person to be called; yellow pages search criteria such as the type of business service provided.

Novell recognized early that to be useful a global computing network would also require an extremely robust directory system. Following the industry standard X.500 directory architecture, Novell developed a viable directory that could be implemented on the relatively modest computer hardware of a PC-LAN. Novell Directory Services (NDS) provides the infrastructure upon which the global directory will be built and the methods to support a variety of networked services that will operate on that global network.

This dramatic NDS transition to the limitless networks of the future will require us as network administrators and managers to alter our fundamental ways of thinking and to view the network in a whole new light. In their book, *Novell's Guide to IntranetWare Networks*, Jeff Hughes and Blair Thomas take the reader through the logical thought processes necessary to make this transition and through the concrete steps needed to make use of this new functionality. It is an exceptionally insightful guide to the future of Novell's smart global networking technology. Welcome!

Dave Eckert
Product Manager, Novell Directory Services

About the Authors

Jeffrey F. Hughes, Master Certified Novell Engineer, joined Novell in 1993. Blair W. Thomas, Master Certified Novell Engineer, joined Novell in 1986. Both authors are Senior Consultants for Novell Consulting Services and have designed and implemented NetWare 4.1 production sites around the globe. They have over 18 years of combined networking experience. Jeffrey Hughes holds a B.S. degree in Marketing from Brigham Young University. He lives in Sandy, Utah. Blair Thomas holds B.S. degree in Computer Science and an MBA from Brigham Young University. He lives in Orem, Utah.

Preface

Since its release in 1993, Novell's NetWare 4 operating system (now known as IntranetWare) has gained popularity as the network operating system of choice for large and small organizations around the world. Among its many new features, IntranetWare offers Novell Directory Services (NDS), which provides a powerful name service, as well as security, routing, messaging, management, Web publishing, and file and print services. Novell Directory Services is unique in the industry and enables you to organize network resources, provide easy access to those network resources, and centralize the administration of your network. In addition, IntranetWare offers the Netscape Navigator Browser, FTP services for NetWare, Novell's IPX/IP Gateway, and a multiprotocol router for wide area network (WAN) and Internet connections. IntranetWare also provides the platform for incorporating other advanced services such as telephony and multimedia.

This book is your comprehensive design and implementation guide to the NetWare portion of IntranetWare. Topics cover the fundamentals of IntranetWare to managing the internal operations of Novell Directory Services. The information presented in this book will help you design, implement, maintain, and troubleshoot all aspects of IntranetWare and related applications.

Although IntranetWare offers a new and different approach to networking, its capabilities are enormous. The Novell Directory is still in its infancy as users, administrators, and vendors realize the potential of a name service. More and more, applications are being created for this technology.

What You'll Learn from Reading this Book

This book is written for all LAN administrators, system administrators, consultants, resellers, and any others who design, implement, and support IntranetWare networks.

Using this book you will learn basic to complex concepts and rules on the aspects of IntranetWare. Whether your interest lies solely in designing an IntranetWare tree or in understanding the internal functions and components of Novell Directory Services, you will find this book to be the definitive source.

How this Book Is Organized

This book is organized into four conceptual parts: Basic IntranetWare information, NDS design topics, internal operations and maintenance of IntranetWare, and using IntranetWare as a complete system.

Part I, The Basics of IntranetWare, includes information on the IntranetWare operating system, Novell Directory Services, and other new features. Novell's IntranetWare utilities are covered so that readers will be familiar with new utilities that have been created for IntranetWare. Part I also provides readers a comprehensive look at NDS objects and how these objects are used to build the Directory tree. An understanding of NDS objects is a prerequisite to utilizing the full potential of NDS. NDS naming conventions are covered in the last chapter of Part I.

Part II, Designing Novell Directory Services, describes in great detail the steps required to design an NDS tree and covers design options for NDS trees, with many examples based on the fictitious ACME company case study. In addition, the design topics include a thorough discussion of partitioning and replication of your NDS tree. The last chapter of Part II provides clear explanations and examples of how to design your NDS tree for time synchronization.

Part III, Operations and Maintenance of IntranetWare, provides a much-needed look at the internal operations of Novell Directory Services. Internal operations of NDS in a single-server environment, as well as the steps that occur during the first IntranetWare server installation, are discussed in detail. In addition, this part explains and thoroughly discusses the background processes of NDS through definitions and examples.

Next, we move on to more complicated multiple server operations that include partitioning operations and managing this complex network environment. The first two chapters in Part III provide a thorough discussion on troubleshooting Novell Directory Services internal operations. Effective troubleshooting requires an understanding of NDS internal processes and the tools you can use to make adjustments to NDS. Refer to Chapter 10 for a detailed description on how to use the DSREPAIR and DSTRACE utilities during troubleshooting operations.

We conclude this section by discussing the tuning parameters you can use to maximize stability and performance of your IntranetWare network.

Part IV, Administration of IntranetWare, rounds out the many day-to-day aspects of IntranetWare that you will need to know in order to install, manage, and support your network. Topics include designing login scripts and access for IntranetWare and providing a comprehensive security plan for your network.

In addition, Part IV discusses NetWare printing in mixed NetWare 3 and NetWare 4 environments as well as printing in a pure IntranetWare network. This part presents valuable information on preparing for an IntranetWare migration, including creating an implementation schedule, gaining lab experience, and readying your NetWare 3 servers. Also covered are the migration options available to you, the advantages and disadvantages of these options, and migration strategies to move you from other operating systems such as Banyan, LAN Server, LAN Manager and NT. Client migration options are also discussed in terms of the different approaches that are available to move workstations into Novell's Virtual Loadable Module technology.

Novell's latest Client32 software includes the NetWare Application Manager, which allows users to access applications that have been represented as NDS objects. We discuss the installation and use of this product in terms of administration and end user capabilities.

The final chapters of this book discuss Novell's IntranetWare technology and how companies can use this exciting product. NetWare has the speed and reliability to serve as a platform for emerging intranetworks.

The four appendixes in Part V include valuable information that can be used as a handy reference. Appendix A lists, with descriptions and actions, the Novell Directory Services error codes. Use Appendix A in conjunction with Part III of this book for more information on troubleshooting NDS.

Appendix B covers the server console commands. Server console commands enable you to change server parameters, monitor the server's utilization, and control the allocation of its resources.

Appendix C provides information on Novell's internal debugger and can be used to diagnose IntranetWare operating system problems.

Appendix D outlines the many client parameters that can be placed in the user's NET.CFG file for greater performance of memory at the workstation.

Special Features in this Book

Throughout this book we use a fictitious company by the name of ACME, which serves as the basis for many of the examples illustrated in the book. We chose as an NDS tree a large, worldwide company with wide area connections. Our intent is not to preclude smaller companies, but to demonstrate as closely as possible the many concepts of IntranetWare. Regardless of the size of your IntranetWare installation, the design strategies are the same. You may have fewer wide area connections or no WAN at all. As you read through the chapters (especially the design chapters), you will understand how to design a tree that meets your particular needs.

We have also, where appropriate, included Consulting Experiences based on actual consulting visits with our customers. These Consulting Experiences emphasize particular points or examples and demonstrate concepts and approaches to Novell Directory Services design.

Finally, this book contains a value-packed CD-ROM containing a two-user version of the NetWare 4.11 operating system upon which IntranetWare runs. If you are new to IntranetWare, we encourage you to install this CD-ROM to learn and gain experience as you read through the book.

Sources

In the process of researching this book, we gratefully acknowledge the following Novell sources:

"Backing up and Restoring NetWare Directory Services in NetWare 4" (Novell Application Notes, August 1995, Dorothy Bowers, Michael Fairbanks, Kerry Loveless, Dale Maughan, and Ken Neff)

"Tuning the Server Memory Calculation Worksheet" (Novell Application Notes, November 1995, Ron Lee)

Acknowledgments

This book reflects the experience and information gathered from the members of Novell Consulting Services group and Novell companywide. We wish to thank in particular Gary Hein, Todd Hogan, Maria Eliason, Kyrt Nay, Paul Reiner, Carl Seaver, J. Orland Seaver, Jim Sorenson, Paula Moreira, Dean Payne, Todd Powell, and Cindy Comstock. All have been contributors in one way or another to this effort.

A very special thanks to Jim Sumser at IDG Books who kept this project focused to its completion. His sense of humor and wit made this project possible. Thanks for your constant words of encouragement.

We thank Carolyn Welch from IDG Books who diligently worked with us to edit and re-edit this manuscript. Thanks for keeping up with all the little details of this book and keeping everything moving through production.

We also want to thank DeeAnne Higley who provided a careful technical review of this work. Her expertise and enthusiasm for Novell Directory Services is unsurpassed. Thanks for spending so much time working with us on this project.

Thanks to Behzad Anaraki and the others in Novell Technical Support groups for their knowledge of IntranetWare and their technical insights into troubleshooting Novell Directory Services. Keep up the good work.

We also want to thank all the others from the IDG team, including Anne Hamilton and David Kolodney, who have been very instrumental with all the logistical aspects of producing this book. We appreciate your support and encouragement.

Thanks to Rose Kearsley, Marcy Shanti, and Colleen Bluhm of Novell Press who have been our constant advocates in producing this book and in making Novell information available to our readers.

Thanks to David James Clarke, IV for collaborating with us to produce an NDS tree based on the ACME case study.

And, as always, we thank our NetWare customers around the world who constantly push Novell's products to their limits. We must continually press forward with your help to make Novell's products the very best in the industry.

Contents at a Glance

Table of Contents

Chapter 3 • Novell Directory Services Objects and Properties   129

Chapter 4 • Directory Services Naming Conventions   181

Part II • Designing Novell Directory Services

Chapter 5 • Novell Directory Services Tree   **225**

Chapter 6 • Designing and Using NDS Partitions and Replicas   **279**

PART I

The Basics of IntranetWare

CHAPTER 1

Introduction to IntranetWare

"The only way round is through." Robert Frost

NetWare is the world's most popular network operating system. With IntranetWare, Novell has incorporated all the advantages of previous versions of NetWare and has added new features that build on the foundation to provide a distributed computing infrastructure. IntranetWare increases productivity, reduces costs, and simplifies installing and maintaining your network.

Key to IntranetWare is Novell Directory Services (NDS), which is a special purpose name service that enables you to find and use network resources and data as a single integrated system. NDS provides this powerful operating system with the same speed and reliability that you've come to expect with NetWare 3.

Many corporations have embraced and implemented NetWare as an integral part of everyday business computing solutions. Today, local and wide area networks are running business-critical applications once considered the sole domain of mainframe computers. More and more businesses are finding that they can operate more efficiently and cost-effectively on NetWare networks and still receive the same security and administrative benefits of larger systems.

With the advent of IntranetWare, NetWare has become more powerful, scaleable, and flexible than any other network operating system available today. Before understanding what IntranetWare is, it helps to understand the purpose and function of a network operating system. From this starting point we will begin an extremely comprehensive look at the fastest growing network operating system currently available.

Network Operating Systems

A network consists of resources such as servers, workstations, printers, bridges, routers, gateways, and other peripheral computer equipment (CD-ROMs or jukeboxes, modems, and so on).

The network operating system (NOS) is software that communicates with each of these devices to form an integrated system. Some of the resources tied together by Novell Directory Services are shown in Figure 1.1.

The primary goal of the network operating system and all the other resources on the network is to build an infrastructure that distributes the processing power among all the network devices. The major network components or devices are the server and client. The architecture that distributes the processing between these machines is called distributed processing. The following sections describe the server, then the client, and finally explain how processing can be distributed between each.

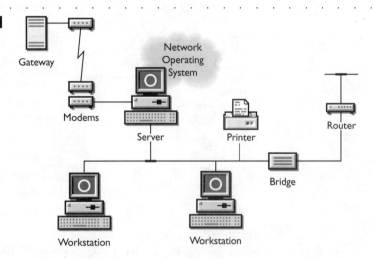

Gateway

Network Operating System

Modems

Server

Printer

Router

Bridge

Workstation

Workstation

SERVER

The network operating system (NOS) is simply the software program that is loaded and runs on the main computers called servers. The NOS enables the local resources of the server to be shared among all the network users. The NOS controls the following resources:

▸ Memory

▸ File System (disk drives)

▸ CPU scheduling

▸ Input/output to shared network devices (CD-ROM, modems, and so on)

▸ Workstation connectivity and access to file system resources

▸ Loading and distributing application programs

Figure 1.2 shows the local server resources that are managed by the NOS.

F I G U R E   1.2

The NOS manages the sharing of the server's local resources.

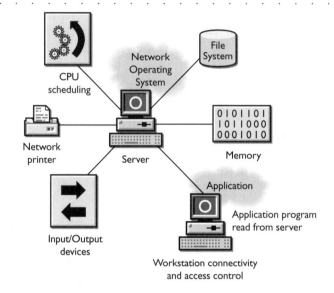

The NOS software runs as either a dedicated machine or can be distributed equally across all nodes on the network. An NOS that is distributed among all network nodes is called a peer-to-peer NOS. NetWare Lite is an example of a peer-to-peer NOS. A NOS whose major portion runs on a hardware platform is a centralized NOS. IntranetWare is an example of a dedicated NOS in which the central node is called the server.

CLIENT

The portion of the NOS that connects the workstations to the server is called the client software. The client software runs on the workstations and is the consumer of services provided by the NetWare server. It also enables the workstation to load applications or share resources from the server. Figure 1.3 illustrates the relationship between the NOS running at the server and the client software running at the workstation.

Workstations that load the client portion of the network operating system are often referred to as clients. In this book, we will use the terms workstation and client interchangeably. Technically, only the workstations that load the client software and make use of the services provided by the servers should be called clients. NDS servers also act as clients of other NDS servers in the tree, but not in the same way as a workstation. For example, an NDS server may communicate with other NDS servers during a login process.

FIGURE 1.3

Client software loads on the workstation and enables it to connect to the server.

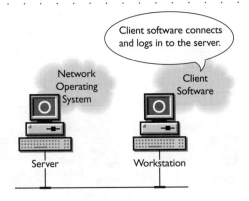

Distributed Processing

Distributed processing occurs when the NOS coordinates the processing in a decentralized fashion. Applications running on the network are a type of distributed processing. For example, each workstation requests from the operating system its own copy of an application. The application is then loaded and run entirely on the workstation. The workstation runs the application independently, and the network operating system simply coordinates access to the shared resources. In the network, application processing can be distributed (client-based) or centralized (server-based) or both (client/server-based). Each of these methods offers advantages and disadvantages that make them right for certain applications and wrong for others.

CLIENT-BASED APPLICATIONS

The types of applications that run entirely on the workstation are called client-based applications. For example, all the clients may use the same word-processing application, but separate copies of the application are executed in each workstation. A copy of the application is transmitted from the server to the client but is executed at the client workstation. In general, applications that are keyboard and display intensive with minimal disk I/O are well suited for the client.

Spreadsheets and word-processing software are examples of client-based applications because they are heavy users of the display and keyboard with infrequent disk or file access. There is no benefit in running any part of these applications

outside the workstation once the program has been loaded into workstation memory from the server. Figure 1.4 illustrates client-based application processing in which the application is loaded from the server.

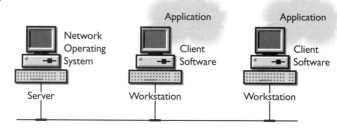

F I G U R E   1.4

Client-based application processing. The application is loaded from the server.

SERVER-BASED APPLICATIONS

Applications that do all the processing locally at the server are known as server-based applications. These applications are usually specialized applications that execute only on the server. For example, backup/restore software needs to read the file system and write it to the local tape device (on the server) and may not need to transfer data across the network. Other types of backup software run as clients on a server and transfer files from other servers. Another example is network management software that controls or monitors the operation of the operating system. In addition, NetWare Loadable Modules are primarily server-based applications, although some have a client counterpart that does some of the processing. Figure 1.5 illustrates server-based application processing.

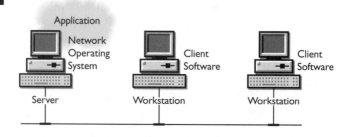

F I G U R E   1.5

Server-based application processing

CLIENT/SERVER-BASED APPLICATIONS

Client/server-based applications split the responsibility of the processing between the client and the server. The client and server work together to execute the application even though it is running on different machines. The fact that the parts of the application are running on different machines is entirely transparent to the user. The software that runs on the server is called the back-end and manages the shared information. The client portion of the application is called the front-end and allows communication and access to the server (or back-end). Figure 1.6 illustrates client/server application processing.

FIGURE 1.6

Client/Server application processing

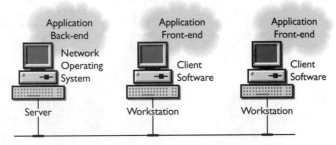

What is IntranetWare?

IntranetWare offers the widest range of distributed applications or network services in the industry. In Figure 1.7, you can see that IntranetWare provides file, print, directory service, database, communication (includes host connectivity), messaging, network management, software distribution, imaging, and telephony.

FIGURE 1.7

IntranetWare is defined as a complete range of network services.

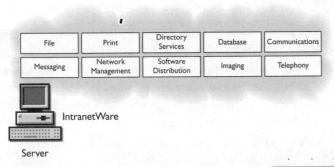

These network services are provided to the users regardless of their type of desktop. The goal of IntranetWare is to tie users running DOS, MS Windows, OS/2, Macintosh, UNIX, or Windows NT into a distributed information system, as shown in Figure 1.8.

IntranetWare connects desktops running DOS, Windows, OS/2, Macintosh, UNIX, and Windows NT operating systems.

IntranetWare allows these diverse workstations to access NetWare services and perform distributed processing in their native environments. Figure 1.9 shows how it is possible for users to choose the desktop system that best fits their needs and still share services and information with other network users using different platforms.

In addition to the integration of desktops, IntranetWare also integrates larger host computers from vendors such as IBM, Digital, and Hewlett-Packard. Regardless of where information is located on the network, users can access host-based resources and information from their desktops.

Applications that can benefit from client/server-based implementation are database, communication, and transactional applications that require frequent access to disk storage. Consider a database that searches, sorts, generates reports, and so forth. The database will perform better if you place the database engine on the server (where the disk I/O is intensive) and process the data entry and user interface at the client. The client simply passes the data request to the database engine, which performs the action and responds accordingly.

FIGURE 1.9

IntranetWare offers distributed processing among workstations running DOS, Windows, OS/2, Macintosh, UNIX, and Windows NT operating systems.

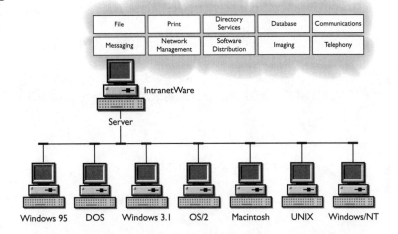

Another example would be an e-mail system in which the user reads and composes mail messages at the client and then passes the responsibility for delivery to a server process. Thus, while the server is delivering the messages to the other mail users, the client (or sender) can continue other activities.

IntranetWare Features

IntranetWare is the next generation of the NetWare operating system and thus inherits all features from previous versions, namely NetWare 3. Some the features shared by both NetWare 3 and IntranetWare are listed below; however, we will not discuss these features in detail in this chapter because they are well known. Here is the list:

- ▸ File and Print

- ▸ Desktop Heterogeneity of DOS, Windows 3.1, Windows 95, OS/2, Macintosh, UNIX (NetWare 4), and NT (NetWare 4)

- ▸ Performance with a 32-bit multitasking operating system

▸ Modular design using NetWare Loadable Modules (NLMs)

▸ Fault Tolerance with NetWare SFT III

▸ Transport protocol support of IPX, TCP/IP, Appletalk, OSI, SNA

▸ Name space support for DOS, OS/2, Macintosh, Network File System (NFS), OSI's File Transfer Access Management (FTAM)

▸ Security

▸ Server-based backup architecture on SBACKUP.NLM

▸ Common transport interface, such as STREAMS, TLI, and BSD sockets

▸ Remote Management Facility (RCONSOLE)

▸ Host Connectivity

In addition, IntranetWare introduces many improvements and features not available in previous versions of NetWare. These features include improvements to the existing services such as file systems (suballocation, data compression, read ahead, and data migration), print services, security, auditing, server memory, client software, and others. The most notably new feature is Novell Directory Services, which provides an easy, intuitive, and integrated view of the network resources to both the user and administrator.

IntranetWare also offers Web publishing, Netscape Navigator, FTP services for NetWare, Novell's IPX/IP gateway, and multiprotocol router for wide area network and Internet connections. For more information on the features of IntranetWare, see Chapters 21 and 22.

NOVELL DIRECTORY SERVICES

Novell Directory Services (NDS) is an information name service in IntranetWare that organizes network resources — users, groups, printers, servers, volumes, and other physical network devices — into a hierarchical tree structure. Figure 1.10 illustrates the structure of an NDS tree. We will use many examples of NDS trees in this book.

FIGURE 1.10

*The structure of an
NDS tree*

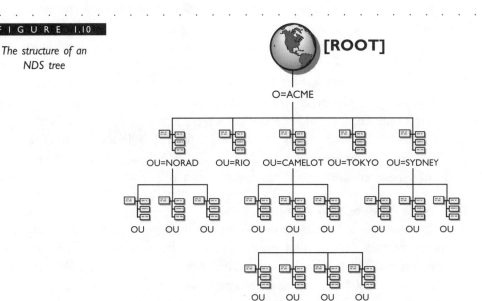

The NDS tree, also known as the Directory tree, allows resources to be managed and displayed as a single view. By contrast, NetWare 3 provides only a server centric view. You can manage the tree including objects and their various properties by providing varying degrees of security access, giving your network enormous flexibility as it expands and changes.

NDS replaces the bindery found in NetWare 3 networks. A major difference between the two methods is that the Directory is distributed and can be replicated on multiple servers for increased fault tolerance and performance. The bindery in NetWare 3 is a flat structure in which the resources belong to a single server. Compatibility with the bindery is available in IntranetWare for applications requiring bindery services. This feature in IntranetWare is known as Bindery Services and is discussed in great detail in subsequent chapters.

NDS provides capabilities unique to IntranetWare. These capabilities are single login, easy administration, and scaleability.

NDS Provides Single Point of Login

The users log in to the network once using one username and password to access all authorized network resources. This means that the users log in to the network, and NDS will process other connections to NetWare 3 and IntranetWare servers if the username and password are the same.

By contrast, NetWare 3 bindery users must log in to each network server individually with a username and password. This could mean that the users would have to provide a different ID and password for each additional server connection. Single user login also makes your job easier as an administrator. You create each user account only once for all IntranetWare servers in the Directory tree. Multiple user accounts on multiple servers are no longer needed in IntranetWare. This feature alone can save you hours of work. As you will see, NDS serves as the central point of management, eliminating tedious duplication and increased administrative costs.

NDS Provides Easy Administration

IntranetWare consolidates most NDS administrative functions into a single, easy-to-use graphics utility that greatly reduces the time you spend on network administration. The Novell utility, called NWADMIN.EXE, is a Windows-based utility that enables you to make changes to the Directory with an easy point-and-click of the mouse. You can get information about a particular object by clicking on its icon. The icon will bring up a dialog box that displays object details that can be modified. This utility is also available in a DOS version known as NetADMIN.

This object-oriented view of the NDS tree is what lets you perform many routine administrative functions easily. NDS objects, files, directories, and server functions can be controlled through the NWADMIN utility. When users change departments, for example, you simply drag and drop the users to a new location to give them appropriate directory rights, or move users with the move command. Adding file system directory rights for a user in previous versions of NetWare requires a multilayered menu and a somewhat tedious process of adding each new user. With IntranetWare all that is required to add directory rights is to drag the user's icon to the specific directory or object, and the NWADMIN utility will ask you for a confirmation prior to completing the request.

NDS is Scaleable

NDS is an object hierarchy that can be divided into smaller sections that can be distributed to any number of network servers. We say it is scaleable because one server does not need to contain all Directory information. With NDS, the information can be distributed and also replicated on multiple servers to provide increased accessibility and reliability. Figure 1.11 shows how NDS can be distributed across the servers in the network.

FIGURE 1.11

*NDS provides distribution
of the information across
the network servers.*

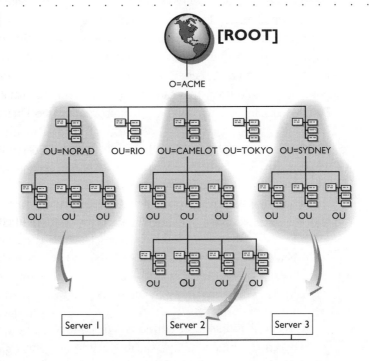

The feature that divides the hierarchy into smaller pieces is called partitioning. Replication is the mechanism that makes the partition redundant. The partitions and replicas are completely transparent to the users and can be scattered across multiple IntranetWare servers. These features make NDS a powerful facility for storing, accessing, managing, and using information about the network resources regardless of where they are physically located. This means that your NDS tree can easily grow to meet the demands of your environment. Another benefit is that your NDS tree design can be easily modified to reflect both the organizational and functional changes in your company.

New NDS Features

IntranetWare has added new utilities and features that help simplify your administration of the network. These new features are unique to IntranetWare; previous versions of NetWare 4 (v4.01 and v4.02) did not have them. These features and utilities include: merge tree, rename tree, move subtree, rename container, NETSYNC, DSMAINT, and DUPGRADE. For more information regarding IntranetWare utilities refer to Chapter 2.

Merge Tree   The DSMERGE utility gives you the ability to merge two separate IntranetWare Directory trees. This feature also gives you greater flexibility during your implementation of IntranetWare and eliminates the task of having to always install every IntranetWare server to the same NDS tree. If a department with an existing NetWare 3 server wants to upgrade their server (for example, from a NetWare 3.12 250-user to an IntranetWare 1,000-user), they can upgrade the server and create their own departmental NDS tree that can be merged into the main corporate tree when appropriate.

Rename Tree   One feature of the DSMERGE utility enables you to rename a Directory tree. This is helpful if you are merging together two trees with the same name. The DSMERGE utility requires that each tree have a separate name.

In addition, if two trees from different networks are joined to the same network, one of the trees will have to change its name by using the DSMERGE utility.

New NetWare Administrator (NWADMIN)   The primary utility used to manage the NDS tree is a graphical and easy-to-use NetWare Administrator utility (NWADMIN). This new utility includes the following features and enhancements:

▸ NetWare Administrator supports Windows 95. There is no difference between the functionality available in the Windows 3.1 and the Windows 95 versions of NWADMIN. The executable path and filename for the Windows 95 version of NetWare Administrator is:

`SYS:PUBLIC\WIN95\NWADMN95.EXE`

▸ The menu in NetWare Administrator has been improved with a configurable toolbar, which provides shortcuts to the menu options, a configurable status bar, and the capability to hide and sort property pages for individual Directory objects.

In addition, the NetWare Administrator utility lets you do the following:

▸ You can now print the entire Directory tree structure for a paper reference.

▸ You can manage multiple NDS trees simultaneously by opening browse windows for multiple trees at once and dragging and dropping NDS objects between browse windows.

▸ You can set property values for multiple objects at the same time with the Details on Multiple Users option. This features enables you to change values for multiple users, containers, templates, or groups.

▸ You can use the Move Subtree option to move an entire subtree (or partition) to another location in the tree. The container object you select to be moved has to be the top-most object (or partition root object) in an NDS partition. The Move Subtree feature gives you the flexibility to reorganize your tree to match the dynamic organization of your company.

▸ You can use the Rename Subtree option to rename any container object in the tree (excluding the [ROOT] object). This feature has been highly requested because it gives you greater flexibility in naming your tree structure.

CONSULTING EXPERIENCE — RENAMING CONTAINER OBJECTS THAT ARE HIGH IN THE TREE

When you rename a container object that is high in the tree (such as the O=Organization object), you are in reality renaming every object below the O=Organization. The renaming process has to change every object's *distinguished name* below the current container. (See Chapter 4 for more information about distinguished names.) Your tree size will determine how long this operation will take.

NDS Manager   With IntranetWare, the NDS Manager utility replaces the Partition Manager utility that was available from the NetWare Administrator (NWADMIN) Tools menu in earlier versions of NetWare 4. The NDS Manager utility has a graphical hierarchical browser and includes many new, powerful features that were not available in Partition Manager. The NDS Manager has the following capabilities:

▸ Runs as a standalone application or as an integrated part of the NWADMIN utility

▸ Provides partitioning and replication services for the Directory database

▸ Repairs the Directory database from a client workstation

▸ Includes a version update capability so that any or all NetWare servers in a network can be updated to a newer version of the DS.NLM file

▸ Provides context-sensitive help for synchronization errors detected by the Partition Continuity option

User Template Object   The User Template is now a specific object in NDS that can be created and defined or used anywhere in the tree structure. The User Template object facilitates the creation of new user objects. (The User Template object is used only during the creation of the users and cannot be used to modify existing users.) The User Template used to be just a special User object with a specific name and attributes.

As an NDS object the User Template gives you greater flexibility when creating your users in the tree because it enables you to create the users quickly and with more consistency. When defining the User Template, you can specify a set of default values for the users, including rights to the file system and other NDS objects and properties. You can also define a setup script for copying files into the new user's home directory.

Audit Log File Object   The Audit Log files created during auditing can now be represented and managed as NDS objects. This enables you to control the access to Audit Log files using simply NDS rights assignments.

NetWare Application Manager   The NetWare Application Manager (NAM) utility enables you to represent applications as objects in the NetWare Directory. You can manage network applications as NDS objects the same way you manage other objects, using the NetWare Administrator utility. NAM also enables you to centrally manage the desktop of the users by defining which network applications they can use through Novell Directory Services.

When the client is started, it displays a desktop that contains the associated Application object icons. When the network user clicks on an icon, the NetWare Application Launcher sets up the workstation and starts the application as defined in the Application object's properties. As a network administrator, you can control which applications the network user has access to and the user's ability to adjust the NAL desktop.

The NAL utility is available in a 16-bit version (NAL.EXE and NALW31.EXE) and a 32-bit version (NALW95.EXE), which supports DOS, Windows 3.1, Windows 95, and Windows NT. Support for OS/2 is currently under development.

Using NAL, you can:

▸ Create Application objects in NDS that define a network application's path, icon, command-line parameters, and other attributes in NDS

▸ Give users access to Application objects through trustee assignments to individual users, groups, and containers

▸ Define startup scripts that establish the appropriate network environment for the application (drive mappings, print captures, and so on) and cleanup scripts that restore the workstation's environment

For more information on setup and installation, see Chapter 20.

NETSYNC Utility   You can make changes to an IntranetWare server's users or groups and have those changes automatically reflected on the NetWare 3 servers by using the IntranetWare utility called NETSYNC. NETSYNC automatically synchronizes updates to user and group objects made on the IntranetWare server to selected NetWare 3 servers. For example, you can add a user to the IntranetWare server and that user will be automatically added to the appropriate NetWare 3 server's bindery.

NETSYNC is a set of NLMs that runs on both IntranetWare and NetWare 3 servers. With NETSYNC installed, up to 12 NetWare 3 servers can be administered from one IntranetWare server. All user, disk, and printer information normally controlled by SYSCON utility under NetWare 3 can be created or modified in NWADMIN on the IntranetWare server. You can manage both versions of NetWare with one utility.

NETSYNC allows you to gradually migrate from NetWare 3 to IntranetWare but still centrally manage mixed network environments.

DSMAINT Utility   This utility enables you to change the server hardware without completely reinstalling NDS. For example, if you need to upgrade or rebuild the SYS volume on your IntranetWare server, you can use this utility to copy NDS to another device, replace the SYS volume hardware, reinstall the operating system, and then copy the NDS files back on to the newly created SYS volume. All the current object IDs are maintained.

DUPGRADE Utility   NDS has been separated from the operating system (SERVER.EXE) so that new versions of NDS can be easily implemented on your IntranetWare servers. This utility helps you distribute a new version of NDS (DS.NLM) to all servers in a tree. DSUPGRADE copies a specified DS.NLM to the SYS:SYSTEM on all the servers located in the selected portion of the tree.

FILE SYSTEM IMPROVEMENTS

IntranetWare optimizes the use of the server file system with several new improvements over previous versions of NetWare. These improvements are: suballocation, data compression, read ahead, and data migration. These improvements enable NetWare to take full advantage of the available disk space and offer speed improvements as well as savings in server memory.

Suballocation

One of the cost benefits to migrating to IntranetWare is the use of volume block suballocation. Suballocation in IntranetWare subdivides the volume blocks (regardless of size) into smaller suballocation units of 512 bytes. This process ensures that you will never waste more than 511 bytes when saving any file to disk. You now have the flexibility to set your IntranetWare volume block size to the recommended maximum of 64K without sacrificing valuable hard disk space, thus ensuring that disk space is more efficiently used.

Previous versions of NetWare worked with a fixed volume block size determined at the time of installation. The block size became the smallest unit of storage on the NetWare volume and server's hard drive. Generally, the larger the block size, the better the throughput between the file server's hard drive and the file server's RAM or cache. But the large block sizes also had the greatest potential of wasting disk space or creating disk slack.

For example, if your block size is 16K (without suballocation) and you save a small file of 1K, the remaining 15K in the disk block is not used (slack). Figure 1.12 shows that large block sizes without suballocation create slack. Figure 1.13 shows the same example but with suballocation, which reduces slack.

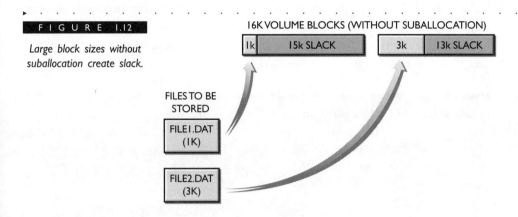

F I G U R E   1.12

Large block sizes without suballocation create slack.

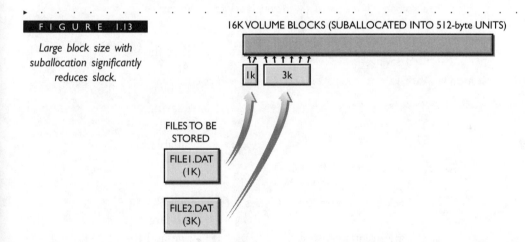

F I G U R E   1.13

Large block size with suballocation significantly reduces slack.

You will notice that in Figure 1.13 the volume block size is still 16K, but the block has been suballocated by the IntranetWare operating system into 512 byte blocks. FILE1.DAT, a 1K file that would ordinarily allocate a full 16K, only takes the required 1K using two suballocated blocks. The other 15K is not wasted but can be used by other files written to the disk. Another file, FILE2.DAT (3K file), is written to disk and starts in the middle of the volume block using six more suballocated blocks. There is no slack in this example.

New files can start in the middle of a volume block that has been suballocated. They do not have to start on the volume block boundary. This means that if you select the recommended 64K volume block size, then several files can be started and stored in the middle of the 64K block.

CONSULTING EXPERIENCE

Some customers will see a return as high as 50 percent of a server's hard disk space by simply migrating to IntranetWare. This savings does not include file compression; server data is simply being migrated to IntranetWare.

This implies that NetWare 3 servers may have up to 50 percent slack. Slack space is automatically reduced by moving to IntranetWare.

The slack can be estimated to equal the total number of files * (volume block size /2). The total savings in disk space from doing the migration from NetWare 3 to IntranetWare can be estimated using the following equation:

```
Savings = total number of files * ((old block size / 2) -
( new block size / 2)).
```

Some example numbers follow:

1 • Slack in NetWare 3: 50,000 files * (4096 bytes / 2) = 102.4 Mb

2 • Slack in IntranetWare: 50,000 files * (512 bytes / 2) = 12.8 Mb

3 • Savings for migrating to IntranetWare from NetWare 3 is:

```
50,000 * ((4096 / 2) - (512 / 2)) = 89.6 Mb
```

File Compression
IntranetWare provides the capability to automatically compress any files on the server that have not been used for a period of time. This compression can result in space savings of up to 50 to 60 percent of a volume in some cases. The File Allocation Table

(FAT) continues to show the files as if no change has occurred. When the user wants to retrieve the file, the operating system automatically decompresses the file. This file compression and decompression process is completely transparent to the user.

The file compression feature in IntranetWare is optional, and you can determine which servers can benefit from its use. You can choose which files, directories, or volumes to compress. The compression process runs as a background task, which means that it will never affect the performance of the file server. To enable file compression, use the following SET parameter (all the following SET parameters can be set in the SERVMAN console utility):

```
SET ENABLE FILE COMPRESSION = ON
```

You can decide the hours during the day when you want the file compression process to start and stop scanning for files that meet the compression criteria. To set the hour in the day to start scanning type:

```
SET COMPRESSION DAILY CHECK STARTING HOUR = 0
```

The default start time is 0, which represents 12:00 PM The possible range is 0 through 23, which represents each hour of the day. To stop scanning type (default is 6 or 6:00 AM):

```
SET COMPRESSION DAILY CHECK STOP HOUR = 6
```

If the "check starting hour" is the same as the "check stop hour," then it starts each day at that time and runs as long as necessary to finish all files that meet the criteria.

You can also set a parameter at the server that specifies the period of time the file has not been accessed before the system compresses it by typing:

```
SET DAYS UNTOUCHED BEFORE COMPRESSION = 7
```

The default setting is seven days.

You can control the minimum space savings that must be accomplished before the compressed file is saved. If the operating system cannot gain a given amount of space from the compression of a file, it does not compress the file. The default is 2 percent.

```
SET MINIMUM COMPRESSION PERCENTAGE GAIN = 2
```

Decompression is automatic when the user requests a compressed file. The algorithms provided are extremely fast and do not affect either the client's or the server's performance. By default, compression runs as a background process. You can also control the decompression options when the compressed file is accessed by the users. The default setting is 1 but the range is (0 to 2).

```
SET CONVERT COMPRESSION TO UNCOMPRESSED OPTION = 1
```

0 means that the operating system will always leave compressed.

1 means leave compressed if it has been read only once in the last seven days (or DAYS UNTOUCHED BEFORE COMPRESSION; see parameter above).

2 means always decompress.

IntranetWare also enables you to control the percentage of disk space that must be present before the system attempts to decompress a file. The default is 10 percent.

```
SET DECOMPRESS PERCENT DISK SPACE FREE TO ALLOW COMMIT = 10
```

IntranetWare provides you with new file attributes that define files and when they should be compressed. Chapter 13 shows a complete listing of all the file attributes and their meanings.

Read Ahead

The read ahead feature in IntranetWare provides the requesting workstation faster response when it is reading files from the server. The operating system anticipates the read requests from the workstation and caches the next disk block of a file, providing a client with faster access.

For example, when the workstation makes a request for a file open, the operating system opens the file and assumes that the next request from the workstation is going be a read request. In anticipation of the read request, the read ahead feature caches (places into file cache) the first block of the file. The result is that when the request from the workstation comes in for the first block, the server already has the block available in cache. The workstation request is serviced immediately instead of waiting for hard disk access. As the workstation reads the information out of the block in cache, the operating system will fetch the next block of the file and place it in cache anticipating more read requests. When the workstation has read one-half of the current block in memory (or cache), the operating system determines that the next block is needed. Using this algorithm, the operating system calculates when the next blocks are needed and reads them from disk before the request is made.

This read ahead feature is a low-priority task, which will not be executed when the server is busy handling other processes. The greatest benefit of read ahead is when you are accessing optical media. A CD-ROM drive, for example, is not as fast as a hard drive. Read ahead pulls the next block into cache so that it is ready when the workstation needs it.

Data Migration

Data migration automatically transfers infrequently accessed files off the file server and places them onto another media such as read/write optical disk or tape. The migrated files are removed from the hard drive of the server but can be viewed in the directory listing. The benefit of data migration is that it saves more expensive online hard drive storage and moves data to less expensive, near-line optical or off-line tape storage.

Even though the file has been migrated, it is automatically brought back to the primary storage when a user requests the file. If the near-line media is not mounted, then the server displays a message indicating which media volume needs to be mounted. After the media is available, the migrated file is retrieved and copied back to the server's hard drive. This operation is transparent to the user. However, if the file is on a media that takes time to mount, there will be a delay noticed by the user. You can set a capacity threshold for the volume so that files are migrated (starting with the oldest unused files) until the threshold is met.

NEW FILE SYSTEM FEATURES IN INTRANETWARE

With IntranetWare, the NetWare file system more effectively supports extended name spaces and can hold 16 million directory entries per volume (16 million on DOS-only volumes). In addition, NetWare volumes mount much faster than before, and the file system automatically monitors volume space.

Support for Long Filenames

With IntranetWare, LONG.NAM provides the extended name spaces available with the Windows 95, Windows NT, and OS/2 workstation platforms on a NetWare volume. LONG.NAM is a special type of NetWare Loadable Module that enables non-DOS filenames on a NetWare volume. Because extended name spaces are used more often now, LONG.NAM is loaded as part of the default server configuration.

In previous versions of NetWare 4, the OS/2 name space was provided by OS2.NAM. LONG.NAM replaces OS2.NAM.

Volume Capacity Supports 16 Million Directory Entries

With IntranetWare, each NetWare server volume can support 16 million directory entries by default and up to 16 million directory entries on volumes that use only the DOS name space. With previous versions of NetWare 4, the limit was 2 million entries per volume. Each additional name space requires an additional entry per file. For example, using only the DOS name space requires one directory entry per file. With the DOS and longname spaces loaded, two directory entries are required.

Faster Volume Mounting

The software responsible for mounting NetWare volumes has been rewritten and optimized for faster volume mounting. The result is that volumes mount much faster, sometimes more than twice as fast as in NetWare 3. As hardware sizes increase and prices go down, larger NetWare volumes are being implemented. This feature will reduce the total amount of time needed to bring the servers up.

The file system monitors NetWare volume space use and proactively purges deleted files to free up volume space when needed.

The file system responds more efficiently to the new 32-bit NetWare client architecture, delivering a higher level of performance to workstations using the new 32-bit NetWare client software.

Backup and Restore Improvements

With IntranetWare, SBACKUP and the NDS Target Service Agent (TSA) provide more effective backup and restore capabilities than before. Until now, the NDS schema extensions and the mechanisms that enabled you to manage file trustee assignments from the Directory were not effectively backed up, and the restoration process involved recreating a server's private key, User object IDs and rights, and replica information on a per-volume basis. With IntranetWare, a server's private key, User object IDs and file trustee assignments, and replica information are effectively maintained throughout the backup and restore process.

Additional Backup and Restore Target Service Agents

With IntranetWare, Novell is shipping the following new Target Service Agents:

▸ Windows 95 TSA — backs up and restores information on workstations running the Windows 95 operating system and the new NetWare Client 32 for Windows 95 software

▸ Macintosh TSA — backs up and restores information on workstations running the Macintosh operating system and the new NetWare Client for Mac OS software

PRINT SERVICES IMPROVEMENTS

IntranetWare has the capability of attaching and sharing printer devices that are attached directly to the server, workstation, or the network. Although these features are supported by NetWare 3, major changes have been made to the print services in IntranetWare. These improvements include:

▸ PSERVER supports 256 printers.

▸ RPRINTER has been replaced with NPRINTER. If the printer is attached to the server, then load NPRINTER.NLM. If the printer is attached to the workstation run NPRINTER.EXE. NPRINTER.EXE can be loaded multiple times on a single workstation to support multiple attached printers.

▸ NPRINTER.EXE runs on DOS, Windows, and OS/2.

▸ PSERVER runs only as an NLM. The PSERVER.EXE is no longer needed or supported because the PSERVER supports more printers and NPRINTER.EXE can be loaded multiple times to service multiple printers attached to a single workstation.

▸ PSERVER performance has been enhanced.

▸ Quick Setup option in PCONSOLE enables you to create new print objects, such as a print server, printers, and print queues, from a single screen. It then establishes the printing relationship between these new print objects.

▸ Printer is now an object in NDS and no longer an attribute of a print server. The user can now send the print job directly to the printer without having to know anything about print queues.

- Network users no longer need to be familiar with print servers or print queues; they can send their print jobs directly to the printer by specifying the printer name.

- You can configure the print queue polling time.

- There is now support for Macintosh and NFS clients.

- You can have an unlimited number of print job configurations.

- IntranetWare print services now has Autoconnect for lost printer connections.

The improved functionality of the print services in IntranetWare increases ease of use for each of your network users.

New Print Services in IntranetWare

With IntranetWare, traditional NetWare print services have been improved, and Novell is introducing the next generation of network printing — NetWare Distributed Print Services (NDPS). With the introduction of NDPS, traditional print services are frequently referred to as queue-based printing. With IntranetWare, queue-based printing has been improved in the following ways:

- The NetWare Administrator utility now includes a Print Services Quick Setup option on the Tools menu. This option provides functionality similar to the Printing Quick Setup option in the PCONSOLE utility. The Print Services Quick Setup option enables you to easily create and associate Print Server, Printer, and Print Queue objects in the Directory.

- You can use the new graphical NPRINTER Manager (NPTWIN95.EXE) to enable network users to share a printer attached to a Windows 95 workstation. NPRINTER Manager and its associated files provide the same functionality that NPRINTER.EXE provides on a DOS or OS/2 workstation.

NetWare Distributed Print Services

NetWare Distributed Print Services, Novell's next generation print service, is designed for complex print management and production requirements. It is an ideal printing solution for users in diverse environments ranging from small workgroups to enterprisewide systems.

NDPS is a distributed service consisting of client, server, and connectivity components seamlessly linking and sharing network printers with applications. It eliminates the need to create and configure Print Queue, Printer, and Print Server objects. In fact, NDPS doesn't require you to manage print queues at all.

A single graphical administration utility (NetWare Administrator) provides comprehensive management and control of all major brands and models of printers.

NDPS gives users greater control over network printing through such capabilities as:

▶ Centralized, simplified, single-source administration

▶ Bidirectional feedback and control

▶ Configurable notification profiles

▶ Automatic printer driver download and installation

▶ Tight integration with Novell Directory Services

▶ New job submission, scheduling, and notification options

▶ Compatibility with multiple clients, applications, and operating systems

▶ Support for existing printers and other output devices

▶ Adaptability to downsizing and organizational growth

WORKSTATION/CLIENT IMPROVEMENTS

NetWare DOS Requester

With the advent of IntranetWare, Novell improved its DOS workstation software by introducing the Virtual Loadable Module (VLM) architecture. The VLM architecture is based on a set of VLMs (or modules) that is loaded and managed by the VLM.EXE. The VLMs work as a DOS requester to share the DOS environment.

The VLM.EXE is a terminate and stay resident (TSR), which manages the loading of the individual VLMs by placing them in either conventional memory, upper memory, or extended memory.

The VLM.EXE automatically detects the presence of upper and extended memory managers and tries to load most of the VLM modules into those memory regions. Although VLM.EXE tries to load its modules high, you can configure which VLM module gets loaded and in which memory space. Typically, you will want the VLMs loaded high because you can save conventional memory for your workstation applications.

The following additional features are now included in the VLM architecture:

- ▸ The system supports up to 50 connections to different file servers.

- ▸ An auto reconnect feature automatically reestablishes a lost server connection.

- ▸ Users can now log in and log out while running Microsoft Windows.

- ▸ Login scripts are supported when users log in while running Microsoft Windows.

- ▸ Packet Burst provides quicker server responses especially across a wide area network (WAN) link.

- ▸ LIP (Large Internet Packets) is automatically supported.

- ▸ Language support can be customized for the workstation.

- ▸ Packet Signatures are provided for increased security of client to server communication.

The VLM client architecture provides you with more flexibility in terms of adjusting the software parameters for performance and workstation memory. For more information on the VLM architecture, see Chapter 18.

NetWare Client32

Novell's new 32-bit clients are based on the new and advanced NetWare Client32 architecture, which departs from the NetWare DOS Requester software (the VLM-based client). Client32 enables the client software to run in protected mode and, in addition, requires less than 5KB of conventional memory while providing a larger cache.

The Client32 architecture, designed for robust connectivity and easy maintenance, provides the following features:

▸ Client32 detects changes in a workstation's network environment and restores connections to the network when the relevant network service is restored. This makes Client32 the most reliable NetWare client available. And, when a computer loses its connection to the network, the computer continues to run without having to reboot.

▸ Client32 caches frequently used data, such as file content and network information, resulting in less traffic on the network and faster response times on the client.

▸ Client32 supports multiple Directory tree access and complete Novell Directory Services access.

NetWare Client32 for DOS and Windows 3.1

In addition to all the benefits of the Client32 architecture, the NetWare Client32 for DOS and Windows 3.1 software provides the following capabilities:

▸ The familiar graphical NetWare User Tools utility is available in Windows to enable network users to manage their network environment.

▸ Support for Novell's 32-bit TCP/IP transport is included.

▸ Integrated support for the NetWare/IP software is included.

▸ The same Target Service Agent used to enable backup and restore on workstations using the NetWare DOS Requester software works on workstations using the Client32 for DOS and Windows 3.1 software.

NetWare Client32 for DOS and Windows 3.1 differs from the NetWare Client32 for Windows 95 software in the following ways:

▸ The core Client32 component, NIOS, runs as an executable file rather than as a virtual device driver (VXD).

▸ NIOS uses a text configuration file (NET.CFG) rather than the registry.

▸ There is no graphical interface for changing configuration parameters. You have to edit the NET.CFG file manually and restart the client software to implement the changes.

NetWare Client32 for Windows 95

NetWare Client32 for Windows 95 differs from the NetWare DOS Requester and the NetWare Client32 for DOS and Windows 3.1 software in the following ways:

▸ The core Client32 component, NIOS, runs as a virtual device driver (VXD) rather than as an executable file.

▸ There is usually no STARTNET.BAT file. Windows 95 loads the client at startup.

▸ There is no NET.CFG file. Configuration settings are saved in the Windows 95 registry. Because configuration settings are saved in the registry, you can manage Client32 parameters using the Windows 95 System Policies Editor.

▸ You can upgrade Windows 3.1x workstations to Windows 95 and NetWare Client32 for Windows 95 in one installation process called the Batch Install.

▸ Client32 for Windows 95 is fully integrated into the Explorer and Network Neighborhood utilities. In addition, you can log in to NetWare networks and run login scripts from the Windows 95 desktop environment.

▸ Client32 for Windows 95 supports long filenames.

▸ Client32 for Windows 95 supports the following industry standard
protocols:

 ▸ Windows 95 implementations of TCP/IP, Winsock, Named Pipes,
 and NetBIOS

 ▸ The Windows 95 WSOCK32.DLL (supported by the Client32 IPX
 protocol stack)

 ▸ Simple Network Management Protocol (SNMP)

 ▸ The Microsoft Client for Microsoft Networks

NetWare Client for Mac OS

For the first time, NetWare has completely folded the Macintosh into NetWare
as a client. With a new product called NetWare Client for Mac OS, the Macintosh
receives a complete Novell IPX protocol stack. With this support the Macintosh
can participate as a full NDS member.

The new NetWare Client for Mac OS software enables workstations using the
Mac OS to communicate with a network via the IPX or IP transport protocols
instead of or in addition to the AppleTalk protocol. This new software lets you use
a single protocol on a network that includes workstations using the Mac OS and
other NetWare clients. In addition, you can browse a Novell Directory Services
tree and log in to Novell Directory Services, change passwords, log out, and manage
Directory connections.

The NetWare Client for Mac OS software includes the following features:

▸ The NetWare Client for Mac OS software fully supports simultaneous
connections to multiple Directory trees and NetWare/IP networks.

▸ The software communicates via the AppleTalk, IPX TM, or TCP/IP
transports. You can use AppleTalk, IPX, and TCP/IP at the same time.

▸ Workstations using the NetWare Client for Mac OS software can access NetWare volumes that do not have the Mac name space or AppleTalk Filing Protocol NLMs loaded. However, these workstations are limited to the 8.3 DOS file naming format.

▸ The NetWare Client for Mac OS software lets place a drive mapping to a NetWare volume on the Macintosh desktop, and you can access files stored on a NetWare server and use a NetWare printer or queue.

▸ The NetWare Client for Mac OS software enables you to open one or more remote connections to one or more NetWare server consoles.

NetWare Client for OS/2

OS/2 is also supported as a client, with the Requester software for OS/2 included with all the other client programs. In addition, the standard version of IntranetWare allows an OS/2 machine to be a nondedicated NetWare server. This might appeal to customers with small branch networks that can't afford a full, dedicated NetWare server.

The NetWare Client for OS/2 software enables OS/2 workstations to connect to NetWare networks. With IntranetWare, the NetWare Client for OS/2 software has been enhanced to include the following features:

▸ The software supports full NDS connectivity during Global DOS and Windows sessions. You no longer need to load NETX during a DOS session to get a bindery connection to a server running NetWare 4. Full NDS connectivity is not possible, however, during Private DOS or Windows sessions.

▸ With the DISCONNECT ON parameter in the NET.CFG file and the NWSTART and NWSTOP utilities, you can control network connectivity during the system boot process. When an OS/2 workstation boots up with the DISCONNECT ON parameter in the NET.CFG file, the NetWare Client software is loaded but no network connections are made. To establish a network connection, use the NWSTART utility. To suspend your network connections, use the NWSTOP utility.

SECURITY AND AUDITING IMPROVEMENTS

IntranetWare security provides you with the solutions to build a trusted network using components such as client, server, and medium. The IntranetWare network will be the first network operating system to receive the National Computer Security Council's C2 rating. It is currently being evaluated as an entire network, which will result in Red Book C2/E2 status rather than the less stringent Orange Book status of other systems.

IntranetWare accomplishes this level of security by providing client authentication for the login process, NCP packet signature for communications, NDS objects and property rights, and auditing of server events.

Client Authentication

IntranetWare and Novell Directory Services use the RSA public and private key encryption technology to authenticate the network users. The workstation proves its identity during login and establishes the necessary authentication pieces necessary for background authentication. Once the users are logged in, NDS's background authentication is used to transparently provide access to other privileged network resources. This combination of NDS and authentication services means the user only has to provide a username and password once for servers in a single tree. The rights authorization process to the individual resources such as servers and printers occurs after background authentication has been completed. For more information relating to client authentication, review Chapter 10.

The net effect of a login and background authentication is that neither the passwords nor unencrypted keys are sent across the network. The connection established by the client is unique only for the current session and cannot be forged.

NCP Packet Signatures

NCP (NetWare Core Protocol) Packet Signature is a security feature that protects servers and clients when they communicate via NCP. NCP packet signatures secure the communication between the client and server by forcing each device to stamp each packet with an electronic signature. This process prevents unauthorized users from capturing packets on the wire and regenerating them to seize a user's session. Capturing and regenerating packets that are not from the original sender is known as packet forgery. NCP packet signatures secure the network against intruders.

In order to enable NCP packets at the server console type:

```
SET NCP PACKET SIGNATURE OPTION = 1
```

The default is 1.
The options are:

▸ 0 — turn packet signature off

▸ 1 — do packet signature only if client requires it

▸ 2 — do packet signature if client can support it

▸ 3 — packet signature is required

NDS Object and Property Rights

Novell Directory Services provides access control to NDS objects and properties. The file system provides its own access; however, both NDS and file system access use the identity that was established during authentication. IntranetWare provides the flexibility for users to manage other objects in the NDS tree. By contrast, NetWare 3 had only the Supervisor (or an operator) who could manage other objects. This access control feature reveals additional functionality for administering security and defining access to your users. For detailed information on security please refer to Chapter 13.

Auditing

Novell provides an auditing capability that allows an auditor to record file system or NDS events, which are stored in an audit log file. Auditing is accomplished through the AUDITCON utility. Some auditable events include:

▸ Changing a user's password

▸ Adding a user

▸ Deleting a user

▸ Creating files

▸ Deleting files

▸ Granting access rights to a user or other object

In order to perform auditing, you must first enable it on an IntranetWare server or on a container independent of a specific server. After auditing is enabled, it can be delegated to another user. This user can then change the password and become an independent auditor. Auditing may best be used for accounts in which such audit trails are required by law or by some other governing body. For more details on auditing, refer to Chapter 2.

New Security Services in IntranetWare

With IntranetWare, Novell is introducing NetWare Enhanced Security. NetWare Enhanced Security is designed to meet the Class C2 requirements.

To facilitate the configuration of NetWare Enhanced Security, the following features are provided:

▸ The AUDITCON utility has been significantly improved to enable C2 compliant auditing.

▸ Audit Log files are now represented by and managed as NDS objects. This lets you control access to the Audit Log files by using the object and property right assignments in NDS.

▸ The NetWare server can be configured as an Enhanced Security server by using an updated group of SET parameters.

▸ The Enable SECURE.NCF SET parameter enables you to specify that a server should be configured automatically during system boot as an Enhanced Security server.

▸ The SECURE.NCF file provides a script that configures a server as an Enhanced Security server. You can run this script at any time from an IntranetWare server console prompt.

MEMORY IMPROVEMENTS

IntranetWare is the first network operating system to offer memory protection as an option. You can create a secure domain in which to run the NetWare Loadable Modules and protect all other server operations from a failing module. If an NLM has proven its reliability, you can choose to run the module at a lower domain, which will increase its performance. The lower domain is not protected. Testing of such NLMs requires that they first be written to run in the secure domain.

IntranetWare also manages the server memory more efficiently by allocating the memory from a single memory pool. Having a single memory pool enables the operating system to recover NLM resources more efficiently when they are unloaded. The IntranetWare single memory pool performs all of the functions that five or more memory pools performed in previous versions of NetWare. These improvements in memory allow the server to load and unload server-based applications without running out of memory and prolong the server's total uptime.

WIDE AREA COMMUNICATION IMPROVEMENTS

IntranetWare has made improvements in WAN communications in the areas of multiprotocol routing, TCP/IP transport protocol support, NetWare Link Services Protocol, packet burst, and large internet packets.

Multiprotocol Routing

IntranetWare provides built-in multiprotocol routing services using the NetWare Multi Protocol Router (MPR). MPR is Novell's software bridge/router that runs on Intel-based personal computers. The bridge/router enables customers to connect remote offices using familiar transport protocols and PC technology. The NetWare MPR is ideal for connecting local area networks by routing and source-route bridging over leased lines, Frame Relay, X.25, and Point-to-Point (PPP). NetWare MPR also functions with third-party dedicated routers in a multirouter network.

NetWare/IP and TCP/IP Protocol Support

IntranetWare can tightly integrate into existing TCP/IP environments using NetWare/IP. By installing NetWare/IP on IntranetWare servers, customers can create an environment that supports both the TCP/IP and IPX transport protocols, or one that uses only TCP/IP.

NetWare/IP is ideal for wide area networks that already use TCP/IP. Many large companies with networks based on NetWare have standardized TCP/IP on their WANs. These companies need efficient integration between TCP/IP and NetWare across their multiple geographic sites. NetWare/IP provides this integration and reduces the number of protocols required to run on a WAN.

With IntranetWare, Novell is incorporating the NetWare/IP software into the NetWare product. NetWare/IP is a set of server and client software modules providing access to a NetWare network using the TCP/IP transport instead of or in addition to the IPX protocol used in traditional NetWare networks. NetWare/IP enables you to:

- Extend NetWare services and applications to nodes on an existing IP network in a manner that is transparent to users.

- Migrate a network from IPX to TCP/IP.

- Interconnect TCP/IP and IPX networks, enabling users on both networks to access NetWare resources on either network.

- Easily manage TCP/IP addresses using the Dynamic Host Configuration Protocol (DHCP).

- Provide access to network printers attached to UNIX hosts using the LPR protocol.

To use NetWare/IP in an IP-only environment, you need to use network client software that supports the TCP/IP transport. The following NetWare clients can access a NetWare/IP network:

- The NetWare/IP version of the NetWare DOS Requester software

- NetWare Client 32 for Windows 95

- NetWare Client 32 for DOS and Windows 3.1

- NetWare Client for Windows NT

- NetWare Client for Mac OS

NetWare Link Services Protocol

NetWare Link Services Protocol (NLSP) is a link state routing protocol for IPX. This routing technology — based on Open Shortest Path First (OSPF) — overcomes the limitations of the Routing Information Protocol (RIP) and the Service Advertising Protocol (SAP) in local area and wide area IPX networks.

NLSP improves overall network efficiency through better utilization of existing bandwidth. It substantially reduces the overhead traffic commonly generated by RIP and SAP, provides load sharing across redundant traffic commonly generated by RIP and SAP, and provides load sharing across redundant paths.

Packet Burst

IntranetWare automatically supports packet burst, which improves data delivery over latent links. Packet burst technology eliminates the ping-pong effect of the send/return packets during communication. For example, the client sends a request via packet burst to the server. The server responds to the client with multiple packets that don't require a return receipt for every packet. The server accepts a return receipt for the entire transmission, thus reducing the total transmission time and minimizing the "chattiness" of the NCP protocol. Packet burst is particularly beneficial to communication across WANs in which line speeds can often result in bottleneck.

Large Internet Packets (LIP)

In previous versions of NetWare, data packets that were passed through a router were automatically sized to 512 bytes. This sizing was done regardless of whether the workstation, server, and router were able to receive larger packets.

IntranetWare provides large packet capability through routers and over wide area links. The largest packet that both the workstation and server can support is negotiated and used for all communication transmissions. Having a large packet for communications reduces the total number of packets and increases the throughput of the network. IntranetWare servers also use LIP for server-to-server communications.

In order to enable LIP type:

```
SET ALLOW LIP = ON
```

CONSULTING EXPERIENCE

When a workstation first attaches to a server, both the workstation and the server negotiate a physical packet size that they will use for communications. If the server and workstation are on the same token ring segment, they will establish a physical packet size of 4202 (the maximum size used for token ring). In previous versions of NetWare, when the workstation had to go through a router to reach the server, the server did not know what type of network topology was on the other side of the router. The server had to default to the least common denominator — ARCnet with 512-byte packets. Today, ARCnet is seldom used.

With Large Internet Packets, this 512-byte ARCnet limit is not assumed, and the workstation and server negotiate their packet size at 1514 bytes for Ethernet or 4202 bytes for token ring.

MESSAGING AND E-MAIL

IntranetWare now comes with NetWare Message Handling Service (MHS) built in. MHS provides message storage and forward transfer services that can be tightly integrated with NDS. This messaging service may be configured to run on any IntranetWare server and is the basis for building a fully interconnected message infrastructure for distributing e-mail. This infrastructure supports all of the popular e-mail programs such as Novell's GroupWise, Microsoft Mail, Lotus CC:Mail, or DaVinci.

IntranetWare includes an e-mail solution called FirstMail, which is a basic NetWare MHS software package. The new FirstMail application provides basic functions for DOS e-mail users on the local network. It will support only the least demanding LAN e-mail users.

NETWORK MANAGEMENT

IntranetWare provides powerful network and server management facilities. Novell has instrumented all of its core modules with built-in management logic, which enables the system to more easily manage each component. IntranetWare is remotely manageable by providing Simple Network Management Protocol (SNMP) alert information directly to management consoles. These management consoles range from Novell's NMS console, IBM's NetView to NetWare for SAA, or Hewlett-Packard's HP Open View.

OTHER NEW FEATURES

Additive Licensing

IntranetWare provides you with increased flexibility to control the number of user connections supported by the system. Additive licensing enables you to add IntranetWare licenses together on the server to support more connections. Additive licensing also lets you build the size of the network you need. The licenses increment in a range from 5 to 1,000.

For example, if you have an IntranetWare 500-user server in production and you need more connections, you can add 5 more connections totaling a 505-user server, or you can add 1,000 more connections totaling a 1,500-user server, or any combination in between.

NetWare Licensing Services

With IntranetWare, Novell is introducing NetWare Licensing Services.

NetWare Licensing Services (NLS) is a distributed, enterprise network service that enables administrators to monitor and control the use of licensed applications on a network. NLS is tightly integrated with the Novell Directory Services technology and is based on an enterprise service architecture. This architecture consists of client components that support different platforms and system components that reside on IntranetWare servers. NLS also provides a basic license metering tool and libraries that export licensing service functionality to developers of other licensing systems.

Easier Installation and CD-ROM Support

IntranetWare is distributed on two CD-ROMs for easy installation. In order to install IntranetWare from a CD-ROM, make sure that you have a DOS partition (we recommend 15 to 30 megabytes), that DOS is installed, and that the CD-ROM drivers for DOS are loaded. You then simply insert the NetWare CD-ROM into the drive, type **INSTALL**, and the bulk of the work is done for you. You then have two options for installation: Simple or Custom Installation.

CONSULTING EXPERIENCE

With IntranetWare you have a choice of Simple Installation or Custom Installation. Whichever one you choose depends on your configuration. Using the Simple Installation option will limit your hands-on involvement to about five minutes. Copying all the files from the CD-ROM to the server will take about one hour. Using the Custom Installation takes less than 10 minutes of hands-on time. But, if you are adding servers to networks and want them in different places in the NDS tree or need multiple NDS trees, you will need to use Custom Installation.

Choose the Simple Installation if:

- Your network consists of fewer servers (one to three) and fewer than 1,000 users.

- All network resources and users will reside in a single NDS container (O=Organization).

- The hard disk has an existing 15MB (or larger) DOS partition.

- The server will boot from the hard disk.

- You will not use disk mirroring or disk duplexing (fault-tolerant features included with IntranetWare).

- Each disk will contain a single NetWare volume.

- IPX will be the only protocol used.

Choose Custom Installation if:

- Your network consists of more than a couple of servers and more than 1,000 users.

- Network resources and users will be placed in different NDS containers.

- The server could be booted from a floppy diskette.

- The hard disk will be partitioned (more than one NetWare volume per disk).

(continued)

> ▸ You will use disk mirroring or disk duplexing.
>
> ▸ Volumes will span across multiple hard disks.
>
> ▸ You will use more protocols such as TCP/IP or AppleTalk.
>
> Although the stated minimum hardware configuration for an IntranetWare file server is a clone 386/33 with only 8MB of RAM and a 380MB SCSI, our experience has shown otherwise. We recommend a minimum 486/50 with 32MB of RAM and 300MB SCSI hard disk for implementing any tree with multiple IntranetWare servers.

IntranetWare ships on two CD-ROM disks: one for the operating system and one for the documentation, making it easier to perform subsequent installation and to access the online documentation.

You can take advantage of IntranetWare's CD-ROM support to simplify installation on the network. Once the product is installed on the local server, the installation files can be copied to the server's hard disk for subsequent installations or the CD-ROM can be mounted as a NetWare volume. This capability is referred to as server-to-server installation and is one of the major improvements in IntranetWare installations.

IntranetWare documentation can also be made available electronically by mounting the online documentation CD-ROM as a volume. Another option, if you have room on the server's hard disk, is to copy or install the documentation files onto the server.

CONSULTING EXPERIENCE

In order to mount your CD-ROM drive as a NetWare volume, you need to have a full SCSI controller for the CD-ROM. If your CD-ROM is nonstandard SCSI, such as the new IDE combination controllers for hard disks and CD-ROM, the CD-ROM drive will work fine for installation but cannot be configured later as a NetWare volume.

International Language Support

IntranetWare ships with English, Spanish, German, French, and Italian language support. On the workstation, you set a DOS environment variable NWLANGUAGE = xxx, where xxx is the desired language. The result is that the NetWare utilities, menus, messages, and help screens will be in the proper language.

A new command, LANGUAGE, can be set on the server console to select the proper language at the server. All the Novell server utilities will be viewed in the selected language. You can also run the installation program in the proper language by choosing the correct language subdirectory before invoking the INSTALL.EXE program.

Hardware Detection During Installation

During an IntranetWare installation, the Install utility automatically detects hardware devices in a server, including hard disks, CD-ROM drives, LAN cards, and so on. It then scans the server for the appropriate drivers and selects applicable device drivers (.DSK and .HAM files) for the hardware.

If the server does not have an advanced bus architecture (EISA, PCI, PNPISA, PCMCIA, or MCA) or device type (SCSI and IDE devices), the Install utility might not select the appropriate drivers for the server. In this case, you will need to manually select the appropriate device drivers for hardware in the server.

Additional Upgrade Utilities

To provide NetWare customers with a more complete upgrade solution, Novell has partnered with Preferred Systems, Inc., to develop and deliver two additional upgrade utilities in IntranetWare — DS Migrate and NetWare File Migration.

DS Migrate Utility　　DS Migrate is a new migration and modeling solution that is provided through an agreement between Novell, Inc., and Preferred Systems, Inc., the makers of DS Standard (the utility upon which DS Migrate is based). The graphical DS Migrate utility is incorporated into the NetWare Administrator utility.

DS Migrate enables you to upgrade a NetWare 2.1x or NetWare 3.1x server bindery by migrating modeled bindery information to an existing NetWare 4 tree. DS Migrate migrates only bindery information, and the new graphical NetWare File Migration utility or the DOS menu-based MIGRATE utility migrates data files.

NetWare File Migration Utility   The NetWare File Migration utility is a new utility that migrates files from NetWare 3 servers to IntranetWare servers. The NetWare File Migration utility is used in conjunction with the new DS Migrate utility after a NetWare 3 bindery migration. The graphical NetWare File Migration utility is incorporated into the NetWare Administrator utility.

IntranetWare

IntranetWare is a software-based solution for existing LAN users who want to transparently connect NetWare networks to the Internet and other corporate intranets. IntranetWare is the on-ramp for the existing NetWare users. It provides a foundation or platform for complete and secure Internet and intranet access. Because IntranetWare is a complete server operating environment, it has the following components:

▸ NetWare Web Server 2.5

▸ Netscape Navigator Browser

▸ NetWare MultiProtocol Router 3.1

▸ Novell's IPX/IP gateway

NetWare Web Server 2.5   NetWare Web Server (version 2.5) is a NetWare Loadable Module (NLM) for IntranetWare that fulfills requests for documents received from World Wide Web (WWW) clients on a TCP/IP network. A client requests a document by sending a HyperText Transfer Protocol (HTTP) request that identifies the document by a Uniform Resource Locator (URL). Although the document can be of any type, the client and server will generally exchange HyperText Markup Language (HTML) documents.

The NetWare Web Server software lets you publish HTML documents on internal corporate networks and the World Wide Web. Implemented as a set of NetWare Loadable Modules, the NetWare Web Server quickly and easily converts your IntranetWare server into a Web server. Once you've created your Web server, you can connect it to the World Wide Web and establish an Internet presence. Or, you can shield it from outside access and use it as an intranet server, enhancing your NetWare network with Internet/Intranet technology.

NetWare Web Server leverages NetWare and TCP/IP security functions. Among them is Novell Directory Services (NDS) Authentication, a feature that provides secure access to your server and directories. NetWare Web Server also lets you browse the NDS directory, making it easier than ever before to find the information you need. What's more, access controls — based on IP addresses, user name, host name, directory, document, users or groups — let you limit access to specific Web documents. These access control features let you publish documents and still control who views them.

NetWare Web Server also supports fault tolerance. Fully compatible with NetWare SFT III, it enables users to mirror their NetWare Web Server site on another system. The result is a robust publishing platform that's up and running all day, every day.

NetWare Web Server supports all the common features of the World Wide Web, including:

▶ Java applet support. Java applets are particularly useful for including processing-intensive or time-sensitive elements, like multimedia and animation, on a Web page.

▶ NDS browsing capabilities. Users can browse the Novell Directory Services tree using an HTML browser and view objects and their attributes within the tree.

▶ The Local Common Gateway Interface (LCGI) and Remote Common Gateway Interface (R-CGI). This feature allows the NetWare Web Server to publish dynamic Web documents.

▶ BASIC and PERL script interpreters.

Netscape Navigator Browser Netscape Navigator is included in both the 32-bit (Windows 95 and Windows NT) and 16-bit (Windows 3.1x) versions. Netscape Navigator is the world's most popular Web browser. Its graphical interface and pop-up menus let you navigate your intranet with point-and-click ease. It includes the Java Class Loader, the Java Applet Security Manager, an integrated e-mail and news reader, a bookmark facility, and plug-in architecture that can extend its capabilities.

TIP

For more detailed information on the Netscape Navigator software, you can point your browser to the URL of http://www.netscape.com.

The Netscape Navigator supports the following Intel-based (x86) platforms:

- Windows 3.1 and 3.11

- Windows for Workgroups 3.11

- Windows 95

- Windows NT (3.5 or higher)

The Netscape Navigator supports the following Apple Macintosh platforms:

- Macintosh System 7 or later

- Mac OS

- PowerPC

The Netscape Navigator supports the following UNIX platforms:

- Digital Equipment Corp. Alpha (OSF/1 2.0 or higher)

- Hewlett-Packard 700-series (HP-UX 9.03)

- IBM RS/6000 AIX 3.2

- Silicon Graphics (IRIX 5.2)

- Sun SPARC (Solaris 2.4, SunOS 4.1.3)

- 386/486/Pentium (BSDI)

Novell MultiProtocol Router (MPR)   The NetWare MultiProtocol Router (version 3.1) software is a family of software-based routing products that operate on standard 386-, 486-, and Pentium-based PCs. NetWare MultiProtocol Router 3.1 provides concurrent routing of IPX, TCP/IP, AppleTalk and SNA protocols, and source-route bridging for NetBIOS and LLC2 applications. MPR supports a wide range of LAN topologies and WAN connection types, including dedicated leased lines, dial-on-demand voice-grade circuits, frame relay, X.25, ISDN, SMDS, and ATM.

IPX/IP Gateway   The Novell IPX to IP gateways translate the IPX transport in a data communications to an IP transport (and back again). The IPX/IP gateway allows clients located on an IPX (NetWare) LAN to communicate with the Internet or TCP/IP-based applications on their intranet without the need for IP address management or the security risks involved in enabling network clients to offer TCP/IP services. The IPX/IP gateways enable the network administrator to easily implement access controls for the Internet or TCP/IP applications.

Because the language of the Internet is TCP/IP, a network administrator providing Internet access for the LAN users normally installs and configures a full TCP/IP protocol stack at each client. The traditional configuration requires that each client be configured with a Unique IP address, Subnet mast, Default router, Domain, and Domain Name Server list.

Since an IP address is associated with a network card and not a particular user, any move to another network requires a reconfiguration of some or all of the parameters. A growing scarcity of IP addresses (because of Internet growth) and nonportable IP addresses assigned by Internet Service Providers further complicate the situation. (Change ISPs and reconfigure every client on your network!)

IPX/IP gateways use a single address to represent all of your IPX clients to the TCP/IP hosts they wish to communicate with. IPX clients communicating to the gateway have their IPX network address in every packet. By building a table associating the IPX clients and a unique port number (the port number is used to communicate with the TCP/IP host), the gateway can substitute IPX and IP headers and pass the communications between LAN client and Internet server. All packets passing onto the Internet contain the IP address of the gateway.

Since no IP addresses are needed for LAN clients, this greatly eases the IP address maintenance tasks for network administrators. The single IP address is one of the greatest advantages of the IPX/IP gateway. Since the gateway has only a single IP address, it provides a natural fire wall or security barrier. Remember, at some point, every Internet communication resolves down to locating resources by their IP address. If you don't know the IP address of a resource or are unable to resolve a domain name to an IP address, you cannot access the services on that resource. Network managers may find it difficult to prevent LAN clients from running TCP/IP services (FTP server for example), but if the station has no IP address of its own it cannot provide services because a remote host will never be able to send to the IP address of LAN-based clients and servers. The LAN-based clients will be able to access services on other hosts because the gateway resolves the remote hosts IP address. But a remote system can only talk to the gateway and has no way to uniquely identify a system on the LAN through the gateway. In essence, the gateway creates a one-way door for providing services from the Internet to LAN-based clients.

Installation and Management Utilities for IntranetWare

"The question of common sense is always 'What is it good for?' — a question which would abolish the rose and be answered triumphantly by the cabbage." J. R. Lowell

The IntranetWare utilities help you install and manage IntranetWare. Your job as an administrator is made easier by being familiar with the utilities and their functions. This chapter will focus on the utilities that are new to IntranetWare and will not attempt to cover utilities that were also available from previous versions of NetWare. For information on NetWare 3 utilities also being used in IntranetWare refer to Novell's IntranetWare documentation.

For reference, the IntranetWare utilities are separated into two categories: Server utilities and the workstation utilities.

Server Utilities

Server utilities enable you to change server parameters, monitor the load on the server, and control its allocation of resources. The following list shows all the IntranetWare server utilities. The menu-driven server utilities that are new to IntranetWare are highlighted in bold. All of the server utilities can be run from the IntranetWare server console using the LOAD <utility name> command. The server utilities include both the menu-driven utilities and the server console commands. In this chapter, we will focus mainly on the menu driven utilities. For a complete description of the server console commands, see Appendix B.

- DSMAINT (Included as part of the INSTALL.NLM in IntranetWare)

- DSMERGE

- DSREPAIR

- INSTALL

- MONITOR

- NETSYNC

- PSERVER

- SERVMAN

- **NETBASIC**

Table 2.1 lists and briefly describes all the new server utilities that have been created since NetWare 3.x.

TABLE 2.1 *New Server Utilities*	UTILITY	DESCRIPTION
	ACTIVATE SERVER	Loads the MSEngine for the IntranetWare SFT III system, synchronizes the memory of both SFT III servers, and executes the MSSTART.NCF and MSAUTO.NCF scripts.
	AFPCON	Configures the AFP module on a server.
	ATCON	Monitors the activity of AppleTalk network segments.
	ATCONFIG	Configures NetWare for Macintosh after installation.
	ATPSCON	Configures the ATPS module on a server.
	ATXRP	Works with PSERVER to send a print job to an AppleTalk network printer from a NetWare print queue.
	BRGCON	Views bridge configuration information for a NetWare Server for an OS/2 bridge.
	CD	Monitors and administers a CD-ROM disk used as a read-only NetWare volume.
	CONLOG	Captures console messages generated by modules during system initialization and writes the messages to the default file, SYS:\ETC\CONSOLE.LOG, or to another file.
	DOMAIN	Included with NetWare 4.1 to enable a protected memory domain. This utility is not included with IntranetWare because improved abend recovery options are now offered as part of IntranetWare.
	DHCPCFG	Manages the NetWare Dynamic Host Configuration Protocol (DHCP) service.
	DSMERGE	Renames and merges Novell Directory Services (NDS) trees.
	DSREPAIR	Maintains and repairs the NDS database on a server.

(continued)

TABLE 2.1

New Server Utilities
(continued)

UTILITY	DESCRIPTION
FILTCFG	Defines filters for the Internetwork Packet Exchange (IPX), TCP/IP, and AppleTalk protocols.
HALT	Used at an IntranetWare SFT III server console to bring down an IOEngine on one SFT III server while leaving the other IOEngine running.
HCSS	Views and changes a list of High Capacity Storage System (HCSS) commands and current settings.
HFSCD	Provides support for Apple Computer's HFS format for CD-ROM drives.
HFSCDCON	Configures the HFSCD module on a server.
INETCFG	Defines an internetworking configuration for the IPX, TCP/IP, and AppleTalk protocols, simplifying the process of configuring local area networks using network and routing protocols supported by IntranetWare.
IPXCON	Monitors and troubleshoots IPX routers and network segments.
IPXPING	Sends an IPX ping packet to an IPX server or workstation to determine whether the node is reachable.
MACFILE	Provides Mac OS file support on a NetWare server and helps to maintain the Mac OS desktop database.
MPDRIVER	Enables processors in a multiprocessor server running NetWare Symmetric MultiProcessing (SMP) software.
MSERVER	Loads the IOEngine on each IntranetWare SFT III server.
NETSYNC3	Loads on a NetWare 3.x server to make it part of a NetSync managed network. This utility works in conjunction with an IntranetWare server to synchronize users and passwords.
NETSYNC4	Loads on a NetWare 4.x server to manage the NetWare 3.x servers in a NetSync environment.
NPAMS	Enables the mounting of a CD-ROM disk as a read-only NetWare volume on an IntranetWare SFT III server.
NPRINTER	Enables a printer attached to any server to be a network printer.
NUT	Used with NetWare 3.11 NLMs that require NUT's library.

UTILITY	DESCRIPTION
NWIPCFG	Used to configure and manage the NetWare/IP server software.
NWSNUT	(NLM utility user interface) Provides a library of routines used by certain NLM programs, such as MONITOR or SERVMAN.
PING	Determines whether an IP node on the network is reachable and provides statistics about the route between nodes. PING sends an Internet Control Message Protocol echo request packet to an IP node and notifies you when it receives a reply.
PMMON	Used to monitor CPU usage on a server running the NetWare Server for OS/2 software.
PUPGRADE	Upgrades NetWare 3.1x printing objects, print job configurations, and printer definitions.
REMAPID	Loads on a NetWare 3.x server to handle passwords correctly in a NetSync environment.
RPL	(Remote Program Load) Enables remote booting of IBM PC-compatible diskless workstations that have network boards installed.
RTDM	(Real Time Data Migration) Enables data migration at the server console.
SBACKUP	Used to back up and restore specified NDS and file system data on a server, workstation, or service that you select.
SCHDELAY	Enables you to prioritize and schedule server processes to use less of the server's CPU. This utility also enables you to slow processes when the server is busy.
SERVMAN	Changes SET parameters in the .NCF files. This utility also displays IPX/SPX, device, volume, and network information.
TCPCON	Enables you to monitor activity in the TCP/IP segments of the network.
TIMESYNC	Controls time synchronization on servers running NDS.
TPING	(Trivial PING) Enables you to determine whether an IP node on the network is reachable. TPING requires a hostname parameter.

(continued)

CHAPTER 2
. . . . .
N O V E L L ' S
G U I D E   T O
I N T R A N E T W A R E
N E T W O R K S

UTILITY	DESCRIPTION
UNICON	Used at the server console to manage certain NetWare/IP products installed on a server, such as the NetWare Domain Name System (DNS) and the NetWare/IP Domain SAP/RIP Service (DSS).

Workstation Utilities

Workstation utilities for IntranetWare are generally stored on a IntranetWare server and run from a DOS, Windows, or OS/2 workstation. NetWare provides several graphical utilities to assist you in managing the IntranetWare environment. The NWADMIN.EXE NetWare Administrator utility enables you to manage your NDS tree by creating, moving, deleting, changing, and renaming objects and containers. The DOS equivalent to the graphics NWADMIN utility is the menu-driven NETADMIN utility.

Another utility in IntranetWare is the NetWare User Tool called NWUSER.EXE, which is available in both Windows and OS/2. Using this utility your users can display and modify or add to their workstation's drive mappings, server attachments, print queues, and so on.

Table 2.2 lists all the IntranetWare workstation utilities, which include not only the command line utilities for DOS and OS/2 but also the menu-driven utilities for DOS and Windows. All of these utilities are executed from a workstation that is logged in to the IntranetWare network. Some utilities (for example, CX and LOGIN) only require an attachment to a IntranetWare server. The utilities that are new to NetWare 4 are highlighted in bold.

UTILITY	DESCRIPTION
AUDITCON	Audits file system and NDS events on the network.
ADDICON	Used at the DOS prompt or in login scripts to add icons to a Windows 3.1x Program Manager group.
ATOTAL	Used to total the accounting charges on your network.
CX	Allows you to change your context in the Directory tree.

UTILITY	DESCRIPTION
DOSGEN	Used to boot a DOS workstation from remote boot image files on the server (rather than booting from a local drive).
DS Migrate	A migration utility that is used on a Windows 3.x or Windows 95 workstation to upgrade a NetWare 2.1x or 3.1x server bindery by migrating bindery information to an existing Directory tree.
NCUPDATE	Updates any number of users' NET.CFG files with a new name context after a container object has been moved or renamed.
NDS Manager	Allows you to create, manage, and repair Directory partitions and replicas. This utility includes a superset of the features in the menu-based DSREPAIR utility and replaces the graphical Partition Manager utility available with previous releases of NetWare 4.
NETADMIN	A DOS menu-based utility that provides a subset of the functionality available in the graphical NetWare Administrator utility.
NETUSER	Enables you to perform network tasks, such as setting up print jobs, managing drive mappings and attachments, and sending messages to other network users. This utility replaces the SESSION utility.
NetWare Administrator (NWADMIN)	A graphical utility that enables you to create and manage Directory objects, set up and manage network printing, manage partitions and replicas (via the integrated NDS Manager utility), and manage licensing services (via the integrated NLS Manager utility). NetWare Administrator incorporates all the functions available in FILER, NETADMIN, PARTMGR, and PCONSOLE.
NetWare Application Manager and NetWare Application Launcher	Enable you to manage and access network applications as Directory objects, providing advanced application control and access by network users.
NetWare Directory Browser (Mac OS)	Used at a Mac OS-based workstation to choose objects from the Directory tree.

(continued)

TABLE 2.2

*IntranetWare
Workstation Utilities
(continued)*

UTILITY	DESCRIPTION
NetWare File Migration	A graphical utility that enables you to migrate files from NetWare 3.1x servers to IntranetWare servers. The NetWare File Migration utility should be used after the NetWare 3.1x bindery has been migrated using DS Migrate.
NetWare Login	Used at a Windows 3.1x or Windows 95 workstation to access a NetWare Directory tree or server or to run a login script.
NetWare Print Chooser (Mac OS)	Used at a Mac OS-based workstation to choose and configure a Novell Directory Services printer or print queue.
NetWare Tools (OS/2)	Used to access network resources from an OS/2 workstation. NetWare Tools enable you to perform tasks such as mapping drives, managing printer connections, managing the Directory tree, managing server connections, displaying network users, and sending messages.
NetWare User Tools	Enables users to manage their network environment, including drive mappings, printing, sending broadcasts, and Directory access.
NetWare Volume Mounter (Mac OS)	Used at a Mac OS-based workstation to mount a NetWare volume.
NLIST	Enables you to view information about files, directories, users, groups, volumes, servers, and queues.
NLS Manager	Used to manage NetWare Licensing Services (NLS).
NMENU	Enables you to create a working environment for network users. This newer utility is easier to use and requires less memory than previous versions.
NPATH	Enables you to determine the search sequence that NetWare uses to find message files so you can troubleshoot why a user's workstation can't find a particular file, why the workstation is finding an incorrect version of a file, or why the workstation is displaying a foreign language.
NPRINTER	Enables a printer attached to a DOS, Windows 3.1x, or OS/2 workstation to be a network printer.

UTILITY	DESCRIPTION
NPTWIN95	Enables a printer attached to a Windows 95 workstation to be a network printer.
NWSTART (OS/2)	Starts NetWare Client for OS/2 on an OS/2 workstation if the DISCONNECT ON parameter is included in the NET.CFG file. The DISCONNECT ON parameter prevents NetWare Client for OS/2 from making a network connection when the workstation is started.
NWSTOP (OS/2)	Disconnects NetWare Client for OS/2 without turning off your computer.
NWXTRACT	Used to extract and copy files from the NetWare Installation CD-ROM to the network or to local drives.
PARTMGR	Used to create and manage partitions and replicas of the NDS database. This utility provides a subset of the features available in the graphical NDS Manager utility.
Remote Console (Mac OS)	Used to view and control one or more server consoles from a Mac OS-based workstation.
SETUPDOC	Used at a Windows 3.1x workstation to install and delete document collections and DynaText viewers, configure viewers to access document collections in various ways, and create viewer icons at individual workstations.
UIMPORT	Enables you to import data from an existing database into the NDS database.
/VER	Enables you to view the version number of a utility and the files the utility requires.
WSUPGRADE	Enables you to upgrade the IPX LAN driver on the workstation to the corresponding Open Data-Link Interface (ODI) driver

INSTALLING THE INTRANETWARE SERVER

The first utility that you need to become familiar with is the IntranetWare INSTALL.EXE installation program. This installation program loads the server INSTALL.NLM program. Both of these installation programs are found on the IntranetWare CD-ROM.

However, before you perform the installation of IntranetWare hardware and software you should plan or design the NDS tree. We have found that well-designed trees, including partitions, replicas, and time synchronization design, are much easier to manage and support. The design decisions you make before installation will affect how the users interact with the network resources.

The NDS tree is a representation of the network resources in your company. You should think through how your users will access the network resources and design your NDS tree accordingly. Although you can move the NDS objects after the tree is installed, a good tree design will reduce the number of changes. For more information on NDS tree design, refer to Chapter 5.

Server Hardware Requirements for IntranetWare

The minimum hardware recommendations given in the Novell manuals are the absolute bare minimum to install IntranetWare.

Novell recommends the following minimum hardware:

▸ A PC with a 386 or 486 (SX or DX) processor

▸ 8MB RAM

▸ 90MB of hard disk space on SYS for the Novell Directory Services and utilities

▸ A CD-ROM drive

▸ 3.5-inch drive

▸ One network board

▸ Low-cost VGA monitor and card

▸ Network cabling

 For more exact calculations on RAM requirements for your system you can refer to the memory calculation worksheet in Chapter 11.

NOTE

CONSULTING EXPERIENCE

Our recommendations for the minimum hardware for IntranetWare are:

- ▸ A PC with at least a 486/66 Mhz processor
- ▸ 32MB of RAM
- ▸ 500MB of hard disk space on SYS for IntraNovell Directory Services and utilities
- ▸ 30MB partition for DOS
- ▸ Quad speed CD-ROM drive
- ▸ 3.5-inch drive
- ▸ One network card that is at least a 16-bit card
- ▸ Low-cost VGA monitor and card
- ▸ Network cabling

IntranetWare Simple Installation

The following step-by-step instructions are for installing a new IntranetWare server using the simplified installation option. This section assumes that you intend to boot the NetWare server from the DOS partition and install the software from a CD-ROM.

1 • Create a minimum 30MB DOS partition on the machine that will be the IntranetWare server. Refer to your DOS manual for detailed instructions on creating a DOS partition.

2 • Insert the IntranetWare CD-ROM into a CD-ROM drive installed as a DOS device or a network device. For information on setting up your CD-ROM refer to your Novell or CD-ROM vendor documentation.

3 • Change to the root of the CD-ROM drive and run the IntranetWare INSTALL program by typing **INSTALL** at the root.

4 • Choose NetWare Server Installation from the main menu as shown in Figure 2.1 below.

*NetWare Server Installation
main menu screen*

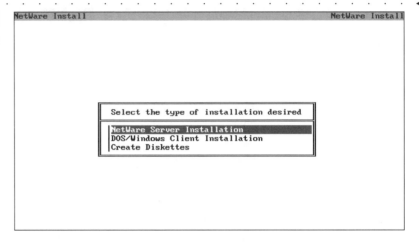

```
NetWare Install                                        NetWare Install




              ┌─────────────────────────────────────────┐
              │  Select the type of installation desired │
              ├─────────────────────────────────────────┤
              │ NetWare Server Installation              │
              │ DOS/Windows Client Installation          │
              │ Create Diskettes                         │
              └─────────────────────────────────────────┘
```

5 • Select Install NetWare Server from the installation screen, and then select Simple Installation of NetWare from the installation screen. This section will review the Simple Installation method.

6 • Choose the server disk drivers. Select a driver that corresponds to the disk controller in your server hardware. If the required driver is not in the list, press <INS>, insert the appropriate diskette that contains the required disk driver, and select the driver.

7 • Select the appropriate parameters for your hardware configuration. You can usually select the hardware parameters from the installation menu unless the hardware settings on your hard disk controller have been changed from the manufacturer's default. If the hardware settings have been changed, please refer to your hard disk controller documentation for more information.

8 • After you have finished selecting your disk driver, select "No" to the prompt "Do you want to select an additional driver?"

9 • Choose the server network or LAN drivers that correspond to the network card in your server and press Enter. Verify the parameters to ensure they match the hardware in your server. You may need to make modifications as necessary.

10 • Install the Server License file by inserting the license diskette that came with the IntranetWare operating system in drive A.

11 • The preliminary file copy for the IntranetWare boot and startup files will now be copied.

12 • Install NDS. You would typically design or plan the NDS tree before installing the server. However, the simplified option automatically makes the decision that all the resources will be installed to a single O=Organization. This means that you do not have to plan the placement of the server in the tree.

Figure 2.2 shows the installation screen option for NDS.

F I G U R E 2.2

Novell Directory Services installation main screen

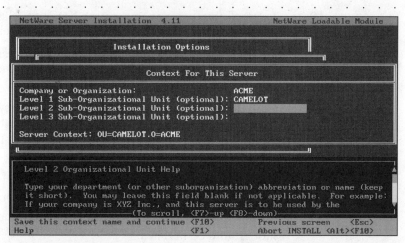

```
NetWare Server Installation  4.11                      NetWare Loadable Module
┌──────────────────────────────────────────────────────────────────────┐
│                         Installation Options                           │
└──────────────────────────────────────────────────────────────────────┘
┌──────────────────────────────────────────────────────────────────────┐
│                       Context For This Server                          │
│  Company or Organization:                      ACME                    │
│  Level 1 Sub-Organizational Unit (optional):  CAMELOT                  │
│  Level 2 Sub-Organizational Unit (optional):                           │
│  Level 3 Sub-Organizational Unit (optional):                           │
│                                                                        │
│  Server Context: OU=CAMELOT.O=ACME                                     │
└──────────────────────────────────────────────────────────────────────┘
┌──────────────────────────────────────────────────────────────────────┐
│  Level 2 Organizational Unit Help                                      │
│                                                                        │
│  Type your department (or other suborganization) abbreviation or name (keep│
│  it short).  You may leave this field blank if not applicable.  For example:│
│  If your company is XYZ Inc., and this server is to be used by the     │
│  ─────────────────────(To scroll, <F7>-up <F8>-down)──────────────────│
│ Save this context name and continue <F10>        Previous screen    <Esc>│
│ Help                                <F1>         Abort INSTALL <Alt><F10>│
└──────────────────────────────────────────────────────────────────────┘
```

If this is the first IntranetWare server on the network and you are installing a new NDS tree, follow the directions in step 13.

If this server is not the first IntranetWare server and an NDS tree already exists, then skip the next steps and move to step 19.

13 • To install the First IntranetWare server, choose the menu item "Is this the first NetWare 4 server?" (You will only see this item if there are no other trees advertising on your network.)

14 • Choose the time zone parameters by using the arrow keys to select the time zone where this server will be installed. You will be presented with another time zone menu for a Daylight Savings Time default.

15 • Next, enter the name of your organization in the field marked Organization Name. You can abbreviate the name as necessary.

16 • Enter the ADMIN password. You'll need to retype the ADMIN password.

17 • NDS installation should now be complete.

18 • Skip to step 22.

19 • To install this server in an existing NDS tree, choose the tree name from the list of NDS trees. If you have only one NDS tree installed on the network, it will be the only name that appears. If no NDS trees are displayed, check the network connection.

20 • Next, choose a time zone by using the arrow keys to select the time zone where this server will be installed. You will then be presented with another time menu to accept Daylight Savings Time. You can accept the default here.

21 • Enter the ADMIN password. This is the password assigned to the user ADMIN that is created when the first server is installed into this tree. NDS should now be installed.

22 • When the NDS installation is complete, the main IntranetWare files will be copied. This procedure will last approximately 15 to 25 minutes depending on the server hardware you are running on.

23 • Next, you have the option to install other options. Please refer to the appropriate documentation for more details.

24 • Exit to the server console and restart the server by typing **DOWN** and then **RESTART SERVER**. Your installation of IntranetWare is now complete.

NOTE

You can use the Custom Installation method to control the server setup and parameters for the new IntranetWare server. The Custom Installation method gives you the most flexibility to change the defaults set by the installation program. For example, you can change the volume block setting before placing the server into the NDS tree. For more information about a custom installation, refer to your Novell documentation.

For more information about migration strategies using INSTALL and MIGRATE.EXE, refer to Chapter 16.

NETWARE ADMINISTRATION (NWADMIN.EXE)

IntranetWare consolidates many of the NDS administrative functions into a graphical, easy-to-use new 32-bit utility that greatly reduces the time you spend administering the network. The NetWare Administration utility, or NWADMIN.EXE, is a Windows-based utility that enables you to make changes to the Directory as easy as a point and click of a mouse. This utility is used by system administrators to manage objects in the NDS tree. Figure 2.3 shows the main screen or window for the 32-bit NWADMIN utility.

Because the NWADMIN.EXE is a Windows-based utility it enables you to graphically manage all objects and properties in the NDS tree. The NDS tree can be created, changed, and browsed by selecting or clicking on the individual NDS objects.

The NWADMIN utility is executed at a client workstation from Windows. With this utility you can view, create, move, delete, and assign rights to the individual objects in the NDS tree. Typically, the individuals using NWADMIN will be system administrators with Supervisor rights over their container objects.

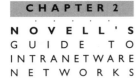
FIGURE 2.3

The main screen or window for the 32-bit NWADMIN utility

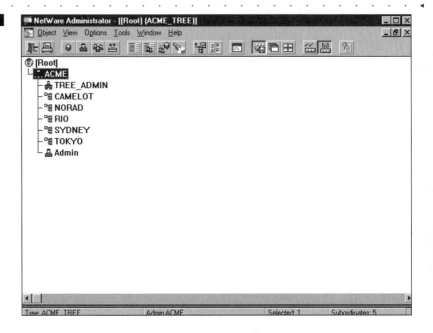

You may limit access to the NWADMIN utility by moving the utility from the SYS:\PUBLIC subdirectory to another subdirectory that only the administrators have access to. Most of your users will not need to use this utility.

TIP

In order to execute this utility, you must have the NetWare DOS Requester, VLMs, or Client32 software running on the workstation. Make sure that you have loaded the appropriate client software or the NWADMIN utility will not load. (For more information on client software, see Chapter 18.) The 32-bit NWADMIN works with Novell's Client32 for DOS/Windows and Windows 95.

You can use this utility to organize, manage, and browse the NDS objects that are contained in the tree by performing any of the following functions:

▶ Create and manage NDS objects

▶ Assign rights in the NDS tree and file system

▶ Set up the print services

▸ Display or browse object and property information stored in the tree

▸ Set up and manage the NDS partitions and replicas through NDS Manager as a snap-in utility

Using NWADMIN to Create and Manage NDS Objects

You can use NWADMIN to create, delete, modify, rename, move, and get detailed information about NDS objects. In order to create an NDS object you must first be logged in to the tree as an individual who has rights, such as the ADMIN (or other administrative) user at the container where you want to create the object.

For example, in order to create the user CN=GWASHINGTON in the container OU=RIO.O=ACME, move to that container in the tree and select the Create option from the Object menu. Figure 2.4 illustrates the New Object screen that is displayed after the Create option is selected.

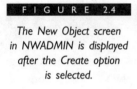

FIGURE 2.4

The New Object screen in NWADMIN is displayed after the Create option is selected.

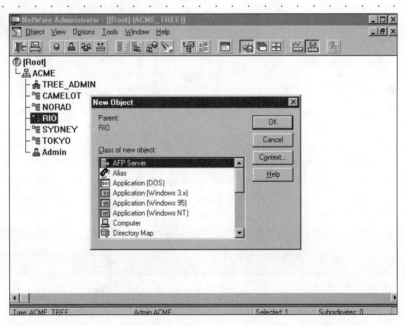

You can then select the User object from the list of objects, and you will be presented with the Create User screen to fill out. Figure 2.5 displays the Create User option for the user GWASHINGTON in the container RIO.ACME.

FIGURE 2.5

*The Detail
information screen in
NWADMIN for the user
GWASHINGTON.RIO.ACME*

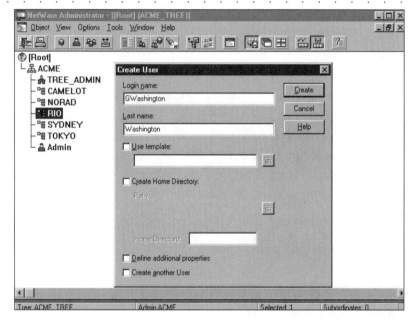

You can also use this utility to delete or rename any of the NDS objects. You can also move a selected NDS object from one location in the NDS tree to another. Figure 2.6 shows how the move operation for ALINCOLN might look. In this figure we are moving CN=ALINCOLN from the ADMIN.RIO.ACME to AUDIT.ADMIN.RIO.O=ACME.

Using NWADMIN to Assign Rights to the NDS Tree and File System

This object-oriented look of the utility enables you to make the assignment of rights much easier. Rights to users, groups, containers (OUs), files, and directories can be accomplished by simply dragging and dropping one icon onto the other. For example, when a user changes departments, you simply drag and drop the user to give that user the appropriate rights or move the user with the move command. Figure 2.7 shows the operation of dragging and dropping one object onto another to give it rights.

FIGURE 2.6

The NWADMIN screen for moving CN=ALINCOLN from the ADMIN.RIO.ACME to AUDIT.ADMIN.RIO.ACME

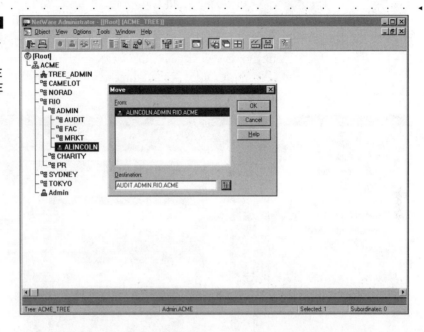

FIGURE 2.7

The NWADMIN screens associated with the operation of dragging and dropping one object onto another to give it rights

The operation of dragging and dropping is also used to assign rights to the files and directories in the file system. You can also enter into the Details screen for the object and assign file and directories rights in that screen. For example, in Figure 2.8, the NDS group object called CN=COMMON in the container ADMIN.RIO.ACME is granted rights to the COMMON subdirectory stored on the server CAM-SRV1.

FIGURE 2.8

The NDS group object called CN=COMMON in the container ADMIN.RIO.ACME is granted rights to the COMMON subdirectory stored on the server CAM-SRV1.

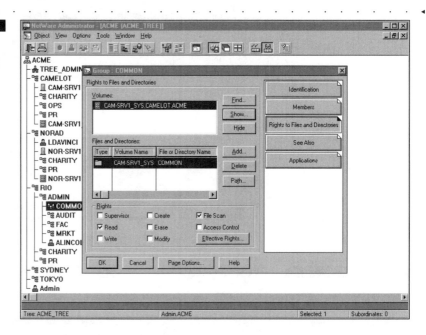

Adding file system directory or object rights in previous versions of NetWare used to require a multilayered menu utility and a tedious process of adding each user. Now all that is needed to add file system directory rights is to drag the user's icon over to the specific directory or object, and NetWare will simply ask you for a confirmation.

Because all the network resources in the NDS tree are represented by NWADMIN, managing multiple IntranetWare servers is greatly simplified. Instead of managing a single server, you can focus your management efforts on a group of servers.

For more information on assigning rights, refer to Chapter 13.

Using NWADMIN to Set Up the Print Services

The NWADMIN utility can also be used to set up and manage the printing environment. NWADMIN is a functional equivalent to the PCONSOLE utility in DOS. For example, in order to create a printer, select the desired container where the printer will be located. Select Create from the Option menu and then select Printer as the object to create. Figure 2.9 shows the dialog box that appears.

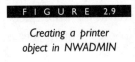

F I G U R E 2.9

*Creating a printer
object in NWADMIN*

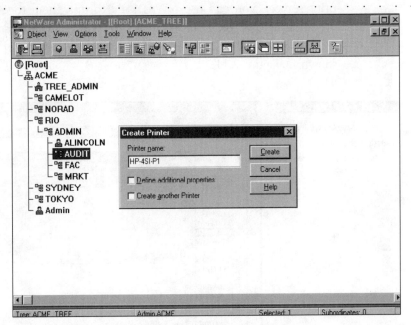

From the screen shown above, you can click on the Define Additional Properties button to define characteristics of the printer. If you select the additional properties, the Printer dialog box appears.

In order to create a print queue and print server object, you follow the same steps that you used to create the printer object. However, you select Print Queue and Print Server as the objects to create instead of Printer. The dialog boxes that are presented are very similar.

NOTE

For the print queues, IntranetWare creates a subdirectory immediately under the root of the volume called QUEUES. Under this subdirectory, the operating system creates a numbered directory that matches the ID number of the queue. If the directory is created remotely it does not use the ID of the queue object at all.

Once all the corresponding print objects are created (printer, print queue, and print server), you can use NWADMIN to link them together. You perform this operation in a two-step process. First, you assign the print server to the print queue as shown in Figure 2.10. Second, you assign the printer to the print queue as shown in Figure 2.11.

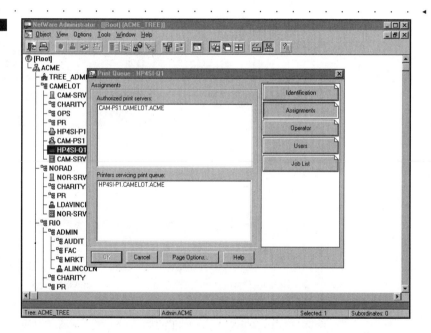

F I G U R E   2.10

Using NWADMIN to assign the print server to the print queue

You can check the status of the printing setup using a new feature of IntranetWare, which displays the print layout. This feature is called Print Layout Page and is illustrated in Figure 2.12.

F I G U R E   2.11

*Using NWADMIN to
assign the printer to
the print queue*

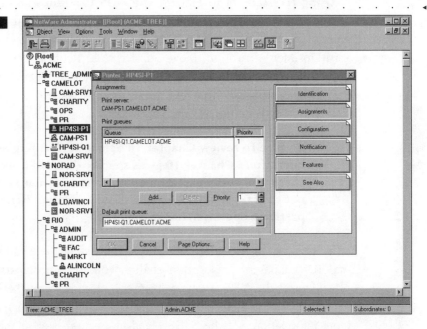

F I G U R E   2.12

*Using NWADMIN
to display the
Print Layout page*

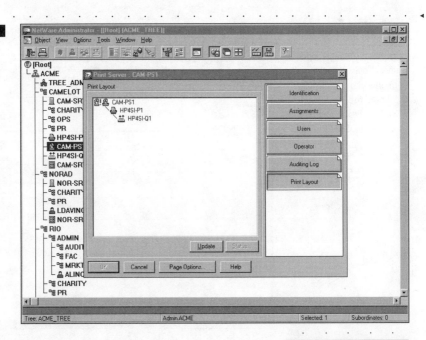

Using NWADMIN to Manage the NDS Partitions and Replicas

In order to manage your NDS partitions and replicas properly, there are several types of operations that you need to be able to perform. These operations are Create Partition, Merge Partition, Move Subtree, Add Replica, Remove Replicas, Change Replica Type, and Abort Partition. You can also delete a server object after removing the replicas from the tree. All these operations can be performed using the NWADMIN.EXE utility and the new NDS Manager utility.

 NOTE

Be sure to review Chapter 10 before performing any partitioning operations. Chapter 10 gives specific detailed instructions on how to check and verify partition operations and their states. It is important not to start an additional partition operation before the first partition operation has completed.

In the Tools menu of the NWADMIN.EXE utility, there can be an item known as the NDS Manager. This option enables you to control partitioning and replica placement of the NDS database. Figure 2.13 shows you the NDS Manager utility that can be run as a stand-alone under Tools in the main menu of NWADMIN. For more information, see the "NDS Manager" section later in this chapter.

F I G U R E 2.13

The NDS Manager option under Tools in the main menu of NWADMIN controls the partitioning and replica placement of the NDS database.

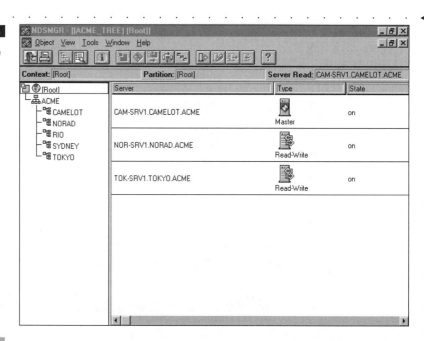

CHAPTER 2
. . . . .
INSTALLATION
AND MANAGEMENT
UTILITIES FOR
INTRANETWARE

In Figure 2.14 you can see that the partitions are denoted with a small box icon to the left of the OU container object. In this example, the OU=NORAD and OU=CAMELOT are partitions.

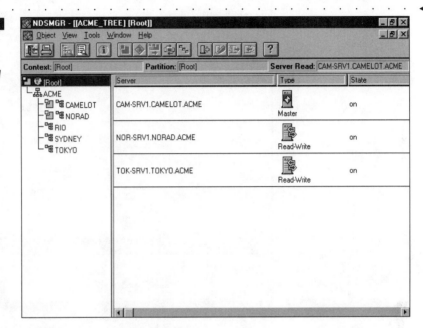

FIGURE 2.14

Using the NDS Manager in NWADMIN, you can see the partitions denoted with a small box icon to the left of the OU container. OU=NORAD and OU=CAMELOT are shown as partitions.

Using NWADMIN to Browse the NDS Tree

The NetWare Administration utility runs as a multiple-document interface application, which enables you to display up to nine different browsing windows at one time. The primary window illustrated in Figure 2.15 provides a background for viewing one or more secondary windows. The secondary windows support that browsing feature.

The browsers in NWADMIN are the secondary windows that appear in the utility. To open or enable a browser window, you need to select a container object from the primary window, and then select the Browse option from the Tools menu.

The new window is the browser window that displays the NDS objects from the selected container or current context. You can then select objects, directories, and files to perform the administrative tasks. Figure 2.16 shows an example of a browser window for the objects in the ACME tree.

FIGURE 2.15

The main screen or window
for the NWADMIN utility

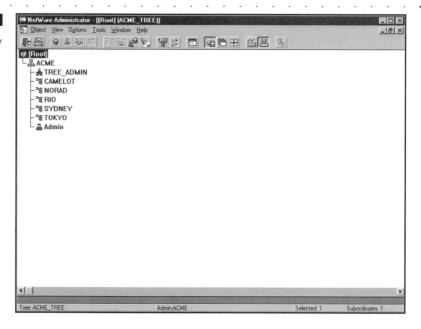

FIGURE 2.16

A browser window in
NWADMIN for the
ACME tree

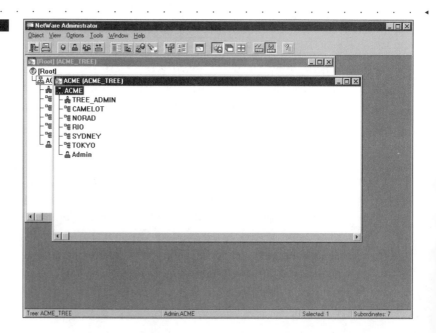

You can open up to nine browser windows, which enable you to view the individual container objects. To view multiple browser windows at the same time, select the Tile option from the Windows menu. Figure 2.17 shows three browser windows tiled for the objects in the ACME tree.

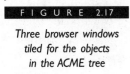

FIGURE 2.17

Three browser windows tiled for the objects in the ACME tree

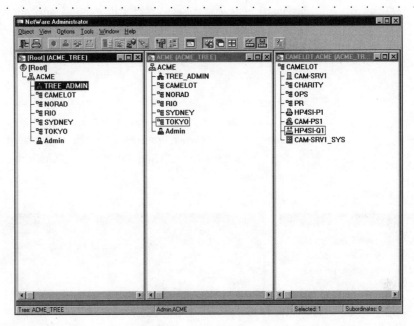

The title for each of the browser windows displays the context of the container where the browse windows is set. These will help you remember and organize the browser window on your screen.

Browse the NDS Tree Using the Container Objects in NWADMIN You can browse the NDS tree by walking through the container objects. The container objects can be browsed by expanding or opening them and displaying their contents. There are several ways to expand the container objects within the NWADMIN utility:

▸ Double-click on the object. By double-clicking on the object the container will expand to show its contents and the subordinate objects. If the container is expanded, you can collapse the container by double-clicking again.

▸ Select a container object in the tree and choose the Expand option from the View menu to expand the contents of the container. You can collapse the container using the Collapse option from the same menu.

▸ Select a container object and press the "+" key on the keypad of the keyboard. The container object will expand and show its contents. (The "+" key above the "=" equal sign on your keyboard will not work for this operation.) You can collapse the container by pressing the "-" key on the keypad.

▸ Select a container object and press the right mouse button (or right click). Select the Browse option from the short menu that appears. This option launches a new browser window with the contents of the container object. Figure 2.18 shows the short menu that appears after you press the right mouse button.

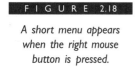

F I G U R E   2.18

A short menu appears when the right mouse button is pressed.

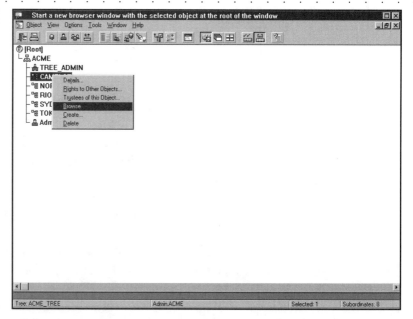

Figure 2.19 illustrates several container objects that have been expanded for the ACME tree.

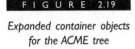

FIGURE 2.19

Expanded container objects for the ACME tree

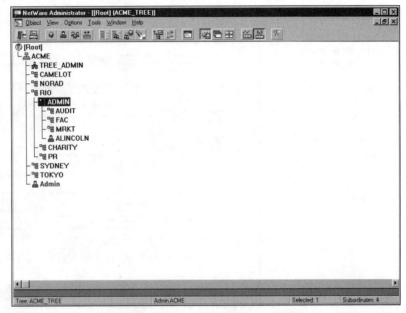

Browsing the Properties in NWADMIN   You can browse the properties for the individual object by opening the Object dialog box or selecting the Details option from the Object menu. You can open the Object dialog box using any of the following methods:

▶ Double-click on the object.

▶ Select the object and then choose the Details option from the Object menu.

▶ Select the object and press the right mouse button. Choose Details from the short menu that appears.

The Object dialog box is organized or divided into pages that you select individually. The "Identification" page is the default or first page shown. Figure 2.20 shows the dialog screen for an object in the ACME tree.

FIGURE 2.20

The object or Details dialog screen for an object in the ACME tree

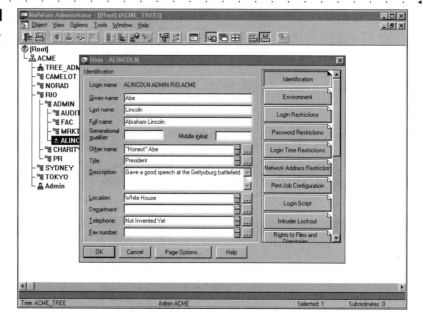

You can browse the specific information for an object by selecting the corresponding page. The page icons are located on the right-hand side of the Object dialog box and are specific to the type of object being displayed.

TIP

The pages in the Object dialog box are all part of the same dialog box. When you select a different page you are still in the same dialog box. If you press OK or Cancel on any page you are affecting the entire dialog box, not just the individual page. Pressing OK will save modifications to all the pages and pressing Cancel will exit the dialog box without saving any changes to any page. In order to move between pages of the dialog box, select the desired page.

Searching for Objects and Properties in NWADMIN   You can find object and property information in the NDS tree using the Search feature. You can perform this function without having to expand each of the container objects. The search operation will check each of the objects in the tree unless you restrict or narrow the search criteria.

For example, in Figure 2.21, the search criteria is set up to find all the users in the ACME tree that have the department property equal to OU=CHARITY.

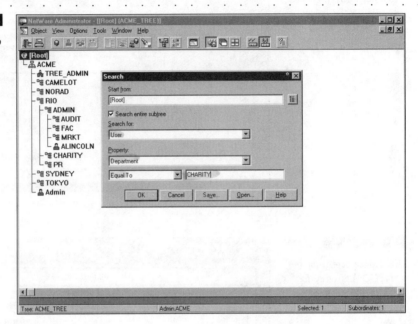

NETADMIN UTILITY

The NETADMIN.EXE is a DOS-based utility that enables you to manage NDS objects and properties in the Directory tree. With this utility you can view, create, move, delete, and assign rights to the individual objects in the NDS tree. This utility, like the NWADMIN utility, is intended to be used by the system administrators with access rights over their container objects. Figure 2.22 shows the main screen of the NETADMIN utility.

The NETADMIN utility has a browse screen that enables you to navigate the Directory tree and manage the objects. Figure 2.23 shows the browse screen for the NETADMIN utility for the ACME tree.

In order to browse down the NDS tree, you select the container objects and press Enter. The container objects are marked with a "+" character in front of the name. Objects without a "+" sign are leaf objects and do not contain other objects.

In Figure 2.23 shown above, the CAMELOT, NORAD, RIO, SYNDEY, and TOKYO objects are the container objects. The user ADMIN is a leaf object.

FIGURE 2.22

The main screen of the
NETADMIN utility

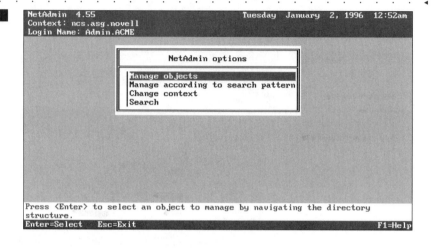

FIGURE 2.23

The browse screen for the
NETADMIN utility for
the ACME tree

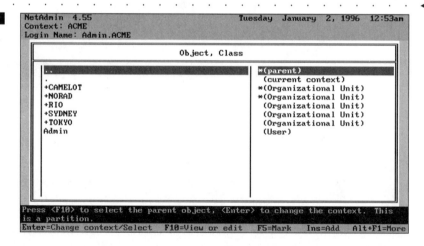

To browse up the NDS tree to the parent container, select the ".." or parent marker. To view or edit the properties of the current container object select the "." or current container marker.

NDS MANAGER

With IntranetWare, the NDS Manager utility replaces the Partition Manager utility that was available from the NetWare Administrator Tools menu in previous versions of NetWare 4.

NDS Manager is a graphical hierarchical browser that offers many new features that were not available in Partition Manager. For example, NDS Manager has the following capabilities:

▸ Can run as a stand-alone application or as an integrated part of the NetWare Administrator utility (NWADMIN)

▸ Provides partitioning and replication capabilities for Novell's Directory Services

▸ Provides the capability to repair the Directory from a client workstation running NDS Manager

▸ Includes a version update capability so that any or all NetWare servers in a network can be updated to a newer version of the DS.NLM file

▸ Provides context-sensitive help for synchronization errors detected by the Partition Continuity option

As shown in Figure 2.23-A, NDS manager is part of Novell's IntranetWare product. This utility can be run as a stand-alone utility or snapped into the NWADMIN utility. It takes some of the best features found in DSREPAIR and Partition Manager and adds a graphical interface for easy operation.

Most operations can be performed from either the hierarchical Tree view or the list of Partitions and Servers. They are represented on the button bar by the icons so you can toggle between views of partitions and servers and the NDS trees.

The other view from which you work in NDS Manager is the Partition Continuity view, which allows you to view the condition of your tree and perform repair operations if necessary. Before using NDS Manager, you should access these views and become familiar with their features and options. An example of a server and partition view is shown in Figure 2.23-B.

FIGURE 2.23-A

NDS Manager can be run as a stand-alone utility or snapped into the NWADMIN Tools menu as a replacement for the NWADMIN Partition Manager utility.

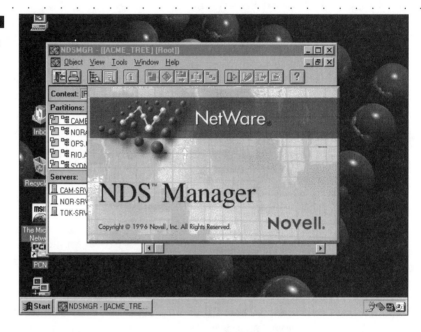

FIGURE 2.23-B

A view of your NDS tree can be seen from two vantage points: partitions and the servers they are stored on or servers and the partitions they contain.

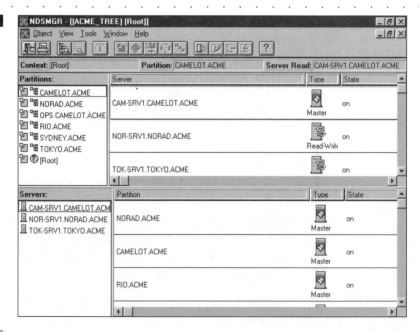

As shown in Figure 2.23-C, after you select a particular partition you can right click on the mouse or select the icons from the tool bar to pull up a series of options, which include:

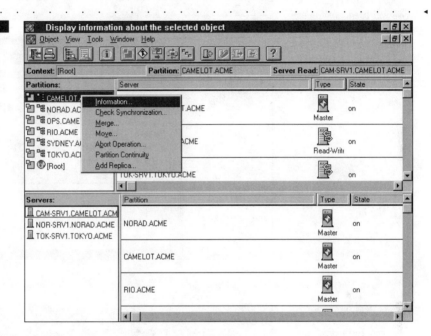

▸ **Information:** Displays information about the partition such as where the master replica is stored, the number of read/write replicas, and the time of the last replica synchronization. See Figure 2.23-D.

▸ **Check Synchronization:** Reads the partition synchronization status of the selected partition or partition list. See Figure 2.23-E.

▸ **Merge:** Merges the selected partition with its parent partition.

▸ **Move:** Moves the selected container (partition) to a new context that you specify.

▸ **Abort Operation:** Attempts to abort a partition operation that has been initiated on the selected partition.

Selecting the information option on a partition will give you useful information such as the last time the partition was synchronized.

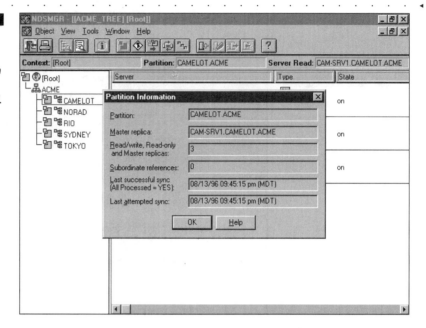

You can easily check the synchronization status of a partition before starting any type of partitioning operation.

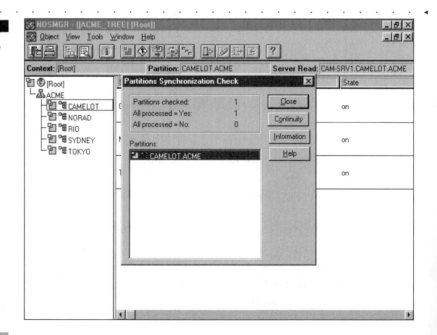

▸ **Partition Continuity:** Helps you identify whether any of a partition's replicas are experiencing synchronization errors. This operation is also known as "walking the replica ring" as shown in Figure 2.23-F.

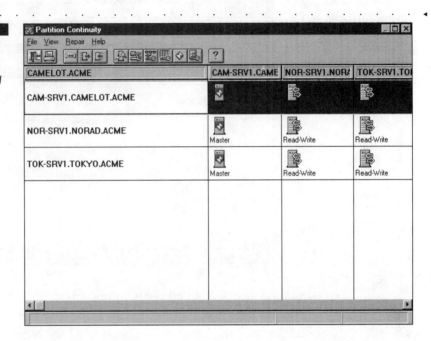

FIGURE 2.23-F

The Partition Continuity Check will show you the state of partitions stored on servers in your tree.

After you run the Partition Continuity option you will be presented with the results of the check, mainly if all servers were able to "talk" in the replica list. This screen also provides another menu bar with the REPAIR option. Before running DSREPAIR the utility will prompt you as shown in Figure 2.23-G.

The REPAIR menu option allows you to perform the following DSREPAIR functions on your servers:

▸ **Synchronize Immediately:** Performs an immediate synchronization on every server that contains a copy of the replica selected for synchronization.

▸ **Receive Updates:** Deletes the Directory data of a replica and replaces it with data from the master replica of the partition. Choose this option if the replica is corrupted or has not received updated data for an extended period of time.

*The REPAIR option runs
DSREPAIR on the local
server's NDS database
and issues a warning before
performing the operation.*

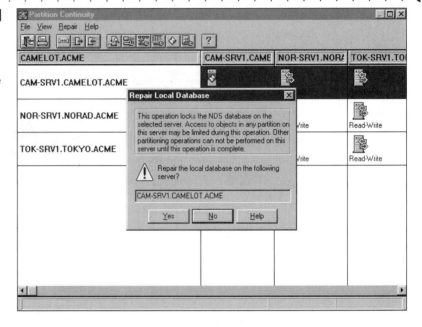

▸ **Send Updates:** Sends updates from one replica to another on the partition. When you send updates from a replica, the Directory data in that replica is broadcast from the server it resides on to all the other replicas of the partition, including the master replica. The other replicas combine the new information you sent with the data they already have. If the replicas have data besides the data sent to them, they will retain that data.

▸ **Information:** Provides information on partitions, replicas, servers, and synchronization errors.

▸ **Verify Remote Server IDs:** This operation verifies:

  ▸ The remote server's name

  ▸ The remote server's ID in a server's database

▸ The remote ID, which is this server's ID as it is found in the remote server's database

If any errors are detected, this operation will attempt to repair the server IDs.

▸ **Repair Replica:** Repairs a replica on a server. Repairing a replica consists of checking the replica ring information on each server that contains a replica and validating the remote ID. This operation repairs only the chosen replica on the server you select.

▸ **Repair Network Addresses:** Repairs network addresses to ensure that the servers in your network are broadcasting correct addresses.

▸ **Repair Local Database:** Repairs local database records when your NDS database is corrupted. This operation resolves inconsistencies in the local Directory Database so that it can be opened and accessed.

▸ **Assign New Master:** A repair feature that should be used only when the current master replica is corrupted, when the server on which the current master replica resides has lost data integrity, and when the server on which the current master replica resides has had an unrecoverable hard disk failure. Do not use this feature to change a replica type.

▸ **Remove Server:** Removes a server from an NDS tree.

WARNING

Misuse of the Remove Server operation can cause irrevocable damage to the NDS tree. If a server that is no longer in the tree appears in the replica ring, instead of using the Remove Server operation, perform a Delete Server operation to delete the server's object.

► **Repair Volume Objects:** Checks the association of all the mounted volumes with Volume objects in the Directory. If the volume is not associated with a Volume object, this operation looks for one in the context of the NetWare Server object. If the volume is found, the Volume object is attached to the volume. If the volume is not found, this operation attempts to create one.

► **Abort Operation:** Attempts to abort a partition operation that has been initiated on the selected partition.

As an administrator, NDS Manager allows you to perform the operations indicated above from a single utility. After running DSREPAIR you can view the error log for any synchronization errors or other errors that may have occurred during the repair. An example of the log file is shown in Figure 2.23-H.

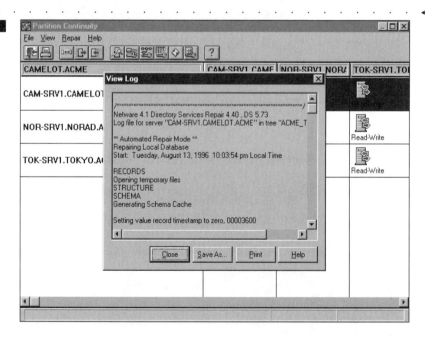

F I G U R E 2.23-H

After running DSREPAIR from the NDS Manager utility you can view the error log file generated by DSREPAIR.

One other useful feature of the NDS Manager utility checks versions of the DS.NLM and then updates the server with a later version if necessary. An example of viewing the DS.NLM version is shown in Figure 2.23-I.

F I G U R E 2.23-I

Prior to updating your servers to a newer version of the DS.NLM you can check the version number through NDS Manager.

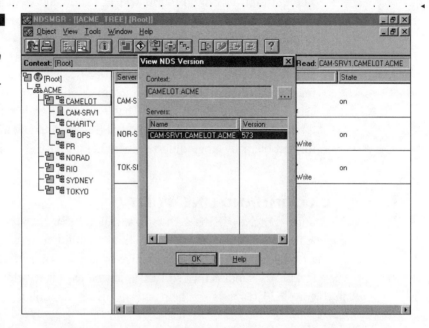

GENERAL RECOMMENDATIONS FOR USING NDS MANAGER

Keep in mind the following guidelines when using the NDS Manager utility:

▸ The NetWare Client32 for DOS/Windows or Windows 95 is recommended when running NDS Manager.

▸ NDS Manager fully supports NDS v4.89a and above as well as DSREPAIR.NLM v4.31 and above.

▸ NDS Manager does not support DSREPAIR.NLM versions prior to 4.31.

▸ Partition and Replica Information will not display information for some fields if the information for the partition or replica is read from a server running NDS versions prior to 4.89a.

▶ The Partition Continuity Grid will not show any synchronization errors (even if they exist) for replicas stored on servers running NDS versions prior to 4.89a.

▶ When running NDS Manager on VLMs, be aware that VLMs default to a maximum of eight simultaneous connections to servers. This default can cause "Unable to attach" and "Unable to read" error messages (often in the form of statuses -321, x8801, and x8809) in NDS Manager. You can avoid this problem by upgrading to Client32.

CX COMMAND LINE UTILITY

Change conteXt (CX) is a DOS-based utility that helps the user set the current context in the NDS tree. You can only use this utility to view the container hierarchy and leaf objects in the tree or to change to a new context. This utility is placed in the SYS:LOGIN subdirectory so that it can be executed before the users are logged in. Figure 2.24 displays the help screen for the CX utility

F I G U R E   2.24

The CX help screen shows the options available to browse the NDS tree.

```
CX                          Options Help                         4.20

Syntax:  CX [new context ¦ /VER] [/R] [/[T ¦ CONT] [/A]] [/C] [/?]

To:                                                Use:
  View all container objects below the              /T
    current or specified context.
  View container objects at the current             /CONT
    or specified level.
  Modify /T or /CONT to view All objects            /A
    at or below the context
  Change context or view objects relative to root   /R
  Display version information                        /VER
  Scroll continuously                                /C

For example, to:                         Type:
  View directory tree below the current context   CX /T
  View containers within a specific context       CX .O=Novell /CONT

>>> Enter = More    C = Continuous    Esc = Cancel
```

This section will not discuss how to set the context using CX, but will focus instead on the options available to you to browse the NDS tree. The browse options that display the tree information are:

▶ /CONT — Lists just the container objects at the current context.

CHAPTER 2
. . . . .
INSTALLATION
AND MANAGEMENT
UTILITIES FOR
INTRANETWARE

▸ /R — Lists objects relative to the [ROOT] object. This option also can change the context to the [ROOT].

▸ /T — Lists all the container objects below the current context.

▸ /A — Lists all the objects, including all the leaf objects.

Figure 2.25 displays the output of the CX /CONT command for the ACME tree when the current context is set to [ROOT].

F I G U R E 2.25

The output of the CX /
CONT command for
the ACME tree when
the current context is
set to [ROOT]

```
*** Directory Services Mapping ***

ACME
   ┣CAMELOT
   ┣NORAD
   ┣SYDNEY
   ┣RIO
   ┗TOKYO
C:\>
```

F I G U R E 2.26

The output of the CX /T
command for the ACME
tree when the current
context is set to [ROOT]

```
*** Directory Services Mapping ***

[ROOT]
  ┗ACME
      ┣CAMELOT
      ┃   ┣CHARITY
      ┃   ┣PR
      ┃   ┗OPS
      ┃       ┣FIN
      ┃       ┗DIST
      ┣NORAD
      ┃   ┣CHARITY
      ┃   ┣PR
      ┃   ┗LABS
      ┃       ┣R&D
      ┃       ┗WHI
      ┣SYDNEY
      ┃   ┣CHARITY
      ┃   ┣PR
      ┃   ┗HR
      ┃       ┣MEDICAL
      ┃       ┣FOOD
      ┃       ┗SHELTER
      ┣RIO
>>> Enter = More   C = Continuous   Esc = Cancel
```

Figure 2.26 displays the output of the CX /T command for the ACME tree when the current context is set to [ROOT].

NLIST UTILITY

The NLIST utility in IntranetWare enables you to browse the information in the NDS tree and replaces a number of NetWare 3 utilities, including USERLIST, SLIST, SECURITY, and others.

The NLIST utility enables any user to search and view information for most of the NDS objects such as the following:

- ▸ AFP Server

- ▸ Alias

- ▸ Computer

- ▸ Directory Map

- ▸ Group

- ▸ Organization

- ▸ Organizational Unit

- ▸ Print Queue

- ▸ Print Server

- ▸ Printer

- ▸ Profile

- ▸ Server

- ▸ User

- ▸ Volume

In order to search the Directory tree there are several options. Figure 2.27 displays one of the help screens for NLIST, which lists the display options for the objects in the tree.

NLIST help screen that lists the display options for the objects in the tree

```
NLIST                    General Help Screen                    4.19

Purpose: View information about users, groups and other objects.
Syntax: NLIST class type [property search option]
                         [display option] [basic option]

For details on:                            Type:
  Property search options                  NLIST /? R
  Properties                               NLIST /? P
  Display options                          NLIST /? D
  Basic options                            NLIST /? B
  All Help Screens                         NLIST /? ALL

Class types:
  * (all class types)      User            Print Queue
  Server                   Group           Printer
  Computer                 Volume          Print Server
  Directory Map            Profile         Organization
  Organizational Unit      Alias           AFP Server

Enclose in double quotes all class types or properties containing spaces.

C:\>
```

The proper syntax must be entered for the NLIST utility to execute. The syntax is as follows:

```
NLIST [object type] [=object name] [/options]
```

Examples:

▶ NLIST User /R /S — Searches for all user objects in the tree starting at [ROOT]

▶ NLIST Server /B — Displays all the servers using bindery calls just like the NetWare 3 SLIST command

You can also use NLIST to search for and display information about the properties for each of the objects. You will use the WHERE and SHOW options in the command line to accomplish the browsing. For example, the syntax for the WHERE and SHOW options for an object is as follows:

```
NLIST object class [=object name] [WHERE

[property]operator [value]]
```

CHAPTER 2
. . . .
NOVELL'S
GUIDE TO
INTRANETWARE
NETWORKS

```
[SHOW property[,property . . .]]
```

Examples:

▸ NLIST user=AEINSTEIN /D — Displays all properties for the user AEINSTEIN in the ACME tree

▸ NLIST user WHERE "Security Equal To" EQ CAMELOT_ADMIN — Shows all the users that are security equivalent to the CAMELOT_ADMIN Organizational Role relative to the current context in the ACME tree

NWUSER AND NETUSER UTILITIES

The Windows-based NWUSER and the DOS-based NETUSER utilities enable the users to manage their own network environment and browse the NDS tree and its resources. Using these utilities the users can change their own context, manage server connections, manage the drive and search mappings, change passwords, change login scripts, capture printers and print queues, and send messages. Each user that has loaded at least the VLM client software will have installed these utilities automatically on his workstation.

Figure 2.28 illustrates the main screen for the Windows-based NWUSER utility.

FIGURE 2.28

The main screen for NWUSER utility

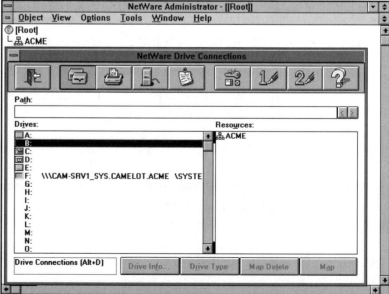

NETWARE APPLICATION LAUNCHER

The NetWare Application Launcher (NAL) manages application objects at a user's desktop. The product currently consists of two components: an administration tool that snaps-in to NWADMIN and client software known as the NetWare Application Launcher.

The NAL enables users to run applications that were previously configured by a system administrator, and whose setup information is stored as an application object in the NetWare Directory tree. NAL displays icons for all available applications in a Windows group, and users double-click an icon to launch particular applications. Users do not need to worry about drive mappings, paths, or rights; the administrator can manage the application launcher on a Container, Group, or User object level through the snap-in utility. This utility greatly simplifies the need for common applications and allows the user desktop configuration greater flexibility.

By creating application objects for your applications, you can manage which applications appear on the user's desktop. Using application objects simplifies the administrative tasks of assigning rights, customizing login scripts, and providing application support. Using NetWare Administrator, applications for an entire organization, group, or user can be centrally administered. By configuring executables as application objects, your administrators can perform upgrades and control versions of applications on the network very easily.

Assigning an application object to a container, group, or user object makes the application available to users who are trustees of the container, group, or user object. When launching the application, all network drive mappings, printer ports, and additional parameters are automatically configured. When the user exits the application, drive mappings and printer ports are returned to their original configuration.

Because application objects configure their required resources when launched, system and user scripts can be reduced. Application information and support contacts can be assigned to each application object. The application information is also available to users on their desktops.

For example, the following scenario illustrates the benefits of using the NetWare Application Launcher utility. A NetWare administrator of a company with 300 employees installs a new application and wants to distribute it to the employees who need it. The application is a spreadsheet program that performs specific business macros unique to the company. The spreadsheet application requires no special drive mappings, printer ports, environment variables, or user configuration files.

Solution #1 Using Local Computer Resources

The administrator installs the application on each user's hard drive. This option is the most time-intensive; it requires the administrator to install, upgrade, and support the application and computer hardware at each user's location.

Solution #2 Using the Network

The administrator installs the spreadsheet on a NetWare server called APPS in the SYS:\APPS\SPREDSHT\V1.0 directory. Using the NWADMIN utility, the administrator creates a group object called SPDSHEET GROUP. File system rights are granted to the group in the directory where the application is installed. Users requiring access to the application are made members of SPDSHEET GROUP. Though the application is now available, an icon representing the spreadsheet application may not appear on the desktop unless it is manually configured for each desktop. The administrator must either communicate that the application is available and explain where the application is located and how to set it up, or physically visit each desktop. This is a better solution but not the best because there are still a few problems:

- ► Even though the application icon may appear on the user's workstation, the application actually resides on the network. If the user is not logged in when he double-clicks an application icon, an error message will be displayed stating that the path is invalid.

- ► The user may delete the icon, then need the administrator's help to restore it.

- ► The icon references the executable file (quattro.exe) in the \\PRODUCTS\SYS\APPS\SPDSHEET\V1.0 directory. To move or rename the executable, or to upgrade to version 2.0 without removing version 1.0, the path must be changed at each workstation.

Solution #3 Using the NetWare Application Launcher

The administrator installs the spreadsheet application on server APPS in the SYS\APPS\SPDSHEET\V1.0 directory, creates the SPDSHEET group, and adds as a member of the group each user who needs the application. Using NWADMIN, the administrator creates an application object called SPDSHEET. The new object contains the path to the program file and other information such as command-line parameters, the working directory, and a description of the application's purpose. The administrator associates the SPDSHEET application object with the SPDSHEET group. The SPDSHEET application icon appears on each user's workstation automatically. No setup is required at the user's workstation. The application may now be launched by double-clicking the icon.

Other benefits of the NetWare Application Launcher are listed below:

▶ If the user is not logged in to the network, the icon is not displayed.

▶ The user cannot delete the icon or change any of the path information.

▶ If the administrator wants to move or rename the executable file, only the SPDSHEET object must be modified, and the user is unaware of any changes.

▶ The upgrade can be installed anywhere (that is, \\PRODUCTS\SYS\APPS\SPDSHEET\V2.0).Using the NWADMIN utility, version 1.0 can be replaced by modifying the path to the new application executable.

▶ Both versions can be available by creating a new SPRDSHT2 application object and associating it with SPDSHEET group.

For a detailed discussion regarding installation and use of the NetWare Application Manager and Application Launcher, see Chapter 20.

PARTMGR UTILITY

The Partition Manager utility known as PARTMGR.EXE enables you to manage your NDS partitions and replicas. There are several types of operations that you need to understand and use. The NDS partition and replica operations are Create Partition, Merge Partition, Move Subtree, Add Replica, Remove Replicas, Change Replica Type, and Abort Partition. You can use the PARTMGR utility to perform the NDS partition and replica operations on the NDS tree. You can also use the Partition Manager option in NWADMIN to perform partition operations.

The PARTMGR.EXE utility is a DOS-based program that performs partition operations on the NDS database. The partition operations are create, merge, move subtree, add replicas, remove replicas, and change replica type. Figure 2.29 displays the main menu of the PARTMGR utility.

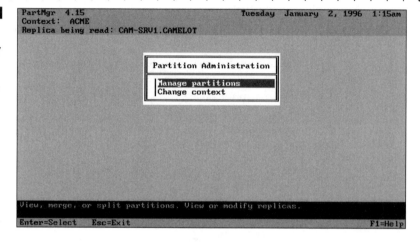

FIGURE 2.29

The main menu of the PARTMGR utility. This utility can perform partition operations such as create, merge, move subtree, add replicas, remove replicas, and change replica type.

Refer to Chapters 6 and 11 for more information regarding partitioning and replication.

UIMPORT UTILITY

The UIMPORT utility enables you to import users from a database application to NDS. This utility can also create, delete, and update user objects and their existing properties. If you are using a database that has the capability to convert records to a comma-separated ASCII file, you can use UIMPORT to migrate this data to the NetWare Directory.

This utility is used primarily to create NDS user objects using records from another database, typically a database application that may contain lists of users. The process of using UIMPORT occurs in three phases:

1 • Create a data file based on your existing database.

2 • Create a control file to interpret and act on the data file.

3 • Import the records into NDS.

The UIMPORT utility consists of two files, the data file and the import control file. The creation of your data file is simply the generation of your ASCII comma-separated file from your previous database. The control file consists of some control parameters and field definitions to define where in NDS the information should be placed.

The Data File

The creation of a data file is accomplished by your database application when you save the information in a comma-separated ASCII file. A comma in the data file indicates a separation of fields in the NDS database. When a record is read through UIMPORT, a comma indicates a new property to be added in the user object. An example of the structure of your database might be as follows:

Last Name:
First Name:
Local Address
   Street:
   City:
   State of Country:
   Zip Code:
Description:
Job Title:

After you have created a data file in delimited ASCII format with any DOS editor you will have a file with records that look like the following:

```
Madison,James,"111  Calle  de  Carnival","Rio  de
Janeiro",Brazil,56665,Facilities,Administrator
```

We have named our file ACMEDATA as we exit and save from our DOS editor.

The Import Control File

The next file you need to create is the import control file. The import control file actually controls how the data file information will be written to NDS. The control file can be written using any DOS text editor. You will enter a set of control parameters first, followed by a list of field definitions. Control parameters define how the information in the data file is separated. The field parameters define how the information is to be written to NDS. Table 2.3 lists the control parameters and their functions.

TABLE 2.3

Control Parameters

CONTROL PARAMETER	EXPLANATION
Separator	Defines the type of separator used in the data file, such as a comma or a semicolon.
Quote	Defines the character used for string data in the data file.
Name Context	Defines the NDS context where the users will be created.
Replace Value	Enables you to overwrite or add data to multi-value fields, such as overwrite an existing telephone number in a user object.
User Template	Specifies the use of a user template in the creation of your NDS user objects.
Import Mode	Defines how user objects will be created. C = Create, B = Create and Update, and U = update data for existing objects.
Delete Property	Enables you to delete a property from a user object in NDS.
Create Home Directory	Enables the creation of a home directory for user objects.
Home Directory Path	Required if you create a home directory for users. The volume name is not necessary in the inclusion.
Home Directory Volume	Required if you create a home directory for users.

The field definitions define which fields should be used in NDS with the incoming data. The following fields can be selected based on your particular needs:

▸ Name

▸ Last Name

▸ Other Name

- ▶ Postal Address

- ▶ E-Mail Address

- ▶ Telephone

- ▶ Fax Number

- ▶ Job Title

- ▶ Description

- ▶ Department

- ▶ Location

- ▶ Group Membership

- ▶ See Also

- ▶ Skip

- ▶ Login Script

Using our previous data file as an example, we would have an import control file that could appear as the following created with any DOS editor utility (note that the Name Context is in the correct order):

```
Import Control

Name Context="O=ACME.OU=RIO.OU=ADMIN.OU=FAC"

User Template=y

Fields

Last Name

Other Name

Postal Address
```

C H A P T E R 2
. . . . .
N O V E L L ' S
G U I D E   T O
I N T R A N E T W A R E
N E T W O R K S

Postal Address

Postal Address

Postal Address

Department

Job Title

We have named our file ACMECTRL as we exit and save from our DOS editor.

Importing Records into NDS

Once you have created a data file and a control file, you are ready to run the UIMPORT utility. At the DOS prompt of your workstation you simply type the following:

```
UIMPORT control_file data_file <enter>
```

In our example we type:

```
UIMPORT ACMECTRL ACMEDATA <enter>
```

The process will then initiate. Keep in mind that you must have Supervisor rights to the container of the context you have specified in the utility. Supervisor rights are necessary for security purposes and will prevent someone from creating objects and then populating them to the NDS database with approval.

If errors should occur during the process, you will receive error messages on your DOS workstation. You can use the > filename command to pipe error messages to a file. So, in our example we could type:

```
UIMPORT ACMECTRL ACMEDATA >LOGFILE
```

NCUPDATE

The NCUPDATE utility provides a network administrator with the ability to update the user's NET.CFG file if a change needs to be made to a container that affects the user's NET.CFG file. It is a convenient way to update the NET.CFG file with a new file that reflects the changes for a group of users.

AUDITCON

For some organizations it may be necessary to maintain an audit of network activity for a given server or perhaps a group of servers. This capability is provided in IntranetWare by the the auditing utility. The AUDITCON utility allows independent auditors apart from your network administrators to audit network events. Network events that can be audited include the following:

▸ File and Directory Activities

 ▸ Creating, modifying, deleting, salvaging, moving, or renaming

▸ Print Queue

 ▸ Creating, deleting, and maintaining other activities

▸ Server Events

 ▸ Downing a server, mounting or dismounting volumes

▸ NDS Events

 ▸ Creating, deleting, moving, renaming operations, and changing to object security.

For more information on the AUDITCON utility refer to your Novell documentation for IntranetWare or Novell's Dynatext under the topic "Auditing."

NPRINTER

NPRINTER.EXE is the replacement program for RPRINTER.EXE, which is no longer used. If you use the NLM-based print server, you will need to use the new NetWare printer program called NPRINTER to enable the print server to send jobs to a network printer. This printer can either be physically attached to the back of the NetWare server, attached to a DOS or OS/2 workstation, or directly to the network itself. Each printer requires the NPRINTER program in order to attach to the printer server and service print jobs.

There are a couple of different versions of the NPRINTER printer program that can be loaded in several different situations. For instance, NPRINTER can be loaded as a terminate-and-stay resident (TSR) program, as a NetWare Loadable Module (NLM), or in the memory of the printer device itself. NPRINTER can be loaded in the following three ways according to the printer configuration:

▸ Workstations with printer devices connected should run NPRINTER.EXE as a TSR to support the network printer. The printer is cabled to the parallel or serial port of the workstation.

▸ Printer devices that are connected to a NetWare server use the NPRINTER.NLM. The printer is cabled to the parallel or serial port of the NetWare server.

▸ Printer devices connected directly to the network run the NPRINTER program from firmware or flash-memory.

With NPRINTER loaded on a workstation, the user of that workstation can run applications and function normally. The user can even access the printer device as a local printer in stand-alone fashion, as well as a network printer. However, the users are not encouraged to use the printer as a local printer because it might conflict with the network printing activities. Naturally, the type of workstation and CPU speed affects the printing performance. For most large network sites this type of configuration is not used.

New to IntranetWare is the ability of the users to specify a printer instead of a print queue when sending their print jobs. Users no longer have to know about print queues; they can simply send their print jobs to a printer by specifying the printer name. The network takes care of all print queue and print server activities. Sending a print job to a printer instead of a print queue is more intuitive to the user.

NMENU

The NMENU.BAT program is a descendent of the older MENU.BAT program and is backward compatible with the older NetWare operating systems. This utility enables you to provide a menu for your IntranetWare users if you do not want to use DOS. Because so many workstations now use MS Windows, the use of menus is not as common. For Windows-based users it usually makes more sense to look at Novell's Application Launcher, which enables you to create an NDS application icon in a Windows group. The user can simply click on the icon to execute the application. For more information on the NetWare Application Manager, see the "NetWare Application Manager" section earlier in this chapter.

IntranetWare Server Utilities

The following section explains the more commonly used IntranetWare server utilities and SET parameters available for network administrators. For information on DSREPAIR and DSTRACE set commands, see Chapter 10.

DSMAINT UTILITY

The DSMAINT.NLM utility (currently available in the INSTALL.NLM utility) provides control of NDS when certain hardware maintenance operations are necessary. Because it deals with the Directory information on a specific server, the utility is run from that server's console. You may want to copy it to the SYS:\SYSTEM directory so it is available if needed.

An example of the DSMAINT main screen is shown in Figure 2.30.

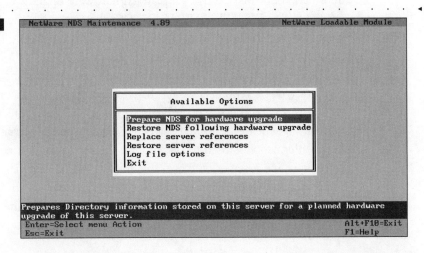

```
NetWare NDS Maintenance  4.89                    NetWare Loadable Module




                           Available Options
                  ┌──────────────────────────────────────┐
                  │ Prepare NDS for hardware upgrade       │
                  │ Restore NDS following hardware upgrade │
                  │ Replace server references              │
                  │ Restore server references              │
                  │ Log file options                       │
                  │ Exit                                   │
                  └──────────────────────────────────────┘


  Prepares Directory information stored on this server for a planned hardware
  upgrade of this server.
   Enter=Select menu Action                          Alt+F10=Exit
   Esc=Exit                                          F1=Help
```

You can also use DSMAINT to maintain server references during a brief server shutdown and to more easily handle the transfer of NDS data when replacing an old SYS volume disk drive. Refer to the documentation that comes with DSMAINT.NLM for detailed instructions.

DSMAINT is included as part of the DS Enhancement Pack, which is available from NetWire and from Novell's Web server on the World Wide Web. The DS Enhancement Pack also contains a number of other utilities and tools to assist you in working with NDS.

The DSMAINT utility provides functionality to address two specific scenarios that NetWare administrators may experience. Each specific situation is addressed by a pair of features in the utility that work together. One command begins a process; another completes it.

Scenario One: NDS and Upgrading Server Hardware

There are times when a server requires an upgrade that does not affect the server as a Directory object. For example, the SYS: volume may be physically located on an old hard disk drive that needs to be upgraded.

In this situation, you no longer need to remove NDS from the server. You can use DSMAINT to prepare Directory information on the server for the upgrade. Then, after you have completed the upgrade, you can restore Directory information to the server with DSMAINT.

The Prepare NDS for a hardware upgrade option prepares the Directory information on this server for a planned hardware upgrade of this server. DSMAINT creates a file (SYS:\SYSTEM\BACKUP.DS) that stores all the Directory information on this server, including replica information. This file should be included in backup procedures before bringing the server down.

The Prepare NDS for a hardware upgrade option locks and disables the Directory on this server, preventing any data change. To other servers that normally communicate with this server, the server appears to be down. Any Directory information that normally is sent to the locked server is stored by other servers in the Directory; the stored information is used to synchronize the server when it comes back online. This is true anytime a server is unavailable for any period of time.

Because the global Directory is expecting the server to come back online quickly, you should not plan on taking several days to upgrade the server. Complete the upgrade promptly and restore Directory information on the server as soon as possible.

The Restore NDS after a hardware upgrade option uses the file created by the Prepare NDS for a hardware upgrade option (SYS:\SYSTEM\BACKUP.DS) to restore Directory information on this server. Before the Directory is restored, DSMAINT ensures that the server is in the same relative state as it was before the upgrade. DSMAINT ensures that the server's object and authentication keys are the same and that the server still exists in all the replica rings for copies that were on this server before the upgrade and as the same replica type.

CONSULTING EXPERIENCE

If you use backup software that needs to be logged in to the Directory, log it in before you use the Restore NDS after a hardware upgrade option. Because the option disables the Directory on this server, you cannot authenticate to this server after performing the option.

To upgrade the hardware, complete the following steps:

1 • Log in your backup software or if you have a current backup log in as ADMIN or administrative user. This step ensures that there is an authenticated connection with ADMIN rights to SYS:SYSTEM.

2 • Load DSMAINT and use the Prepare NDS for a hardware upgrade option; then, back up the server. If a backup was already performed, the BACKUP.DS file will need to be copied to the client's hard drive or to some location other than the server.

This step not only backs up the data, but it also gets a backup of the BACKUP.DS file in the SYS:SYSTEM subdirectory, which was created by DSMAINT.

3 • Bring down the server and perform the upgrade.

4 • Use the INSTALL utility to reinstall NetWare and place a temporary Directory on the server. Install the server to its own temporary Directory tree, not to your normal Directory tree.

The temporary Directory tree will be replaced in step 7.

5 • Copy the DSMAINT.NLM and restore BACKUP.DS to the SYS:\SYSTEM directory.

6 • Use the INSTALL utility to remove NDS from this server. This option is located under INSTALL's Directory options menu.

7 • Load DSMAINT.NLM at the server console and use the Restore NDS after a hardware upgrade option to restore the correct Directory information to the server.

8 • Restore data from backup performed in step 2.

9 • Load INSTALL and upgrade mounted volumes.

CONSULTING EXPERIENCE

This procedure may create a trustee assignment that did not exist before the upgrade. By default, the container object into which the server is installed receives Read and File Scan rights to the server's SYS:\PUBLIC directory. If these rights were previously removed you will need to remove them again.

Scenario Two: Maintaining Server References During a Brief Shutdown

At times, it is necessary to remove a IntranetWare server object from the Directory for a brief period of time. For example, in the case of a corrupt authentication key, it is necessary to reinstall NDS on the server. During the remove NDS process, the IntranetWare server object is removed from the Directory. When the IntranetWare server object is removed from the Directory, objects that reference it in their required attributes can become Unknown objects. A similar type of problem can occur with

CHAPTER 2
. . . . .
INSTALLATION
AND MANAGEMENT
UTILITIES FOR
INTRANETWARE

services like printing that are associated with a physical server. Queues, for example, have a host server attribute. This attribute tells the printing utilities where to find the queue directory. When the host server is deleted, the queue becomes unusable because the location of the queue directory is not known.

With DSMAINT you can avoid losing objects and ease reinstallation by replacing references to the server with references to another object that you create for this purpose. After installing NDS on the server again, you can use DSMAINT to replace these references to the server in other objects' Host Server, Host Device, or Message (Default) Server attributes.

The Replace server references option searches the Directory and replaces references to this server's IntranetWare server object in other objects' Host Server, Host Device, or Message (Default) Server attributes with a reference to another Directory object.

The Restore server references option restores references to this server in other objects' Host Server, Host Device, or Message (Default) Server attributes. This option reverses the replacements made by the Replace server references option.

To reinstall NDS on the server, follow these steps:

1 • Begin by selecting an object for "holding" the references. This object can be an existing User object, but must not be a IntranetWare server object. The user object you have logged in would be appropriate.

2 • Now select the Replace server references option. You are required to enter the full name of the container where you want to begin searching for objects that reference this server's IntranetWare server object. You also need to enter the full name of the object you want DSMAINT to use as a replacement value (such as a TEMP User object).

3 • At this point, you can remove and reinstall NDS.

4 • Once NDS is properly operating, you can select the Restore server references option to reverse the replacements made by the Replace server references option. You will again be required to provide the full name of the temporary object that is holding the references.

DSMAINT automatically removes volume IDs from the physical volumes on the server so that Volume objects are not removed during a remove **NDS** procedure.

NOTE

DSMERGE UTILITY

The DSMERGE utility enables you to merge NDS trees into the same tree. The DSMERGE.NLM provides the mechanism for combining two trees through four basic functions:

▸ Checks status of IntranetWare servers in the Directory Tree before the merge

▸ Checks time synchronization status of IntranetWare servers before the merge

▸ Renames a directory tree when necessary

▸ Performs the merge of two trees when the previous criteria are satisfied

The main screen of DSMERGE enables you to perform these operations and is displayed in Figure 2.31.

FIGURE 2.31

The main
DSMERGE screen

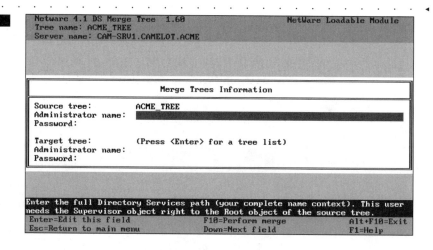

Check Status of IntranetWare Servers

Before and after the merge of two trees it is important to check the status of your IntranetWare servers. Before the merge, you want to check the versions of each IntranetWare server and their current status. Table 2.4 lists the possible statuses and brief descriptions.

	SERVER STATUS	DESCRIPTION
T A B L E 2.4 *IntranetWare server statuses*	DS Locked	The server responds with an error message indicating that the NDS name service is locked and not accessible.
	Inaccessible/Down	The server does not respond and is considered to be inaccessible.
	Error <-N>	N is the Directory Services error code number. This status indicates that the server is not responding because of the error condition listed in the value N.
	Wrong Tree	The server is responding with a tree name that does not match the tree name of the local server container the master replica of [ROOT].
	UP	The server is up and functioning.

The check phase of DSMERGE also ensures that the current server on which you are running this utility holds a replica of the [ROOT] partition. If it cannot find a replica of [ROOT] the operation will abort.

Next, the DSMERGE utility will attempt to find all IntranetWare servers in the tree by searching a list of servers to collect the server name, version of NDS, and tree name. If a server in the list cannot be found or has an incorrect tree name, the utility will issue an error message.Once all the servers have been contacted, the operation will display the list of servers on the screen and their statuses. An example of checking the servers before a DSMERGE operation is shown in Figure 2.32.

Check Time Synchronization

Another important check that the DSMERGE utility performs is the status of time synchronization on all servers to be merged. Both trees must be synchronized and they must refer to the same time source. Once DSMERGE is loaded on a server containing a replica of the [ROOT] partition, you can initiate the time synchronization command as shown in Figure 2.33.

FIGURE 2.32

DSMERGE will check the status of servers before the merge operation begins.

FIGURE 2.33

Time synchronization status screen in the DSMERGE utility

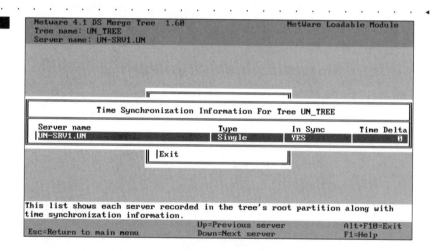

```
Netware 4.1 DS Merge Tree   1.60                    NetWare Loadable Module
Tree name: ACME_TREE
Server name: CAM-SRU1.CAMELOT.ACME


              Time Synchronization Information For Tree ACME_TREE

      Server name                    Type          In Sync        Time Delta
      CAM-SRU1.CAMELOT.ACME          Single        YES                     0
      TOK-SRU1.TOKYO.ACME            Secondary     YES                     0


This list shows each server recorded in the tree's root partition along with
time synchronization information.
                                    Up=Previous server              Alt+F10=Exit
Esc=Return to main menu             Down=Next server                F1=Help
```

```
Netware 4.1 DS Merge Tree   1.60                    NetWare Loadable Module
Tree name: UN_TREE
Server name: UN-SRU1.UN


              Time Synchronization Information For Tree UN_TREE

      Server name                    Type          In Sync        Time Delta
      UN-SRU1.UN                     Single        YES                     0
                          |Exit


This list shows each server recorded in the tree's root partition along with
time synchronization information.
                                    Up=Previous server              Alt+F10=Exit
Esc=Return to main menu             Down=Next server                F1=Help
```

The option will check the time status of all servers for server name, NDS version, and the time synchronization status. If there is a time delta between a IntranetWare server and the local server running DSMERGE, the difference is displayed as shown in Figure 2.34.

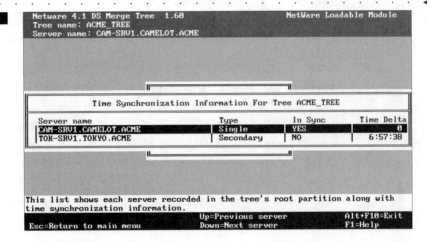

FIGURE 2.34

If time synchronization differs, the DSMERGE utility will show the time delta between servers.

```
Netware 4.1 DS Merge Tree  1.60                      NetWare Loadable Module
Tree name: ACME_TREE
Server name: CAM-SRV1.CAMELOT.ACME




                   Time Synchronization Information For Tree ACME_TREE

       Server name                          Type          In Sync      Time Delta
       CAM-SRV1.CAMELOT.ACME                 Single        YES                  0
       TOK-SRV1.TOKYO.ACME                   Secondary     NO             6:57:38




    This list shows each server recorded in the tree's root partition along with
    time synchronization information.
                                       Up=Previous server          Alt+F10=Exit
    Esc=Return to main menu            Down=Next server             F1=Help
```

Your merged Directory tree must only have one reference or single reference time source. If the two trees you are merging both have a reference or a single reference server, you must assign one of them as a secondary server prior to initiating the merge.

Rename a Directory Tree

Another useful feature found in the DSMERGE utility is the capability to rename an NDS tree. You must use this option if you are merging two trees that have the same name. Keep in mind that currently this is the only Novell utility that will enable you to change the name of your NDS tree. You must load the DSMERGE.NLM on the server that contains the master replica of the [ROOT] partition. The utility will first verify that you are running on the server containing the master replica of [ROOT].The master replica can calculate a list of servers that the utility can contact to change the names of servers holding a replica of [ROOT].

If a server in the list cannot be contacted, a warning message will be issued. You can proceed to rename the tree if servers are unavailable, but you must enter a confirmation to continue the operation.

The operation actually begins by changing the name of the local tree's [ROOT] object to the new tree name. If an error should occur during this process, the operation is aborted. After the local server has changed the name of the [ROOT] object, a command is issued to change all servers in the local tree to the new tree name. Keep in mind that once this process has completed there are many more synchronization activities being performed in the background. Once initiated, this process is irrevocable. After completion of the operation, you should check the status of the servers once again to verify that all servers have received the new name.

Perform the Merge Operation

Once you have checked and verified the status of your IntranetWare servers, along with time synchronization, you are ready to perform the merge operation. After the completion of DSMERGE, you will have a single tree with a common [ROOT]. The operation merges the selected source tree with a target tree. The end result is a tree with the target tree's name of [ROOT].

The DSMERGE.NLM must be loaded on a server containing the master replica of [ROOT] of the source tree. The operation occurs in four phases:

Phase I: Merge Check   This check ensures that your source server running DSMERGE.NLM contains the master replica of the [ROOT] partition. If this check is successful you will see a screen similar to the one shown in Figure 2.35. This screen asks for the tree name of both the source and target trees along with their administrative names and passwords.

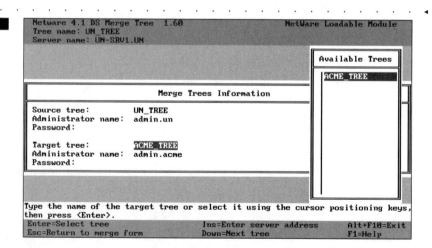

F I G U R E   2.35

The Merge Trees
Information screen

Phase 2: Merge Preparation   This phase modifies the source tree partitions. The utility will do a schema comparison. If the schemas do not match, you will need to use DSREPAIR to import a remote schema from the other tree. It will also split the [ROOT] partition from all other objects in the tree, making a partition that contains only the [ROOT] object. All other Read/Write or Read Only replicas of [ROOT] will also be removed from any servers in the tree. Once this operation is completed the utility can actually merge the trees. Keep in mind that the partitioning operations mentioned here could also be performed beforehand with the Partition Manager or PARTMGR utilities. The first two phases are displayed in the utility before you continue as shown in Figure 2.36.

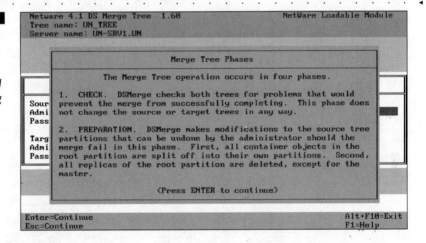

Phase 3: Merge Trees   Once the first two phases are completed, the merge operation will begin. Once again, the operation will gather the list of servers known by the source server. Each server in the source tree will be contacted to obtain its server address and distinguished name in preparation for merging the source tree to the target tree.

The merge operation actually changes the name of the source tree [ROOT] object to that of the [ROOT] in the target tree. Once this process occurs the source server receives a new name and issues a command to change the tree name of all servers in the source tree.

Phase 4: Merge Completion   The merge completion phase includes the continuation of renaming the tree and servers in the source tree. A copy of the target tree's [ROOT] replica will then be copied over to the source server. This operation may take some time depending on the size of the target's [ROOT] replica. Any objects that are no longer needed will be removed by the background synchronization processes.

Some manual tasks may have to be completed after the two trees are merged together. These tasks would include placing copies of the [ROOT] replica where needed in your tree. You may have to restore any objects that were deleted before the DSMERGE utility was run. Because the source tree has had significant changes to the partitions below [ROOT], you will have to use the Partition Manager or PARTMGR utilities to place partitions back again. Follow the guidelines discussed in Chapter 6 of this book.

Finally, you may have to check workstations that have the PREFERRED TREE statement set in their NET.CFG. Each workstation with the source tree name will have to be changed to reflect the target tree name. This can be accomplished through the use of batch files or an update program, such as the UCUPDATE utility, contained in the user's container login script.

NETSYNC UTILITY

NETSYNC is a management utility designed to expand the benefits of NDS to NetWare 3 file servers. With NETSYNC you have the ability to synchronize NetWare 3 users and groups with objects that are contained in a IntranetWare server's bindery context. Therefore, when you create or modify a user in the bindery of a IntranetWare server, the changes are synchronized with all NetWare 3 servers participating in the NETSYNC cluster.

A IntranetWare server can have up to 12 NetWare 3 servers attached in what is known as a cluster. Because all servers in the cluster are synchronized you need to create a user only once because the user will exist on all NetWare 3 servers that are actively attached. An example of a cluster of five NetWare 3 servers is shown in Figure 2.37.

You can also use the NWADMIN or NETADMIN utilities found in IntranetWare to easily manage NetWare 3 users and groups. Printing is also manageable with the IntranetWare versions of PCONSOLE and NWADMIN.

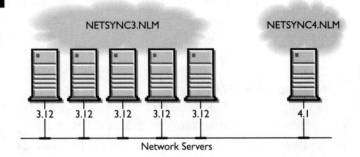

FIGURE 2.37

A cluster of five NetWare 3.12 servers is connected to a single IntranetWare server. The IntranetWare server can have up to 12 NetWare 3.12 servers attached.

Using NETSYNC

NETSYNC is intended as a temporary solution for central administration of a mixed NetWare 3 and IntranetWare environment. For those servers running versions of NetWare 3 that cannot immediately be moved to IntranetWare, this utility provides a good, albeit, temporary solution. It can also be used in environments that are running Novell's NetWare Name Service domain and cannot move all the servers in the domain to IntranetWare immediately.

The NETSYNC NetWare Loadable Module can be loaded on a single IntranetWare server and up to 12 NetWare 3 servers to provide communication between the binderies of the NetWare 3 servers and the emulated bindery of IntranetWare. NETSYNC on the IntranetWare server performs the following functions:

▸ Copies all users and groups from the NetWare 3 server's binderies into the bindery context of the IntranetWare server when NETSYNC.NLM is first enabled on the IntranetWare server.

▸ Downloads all objects in the IntranetWare bindery context to the connected NetWare 3 servers. A combined bindery of NDS users and groups along with the NetWare 3 binderies is downloaded to each NetWare 3 server. This process gives all servers (NetWare 3 and the IntranetWare server) a common, synchronized bindery.

▸ Monitors any changes to the bindery context of the IntranetWare server. The NETSYNC utility will monitor any user or group changes made on the IntranetWare server and synchronize these changes with all NetWare 3 servers connected in the cluster.

▸ Synchronizes bindery information from any NetWare 3 server that has been temporarily removed from the cluster. Any changes that may have been made to the bindery during the server's absence will be sent down by the IntranetWare server.

Installing **NETSYNC**

Installing NETSYNC is not difficult. All of the components are already stored on your IntranetWare file server. The SYS:SYSTEM directory contains the necessary IntranetWare files, and the SYS:SYSTE\NETSYNC directory contains the NetWare 3 files. At least one IntranetWare server is required but you can have up to 12 NetWare 3 servers connected to one IntranetWare server. For authentication of each NetWare 3 server you will also need an available licensed connection to the IntranetWare server.

To load NETSYNC simply type **LOAD NETSYNC4** at the IntranetWare server console. Always load NETSYNC4 server first and authorize the NetWare 3 servers before beginning the installation of NETSYNC3 on the NetWare 3 server. If you don't load the NETSYNC4 server first, the NetWare 3 servers are not authorized to connect to the NETSYNC cluster. This installation program will automatically create the SYS:SYSTEM\NETSYNC directory that contains log files and the other NETSYNC file that will be copied automatically when each NETSYNC module is loaded on the NetWare 3 servers.

The loading of your NetWare 3 servers requires you to first authorize each server to connect to the IntranetWare network. When you have loaded NETSYNC4, you will see the screen shown in Figure 2.38. Pressing Enter to the Edit Server List option enables you to enter NetWare 3 servers by name to begin the authorization process. You can enter up to 12 NetWare 3 servers on the list.

As an added measure of security you will also need to enter a NETSYNC password. This password will then be required as each NetWare 3 server initially requests entry into the cluster. The password is used only once.

You can use a different password for each NetWare 3 server. However, since this password is used only once, for simplicity we recommend the same password for all NetWare 3 servers in the cluster. In addition, do NOT use your ADMIN or Supervisor password as your NETSYNC password as this may pose a security risk.

TIP

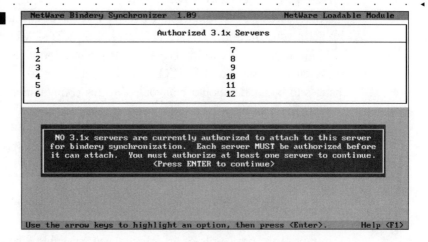

FIGURE 2.38

The NETSYNC4 utility enables you to authorize NetWare 3.1 servers for synchronization with a IntranetWare host server.

Next, you will be asked if you want to copy the program files to the NetWare 3 server by pressing the Down arrow key. This option appears when you first authorize a NetWare 3 server for installation of NETSYNC.

Loading NETSYNC3

Every NetWare 3 server that participates in the cluster must load the program NETSYNC3. Again, be sure that you have completed the steps to loading NETSYNC4 on your IntranetWare server before starting this phase. The first step is to reboot the NetWare 3 servers because they will execute some new files that have been downloaded by the NETSYNC4 process earlier. Once your NetWare 3 server is back up and running you can now type **LOAD NETSYNC3** at the server's console.

Once the NETSYNC3 program is loaded you will be asked a couple of questions regarding NetWare Name Services. If you are not running NNS, select NO to these questions and proceed. If you are running NNS, refer to Novell's documentation for information.

The utility will ask you to enter the name of the IntranetWare host and the password. After successful entry of your password the utility will upload the NetWare 3 bindery information to the IntranetWare bindery context. The bindery type objects at the bindery context are in turn loaded onto the NetWare 3 server.

For further configurations of NETSYNC you can use the NETSYNC Options menus for NETSYNC3 and NETSYNC4, such as viewing or editing the log file, editing a server list, and other activities.

Managing Objects with **NETSYNC**

Upon successful installation of NETSYNC, you will be able to manage your NetWare 3 objects with the IntranetWare NWADMIN or NETADMIN utilities. DO NOT go back and use SYSCON to modify user and group information on NetWare 3 servers in the cluster. The use of SYSCON on the NetWare 3 server will not synchronize changes to NDS and should be avoided in this configuration.

NETSYNC also provides printing support. After you have completed your installation of NETSYNC3 and NETSYNC4, all workstation print utilities are copied to the NetWare 3 servers, and PRINTCON and PRINTDEF databases are updated to the IntranetWare formats. You can also choose to move your NetWare 3 print servers into a single print server on the IntranetWare server. Your printers are moved into Directory Services where they can be managed from a single IntranetWare print server.

IntranetWare print utilities are immediately available for use in your NetWare 3 environment once NETSYNC is operational. For more information on using print utilities with NETSYNC, refer to your Novell documentation.

NETSYNC and the Bindery Context

NDS provides compatibility to NetWare 2 and NetWare 3 using a feature called bindery services. This feature enables bindery versions of NetWare and other bindery-based applications to access the NDS tree as if it were the bindery. Bindery services is accomplished by setting a bindery context on the server, which specifies the name of the NDS tree container(s) to search as the bindery.

In order to set the bindery context on a server, you can enter SET BINDERY CONTEXT = "OU=OPS.OU=CAMELOT.O=ACME" at the server console. The server bindery context can also be set using the server-based SERVMAN utility.

TIP

Prior to NetWare 4, object information was not available from a distributed directory. A NetWare 3 server stored only information related to its own server in the bindery. Therefore, applications were written that accessed each NetWare 3 server's bindery for user or connection information. NDS provides bindery services that enable objects in a container to be accessed by bindery-based servers and clients as well as NDS objects. When a bindery-based application makes bindery calls to the server, the server sees the objects in the container where the server bindery context is set.

TIP

In terms of bindery context on the server, NDS will see only the objects that previously existed in a NetWare 3 bindery as the bindery objects. These objects are limited to user, group, print queue, and print server. In addition, IntranetWare has added the profile object to assist with migrations from NetWare Name Services (NNS).

The default server bindery context is set to the container where the server was installed. The context can be changed to look to another container or OU if you want. Previous versions of NetWare 4, up to and including NetWare 4.02, allow you to set only a single context for your server. IntranetWare enables you to set up to 16 contexts for a single server.

Since NetSync synchronizes NetWare 3 user and groups with objects in a IntranetWare bindery context, you must enable the host 4.1 server with bindery services. The IntranetWare server periodically queues up and signals the NetWare 3 servers to retrieve the changes in the cluster. If more than one IntranetWare server is using the same bindery context, you will have all servers with the same context synchronizing with the NetWare 3 servers in the cluster. Although there is no theoretical limit on how many servers can be using the same bindery context, the NetSync operation is CPU intensive. Thus, the more objects to synchronize, the more overhead is placed on a server.

In addition, if you desire to set multiple bindery contexts for a server, the process is also governed by the number of objects and the speed of your links during synchronization.

SERVMAN

The SERVMAN utility monitors your IntranetWare servers and is broken down into four main parameter groupings. Keep in mind that the SERVMAN utility is a menu interface for all the IntranetWare SET parameters and makes administration of these parameters a little easier. The four groups are listed below.

Server Parameters

Server parameters enable you to view and modify operating system parameters. Server parameters include packet communication options such as maximum and minimum packet receive buffers and watchdog packets. Figure 2.39 shows the main screen for server parameters. To make a change to any of these options, simply highlight the option and press Enter. You can then backspace over the old option

and enter the new one. If the option is toggled, then simply highlight the option and press Enter to toggle to the desired value.

FIGURE 2.39

The Server
Parameters screen

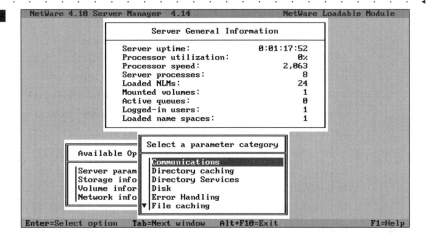

```
NetWare 4.10 Server Manager  4.14                    NetWare Loadable Module

                    ┌─────────────────────────────────────────┐
                    │       Server General Information          │
                    │                                           │
                    │ Server uptime:              0:01:17:52    │
                    │ Processor utilization:             0%     │
                    │ Processor speed:                2,063     │
                    │ Server processes:                   8     │
                    │ Loaded NLMs:                       24     │
                    │ Mounted volumes:                    1     │
                    │ Active queues:                      0     │
                    │ Logged-in users:                    1     │
                    │ Loaded name spaces:                 1     │
                    └─────────────────────────────────────────┘

              ┌──────────────┬────────────────────────────────┐
              │ Available Op │ Select a parameter category    │
              │              ├────────────────────────────────┤
              │ Server param │ Communications                 │
              │ Storage info │ Directory caching              │
              │ Volume infor │ Directory Services             │
              │ Network info │ Disk                           │
              │              │ Error Handling                 │
              │            ▼ │ File caching                   │
              └──────────────┴────────────────────────────────┘

  Enter=Select option    Tab=Next window    Alt+F10=Exit              F1=Help
```

NOTE   **For a detailed description of using SERVMAN for time synchronization control found under the SERVER PARAMETERS screen, refer to Chapter 7.**

Storage Information

The storage information option enables you to view adapter, device, and NetWare partition information. An example of the main screen for storage information is shown in Figure 2.40.

Volume Information

The volume information option displays the NetWare volume statistics for currently mounted volumes. These statistics provide information such as compression status, number of directory entries, and size of suballocation units. An example of a volume information screen is shown in Figure 2.41.

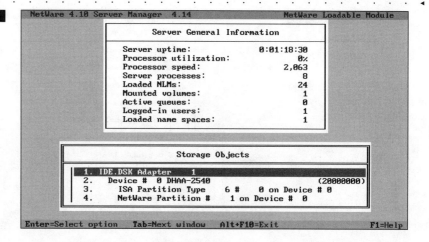

*The Storage
Information screen*

*Volume Information screen
for the SYS volume*

Network Information

The network information parameters enable you to view packet information such as the numbers of packets transmitted and received. This information is helpful if you are trying to diagnose a problem with network traffic. An example of this statistics screen is found in Figure 2.42.

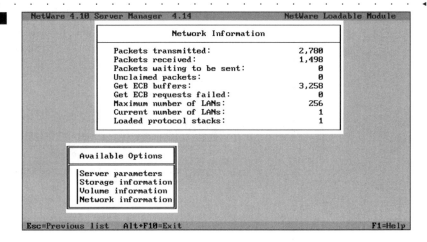

NETBASIC

NETBASIC is a scripting language specifically designed for the IntranetWare environment. It creates BASIC language scripts that can be run on your server platform as interpreted BASIC programs and also compiled as NetWare Loadable Modules (NLMs) for server execution. NETBASIC ships with a suite of utility scripts and example programs demonstrating how the language is used. NETBASIC scripts can be written to query information from NDS as well as perform various management functions on your IntranetWare servers. In fact, any Net2000 compliant component APIs are accessible, including NetWare and Novell Directory Services APIs.

NETBASIC is licensed from HiTecSoft, Inc., and offers three basic features:

▸ The Network Management Extensions engine. This tool loads and unloads components, such as NLMs and BASIC scripts from an operational server on demand.

▸ A BASIC script interpreter for IntranetWare compatible with Visual Basic that allows an administrator to easily and quickly develop scripts for your servers, such as new utilities and automate tasks.

▸ Provides BASIC scripting APIs for the Internet. With these APIs, an administrator can develop advanced Internet and Intranet services, such as dynamic HTML pages and sites that access Novell services or Oracle databases.

NETBASIC provides the capability to create Web pages to output HTML source code. The output from a BASIC script is written to the Web server, which then routes the data back to the Web browser.

NETBASIC also provides a document management component known as DOC.NLM that allows you to write BASIC language scripts to generate HTML documents quickly and easily on the fly. You can then link a NETBASIC script to an HTML document.

CHAPTER 3

Novell Directory Services Objects and Properties

"If two objects have the same logical form, the only distinction between them, apart from their external properties, is that they are different." Wittgenstein

Novell Directory Services (NDS) is a collection of objects that follows a set of rules regarding how they are created and used. Becoming familiar with NDS objects and properties and the ways in which they are used to build the NDS tree structure will enhance your use of IntranetWare. Your understanding of the schema will help you to determine the structure of additional objects that may be added to your NDS schema through the installation of add-on or third-party applications. In addition, an understanding of the internal structure of both the NDS objects and the schema will give you greater flexibility in managing and designing your IntranetWare network.

This chapter first begins with a basic discussion of the NDS objects and properties (or attributes). Next, we will explain the NDS schema — its components and rules and how the NDS objects are created. Schema extensions are discussed to help you understand what happens when additional object classes or properties or modifications are added to existing classes. We will then explore the purpose and use of each individual NDS object with examples of how they can effectively be used in your tree. Where pertinent we have also included consulting experiences that will help you in understanding how various objects have been used in actual customer environments.

Introduction to NDS Objects

Your primary responsibility as a network administrator is to maintain the servers, volumes, users, groups, printers, and other resources in the network. In order to help with this task, NDS enables you to view all the network resources as objects within a distributed or network-wide name service known as the NDS tree. You decide which network resources are created and placed as objects in the name service. These objects might include users, groups, printers, servers, volumes, computers, and so on.

Each of the entries in the NDS tree consists of the object and the properties or data stored as a property. For example, the User object has up to 75 properties, and some of the properties have multiple values. Table 3.1 shows an example of a User object. This table is not a complete list of all the properties, but notice that some of the properties have multiple values.

	OBJECT	PROPERTY	VALUE(S)
T A B L E 3.1	User	Login Name	GWASHINGTON
Example of a User object		Given Name	George
		Last Name	Washington
		Title	President, Statesman, Farmer, Cherry Tree Killer
		Location	Washington D.C, Mount Vernon
		Telephone	(not invented)
		Fax Number	(not invented)
		Description	President of the United States

NDS Objects

The NDS objects are the entities that store the information or data about a network resource. The NDS objects represent both physical and logical entities on the network. Table 3.2 illustrates examples of both logical and physical network resources that can be represented by NDS.

	LOGICAL ENTITIES	PHYSICAL ENTITIES
T A B L E 3.2	User	Printer
Example of logical and physical entities	Group	NetWare Server
	Print Queue	Volume
	Alias	Computer

Since there can be many NDS objects in the network, the objects are organized into a hierarchical structure called the NDS tree. A good analogy here is a file system. The file system is a hierarchy of subdirectories and files. The reason for the hierarchy is that the files are more manageable with this structure than storing them at the same level. The same is true with Novell Directory Services.

Novell Directory Services classifies all objects as either *container* or *leaf objects* (*non-container objects*). The container objects are analogous to subdirectories in a file system, and leaf objects are analogous to the files.

CONTAINER OBJECTS

The container objects are those objects that are allowed subordinate objects. The container objects form the hierarchy of the NDS tree and are typically named after the locations, divisions, departments, and workgroups in your company. The container objects enable you to group the other NDS objects together in the tree. A branch or subtree of the NDS tree consists of a container object and all the objects it holds, which can include other container objects.

There are several types of container objects defined for your use. The container object base classes are as follows:

▸ TOP [ROOT] — a special object at the top of the NDS tree

▸ Organization (O=) — represents the name of your company

▸ Organization Unit (OU=) — represents locations, departments, divisions, or workgroups

▸ Country (C=) — represents a 2-letter country object

▸ Locality (L=) — is named by "L" or "S" for state or both. Currently the Locality is not enabled by the Novell utilities.

Although, the IntranetWare Directory defines five container objects, the current utilities support only the O=Organization, OU=Organizational Unit, and C=Country. The TOP [ROOT] class is supported but only the NDS system can create it. Future releases of the NetWare utilities might implement the L=Locality and S=State, as well as third-party products. Both can also be currently represented by using the OU=Organizational Units, which serve the same purpose.

Figure 3.1 illustrates how the container objects are the building blocks of the NDS tree. The container objects also help you organize and manage the leaf objects or non-container objects.

FIGURE 3.1

*The container objects are
organized into a hierarchical
structure called the
NDS tree.*

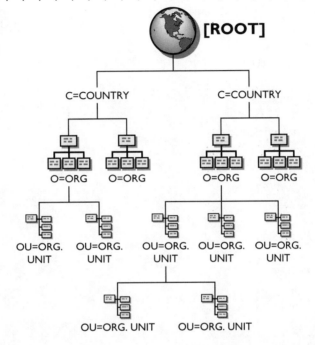

LEAF OBJECTS (NON-CONTAINER OBJECTS)

The leaf objects are located at the ends of the NDS tree branches and don't contain any other objects. These are the objects that are used to represent the network resources. The following is a list of some of the leaf objects for IntranetWare.

- ▸ AFP Server

- ▸ Application Object

- ▸ Alias

- ▸ Bindery Object

- ▸ Bindery Queue

- ▸ Computer

- ▸ Directory Map

- ▸ Group

- ▸ NCP Server

- ▸ CommExec

- ▸ External Entity

- ▸ Organization Role

- ▸ Queue

- ▸ Print Server

- ▸ Printer

- ▸ Profile

- ▸ User

- ▸ Unknown

- ▸ Volume

- ▸ Messaging Server

- ▸ Message Routing Group

- ▸ List

In the NDS tree, you can place container objects and leaf objects in different arrangements, according to your company's needs. Figure 3.2 illustrates how container objects organize the leaf objects.

The container objects organize the leaf objects in the NDS tree.

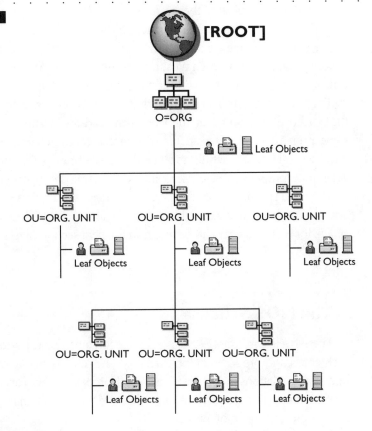

NDS PROPERTIES

The properties (also referred to as attributes) of the objects specify the type of information that the object can store. The terms property and attribute share the same concept and are used interchangeably throughout the rest of this book.

Different types of objects have different types of properties. Thus, it can be said that the properties define or describe the object. For example, a User object has the following properties: Login Name, Last Name, Group Membership, Telephone, Fax Number, and so on. On the other hand, a Printer object has the properties: Name, Network Address, Location, Print Server and so on.

There are two categories of properties for the object: mandatory and optional property. The mandatory properties are required during the object creation and cannot be removed. The Novell utilities enforce the data entry for properties that are mandatory. Typically, these are properties that name the object necessary for operation. Many properties are mandatory to comply with the X.500 standard. For instance, the surname (or last name) of a User object is mandatory. The host server property is mandatory when creating a Volume object. An object's optional properties can be entered as the network administrator deems appropriate.

The value of the property is the data information stored in each property. This is the object information that the users can read and write in many cases, although some properties are not readable or writable by the client. One property type can have a single value, while another can have multiple values. For example, the Telephone property of the user can hold several different telephone numbers.

There is a specific syntax for the value or data type of each property. One use of the syntax is to define the acceptable characters for the value field(s). More details on the syntax for each property can be found in the next section of this chapter.

The NDS Schema

The Novell Directory Services schema contains the rules to create and maintain each object and property in the Directory. The schema rules dictate the requirements, limits, and relationship of the objects and properties that can exist in the Directory. NDS enforces those rules for each client request to change (add, delete, modify, and so on) an object or property.

The NDS schema is automatically stored on every IntranetWare server you install, even if you don't have NDS replicas stored on that server. The IntranetWare installation automatically places the schema on the server for the following reasons:

- ▸ The schema enables each server to know how to create and maintain all the NDS objects and properties.

- ▸ The schema placed on each server permits the administration utilities to access the schema during the creation of an object or objects.

The schema consists of three major components: the object class, the property or attribute type definitions, and the attribute syntaxes. These three components work together to establish the rules that control the creation of a particular object type in the Directory. In Figure 3.3, you can see the relationship between these components. For instance, each object class is defined in terms of attribute or property definitions. The attribute types, in turn, are defined in terms of the attribute syntaxes. The attribute syntaxes are the data type of the values or information that can be stored in the attribute.

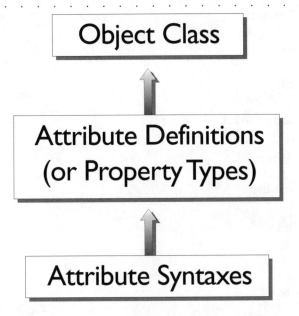

Keep in mind that, for the most part, the objects defined in the base schema for IntranetWare are taken from the X.500 specifications for appropriate objects in a directory service. Other objects were defined that describe existing NetWare 3 bindery objects. Some objects may currently have little use and are intended for future enhancements to the Directory and thus were placed in the schema for future use.

OBJECT CLASSES

The object class defines the types of NDS objects that can be created and stored in the Directory. The object class is used as a set of rules to create the individual objects and to determine its set of characteristics. This means that every object in the tree belongs to an object class that specifies which attributes can be used or must be used as well as where objects can be created in relation to other objects. Figure 3.3 illustrates how the object classes are constructed from the attributes types. Keep in mind that object classes can refer to other object classes as well.

The base schema that ships with IntranetWare contains 32 object classes. These object classes cannot be removed or deleted. The following is a list of 32 object classes stored in the schema.

- AFP Server

- Alias

- Application

- Bindery Object

- Bindery Queue

- CommExec

- Computer

- Country

- Device

- Directory Map

- External Entity

- Group

- Locality

- Message Routing Group

- Messaging Server

- NCP Server

▸ Organization

▸ Organizational Person

▸ Organizational Role

▸ Organizational Unit

▸ Partition

▸ Person

▸ Printer

▸ Print Server

▸ Profile

▸ Queue

▸ Resource

▸ Server

▸ Top

▸ Unknown

▸ User

▸ Volume

▸ List

Each of the object classes in the schema is determined by the distinctive information held in five components. The five components or type of information that make up an object class definition are:

▸ Structure Rules — Defines the relationship of the objects in the Directory tree. The relationship is constructed based on two items: Naming Attributes (how the object is named) and Containment Class (which object classes the object can be subordinate to).

▸ Super Classes — Builds the internal structure of the schema by relating the object classes to each other. Some object classes are simply the building blocks for the other object classes, or are classes from which the object class inherits its definition.

▸ Mandatory Attributes — The attributes listed in the mandatory attribute list for the object class are the attributes required during the object's creation and throughout the life of the object.

▸ Optional Attributes — The attributes listed in the optional attribute list for the object class are the attributes that are not required but may be added.

▸ Object Class Flags — There are five object class flags that are either set to ON or OFF. These object class flags include the container flag, effective status, and nonremovable flag.

As an example, the following is the definition of the Group object class:

Object Class: GROUP
Class Flags: Effective Class
Super Classes: Top
Named By: CN (Common Name)
Containment: Organization
Organizational Unit
Mandatory Attributes: CN
Optional Attributes: Description
Full Name
GID
Locality Name
Member
etc.

The following is the definition of the Organization object class:

Object Class:	ORGANIZATION
Class Flags:	Effective Class, Container Class
Super Classes:	Top
Named By:	O (Organization Name)
Containment:	Country
	Locality
	Top
Mandatory Attributes:	O
Optional Attributes:	Description
	Detect Intruder
	E-Mail Address
	Facsimile Telephone Number
	etc.

Structure Rules

The structure rules for an object define the relationship between the objects in the NDS tree. The relationship between object classes is determined by two items. These items are Naming Attributes and Containment Class. The naming attributes determine how the object is named. The containment class determines where the object may appear in the Directory tree relative to the other object classes.

Naming Attributes   The naming attributes (or properties) determine how an object is named in the NDS tree. An Object is identified in the tree by its common name and also by the names of all its parent containers. An object's name includes the object name type and a value connected together with an equal (=) sign. Some object classes are container objects while other objects are the leaf objects (or non-container objects). Table 3.3 lists the object name types that are currently used in the naming attribute of the object class definition.

The first four name types — C=Country Name, L=Locality Name (S=State or Province), O=Organization Name, and OU=Organizational Unit Name — are all the container objects. The CN=Common Name and Bindery Type are used for the leaf objects.

An object's leaf-most name is referred to as its partial name or Relative Distinguished Name (RDN). For example, the user, MTERESA, in the ACME tree has an RDN of CN=MTERESA. If we refer to the user's distinguished name or full name, it would be defined as the RDN, MTERESA, plus the names of all the parent containers above the user MTERESA. The distinguished name would be written as follows:

```
CN=MTERESA.OU=FOOD.OU=SYDNEY.O=ACME
```

List of the object name types that are available for use in object name type definitions

NAME TYPE		NAME VALUE
C	=	Country Name
L	=	Locality Name
S	=	State or Province Name
O	=	Organization Name
OU	=	Organizational Unit Name
CN	=	Common Name
Bindery Type	=	Bindery Type

Therefore, the structure rules effectively control the formation of the distinguished names and relative distinguished names for each of the objects created in the NDS tree.

Nearly every object class will have one or more object name types defined in the Naming portion of the object class definition unless inherited by a super class. For example, the Organization object class is named by the "O" name type. The naming attribute of the Organizational Unit object class is defined as an "OU" name type. The Country object class has the "C" name type. It is mandatory that at least one naming attribute be defined or inherited.

The Named By attribute is not always a reflection of the class to which an object belongs. For example, leaf objects such as User or Printer are named by the Common Name (CN). The CN= name attribute does not by itself give you any indication to which class the object belongs.

An object class can allow for multiple object name types in the Named By attribute in the definition. In these cases any one of the object name types can be used to name the object. For classes having multiple naming attributes, any combination of the naming attributes can be used. The attribute values are connected together using the plus (+) sign.

A common occurrence of this peculiar naming convention occurs in the case of Bindery Objects. In the definition of the bindery object class, there are two object name type attributes called Bindery Type and Common Name (CN). A bindery object would then be defined as:

```
CN=ATPSUSER+BINDERY TYPE=83
```

The Locality object class definition also has a multivalued Named By attribute definition. It is named by either the name type L=Locality Name, or S=State or Province Name. Therefore, the RDN for a Locality object could appear as:

```
L=NORAD+S=COLORADO
```

Containment Classes   As we mentioned earlier in this chapter, some object classes are designed to contain other objects. The containment class list specifies where the individual object classes may appear in the NDS tree. Each object class has a definition or list of the container objects that it may be created in or subordinate to. This list, called the containment class list, builds the relationship between the object classes in the NDS tree.

An individual object can only reside or be created directly in a container that is found in its containment class list. For example, the Group object class can only be placed in or created subordinate to an Organization or Organizational Unit object. The containment class list for the Group object lists this relationship as illustrated in the list of Group object classes shown above. The following example for the Group object class is taken from the list of Group object classes:

Object Class: GROUP
Named By: CN (Common Name)
Containment: Organization
Organizational Unit

The containment class list simply specifies that the Group objects can be placed under either the Organization or Organizational Unit objects in the tree. Therefore, the containment class specifies where an individual object may appear in the Directory tree. The schema prohibits objects from being created directly below or subordinate to container objects whose class definition is not in the new object's containment list.

The following is a list of the container objects that are used in the containment class lists for each of the object class definitions:

▸ Top

▸ Country

▸ Locality

▸ Organization

▸ Organizational Unit

The containment class dictates the structure of the NDS tree and changes as the tree expands toward the bottom. For example, the Organization and Country object classes are the only object definitions that have Top in their containment class list. The Top object class is implemented as the [ROOT] object in the tree. This means that only Organization and Country objects can be subordinate objects to [ROOT]. The Organization and Locality object class definitions are the only object classes that have the Country object listed in their containment class. Thus, Organization and Locality objects can only be subordinate objects to Country. Continuing down the tree, the Organizational Unit has the Organization, Locality, and Organizational Unit (itself) defined in its containment class.

As the tree expands toward the bottom most of the leaf object class definitions have the containment class for both Organization and Organizational Unit. This means that most leaf objects will reside either within the Organization or Organizational Unit container objects.

Super Classes

The internal structure of the schema is built using the super classes specification for the object class. The super classes help designate the structure of the schema internally and do not dictate the hierarchical structure for the NDS tree. As stated above, the NDS tree structure is dictated by each object's definition of the containment class.

The super classes are those object class definitions in the schema from which other objects classes may be constructed. A complete definition for an object class is derived from the components of the object class itself plus all the components of its super class objects. An example of the super class structure for a User object class is illustrated in Figure 3.4.

The NDS Directory allows for classes to inherit from other class objects in a unidirectional manner. This means that object class B can inherit from object class A, but object class A cannot inherit from object class B. The concept of inheritance among objects in the schema stipulates that an object class inherits the features of its super classes. This means that all the definitions of the super class objects are inherited in the new object class. If object class B inherits from object class A, B must receive all the definitions from A. The Directory does not have the capability to inherit only parts of the super class definition. A class may inherit from multiple super classes.

FIGURE 3.4

Super class structure for the User object class as defined in the schema

Top
Effective Class
Super Classes:	(none)
Containment:	(none)
Named by:	(none)
Mandatory:	Object Class
Optional:	ACL
	Back Link
	Bindery Property
	Obituary
	Reference

Person
Non-Effective Class
Super Classes:	Top
Containment:	(none)
Named by:	(none)
Mandatory:	CN
	Surname
Optional:	Description
	Full Name
	See Also
	Telephone Number

Organizational Person
Non-Effective Class
Super Classes:	Person	
Containment:	Organization	
	Organizational Unit	
Named by:	CN	
	OU	
Mandatory:	(none)	
Optional:	EMail Address	Postal Address
	Facsimile Telephone No.	Postal Code
	Locality Name	Postal Office Box
	OU	S
	Physical Delivery Office	SA
	Name	Title

Organizational User
Effective Class
Super Classes:	Organizational Person	Login Grace Remaining	Password Expiration
Containment:	(none)	Login Intruder Address	Time
Named by:	(none)	Login Intruder Attempts	Password Minimum
Mandatory:	(none)	Login Intruder Reset	Length
Optional:	Account Balance	Time	Password Required
	Allow Unlimited Credit	Login Maximum	Password Unique
	Group Membership	Simultaneous	Required
	Higher Privileges	Login Script	Password Used
	Home Directory	Login Time	Print Job Configuration
	Language	Message Server	Private Key
	Last Login Time	Minimum Account	Profile
	Locked By Intruder	Balance	Public Key
	Login Allowed Time Map	Network Address	Security Equals
	Login Disabled	Network Address	Server Holds
	Login Expiration Time	Restriction	Type Creator Map
	Login Grace Limit	Password Allow	UID
		Change	
		Password Allow	
		Interval	

Mandatory Attributes

The attributes listed in the mandatory attribute list for the object class are the attributes that are required. If an attribute is mandatory, every object created from the class must have at least one assigned value for each mandatory attribute.

Optional Attributes

The attributes listed in the optional attribute list for the object class are the attributes that are not required. If an attribute is listed as optional, then when the object is created the attributes may or may not be created.

Object Class Flags

There are several object class flags that are either set to ON or OFF. These object class flags include the container flag, effective status, and nonremovable flag among others.

Container Flag   The container flag is set to ON only for those object classes that are designated as the container object classes in the Directory tree. The container flag would be set to ON for the following object classes: Top, Country, Locality, Organization, and Organizational Unit.

The container flag is set to OFF for all the object classes that are the leaf objects in the schema or non-effective classes.

Effective and Non-Effective Status   Each object class is categorized as an effective or non-effective class. Effective classes are visible in the utilities and are used to create new objects in your NDS tree.

Non-effective object classes are used as super classes to build the other object class information. Therefore, non-effective classes are used only in the definition of other objects and not to create objects in the Directory tree. The non-effective object classes are not visible using the management utilities. Non-effective object classes in the schema are used to create other object classes in the Directory tree. (Later in this section where each object is listed is a notation of each object's effective or non-effective class.)

Nonremovable Flag   The nonremovable flag determines if the object class can be removed from the schema definitions. The nonremovable flag is set to ON for all the object classes that are defined in the base schema that is shipped with IntranetWare. The object classes added later to extend the schema have the nonremovable set to OFF.

PROPERTY OR ATTRIBUTE TYPE DEFINITIONS

All the properties or attributes found in the Directory consist of an attribute type and an attribute value. The attribute identifies the nature of the information that will be stored by the attribute and dictates the syntax used to enter the value.

An attribute definition is based on special constraints and on a specific attribute syntax that determines the values the attribute can store. There is a one-to-one relationship between attributes and their syntaxes. There are approximately 142 available attributes that are defined in the base NDS schema that ships with IntranetWare. Various combinations of these attributes apply to all object classes. You can view some of the available attributes or properties for each object through the use of the NWADMIN utility. The following is a list of the attributes defined for the Group object class:

- Access Control List

- Authority Revocation

- Auto Start

- Back Link

- Bindery Property

- CA Public Key

- Certificate Validity Interval

- Common Name

- Default Queue

- Department

- Description

- Desktop

- E-mail Address

▸ Equivalent To Me

▸ Full Name

▸ GID

▸ Last Referenced Time

▸ Location

▸ Mailbox ID

▸ Mailbox Location

▸ Member

▸ Object Class

▸ Obituary

▸ Organization

▸ Other Name (other values of common name)

▸ Owner

▸ Reference

▸ Revision

▸ See Also

The attribute type definition consists of Attribute Syntax and Attribute Constraints.

Attribute Syntax

The attribute syntaxes are data types for values that will be stored in the Directory. The attribute syntaxes are predefined. The NDS schema is extensible, as discussed in the next section, meaning that you can create new object classes and attributes based on the attribute syntaxes. You can also add attributes to existing class definitions. Although the schema is extensible, the attribute syntaxes cannot be alternated. There are currently 28 static attribute syntaxes defined in the schema. The following is a list of the attribute syntaxes that are defined in the schema:

- ► Back Link

- ► Boolean

- ► Case Exact String

- ► Case Ignore List

- ► Case Ignore String

- ► Class Name

- ► Counter

- ► Distinguished Name

- ► E-mail Address

- ► Facsimile Telephone Number

- ► Hold

- ► Integer

- ► Interval

- ► Net Address

- ► Numeric String

- ► Object ACL

- ► Octet List

- ▸ Octet String

- ▸ Path

- ▸ Postal Address

- ▸ Printable String

- ▸ Replica Pointer

- ▸ Stream

- ▸ Telephone Number

- ▸ Time

- ▸ Timestamp

- ▸ Typed Name

- ▸ Unknown

ATTRIBUTE CONSTRAINTS

Attribute constraints are all restrictions that affect the attribute values for each of the attributes. These constraints include whether the attribute values can have a single value or multiple values, whether the attribute values are immediately synchronized between replicas, or whether the attribute is hidden or nonremovable. The constraints also manage access control to the attribute value. For example, an attribute can be constrained to allow only someone with sufficient rights to the object to add an attribute.

The attribute syntax also dictates the matching rules that are used when comparing two values of the same syntax. The primary matching rules are: equality, substrings, and ordering. The equality checks for equal values of the attribute values and only applies if the attribute types are the same. It can't compare unless the attribute is the same. Therefore, the syntax would be the same. The substring compares two string attribute values where a wildcard "*" can be used. The ordering rules compare for "less than," "equal to," and "greater than."

For a complete definition of the attribute syntax IDs, data formats, and matching rules, please refer to Novell's Software Developer's Kit (SDK).

SCHEMA STRUCTURE

Each object class along with its properties or attributes and the attribute syntaxes form what is called the NDS Base Schema. As shown in Figure 3.5, the schema structure can be represented as a pyramid in which the foundation consists of the attribute syntaxes. These attribute syntaxes are used to define an attribute; in turn the attribute defines the object classes, and the object classes determine the schema structure.

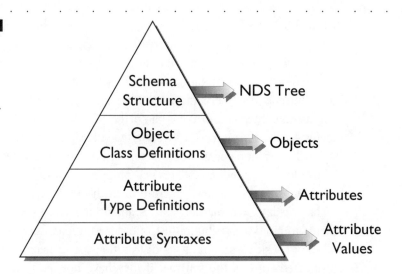

F.I G U R E   3.5

The schema structure is represented as a pyramid in which the foundation is the attribute syntaxes, which define the attributes. The attributes define the object classes, and the object classes determine the schema structure.

THE NDS SCHEMA IS EXTENSIBLE

NDS provides a mechanism for making changes or extensions to the schema. The purpose of this section is to give an overview of how this can be accomplished in your IntranetWare environment. For specific information on API functions and making API calls, see the Novell Directory Services API Reference Manual from Novell. By using the client Application Programming Interface (API), the schema can be expanded beyond the base schema, which is provided by Novell. Attributes can be added to existing object classes, or new object classes or attributes can be created.

The first step to extending the schema is to create new attribute definitions and/or new object class definitions. The extensions to the schema can be accomplished through the use of programming, with Novell's API calls designed for this purpose. After completing this task, you have modified the schema. All changes or extensions are automatically replicated on all IntranetWare servers in the Directory tree.

Third-party applications will also provide a means for extending the schema. Novell's NetWare Application Launcher, for example, will make an extension to the schema to define an Application icon. Prefixes for schema extensions can be registered with Novell Developer Support. This registry ensures that schema prefixes among vendors are not duplicated on the schema.

Any user performing modifications to the schema must have write rights on the [ROOT] object. Before you create a new attribute or object class, determine first if the attribute or object class already exists in the schema. If you cannot find the attribute or object class you need or if the class is missing an attribute, you can then take the steps necessary to extend the schema.

Each time there are modifications to the schema, these changes will be synchronized on all IntranetWare servers in the tree. The synchronization process requires no administrator intervention as it is part of the NDS background processes that occur. The schema synchronization occurs through the use of the trickle-down algorithm because the synchronization occurs from the top and proceeds downward.

Therefore, the schema updates will propagate across replicas of the same partition and downward in the tree structure from the [ROOT].

The trickle-down method causes an IntranetWare server receiving an updated schema to build a distribution list in order to update servers that it knows about. It will then check all servers in its distribution list to determine if they have received an updated copy of the schema. If they have not received a copy, that server will send an updated copy of the latest schema to other servers. This process extends only down and across, not up.

NDS Objects and Their Uses

You will discover if you haven't already that some NDS objects will be used much more than others. Obviously, the User object will be the most commonly used object in your tree. Some other leaf objects may never be used in your tree. That's okay. There are probably no IntranetWare networks that will have a need for all the objects defined in NDS. But, they are in the schema for a general audience that may need them at some point.

To make your job easier, we have first grouped the objects in the following sections according to how they are used.

▸ Required Objects — These are the objects that either you must define or are defined for you during the installation of IntranetWare.

▸ Commonly Used Objects — These objects include both the container and non-container objects along with examples of how the objects can be used. These examples are based on actual consulting experiences.

▸ Less Commonly Used Objects — These are the objects that may have less importance for you. Where appropriate we have listed consulting recommendations with these objects as well.

REQUIRED OBJECTS

The following objects are required in your NDS tree. When you install your first IntranetWare server, these objects will be present in your NDS tree. All of these objects will require you to name them at some point in the IntranetWare installation.

As shown in Figure 3.6 of Novell's installation utility, you will be prompted for a name of the tree, organization, and organizational units. You can also create a Country object, which is not mandatory.

Top and [ROOT]

Effective Class

Purpose   The Top object class is the super class of all other object classes in the schema. This object is also the container object for all other objects in the Directory hierarchy. The Top class is an effective class object. The only instance of the Top object is the [ROOT] object.

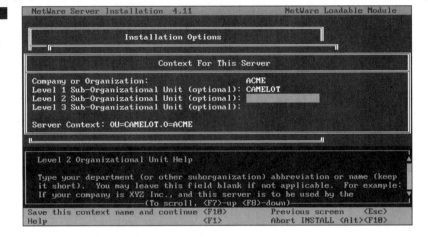

F I G U R E   3.6

*Novell's Install utility
requires you to name all
required objects during
the installation.*

The [ROOT] object is at the top of your inverted tree structure. The [ROOT], from a visual standpoint in the utilities, is the starting point of your tree and branches downward as shown in Figure 3.7. The name of the [ROOT] object is your tree name, although this name is not indicated or displayed in the utilities. When you install the first IntranetWare server in a tree, you are prompted for a tree name, which means that you actually assign a name to the [ROOT] object. Each tree will contain one and only one [ROOT] object.

The [ROOT] object's name, which is the tree name, is broadcast on your network using the Service Advertising Protocol. If you have multiple trees running on the same network infrastructure, you must ensure that the names are unique.

Sample Uses   Choose a name for [ROOT] that will clearly identify the organization or company for the tree. Keep in mind that renaming the [ROOT] object or tree name can only be done with the DSMERGE.

Example Uses   Again, [ROOT] is the only instance of the Top object class in the NDS tree. However, in the schema, all object classes must have the super class of Top defined, including any new classes created by extending the schema. Top is the only object that has no super class. All object classes inherit from the class Top. All object classes that you may define through schema extensions must contain the Top class.

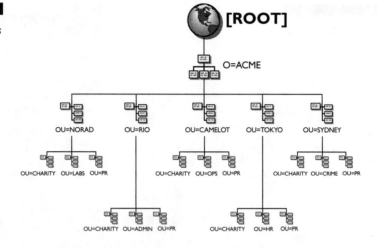

F I G U R E   3.7

ACME tree structure shows
the [ROOT] object at
the top of the inverted
tree structure.

CONSULTING EXPERIENCE

Most companies simply use the same name as their company or Organization object and add an _TREE. For example, our tree name for ACME is ACME_TREE. The organ-ization name is O=ACME. You want to choose a name that you can recognize as the tree name if you are using software analysis tools on your network and looking at server-to-server communications. Figure 3.8 illustrates how the NDS tree for ACME has been named.

Organization

Effective Class

Purpose   This object class is used to define organization objects in the tree. An organization is located directly under the [ROOT] object or C=Country object. This object is used to define the name of a company, and you are required to define at least one organization in your NDS tree. Multiple O=Organization objects may be used directly below [ROOT] or Country as shown in Figure 3.9.

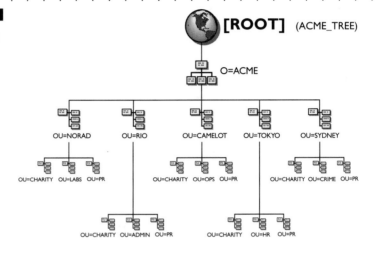

F I G U R E   3.8

The NDS tree for ACME is
named ACME_TREE.

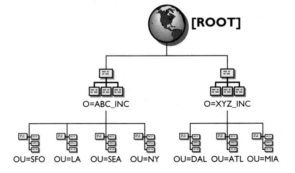

F I G U R E   3.9

Multiple O=Organization
objects defined for a large
conglomerate company

Sample Uses   The ACME tree is defined as the name of its organization O=ACME.
The organization represents the name of your company or organization and should
be an overall descriptor of the business. If you are a member of a nonprofit group or
university, the name of your Organization object can be the same name as your
university or group.

CONSULTING EXPERIENCE

Most companies typically define only one Organization object in their NDS tree. If all your business units are connected with the same network, then a single Organization object more accurately represents your network. Our guideline for using multiple Organization objects is based on the network infrastructure in which you operate. For example, if you are a large conglomerate with varied businesses that have decided to communicate information together using IntranetWare for the exchange of information, you can use multiple Organization objects as shown in Figure 3.9 above. If each company is separately managed with a separate network infrastructure, you can create multiple Organization objects for each business unit under the [ROOT] object. You can also use the Organizational Unit objects to represent your business units.

For more information on designing multiple Organization objects, see Chapter 5.

User

Effective Class

Purpose Obviously, the most common object in your tree, the User object represents every user that is part of your IntranetWare network. The User object is similar to the user object found in NetWare 3 environments but contains more attributes.

Sample Uses During the installation of your first IntranetWare server, you will be prompted to assign a password for the first user ADMIN created on the network. This user, named ADMIN, has object Supervisor rights assigned to the [ROOT] object of your tree. The ADMIN user has all rights (NDS and File System) initially to the entire tree. At this point in your installation, it is the only object with such complete and extensive access to your network. The importance of maintaining the ADMIN user or another object with the same rights at [ROOT] is well known. If you should delete this object without making other rights assignments, say to an organizational role, your access to the tree is lost. Your options in this situation would be to reinstall NDS or call Novell Technical Support to provide you with reentrance into your tree.

CONSULTING EXPERIENCE

After you have installed the first couple of IntranetWare servers, ensure that the ADMIN password is protected. Following these steps will diminish the likelihood of losing access to your tree:

1 • Your first IntranetWare server installation will prompt you for a password for the ADMIN user. Remember that the first password you assign to the NDS for ADMIN is also assigned to the bindery Supervisor object created by the install utility. If you are doing a bindery upgrade, the supervisor's password is taken from the bindery. If the bindery supervisor's password does not exist, then the NDS ADMIN password is used. If you later change the ADMIN user's password, the bindery Supervisor password does not change. Choose a password that will not easily be guessed. Change your passwords periodically for greater security. The ADMIN user password is changed through NWADMIN or NETADMIN utilities. The bindery Supervisor password can be changed through the NetWare 3 SYSCON utility.

2 • Create an organizational role in the O=Organization level of your tree and assign this role object Supervisor rights at the [ROOT] object of your tree.

3 • Do not make this organizational role object a security equivalent to the original ADMIN user. If the original ADMIN were to be deleted, your organizational role would have no access to the tree because the security equivalency would be lost. For more information on how to define security for organizational roles, refer to Chapter 13.

NCP Server

Effective Class

Purpose   A NetWare (NCP) server object will automatically be created for any IntranetWare server being installed or upgraded to IntranetWare. The server object holds key information such as the network address and the version of NetWare you are running on that machine. This object type is used to represent any server that provides NCP (NetWare Core Protocol) transport and session services and can represent either bindery or NDS-based NCP servers. This subclass of the Server object provides further definition of NCP services available on a particular server.

Sample Uses   The supported Services attribute can be used to list NCP-based features and services available for this network address. As part of an NDS search engine, you can search for available NCP services.

Another useful feature is the Operator attribute, which is used by an NCP server as an access control list. If a particular object is part of this access control list, that object can perform remote console operations. These remote operations do not mean using RCONSOLE; they have the capability to exercise the console APIs, which RCONSOLE does not use.

The server object is basically managed by NDS and requires little attention from the administrator.

CONSULTING EXPERIENCE

Be sure to follow the naming standards presented in Chapter 4. This is a resource on which you will no doubt want to perform Directory queries. Consistent and appropriate naming will help this process considerably.

Volume

Effective Class

Purpose   The server volume object is automatically created when you install an IntranetWare server into the tree. A file server must have at least one volume called the SYS volume. The server may have additional volumes that are defined during the installation of IntranetWare. A volume object will be created for each mounted volume during the installation. The naming convention is <file server name> _ <volume name>.

Sample Uses   This object type exists primarily to differentiate it from other types of resource objects and to allow greater flexibility for volume management if needed. It is also used in MAP commands and is required by the FILER utility to grant file system rights.

CONSULTING EXPERIENCE

IntranetWare gives you flexibility to place print queues on any IntranetWare volume. We recommend that you always create at least one other volume in addition to the SYS volume so that your print queue will not fill up the SYS volume and cause NDS to become disabled.

Use the volume restrictions to limit the size of your volumes before they fill up completely. You can also limit the disk space used on the Home Directory if you are short on space or want to limit each user on the volume.

COMMONLY USED OBJECTS

Below is a list of the most commonly used NDS objects. Most, if not all, of these objects will be used in your NDS tree. Small sites with perhaps one server may not use all of these objects. In fact, it is only necessary to make use of the objects that will best serve the purposes of your network environment.

> **NOTE** The following objects are schema extensions for the NetWare Application Launcher (NAL) version 1.0. These extensions occur during the installation of IntranetWare automatically.

Application Object

Non-Effective Class

Purpose   The purpose of this object is to define other application objects for the NetWare Application Launcher.

DOS Application Object

Effective Class

Purpose   The purpose of the DOS application object is to represent applications that use the DOS operating system.

Sample Uses   You can use this object for any application that runs on DOS that you wish to represent with an NDS object.

Example Uses   The most likely use of this object is with legacy applications that are written to run only on DOS. This object can also be used to represent DOS-based utilities such as RCONSOLE.

Windows 3.1x Application Object

Effective Class

Purpose   This object is used to represent objects that are written for the Windows 3.1x platform.

Sample Uses   Use this object to represent any Windows-based application that you want to access from Directory Services such as the NWADMIN utility or NDS-MANAGER.

Windows 95 Application Object

Effective Class

Purpose   This object is used to represent an application that is running on Windows 95.

Sample Uses   Applications such as the 32-bit NWADMIN can be represented with this object.

NT Application Object

Effective Class

Purpose   This object is used to represent any application that is using NT as the workstation platform.

Bindery Object

Effective Class

Purpose   This leaf object represents any object other than user, group, queue, profile, and print server created through bindery services. The bindery object has the format of Common Name + Object Type and is used to provide backward compatibility for bindery-oriented applications or utilities.

Sample Uses   You will see bindery objects appear after a migration from NetWare 3 to IntranetWare if an object is not identifiable by NDS. Some applications will create bindery objects to suite their particular purposes. For applications that still require the bindery services, a bindery object could exist in the tree. Although these objects appear in utilities such as NWADMIN, they are nonmanageable from NWADMIN or NETADMIN and are present only for information purposes.

CONSULTING EXPERIENCE

Do not delete any bindery object until you verify its purpose in the Directory. Some installation utilities will create a bindery object that if removed will cause problems for the application. Always check first before deleting bindery objects that appear in your containers.

Organizational Unit

Effective Class

Purpose   Nearly all NDS trees, except environments with a single IntranetWare server, will use Organizational Units. They are, however, optional. Organizational Units subdivide the tree into either locations or organizations, which could be departments, divisions, or workgroups. The Organizational Unit is also referred to as a container and contains the login script property, also known as the container login script. All users in a container will execute that container's script if it is available.

Sample Uses As shown in Figure 3.10 the ACME tree uses containers to make logical divisions in the tree. Notice that the first level of OU's represent geographic sites based on the network infrastructure, and the subsequent levels represent the departments of ACME. Many trees will be designed in this fashion with several levels of nested organizational units. For more information on designing an IntranetWare tree, see Chapter 5.

FIGURE 3.10

The use of organizational units makes NDS tree subdivision clear and logical.

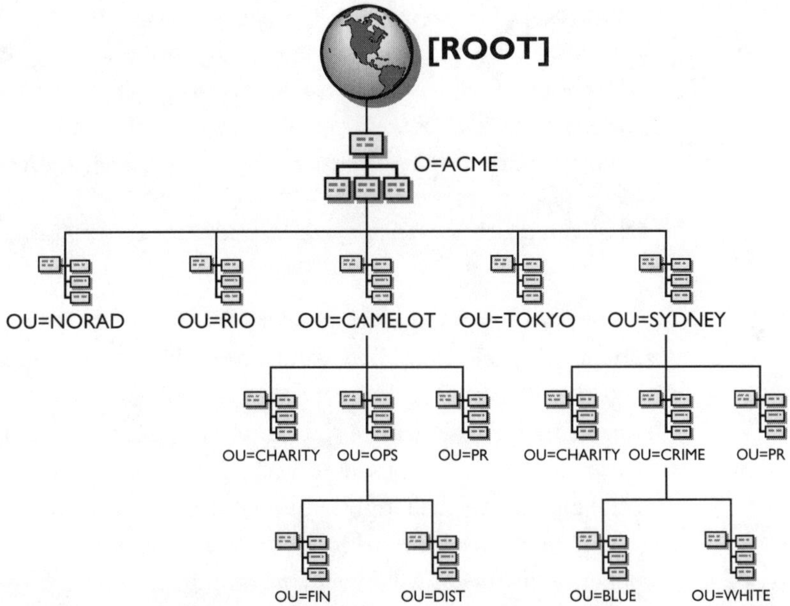

Organizational Role

Effective Class

Purpose An Organizational Role object is typically used to define a role or position within an organization object or container object. The role is extremely useful because the object or file rights are granted to the role itself and not to the occupants who may belong to the role.

However, this rule is different for object creation. For example, an object is created by a user assigned to the organizational role. The object creation rights to the new object go to the user creating the object, not to the organizational role.

NOTE

CONSULTING EXPERIENCE

Most companies use the Organizational Unit to represent geographic locations, divisions, and workgroups. You generally use an Organizational Unit to group common users and resources in the same container. Organizational Units should not be created to represent a single person or a single resource. They are used to provide access to a group of users in a particular part of the tree. IntranetWare does provide the capability to move containers to new locations in the tree should your needs change.

Sample Uses Organizational Roles are especially useful in maintaining sub-administrators. The occupant can be moved in and out of the role quickly to facilitate short-term assignments. For example, if the regular administrator is absent for any length of time, another user can be moved into the role temporarily to manage the network. The implementation of this object is just like a group. The organizational role occupants derive their rights through security equivalence to the role object.

As shown in Figure 3.11, we have created an organizational role for each city contained in the ACME tree. This administrator will have rights to manage their entire container, such as adding and deleting users or servers.

Group

Effective Class

Purpose This class is used to represent a set of users from any part of the NDS tree. The membership of the group is static and is only modified by your administrative action.

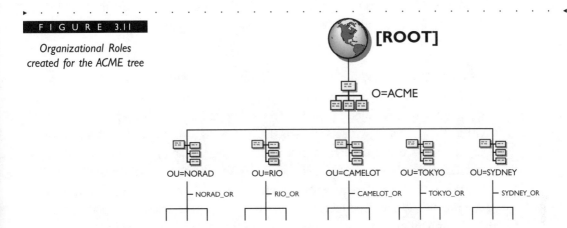

*Organizational Roles
created for the ACME tree*

Groups function the same way they did in NetWare 3. There is very little difference between using group objects and organizational unit (OU) objects. Both have the same function, which is to place common users close together. It is true that users who are members of both objects receive rights by security equivalence, but there are some differences. Because of security equivalency, any member of an OU will receive whatever rights the OU possesses. Users inside groups also receive whatever rights the group possesses, and just like a container there is no IRF provision. For more information on NDS security refer to Chapter 13.

CONSULTING EXPERIENCE

The use of an organizational role is highly recommended as a way to administer rights in your network to various administrators in your network. You can more easily track who has received rights as administrators in your tree by checking who has been made an occupant of a role. Assigning rights to individuals through means other than the organizational role is not recommended because it is more difficult to track which individuals have been granted rights in your tree. After a few months or even weeks, you'll forget who has been assigned rights. For more details on setting up an organizational role for your tree, see Chapter 13.

Groups are used to differentiate rights within a particular Organizational Unit. Rather than create multiple subcontainers, you can simply use groups within a container for users that need a specific environment created.

Sample Use   In order to provide rights to a smaller subset of users in the CHARITY.SYDNEY.ACME OU, you can use a group. Figure 3.12 shows an organizational unit called OU=Charity and is populated with users and resources. Within this OU are two sets of users. Each group is accessing different software on the server and needs different rights assignments. Within the container or OU login script (known as the system login script in NetWare 3), the IF MEMBER OF GROUP statements are used to determine which group a user belongs to for rights assignments. When each user logs into the network, the login script determines if a user is a member of a group and sets the appropriate environment variables.

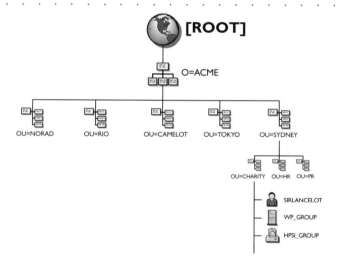

FIGURE 3.12

*The Organization Unit
Charity with two groups
created to differentiate
users within the
same container*

Directory Map

Effective Class

Purpose   The Directory Map object is a pointer that refers to a file system directory on a NetWare volume. It is used in login scripts or by the MAP command to point to a directory that contains a particular application.

CONSULTING EXPERIENCE

Groups are great to use in a container to provide further differentiation of rights to a subset of users. We recommend that groups be used in a container instead of creating more containers. Additional containers would require the use of additional container login scripts. Limit the number of groups to fewer than 15 in a container login script, if possible. The more groups, the longer the container login script will be, and a slower login will occur. However, if you have 15 or more groups you should create additional containers because the login script must check your users against each group membership list. Groups should be contained locally. Avoid the use of groups that contain users from multiple organizational units.

Sample Use   Let's assume you have WordPerfect installed in a directory called WP60. If you were to upgrade your software to WordPerfect 6.1, you could choose to rename the subdirectory to WP61. You would also have to change every login script to reflect this change for the new subdirectory. Through the use of a directory map you can eliminate making changes to your login scripts. Your directory map object is used in your login scripts and points to a subdirectory on a NetWare volume. Your only change is to have the directory map point to WP61. All container login scripts are left intact.

Alias

Effective Class

Purpose   An alias is another name for an object. An alias is an object that points to another object you specify in the Directory tree. An alias can point to either a container object (an object that holds other containers) or a non-container object (one that does not have any other containers).

Sample Uses   An alias is a name containing at least one Relative Distinguished Name. As a network administrator you may grant users access to a particular resource contained in another OU, such as a printer. You can create an alias to reference that printer, for example. The alias can be considered a relay to another object in a different part of the tree.

CONSULTING EXPERIENCE

Directory map objects are useful for providing a standard container login script on multiple servers. We recommend that you have standard file structures for all your IntranetWare file servers so that you can facilitate easier use of directory maps. If you maintain a directory map for an application, you can make a change to the directory map pointer and have it be effective for many servers. The directory map requires the administrator to make each user security equivalent to the map object and for containers with large numbers of users. This could be a drawback from an administration standpoint. You can, however, grant rights on the directory pointed to by the directory map to the container to simplify this situation.

You can also alias one OU to another OU, giving one OU to the other OU's resources. It appears as if the alias places the alias's container inside of the other container.

The object being aliased is known as the primary object. When you create an alias object you may or may not name it with some indication that it is an alias to another object. For example, the name might include the word "alias," such as Alias_Blair.

CONSULTING EXPERIENCE

The alias object is very useful in moving subtrees or renaming containers so that you can easily make the transition. The alias can assist you in this migration path. In addition, the alias can be useful for some companies wanting to create mobile users who do not want to remember their user context. The alias can be created at the top of the tree below the Organization object, for example, to shorten the user's context. If user DAVID wants to log in to the network he only has to remember that his context is DAVID.Acme because that alias points to his actual context in the tree. This example is shown in Figure 3.13. Keep in mind that this example refers to a very limited number of users, such as mobile users. We are not implying that you alias every user in your tree.

*Mobile user DAVID has a
shortened context through
the use of aliasing.*

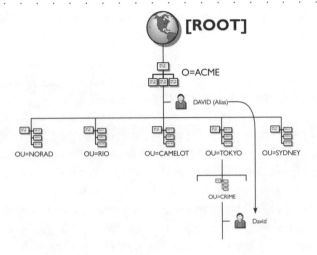

Print Server

Effective Class

Purpose   The print server leaf object represents a server that takes print jobs out of a print queue and sends them to a network printer. This object is used in conjunction with the Printer and Print Queue objects. A print server object must be created for every actual print server that exists on the IntranetWare network.

Sample Uses   All IntranetWare networks using printers will have at least one print server object. You can use this object to define which printers to assign to users based on their position or location in the NDS tree. You can also define the print server operators.

Printer

Effective Class

Purpose   The Printer object is used in conjunction with the print server object. You use this object to manage a printer. The assignment for a print queue can be made within the object.

Sample Uses   You can attach printers in several different ways to the network, namely, directly to the network, to a printer port of a NetWare server, or to a printer port of a PC.

CONSULTING EXPERIENCE

You can place the Printer object along with the Print Queue object as high as possible in your NDS tree to support many users. If your printer is for only your container, then place the printer in your container. If more containers need access to the printer, place the object in the next highest level in your tree. Keep in mind that the placement of printers higher in the tree also adds overhead to NDS in terms of name resolution. We also recommend that you configure printers as network-direct printers in queue server mode as explained in Chapter 14.

Queue

Effective Class

Purpose   This object represents a print queue defined on an IntranetWare server. The queue actually represents the directories where the print jobs are sent to be serviced by a printer.

Sample Uses   Place Print Queue object along with the Print object at the highest level possible in your tree to service the most users.

CONSULTING EXPERIENCE

All IntranetWare print queues should be placed on a volume other than the SYS volume for greater fault tolerance of the server. A queue object must be created for IntranetWare printing. A Print Queue object is assigned to a printer.

Profile

Effective Class

Purpose   The Profile object is used as a special purpose scripting object that is executed by LOGIN.EXE and is a shared login script after the execution of your container login script. The profile script can contain special drive mappings or environment settings you want a select group of people to receive.

One of the properties of a user object is the profile. When a user is first created using the NWADMIN utility, you can specify that the user be part of a profile. You can also add a user to a profile anytime after by going back and adding the profile to a user object's properties.

Sample Uses   There are three notable uses for a profile script:

- ▸ Creating a global login script

- ▸ Creating a location login script

- ▸ Creating a special function login script

Creating Global Login Scripts

NetWare 4 does not use a global system login script. Each Organizational Unit created will have its own login script referred to as the OU login script. The order of execution of login scripts is:

1 • OU login script

2 • Profile login script, if used

3 • User login script, or

4 • Default login script if no other script is available

Therefore, if you want to create a more global login script and include multiple Organizational Units, you could employ the profile object to set up a specific environment for a group of users. Keep in mind that this type of solution is expensive in terms of NDS overhead that will be created on your network.

Location Login Scripts

A profile can also be used for determining allocation of resources based on location. For example, each department of a company may have three printers and three print queues. A profile enables you to assign a particular group of users to a specific print queue. You can use a profile login script to capture to a particular print queue and the users will automatically capture to that print queue.

Special Function Scripts

A profile can be used as a special function script to assign users access for applications. For example, you can create a profile script that will be used by only administrators. This script may give these users a specific drive assignment to a help desk utility. In this scenario, you would move the help desk utility out of the SYS:Public directory into a new subdirectory you create called HELPDESK. When a user logs into the network, the admin Profile object is executed, and the user is assigned a drive mapping to the HELPDESK directory. Only users who execute the profile script will be assigned rights to access the help desk utility.

CONSULTING EXPERIENCE

Typically, the profile object is used as a global login script for a workgroup or organization. Keep in mind that the profile object will execute from one container, although users may be participating from other containers and may see some performance issues if the script is executing over a wide-area connection. In addition, you will notice increased overhead of NDS traffic as NDS searches the tree to locate a particular object.

Unknown

Effective Class

Purpose   This object class represents any object created by the server to restore any object whose base class is currently undefined in the schema. Objects of this class type are created by only the server, not the client, and usually occur when a mandatory property of an object has been lost.

Unknown objects are created during synchronization of objects as placeholders, when a mandatory attribute of an object has been lost, and when an object class has been deleted and the server had an object of that class.

Sample Uses   This object is automatically created by NDS. If an unknown object appears in your tree, check to see if some other object has been deleted. In the case of a deleted server object, the server's volume objects will appear as unknown objects and must be deleted by an administrator. In other circumstances an unknown object may appear temporarily as the NDS background processes work through a synchronization process.

CONSULTING EXPERIENCE

Before deleting an unknown object, first check to make sure it is not needed. When you have verified that the object is not needed, then remove it from your tree. There is no point in maintaining unknown and unused objects.

LESS COMMONLY USED OBJECTS

AFP Server

Effective Class

Purpose   The AFP Server object represents an Appletalk Filing Protocol-based server that is part of your IntranetWare network as a server node or router for connected Macintosh workstations.

Sample Use   This object serves only as a descriptor object and does not provide any management capability for your AFP server in an IntranetWare environment. You can use this object for informational purposes about Appletalk in your IntranetWare environment.

Bindery Queue

Effective Class

Purpose   The Bindery Queue object represents a leaf object queue that has been placed in the Directory through an upgrade or migration to IntranetWare.

Sample Use   A bindery queue is used to support other queues upgraded from NetWare 3.

Country

Effective Class

Purpose   This object is used to define country entries in your NDS tree. The Country Name attribute is restricted to two characters as defined by the ISO3166 standard. Directory Services does not check to see if characters are correctly defined, just if there are two.

Sample Uses   For companies desiring to use the Country object, there are several considerations. First, the object must be placed directly below the [ROOT] object. Specifying this option during installation of IntranetWare is shown in Chapter 16. Second, consider the ramifications of adding the Country object to your tree in terms of adding another layer to your tree and lengthening your users' context. Also, carefully plan your tree design so that your users' context will be logical and make sense. For example, let's assume we added the Country object to the ACME tree under [ROOT]. Since our company is global in nature, which country do we choose? If we say that C=US, notice what the context would be for users not reporting under the US region. This example is shown in Figure 3.14.

CommExec

Effective Class

Purpose   The CommExec object is used to manage Novell's NetWare for SAA NetWare Loadable Module on an IntranetWare Server.

Sample Use   This object is used only with NetWare SAA and provides management capabilities and rights privileges for the [ROOT] level of your NDS tree.

FIGURE 3.14

The Country object can cause your users' context to look different than the context you are actually trying to represent.

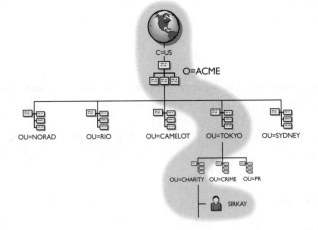

Distinguished name: CN=SIRKAY.OU=CHARITY.OU=TOKYO.O=ACME.C=US

CONSULTING EXPERIENCE

Our recommendation is to avoid using the Country object in your tree. Even with emerging gateway technology to interconnect disparate directory databases, the gateway will handle the distinction between databases using and not using the Country object. The Country object is also not necessary for companies wanting to connect to a public data provider for Directory Services.

Locality

Effective Class

Purpose   The Locality object is used to define geographic locations in the NDS tree such as states or regions or counties. The Locality object is currently not enabled by Novell's NWADMIN or NETADMIN utilities and therefore is not visible through the current utilities. Programs are available to define and view this object class.

Sample Uses This object must be named by one or both of its attributes L=Locality Name or S=State or Province Name. Most companies will not need to use this object. Some Directory Services that provide connection services through NDS will use the Locality object.

CONSULTING EXPERIENCE

The Locality object exists in the NDS schema.

Computer

Effective Class

Purpose This object class can represent both computers used as NetWare servers and computers used as client workstations.

Sample Use A key attribute of this object is the Operator, which can be used to identify individuals or groups that typically handle the day-to-day hardware maintenance of this computer.

Device

Non-Effective Class

Purpose This object subclass is used to represent a physical device such as a modem or printer that you want to have defined in your tree.

Sample Uses One attribute contained in this object is the Locality Name, which can be used to identify the physical location of a device. In addition, as more devices become NDS enabled, the Device object will possibly come into greater use for managing those objects.

External Entity

Effective Class

Purpose This object is used to store information about non-native NDS objects in the Directory tree.

Sample Use Some situations may require that an NDS object have information about another object that does not exist on the Directory Tree. A messaging service, for example, can use the External Entity class to store information about e-mail users who exist on other systems outside of the IntranetWare tree.

List

Effective Class

Purpose This object is used to represent an unordered set of object names in the Directory. It could be a list of leaf objects or other objects that you want to logically group together based on some type of search criteria.

Sample Use The Member attribute is used to define the objects that are members of the list. The members can be any individual objects, even including Group objects. However, the key difference between this object and a group object is that membership in a list does not imply security equivalence as it does in a group. This object can be used to logically list objects for NDS searches.

Message Routing Group

Effective Class

Purpose Closely related to the Messaging Server, the Message Routing Group object is used to represent a group of messaging servers that communicate with each other to transfer messages.

Sample Use The Member attribute is used to define the messaging servers that belong to the Message Routing Group.

Messaging Server

Effective Class

Purpose   This object is used to represent messaging servers such as Novell's MHS servers that may exist in the Directory tree.

Sample Uses   If you are using Novell's MHS services for IntranetWare you will use this object. Important attributes such as the Message Routing Group, Messaging Server Type, and Supported Gateway will be configured to define the types of services provided for e-mail communications on your network.

Organizational Person

Non-Effective Class

Purpose   This object defines anyone who either represents or is in some way associated with a particular organization, such as an employee. This object is part of two subclasses defined in the X.500 standard: Organizational Person and Residential Person.

Sample Uses   The User object is a subclass of the Organizational Person. The user class inherits from the organizational person.

Person

Non-Effective Class

Purpose   This object contains the more common attributes of the Organizational Person and Residential Person objects.

Sample Uses   The X.500 specification defines two subclasses of Person: Organization Person and Residential Person. The current IntranetWare schema does not include Residential Person. The separation of Person from Organizational Person has been done for future compatibility with x.500.

Resource

Non-Effective Class

 Purpose   This object class is used to identify the logical resources available on your network. The resource class is similar to the device class in that a device is a physical unit, and a resource is a nonphysical or logical unit.

Sample Uses   A very useful attribute in this object is the Host Resource Name, which can be used if a host's local identification differs from a more global resource identification. If a resource is being used by multiple localities you can define a Locality name, Organization name, and Organization Unit name as separate identifiers. If you define appropriate values, you can initiate NDS searches for a particular resource name, locality, or organization.

This chapter has presented a basis for understanding and using NDS objects in your tree along with the schema structure, which is the foundation of Novell Directory Services. Extensions can be made to the schema to add new object classes or to add properties to existing object classes.

With this information you will be able to create a useful naming standard and to define appropriate objects for use within your tree.

CHAPTER 4

Directory Services Naming Conventions

"It is impossible that every particular thing should have a distinct peculiar name."
John Locke

Closely tied to the NDS structure is the concept of naming. Object naming is fundamental to the Directory because it provides a definition of the objects in the tree as well as their relationship to the other objects in the tree. In addition, resource searching, a key function of the NDS name service, is provided through the use of object naming within the Directory. Good naming implies improved search capabilities now and in the future as more applications take advantage of NDS capabilities.

IntranetWare uses a set of rules known as the Directory schema to define the naming hierarchy for the entire IntranetWare network. The schema is replicated across all IntranetWare servers that exist in the same tree. By contrast, the NetWare 3 bindery is a flat naming structure that is defined by the individual NetWare 3 server and does not provide a hierarchy of bindery objects. A visual example of this concept is shown in Figure 4.1.

FIGURE 4.1

A comparison between the NetWare 3 bindery and the IntranetWare Directory

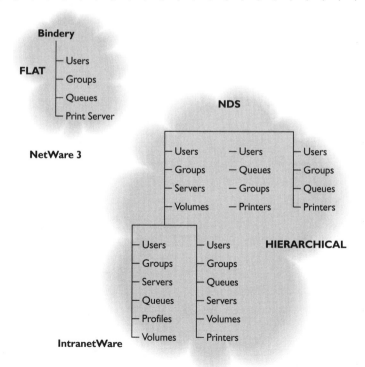

This section will first consider the basic elements provided within NDS for searching and locating objects within the Directory. These elements include the concepts of name types, distinguished names, relative distinguished names, contexts, typeful and typeless naming, and other methods of naming.

Next we will discuss how to create a naming standard for your particular needs and will include sample standards that can be implemented at your organization.

NDS Naming Rules

NDS is a collection of objects that follows a set of rules regarding their creation, naming, and use. Becoming familiar with how each of the NDS objects and properties are used in building the NDS tree structure and how they should be named will improve your NDS tree design.

Your understanding of the schema will help you to understand the internal rules of the objects, including the name types. Also, your understanding of the schema will help you to determine the necessity of creating additional objects through schema extensions or through the use of existing NDS objects and properties.

Next, we will explain briefly the NDS schema — its components, rules, and how the NDS objects are created. For a more detailed understanding of the NDS schema refer to Chapter 3.

NDS SCHEMA

NDS consists of objects and properties that are defined by a set of rules in the Directory called the schema. The schema rules dictate the naming and relationship of the objects and properties that can exist in the Directory.

The NDS schema is automatically stored on every IntranetWare server you install, and any updates to the schema are automatically synchronized to all IntranetWare servers.

The schema consists of three major components: the object class, the property definitions, and the property syntaxes. These three components work together to establish the rules that control the creation of a particular object type in the Directory. For instance, each object is defined in terms of the property definitions and other class definitions.

The property definitions, in turn, are defined in terms of the property syntaxes. The property syntaxes are the data types of the property values and define the type and length of data. Figure 4.2 illustrates the relationship between the components of the schema.

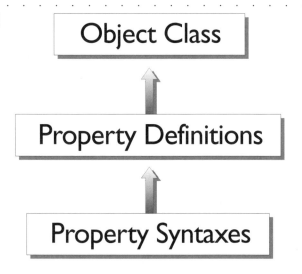

The object class defines the types of NDS objects that can be stored in the Directory. The object class is used as the rules for creating the individual objects and determining that object's set of characteristics. This means that every object in the tree belongs to an object class that specifies what properties are used.

The base schema that ships with IntranetWare contains 32 object classes. These object classes cannot be removed or deleted from the schema.

Novell's INSTALL Utility also makes extensions to the schema to add additional objects. See Chapter 3 for a complete listing of the schema extensions. Each of the object classes in the schema is defined by the relationship of the object's containment in the Directory tree. This relationship is constructed on the basis of the containment class rules.

OBJECT NAME TYPES

Each object consists of a naming attribute and its value. The value is assigned by the administrator during the object creation in the Directory tree. Connecting the naming attribute with the value is an equal (=) sign. The naming attribute determines how the object will be used in the Directory tree. Some objects are container objects while other objects are leaf objects (or non-container objects). Table 4.1 lists the object name attributes that are assigned to each of the NDS objects. Generally, they are abbreviated.

T A B L E 4.1	NAME ATTRIBUTE	NAME DESCRIPTION
List of the object name types that are assigned to each of the NDS objects	C	Country Name
	L	Locality Name
	S	State or Province Name
	O	Organization Name
	OU	Organizational Unit Name
	CN	Common Name (includes all leaf objects)
	Bindery Type	Bindery Type

The name types C=Country Name, L=Locality Name, O=Organization Name, and OU=Organizational Unit Name are naming attributes of container objects. The TOP class is also a container object (containing [ROOT]), although it is not visible by the Novell utilities. State or Province Name is not a base class.

► · ◄

CONSULTING EXPERIENCE

As you may have noticed from the Novell utilities, not all of the object class attributes of the container objects are available to you for use when building your NDS tree. For example, the class L=Locality Name and the S=State or Province Name do not show up in the current versions of the Novell utilities. These object classes are found in the NDS schema but have not been exposed by the utilities. The L=Locality class was placed in the schema for compatibility with the X.500 standard. When building the structure of your NDS tree, you can use the O=Organization and OU=Organizational Unit container classes, which provide you with the same functionality. The Locality container can be enabled through utilities such as the Preferred Systems' DS Standard utility.

The name type CN=Common Name includes all the leaf objects or non-container objects. Therefore, if the object is a user, printer, server, or any other leaf object, it is named by the type CN. The following is a list of all the leaf objects you may use to represent the network resources in your NDS tree. These objects are all named with the "CN=".

▸ Auditor	▸ NLS
▸ AFP Server	▸ Organization Role
▸ Bindery	▸ Print Queue
▸ Bindery Queue	▸ Print Server
▸ Computer	▸ Printer
▸ Directory Map	▸ Profile
▸ Group	▸ User
▸ NetWare Server	▸ Volume

Alias is not shown in this list because it is actually named by the object that it is referencing, such as an Organization, Organizational Unit, or Common Name.

Distinguished Name

Each object in the tree is given a distinguished name during its creation. An object's distinguished name consists of the name of the object plus the names of each of the container objects between itself and the [ROOT] object of the NDS tree. The naming of the object determines the location or position of the object in the tree. The object name attribute, mentioned in the previous section, can be used to help define the distinguished name by specifying the object type for the distinguished name. The distinguished name, therefore, provides a global, complete, and unique name in the Directory tree.

For example, in Figure 4.3 in the ACME tree, the distinguished name for the user Abraham Lincoln is the user object name plus the names of all the containers in which he is a member. It can be viewed as a path back to the top or [ROOT] of the tree. Thus, the distinguished name for the user Abraham Lincoln begins with his common name, CN=ALINCOLN, followed by each of the containers in which he is a member, OU=AUDIT.OU=ADMIN.OU=RIO.O=ACME, back to the [ROOT] object. Therefore, the distinguished name is read from left (lowest level in the tree Common Name) to right (highest level [ROOT]).

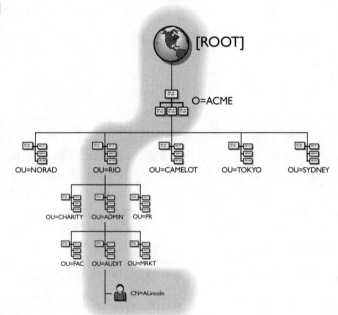

FIGURE 4.3

Each object in the ACME tree has a complete or distinguished name that is unique based on its object name plus the names of each of the container objects all the way back to [ROOT]. For example, CN=ALINCOLN.OU=AUDIT. OU=ADMIN.OU=RIO. O=ACME.

The sequence for writing or displaying the distinguished name of an object is as follows:

```
CN=ALINCOLN.OU=AUDIT.OU=ADMIN.OU=RIO.O=ACME
```

The distinguished name can be separated into segments and each segment of the object's name is separated by periods. Each segment of an object's name consists of two parts: the object name type and the name value. The first segment in the example given above is CN=ALINCOLN where CN is the object name type (abbreviated for Common Name) and ALINCOLN is the object name value.

TIP   **The proper order for writing an object's distinguished name is the least-significant (object deepest in the tree) to the most-significant (object closest to the [ROOT]). The distinguished name is always written left to right.**

NDS will resolve the distinguished names regardless of their character case. For example, ALINCOLN's distinguished name could also be written as follows:

```
cn=alincoln.ou=audit.ou=admin.ou=rio.o=acme
```

as well as:

```
CN=ALincoln.OU=Audit.OU=Admin.OU=Rio.O=Acme
```

Each of the above distinguished names for the user ALINCOLN is equivalent.

Another example of a distinguished name in the ACME tree is for the print queue object known as HP4SI-PQ1. The HP4SI-PQ1 is found in the NDS tree in the container MEDICAL, which is in the container HR, which is in the container SYDNEY, which, in turn, is in container ACME. Figure 4.4 illustrates the distinguished name for this print queue object.

Figure 4.5 shows the distinguished name for two NDS server objects. These server objects are:

```
CN=LABS-SRV1.OU=LABS.OU=NORAD.O=ACME and
```

```
CN=WHITE-SRV1.OU=WHITE.OU=CRIME.OU=TOKYO.O=ACME.
```

NOTE   **Notice that the object [ROOT] is not used in any of the distinguished names. The [ROOT] object is always implied by the NDS system. Therefore, you are not required to supply a [ROOT] object when entering a distinguished name.**

FIGURE 4.4

The distinguished name for a print queue object in the ACME is: CN=HP4SI-PQ1.OU=MEDICAL. OU=HR.OU=SYDNEY. O=ACME.

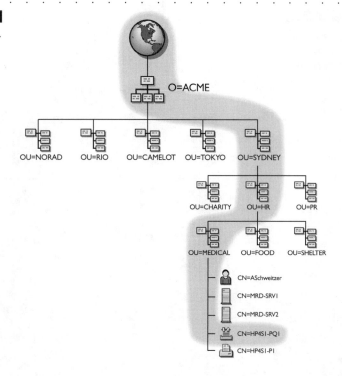

O=ACME

OU=NORAD   OU=RIO   OU=CAMELOT   OU=TOKYO   OU=SYDNEY

OU=CHARITY   OU=HR   OU=PR

OU=MEDICAL   OU=FOOD   OU=SHELTER

CN=ASchweitzer

CN=MRD-SRV1

CN=MRD-SRV2

CN=HP4SI-PQ1

CN=HP4SI-P1

CONSULTING EXPERIENCE

It can be cumbersome to use the distinguished name when referring to the NDS objects. You should become familiar with the use of the relative distinguished name, which is defined as the leaf-most portion of the name in relation to its parent container. A partial name is another commonly used term and is defined as the name in relation to a container. For example, referring back to Figure 4.5, LABS-SRV1.LABS is a partial name in relation to the container NORAD.ACME. The server object LABS-SRV1 is the relative distinguished name in relation to the container LABS.

F I G U R E 4.5

*The distinguished names
for the server object
CN=LABS-SRVI.OU=LABS.
OU=NORAD.O=ACME and
the server object
CN=WHITE-
SRVI.OU=WHITE.
OU=CRIME.OU=TOKYO.
O=ACME*

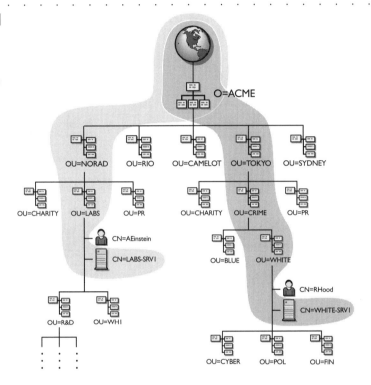

Relative Distinguished Name

A relative distinguished name (RDN) is the individual name assigned to an object otherwise known as the value plus the object naming attribute. The relative distinguished name must be unique only in relation to its parent object. This implies that there cannot be two objects in the same container using the same name.

In Figure 4.6 objects in the R&D department in the NORAD location of the ACME tree have relative distinguished names that are unique in relation to their parent object OU=R&D. The objects are CN=LDAVINCI (user), CN=R&D-SRV1 (server), CN=R&D-SRV1_SYS (volume), and CN=R&D-PSI.

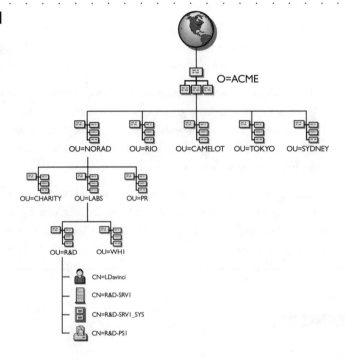

The objects in the R&D container of the ACME tree have unique relative distinguished names.

You can see in Figure 4.7 that you will not be able to create a second user object named CN=LDAVINCI in the same container R&D.LABS.NORAD.ACME. NDS naming does not permit duplicate object names in the same container regardless of the object type.

It may not always be obvious that objects of different types still need unique relative distinguished names in the container. For example, a print queue object and a group object cannot have the same relative distinguished name in the same container for the same reasons discussed above.

CONSULTING EXPERIENCE

If you are migrating from NetWare 3, be aware that you will need to have a unique relative distinguished name for each of the objects that you will be moving to

(continued)

(continued)

IntranetWare and NDS. The NetWare 3 bindery permits you to create objects with the same name as long as the object types are different. This rule does not apply to IntranetWare and NDS.

For example, it is very common for an administrator in NetWare 3 to create a print queue object and the group that will use the print queue with the same name. This is an easy method to administer the printing setup as this form of naming is legal in the NetWare 3 bindery. However, in IntranetWare each object in the container must have a unique relative distinguished name.

During the preparation of migrating from NetWare 3 to IntranetWare, you must resolve any of these duplicate names. If you do not resolve the naming conflicts, the IntranetWare migration utility will migrate the first object and not the second object with the same name.

FIGURE 4.7

Two objects within the same container cannot have the same relative distinguished name. There cannot be two objects named CN=LDAVINCI in the container R&D.LABS.NORAD.ACME.

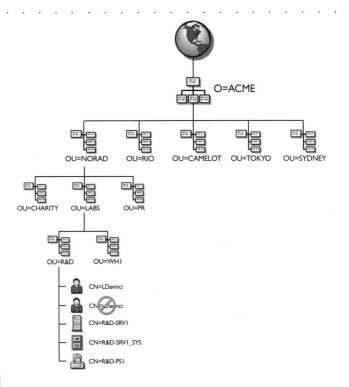

The relative distinguished name has to be unique in only the parent container. The same object name can exist in the tree if the objects are located in different containers because the parent object has a different name, which causes the object to have a unique distinguished name. Thus, the same named object in different containers has a unique relative distinguished name in relation to its parent.

Figure 4.8 illustrates how two different printer objects in the ACME tree can have the same relative distinguished name but still have a unique distinguished name in the Directory. The two printer objects are:

    CN=HP4SI-P1 (in container OU=PR.OU=NORAD.O=ACME)

    CN=HP4SI-P1 (in container OU=CHARITY.OU=TOKYO.O=ACME)

Two separate printer objects in the ACME tree can have the same relative distinguished name only if the printers are in different containers in the tree.

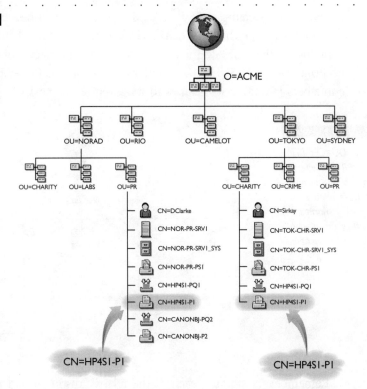

Both the printer objects named HP4SI-P1 are relative distinguished names in relation to their parent container OU=PR.OU=NORAD.O=ACME and OU=CHARITY.OU=TOKYO.O=ACME, respectively.

CONSULTING EXPERIENCE

Although the relative distinguished names for user objects must be unique within one container in the tree, we highly recommend that you create a unique naming standard across the entire NDS tree for users. Having a global naming standard for users reduces name conflicts when users are created and subsequently moved to another container for any reason. Keep in mind that e-mail systems also require unique names as well.

Relative distinguished names are not just reserved for the leaf objects. All objects in the NDS tree have a relative distinguished name in relation to their parent container. For example, in the ACME tree, there cannot exist two OU=NORAD containers under the O=ACME. However, in Figure 4.9, you will notice two containers called CHARITY and PR that are under each of the locations. This is acceptable by NDS because each instance of the OU=CHARITY and OU=PR containers is unique in relation to its parent containers.

F I G U R E   4.9

Each of the OU=CHARITY and OU=PR containers under each of the location OUs have relative distinguished names because they are unique under each of the locations.

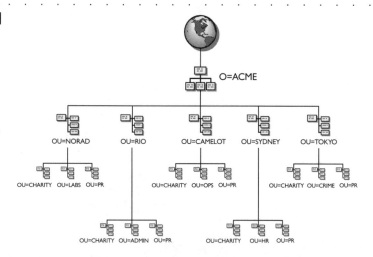

Remember, combining each of the relative distinguished names with its parent object back to [ROOT] creates a distinguished name for the Directory object. Also, both the relative distinguished name and the distinguished name can be entered as *typeful* or *typeless* names.

Typeful Names

Using or placing the object name types in an object's distinguished name is referred to as typeful naming. A couple of examples in the ACME tree of a typeful name are:

```
CN=SIRKAY.OU=CHARITY.OU=TOKYO.O=ACME
```

or

```
CN=TOK-CHR-PS1.OU=CHARITY.OU=TOKYO.O=ACME
```

where the user SIRKAY and print server TOK-CHR-PS1 are in the Charity OU in the Tokyo location.

You can also refer to each of these objects independently as CN=SIRKAY, CN=TOK-CHR-PS1, OU=CHARITY, OU=TOKYO, and O=ACME.

Each of these objects has its object name type plus the object name; hence, the definition of typeful naming. Typeful names, such as the CN designator, help define the object's location in the hierarchy. The CN designator always indicates a leaf object and is the lowest object in the NDS hierarchy.

Typeful names are not required by the Novell utilities or NDS to indicate an object's complete name because you can also use typeless names to write the complete name without using the object types. The Novell client software allows you to use typeless names because it parses the entered name with the appropriate name type.

The typeful naming method is not case sensitive. Using the examples given above, you can see that the following names are equivalent:

```
cn=sirkay.ou=charity.ou=tokyo.o=acme
```

is equivalent to

```
CN=SIRKAY.OU=CHARITY.OU=TOKYO.O=ACME
```

and

```
cn=tok-chr-ps1.ou=charity.ou=tokyo.o=acme
```

is equivalent to

```
CN=TOK-CHR-PS1.OU=CHARITY.OU=TOKYO.O=ACME
```

CONSULTING EXPERIENCE

Using typeful names can obviously be a lengthy method for indicating an object's distinguished name. Thus, this form of naming is not required or recommended for use with the command line utilities, especially LOGIN.EXE. It is cumbersome for the user to learn and use typeful naming. The user should only need to use typeless naming for the NDS objects.

Typeless Names

Typeless names are object names that do not include the object name type in each segment. Using the same examples that we used in the typeful naming from the ACME tree, the typeless names would be:

```
SIRKAY.CHARITY.TOKYO.ACME
```

or

```
TOK-CHR-PS1.CHARITY.TOKYO.ACME
```

where the user SIRKAY and print server TOK-CHR-PS1 are in the Charity OU in the Tokyo location.

Notice that we have removed the object name type from each of the segments in the object. You can now refer to the objects as simply SIRKAY (where the CN= has been removed), TOK-CHR-PS1, CHARITY, TOKYO, and ACME. All the object name types have been removed.

Like the typeful naming method, typeless naming is not case sensitive. Again, using the examples given above, you can see that the following names are equivalent:

```
sirkay.charity.tokyo.acme
```

is equivalent to

```
SIRKAY.CHARITY.TOKYO.ACME
```

and

```
tok-chr-ps1.charity.tokyo.acme
```

is resolved in the same way as

```
TOK-CHR-PS1.CHARITY.TOKYO.ACME
```

TIP

Typeless names are easier to use for both administrators and users because they are shorter and more intuitive. You will use the typeless naming more during your day-to-day operations. You should become very familiar with it.

You can also use this method of typeless naming for indicating either a relative distinguished name or a distinguished name.

Context

An object is identified in the Directory by its distinguished name, which provides the dual benefit of uniqueness and location within the tree. An object's context is its position or location in the NDS tree. If two objects are in the same container, they have the same context because their parent container is identical. In NDS tree terms, the context can be defined as the name of the parent object.

For simplicity, IntranetWare allows the client to shorten or abbreviate a complete object name through the use of a user context.

Figure 4.10 shows CDARWIN's context or location in the ACME tree. CDARWIN is in part of the Pollution department organizational unit (OU=POLL), in the R&D department (OU=R&D), in the LABS division (OU=LABS), in the NORAD office (OU=NORAD), under the ACME tree (O=ACME). The context for CDARWIN is OU=POLL.OU=R&D.OU=LABS.OU=NORAD.O=ACME.

TIP

The best analogy for the context in NDS is the "path" in the DOS file system. The path statement in DOS helps you quickly and automatically find files stored in specific subdirectories. In the same fashion the context in NDS will help you find resources in specific NDS containers.

FIGURE 4.10

*The context in the ACME
tree for the user
CN=CDARWIN is
OU=POLL.OU=R&D.
OU=LABS.OU=NORAD.
O=ACME.*

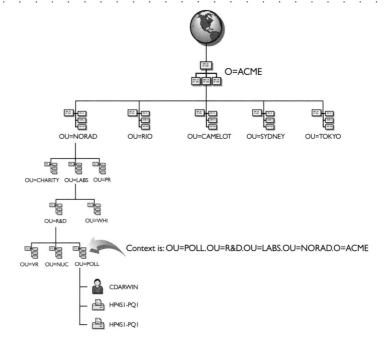

Context is: OU=POLL.OU=R&D.OU=LABS.OU=NORAD.O=ACME

Setting a context helps the user and administrator access NDS objects in the tree more easily. If a context is set, then the user and administrator simply have to enter the relative distinguished name for the resource in the container where the context has been set. Figure 4.11 shows several contexts that exist on the ACME tree:

```
OU=OPS.OU=CAMELOT.O=ACME

OU=FIN.OU=OPS.OU=CAMELOT.O=ACME

OU=DIST.OU=OPS.OU=CAMELOT.O=ACME
```

A context can be set only to a container object. This means that you can set a context to point to either an Organizational Unit (OU=), an Organization (O=), or the [ROOT] object. You cannot set a context to a leaf object.

F I G U R E   4.11

Several contexts at different levels are shown in the ACME tree.

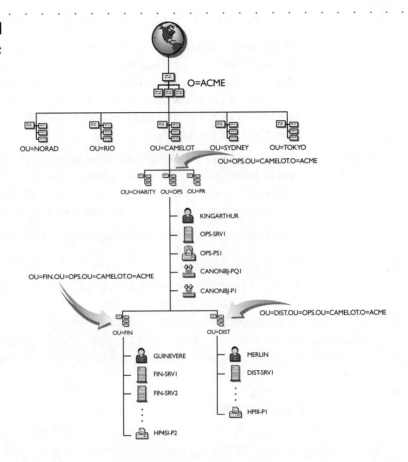

A user can more easily identify an object in the tree if his or her context is set to the appropriate container in the tree. For example, if the user MERLIN wants to search for all printers in the OU=DIST in the OPS division in CAMELOT, he can set his context to OU=DIST.OU=OPS.OU=CAMELOT.O=ACME and search only there for the desired printer using the NWUSER utility.

Using the information in Figure 4.11, in order for the user KINGARTHUR to log in using just the command syntax

`LOGIN KINGARTHUR`

he should set the name context variable in the workstation file NET.CFG to

TIP

```
Name Context = "OU=OPS.OU=CAMELOT.O=ACME"
```

The user KINGARTHUR could also use the Novell CX (Change ConteXt) utility to manually select the same context. Keep in mind that the CX command is valid only during the current session. By selecting the correct context he can simply enter his user name at the LOGIN.EXE command line and NDS will look in the OU=OPS container for his name.

The alternative is not having a context set. This means that the user would have to know his distinguished name and be able to enter it in order to log in. For example, if the user KINGARTHUR did not set a context, he would have to enter the following during login:

```
LOGIN CN=KINGARTHUR.OU=OPS.OU=CAMELOT.O=ACME
```

or

```
LOGIN KINGARTHUR.OPS.CAMELOT.ACME
```

The name context in NDS gives you the functionality of navigating the NDS naming service more easily. The bindery context gives you the functionality to browse the same information as a bindery naming service, which is an entirely different context.

BINDERY CONTEXT

NDS provides compatibility with NetWare 2 and NetWare 3 using a feature called bindery services. This feature allows bindery versions of NetWare and other bindery-based applications to access the NDS tree as if it were the bindery. Bindery services is accomplished by setting a bindery context on the server, which specifies the name of the NDS tree container(s) to search as the bindery.

In order to set the bindery context on a server, you can, for example, enter

```
SET BINDERY CONTEXT = OPS.CAMELOT.ACME
```

at the server console. The server bindery context can also be set using the server-based SERVMAN utility.

Prior to the release of NetWare 4, object information was not available from a distributed directory. A NetWare 3 server stored only information related to its own server in the bindery. Therefore, applications were written that accessed each NetWare 3 server's bindery for a user name or other information. NDS provides bindery services that allow objects in a container to be accessed by bindery-based clients as well as by NDS objects. When a bindery-based application makes bindery calls to the server, the server sees the objects in the container where the server bindery context is set.

NOTE

In terms of bindery context on the server, NDS will see only the objects that previously existed in a NetWare 3 bindery as the bindery objects. These objects are limited to: user, group, print queue, print server. In addition, IntranetWare has added the profile object to assist with migrations from NetWare Name Services (NNS).

The default server bindery context is set to the container where the server was installed. You can change the context to another container or OU if you want. Previous versions of NetWare 4, up to and including NetWare 4.02, allowed you to set only a single context for your server. IntranetWare allows you to set up to 16 contexts for a single server.

You can set multiple contexts by using the SERVMAN utility as shown in Figure 4.12. This utility allows you to separate each context by using a semicolon or a space as shown in this example.

FIGURE 4.12

Use the SERVMAN utility to set multiple bindery contexts.

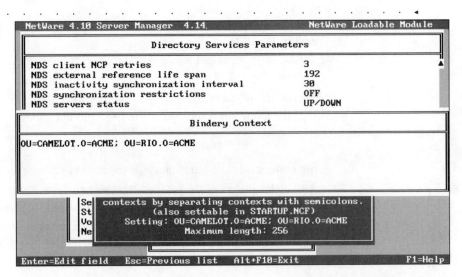

```
NetWare 4.10 Server Manager  4.14.              NetWare Loadable Module

                        Directory Services Parameters

  NDS client NCP retries                         3
  NDS external reference life span               192
  NDS inactivity synchronization interval        30
  NDS synchronization restrictions               OFF
  NDS servers status                             UP/DOWN

                           Bindery Context

  OU=CAMELOT.O=ACME; OU=RIO.O=ACME




         Se   contexts by separating contexts with semicolons.
         St        (also settable in STARTUP.NCF)
         Vo     Setting: OU=CAMELOT.O=ACME; OU=RIO.O=ACME
         Ne           Maximum length: 256


   Enter=Edit field   Esc=Previous list   Alt+F10=Exit           F1=Help
```

LEADING PERIODS

The period (.) separates the individual name segments in distinguished names, relative distinguished names, and user contexts. Through the use of leading and trailing periods in the name sequence, you can quickly navigate to any object in the tree. This is useful for referencing objects located in other portions of the tree from a workstation console.

A name with a leading period instructs the client software to ignore the current context and start the search at the [ROOT] object. This means that any object name with a leading period will be treated as a distinguished name starting at the [ROOT] object.

For example, using the information in Figure 4.13, the current context for a user is set to:

```
OU=R&D.OU=LABS.OU=NORAD.O=ACME
```

Using the Novell CX utility you type the following command (notice the leading period at the beginning of the distinguished name):

```
CX .DIST.OPS.CAMELOT.ACME
```

which will be resolved to the container OU=DIST.OU=OPS.OU=CAMELOT.O=ACME by the NDS client. The leading period causes the name to be treated as a whole name, not a partial name. In other words, start at the [ROOT] and work down.

Using the leading period is simply a shortcut for navigating the tree from the command line utility of your workstation. There can be only one leading period in the object name on the command line.

Trailing Periods

A period after an object name (known as a trailing period) can be used to select a new context. The use of a single trailing period will move the current context up by one container in the tree. For instance, you can use the Novell CX (Change ConteXt) utility and type the following command at the DOS prompt (notice the single trailing period):

```
CX.
```

This command will automatically move you up one layer or container in the tree. Unlike leading periods, you can have as many trailing periods up to the number of relative distinguished names (RDNs) in the current context. If you want to move the current context up two layers in the tree, then you simply supply two trailing periods. You change the context in the tree one layer for every trailing period you supply at the end of the name.

FIGURE 4.13

*A view of the ACME tree
and changing the context*

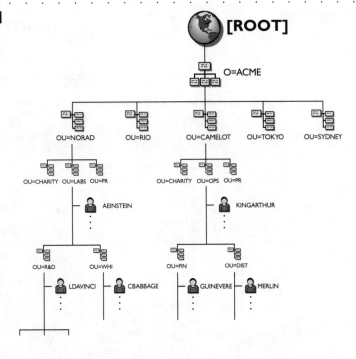

In Figure 4.14, let's assume that the current context is

```
OU=DIST.OU=OPS.OU=CAMELOT.O=ACME
```

and you want to change the context to O=ACME. You simply type the following command (notice the three trailing periods):

```
CX...
```

Trailing periods can be used with relative distinguished names to instruct segments of the context to be replaced. The replacement occurs during the resolution of the full distinguished name.

In Figure 4.14, for example, let's assume that the current context is:

```
OU=DIST.OU=OPS.OU=CAMELOT.O=ACME
```

If we wanted to change our context to the OU=FIN container, which is under OU=OPS, then we would simply type the following command (notice the trailing period):

```
CX OU=FIN.
```

FIGURE 4.14

*Changing the context by
using trailing periods*

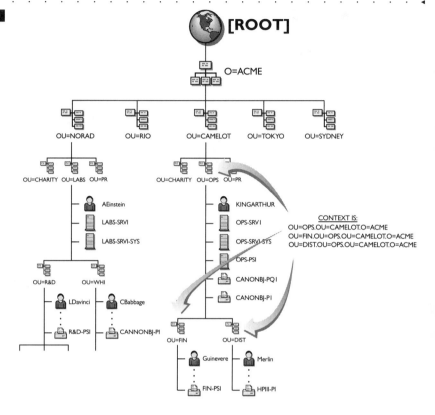

For each trailing period in the RDN, one segment of the context is ignored. This starts at the least-significant segment (deepest in the tree) and proceeds to the most-significant segment or until the trailing periods are exhausted.

Again in Figure 4.14, let's assume the current context is:

```
OU=DIST.OU=OPS.OU=CAMELOT.O=ACME
```

If we wanted to change our context to the OU=WHI container, which is under OU=LABS in the NORAD location, then we would need to type the following command:

```
CX  OU=WHI.OU=LABS.OU=NORAD...
```

Naming Standards Document

Creating a naming standards document need not be difficult or time consuming. The first step is to determine why such a standard should be created. The preceding sections of this chapter have demonstrated that naming is the structure of the Directory tree. As a basis or purpose for why the standard is important, consider the following:

- ▸ How can you provide a Directory structure for your employees that is flexible, easy to use, and meets today's business needs?

- ▸ How can you ensure that you provide a consistent Directory structure within all divisions, locations, and perhaps, operating companies?

- ▸ How can you communicate and implement a consistent standard across an entire company that everyone will follow?

The answers to these questions lie in creating a naming guidelines document that will force you to devise clear and easy-to-remember names and thus make the NDS database a more useful resource.

Naming Guidelines

Create some naming guidelines before installing your first IntranetWare server. Once an installation has begun it becomes more difficult to implement a standard. At a minimum, you should determine how Organizational Units, Servers, and User objects will be defined. These will be the most widely created objects along with your printing objects.

If you have already implemented some existing naming, that's the place to start your review. Many companies already have some guidelines in place for defining their users' names. These guidelines are usually based on an e-mail standard. Review the standard and make modifications where necessary to add or modify your current standard. If your company's network is small, you should still create naming guidelines because the network will most likely grow to include more users and resources in which naming becomes more important. Supporting a network with consistent naming is made easier as well.

Your naming guidelines need to be global in nature. You should strive to implement your naming guidelines consistently across the entire network so that all users and departments can readily and easily access resources anywhere on the LAN. Global naming guidelines can also help your administrators to understand the purpose and use of all objects in the tree.

Most likely you will need the input from others in your company in order to create some naming guidelines. You should gather information from the organizations within your company that must participate to form the naming standard. This information may include input from e-mail administrators, network administrators, and mainframe personnel.

Usually an established host environment will have user naming standards in place. Review these standards as a basis for your IntranetWare user naming guidelines. Some customers prefer to maintain their host userids on the LAN rather than create a new standard at the network level. Others can't wait to change their host userids!

Consider all other naming guidelines that you may already have in place from a NetWare 3 environment to determine how well they might fit into the IntranetWare environment. Your NetWare 3 printers and servers may already have names defined that will work just fine after migration to an IntranetWare tree. If your organization has sufficient or acceptable guidelines, then there is no need to change them.

As mentioned previously many sites already have e-mail addresses set up that require a user naming convention, such as the first initial and last name of the user (for example, TJEFFERSON for Thomas Jefferson).

Naming guidelines provide consistency across your network. If your naming standard is already consistent and firmly in place, you are in great shape and can move on to the next phase of designing your NDS tree. If you do not have an existing naming standard then you should consider establishing naming guidelines that meet the goals discussed in the following section.

GOALS FOR THE NAMING GUIDELINES

The goals or objectives for creating naming guidelines for Novell Directory Services should be as follows:

▸ To make browsing and navigation of the NDS tree easier for the users

▸ To make maintenance of the NDS tree easier for the administration staff

▸ To make merging separate NDS trees easier

▸ To keep the NDS object names unique as required by certain services

▸ To avoid special characters reserved by the operating systems

NAMING GUIDELINES HELP NDS BROWSING AND NAVIGATION

Your primary objective for creating the naming guidelines is to provide the network user a simple view of the network resources contained in the tree. You may not see the immediate need for good naming guidelines, which enable the user to easily navigate the tree. But as more applications are written to take advantage of NDS and its searching capabilities, an uncomplicated naming standard will be needed.

Objects named with purpose and consistency will eventually provide you with a solid foundation that benefits your administrators as well as your users. Other benefits will be recognized as applications make more use of the Directory and its services. You will see that the system is much more efficient if users can quickly identify the network resources available to them and minimize the impact on searching NDS across multiple locations.

You should keep the names of all the objects short and simple, yet descriptive enough that the user knows by the name what the object is and the services it provides. For example, the object name HP4SI-P1 is short yet descriptive and lets the user know that this object is an HP4si laser printer. The object name HP4SI-PQ1 is another example of a short name but is different from the previous example. The PQ1 suffix lets the user know that the object is the print queue that supports the printer (P1).

As you can see, there are many instances throughout the book where we have benefited by using the names of containers and network resources from the ACME tree. It has been helpful to have clear and simple names. Some examples of the naming guidelines for ACME are shown in Table 4.2.

TABLE 4.2

Examples of the naming guidelines for ACME

OBJECT	ENTITY	STANDARD
[ROOT]	Tree Name	ACME_TREE
O=Organization	A Cure for Mother Earth	ACME
OU=Organizational Unit	Rio de Janeiro, Brazil	RIO
	Tokyo, Japan	TOKYO
	Sydney, Australia	SYDNEY
	Research and Development	R&D
	World Health Index	WHI
	Facilities	FAC
	Public Relations	PR
Users	George Washington	GWASHINGTON
	Thomas Jefferson	TJEFFERSON
	Leonardo DaVinci	LDAVINCI
	Albert Einstein	AEINSTEIN
Servers	Server in Labs	LABS-SRV1
	Server in White	WHITE-SRV1
	Server in NORAD/PR	NOR-PR-SRV1
Printers	HP 4si in NORAD/PR	HP4SI-P1
Print Queues	Queue in NORAD/PR	HP4SI-PQ1

NAMING GUIDELINES HELP MAINTAIN NETWORKS AND NDS

Consistent naming provides a framework for the network administrators to monitor and maintain the network and NDS. The administrators will be installing file servers, creating users and printers, modifying existing objects, and moving objects within the tree. The administrators will also set up all the user configuration files at the workstation to connect to NDS in the predetermined fashion. The administrator's job is going to be much easier if there are naming guidelines in place.

NAMING STANDARDS HELP MERGE NDS TREES

The capability to merge multiple NDS trees is a feature introduced in NetWare 4.1. However, two trees being merged within the company will be made much easier if the trees are based on the same naming standards for container and leaf objects. The tree merge will be seamless to users because their workstation configuration files will not have to be modified, even though the NDS trees are merged.

NAMING GUIDELINES HELP KEEP NDS OBJECT NAMES UNIQUE

Some of the NDS tree objects are required to have unique object names in order for the network to work properly. For instance, the file server and print server objects stored in NDS broadcast their services using the Service Advertising Protocol (SAP). While the file server and print server objects are not required to have unique names on the network, it is highly recommended in order to avoid confusion for users and administrators.

Establishing and dictating the naming guidelines to all the network administrators in the network will help keep the NDS objects unique. As stated previously, it is recommended that the user objects have unique names throughout the network. This way users can be moved or new users added without conflict, in your containers.

Not all the objects in the NDS tree will need unique names throughout the network. You decide which NDS objects have unique names. The SAP requires that file server object names be unique on the network.

NOTE

All network devices on the network that communicate using the Service Advertising Protocol should have unique object names in the entire network. Therefore, all file servers and print servers should have unique names on the wire. The maximum length of the names of the objects that use SAP is 47 characters. The space character is illegal for server names.

NAMING GUIDELINES SHOULD AVOID SPECIAL OR RESERVED CHARACTERS

NDS requires the use of the escape character with some characters and therefore we recommend you avoid using them in your naming guidelines. The characters are:

▸ Period (.) — The period is used by NDS to separate the name segments of distinguished names. For example, the distinguished name for the user George Washington is:

```
CN=GWASHINGTON.OU=ADMIN.OU=RIO.O=ACME
```

‣ Commas (,) — The comma is allowed by NDS naming rules. However, it is very confusing and generally should be avoided.

‣ Plus (+) — The plus sign is used by NDS to represent objects with multiple naming attributes such as the bindery objects. A common use of the plus sign is for bindery objects placed in the NDS database. For example, a bindery object with the plus sign in the name is seen as CN=BinderyObject+Name. In the case of an Appletalk print server it might appear as:

```
CN=AtpsQuser+83
```

‣ Equals (=) — The equals sign is used by NDS to tie name types and object names together. For example, the object type O=Organization would appear as:

```
O=ACME
```

‣ Backslash (\) — The backslash precedes the special characters above if they are used as part of an object name. For example, you want to use the name ACME Inc., which has a period at the end. In order to make it a legal NDS name, you would need to enter:

```
ACME Inc\.
```

It is also recommended that you understand the following guidelines if you use spaces in any of the object names. You may want to use the underscore character instead. Spaces are used as delimiters for all the command line parameters. If you use spaces in the NDS object names and need to use the name with a command line utility, then you will need to enclose the name in quotes.

For example, the user George Washington is named "George Washington" in NDS with a space separating the first and last name. In order to use the relative distinguished name with the LOGIN.EXE program, the name would have to be entered with quotes around it:

```
LOGIN "George Washington"
```

and not

```
LOGIN George Washington
```

If you were required to provide the full distinguished name during login, the name would then appear as:

```
LOGIN "GEORGE WASHINGTON.ADMIN.RIO.ACME"
```

You can also use the underscore character as a replacement for the space character because NDS interprets the space and underscore in the same way. In the example of the user George Washington, his name would appear as:

```
George_Washington
```

When the name is used during login, it would be entered without the quotes:

```
LOGIN George_Washington
```

You should also avoid the use of the forward slash (/) in your naming of any container or leaf object. Novell's Windows-based NWUSER utility will fail if you map permanent drives or capture a print queue. This is an MS Windows issue that does not allow for the use of the forward slash in any object name.

Producing a Naming Standards Document

Producing a naming standards document is not very glamorous, but it shouldn't require a great deal of time to complete either. Here are some steps you can take to produce your naming standards document as quickly and efficiently as possible:

▸ Document the naming standard for each object to be used in the NDS tree.

▸ Provide an example for each object used.

▸ Specify properties for each of the objects selected.

DETERMINE THE NAMING STANDARD FOR EACH OBJECT USED IN THE TREE

In order to create the naming guidelines, review which NDS objects you will use in your NDS tree. Typically, these objects include organizational units, servers, users, printers, print queues, groups, organizational roles, directory maps, and profiles.

Other possible areas for naming consistency include the properties associated with each object you define in the NDS tree. In short, any information you plan on using to search the NDS database needs a naming standard for consistency.

The naming standard for each of the objects used in the ACME tree is included in Table 4.3.

T A B L E 4.3	NDS OBJECTS	STANDARD
NDS object naming standard for the ACME tree	Users	First character of the first name plus the entire last name. All titles are spelled out.
	Organization	Abbreviation of the company name.
	Organizational Unit	Location, division, or department name. Abbreviate the names if they are over eight characters long.
	NetWare Server	Department-SRV#. Exception is the Location-Department-SRV#, which is for the CHARITY and PR departments. The difference is because of the duplication of container names for all locations of CHARITY and PR.
	Volumes	ServerName_VolumeName.
	Print Server	Department-PS#. Exception is the Location-Department-PS#, which is for the CHARITY and PR departments.
	Printer	PrinterType-P#.
	Print Queue	PrinterType-PQ#.
	Computer	No standard because it is not used.

PROVIDE AN EXAMPLE FOR EACH OBJECT USED

You may have noticed when reading Table 4.3 that there were no examples of the object naming standards. Remember, a picture is worth a thousand words. An example can convey the meaning of an entire written page. Therefore, include some brief examples in your naming guidelines document. As shown below in Table 4.4, you can convey your meaning more quickly and easily by providing an example.

Table 4.4 is simply a reprint of Table 4.3, but examples for each of the object's naming standard have been added for clarity.

T A B L E   4.4

*NDS object naming
standard for the ACME tree*

NDS OBJECTS	STANDARD
Users	First character of the first name plus the entire last name. All titles are spelled out.
	Examples: GWASHINGTON, SIRGAWAIN
Organization	Abbreviation of the company name, which is "A Cure for Mother Earth."
	Example: ACME
Organizational Unit	Location, division, or department name. Abbreviate the names if they are over eight characters long.
	Example: NORAD, R&D, ADMIN
NetWare Server	Department-SRV#. Exception is Location-Department-SRV#, which is for the CHARITY and PR departments.
	Examples: LABS-SRV1, NOR-CHR-SRV1
Volumes	ServerName_VolumeName.
	Examples: LABS-SRV1_SYS, NOR-CHR-SRV1_SYS
Print Server	Department-PS#. Exception for the CHARITY and PR departments, which is Location-Department-PS#.
	Examples: FAC-PS1, TOK-PR-PS1
Printer	PrinterType-P#.
	Examples: HP4SI-P1, CANONBJ-P2
Print Queue	PrinterType-PQ#.
	Examples: HP4SI-PQ1, CANONBJ-PQ2
Computer	No standard because it is not used.

SPECIFY PROPERTIES FOR EACH OBJECT CLASS SELECTED

For some installations it may be necessary to determine which properties will be required for the selected objects. Some properties are mandated by the NDS schema when you create the object. This means that if the mandatory properties are not filled in then the NDS utilities will not create the object. For example, during the creation of a user object, you are required to specify the Login Name and Last Name properties.

You may have additional properties that you would like all your administrators to include when they create a new object. This type of information might include addresses, fax numbers, department names, and so on. Table 4.5 illustrates the naming standards for a user object with additional properties you want filled in when the users are created. Not all the properties for the user are represented in the table. Some properties are required and a value must be entered at creation, while other properties are optional and are left up to you to determine if they should be used. System properties are those properties that NDS automatically populates during the creation of the object.

TABLE 4.5

NDS property naming standards for a user object in the ACME tree

PROPERTY	REQ/OPT/SYSTEM	STANDARDS
Login Name	Required	First character of the first name plus the entire last name. Add a middle initial to resolve name conflicts.
Given Name	Optional	First name of the user.
Last Name	Required	Last name of the user.
Full Name	Optional	First and last name of the user.
Generational Qual.	Optional	
Middle Initial	Optional	Middle initial of the user, if known.
Other Name	Optional	
Title	Optional	Job title.
Description	Optional	
Location	Optional	City or site location (NORAD, RIO).
Department	Optional	
Telephone	Optional	Business phone number with area code.
Fax Number	Optional	Fax phone number with area code.
Language	Optional	Preferred language of the user.

T A B L E 4.5		
PROPERTY	**REQ/OPT/SYSTEM**	**STANDARDS**
Network Address	System	
Default Server	Optional	Enter the same server as the home directory.
Home Directory	Optional	Enter the volume/subdirectory/user path.
Require Password	Optional	Force the user to have a password.
Account Balance	Optional	
Login Script	Optional	Determined by the site administrators.
Print Job Config.	Optional	Determined by site administrators.
Post Office Box	Optional	
Street	Optional	
City	Optional	
State or Province	Optional	
Zip Code	Optional	
See Also	Optional	

NDS property naming standards for a user object in the ACME tree (continued)

CONSULTING EXPERIENCE

Currently the Novell utilities do not enforce additional required properties that you define as an administrator. However, we recommend a well-documented guideline in which you explain your reason for including a particular property. Your administrators will be more likely to adhere to the guideline if they understand the reasoning behind the inclusion of an object's attribute.

MORE IDEAS FOR NAMING STANDARDS

User Accounts

When you create a naming standard, one of the first steps is to decide how to standardize your usernames. IntranetWare allows usernames to be up to 64 characters long. However, a 64-character username is a very long name and not easy to use.

In the example of ACME, the username was limited to the first character of the first name plus the entire last name. If there are duplicate names within a single container, then the middle initial is added to resolve the name conflict. This type of username may not be used globally because of the number of username conflicts.

Some companies have limited the length of the username to eight characters. This naming convention for the user accounts matches the naming of the user's DOS home directory. Since DOS is limited to just eight characters for subdirectory names, limiting the usernames to eight characters will automatically match the name of the DOS subdirectory assigned to the user. For example, if you use eight characters for the user, Thomas Jefferson, his name could be defined as:

TJEFFERS

which is the first character of his first name and the first seven characters of his last name.

Another way to represent a user is to take the first six characters of his last name and the first two characters of his first name. This name would appear as:

JEFFERTH

Duplicate names can be handled by specifying a middle initial in one of the two names such as:

TQJEFFER

(Thomas Q. Jefferson)

or

QJEFFETH

(Q. Jefferson Thomas)

TIP

Remember, object names within the same container must be unique. Duplicate names are allowed only if the objects are in different containers. However, it is still recommended that you keep object names unique across the entire tree.

Organization and Organizational Unit Names

Your organization name should reflect your company name. The company name "A Cure for Mother Earth" is abbreviated to ACME. Thus, the O=Organization is called O=ACME. For the Organizational Units, the locations and departments with short but descriptive names are used. For instance, OU=SYDNEY and OU=TOKYO are examples of the location OUs. They could have been abbreviated to SYD and TOK but their names are already short. Examples of the division and department Organizational Units are OU=R&D for the Research and Development department and OU=MRKT for the Marketing department.

NOTE

The tree name can be named with the company name plus _TREE. We have chosen as our tree name for the ACME company ACME_TREE and O=ACME for the organization. Notice the difference between tree name and the organization name is simply the addition of the "_TREE."

Server Names

Server names should be unique on the entire network because each server name is broadcast through the Service Advertising Protocol. You may wish to consider a server name that signifies a location and department.

For ACME, a NetWare server in the CHARITY department of NORAD is called NOR-CHR-SRV1, and a print server is called NOR-CHR-PS1. A server in the R&D department in NORAD is called SRV1. You may wonder why the naming standards seem different for different departments. Notice that the R&D department is a unique department within the ACME tree and that there is no need for the location name in the server name. However, the CHARITY and PR departments are not unique departments within the ACME tree. These two departments are placed as OUs beneath every location, and the servers in those containers should have the location name in order to be unique.

Printer and Print Queue Names

Printers and print queue names do not have to be unique on the network. The department and location information is obtained by where the printer and print queue are placed in the tree. The distinguished name of the printer or print queue object is used to discover the location and department in which the printer is placed. Thus, the individual object name for the printer and print queue should show the functionality of the printer.

For example, in the ACME tree an HP4si printer is named HP4SI-P1, and the print queue that supports the printer is called HP4SI-PQ1. A Canon Bubble Jet printer is named CANONBJ-P2, and the print queue is named CANONBJ-PQ2. This type of naming provides users with fundamental information about the printer they will be using.

The user can obtain the location and department in which the printer has been placed from the distinguished name or location in the ACME tree. For example, a Canon Bubble Jet printer (CANONBJ-P1) in the Operations (OPS) department in Camelot (CAMELOT) has a distinguished name of CANONBJ-P1.OPS.CAMELOT.ACME.

The difference between the printer object and the print queue object is defined by the object suffix. For instance, the "P" is for the printer object and the "PQ" is for print queue object.

NOTE

A printer that connects directly to the network and services a print queue on the file server is called a queue server. A queue server is a special-purpose print server that needs to have a unique name to broadcast using SAP. All queue servers use SAP to advertise their services on the network.

Sample of a Basic Naming Standard

The following table is another example of how you can create a naming standard document that is simple but very useful. Table 4.6 shows the document with the object type, the naming syntax, and an example. Keep in mind that, although we have already demonstrated our naming standard in previous sections of this chapter, the following naming standard is another one for your review.

	OBJECT TYPE	SYNTAX	EXAMPLE
T A B L E 4.6 *Sample of a Basic Naming Standard*	[ROOT] or Tree Name	AAAA_TREE	ACME_TREE
	Organization	AAAA = Company Name	O=ACME
	Organizational Units	XXXXXX, YYYYYY XXXXX = Location YYYYY = Department	OU=RIO, OU=FIN
	NetWare Servers	XXXYYZ##	RIO-ADM-F01
	Print Servers	XXXYYZ##	NOR-CHR-P04
	Volume Names	Server_Volume XXX = Location (NOR, RIO, CAM, TOK, SYD) YYY = Department (LAB, CHR, PR, ADM, OPS, FIN) Z = Server type where: F=File Server, T=Test Server, P=Print Server, C=Comm Server, etc. ## = Quantity (01, 02, 03, . . . , 99) Volumes are: SYS, APPS, DATA, USERS, SHARE	RIO-ADM-F01_SYS
	Printers	YYYTTLL##P	FIN-LJPS01-P
	Queues	YYYTTLL##Q	FIN-LJPS01-Q
	Queue Server	YYYTTLL##QS YY = Department (LAB, CHR, PR, ADM, OPS, FIN, HR)	FIN-LJPS01-QS

(continued)

OBJECT TYPE	**SYNTAX**	**EXAMPLE**
Queue Server	TT = Type of printer (LJ for LaserJet, BJ for BubbleJet, PL for plotter)	
	LL = Language (PS for PostScript, PC for PCL, etc.)	
	## = Number of printer, queue, or queue server (01, 02, 03, . . . , and so on)	
	P = Printer	
	Q = Queue	
	QS = Queue Server	
Group HelpDesk	Function Function (the activity that the group will perform)	WP_Group
Organizational Roles	Name_Function Function (the administrative activity or role that the Organizational Role performs)	RIO_Admin_OR
Profiles	Name_P Name (the purpose of the Profile object)	Mobile_P
Directory Maps	Directory Name Directory Name (the DOS directory name in which the application has been installed)	WP61

Network Addressing Standards

SERVER INTERNAL NETWORK ADDRESS

The IPX cable address defines the physical cable segment for your file servers. The cable segment may be your entire network or you may have many segments based on locations in your network infrastructure. If you do not already have a standard for cable segments, you should implement one. A brief example of a cable segment standard is:

XXXSSSSN

For example: 20025451 represents the Norad (200) facility building 2545, segment number 1, where:

- ▸ XXX = Numeric value that represents a location such as NOR, CAM, TOK

- ▸ SSSS = Numeric identifier for a wiring closet or building

- ▸ N = Numeric value that represents a number for the specific segment. This value is useful if you have more than one segment in that location.

IPX NETWORK ADDRESS

Most sites using NetWare 3 will have an IPX network address in place for the existing NetWare 3 servers. If you have an IPX network address, you can continue to use the same standard in IntranetWare. The important point is to maintain unique network addresses for all your NetWare servers because duplicate addresses will obviously cause great difficulties for your network. The IPX network address must be unique for the cable segment address as well.

A sample network address may appear as the following convention:

ARRSSSSN

where:

▸ A = Indicates that this is an internal IPX number

▸ RR = Indicates a numeric value designating a state or other region

▸ SSSS = Indicates a location

▸ N = Indicates the server number such as 1 to 10

With a naming standard in place, you are ready to begin the design of your NDS tree. Remember that your naming standard will make administration of your tree easier and will provide you with consistent naming across your entire organization.

PART II

Designing Novell Directory Services

CHAPTER 5

Novell Directory
Services Tree

"He that plants trees loves others beside himself." Thomas Fuller (Gnomolgia 1732)

After you are familiar with NDS objects and have devised a naming standard, you are ready to begin designing your IntranetWare tree. This section will outline the steps involved in the design of your NDS tree and explore different design options. Once you have a design that meets your needs you can begin the installation or migration to IntranetWare. Keep in mind that you can always make changes to your tree later, but a properly designed tree will almost never need significant changes. Modifications may be necessary at some point to meet the needs of your changing organization.

When designing your NDS tree, three goals should help drive the design decisions you make. The three goals are:

▸ Organize the network resources in your company for ease of access.

▸ Provide a blueprint for a consistent rollout of IntranetWare.

▸ Provide flexibility to the design to reflect corporate changes.

Organize the Network Resources in Your Company

The primary objective for designing the NDS tree is to organize the network resources in your company. The NDS tree should be arranged to reflect the location and placement of the network resources in the network. The network resources should also be placed in the tree to provide easy access to both users and administrators. The goal of the NDS tree design then is not to reproduce the organization chart of the company but to represent all users and resources in such a way that allows them to work efficiently and easily. Notice in Figure 5.1 how users and resources are grouped together for ease of access. Some users need access to a particular printer or server while a larger group may need access to an e-mail server. The e-mail server can be placed higher in the tree so that all users needing that resource have easier access to it.

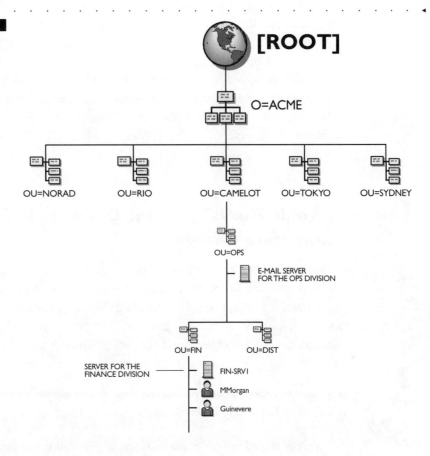

F I G U R E   5.1

Resources and users are grouped near each other in the ACME tree. The OPS division has an IntranetWare server dedicated for e-mail.

Provide a Blueprint for the Consistent Rollout of IntranetWare

Your blueprint for NDS installation includes your naming standard, tree design, and migration strategies. With this information in hand, you will have a guide for the installation of all your IntranetWare servers. For example, the tree design will give you the location where an NDS server should be installed. An administrator can review the naming standards and know exactly how a server should be named.

During the rollout of IntranetWare, some companies may be forced to implement more than one NDS tree on the network, with the intent to merge them together in the future. Creating more than one NDS tree is made much easier if the multiple trees are based on a similar NDS tree design.

In addition, your blueprint gives you a clear map of how to migrate an entire corporation to IntranetWare. Initially, your migration will begin with a few servers and may eventually involve hundreds. Your design can be the master plan for migration of all servers to IntranetWare.

Provide Flexibility to the Design to Reflect Corporate Changes

Another objective of the NDS tree design is to provide flexibility for both users and administrators. This simply means that as the corporation changes, both organizationally and physically, you will be able to facilitate those changes easily without making large modifications to your tree structure. For example, you may want a design that allows for easy moves of users and containers. This objective can be met by designing the NDS tree as described in the following sections.

CONSULTING EXPERIENCE

Politics should not get in the way of your tree design, but sometimes it does. Not long ago an agency was in the process of designing its NetWare 4.1 tree. During the design process, some individuals insisted that they be represented as their own organizational units in the tree because of where they appeared organizationally in their agency. They incorrectly assumed that managerial positions or positions of authority should receive special attention in the design of the tree. As important as these individuals may be, they do not function as their own organizational units in the tree. Regardless of their titles, they are users and, thus, share resources with other individuals on the same floor or building.

These goals seem trivial but they become very important when you are considering all the NDS design issues. One classic example that seems to always come up is that different groups or individuals in your organization will want the NDS tree designed to meet their specific needs or situation. These political issues can best be handled by referring back to your design goals. For example, how does a particular design approach help you organize your network resources? In other words, if you have specific goals to fall back on, you can deal with the political issues by applying each issue against your design goals. Keep in mind that the network is installed to serve a business purpose and your job as an administrator is to see that that purpose is being met. If you design your NDS tree with this in mind, many of the political issues can be removed from this process.

NDS Tree Design Tasks

This section introduces the tasks associated with the NDS tree design. The tasks or steps provide an easy-to-understand and effective method for designing your NDS tree. The tree design consists of five steps:

1 • Gather your network and company documents.

2 • Design your tree in the shape of a pyramid.

3 • Design the top level of your tree.

4 • Design the bottom level of your tree.

5 • Make modifications to the tree based on your needs.

While there is no absolute or exact way to design an NDS tree, some methods are definitely more efficient than others. Efficiency is achieved when the tree is stable, and the design provides for the least amount of NDS traffic possible.

These methods are presented in the following sections to help you design an efficient NDS tree. The methods presented here have been developed by Novell Consulting and have been successfully implemented by hundreds of their large and small customers. The design guidelines presented here work for small and large companies regardless of any unique requirements.

It is important to define what we mean by a small and large company. For the purposes of the examples given in this chapter, a small company consists of 5 servers or fewer (with no wide area network (WAN) connections) and fewer than 500 users. Certainly, there is no written law that this definition is always true; however, a network of this size has fewer design ramifications than a network with thousands of users and a very complicated network infrastructure.

A large network then is anything greater than 5 servers *with* a WAN connection and greater than 500 users. As you read through this chapter, you will be able to determine which category (small or large) you fall into. So, let's begin the design.

GATHER THE CORPORATE DOCUMENTS

Some company information or documentation is necessary to help you initiate an NDS tree design for your corporation. The following documents are listed and discussed below in order of importance.

The Wide Area Network (WAN) Diagrams for Your Company

Figure 5.2 shows the ACME WAN layout map. The WAN layout or physical layout usually consists of all your major hub locations that are interconnected with routers and bridges. Notice in ACME's WAN layout map that all five main sites are shown with their router connections and the speed of these links in kilobits per second. Your WAN layout map may look similar or it may include the link speeds of your satellite offices.

Your WAN documentation may consist of more than one compact diagram. Don't worry if your documentation consists of many pages of information. The key here is to understand how your infrastructure is organized and where the major hub locations exist. These documents are necessary for the upper layer design of your tree as we will explain. Most large companies have some sort of wide area network diagrams available. We recognize that a WAN network diagram is a document always in flux at most companies. However, try to obtain the latest WAN map from your staff that manages your network infrastructure.

The Campus Network Maps for All Your Individual Locations

Along with your WAN layout maps, campus diagrams will provide a further breakout of locations of your hub sites. This type of documentation varies from company to company. Some companies show the entire hub and campus diagrams together, while others separate the information because of the size of their network. A campus network map may show you a campus, such as the NORAD campus shown in Figure 5.3.

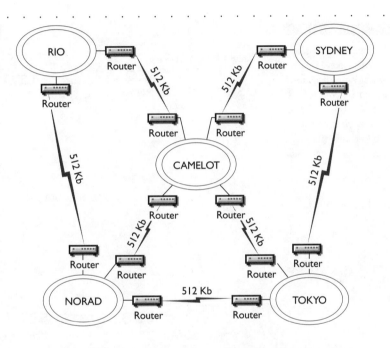

FIGURE 5.2

The ACME Physical WAN layout map includes important information such as the major hub locations of its network as well as router connections and link speeds.

The ACME campus map for NORAD shows information such as an FDDI ring and routers connecting this site's buildings. The campus diagram may also show buildings and their interconnections. Again, this information, along with the physical WAN map, describes your WAN/LAN infrastructure. This preliminary information is necessary to build the foundation for your IntranetWare environment.

A List of Sites or Locations Within Your Company

The next item to obtain for your tree design is a list of sites or locations of your network. Sometimes this information is included with your other documentation discussed previously. In large companies, there is usually a list of sites with their locations. For example, the ACME network has a site known as CAMELOT, which is shown as a single site on the WAN map for ACME. Further documentation, however, shows sites within the CAMELOT area, such as an operations center

(OPS) located at the south end of the city and a public relations office (PR) center located in the downtown district. An office for charitable contributions (CHARITY) is also found at the downtown location. Figure 5.4 shows an example of the sites for the CAMELOT location.

FIGURE 5.3

The campus diagrams show a continuation of your physical WAN diagrams. Information can include connection types between buildings such as FDDI, bridged token rings, 10baseT, fiber, and so on.

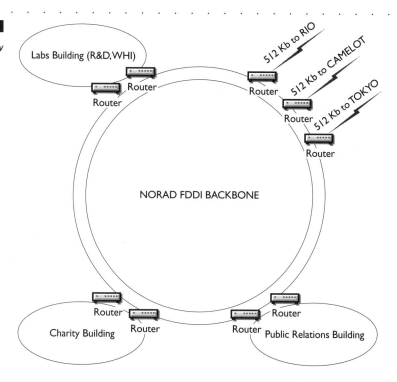

Resource List That Includes Your File Servers, Printers, and Other Major Network Resources

A resource list may be included with your LAN maps for each site. This list gives important information about the servers and printers found in each region, site, building, or department. Table 5.1 shows the resource list for ACME with its servers, printers, and print queues. This information is later used in your tree design for the placement of these resources.

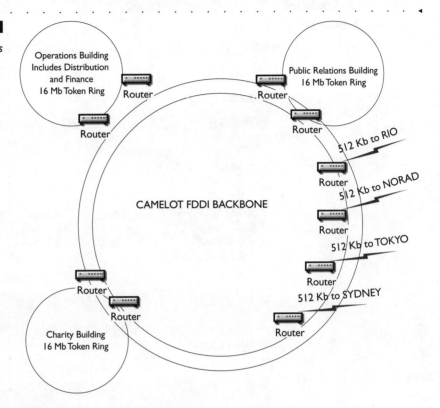

FIGURE 5.4

The CAMELOT site includes three buildings under its designation: Operations (OPS), Public Relations (PR), and CHARITY.

NOTE

Keep in mind that the information we are referring to in this resource list will be either NetWare 3 server information or other operating systems that will be migrated to IntranetWare. This list enables you to know beforehand where objects need to be created in the NDS tree. Notice also that some of the naming standards shown in the list can be used in your IntranetWare environment while others may need some slight changes.

LOC/DIV	SERVER NAME	PRINTERS/QUEUES
NORAD	NOR-SRV1	
CHARITY	NOR-CHR-SRV1	HP4SI-PQ1
		HP4SI-P1
LABS	LABS-SRV1	
R&D.LABS	R&D-SRV1	HP4SI-PQ1
	R&D-PS1	HP4SI-P1
POLL.R&D.LABS		HP4SI-PQ2
		HP4SI-P2
NUC.R&D.LABS		HP4SI-PQ3
		HP4SI-P3
VR.R&D.LABS		HP4SI-PQ2
		HP4SI-P2
WHI.LABS	WHI-SRV1	CANONBJ-PQ1
	WHI-SRV2	CANONBJ-P1
WHI.LABS	WHI-SRV3	
	WHI-PS1	
PR	NOR-PR-SRV1	HP4SI-PQ1
	NOR-PR-PS1	HP4SI-P1
		CANONBJ-PQ2
		CANONBJ-P2
RIO	RIO-SRV1	
CHARITY	*RIO-CHR-SRV1*	*HP4SI-PQ1*
	RIO-CHR-PS1	*HP4SI-P1*
ADMIN	*ADMIN-SRV1*	*CANONBJ-PQ1*
	ADMIN-SRV2	*CANONBJ-P1*
	ADMIN-ADM-PS1	
FAC.ADMIN	*FAC-SRV1*	*HP4SI-PQ1*
	FAC-PS1	*HP4SI-P1*

	LOC/DIV	SERVER NAME	PRINTERS/QUEUES
TABLE 5.1 *ACME Resource List* *(continued)*	**AUDIT.ADMIN**	*AUDIT-SRV1*	*HP4S1-PQ1*
			HP4S1-P2
	MRKT.ADMIN	*MRKT-SRV1*	*HPIII-PQ1*
			HPIII-P2
	PR	*RIO-PR-SRV1*	*HP4S1-PQ1*
		RIO-PR-PS1	*HP4S1-P1*
			CANONBJ-PQ2
			CANONBJ-P2
	CAMELOT	*CAM-SRV1*	
	CHARITY	*CAM-CHR-SRV1*	*HP4S1-PQ1*
		CAM-CHR-PS1	*HP4S1-P1*
	OPS	*OPS-SRV1*	*CANONBJ-PQ1*
		OPS-PS1	*CANONBJ-P1*
	FIN.OPS	*FIN-SRV1*	*HP4SI-PQ1*
		FIN-SRV2	*HP4S1-PQ2*
		FIN-SRV3	*HP4SI-P1*
		FIN-PS1	*HP4S1-P2*
		FIN-PS2	
	DIST.OPS	*DIST-SRV1*	*HPIII-PS1*
		DIST-SRV2	*HPIII-PQ1*
			HPIII-P1
	PR	*CAM-PR-SRV1*	*HP4S1-PQ1*
		CAM-PR-PS1	*HP4S1-P1*
	SYDNEY	*SYD-SRV1*	
	CHARITY	*SYD-CHR-SRV1*	*HP4S1-PQ1*
		SYD-CHR-SRV1	*HP4S1-P1*
		SYD-CHR-PS1	

(continued)

ACME Resource List
(continued)

LOC/DIV	SERVER NAME	PRINTERS/QUEUES
HR	*HR-SRV1*	*HP4S1-PQ1*
	HR-SRV2	*HP4S1-P1*
	HR-PS1	
MEDICAL.HR	*MED-SRV1*	*HP4SI-PQ1*
	MED-SRV2	*HP4S1-P1*
FOOD.HR	*FOOD-SRV1*	*HP4SI-PQ2*
	FOOD-SRV2	*HP4S1-P2*
SHELTER.HR	*SHELT-SRV1*	*HP4SI-PQ3*
	SHELT-SRV2	*HP4S1-P3*
PEACE.HR	*PEACE-SRV1*	*HPIII-PQ4*
		HPIII-P4
PR	*SYD-PR-SRV1*	*HP4S1-PQ1*
	SYD-PR-PS1	*HP4S1-P1*
TOKYO	*TOK-SRV1*	
CHARITY	*TOK-CHR-SRV1*	*HP4S1-PQ1*
	TOK-CHR-SRV1	*HP4S1-P1*
	TOK-CHR-PS1	
CRIME	*CRIMEI-SRV1*	*HP5-PQ1*
	CRIME1-SRV2	*HP5-PQ1*
	CRIMEI-PS1	*HP4FI-P2*
BLUE.CRIME	*BLUE-SRV1*	*HPIII-PQ1*
	BLUE-PS1	*HPIII-P1*
VIO.BLUE.CRIME	*VIO-SRV1*	*HP4SI-PQ2*
	VIO-SRV2	*HP4S1-P2*
ENV.BLUE.CRIME	*ENV-SRV1*	*HP4S1-PQ3*
		HP4S1-P3
THEFT.BLUE.CRIME	*THEFT-SRV1*	*HP4SI-PQ4*
		HP4SI-P4

TABLE   5.1

ACME Resource List
(continued)

LOC/DIV	SERVER NAME	PRINTERS/QUEUES
WHITE.CRIME	*WHITE-SRV1*	*CANONBJ-PQ1*
	WHITE-SRV2	*CANONBJ-P1*
	WHITE-PS1	
CYBER.WHITE.CRIME	*CYBER-SRV1*	*HPIII-PQ2*
		HPIII-P1
POL.WHITE.CRIME	*POL-SRV1*	*HP4SI-PQ3*
		HP4SI-P3
FIN.WHITE.CRIME	*CRIMEI-FIN-SRV1*	*HP4SI-PQ4*
		HP4SI-P4
		HP4SI-P5
PR	*TOK-PR-SRV1*	*HP4S1-PQ1*
	TOK-PR-PS1	*HP4S1-P1*

The Organizational Chart or Similar Document for Your Company

The last piece of information that is helpful in designing your tree is your company's organization charts. Your company may have many pages of organizational charts or a single chart. Your main purpose in obtaining the organization chart is to determine what divisions, departments, or other groups need to be created at the bottom layer of your tree. Figure 5.5 shows ACME's organizational structure. It is the input from this structure that will determine the lower layers of the NDS trees.

Typically, the most difficult task in designing the NDS tree is gathering all these corporate documents. Yet, an even more difficult task is trying to design the tree without them. These documents are the inputs into the NDS tree design process. Try to obtain as many of them as you can.

Each of the documents is used during different phases of the design process, and some documents are more important than others. The most important company document is the WAN layout or map. The WAN map is required before starting the NDS design for your company because it is used to design the top of the NDS tree. If your company has campus networks at one or more locations, documentation of the physical campus network is also needed. If you have a small network (based on our previous definition of a small company), you may not have a WAN map, but you will probably have an organizational chart.

The organizational structure for ACME gives us information about departments, divisions, and workgroups that may need to be represented in your NDS tree structure.

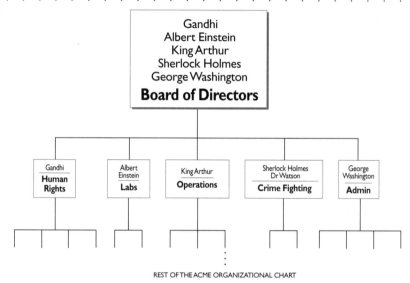

REST OF THE ACME ORGANIZATIONAL CHART

The organizational chart is also an important document. But, as you will see, the organizational chart is used only during the design of the bottom of the tree. After you have gathered the corporate documents, you are ready to start the planning of the NDS tree.

DESIGN THE TREE IN THE SHAPE OF A PYRAMID

The design of the NDS tree should take the shape of a pyramid or inverted tree. The pyramid design implies that you place most of the containers and objects at the bottom of the structure with fewer containers at the top. The pyramid design shape of the tree is logically split into two sections. First, you will design the top of the tree, with its appropriate containers, and second, design the bottom of the tree. Figure 5.6 illustrates how the pyramid design is split into the top and bottom sections of the tree.

The advantage of a pyramid-shaped tree layout is that the top layers become the foundation (or static layers) upon which the bottom layers can be established. The bottom layers of the tree will be more dynamic, allowing for greater flexibility to change when your company changes. This design approach enables you to more easily make changes, such as moving users or subtrees.

*The NDS tree should be
designed like a pyramid
with a top and bottom
portion of the tree.*

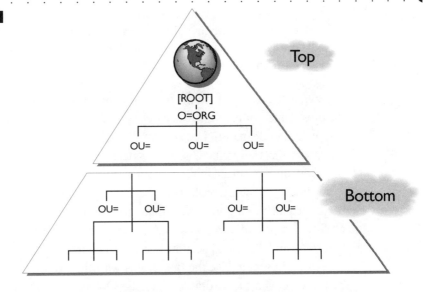

Another advantage of the pyramid tree design is that the partitioning of the NDS database is more natural. The alternative to the pyramid design is to create a flat tree layout or structure that places all the objects in the top layers of the tree. As shown in Figure 5.7, a very flat and wide tree is not an efficient design approach because of how NDS communicates with its subordinate levels.

*A very flat and wide tree
is not as efficient as
designing an NDS tree
with the pyramid shape.
The design in this figure
is not recommended
because it shows 150
locations at one level.*

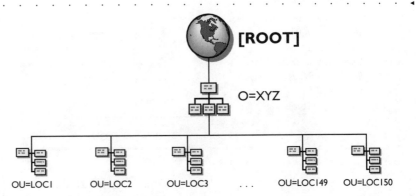

TIP

An efficient NDS tree will have more organizational units at the bottom and less at the top. Our recommendation is to have only 10 to 15 OUs per level in the tree. Even the largest companies with many branch offices will usually meet this requirement as explained later in this chapter.

Having all the objects in the top of the tree also makes the tree rigid and inefficient for most large companies. A flat tree is not recommended primarily because of the way it has to be partitioned and replicated. Synchronization traffic of NDS on all servers in the tree is increased considerably with this type of approach. The tree partition and replica layout becomes extremely flat, which could cause many subordinate reference replicas to be created. Subordinate references are pointers between partitions and subordinate partitions and are automatically created by NDS. For more information about subordinate reference replicas, refer to the "NDS Partitions and Replicas" section later in this chapter.

As seen in Figure 5.8, the tree begins with the [ROOT] object at the top followed by the O=Organization object. After the O=Organization object(s), the next level is a layer of OU=Organization Unit(s). Typically, only a selected set of users and network resources is located in the top layers of the tree. For example, the ADMIN user object is located in the O=Organization object because the installation program automatically creates it.

FIGURE 5.8

The top of the tree includes the [ROOT] object, O=Organization, and the first layer of OUs. The first layer of OUs should be based on the network infrastructure.

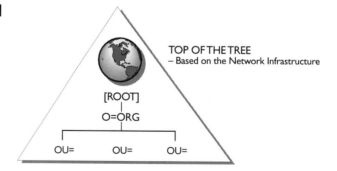

TOP OF THE TREE
– Based on the Network Infrastructure

[ROOT]
O=ORG
OU=   OU=   OU=

The bottom of the tree is defined by the local area network (LAN) and is based on the actual organization of your company from a departmental or divisional standpoint. In Figure 5.9, the bottom layers in the tree are most flexible if they represent the organizational structure of your company. This can be accomplished by using the divisions, departments, and workgroups in the corporation. The bottom layer OUs will hold the majority of your leaf objects such as the users, file servers, printers, queues, and other network resources. This approach provides the greatest flexibility because when you make changes to a department you will only affect the container(s) of that department. The rest of the tree is left unchanged. In contrast, if you have organizations represented at the top of your tree and you make changes to an organization, these changes can possibly affect your containers that are subordinate to the container you initially changed.

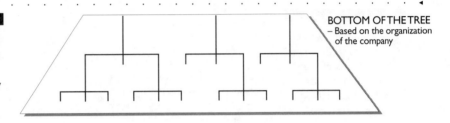

FIGURE 5.9

The bottom of the tree is based on the organization of the company. These lower layers offer flexibility to the tree design for moves and other changes.

BOTTOM OF THE TREE
– Based on the organization
of the company

Both the top and the bottom of the tree are illustrated in Figure 5.10 and will be discussed in the following sections in greater detail.

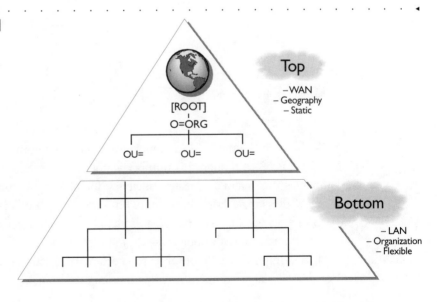

FIGURE 5.10

The top of the NDS tree is based on the WAN or locations of your company and becomes the static portion of the tree. The bottom of the tree is based on the LAN and organization of your company and gives you the flexibility to make moves and other changes.

[ROOT]
O=ORG
OU=   OU=   OU=

Top
– WAN
– Geography
– Static

Bottom
– LAN
– Organization
– Flexible

DESIGN THE TOP LEVEL OF THE TREE

The design of the top of the NDS tree is the most important because it is the foundation of the NDS tree. The rest of the tree will branch downward from the top. As we mentioned earlier in this chapter, the top level of the tree includes the tree name, which is the [ROOT] object, the O=Organization object, and the first layer of OU=Organization Units which, for most companies, will be based on your WAN infrastructure and locations. Figure 5.11 illustrates how we are taking the information from the WAN diagrams and designing the upper layer of the tree.

For the upper layer of the tree, match the major hub locations of your nework to the first level of organizational units in your tree.

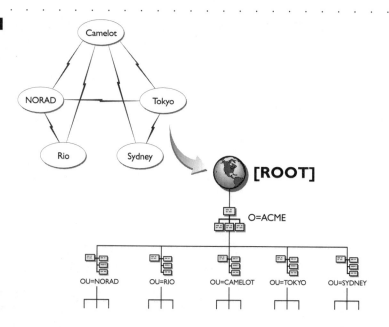

As shown in Figure 5.12, a guideline for the maximum number of containers at each level is 50. Although this number is not a strict rule, we have found that most companies can maintain greater efficiency for NDS synchronization if they stay at or below this range. For companies with many branch offices exceeding this value, try to insert a level of regional organizational units one level above to distribute the load of branch offices under these regional containers.

Most companies will be able to work within this guideline. However, for exceptionally large companies with thousands of branch offices, you may have no choice but to exceed this recommendation. If you must, pay special attention to partitioning and replication guidelines as presented in Chapter 6.

FIGURE 5.12

The appropriate number of subordinate containers is 10 to 15 at each level in the tree. Beyond this number you should consider adding another level in your tree to distribute your containers.

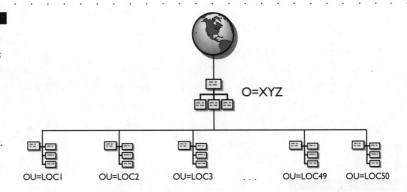

O=XYZ

OU=LOCl   OU=LOC2   OU=LOC3   . . .   OU=LOC49   OU=LOC50

For synchronization efficiency do not exceed
10 to15 containers at each level in the tree.

Tree Name or [ROOT] Object

The first entity that needs to be named in NDS is the tree itself. The tree name is also the name of the [ROOT] object, which is placed as the top-most object in your tree. The NDS tree name is displayed in many of the current NetWare utilities such as MONITOR, SERVMAN, and INSTALL. The tree name you choose can represent the company name plus _TREE. For example, our company is called ACME, so we chose to name the tree ACME_TREE, as shown in Figure 5.13.

FIGURE 5.13

Another name for the [ROOT] object is ACME_TREE.

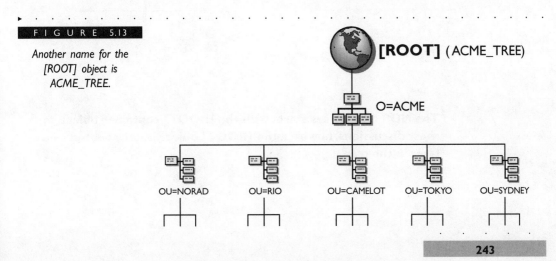

[ROOT] (ACME_TREE)

O=ACME

OU=NORAD   OU=RIO   OU=CAMELOT   OU=TOKYO   OU=SYDNEY

The name of the tree should be a unique value on the network wire because the tree uses SAP to broadcast to the client or workstations where the tree can be found. SAP bootstraps clients and all applications requiring NDS to find the NDS database very efficiently. If you need to install more than one physical NDS tree make sure that the trees have different names. An example of this important point is illustrated in Figure 5.14.

The company name plus _TREE is recommended because it clearly identifies the tree SAP as an NDS tree when you DISPLAY SERVERS at a console. Be careful not to make this name too long. Also, the SAP does not support spaces in the name, which is advertised via SAP, and the NetWare 4.1 INSTALL utility will not let you place spaces in the tree name.

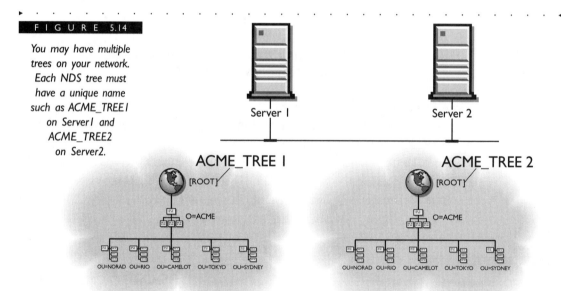

The NDS tree always starts with the [ROOT] container object. In most discussions, however, the [ROOT] object is not counted as a layer in the tree.

TIP

The object class definition in the schema that defines the [ROOT] is the object class TOP. The [ROOT] object is the only instance of the object class TOP and for this reason TOP is known as an effective class.

The [ROOT] object is parent to either the C=Country and/or O=Organization. Novell Consulting recommends that you use the O=Organization below [ROOT] rather than the C=Country object.

To Use or Not to Use the C=Country Object

The C=Country designator is used to specify a particular country code based on the X.500 standard. Public network providers, such as NetWare Connect Services (NCS) being offered with the cooperation of Novell, will make use of the Country object in their tree. The question often asked is, "If a company wants to connect to a public service provider, is it required to use the C=Country code in the NDS tree?" Most companies are not required to use the country object for their corporate tree. Instead, they can create a separate tree used for connecting to the public data network or through a 32-bit client that can connect to multiple trees.

If you choose to use the Country object, keep in mind that it will add an additional layer to your NDS tree and it will also create some rather odd distinguished names for your objects. Consider the example below in Figure 5.15. If we were to add the Country object to the ACME tree, which country do we choose? Do we use multiple country codes? For our example, ACME is headquartered primarily in CAMELOT; therefore, our Country object will be C=UK for England in this example.

Let's look at some of the user's contexts that would be created in other locations if we used only the C-UK COUNTRY designator. Abe Lincoln resides in the RIO location and so his context would be:

```
CN=ALINCOLN.OU=AUDIT.OU=ADMIN.OU=RIO.O=ACME.C=UK
```

User Sherlock Holmes in the TOKYO location would have the following context:

```
CN=SHOLMES.OU=CRIME.OU=TOKYO.O=ACME.C=UK
```

Now, if your names are supposed to adequately describe and identify a user's location in the tree, these examples are a little confusing and add more length to the context. Also, for some users who work in both the UK and the United States, it is difficult, if not impossible, to determine where in the tree they belong.

FIGURE 5.15

The use of the Country object can create some odd contexts in your tree.

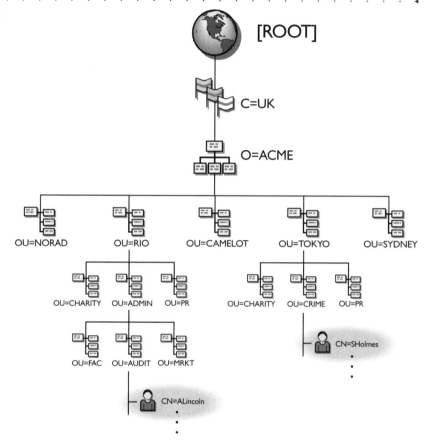

If you have already implemented the Country object in your tree, not to worry. It does not cause any serious consequences, but keep in mind the previous considerations.

Name the O=Organization for Your Company

After the [ROOT] object at the top, you will provide the NDS tree with at least one O=Organization. At least one O=Organization object is required for all NDS trees. The subsequent layers in the tree (the OUs) will be placed directly below the O=Organization.

We recommend that you name the O=Organization the same name as your company or use an abbreviation. Most companies use an abbreviation for the company name because it is easier when you are typing an object's context. For example, our company is named A Cure for Mother Earth, which is abbreviated to ACME. In almost every case, the Organization layer in the tree contains only one O=Organization, which gives you a single object to represent the entire company. Figure 5.16 shows how we have named our organization to represent our company name ACME.

FIGURE 5.16

ACME is representative of our entire company and is used as our organization name in our NDS tree.

[ROOT]

O=ACME — Organization name

OU=NORAD   OU=RIO   OU=CAMELOT   OU=TOKYO   OU=SYDNEY

CONSULTING EXPERIENCE

We recommend that you not name the O=Organization the same name that you used for the NDS tree. For troubleshooting purposes, the NDS tree should be named with the company name plus _TREE, and the O=Organization should be named with just the company name or an abbreviated company name. The ACME corporation would therefore be named O=ACME, with a tree name ACME_TREE.

Your company may want to use more than one O=Organization if your corporation has multiple companies that do not share the same network infrastructure. For example, the large conglomerate shown in Figure 5.17 uses multiple O=Organization objects because there are two separate companies (separate network infrastructures) included in a single NDS tree.

FIGURE 5.17

A large conglomerate company with multiple O=Organization objects

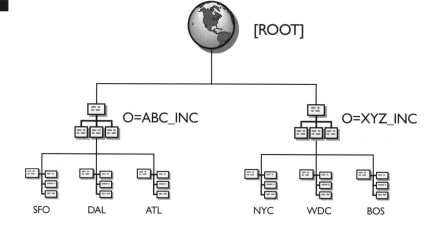

CONSULTING EXPERIENCE

A single NDS tree with two or more O=Organization objects is rarely used and is not usually recommended. This configuration is not often used because one of the design goals is to represent the entire corporation in the single tree with the same organization name. NDS will operate either way without difficulty, however.

Small Companies

In some cases the tree design can be finished very easily for small companies at this point because most servers, users, and other resources can be placed in the Organization container without creating any more containers. If you are the network manager responsible for all users, printers, and servers, you can simply group everyone in the same container, which can be the Organization container.

Figure 5.18 shows how a tree design can be very simple for a small company. If ACME had only a few servers in a single location, its tree could appear as shown in the figure. You may still want to subdivide the tree a little more if you have separate groups.

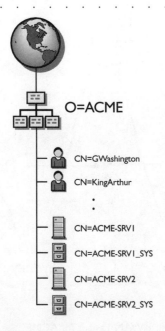

FIGURE 5.18

Small companies can group all their resources in the organization container if they have only a single network administrator managing all resources.

O=ACME

CN=GWashington

CN=KingArthur

CN=ACME-SRV1

CN=ACME-SRV1_SYS

CN=ACME-SRV2

CN=ACME-SRV2_SYS

The Geographic Design: Top Layers of the Tree are the OU=Organizational Units

As mentioned previously, the layer below the O=Organization is the first layer of OU=Organizational Units in the NDS tree. This layer of OUs is the most important layer of the NDS tree because it represents the geographical locations of your company. Using your company WAN maps or WAN documentation you can carefully design the contents of this layer, which becomes the foundation for the entire tree. This method is often referred to as the geographical design approach because you use your company's geographic or location information for the design at the top of the tree.

The key to designing the top of the tree is to match the WAN infrastructure or locations of your company with the first OU layers or containers. Based on our experience at many sites, the design of the top of the tree should be completely based on the WAN infrastructure. You will have a successful NDS tree design if you follow the guideline of representing the sites of your company with the top-most OUs. Figure 5.19 and Figure 5.20 illustrate how the top layer of the ACME tree is designed based on the physical WAN layout of the company.

FIGURE 5.19

Physical WAN layout for ACME

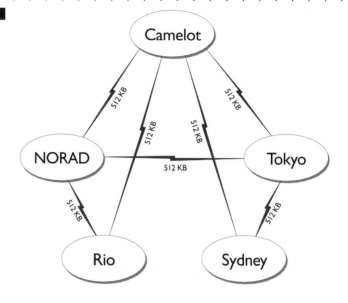

Physical WAN Layout for ACME

FIGURE 5.20

Top layer of the tree design for ACME, which is based on the physical or geographical WAN sites

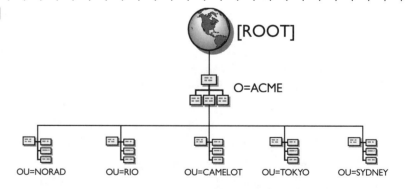

If you are a small company (no WAN, 5 servers or fewer), you can simply use the first Organization container you created to name your company. This container will hold all your objects including printers, servers, and users. Administration of a single container is very easy and requires very little maintenance. You can also create a container beneath the Organization container and place the resources there.

In general, if your company has multiple geographic sites or locations, you should represent the locations in the NDS tree at the top of your tree. The organizational structure of departments, divisions, and workgroups will be placed under each of these locations. Keep in mind that one of our design goals is to design a flexible tree in which changes are easily made. As you might expect, there are a few exceptions to the practice of designing geographically:

▶ Companies with a single site or campus-connected network are not dependent upon the geographic design approach. Since this configuration does not have physical locations that can be placed under or created as OUs, you will skip the geographical design approach at the top of the tree and proceed directly to the departmental design approach. Some companies with few servers and users may not need to create additional containers. Rather, they can place all the NDS objects under the single O=Organization.

▶ For companies with WAN sites or locations connected with very high speed links, such as T-3 or greater, the location OUs are less important because the limitation of the WAN has been removed. This is because WAN speeds are approaching LAN speeds. For the purpose of NDS tree design, the high-speed WAN connections really represent LAN bandwidths. However, we still recommend that you use the geographic design approach. See the section "Design the Bottom Level of the Tree" later in this chapter.

CONSULTING EXPERIENCE

Many companies still choose to use geographic containers even though they have very high speed WAN links. One company, for example, has a metropolitan area network (MAN) running FDDI to connect 12 buildings together across a city. The basis for the company's decision to use geographic sites at the top of the tree was twofold. First, for administrative purposes, the company wanted a single administrator to support each site. The sites gave the tree a good place to break out security administration. Second, the company was installing an e-mail application on its servers at each geographic location. So, even though the company has high-speed links, it still chose to design geographically.

When considering a campus network layout, such as a research park or university, consider first the speed of the links between the buildings or floors of the campus network. The locations in the campus network, such as buildings, could be used to represent minor sites in the network infrastructure and in the NDS tree. The buildings in the campus network can be useful container objects if they help organize your network resources and the NDS tree. The ability to effectively organize network resources is one of your design goals. The ACME tree NORAD location as shown in Figure 5.21 has used buildings named by function as its organizational units. Either design approach is acceptable. You must determine which one provides the best description of your environment.

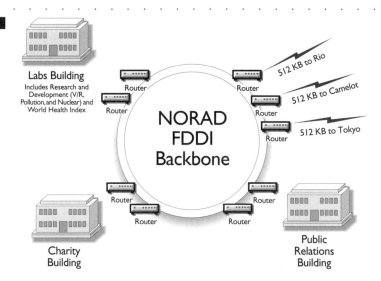

FIGURE 5.21

The ACME NORAD organization units are named based on their functions, which are also the building names such as OU=CHARITY, OU=LABS, and OU=PR.

Labs Building
Includes Research and Development (V/R, Pollution, and Nuclear) and World Health Index

Router

Router

Router

512 KB to Rio

512 KB to Camelot

Router

512 KB to Tokyo

Router

NORAD FDDI Backbone

Router

Router

Router

Router

Charity Building

Public Relations Building

If your company does not have a WAN infrastructure but only a LAN network, then you can skip the geographical design approach and go directly to the departmental design discussed later in this section.

Regional Layer of Organizational Units Helps Distribute the Location OUs

In some cases, it will be necessary to place regional containers directly below the O=Organization in the NDS tree to more fully distribute the total number of locations or geographical sites. Placing regional OUs under the O=Organization, but before the actual location OUs, will increase NDS operating efficiency and give the tree a closer pyramid shape.

As an example, consider the company ACME as we change the WAN layout to include more offices or cities around the world. We are changing ACME's WAN infrastructure only for this example. Figure 5.22 illustrates the offices or cities that are connected together via 56K links. Each of the cities added to the WAN layout is connected to its appropriate regional hub. Using the WAN infrastructure, we have designed a new tree, which includes regional OUs named North America (NA), South America (SA), Europe (EUR), Asia (ASIA), and Australia (AUST). These regional OUs group the appropriate cities and help keep the NDS tree design closer to a pyramid shape. See Figure 5.23 for the new ACME tree based on regional containers. Notice how the physical WAN layout in Figure 5.22 is driving the tree design in Figure 5.23.

FIGURE 5.22

Example of ACME with regions and cities. This is typically called a "hub and spoke" WAN infrastructure.

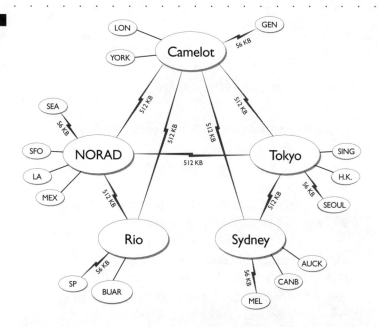

If your network utilizes a WAN infrastructure with a number of physical sites or offices, you may want to create regional containers based on those WAN sites at the top layer, which will help distribute the individual offices. Having the regional OUs helps the NDS tree operate more efficiently during all phases of operation.

Example of ACME tree with
the regions and cities as
the top layers

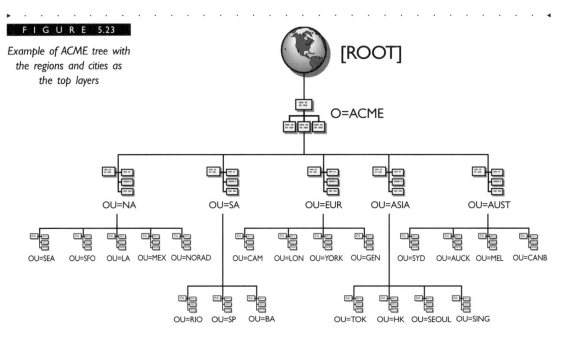

Departmental Design: Top Layers Not Based on Your WAN

The departmental design approach can be used most efficiently at the top of the tree only if your company does not have a WAN infrastructure or other locations to consider. If your company has only a LAN-based network, then you can skip the design of the top layers and go directly to the bottom layer design, which is based solely on the organization of the company.

If you have WAN links you may consider designing your NDS tree by placing the departments, divisions, and workgroups at the top of the tree and placing the physical locations at the bottom. This method is often called the departmental design approach and is not recommended for a company with a WAN infrastructure. Having the organizations placed at the top of the tree is a less efficient tree design because any change to the top organizations will ripple down the entire structure, including the sites locations below.

Consider the example in Figure 5.24 in which we have designed the top of the tree organizationally with locations at the bottom. The first question you need to ask is where do most network changes occur? Most changes will occur in your organization. That's not to say that changes don't occur in geographic sites as well, but they are less frequent. Therefore, when you make changes to the tree you want to impact as few people as possible. This is the third design goal of building flexibility into the tree design. In terms of other design elements, such as administration, partitions, replicas, network resource placement, login scripts, and bindery services, it is apparent that the organization layers at the bottom of the NDS tree more adequately address these factors.

The ACME tree with organizations at the top and geographic sites on the bottom is a less flexible way to design a tree in a network with WAN links and multiple locations. This is not a good tree design.

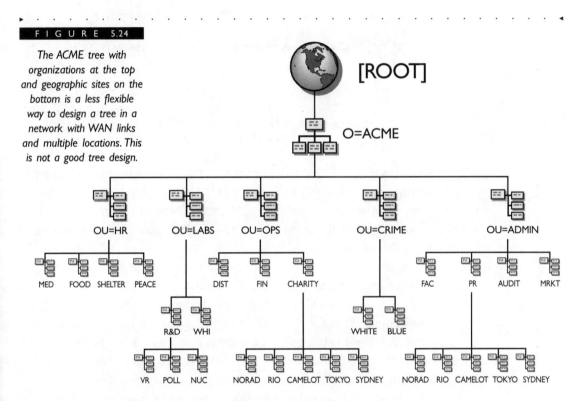

DESIGN THE BOTTOM LEVEL OF THE TREE

You should design the bottom level of the NDS tree along the organizational lines of your company by using your company's organizational charts or similar documents. The bottom layers of the tree are made up of OU containers, which are based on the divisions, departments, workgroups, and teams under each of the various locations defined at the top of the tree. Figure 5.25 shows the ACME organization chart that we will use in our tree.

FIGURE 5.25

The ACME organization chart used in our NDS tree

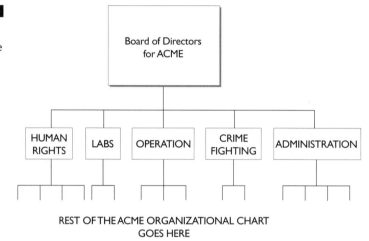

REST OF THE ACME ORGANIZATIONAL CHART
GOES HERE

The bottom layers of the tree should represent the network resources located in the LAN network of the location or site. Since the LAN supports a greater bandwidth or throughput of information than the WAN, the design of the bottom layers is extremely flexible. You, as the designer and administrator, can shape the bottom of the tree to meet your specific needs.

We recommend that you design the bottom of the tree based on the organizational chart documents because the users and administrators are already familiar with that type of layout. Remember that the bottom section is flexible if it is designed around organizations. You will discover through experience that a tree designed with the organizations at the bottom of the tree can more easily adapt to the changing requirements of the corporation. Figure 5.26 shows the bottom layers of the ACME tree based on the organizational charts for each ACME site.

During the design of the bottom of the NDS tree, ensure that there is a place for every user and network resource currently in your company. Remember that the primary goal in designing the NDS tree is to organize the network resources, including the users. If you do not have a place for all the users or network resources then you need to adjust your tree design. The bottom layers are typically the only ones affected. Refer back to Table 5.1 for the ACME resource list. This list has information on servers and printers and provides you with helpful information for placing resources in your tree.

FIGURE 5.26

The ACME tree with the bottom layers of OUs based on the organizational charts of the company

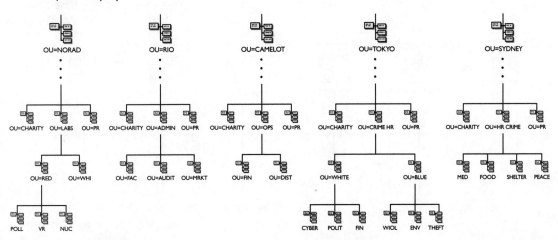

As mentioned earlier, the bottom containers or OUs in the tree are typically the divisions, departments, workgroups, and teams of your company. Do not include as containers any individuals that appear as division or department heads in your company's organizational charts. You simply want to identify the functional groups or departments; the individuals become the users in each container.

The ACME Tree Design

Notice in Figure 5.27 that the top layers of the ACME tree are based solely on the WAN infrastructure and will remain fairly stable or constant. Once the WAN infrastructure for ACME is considered in the design, the design effort shifts to the bottom of the tree. The bottom of the tree is based on the organizational chart for ACME. Most of the network resources will be placed in the bottom of the tree. Figure 5.27 illustrates a clear division between the top and bottom of the tree design phases in which the top is based on locations in the WAN and the bottom is based on the company's organizational information after crossing into the LAN infrastructure.

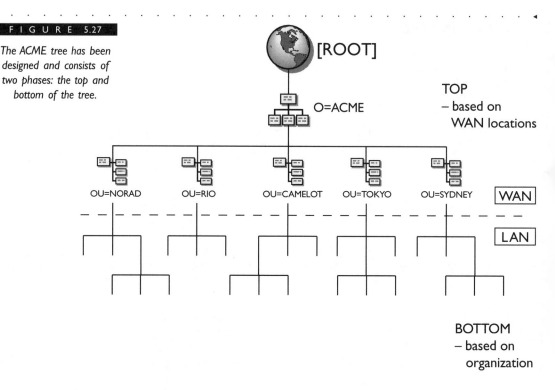

FIGURE 5.27

The ACME tree has been designed and consists of two phases: the top and bottom of the tree.

[ROOT]

O=ACME

TOP
– based on
WAN locations

OU=NORAD   OU=RIO   OU=CAMELOT   OU=TOKYO   OU=SYDNEY   WAN

LAN

BOTTOM
– based on
organization

Placement of Network Resources

The placement of the network resources, such as servers or printers, in the tree can affect how you design the bottom layers. As you decide where to place the physical network resources in the tree, you should consider the needs of the users who willshare these resources. If the network resources are organized according to divisions, departments, and workgroups, they should be placed in the same container with the users. However, if the network resources offer services to multiple departments in one site or location, you should place the resources in the location OU.

The placement of the network resources is an important design consideration for the bottom of the tree because the appropriate containers need to exist to place resources. If the OUs or containers do not exist then they will need to be created. Remember that one of the primary goals for designing the NDS tree is to organize your network resources.

With your resource list in hand, you can place your resources in their appropriate locations in the NDS tree. Below, we display illustrations of the ACME tree's five main sites. Included with each of these illustrations are some examples of how objects can be used in the ACME tree for the greatest impact and efficiency. Figure 5.28 shows the NORAD subtree with its resources.

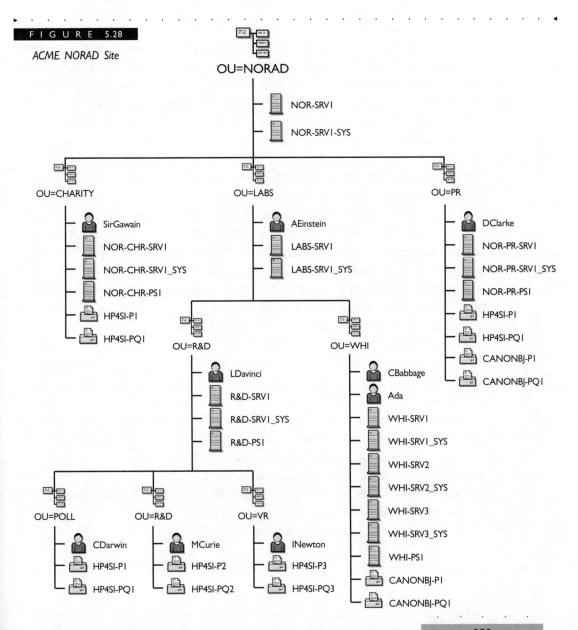

F I G U R E 5.28

ACME NORAD Site

At the NORAD site, as well as all other sites, we have placed a central server at the top OU=NORAD. This server will hold the master replica of the NORAD partition and can also function as an e-mail server for this location. The same process is repeated at all five sites.

Notice that the naming standards follow a very simple pattern based on our naming standards document. Servers are always defined by unique names across the entire tree because of the SAP requirement. Printers and print queues, however, can have the same name as long as they reside in different containers, such as HP4SI-P1, found in both OU=CHARITY and OU=POLL containers.

In Figure 5.29, the RIO location shows the placement of resources in each of the departments. It is not necessary to place all users in your tree using drawings such as these. We have included a user in each location as an example. The primary purpose in placing objects in this fashion is to determine their general placement in the tree. This will give you a better understanding of organizations and their resources.

In addition to creating user and server objects, you will want to create some other objects as well. For the RIO location, as well as all major locations, you should consider creating an organizational role object as the site administrator. Grant supervisor rights at the site location, such as RIO, to the organizational role object. For example, create a role called ADMIN_RIO. You can then move a user or two in as occupants of the role. If you have multiple administrators managing organizations at the same site, you may want to create separate roles for each department.

Since CAMELOT is basically the center of activity for the ACME tree, you may want to maintain control over the ADMIN user object from this location. Change the password frequently and limit the number of users who know the password. An example of the CAMELOT site is shown in Figure 5.30.

You can also use directory map objects to simplify the administration of your users. For example, the SYDNEY office uses directory maps in all their container login scripts. As versions of their specialized software change, the SYDNEY site administrator changes only the pointer of the directory map object to the new software version. This automatically enables all users in SYDNEY to see the new version of software because all container login scripts use the same directory map. An example of this site is shown in Figure 5.31.

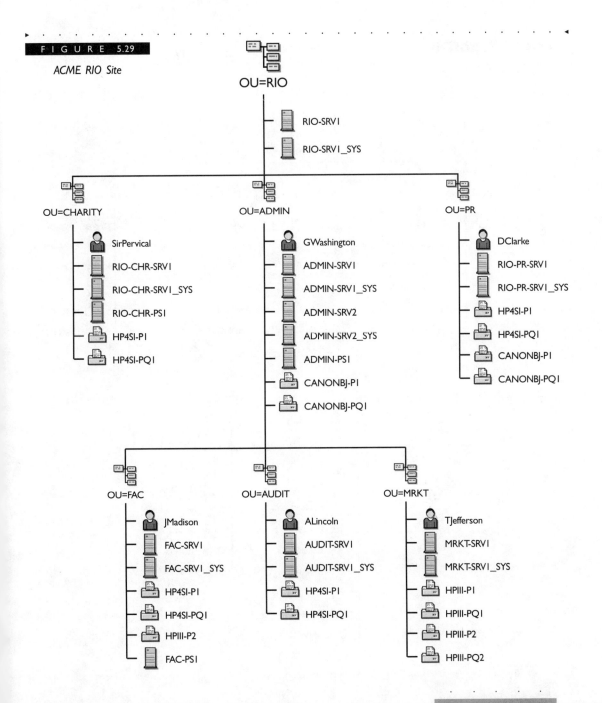

FIGURE 5.29

ACME RIO Site

FIGURE 5.30

ACME CAMELOT Site

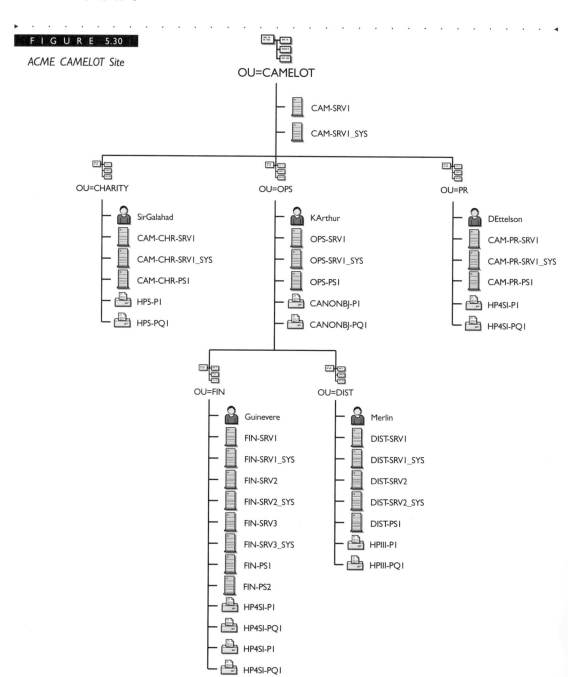

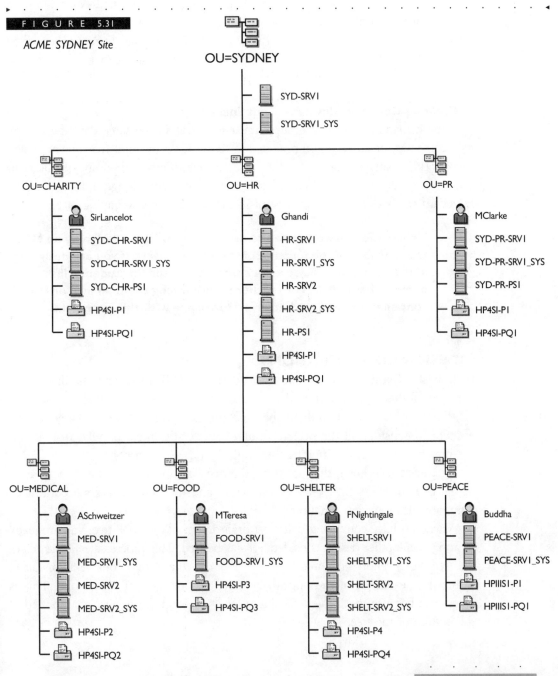

FIGURE 5.31

ACME SYDNEY Site

OU=SYDNEY

SYD-SRVI

SYD-SRVI_SYS

OU=CHARITY

SirLancelot

SYD-CHR-SRVI

SYD-CHR-SRVI_SYS

SYD-CHR-PSI

HP4SI-PI

HP4SI-PQI

OU=HR

Ghandi

HR-SRVI

HR-SRVI_SYS

HR-SRV2

HR-SRV2_SYS

HR-PSI

HP4SI-PI

HP4SI-PQI

OU=PR

MClarke

SYD-PR-SRVI

SYD-PR-SRVI_SYS

SYD-PR-PSI

HP4SI-PI

HP4SI-PQI

OU=MEDICAL

ASchweitzer

MED-SRVI

MED-SRVI_SYS

MED-SRV2

MED-SRV2_SYS

HP4SI-P2

HP4SI-PQ2

OU=FOOD

MTeresa

FOOD-SRVI

FOOD-SRVI_SYS

HP4SI-P3

HP4SI-PQ3

OU=SHELTER

FNightingale

SHELT-SRVI

SHELT-SRVI_SYS

SHELT-SRV2

SHELT-SRV2_SYS

HP4SI-P4

HP4SI-PQ4

OU=PEACE

Buddha

PEACE-SRVI

PEACE-SRVI_SYS

HPIIISI-PI

HPIIISI-PQI

The TOKYO office has traveling users as shown in Figure 5.32. We will create an alias for these users at the top of the tree at O=ACME. With the alias in place a traveling user such as DHOLIDAY in the OU=THEFT only has to remember to log in as DHOLIDAY.ACME. This makes the login process much easier for users who travel but do not carry their own laptop.

Creating Common Resource Containers

Some companies prefer to group similar resources in the same containers, such as a container for all servers, printers, and users. Keep in mind that this approach may work for smaller companies that do not have to group thousands of users in the same container or hundreds of servers together. This design approach works best with smaller companies that want to provide a simple grouping of resources.

NOTE

Universities may also need to use this approach to designing an NDS tree because of the location of servers and users. If you are designing a tree for a university, create containers based on students' last names (that is, A-C, D-F) rather than lumping them all into one container. You will get better performance with this approach.

DESIGN CONSIDERATIONS

Some LAN administrators may try to design the NDS tree and simultaneously consider all the external factors that may affect the design of the tree. Considering all the factors at once is difficult because the tree will shift and change as you attempt to consider all the design inputs. Some of the most popular distractions are bindery services, partitioning, replication, and login scripts.

Experience has shown that designing the tree is simple if you base the top layers of the tree solely on the WAN infrastructure and the bottom layers according to your organizational information.

When you have completed your first draft design of the NDS tree, you are ready to apply some other design considerations as needed. This process greatly simplifies the tree design effort. It is interesting to note that the design considerations affect primarily the design of the bottom of the tree, not the top of the tree. This is acceptable because the greatest flexibility for changes in the design is supported at the bottom of the tree.

FIGURE 5.32

ACME TOKYO Site

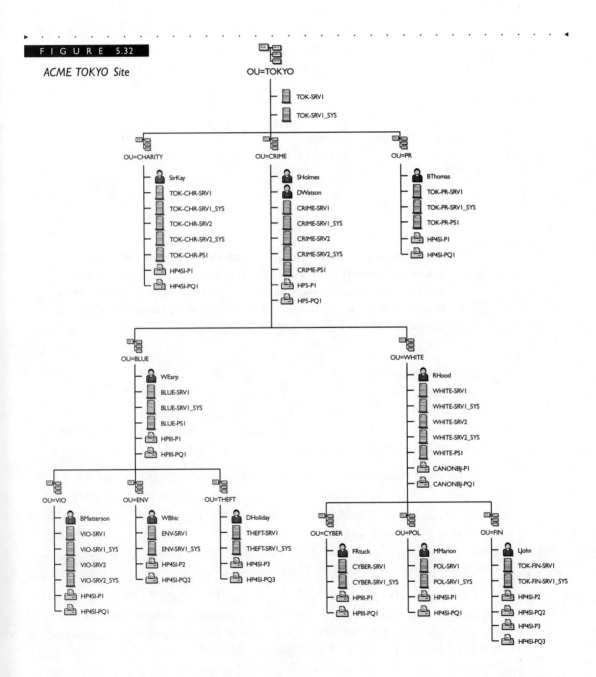

Again, our approach is to design the bottom level of the NDS tree aligned entirely to the organizations of your company. You can then apply the design considerations as needed. The design considerations that affect the bottom of the tree are:

- Administration

- NDS partitions and replicas

- Login scripts

- Bindery services

TIP

Remember that these design considerations apply only to the bottom of the tree; they do not alter the top layers in the tree design. By reviewing each design consideration, you will see how it applies only to the users and other network resources that are contained in the bottom layers.

Administration

One of the most important design considerations is how the NDS tree is going to be managed at your company. Are you going to manage the NDS tree as one Information System (IS) group (the centralized approach) or by several different IS groups (the decentralized approach)?

Centralized Management The entire NDS tree is controlled by one group in the company. This group manages all the additions and deletions of the NDS objects, partitioning, replication, and everything else related to the NDS database. Figure 5.33 shows how you can centrally manage your tree with one IS group having rights to the top of your tree and down. For more information regarding rights assignments, refer to Chapter 13.

Decentralized Management Portions of the NDS tree are delegated to individuals or independent groups in the company for management. These individuals or groups may be administrators for each department or site administrators responsible for all the network resources in a particular location. All subadministrators should, however, adhere to your previously defined naming standards. Figure 5.34 illustrates how you can set up administration for the lower containers in your group. You will have a central IS staff managing the upper layers of the tree, with other administrators being responsible for their respective containers.

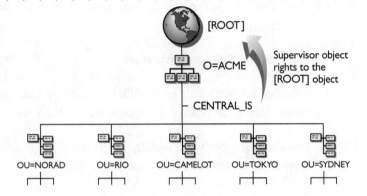

FIGURE 5.33

A centralized management approach with a single group having rights to the entire tree

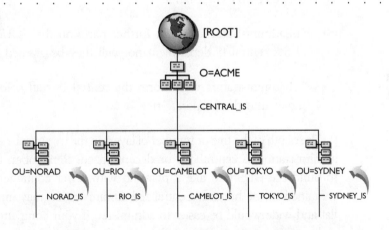

FIGURE 5.34

Creating a distributed administration approach by creating container administrators. Each subadministrator has rights to his or her own organizational unit.

If the NDS tree is going to be centrally managed, it makes sense to further the tree design to the bottom layers. The central team that provides administration has control of all the objects in the tree from top to bottom.

However, if the tree is going to be decentrally managed, each department administrator or site administrator will decide independently how the tree is organized in that portion of the tree. The top administrators have full responsibility to create the tree down to the department or site and then relinquish control at that

layer to each of the independent LAN administrators. Top administrators of the tree will still want to give design guidelines and suggestions to the bottom administrators on organizing the lower containers and grouping network resources. The following is a list of suggestions that you can give your administrators as guidelines. These ideas can also be mandated through the use of access controls as explained in Chapter 13.

Guidelines for Subadministrators

▸ Subadministrators will have sufficient security over their container to create, delete, or change all objects within their subcontainer.

▸ Subadministrators will carefully determine if more levels need to be created beneath their container before making changes.

▸ Subadministrators will do their part to maintain the naming standards as defined by the corporation.

▸ Subadministrators will not further partition their OU without the assistance of the central IS department nor will they be granted rights to do so.

▸ Subadministrators will inform the central IS staff before adding a new server into the corporate tree.

The depth of the tree or number of layers in the tree may be affected by whether your administration is centralized or decentralized. Remember, the recommendation is to build the NDS tree like a pyramid with fewer containers at the top and more containers at the bottom. Centralized administration may imply that a tree designed flat and wide would be easier to administer. If your company has only a few servers and users, you can build a shallow tree that is suited to centralized administration.

This may not be possible if your company is large with many servers, users, and geographic sites. In this case you will need to design the NDS tree with more layers, which means a deeper tree.

For decentralized management of NDS trees, individual administrators along with central administrators can determine the depth of their portion of the tree. Although there is no hard and fast rule regarding the total number of layers in the tree, the NDS tree is more flexible and easier for the user to find information if the tree has three to five layers. Typically, even the largest companies can design a very useful tree with five layers or fewer. Notice in Figure 5.35 that the ACME tree consists of five layers, not including [ROOT].

F I G U R E   5.35

The ACME tree consists of five layers, not including [ROOT].

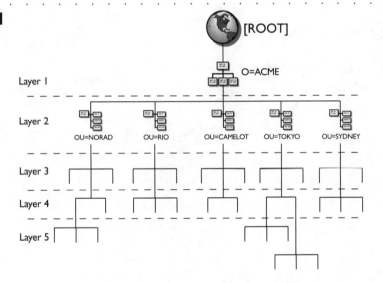

TIP

There is a logical limit to the total number of layers in the tree you can access. For example, **NDS** has a limit of 255 characters for a distinguished name. Thus, the actual limit for the number of layers is dependent on the number of characters in the names of your objects. If your **OU** names are long, your tree will not be able to have as many layers as it would with shorter **OU** names. For example, if all the **OU** names were just two characters then you would be able to have 51 layers (**OU=US**, 256/5 = 51). We recommend that you give the **OU**s in your tree short, descriptive names. For more information on naming standards, see **Chapter 4**.

NDS Partitions and Replicas

The next design consideration you need to address is how you will split the NDS database into partitions. For this discussion, we will consider the size of the partition (total number of objects), the total number of replicas, and where in the tree the partition is to be created. A container object is required for the creation of a partition and is designated the root-most object of the partition. Figure 5.36 shows a partition root called NORAD in the NORAD facility. The partition root is named NORAD because that is the starting point of that partition.

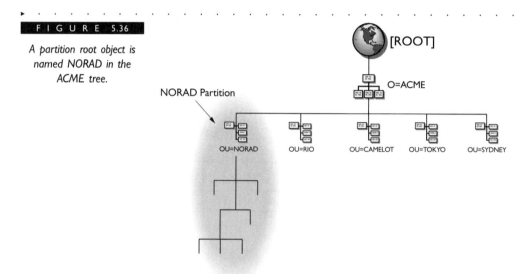

FIGURE 5.36

A partition root object is named NORAD in the ACME tree.

When deciding where to create a partition, you should follow the physical network infrastructure. Like the top layer of the tree, the partitions of the tree should represent the WAN, making each site or location its own partition. The benefit of partitioning the NDS database according to the WAN is that the information needed by the local users stays inside that location. We have partitioned each of the location organizational units by site as illustrated in Figure 5.37.

Each site is its own partition and maintains its portion of the NDS database on its own servers within the site.

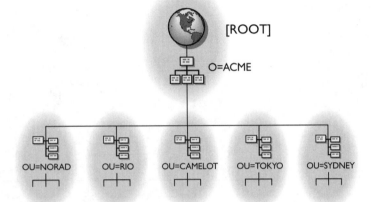

The size of your partitions and the total number of replicas is a design consideration for the bottom of the tree. Typically, partitions consist of fewer than 1,500 objects. If the partition grows to be significantly larger than 1,500 objects you should split the partition. Therefore, in Figure 5.38 we have created a new partition called OPS under CAMELOT because that location's partition has grown beyond 1,500 objects. More partitions in the right places provide greater efficiency in your tree design. Remember, a partition contains all the objects in a defined subtree, not just the objects in a single container.

CONSULTING EXPERIENCE

We are suggesting that NDS is more efficient using partitions less than 1,500 objects. Therefore, when your partitions reach this size you can begin to assess the need to split the partitions. Check your user and synchronization performance and use that as a guide. These recommendations are dependent upon the speed of your server hardware. We recommend that your server hardware be a Pentium class machine with 64MB of RAM if you exceed 1,500 objects.

F I G U R E   5.38

A new partition is created in the OPS department. It is now a child partition of its parent named CAMELOT.

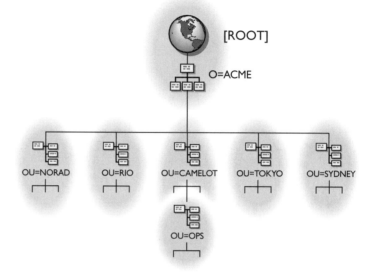

The next consideration is the total number of replicas of a partition. If the number of replicas is greater than 10, consider creating additional partitions to reduce the total number of replicas. Novell recommends three replicas for each partition. The primary reason you would need more than three replicas of any partition is for bindery services. Bindery services requires a writable copy of the replica. Refer to the "Bindery Services" section later in this chapter.

Decide who is responsible for the partitioning of the NDS tree. If you manage the tree centrally, all the partitioning decisions are made by the central IS department. If the tree is decentralized then you may turn over the rights of partitioning the tree to each of the local site or facility administrators. Whichever way you decide to handle partitioning, make sure you decide before installation of IntranetWare begins and make a company policy stating who will handle the partitioning.

Login Scripts

Another design consideration for the bottom of the tree is designing how the users will access the information in the tree. The users will primarily access NDS through the use of login scripts. Remember, the users need login scripts to map network drives and applications, capture to print queues, and set other variables. Thus, the login scripts become a very important design consideration. Typically, the users needing the same login script will be grouped together in the same OU container. You can then use the OU login script to provide users access to the NDS tree. Figure 5.39 shows a container login script that will be used by everyone in the container.

F I G U R E   5.39

*All users execute the login
script in the container
where they reside.*

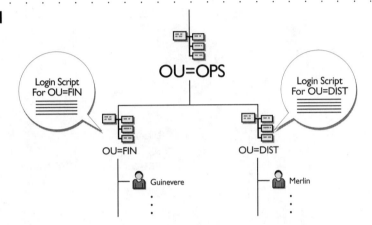

You will separate the users that need different login scripts for the same reason. As you design the login scripts for your users, you are in fact designing the organization of the bottom level of the tree.

Another strategy for organizing the login scripts is to have the same login script for all users and copy it to multiple containers. In this manner, the user placement in the tree is not affected. However, this strategy requires that the network administrator be responsible for keeping all copies of the login script the same.

It is recommended that you use the OU container login script to replace the functionality of the NetWare 3 system login script. This will help you organize the bottom layers and containers in your tree.

You can also make use of the profile login script whenever possible for configuring the users for access to resources that are more global in nature. The profile login script enables you to span a single login script across multiple OU containers and assign it to specific users. For example, the container SYDNEY has a profile script created for the HR department, and its subordinate departments of MEDICAL, FOOD, and SHELTER as shown in Figure 5.40 all use the script. The script can reside in any container, and users from any container can execute it.

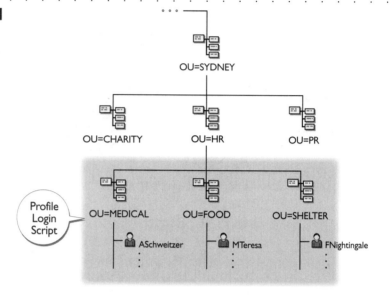

FIGURE 5.40

A profile script used by users from MEDICAL, FOOD, and SHELTER

OU=SYDNEY

OU=CHARITY   OU=HR   OU=PR

Profile Login Script

OU=MEDICAL   OU=FOOD   OU=SHELTER

ASchweitzer   MTeresa   FNightingale

Through the login script, each user maps network drives to the appropriate network server and establishes access to specific network applications and services. Most login scripts depend on groups and directory map objects for these drive mappings. These groups and directory map objects must be accessible so that any users needing them can find them during the login process.

In order to simplify the mapping to generic network applications (ones needed by all network users), it is appropriate to place the applications in the same subdirectory structure on all the servers. In other words, use the same file structure for all servers. Then when a user maps the drive, he or she does not care which server responds.

For example, assume that each network user needs to have drive mappings to both a word processor and spreadsheet software. These two software packages are installed on all file servers in the same place on the file system (SYS:APPS\WP and SYS:APPS\QPRO). All servers that have a generic file system structure enable the users to map these applications regardless of their location or the server to which they are physically attached. An example of how you can standardize your file system is shown in Figure 5.41.

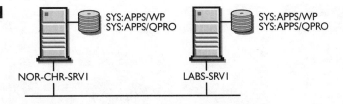

FIGURE 5.41

A standard file system on all your IntranetWare servers will make administration of your network easier.

Bindery Services

NDS provides compatibility with NetWare 2 and NetWare 3 using a feature called bindery services. This feature allows bindery versions of NetWare applications and other third-party software that require the bindery to access the NDS database as if it were the bindery. For example, a client can use the NETX shell (NetWare 3 client) to log in to an IntranetWare server and run any bindery-based application that may exist on the IntranetWare server.

Bindery services can be enabled through the server SET Server Bindery Context command. The server can select one OU, Organization, or Locality container or many containers as the bindery context. The server bindery context is simply the containers the server sees as the bindery. All the leaf objects in the NDS container(s) that are also objects in the NetWare 3 bindery (for example, users, groups, queues, print servers, and profiles) are seen as objects through the bindery application programming interfaces (APIs). The following figures show how you can set a server's bindery context(s). Figure 5.42 shows how you can use the SERVMAN utility to set the bindery context(s). Figure 5.43 shows how you can verify on a server that the bindery context(s) have been set.

Typing Set Bindery Context at a server shows the string of contexts as valid or invalid. If you want to see only the valid (effective and active) contexts you must type CONFIG at the server console.

TIP

Bindery services in IntranetWare lets you select up to 16 containers as the server bindery context. The major requirement for bindery services is that the server must store at least a read/write replica of the partition where the bindery context is set. If a server has the maximum 16 bindery contexts set, the server would have to store 16 separate replicas just to support bindery services on all contexts. Figure 5.44 shows how we have set multiple bindery contexts on a server in TOKYO to search the organizational units of CRIME, BLUE, and WHITE when a bindery request is made.

FIGURE 5.42

Using the SERVMAN
utility to set the server
context at OU=CRIME.
OU=TOKYO. O=ACME

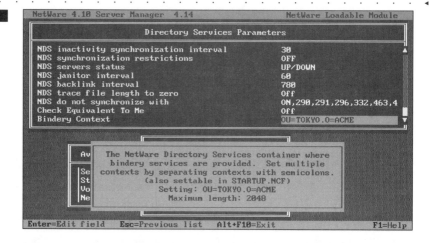

```
NetWare 4.10 Server Manager  4.14                    NetWare Loadable Module
┌──────────────────────────────────────────────────────────────────────────┐
│                      Directory Services Parameters                         │
│ NDS inactivity synchronization interval           30                       │
│ NDS synchronization restrictions                  OFF                      │
│ NDS servers status                                UP/DOWN                  │
│ NDS janitor interval                              60                       │
│ NDS backlink interval                             780                      │
│ NDS trace file length to zero                     Off                      │
│ NDS do not synchronize with                       ON,290,291,296,332,463,4 │
│ Check Equivalent To Me                            Off                      │
│ Bindery Context                                   OU=TOKYO.O=ACME          │
│                                                                            │
│       ┌────────────────────────────────────────────────────┐             │
│    Av │  The NetWare Directory Services container where     │             │
│       │  bindery services are provided.  Set multiple       │             │
│    Se │ contexts by separating contexts with semicolons.    │             │
│    St │        (also settable in STARTUP.NCF)                │             │
│    Vo │          Setting: OU=TOKYO.O=ACME                   │             │
│    Ne │          Maximum length: 2048                        │             │
│       └────────────────────────────────────────────────────┘             │
│ Enter=Edit field    Esc=Previous list    Alt+F10=Exit           F1=Help   │
└──────────────────────────────────────────────────────────────────────────┘
```

FIGURE 5.43

Typing **SET BINDERY
CONTEXT** at an
IntranetWare server
console will display
a server's bindery
context(s) if set.

```
CAM-SRU1:set bindery context
Bindery Context:  OU=CAMELOT.O=ACME
Maximum length:  2047
    Can be set in the startup ncf file
    Description:  The NetWare Directory Services container where bindery
                  services are provided.  Set multiple contexts by separating
                  contexts with semicolons.
CAM-SRU1:
```

As you can see, placing replicas on servers to support bindery services will increase
the total number of replicas for each partition. This will affect the tree design because
you may be forced to split a partition to reduce the number of replicas. Bindery
services is the principal reason for maintaining more than a few replicas of any
partition. Refer back to the section "NDS Partitions and Replicas" earlier in this
chapter.

FIGURE 5.44

Multiple bindery contexts are separated by semicolons on a server in TOKYO, which will view the CRIME, BLUE, and WHITE containers as its bindery.

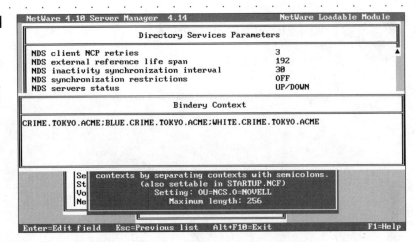

```
NetWare 4.10 Server Manager  4.14              NetWare Loadable Module
┌────────────────────────────────────────────────────────────────────┐
│                     Directory Services Parameters                     │
│ NDS client NCP retries                        3                      │
│ NDS external reference life span              192                    │
│ NDS inactivity synchronization interval       30                     │
│ NDS synchronization restrictions              OFF                    │
│ NDS servers status                            UP/DOWN                │
├────────────────────────────────────────────────────────────────────┤
│                          Bindery Context                             │
│ CRIME.TOKYO.ACME;BLUE.CRIME.TOKYO.ACME;WHITE.CRIME.TOKYO.ACME        │
│                                                                      │
│                                                                      │
│                                                                      │
│        ┌──────────────────────────────────────────────────┐        │
│        │Se  contexts by separating contexts with semicolons.│       │
│        │St       (also settable in STARTUP.NCF)             │        │
│        │Vo          Setting: OU=NCS.O=NOVELL                │        │
│        │Ne            Maximum length: 256                   │        │
│        └──────────────────────────────────────────────────┘        │
│ Enter=Edit field   Esc=Previous list   Alt+F10=Exit          F1=Help │
└────────────────────────────────────────────────────────────────────┘
```

Another design consideration is that you should place all the clients or users requiring bindery services from a particular file server in the OU container where you have set the server bindery context. This consideration can affect the NDS tree design at the bottom level because it may require you to combine users and resources of multiple departments or workgroup into one OU. You may need to separate users from the resources they don't use for the same reason. In any event, the organization of the bottom layers of the tree may be affected because the users and resources need to be arranged for bindery services.

NOTE

Before you change the bottom of the tree design to accommodate bindery services, determine whether you even need bindery services for the servers. Remember, bindery services is an optional feature that does not have to be enabled at each server. You should determine if the clients are using NETX or applications that require bindery services. You could also identify the users and key applications and force them to use bindery services on specific servers.

With an NDS tree design roughed out you are now ready to design for partitioning and replication.

CONSULTING EXPERIENCE

Here is a brief list of some of the applications you may encounter that make bindery calls. This is a brief list, and you need to check all your applications to determine if they require the bindery.

- NetWare 3 Print Services
- Backup Utilities
- Host Connectivity Products
- Menuing Systems
- Network Management Utilities
- Other NetWare 3-Based Applications and Utilities

Designing and Using NDS Partitions and Replicas

"The beginning is the most important part of the work." Plato

The NDS tree information is stored on the servers in data files. These data files may be either centralized on one or two network servers or be distributed across all the network servers in the company. Although the NDS tree can be distributed to servers across the network, the users are provided a single view of its resources. With NDS, the information is not only distributed but also replicated on multiple servers to provide increased reliability. Figure 6.1 shows how NDS might be distributed across a few servers in the network for the ACME company while still providing the user with a single view of the network resources.

F I G U R E 6.1

NDS provides distribution of the information across a few of the network servers for ACME while still providing the user with a single view of the network resources.

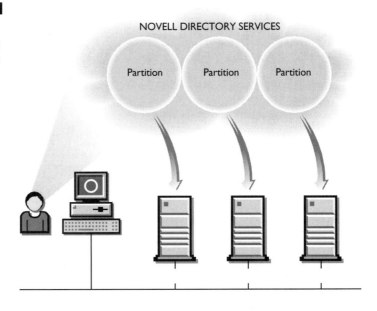

NOVELL DIRECTORY SERVICES

Partition   Partition   Partition

In a company with a small number of servers, the NDS tree information could be centralized with all the information residing on one or two network servers. The benefit of having the data files centralized on just a couple of servers is that the administration is easier. The NDS tree will perform efficiently as long as the total number of users and network resources for the entire company remains small.

In a small company, you can place all of its resources into a single O=Organization in the NDS tree structure for simplicity or create an OU under the O=Organization.

TIP

Companies that have large networks with a large number of servers should split the NDS tree (or object hierarchy) into sections and distribute them to the appropriate network servers.

NDS Partitions

NDS is represented as a hierarchical structure called a tree into which all the network resources are placed. Figure 6.2 illustrates how the NDS database is viewed as a hierarchical tree. The NDS partitions are also hierarchical and follow the same structure as the tree.

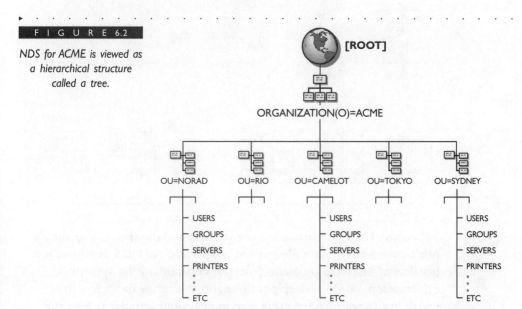

[ROOT]

ORGANIZATION(O)=ACME

OU=NORAD   OU=RIO   OU=CAMELOT   OU=TOKYO   OU=SYDNEY

- USERS
- GROUPS
- SERVERS
- PRINTERS
- ○
- ○
- ETC

- USERS
- GROUPS
- SERVERS
- PRINTERS
- ○
- ○
- ETC

- USERS
- GROUPS
- SERVERS
- PRINTERS
- ○
- ○
- ETC

NDS partitions are logical sections of the NDS tree. The NDS partitions are based on the same structure as the NDS tree. Partitioning is the process of splitting the NDS hierarchy or tree into smaller parts or subtrees. These subtrees can then be physically stored on your network servers as replicas of the partition. Partitioning the NDS tree enables you to selectively distribute the NDS tree information to the areas in the network that need the information. Figure 6.3 illustrates how the NDS hierarchy or tree for ACME can be split into partitions and placed on or copied to the network servers.

FIGURE 6.3

The NDS tree for ACME has been partitioned and placed on or copied to the network servers.

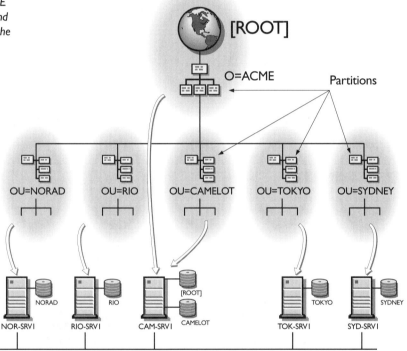

TIP

When the NDS partitions are mentioned and described, you should not confuse them with file system partitions. An NDS partition is a portion of the NDS tree and does not contain any file system information. A file system partition, on the other hand, has the capability to split a hard drive into logical segments for use by the operating system.

NDS partitions and file system partitions serve different purposes and are not related in any way.

Partitioning gives you the ability to scale the NDS tree across the network servers. Splitting up the NDS tree into partitions and storing them on separate network servers will distribute the workload for each of the servers. In addition, the NetWare utilities enable you to select the servers in the network where you want to store the different NDS partitions.

As mentioned earlier, the layout of the NDS partitions is hierarchical, meaning that one partition is parent to subordinate or child partitions. When all partitions are taken together, they form a hierarchical map back to the [ROOT] object. Figure 6.4 illustrates how the individual partitions form a hierarchical map. This map is often called a partition map.

FIGURE 6.4

Individual partitions for the ACME tree form a hierarchical partition map.

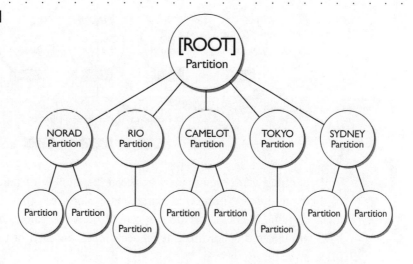

PARENT-CHILD RELATIONSHIP BETWEEN PARTITIONS

The relationship between the individual partitions in the tree is a parent-child relationship. Where the boundaries between the partitions meet, the partition closer to the [ROOT] is considered the parent and the one further away is the child.

TIP

The parent-child relationship is also described in terms of subordinate and superior partitions. A subordinate partition (or child) is the partition that is down the tree or further from the [ROOT]. The superior partition (or parent) is the partition that is closer to the top of the tree than its subordinate partition.

In the ACME partition map, the parent-child relationship between partitions is illustrated in Figure 6.5. In this example, the OU containers that have been partitioned at NORAD, RIO, CAMELOT, TOKYO, and SYDNEY are child partitions to the partition [ROOT], which is the parent. In the case of the CAMELOT partition, it is also a parent partition with the three subordinate partitions as the child partitions.

F I G U R E 6.5

Parent-Child relationship between the partitions in the ACME tree

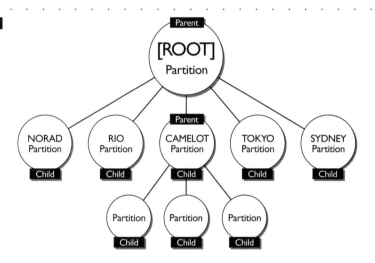

Partitioning can be compared to the responsibility of parents for keeping track of their children. When child partitions are created, their parent must maintain their locations. If the server does not hold both the parent and its child partitions, NDS will create a subordinate reference replica for each of the child partitions and place it on the server.

NDS requires that the location of the subordinate partitions be linked with their parent to form a common set of NDS information. The tree can then be traversed by the users. The parent only needs to know the location of its child partitions if the child partitions are not stored on the same server as the parent. The mechanism that maintains the relationship is called a subordinate reference replica. This topic will be discussed in more detail in the "Subordinate Reference Replicas" section later in this chapter.

If you should create new partitions below the CAMELOT partition as illustrated in Figure 6.6, then CAMELOT becomes a parent partition to the newly formed partitions. Although CAMELOT is a new parent, it is still a child partition of [ROOT]. However, there is not a grandparent relationship, in which a grandparent must know about a grandchild partitions. Only the parent-child relationship exists in the NDS among partitions.

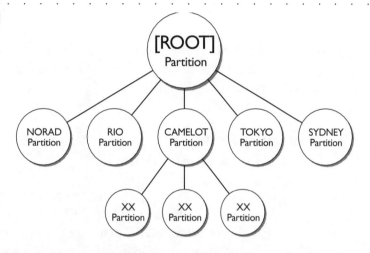

NOTE

NDS maintains the relationship between the parent and child partitions. If a server is holding a parent partition and is not storing the child partition, NDS creates a subordinate reference replica pointing to the child partition. This replica maintains the links in the NDS tree. Again, the subordinate reference replicas are placed on servers where the parent partition is and the child partition is not. Therefore, any server holding a parent partition can end up storing subordinate reference replicas to child partitions.

Servers can also end up holding a large number of subordinate reference replicas depending on how you design the partitions for your NDS tree — for example, creating or partitioning each of the organizational units beneath the [ROOT] partition. If you have too many partitioned organizational units that are immediately below the [ROOT], NDS creates subordinate reference replicas automatically for any servers holding a copy of the [ROOT] partition.

Design your tree so that you minimize each server holding subordinate reference replicas. More on this topic later.

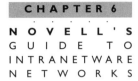

CHAPTER 6
. . . . . .
NOVELL'S
GUIDE   TO
INTRANETWARE
NETWORKS

PARTITIONING IS TRANSPARENT TO THE USERS

Partitioning of the NDS database is completely transparent to the users. The users can access the entire NDS tree regardless of which server they are connected to. For example, a user sitting at a single workstation on the network sees the NDS tree as a single logical entity, even though the NDS tree has been partitioned and distributed across the servers.

Although a specific server may not contain the complete set of NDS data files for the network, the users still have the ability to get the information they request through background processes that NDS establishes and maintains between the separate partitions.

PARTITIONING RULES

The NDS partitions will follow these rules:

▸ The partition is named and requires a single container object at the top (or root) of the partition (not to be confused with the [ROOT] partition). The container object that is used as the start of the partition is called the partition root object. Only one partition root object exists for each partition and is the top-most container object. An example of partition root objects is shown in Figure 6.7.

▸ . . . . ◂

FIGURE 6.7

Several partition root objects in the ACME tree

[ROOT]

O=ACME

OU=NORAD   OU=RIO   OU=CAMELOT   OU=TOKYO   OU=SYDNEY

NORAD Partition

TOKYO Partition

▶ Two organizational unit containers at the same level cannot exist as a partition without a parent container. This rule is very similar to the first rule. Figure 6.8 illustrates how two peer OUs in the ACME tree cannot be contained in the same partition.

F I G U R E 6.8

Two peer OUs in the ACME tree, such as OU=NOR and OU=RIO, cannot be contained in the same partition. A partition must have a single container object to define the top of the partition.

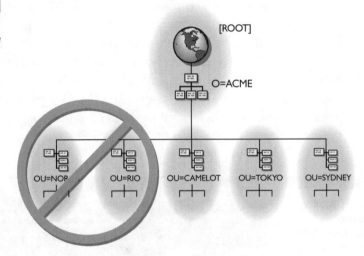

▶ The partitions cannot overlap with any other part of the NDS tree, meaning that one object will never reside in two partitions as illustrated in Figure 6.9.

F I G U R E 6.9

Partition information cannot overlap as shown in this figure. For example, the NORAD and TOKYO partitions cannot contain information that is subordinate to OU=RIO and OU=SYDNEY, respectively. An object can exist in only one partition.

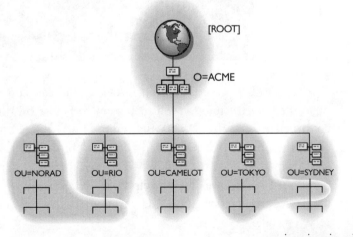

▸ The partition contains all of the information for the connected subtree. Each partition may be thought of as a section or subtree of the entire NDS tree.

THE [ROOT] PARTITION

During the installation of the first NDS server, the [ROOT] partition for the tree is created automatically and placed on the IntranetWare server. A copy (replica) of [ROOT] is placed on this server. In IntranetWare, the [ROOT] partition is the only partition that the installation program will create. Figure 6.10 illustrates the point at which the [ROOT] partition is created during the installation of NDS on the first IntranetWare server. All other partitioning of the NDS database must be created by you or other system administrators. The [ROOT] partition cannot be removed unless you remove NDS from all the IntranetWare servers, which is really removing the entire tree.

F I G U R E 6.10

The [ROOT] partition is created automatically when the first IntranetWare server is installed. In this example, the first server is the CAM-SRV1 server in CAMELOT, which holds the master replica of [ROOT].

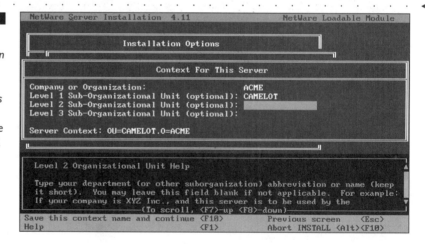

After the first server has been installed, you can add the objects necessary to build the tree structure for your company. In Figure 6.11, the ACME tree has been constructed using the NWADMIN utility to add the necessary container objects.

All the objects that have been added to the ACME tree are initially held by a single partition called the [ROOT] partition. Figure 6.12 illustrates how the [ROOT] partition is holding all the objects in the NDS tree until further partitioning can take place. After installation this partition resides only on the first IntranetWare server installed.

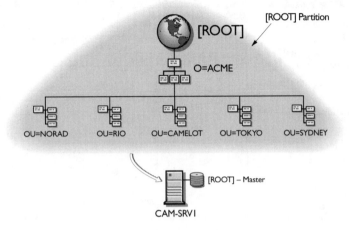

FIGURE 6.11

The ACME tree has been constructed by adding the necessary objects.

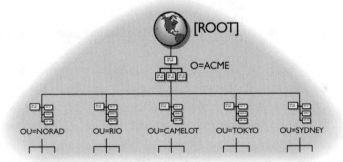

FIGURE 6.12

The [ROOT] partition holds all the objects in the tree until further partitioning takes place.

Since there is only one copy of the [ROOT] partition, you should place the partition on other servers as they are installed in the system. Additional copies of the partition are automatically created by the Novell Installation Program as you add servers. For example, server NOR-SRV1 is installed into the tree and receives a read/write copy of the partition. Figure 6.13 shows that you will have two copies of the [ROOT] partition placed on the servers, NOR-SRV1 and CAM-SRV1.

*Using the NDS Manager
utility, you can see two
copies of the [ROOT]
partition, NOR-SRV1 and
CAM-SRV1, that have been
placed on the servers for
the ACME tree.*

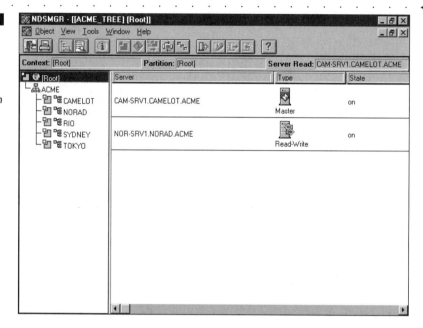

Child partitions can be created from the [ROOT] partition by selecting a subordinate container object, typically an OU, as the top of the partition. A partition can have only one top-most container object (referred to as the partition root object).

When the partition is created, it takes its name from the top-most container object (partition root object). All the objects in the tree that are under the container object comprise the contents of the new partition. Creating a partition does not affect the child partition boundaries. Figure 6.14 shows the creation of the NORAD partition for the ACME tree. All the objects in the subtree under NORAD are included in the partition.

Creating a child partition from the parent partition is an operation called Create partition in the NetWare utilities. The operation is fast and in most cases does not generate a lot of traffic on your network unless you have many replicas of the partition. The operation simply divides one partition into two with all the information staying on the same server that contained the original partition. This Create partition operation will make a new child partition on all the servers that had a copy of the parent partition. Figure 6.15 shows the NORAD partition being created from the [ROOT] partition.

A new partition called
NORAD is created for the
ACME tree.

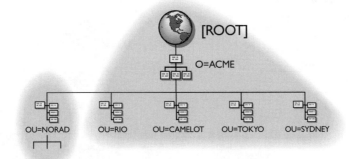

A conceptual view of a
Create partition operation
to create the NORAD
partition. This operation
affects both original copies
of the [ROOT] partition,
which are stored on
CAM-SRV1 and NOR-SRV1.

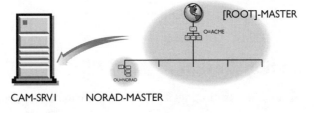

CAM-SRV1   NORAD-MASTER

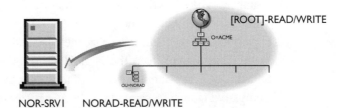

NOR-SRV1   NORAD-READ/WRITE

It is recommended that the [ROOT] partition be kept small with only the [ROOT] object and O=Organization containers and a few objects if necessary. For example, in order to keep the [ROOT] partition small for ACME, further partitioning needs to take place. As illustrated in Figure 6.16, if more partitions are created directly under the [ROOT] partition, then the [ROOT] partition holds only the top-most portions of the tree.

FIGURE 6.16

The [ROOT] partition for
the ACME tree should
hold only the top-most
portion of the tree.

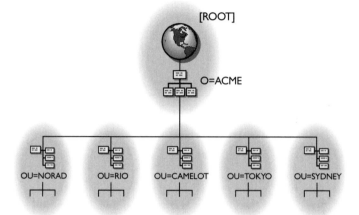

Partition Design

Designing the partitioning of your NDS tree can be very simple if you remember why you create a partition. You create a partition to scale NDS across your network servers. If your network is very small, then you do not need to partition your NDS tree.

The number one design criteria for partitioning is the physical layout of your network infrastructure: the WAN links and the network servers. Using this criteria, your main task is to partition the NDS tree to localize the information. This means that you want to partition the Directory to keep the NORAD information in NORAD, and the RIO information in RIO, and so on. Figure 6.17 illustrates the physical WAN layout for the ACME company. Figure 6.18 shows how the ACME tree has been partitioned to support the physical WAN layout. Note that in our example the [ROOT] partition is very small and includes only the [ROOT] and organization container objects. Keeping the [ROOT] partition small is recommended and will be discussed later when we address replication.

As illustrated in Figure 6.19, you can see that the NORAD partition and its object information have been be placed on the server in NORAD. The same is true for all the locations. By partitioning the NDS tree based on your WAN network layout, you can keep the information local to each location and yet still find and use the resources throughout the entire NDS tree.

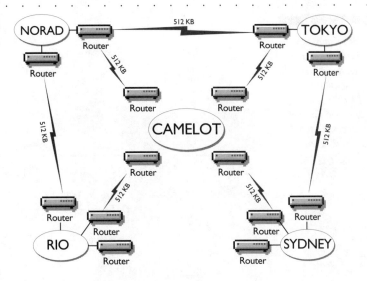

FIGURE 6.17

The physical WAN network
layout for the ACME
company

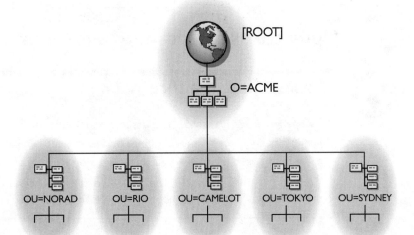

FIGURE 6.18

The ACME tree has been
partitioned according to the
WAN infrastructure.

FIGURE 6.19

NDS distributes the information across the networks servers for ACME. The NORAD partition is stored locally on the NORAD server. Each of the partitions is stored on its local server.

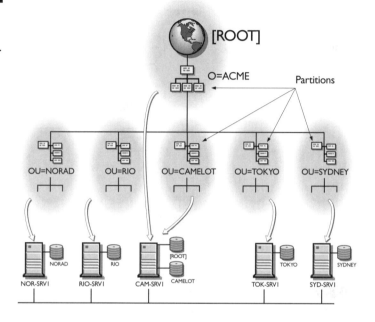

GUIDELINES FOR CREATING PARTITIONS

CONSULTING EXPERIENCE

The guidelines presented here assume that your server hardware is fast, meaning Pentium class PCs operating at 100Mhz or better. Keep in mind that the slowest server in the replica list tends to affect all synchronization activities of even the faster servers in the same partition. If you are operating on slower hardware, you should carefully read the recommendations throughout this section for partitioning guidelines.

The specific guidelines and recommendations for designing your NDS partitions are as follows:

▶ Do not span a WAN link or physical locations with a partition. This design rule is very important and should not be ignored. The reason we don't recommend spanning with the WAN link is that unnecessary NDS traffic will travel between two locations and across your WAN infrastructure. This extra traffic would occur during each of the normal synchronization operations. Spanning a partition across the WAN link is shown in Figure 6.20 and generally should be avoided.

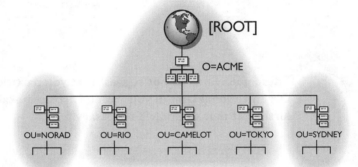

F I G U R E 6.20

Do not span the WAN link as shown in this example of the [ROOT] partition spanning the CAMELOT, RIO, and TOKYO sites.

[ROOT]

O=ACME

OU=NORAD OU=RIO OU=CAMELOT OU=TOKYO OU=SYDNEY

▶ Keep the [ROOT] partition small. The [ROOT] partition should include only the [ROOT] object and the O=Organization object. Do not include additional containers in the [ROOT] partition other than the [ROOT] object and Organization=ACME object as shown in Figure 6.21. This means that you should not include any other subordinate container OUs in the partition with the [ROOT] partition. As illustrated in Figure 6.21, you should avoid partitioning an individual location within the [ROOT] partition.

▶ The top layers of the tree should be partitioned according to the locations in your company. Again, do not span a WAN link with the same partition. Partition locally wherever possible.

FIGURE 6.21

Do not include additional containers in the [ROOT] partition other than [ROOT] object and Organization=ACME as shown in this example. We recommend that you not leave the individual location information in the [ROOT] partition.

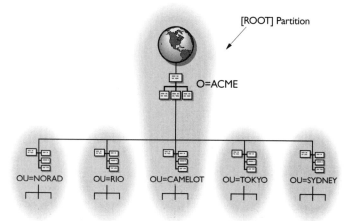

These guidelines do not suggest that you partition every Organizational Unit in your tree. Partition locally, and partition further at that site only if necessary.

TIP

▶ The bottom layers of the tree should be split off into additional partitions only if there are special requirements. The special requirements are either the size of the partition (total number of objects is greater than 3,500), more than 7 to 10 replicas of the same partition, or the need to break out an administrative subtree.

The previous partitioning thresholds assume you are operating on high-end server hardware. For some servers the thresholds may be 1,000 to 2,000 objects per partition and 4 to 5 replicas.

TIP

▶ You will want a small number of partitions at the top layers of the tree and possibly more partitions as you move toward the bottom. If you have designed the tree based on a pyramid shape, as recommended in Chapter 5, then your partition design will naturally follow the tree design.

▸ Do not create a partition for a location (even if it is across a WAN link) if there is no local server to store it on. This situation is common only with small remote offices that do not have servers at their local site. The users in this situation would currently access all the network services across the WAN infrastructure. The access to NDS is not any different. Figure 6.22 shows how these users at the OU=DIST would still be part of a partition contained on a server in OU=DIST because they do not have their own server.

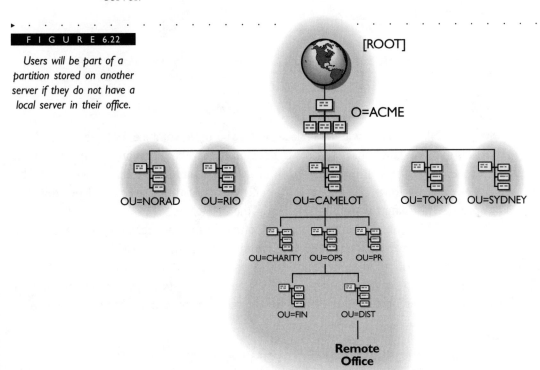

F I G U R E 6.22

Users will be part of a partition stored on another server if they do not have a local server in their office.

PARTITIONING THE TOP LAYERS

As mentioned earlier, the top layers in the tree should be partitioned according to the WAN infrastructure as shown in Figure 6.23. Since the top layers of the tree should already be designed according to the WAN links, then partitioning will naturally follow these boundaries.

FIGURE 6.23

The top layers of the ACME
tree partitioned according
to the WAN infrastructure

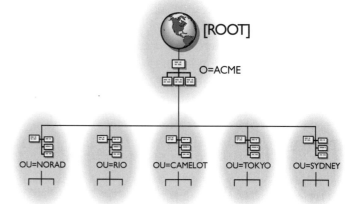

The NDS database will not scale as well if you try to combine multiple geographical sites into one partition. If you try to span more than one location in a partition then the information in the partition will synchronize with the other copies across the slower WAN links. This reduces the efficiencies of the network and destroys the purpose of trying to create a partition in the first place.

If you have implemented regional OU containers in your tree, then you should create a partition for each of the regional OUs and store that partition on a server separate from its parent partition. After the region partitions are defined in your tree, you will need to partition at the locations under each of the regions and store them on separate servers from their parents in order to distribute the subordinate references to multiple servers.

PARTITIONING THE BOTTOM LAYERS

Because the design of the bottom of the tree is based on the divisions, departments, and workgroups within the each location of the WAN, the tree should already be partitioned at the WAN site or location. Further partitioning may not be needed. Follow the partitioning guidelines presented earlier regarding the number of objects in a partition and the number of replicas. The bottom layers of the tree can be partitioned only if there is a special requirement. The special requirements are:

▸ Partition size

▸ Number of replicas

▸ Partition administration

Partition Size

As the partition size grows you should consider creating another partition to help distribute the workload that any one server or set of servers has to handle. A larger sized partition is approximately 1,500 objects on a high-end PC. So as the partition grows to be larger you should then split the partition by creating a new child partition. Remember, a partition contains all the objects in a defined subtree, not just the objects in a single container.

Figure 6.24 depicts the CAMELOT partition being split into two partitions. The OU=OPS container object becomes a new child partition to CAMELOT. It is assumed that this new partition was created because the CAMELOT partition became larger than 1,500 objects and was running on a Pentium class PC. The OU=OPS container and subtree hold a large number of the objects and was split off as a new partition.

Number of Replicas

Another consideration is the total number of replicas of a single partition. If the total number of replicas for the same partition goes beyond 7 to 10, then you should consider splitting the partition just to reduce the total number of replicas for that partition. The primary reason you will need more than three replicas of any partition is to support bindery services at IntranetWare servers for backup and other utilities that need the bindery.

Also, keep in mind that more replicas means more management if a partition should need repairing. Using Novell's utilities to make repairs becomes a bigger task if you have many replicas. Each server holding a replica (and the subordinate replicas) may need to be repaired if you encounter problems. Obviously, the more replicas, the larger the task of repair for you, your administrators, or other outside support personnel.

FIGURE 6.24

*The OU=OPS container
object is created as a new
partition because the
CAMELOT partition
became too large.*

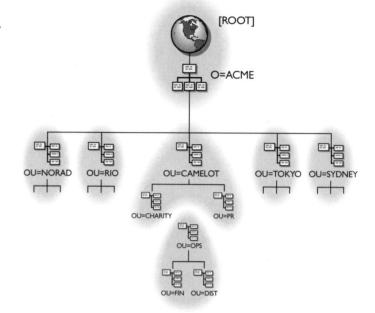

Partition Administration

NDS enables several different administrators to be responsible for the partitioning of the NDS tree. If a departmental or site manager wants the responsibility to manage his or her own partitioning, then you need to plan the parent partitions accordingly. For example, the rights needed to partition the NDS tree are effective write rights to the Access Control List (ACL) of the top container object of the partition. There are several ways to receive this privilege. One way is through the Supervisor object right to the container object that defines the partition. You can also grant explicit write rights to its ACL. Also, if there is a need to create a new partition from the parent partition, then the administrator creating the child also needs full rights to the parent.

In order to perform other partition operations such as Add/Remove replica and Change Replica Type, you are required to have rights to the server object that is being affected. For more information on security and rights, see Chapter 13.

PYRAMID SHAPE FOR THE PARTITIONS

The pyramid-shaped design for the partitions is recommended because it automatically distributes the subordinate reference replicas. Having a smaller number of partitions at the top of the tree with more at the bottom of the tree satisfies the requirement of fewer subordinate reference replicas per server and minimizes the supportability and repairability of your tree if problems should occur.

The pyramid-shaped design can be accomplished if you always create partitions at the top layers according to the WAN infrastructure and then create the bottom layer partitions as specified in the previous guidelines. For example, as illustrated in Figure 6.25, the ACME tree has been partitioned according to the WAN infrastructure with some further partitioning at the lower layers. The partitioning for the ACME is in the shape of a pyramid.

FIGURE 6.25

The ACME tree has been partitioned according to the WAN infrastructure, which naturally takes the shape of a pryamid.

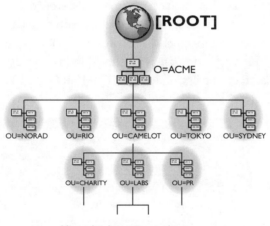

Hierarchical partitions in the map

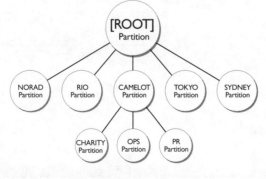

Pyramid-shaped partition map

By following the partitioning guidelines for both the top and bottom layers of your tree, the NDS information will always remain close to the user and other leaf objects because the partitions have been based on the locations. An exception would be the [ROOT] partition, which is created automatically during installation of the first IntranetWare server.

NDS Replicas

As mentioned earlier, NDS is a global name service and can be split into partitions and then distributed to any number of network servers. The feature that distributes NDS is called partitioning and the characteristic that makes it redundant is called replication. An NDS replica is the physical copy of a partition that is stored on a network server. An NDS partition can have multiple replicas or copies stored on different network servers. The group of replicas that exists for a particular partition is called a replica list.

It is important to remember that a partition is a logical structure, while the replica is a physical copy of the partition as illustrated in Figure 6.26. The [ROOT] partition for ACME is placed on servers NOR-SRV1, CAM-SRV1, and TOK-SRV1.

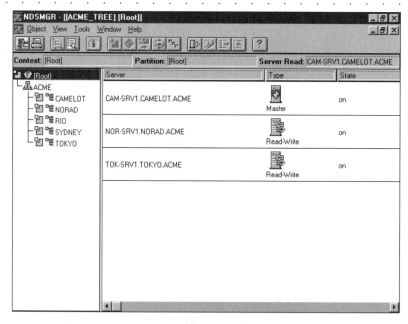

F I G U R E   6.26

NDS replicas for the [ROOT] partition are stored on different servers throughout the network. In this case, the [ROOT] partition for ACME is placed on servers NOR-SRV1, CAM-SRV1, and TOK-SRV1.

The fact that an NDS tree can be partitioned and replicated makes NDS a powerful facility for storing, accessing, managing, and using information about network resources regardless of where they are physically located. Replication increases the availability of NDS, so that any number of servers can be down and the users can still log in and access the network services.

PURPOSE OF NDS REPLICAS

Replication is a major feature and advantage of NDS. Replication of the NDS tree serves three primary purposes:

▸ Fault tolerance — Replication increases the availability of a partition (section of the NDS tree) to the users because the partition now has more than one copy of its information. For example, if a server holding a replica of the partition becomes unavailable, then the users can use another copy or replica for authentication and updates.

▸ Performance — You can increase the performance of the NDS access by the physical placement of the replicas. Replication enables you to have multiple replicas of the partition and to place those replicas local to the users that need the information. Having a local replica will decrease the time needed to authenticate, make changes, do searches, and extract NDS information.

▸ Name Resolution — The mechanism that NDS uses to locate the proper server is name resolution or tree walking. Users requesting NDS information have to first locate the server that stores the information. If the requested information is not found on the server that the user is already connected to, then NDS will automatically connect the user to the proper server.

The primary goal of replication is to eliminate the single point of failure for an NDS partition. Having multiple replicas of a partition protects you against most outages in the network infrastructure such as downed servers, routers, or WAN links.

NOTE

NDS replication does not provide fault tolerance for the file system stored on the IntranetWare servers. Replication only increases the availability of the NDS object and property information stored in the NDS partition.

The IntranetWare installation program will help you replicate the NDS partitions for fault tolerance during the installation of the server. When you are installing additional servers into the tree, the installation program will try to place up to three replicas for a partition. For example, the partition where you are installing the server has less than three total replicas. The installation will place a read/write replica on the new server. Automatic replication applies only to the partition where the server object is being installed and does not affect other partitions in the tree. The purpose for doing this automatic replication is to support fault tolerance of the NDS database. If you are comfortable with the three automatic replicas placed during installation, then you may not need to change the replication of a partition for fault tolerance.

REPLICA TYPES

Proper placement of replicas on the network servers is important to ensure proper operation of the Directory. A server may contain a number of replicas if they are from different partitions. A server also does not have to contain any replicas. In order to understand where and when to place the replicas, you must understand the different types of replicas and their characteristics.

As stated earlier, each partition can have multiple replicas. And each replica will be one of the following four replica types: master, read/write, read only, and subordinate reference.

Master Replica

The master (M) replica of a partition is created when the partition is first created. Although the first replica is always designated as the master, it can be changed as other replicas are added. There can be only one master replica for each partition. The master replica provides the following features:

▶ Accepts client updates to the NDS object and attributes. This is the ability to add, delete, and modify the objects in the partition.

▶ Controls all partitioning operations. These operations include splitting and joining partitions, moving objects and subtrees, adding and removing replicas, and repairing the replicas.

▶ Conforms to the X.500 model. This model enables clients to request the use of only the master replica.

NDS permits only one master replica per partition because the master replica controls all the partitioning operations. The master replica essentially locks the partition during any partition operation, thus ensuring that there is only one operation being performed at a time. This mechanism provides the NDS database integrity.

For example, in order to change the partition structure of the tree through either a create or merge partition operation, you must be able to contact the master for that partition. The master then works with the other replicas to complete the operation. If you are the system administrator, you must have sufficient rights to the partition before NDS will let you do the partitioning.

In addition, the master replica is equal to all other replicas during the replica synchronization. The replica synchronization is a peer-to-peer mechanism, not a master-slave device.

The master replica provides complete access to the object and property information in the partition. This means that the users can log in through this replica and make changes to the information in the replica. The changes include adding, deleting, and renaming NDS objects or modifying the objects and the properties.

Figure 6.27 show the master replicas for the [ROOT], CAMELOT, and NORAD, RIO, TOKYO, and SYDNEY partitions of the ACME tree. The master replicas are stored on the server CAM-SRV1.

F I G U R E   6.27

The master replicas for the [ROOT], CAMELOT, NORAD, RIO, TOKYO, and SYDNEY partitions of the ACME tree are stored on the server CAM-SRV1.

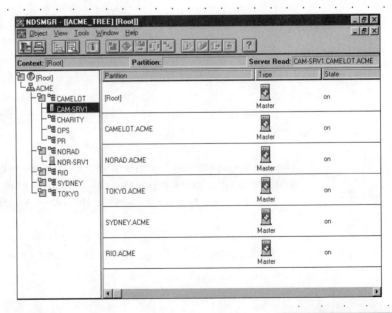

Read/Write Replica

The read/write (R/W) replica is used most often because there can be any number of them for any given partition. Although there is no limit to the number of read/write replicas per partition, we do recommend that you keep the number small, and create a new read/write replica only when needed.

In large networks with many servers, the type of replica that is mostly used is the read/write. The purpose of the read/write replica is to distribute the NDS partition information across the IntranetWare servers on the network for fault tolerance and performance.

A read/write replica provides the following features:

▸ Accepts client updates to the NDS objects and properties. Client updates include adding, deleting, and modifying the objects in the partitions.

▸ Provides fault tolerance for the partition. This means that the read/write replicas improve availability of the information stored in the partition.

▸ Increases performance of the NDS access by the physical placement of the read/write replicas. The read/write replica enables you to have multiple replicas of the partition and to place those replicas local to the users who need the information.

Like the master replica, the read/write replica provides users complete access to the object and property information in the partition. A read/write replica also allows the clients to make modifications. Since updates can be made to a read/write replica, users of the network can use the read/write replica to log in and make authentication requests.

In some of the other documentation on IntranetWare the read/write replica is often referred to as a Secondary replica.

The bindery services feature in IntranetWare requires that at least a read/write or master replica of the partition containing the bindery context exist on the server where the services are needed.

TIP

Figure 6.28 shows the read/write replicas for the [ROOT] partition of the ACME tree. There are several read/write replicas, which are stored on the servers, CAM-SRV1, and TOK-SRV1.

FIGURE 6.28

The read/write replicas for the [ROOT] partition of the ACME tree are stored on the servers CAM-SRV1, and TOK-SRV1.

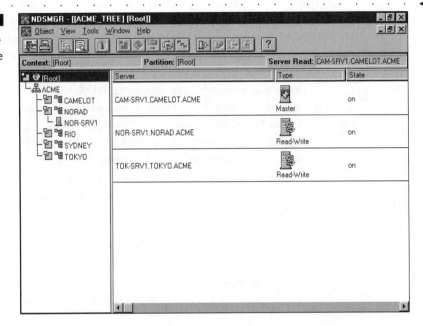

Read Only Replica

The read only (RO) replica, as the name implies, will not accept changes from users. The only way that a read only replica discovers changes is through synchronization with the other replicas (read/write and master).

The read only replica has the following features:

▶ Provides access to the NDS objects and attributes in the partition. This replica does not accept client updates but does accept read requests from the clients.

▶ Provides fault tolerance for the partition. This means that the read only replicas improve availability of the information stored in the partition.

▶ Increases performance of the NDS access by the physical placement of the read only replicas. The read only replica enables you to place those replicas local to the users who need the information.

Because the read only replica cannot be updated, it cannot support login or authentication requests from the users. For this reason, the read only replicas are seldom used or implemented into production. There are currently very few reasons to implement read only partitions.

NOTE

When a network user logs in to NDS, three properties of the user object are updated. These three properties are Network Address, Login Time, and Last Login Time. In order for users to change or update these three properties, they must log in to at least a read/ write or master replica. The read only replica cannot accept user logins because these properties cannot be updated. When a network user logs out of the Directory, the Network Address property for the user object is modified.

One possible use of a read only replica is when you are trying to provide users read access to the NDS information but no update activity. For example, if you want to build an off-site disaster recovery center for the servers, you could implement a read only replica, which would maintain itself through replica synchronization but not let any users connect to that server.

WARNING

Be aware that if you disable login on an IntranetWare server (in this case a server with a read only replica), then the other IntranetWare servers will not be able to connect to the server to perform the replica synchronization. Disabling logins on a server with any replicas should be avoided because it will discontinue the replica synchronization for that server.

Subordinate Reference Replica

A subordinate reference (SR) replica contains only one object — the top-most container object in the partition. The top-most object in the partition defines the partition and is called the partition root object. This container object stores partition information that links the partitions in the tree together. Subordinate reference replicas connect the parent partitions with their child partitions.

Subordinate references replicas are created and managed by NDS and the servers. You do not need to manage them. The NDS system will place a subordinate reference replica on a server that contains a replica of the parent but does not have the child replica. NDS places a subordinate reference replica for each child of the parent on that server. Figure 6.29 illustrates a partitioned tree and its subsequent replica placement on the network servers. Some of the servers have subordinate reference replicas.

F I G U R E 6.29

The ACME tree is partitioned, and subordinate reference replicas are created whenever a parent partition exists on a server without a copy of a child partition.

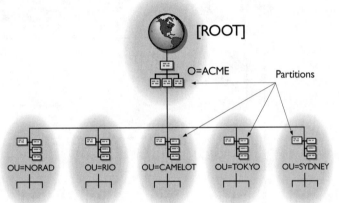

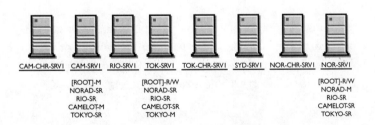

Some of the servers in Figure 6.29 are storing subordinate reference replicas because the servers are holding the parent partition, but not the corresponding child partition. For example, TOK-SRV1 holds a copy of the [ROOT] partition but not the NORAD, CAMELOT, or RIO partitions. So subordinate references are established on TOK-SRV1 to link the parent partition with its child partitions.

The subordinate reference replicas that connect the tree together are visible in Novell's NDS Manager utility and also the DSREPAIR utility. They are not visible from the DOS-based NETADMIN or PARTMGR utilities. Figure 6.30 displays all the replicas on the server NOR-SRV1. Notice the subordinate reference replica for the CAMELOT partition.

F I G U R E 6.30

NDS Manager displays all of the read/write replicas on the server NOR-SVR1.

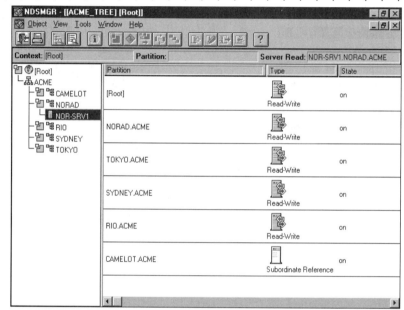

Because a subordinate reference replica does not contain all of the information for each of the objects in the partition, it cannot provide the users access to the object and property information. The user cannot log in through this replica because there is no NDS object information to access.

NDS Replication Design

One of the most important responsibilities of an NDS administrator is to design the placement of the NDS replicas. The replication design includes the distribution and placement of replicas to the specific network servers for each of the partitions. Your replica design should provide fault tolerance for each partition.

Before you complete your replication design there are some basic rules you will need to know. These rules apply to all replicas and will help you understand how replicas are implemented or placed throughout the servers on the network.

▸ **A partition can have multiple replicas.** Multiple copies of a partition are known as replicas and can be stored on separate servers across your network as explained in previous sections.

▸ **A partition can only have one replica designated as the master.** The other partitions will be read/write replicas and in some rare cases read only.

▸ **Only one replica of a partition can be stored on any given server.** An IntranetWare server can hold multiple replicas from different partitions. It cannot hold two replicas of the same partition.

▸ **All replicas will participate in the replica synchronization for a partition.** All replicas are part of the synchronization operations regardless of replica type.

These rules are important because they describe the characteristics of replication. Knowing these rules will help you efficiently design the replica placement during implementation of your IntranetWare network.

GUIDELINES FOR REPLICA PLACEMENT

The design guidelines for replica placement for any partition are the following:

▸ Replicate for fault tolerance

▸ Replicate locally

▸ Replicate for bindery services

▸ Replicate for improved name resolution

We will discuss each of these design considerations in detail in the following sections.

Replicate for Fault Tolerance

A primary goal of replication is to eliminate the single point of failure for an NDS partition. Having multiple replicas of a partition on separate servers increases the availability of object information if one of the servers should become unavailable. In Figure 6.31, the NORAD and CAMELOT partitions have been replicated to multiple servers at their respective sites to provide fault tolerance for each partition. If one of the servers in the partition becomes unavailable, NDS will respond from the other server.

FIGURE 6.31

The NORAD and CAMELOT partitions have been replicated to multiple servers on the network to provide fault tolerance for NDS.

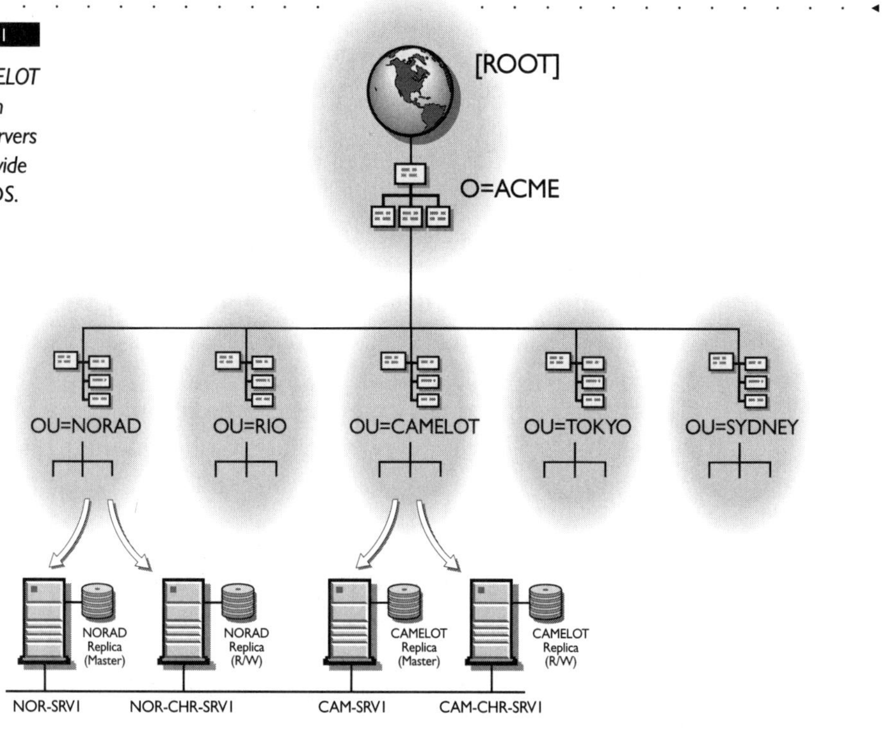

The IntranetWare installation program will automatically create up to three NDS replicas for fault tolerance. When you install additional servers into the tree, the installation program will place up to three replicas of the partition where the server is going to be located in the tree. If the partition where you are installing the server has fewer than three total replicas, the installation will place a read/write replica on the new server in that partition.

If the server being installed is upgraded or has an existing bindery, such as a NetWare 3.12 server, then the installation program will automatically convert the bindery to an NDS replica of the partition where the server is being installed. A NetWare 3.12 server being migrated or upgraded will receive at least a read/write replica of the partition even if there are already three other replicas for that partition.

In Figure 6.32 the NORAD partition has been replicated automatically to the servers NOR-SRV1, NOR-CHR-SRV1, and LABS-SRV1 by the installation program. Because NOR-SRV1 contains the master replica of the [ROOT] partition, it will also receive the master replica for the NORAD partition. The other servers will receive read/write replicas until there are at least three replicas for the NORAD partition. Notice that a fourth server (RD-SRV1) has been installed into the partition but did not automatically receive a replica. The installation program assumes that the RD-SRV1 is a new server that was not migrated from NetWare 3.12 (meaning there was no bindery to convert to a replica).

FIGURE 6.32

The installation program automatically replicates the NORAD partition to the first three servers NOR-SRV1, NOR-CHR-SRV1, and LABS-SRV1. A fourth server (RD-SRV1) was installed into the partition but did not receive an automatic replica.

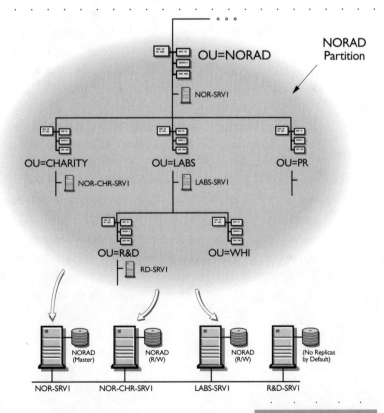

Automatic replication applies only to the partition where the server object is being installed and does not affect other partitions in the tree. The purpose for automatic replication is to support fault tolerance of the NDS tree information. If you are comfortable with where the three automatic replicas were placed during installation, then you need not change the replicas of a partition for fault tolerance.

As a general guideline, you should always have both a master and two read/write replicas for every partition. At a minimum, we recommend two replicas, and three replicas are even better. Again, having two or three replicas eliminates any single point of failure in your network. By placing multiple replicas locally, any IntranetWare server with the same replica can fail without affecting NDS availability for your users.

Replicate Locally

The best method to guarantee efficiency in the replication design is to replicate locally. This means that you would place all the replicas of a partition on local servers. You should not place a replica across a WAN link if you have locally available servers, meaning on the same side of your WAN link. If you follow this guideline, you can be guaranteed that the users will retrieve their object information from the nearest available server. Figure 6.33 is an example of placing a replica that is not local to that partition.

Ideally, you should place the replica containing the user's information on the server that stores the user's home directory. This may not always be possible, but it does improve the users' access to the NDS objects and properties. For example, during the login process the user will map drives to volumes, capture to print queues, and access several of the user object and properties. NDS will execute each of these requests regardless of where the replicas are stored. However, the login speed for the user will be increased if the user finds the requested information on his or her preferred server.

Again, the primary design consideration is that you replicate the NDS partition locally. For example, a partition is created for a specific location, and a master replica is placed on a server in that location. We recommend that you place your read/write replicas of the partition on different servers in the same physical location as the master replica. If you are forced to place the third replica across a WAN link because there are only two servers at the location, then we recommend that you not create the third replica if it is placed across the WAN link. This choice depends upon the level of fault tolerance you want to maintain.

F I G U R E 6.33

You should always try to replicate locally by placing replicas of a partition on the servers at that location or site. Do not place a replica across a WAN link from the original partition.

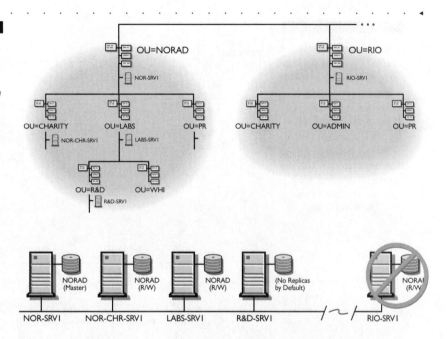

The question is often asked, "What happens if the location or site has only one server? Do I still partition and replicate locally? How do I replicate for fault tolerance?" In the case of a remote site with just one server, you should still partition at that site and place the master replica on that server. A second replica of the partition can be placed on the nearest location for purposes of fault tolerance. Typically, the remote site with just one server contains a small number of user objects. Therefore, although we do not recommend replicating across your WAN, a small replica across your WAN in this case is your only alternative for replication. It is better to replicate a small partition across a WAN than lose the NDS information if the server ever goes down.

Figure 6.34 illustrates how a small remote office in the ACME tree should be replicated. Assume that a small remote site called SLC is connected to the NORAD hub. There is only one server (SLC1) in the remote site of SLC. You should create a small partition and replicate it to SLC1. You should also place a replica in the NORAD location on the server NOR-SRV1.

There is only one server (SLC-SRV1) in the remote site of SLC. You should create a small partition called SLC and replicate it to the SLC-SRV1 and NOR-SRV1 servers in the NORAD location. It is more important to replicate for fault tolerance than to not replicate across the WAN links.

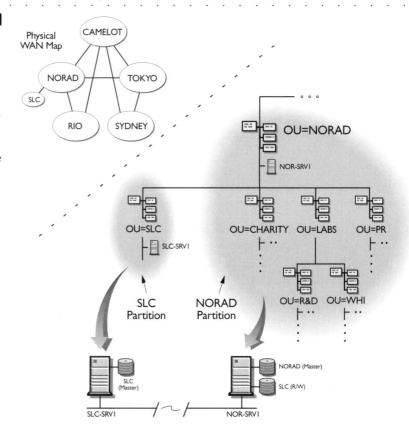

Replica Placement to Support Bindery Services

As mentioned earlier, bindery services does require the placement of a read/write or master replica on the server that sets the bindery context. The bindery context set at the server is officially known as the server bindery context. Figure 6.35 illustrates how the NOR-SRV1 server needs to hold a read/write replica in order to set the server bindery context at OU=NORAD.

The server bindery context can be set at the server console by typing the following:

```
SET SERVER BINDERY CONTEXT = "OU=NORAD.O=ACME"
```

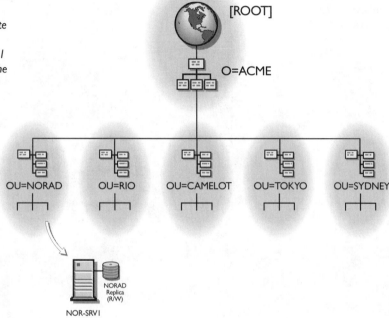

FIGURE 6.35

Setting the bindery services
for partition NORAD
requires that a read/write
or master replica be
stored on the NOR-SRV1
server, which is where the
server sets the server
bindery context.

In Figure 6.36, all the objects in the NORAD container that are NetWare 3 bindery objects are viewed and accessed as if they are in a bindery. The NDS objects available through bindery services include the user, group, print queue, print server, profile, and bindery type objects. This list is included because these are the only objects that were defined in the NetWare 3 bindery. The new NDS objects such as directory map, organizational role, computer, and alias will not show up as bindery objects in your Directory.

In order for an IntranetWare server to support bindery services, it must hold either a read/write or master replica of a partition where the server is installed. You will need to place read/write replicas on the network servers to support bindery services.

The IntranetWare feature known as bindery services enables the IntranetWare server to respond to the bindery calls made by the bindery-based utilities and applications. Bindery services lets these applications run on IntranetWare and NDS without modifications.

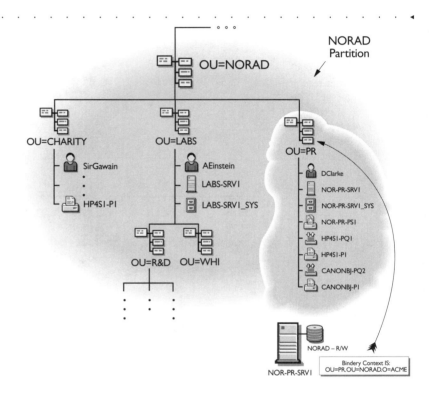

F I G U R E 6.36

Server NOR-PR-SRVI has a bindery context set to "OU=PR.OU=NORAD. O=ACME".

Bindery services is also required during a NetWare 3 to IntranetWare server upgrade. For example, if you are upgrading a NetWare 3 server, a read/write replica of the partition is placed on the upgraded IntranetWare server. The read/write replica is placed on the server regardless of whether there are already three replicas, as described in the "Replicate for Fault Tolerance" section above. The system assumes that since the server is being migrated from NetWare 3, bindery services in IntranetWare will be needed.

Replica Placement for Improved Name Resolution

The mechanism NDS uses to find the object location is referred to as name resolution. If the object information is not stored locally, the server must search the directory tree to find the other servers that have the object information. Every replica maintains a set of pointers to all the other replicas in the same partition. NDS uses these pointers to locate the partitions that are above and below in the Directory tree. With the name resolution mechanism, NDS can follow these pointers to locate the servers holding the requested data.

TIP

For improved speed of name resolution from one side of the tree to the other, you can replicate the [ROOT] partition in a couple of strategic locations, such as hub sites, so that users can search the tree faster. The [ROOT] partition should be small to keep NDS traffic to a minimum. However, unlike other partitions, you should not replicate [ROOT] more than three times.

To speed access to the appropriate server, replicas can be placed closer to the server to help the user find the requested information. For example, if you are trying to locate information from one side of the tree to the other, the partition that will help you is the [ROOT] partition. In this case, you can replicate the [ROOT] partition to that major hub site in your company. Replicating the [ROOT] partition is recommended only if it is set up as a small partition and you only replicate it a couple of times. Small means the [ROOT] partition should include just the [ROOT] object and the O=ACME object. See Figure 6.37 for an illustration of a small [ROOT] partition that is replicated across a WAN link.

F I G U R E 6.37

The [ROOT] partition can be replicated across the WAN links if it is created as a small partition containing just the [ROOT] object and O=ACME object.

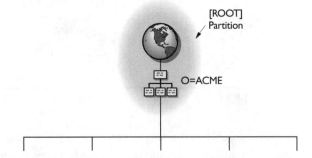

[ROOT] Partition

O=ACME

WARNING

Do not replicate [ROOT] more than three times. Keep in mind your understanding of subordinate reference replicas. Each replica of [ROOT] you create will also create subordinate reference replicas. Spreading around more copies of a partition will increase the number of subordinate references. For example, let's assume you have 10 child partitions created directly below [ROOT] because you have 10 locations. When you replicate [ROOT] three times, you will have 10 subordinate reference replicas on 3 separate servers for a total of 30 subordinate reference replicas. Add two more replicas of [ROOT] and you have 50 servers holding subordinate reference replicas.

Figure 6.38 illustrates how the [ROOT] partition can be replicated to a few strategic locations in the WAN infrastructure to facilitate improved name resolution. In this case, we have placed a copy of [ROOT] in NORAD on the NOR-SRV1 server, in CAMELOT on the CAM-SRV1 server, and in TOKYO on the TOK-SRV1 server.

F I G U R E 6.38

NDS replicas for the [ROOT] partition are stored on different servers throughout the network to faciliate improved name resolution.

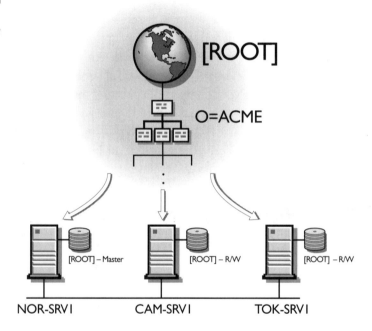

The small [ROOT] partition (containing very few objects) is also fairly static. So the replication of [ROOT] across the WAN links is okay. However, do not go overboard on replicating this partition. Three replicas of the [ROOT] partition are usually sufficient.

We do not recommend that you replicate any other partition across the WAN infrastructure for the purpose of name resolution. Because [ROOT] is at the top of your tree and a lot of name resolution must traverse the [ROOT] partition, it makes sense to replicate [ROOT] only at key hub locations in your tree.

SUMMARY OF NDS PARTITION AND REPLICA DESIGN GUIDELINES

The specific design rules for partitioning and replication of Novell Directory Services can be separated into two different categories depending on your specific implementation requirements, hardware, and knowledge level of the staff. The two categories defined for the partition and replica design rules are the Quick Design and Advanced Design.

Quick Design

The Quick Design rules for partitions and replicas are simple, basic rules that can be implemented in all companies and applied to almost every situation regardless of the WAN or LAN infrastructure. The Quick Design is highly recommended for designers and customers who want to operate their NDS tree structures as effectively as possible. These design rules will minimize the impact of replica synchronization and will provide a good foundation for overall performance.

The Quick Design rules provide everyone with an easy and safe method to design and implement NDS in their network environments. If you follow the recommendations stated below, you will be successful in designing Novell Directory Services. The system will also be much easier to service and maintain.

The following are the specific Quick Design rules for partitioning and replication of NDS:

- ▸ Partition size — 1000 to 1500 objects

- ▸ Number of child partitions/per parent — 10 to 15 partitions

- ▸ Number of replicas/per partition — 2 to 5 replicas (typically 3)

- ▸ Number or replicas/per server — 7 to 10 replicas

- ▸ Minimum server hardware — 486/66 Mhz with 32MB of RAM

There will be only a few situations in which the Quick Design rules will not apply. In the few portions of the tree where these rules cannot be followed, we introduce the more costly Advanced Design rules.

Advanced Design

The Advanced Design rules are simply greater numbers for each of the partition and replica areas. Because these rules will exceed the numbers given in the Quick Design rules, they are going to be more costly in the efficiency of the replica synchronization process on the servers. For this reason, we strongly recommend, if not require, that you or your staff completely understand the effect or impact of the larger numbers. It is safe to say that the Advanced Design rules require the individuals maintaining the system to have a greater in-depth knowledge of NDS and IntranetWare.

For the most part, the Advanced Design rules are targeted at the consultant or administrator who understands the impact or ramification of moving past the Quick Design rules to the larger numbers.

The specific Advanced Design rules, shown in the following list, for partitioning and replication of NDS are the maximum values for each area and should never be exceeded. The Advanced Design rules are:

▸ Partition size — 3,500 to 5,000 objects

▸ Number of child partitions/per parent — 35 to 40 partitions

▸ Number of replicas/per partition — 10 replicas (typically 3)

▸ Number or replicas/per server — 20 replicas

▸ Minimum server hardware — Pentium 100+Mhz with 64MB of RAM

Managing NDS Partitions and Replicas

In order to manage your NDS partitions and replicas properly, there are several types of operations that you need to understand and use. The NDS partition and replica operations are: create new partition, merge partition, move partition, add replica, remove replica, change replica type, and abort partition operation. There is a new utility in IntranetWare that you can use to perform NDS partition and replica operations on the NDS tree. This utility is called NDS Manager.

The NDS Manager utility is the Windows-based administration program. This program is used by the system administrators to manage all the NDS partitions and replicas. Figure 6.39 shows the NDS Manager main option screen or menu.

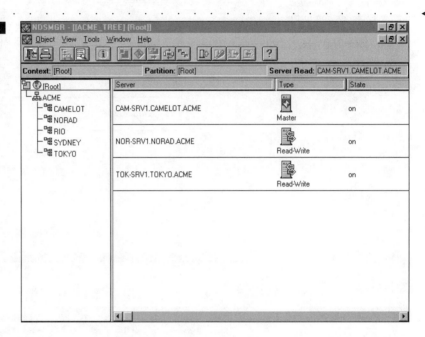

In Figure 6.40 you can see that the partitions are denoted with a small box icon to the left of the OU container object. In this example, OU=CAMELOT, and OU=NORAD are partitions.

The PARTMGR.EXE utility is a DOS-based program that performs partition operations on the NDS database, such as create, merge, move subtree, add replicas, remove replicas, and change replica type. Figure 6.41 displays the main menu of the PARTMGR utility.

FIGURE 6.40

Using the NDS Manager, the partitions are denoted with a small box icon to the left of the OU container. OU=CAMELOT and OU=NORAD are shown as partitions.

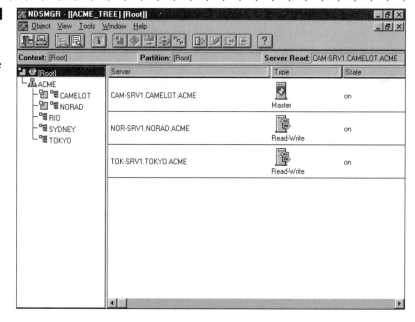

FIGURE 6.41

The main menu of the PARTMGR utility. This DOS-based utility can be used to perform partition operations such as create, merge, move subtree, add replicas, remove replicas, and change replica type.

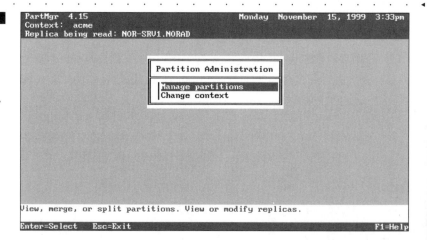

NDS PARTITION AND REPLICA OPERATIONS

All partition and replica operations require that the master replica for the partition be available. As mentioned earlier, the master replica locks the partition before it starts the operation. The only partition operations that do not require the master replica to lock the partition are the add replica and remove replica operations.

All the replicas for a specific partition must be available in order to complete the operation. If a replica is not reachable, the NDS system will wait until it is available.

WARNING

Before you start a partition operation, you should ALWAYS check the status of the replicas of the partition. You can avoid many problems if you check the synchronization status of the replicas before you perform any partition operation. You can use DSREPAIR to check the status of the replicas and synchronization. Make sure that the synchronization process is complete before starting a new operation on that partition. Figure 6.42 displays the status check of the replicas in DSREPAIR. For more information on specific interpretation of each of the items shown, you can refer to our discussion of the DSREPAIR utility in Chapter 10.

F I G U R E 6.42

Use DSREPAIR to check the status of the replicas before starting a partition operation.

```
NetWare 4.1 DS Repair   4.26b                    NetWare Loadable Module
Tree name: ACME_TREE
Server name: NOR-SRV1.NORAD.ACME                         Total errors: 0

        Edit Log File (Last Entry): "SYS:SYSTEM\DSREPAIR.LOG"   (18679)

/******************************************************************************/
Netware 4.1 Directory Services Repair 4.26b, DS 4.89
Log file for server "NOR-SRV1.NORAD.ACME" in tree "ACME_TREE"
Start:  Monday, November 15, 1999   3:39:56 pm Local Time

Synchronizing Replica: [Root]
Performed on server: CAM-SRV1.CAMELOT.ACME

Servers that contain a replica              Replica Type    Status
--------------------------------------------+---------------+-----------
CAM-SRV1.CAMELOT.ACME                        Read Write      Host
TOK-SRV1.TOKYO.ACME                          Read Write      OK
NOR-SRV1.NORAD.ACME                          Master          OK

Synchronizing Replica: [Root]
Performed on server: TOK-SRV1.TOKYO.ACME

Esc=Exit the editor              F1=Help              Alt+F10=Exit
```

CONSULTING EXPERIENCE

If your IntranetWare servers are running the code release of DS.NLM (Version 501 or greater), then you can use DSREPAIR to read the partition status after the partition operation. It will be more accurate than previous releases of DSREPAIR, which often generated the "partition busy" error message.

If you are performing a merge partition operation then you need to check the status of both the parent and child partitions involved in the merge. Again, you should check the status of the partitions before you start the merge operation.

Another operational guideline is that after you have started a partition operation, you should be very patient and wait for all the synchronization work to complete. We mentioned that NDS is a distributed and replicated system that is loosely consistent, and it takes time for the partition changes to be reflected across the network. The synchronization process for a partition with many objects and replicas will naturally take longer than one with just a few objects.

In addition to checking the partition status through the DSREPAIR utility, you can use the DSTRACE utility. Figure 6.43 shows the screen in DSTRACE to check when the synchronization process is completed.

FIGURE 6.43

The Replica screen in DSTRACE shows you when the synchronization process has been completed for a partition.

```
NetWare 4.1 Directory Services  4.89,  8/30/1995

(99/11/15 15:43:19)
SYNC: Start sync of partition <[Root]> state:[0] type:[0]
 SYNC: Start outbound sync with (1) [030000C1]<CAM-SRV1.CAMELOT.ACME>
 SYNC: Start outbound sync with (2) [030000C2]<TOK-SRV1.TOKYO.ACME>
SYNC: End sync of partition <[Root]> All processed = YES.

(99/11/15 15:43:48)
SYNC: Start sync of partition <[Root]> state:[0] type:[0]
 SYNC: Start outbound sync with (1) [030000C1]<CAM-SRV1.CAMELOT.ACME>
 SYNC: Start outbound sync with (2) [030000C2]<TOK-SRV1.TOKYO.ACME>
SYNC: End sync of partition <[Root]> All processed = YES.
```

The DSTRACE information can be difficult to read and interpret because the information is more cryptic than DSREPAIR. For example, in Figure 6.43, we see the synchronization process for the [ROOT] partition stored on this server. The state:[0] means the partition is ON, and type:[0] means that this is the master replica. In this example, an outbound synchronization is started with (2), which is the replica number, stored on [020000D7]<CAM-SRV1.CAMELOT.ACME>. The value of [020000D7] indicates the ID number of the server (CAM-SRV1). All updates are sent and the "All processed = YES" message is displayed, which means that the synchronization is successful.

If possible, we recommend that you centralize the partition operations management. Only one person or a small group of people should be responsible for all of the partitioning and replication for your company. You might decide there is only one workstation on the network that should start the partition operations. This way you can eliminate the possibility that two people or two different workstations are making changes to the partitions simultaneously.

The next several sections discuss each of the partition and replica operations that can be performed. These operations include create new partition, merge partition, move partition or subtree, add replica, remove replica, change replica type, rebuild replicas, and abort partition operations.

Create Partition Operation

Creating a new partition is the same as creating a child partition from the parent partition. This operation is sometimes called a partition split. The terms create and split are used interchangeably. The operation is generally fast because it generates less network traffic than do other partition operations. The traffic is limited to changes to the replica pointers, synchronization, and partitioning control. However, once again, if you have many replicas of the partition before the split, NDS must contact each server holding a replica in order to perform the operation there as well.

The operation simply divides the partition into two with all the information staying on the same servers where the operation originally started. This split operation will create a new child partition on all the servers that had a copy of the parent partition.

When the partition is created, the partition takes its name from the top-most container object (partition root object). All the objects in the tree that are under the container object form the contents of the new partition.

In the following examples, we have installed a third server in the tree called TOK-SRV1. The result of installing the TOK-SRV1 server into the tree is that it will receive a read/write copy of the [ROOT] partition. Figure 6.44 shows how you can use the NDS Manager utility to create a new partition called the TOKYO partition for the ACME company. All the objects in the subtree under TOKYO are included in the partition.

FIGURE 6.44

The OU=TOKYO container
is created as a new
partition for the ACME tree.

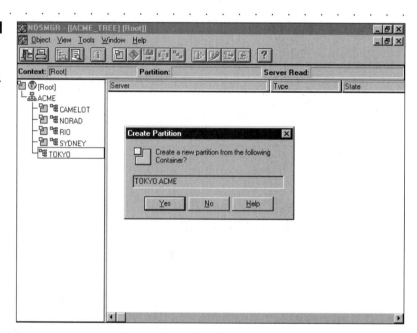

Also in Figure 6.45 notice that the create partition operation for TOKYO placed copies of the new TOKYO partition on all the servers that originally had copies of the parent partition [ROOT]. You can remove the additional copies if they are not placed on the servers you want.

In Figure 6.45 you can see that the TOKYO partition and its information can be placed on the servers in TOKYO. The same is true for all the locations. By partitioning the NDS tree, you can keep the location information in each location and still find and use the resources throughout the entire NDS tree.

The create partition
operation placed copies of
the new TOKYO partition
on all the servers that
orginally had copies of the
[ROOT] partition. These
servers are NOR-SRV1,
CAM-SRV1, TOK-SRV1.

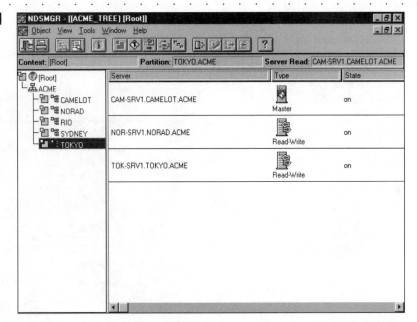

In order to perform the create partition operation, you must have rights to the top of the partition or OU container that defines the partition. The effective rights needed are the write rights to the ACL of the top container object that defines the partition. There are several ways to receive this privilege. You can be granted either the Supervisor object right or the explicit write property right to the ACL. Either of these two rights will enable you to perform the create partition operations on the tree.

Figure 6.46 illustrates the rights needed to perform the future partition operation for the NORAD partition in the ACME tree. Notice that the user, AEinstein, has been given the Supervisor object right to the OU=NORAD. The OU=NORAD is the top of the partition, and is referred to as the partition root object of the NORAD partition.

Merge Partition Operation

The operation used to combine a child partition with its parent is called a merge. This operation is sometimes called a partition join. The terms merge and join are used interchangeably. This operation takes different amounts of time and could generate network traffic depending on which servers the partitions were originally placed.

F I G U R E 6.46

The user AEinstein has been assigned the rights needed to perform the create partition operation for the NORAD partition.

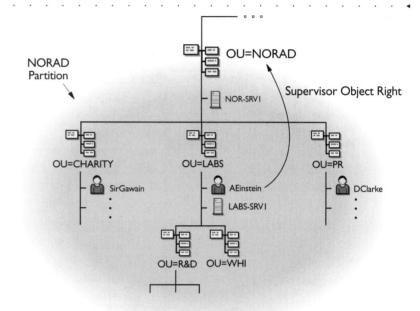

The merge operation requires that each server holding a copy of the parent partition must receive a copy of the child partition before the merge can take place. In return, each server holding a copy of the child partition must receive a copy of the parent before the merge can be completed. The merge operation will attempt to move copies of either the parent or child partitions to the appropriate servers as needed. After the copies have been successfully moved, the merge operation then joins the partitions together.

It is strongly recommended that you manually place copies of the parent partition on all the servers with a child partition before you initiate the merge operation. In turn, you should place copies of each of the child partitions on the servers holding the parent partitions before you start the merge operation.

You will have greater success merging partitions if you manually place copies of the parent and child partitions on appropriate servers. In order to accomplish this task, you must know where each of the copies of the partitions is located. Refer to the "Partition and Replica Matrix" section later in this chapter.

If all the servers have copies of both the child and parent partitions before the merge operation is started, the merge will be quicker and encounter fewer problems, thus enabling the operation to complete. Copies of both child and parent partitions also prevent large amounts of NDS data moving across the network during the operation. Network traffic occurs when you prepare for the merge by placing the appropriate replicas on the servers.

An example of a merge partition operation is illustrated in Figure 6.47, where the OPS partition is merged back with its parent partition CAMELOT. The utility will ask you to confirm the merge operation as shown.

The OPS partition is merged back with its parent partition CAMELOT.

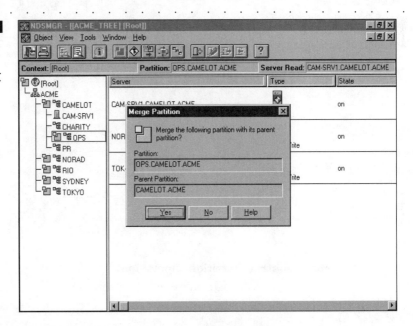

WARNING

Check the synchronization status of all replicas in the partition with DSREPAIR before initiating any partition operation. All replicas must be available and functioning properly before you proceed with the partitioning.

In order to perform the merge partition operation, you must have rights to only the child partitions. The effective rights needed are the write rights to the ACL of the child partitions. There are several ways to receive these privileges. You can be granted either the Supervisor object right or the explicit write property right to the ACL property.

Figure 6.48 illustrates the rights needed to perform the merge partition operation for the CAMELOT and OPS partitions in the ACME tree. Notice that the user, KingArthur, has been given the Supervisor object right to the OU=OPS container.

The user, KingArthur, has been assigned the rights needed to perform the merge partition operation for the OPS and CAMELOT partitions.

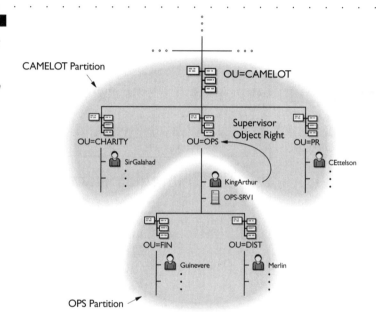

Move Subtree Partition Operation

The operation used to move an OU container and its entire contents or subtree from one location in the NDS tree to another is called a move subtree. This operation is very important when you reorganize the information in your NDS tree because it enables you to move the container objects in the NDS tree. In order to move an OU container, two conditions must exist. The two conditions are:

▸ The OU container object being moved must be a partition. This means that the OU container object must be a partition root object. You will need to create a partition from the OU container before moving it if one does not exist.

▶ The partition or subtree you want to move cannot have any child partitions. You may be forced to merge child partitions with their parent in order to move the subtree.

This operation is essentially moving a partition from one location in the NDS tree to another location. This operation can generate network traffic depending on which servers the parent partitions were originally placed.

In Figure 6.49 we have assumed that the join operation did not occur or was aborted. The NDS Manager move screen for the OPS partition under the CAMELOT location is moved to another location in the NDS tree. In this case, under the NORAD.ACME container.

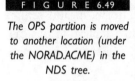

FIGURE 6.49

The OPS partition is moved to another location (under the NORAD.ACME) in the NDS tree.

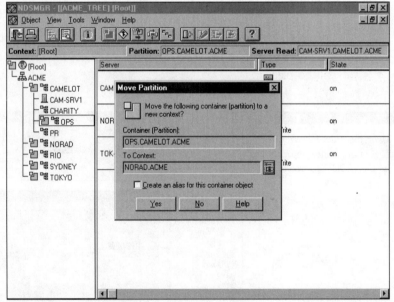

In order to perform the move subtree partition operation, you must have rights to all the partitions involved. The effective rights needed are the write rights to the ACL of the top container object that defines the partition. There are several ways to receive this privilege. You can be granted either the Supervisor object right or the explicit write property right to the ACL property.

Add Replica Operation

The add replica operation is used to create a new copy of the partition information and store it on another server. Adding replicas to other network servers requires that all the data in the partition will be copied to the new servers across the network. This operation will cause network traffic. Because the amount of traffic is dependent on the number of objects in the partition, it is a good idea to schedule this operation during a low usage time in the network.

Figure 6.50 shows the NDS Manager screen used to perform an add replica operation. You first select a partition to which you want to add a replica. In this case the [ROOT] partition is selected. You then select the server on which the new replica will be placed.

Using the NDS Manager utility to add a new replica to the [ROOT] partition

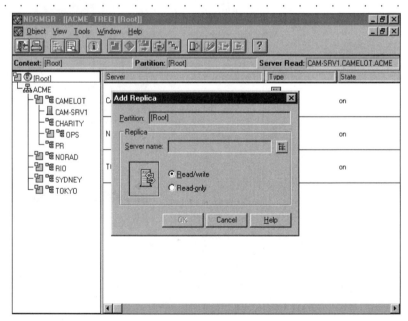

Remove Replica Operation

The remove replica partition operation is used to delete a copy of the partition information from a specific server. You might think this operation to delete the replica happens very quickly because it simply marks the information to be removed from the server. However, every object in the replica must now be set up as an external reference, which is a pointer to the real object in another replica on another server. With the creation of the external references, backlinks, which are pointers back to the external references, are established. Even though the backlinks are checked in the background process, the initial setup will take time. For a complete discussion on external references and backlinks see Chapter 8.

Figure 6.51 shows the NDS Manager screen that is used to remove a replica of a partition. You first select a partition from which you want to remove the replica. In this case the [ROOT] partition is selected. You then select the server from which to remove the replica. In this example, we have selected the TOK-SRV1 as the replica to remove. The result is that there are only two replicas left on the servers, CAM-SRV1 and NOR-SRV1.

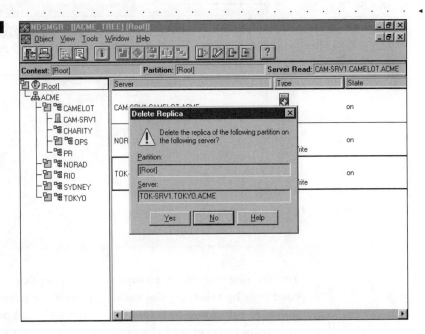

F I G U R E 6.51

Using the NDS Manager utility to remove the TOK-SRV1 replica from the [ROOT] partition.

Change Replica Type Operation

This operation can be performed when a specific type of replica needs to be changed. For example, if you want a different replica to be the master replica for the partition, you highlight which replica you want to be the new master and NDS will change the type and propagate the change to the other replicas. In order to change the master replica, the target server must have a read/write or read only replica.

Figure 6.52 shows the NDS Manager screen used to change the replica type for a partition. You first select a partition for which you want to perform the change replica type operation. In this case the [ROOT] partition is selected. You then select the server on which to change the replica type. We have selected the read/write replica on NOR-SRV1. We can now change its type to master. The result is that the master replica on CAM-SRV1 will change to a read/write replica.

F I G U R E 6.52

Using the NDS Manager utility to change the replica type for the [ROOT] partition.

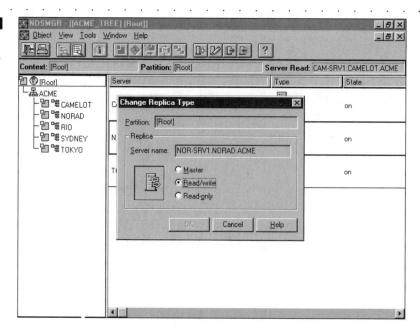

NOTE

You are not allowed to change a master replica to a read/write or read only by selecting the server holding the master replica. The utility requires you to select either a read/write or read only replica on another server and change it to the master replica.

Rebuild Replica Operation

There are a couple of ways you can rebuild the replica information for each of the partitions. The rebuild replica operation is used when the NDS information on the current server is not completely accurate or has become corrupt.

NOTE

The current rebuild replica operation in IntranetWare should not be confused with the older Rebuild Replicas from previous versions of NetWare 4 (specifically NetWare 4.0 and 4.01). The current rebuild replica operation does not destroy the partition information; instead, it sends all information to all the other replicas.

The previous versions of NetWare 4 used the rebuild replica operation to rebuild the timestamps for each object in the partition. The operation to rebuild timestamps is a very aggressive troubleshooting technique and will not be discussed here.

From the NDS Manager utility, there are two ways to update replica information. These two operations are called Send Updates and Receive Updates. Both these functions are network intensive because they move all the partition data across the network to the servers. The Send Updates tries to send the all the object information to all the other replicas in the ring.

The Send Updates operation synchronizes all the other replicas for the partition with the replica you have selected. You would perform this operation when the partition information on some of the servers is not complete or has become corrupted. By selecting the most current replica or the replica that has the best information, you can send its information to all the other replicas in the partition. You can use either NDS Manager (Send Updates) or DSREPAIR (Send all objects to every replica in the ring).

Figure 6.53 shows an example of using NDS Manager to perform the Send Updates operation. In this example, the server CAM-SRV1, which is the master replica of the [ROOT] partition, is selected as the sending replica. The Send Updates operation will send the contents of the selected replica to all the other replicas in the partition.

The Receive Updates operation synchronizes selected replica with the information from the master replica. You would perform this operation when the partition information on one of the servers is not as complete as the master replica. This operation can be performed using both NDS Manager and DSREPAIR utilities.

FIGURE 6.53

The Send Updates replica operation. The CAM.SRV1 server, which holds the master replica of the [ROOT] partition, is selected as the sending replica. This operation will send the contents of the selected replica to all the other replicas in the partition.

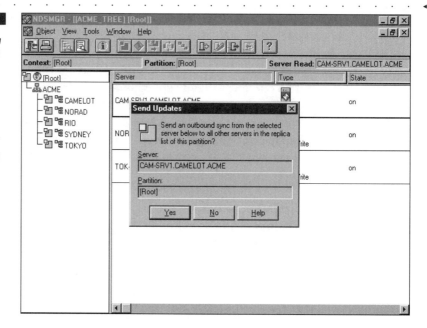

The Receive Updates operation essentially marks the affected replica as a new replica. The operation begins the process of adding the partition information to the replica again.

Figure 6.54 shows an example of the Receive Updates operation using the DSREPAIR utility. In this example, the server named NOR-SRV1 receives the replica information from the master replica of the [ROOT] partition. (Notice that the "Send all objects to every replica in the ring" message is the Send Updates mentioned earlier.)

WARNING **Check the synchronization status of all replicas in the partition with DSREPAIR before initiating any partition operation. All replicas must be available and functioning properly before you proceed with the partitioning.**

Abort Partition Operation

You have the ability to abort a partition operation that was previously started. The abort partition operation is valid only for certain partition operations, including create, merge, move subtree, and change replica type. The abort partition operation cannot be used on add replica and remove replica.

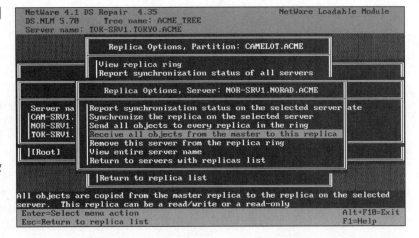

The Receive Updates replica operation. The server named NOR-SRV1 receives the replica information from the master replica of the [ROOT] partition. This operation will send the contents of the master replica to the server holding the selected replica.

This feature is valuable not as an undo function but as a way to back out of partition operations that do not complete. For example, only one partition operation can take place at a time. So if a partition operation starts and does not complete, no other partition operations can be started. A partition operation will wait indefinitely if one of the servers in the replica list of the partition becomes unavailable because of either a downed server or an unavailable communication link. This problem is manifested by the "master replica state is not on for the selected partition" message if you try to start another partition operation. See Figure 6.55. You can also check the status of the replicas using the NDS Manager utility.

If you suspect that a partition operation is having difficulty completing, then you can either wait until the situation causing the problem is cleared up or you can abort the operation. To abort the partition operation you can go to NDS Manager, select the partition, and press the abort button. Figure 6.56 displays the abort partition operation in NDS Manager. In this example, the operation that has not completed is the change replica type operation because the replica state information shows each replica with Change Type 0. This means that the current change state of the replicas is 0. For more information and a complete list of the replica change states, see Chapter 8.

FIGURE 6.55

*The message displayed
from NDS Manager if
another partition operation
is requested before the
first partition operation
is completed.*

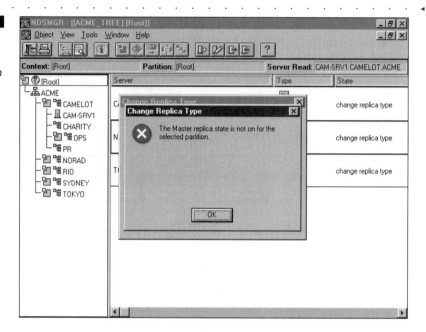

FIGURE 6.56

*The abort partition
operation screen in
NDS Manager*

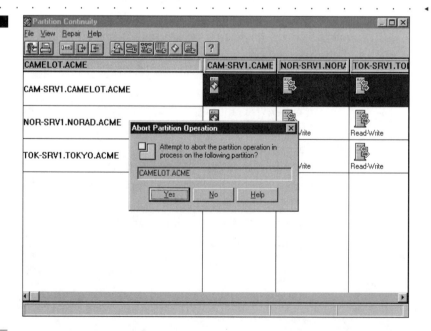

To execute the abort operation press the abort key at the bottom of the screen. After the partition operation has been aborted, the replicas involved will be turned back on as illustrated in Figure 6.57. In this example, each replica state has been set to ON, meaning that the partition is ready once again.

F I G U R E 6.57

The replica states are turned back to ON after the partition operation is aborted.

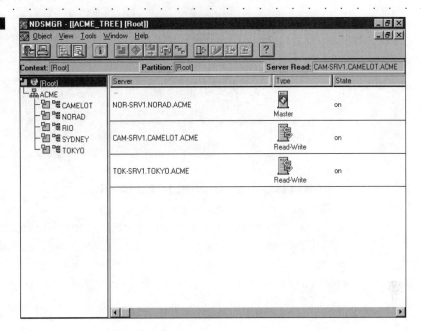

You can also abort a partition operation within the DSREPAIR utility. From the DSREPAIR main menu select the Advanced Options menu. From the Advanced Option menu select the replica and partition operations menu. A list of all the partitions and replicas stored on the server is displayed. After you select the partition that is having problems, the Replica Operations menu is displayed. (See Figure 6.58.) Down the menu is the Cancel partition operation selection. When you select this menu you will be asked to log in to Directory Services as someone who has rights over the partition.

*You can use DSREPAIR
to abort or cancel a
partition operation.*

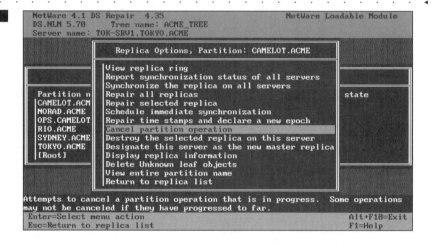

PARTITION AND REPLICA MATRIX

The best method for keeping track of where partitions and replicas are stored in
the NDS is to create a Partition and Replica Matrix. The matrix, as shown in Figure
6.59, helps you document the creation of partitions and the replication of the
partitions. The matrix will help you design and implement the partitions and replicas
more efficiently. If you need to perform any partition operation, you have a quick
and easy tool to refer to.

*You should document your
NDS partitions and replicas
using a Partition and
Replica Matrix.*

M - MASTER R/W - READ/WRITE	RO - READ ONLY SR - SUBORDINATE REF.		PARTITIONS					
DESCRIPTION OF THE SERVER			[ROOT]	NORAD	RIO	CAMELOT	TOKYO	SYDNEY
NAME	LOCATION	NETWORK ADDRESS						
	CAMELOT	ØBØØFADE						
	NORAD	ØFFØBBØØ						
	NORAD	ØFFØBBØØ						
	RIO	ØØØØIØØØ						
	TOKYO	ØØ22ØØØI						
	SYDNEY	2IØØIØØØ						

REPLICA SYNCHRONIZATION

Replication of the NDS database is one of the major features of NDS. However, because a partition can be distributed, any changes or updates to that partition will take place on an individual replica, which, in turn, must pass the latest changes to all the other replicas of that partition. This process of ensuring that all the latest changes or updates to a particular partition are reflected in each of its replicas is called synchronization.

When updates and modifications are made to NDS, the fact that one of the replicas in a partition will change while the other replicas will not receive the updated information is known as loose consistency. Loose consistency simply means that all the replicas are not instantaneously changed as updates to NDS are made. So, as NDS receives updates from users and administrators, all the replicas for the partition are not guaranteed to be completely converged or synchronized at any one time. However, to ensure the integrity of the database, NDS automatically synchronizes all the replicas for a specific partition. Figure 6.60 illustrates how the replicas for the [ROOT] partition will stay synchronized among the servers. This figure should be viewed only as a conceptual illustration. For a complete discussion on how the replicas send and receive data for the partition, see Chapter 9.

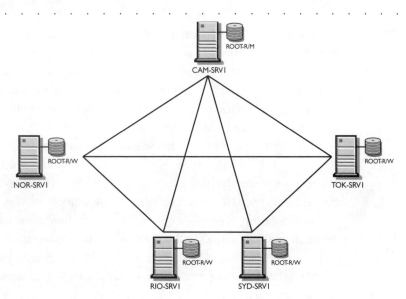

F I G U R E 6.60

The NDS replicas synchronize with each other to maintain consistency of the [ROOT] partition information. The synchronization is loosely consistent because of the timing during the process.

This synchronization process, which runs in the background, introduces a new level of complexity to the network and the traffic it could generate. The information passed between the replicas during the synchronization exchange is limited to just the updates, thus reducing the total amount of network traffic.

Because the synchronization process between replicas could impact the traffic on both the local LAN and WAN networks, you should decide where to place the replicas. You can also control which replicas in the partition will accept client updates by choosing the type of replica to place in service.

Traffic Efficiency Based on Replication Synchronization

The process that synchronizes the data between the replicas needs to be considered during the placement of the replicas. Your goal is to minimize the impact of the synchronization between replicas. In general, you should avoid having too many replicas on a single server and too many total replicas per partition. These two factors go hand in hand to help you reduce the work load of the servers and the network traffic.

We will discuss three issues that you need to consider when organizing the replicas to minimize replica synchronization. The three issues are total number of replicas per partition, total number of replicas per server, and subordinate reference replicas.

Total Number of Replicas Per Partition   The synchronization of information between all the replicas in a partition varies according to several factors. The amount of replica synchronization for one partition depends on the size of the partition (number of objects), the number of updates or changes to the object information, the number of replicas or servers participating in the synchronization, and the speed of the network (LAN and WAN links).

We encourage you to keep the size of the partitions small. We recommend that the partition not hold more than 3,500 objects so that the synchronization process can efficiently update all the replicas. If a partition grows larger, you should split the partition to reduce the total number of objects in the partition. Again, this recommendation assumes high-end Pentium hardware. Scale back to a smaller partition (1,000 to 1,500 objects) if you have slower hardware.

If the object information changes in one of the replicas it needs to change in all the other replicas for that partition. Remember, the NDS database is loosely consistent, which means that not all the replicas are not instantaneously updated. For example, each user object's information changes when the user logs in to NDS. The change is written to the replica on the server that logged the user in. These changes are then synchronized to each of the other replicas in the partition. You can see that replica synchronization increases by simply having more objects in the partition and more replicas per partition.

The installation program will try to create up to three replicas per partition for fault tolerance. (You may, however, need to create more replicas simply to support bindery services on more servers. We recommend that you do not have more than 7 to 10 full replicas.) These are the master, read/write, and read only replicas, and do not include the subordinate reference replicas. If you need to have more than 7 to 10 replicas, then consider creating another partition to reduce the total number of replicas per partition and decrease the load for the NDS synchronization process. Keep in mind supportability and repairability of these partitions.

Number of Replicas Per Server   Another consideration is the total number of replicas per server. A server cannot hold two replicas from the same partition. A server can hold multiple replicas only if the replicas are from different partitions in the NDS tree.

We always recommend that you place the NDS replicas on high-end servers that can keep up with the other servers on the network. The synchronization process between all the replicas is only as fast and efficient as the weakest link. Do not place replicas on a low-performance server because it will impact the entire process.

The number of total replicas per server varies depending on the application or use of the server that is in use. For example, a home directory server is not recommended for holding more than 7 to 10 replicas. An application or e-mail server could hold 20 more replicas. A dedicated NDS replica server could hold up to 100 replicas per server. Again, the other network services that each server provides could affect the total number of replicas per server. We are also assuming a high-end server in all cases.

An extreme case, for example, is one in which a super server is brought in just to maintain the NDS replicas. This server could possibly maintain up to 100 replicas of *different* partitions. This example assumes a very large NDS tree that has at least 100 separate NDS partitions. Such a case would include an NDS tree with many geographically dispersed locations.

Subordinate Reference Replicas   There is a special consideration when it comes to the distribution of subordinate reference replicas. The subordinate reference replicas participate in the synchronization process equal to the other types of replicas for the partition. However, the amount of information for the subordinate reference replicas is very little. Nonetheless, the subordinate reference replicas change timestamps with the other replicas, and no object data is passed.

If you have done a careful job designing your tree and partitions like a pyramid, then a good distribution of the subordinate references will be automatically handled by the NDS system. If you have created only a few replicas per partition, then the subordinate references have been optimized and there is very little else that you need to change.

Remember, the subordinate reference replicas are needed because they provide tree connectivity by linking the parent partitions with their child partitions. A subordinate reference replica is essentially a pointer down the tree to the next layer of partitions. Using the subordinate reference mechanism, NDS operates more efficiently because it does not have to place a full replica (master, read/write, and read only) to provide the tree connectivity. The NDS system will place a subordinate reference replica on a server that contains a replica of the parent but does not have the child replica. Again, subordinate reference replicas are useful because NDS does not require you to connect the tree manually by placing full replicas.

Because the NDS system is responsible for maintaining the subordinate reference replicas, you, as administrators, need to be aware (not beware) of their placement and impact on the synchronization process. Again, keep in mind that supportability and repairability play heavily into this equation. The more subordinate references, the more servers need to be contacted during a repair procedure.

A subordinate reference replica contains only one object, which is the top-most container object in the partition (typically an OU). This top container object, which is called the partition root object, stores the partition information that links the tree together. The partition root object holds a list of all the replicas in the partition (master, read/write, read only, and subordinate references) that participate in the replica synchronization process. The greater the number of subordinate reference replicas, the larger their impact on the synchronization process. You should ascertain where the subordinate references are being created and, if possible, try to reduce them. By reducing the number of subordinate reference replicas you will increase the performance of the synchronization process for each server. One way to reduce subordinate references is to reduce the number of replicas of the parent partition by reducing the number of servers that contain a copy of the parent partition. Another way to reduce subordinate reference replicas is to place the child partitions on the same servers as their parents. The second option is not always feasible.

Example of Subordinate References   A good example with which to illustrate subordinate reference replicas is the [ROOT] partition, which is at the top of the tree. The ACME tree is partitioned as shown in Figure 6.61. In this example, we have 200 cities or locations, each partitioned under the [ROOT] partition.

F I G U R E 6.61

The ACME tree has over 200 cities, each partitioned under the [ROOT] partition.

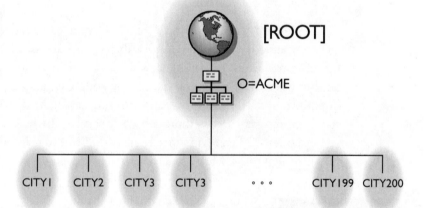

Consider what would happen each time you place a replica of the [ROOT] partition on a server. The NDS system would be forced to create 200 subordinate references replicas on that server, one for each of the child partitions. From the server's perspective, it now has to participate in each one of the 200 partitions' synchronization processes. This amount of work will probably overload the one server, and, as a result, the server will not be able to keep up with all the changes in the network. You can see the problem, especially as you add more replicas of the [ROOT] partition to other servers in the network.

CONSULTING EXPERIENCE

In the example of 200 cities being partitioned off the [ROOT], the issue is not just the traffic between the replicas because very little data is passed between a subordinate reference replica and the other replicas. The bigger concern is the effect that the large number of subordinate reference replicas has on partition operations and completion of partition operations. Remember, each replica of a partition must be contacted before a partition operation can be successfully completed. The other issue once again is supportability and repairability.

The simplest way to eliminate this problem is to design your tree and partitions like a pyramid, which naturally distributes the subordinate references accordingly. For example, to fix the problem with the ACME tree in Figure 6.61, you simply need to change the design of the tree. By adding another layer of partitions or OUs directly under the [ROOT] partition you can help distribute the subordinate reference replicas across more network servers. In Figure 6.62 we have added regional layer OUs and partitions in the ACME tree to help distribute the subordinate reference replicas. Each regional OU is its own partition.

F I G U R E 6.62

Adding a layer of regional OUs and partitions in the ACME tree design will help distribute the subordinate reference replicas.

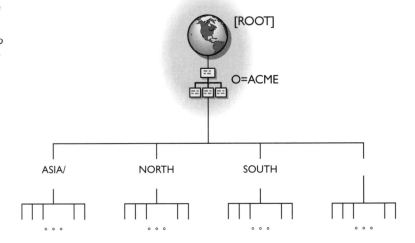

The Effect of Subordinate References on Partitioning Operations   Partitioning operations is another issue that could affect the placement of the subordinate reference replicas. During any partitioning operation all the replicas in the replica list, including the subordinate reference replicas, must be contacted in order for the partitioning operation to complete. If, for any reason, the server with a replica is not available, then the partition operation will not complete. The operation will try to contact the replicas that are unavailable until they can be reached. The total number of subordinate references could affect the efficiency of the partitioning operation.

One design consideration discussed earlier is to distribute the number of subordinate references among more servers, thus reducing the chance that a server containing subordinate references may not be up during partitioning operations.

You may be wondering why the subordinate reference replicas are contacted during a partition operation. Even though subordinate references do not contain all the partition information, they do contain the partition root object, which could change during the operation.

Now with these partitioning and replication guidelines in place you can move to the last step in the NDS design process. This step is NDS time synchronization.

CHAPTER 7

NDS Time Synchronization

"Nothing puzzles me more than time or space; and yet nothing troubles me less, as I never think about them." Charles Lamb

A step in your NDS tree design is to determine the time synchronization configuration for your IntranetWare servers. Time synchronization is the capability of IntranetWare servers to coordinate and maintain consistent time among all servers in the NDS tree. Time synchronization is necessary to ensure that each Novell Directory Service event receives an accurate timestamp.

A time synchronization configuration can be easily and quickly designed for an IntranetWare network of any size. For single-server or small-network environments you can accept the defaults provided by IntranetWare's installation utility. This configuration is commonly referred to as the single reference configuration or default configuration. There are no steps required for the LAN administrator because the setup is handled completely by the IntranetWare installation utility.

For larger networks with more servers or multiple sites, a configuration known as a time provider group is recommended. The time provider group is designed to provide greater fault tolerance and efficiency for communicating time across multiple servers and wide area networks. Both of these approaches are discussed in this chapter.

Once NetWare time has been configured there is very little additional activity required to maintain this function. Time synchronization is both stable and dependable once it has been configured. Both the single reference and the time provider group design options are explained in this section, and background information about how time synchronization functions in a NetWare environment is provided. In addition, the SET commands that relate to time synchronization are discussed here.

Novell Directory Services Time Synchronization

Time synchronization services provided in IntranetWare is the mechanism by which network time is maintained on all IntranetWare servers. IntranetWare uses the TIMESYNC NetWare Loadable Module (NLM) to coordinate the time between servers on the network. TIMESYNC.NLM will maintain each server's time to Universal Coordinated Time (UTC), which is the world time standard. The local time is used as a reference from which servers can calculate their UTC time. LOCAL time will either be ahead of or behind UTC time depending on your geographical location. Each time zone has an offset (+ or −) in relation to the UTC. For example, the United States time zones are behind UTC time and most of Europe's time zones are ahead of UTC.

The TIMESYNC.NLM is automatically loaded each time the server is started. Time synchronization is active only when the TIMESYNC.NLM is loaded. Do not unload this module because you will create problems with resolutions of duplicate event collisions of NDS timestamps.

There is a strict relationship between local time and UTC. Each server uses this relationship to maintain both a UTC and a local time counter. To the extent that an accurate time signal is available both UTC and local time will be accurate, but TIMESYNC does not guarantee accuracy, only consistency. The difference between local time and UTC time is dependent on the time zone and daylight savings time (DST) status of the server as illustrated in the following equation:

```
UTC = LOCAL TIME + (timezone offset) - (current daylight adjustment)
```

For example, consider a server located in Provo, Utah. Provo uses Mountain Standard Time during part of the year and Mountain Daylight Time the rest of the year. Mountain Standard Time is behind UTC by seven hours. When Mountain Daylight Time takes effect local time is adjusted forward by one hour from Mountain Standard Time. So, local time for the server in Provo is ahead of UTC by seven hours when daylight savings time is not in effect and six hours when it is.

```
UTC = LOCAL TIME - (7 hours) + (0 hours) [when DST is not in
effect]
```

```
UTC = LOCAL TIME - (7 hours) + (1 hour) [when DST is in effect]
```

If you want to view time at a server's console you can type **TIME** to display its status. Figure 7.1 shows how you can see the time information from the server, which displays the local server's time as well as the UTC time value.

The time information displayed includes the time zone string, status of daylight savings time (including when it starts and ends), UTC time, local time, whether time synchronization is active, and whether the server's time is synchronized to the network. Using this information you can easily detect whether the server is synchronized to the network time.

Time information is displayed at the server console by entering TIME.

```
NOR-SRV1:time
  Time zone string: "MST7MDT"
  DST status:  OFF
  DST start:    Sunday, April 7, 1996    2:00:00 am MST
  DST end:      Sunday, October 27, 1996   2:00:00 am MDT
  Time synchronization is active.
  Time is synchronized to the network.
Sunday, November 26, 1995    1:04:39 pm UTC
Sunday, November 26, 1995    6:04:39 am MST
NOR-SRV1:
```

Once time is synchronized on all IntranetWare servers, the Directory can accurately timestamp any network event; for example, adding a new user or assigning rights to a new administrator are both considered events. The timestamp ensures that as the Directory tree replicas are synchronized, the correct order of events will be applied during replica synchronization.

Each event that occurs in NDS is marked with a timestamp. The timestamp is a unique value within an NDS partition. The timestamps are used to order the events or changes that occur on multiple servers. The timestamping of events keeps all NDS changes in their proper order. For more information regarding timestamps, refer to Chapter 8.

Timestamps within all the replicas of any partition are unique. As shown in Figure 7.2, the left portion of the timestamp shows the seconds since 1970 of the change based on UTC time. This ensures that there is a unique timestamp for any changes that are at least 1 second apart. The second portion of the timestamp shows the replica number. The replica number will create a unique timestamp for changes occurring within the same second on different replicas. The last portion of the timestamp is called the event counter. The event counter is set to zero at the beginning of each second. It is incremented with each change on a particular replica when changes occur within the same second. This event counter further enables a unique timestamp for events occurring in rapid succession on the same replica within the same second.

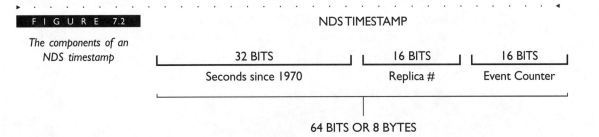

FIGURE 7.2

*The components of an
NDS timestamp*

NDS TIMESTAMP

32 BITS	16 BITS	16 BITS
Seconds since 1970	Replica #	Event Counter

64 BITS OR 8 BYTES

Accurate and automated time of day can also be provided by attaching your IntranetWare server (reference or single reference) to an external time source service such as a radio clock, an atomic clock, or the Internet (a time source provided by connecting to the Internet). Although not mandatory for the operation of an IntranetWare network, the use of an external time source in larger network installations is highly recommended, thus eliminating the manual task for a network administrator to verify time. In addition, the external time source provides accurate time of day for your network, which is required by some NLMs or backup devices. The use of an external time source is shown in Figure 7.3.

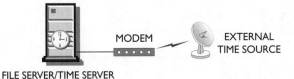

FIGURE 7.3

*Attach your time server to
an external source for
automatic time updates.*

MODEM

EXTERNAL
TIME SOURCE

FILE SERVER/TIME SERVER

TIME SERVER TYPES

Each IntranetWare server is configured as a specific type of time server during installation. All IntranetWare servers perform the same basic time functions including:

- Providing UTC time to any client or NLM making the request

- Providing status information on time synchronization

- Making adjustments to correct discrepancies when time synchronization is active

An IntranetWare server will provide time to any client or NLM making a request for network time. For example, your backup or archival software may require accurate network time to know when to initiate a particular process or function. Client utilities may also query time from an IntranetWare server of any type.

Regardless of the configuration, all IntranetWare servers will provide time status information. Through time synchronization, each IntranetWare server knows the status of its clock with respect to the network.

All IntranetWare servers are time servers and participate as either providers of time or consumers of time. The internal mechanism for querying the time is the same for all types of servers. There are three types of time providers: primary server, reference server, and single reference server. Time providers coordinate time among themselves to determine the "official" network time. Time consumers are known as secondary servers and can request time from any of the three types of time providers. Time consumers will constitute the majority of your IntranetWare servers. Figure 7.4 shows the categories of the time servers.

FIGURE 7.4

Time servers are categorized into one of two classes: the time providers or the time consumers.

TIME PROVIDERS	TIME CONSUMERS
Primary	Secondary
Reference	
Single Reference	

Functionally, all IntranetWare servers are very similar in terms of how they are configured for time. In fact, reference and single reference servers are just special cases of primary servers. Each IntranetWare server on the network is responsible for its own synchronization and status. This means that each server will, at periodic intervals, poll other servers for time, make any necessary adjustments, and wait for the next interval to repeat the process.

Since time synchronization is a server-centric operation, each server determines if its time is within an acceptable limit, known as the *synchronization radius*. A server is synchronized to the time on the network when its time is within the synchronization radius. If the server determines that its time is within the radius, it raises a time synchronization flag. This synchronization flag indicates that this server has a UTC time that can be used by NDS to accurately timestamp events on the network.

Secondary servers are the most common type of server as they will synchronize to either a time provider or another secondary server.

Secondary Time Servers

Secondary time servers rely on other sources to provide them with network time. A secondary server can query another secondary, single reference, reference, or primary time server for the network time.

The secondary server will be the most prevalent type of server on your network because most of your servers do not need to participate in determining network time. During the installation of your file servers, all servers except the first server are designated as secondary servers. The first server is automatically designated a single reference time server as explained later in this section.

During the installation of your file servers, all servers except the first server are designated as secondary servers. The first server is automatically designated a single reference time server as shown in Figure 7.4-A. This is the default configuration. If the UTC time value on the secondary time servers is within the synchronization radius, the synchronization flag can be raised.

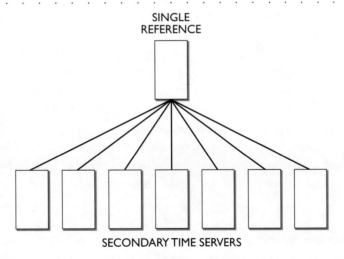

SINGLE
REFERENCE

SECONDARY TIME SERVERS

The secondary server adjusts its clock to make up any difference in the time it receives from the network. The network time will be provided by another server or servers during each polling interval. Therefore, any discrepancies in the secondary server's time will be resolved during each polling interval. The secondary servers can and do provide time to requesting client or server applications.

The secondary time servers do not participate in determining network time. These servers do not negotiate time with any other time servers. They simply get the network time from another source on the network and make the appropriate adjustments to their own clock during each polling interval. The secondary server will raise its synchronization flag once its time discrepancy is less than the synchronization radius set for that server.

Primary Time Servers

The primary time servers are responsible for determining and setting the network time. The primary time servers are known as time providers because they distribute the network time to other requesting servers. The secondary servers will constitute the majority of the requesting servers needing network time.

In order to determine the network time, the primary server will poll other primary and reference servers from its list of servers. This process determines the "official time" for the network as each primary server polls other primary servers to determine any discrepancies between its local clock and the calculated network time. If there is a difference, the primary server will try to adjust its clock to remedy the discrepancy.

Figure 7.4-B illustrates how a primary time server polls the other time providers. In this case, the other time providers are primary servers.

Like all time servers, a primary server will determine if its time is within its synchronization radius. If the server is within the radius, it raises its synchronization flag to indicate that synchronization has occurred.

During the polling process, each primary time server has a weighting factor of one. This weighting factor means that all other primary servers will be given equal consideration during the polling interval. Each primary server will "wake up" on its polling interval and begin checking its time against other time providers.

For example, primary server A begins a polling process of the other primary servers in the group. Its current network time is 10:15 AM. After polling begins primary server B returns a time of 10:20 AM and primary server C returns a time of 10:10 AM. Because each server has a weighting factor of one, they are treated equally and the two times are averaged together to produce a time of 10:15 AM. An example of this process is shown in Figure 7.5.

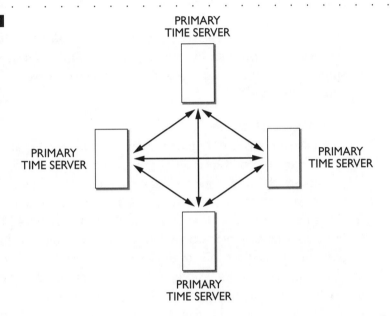

FIGURE 7.4-B

Each primary time server wakes up and begins polling the other time providers on the network during its polling process.

PRIMARY
TIME SERVER

PRIMARY
TIME SERVER

PRIMARY
TIME SERVER

PRIMARY
TIME SERVER

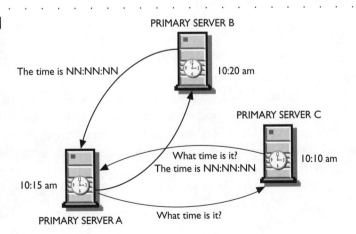

FIGURE 7.5

Each primary time server wakes up and begins polling the other time providers during its polling process.

PRIMARY SERVER B

The time is NN:NN:NN   10:20 am

PRIMARY SERVER C

What time is it?
The time is NN:NN:NN   10:10 am

10:15 am

PRIMARY SERVER A   What time is it?

The polling process is unique and operates independently for all time servers as each server is responsible for its own network time. Although your servers may have the default polling interval of every ten minutes, each server will most likely be polling at different ten-minute intervals as each primary server checks its time against other time providers in the tree.

While primary servers alone can achieve network time, they need the help of a consistent time provider that never makes adjustments to its clock after polling. A special case of the primary server is the reference server, which sets time for the entire network.

Reference Time Server

A reference server is a time provider that adds additional capability to a primary time server. The reference time server works with other time providers, such as primary servers, to provide the network time. The difference between the reference time server and a primary server is that the reference server will always believe that it has network time and will not adjust its internal clock. Therefore, you should place a reference server where you set network time and force all other primary servers to adjust their time to the reference server. The reference server participates in polling intervals just like the primary servers, but does not adjust its clock.

The best configuration is to have one reference server with a few primary servers to provide accurate time. Figure 7.5-A illustrates the configuration of one reference server and multiple primary time servers on the network.

Over time all IntranetWare servers will converge their internal clocks to the time of the reference server. On the other hand, the reference time server will never adjust its clock. This naturally makes the reference time server over time the point of reference for convergence.

During the polling process, the reference time server has a weighting factor of 16. This means that all primary servers will converge their time to that of the reference time server because it has the greatest weighting in terms of time. You will typically want to have only one reference server on your network as it is the definitive time source. The best configuration is to have one reference server with a few primary servers to provide accurate time. Design configuration options are discussed in the following section.

The configuration of one reference server and multiple primary time servers on the network

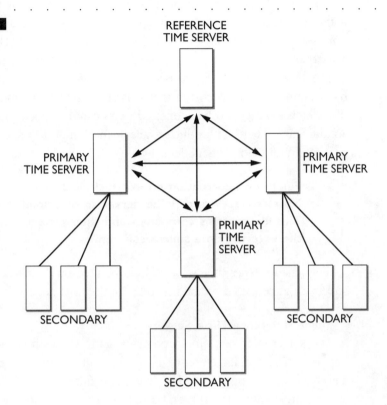

Primary servers work with the reference server to provide fault tolerance and multiple sources for time. The reference server must, like other primary servers, contact another source during the polling process in order to raise its synchronization flag. In addition, if the reference server should fail, multiple primary servers can still provide consistent network time to requesting servers and clients until you restore another reference server. Therefore, the reference server is the supreme authority of time, except when it is not accessible.

Like all time servers, a reference server will determine if its time is within the synchronization radius. If the server is within the radius then it raises its time synchronization flag, which indicates that its time is acceptable for timestamping events.

Because the reference server does not make an adjustment to its internal clock, you can connect it to an external source. Having an external clock accomplishes several important things. First, it provides an accurate and automated mechanism to check time. Some of your applications may require accurate time of day if they initiate a process, such as a backup, in the middle of the night. Second, an automated time source will help ensure that the reference server's clock is not drifting, and consequently is keeping all other servers in your network with accurate time.

The server's own clock can be used as a time source, but time must be verified manually by an administrator to ensure that it is staying accurate and not drifting. Ideally, the reference server can be connected to an external clock source to provide highly accurate time. There are products available that connect PCs to external time sources, such as a radio clock or modem, which can contact an outside source.

TIP For more information on external clock solutions you can contact Novell's NetWire or WEB server to download the TIMESG.TXT file. This file contains companies and their product names that support the external time source solution.

Only one reference time server should be used on the network. Multiple reference servers could be placed on the network, but they will not synchronize with each other.

Single Reference Time Servers

The single reference time server is a stand-alone time provider for the entire network. The single reference is the default configuration and is established automatically during installation. The main difference between a reference server and a single reference server is that the single reference server can raise its synchronization flag without confirming its time with any other time providers. It does, however, go through the polling process like all IntranetWare servers. In this case, the polling does not expect a response from any server. A response from another server would indicate that another time provider has been erroneously placed on the network. This condition would cause the single reference server to report an error to the console screen .

A single reference time server should be the only time provider on the network. The rest of the time servers should be secondary time servers. The secondary time servers simply contact the single reference to get the network time. Figure 7.5-B illustrates a single reference time server, with the others being secondary time servers.

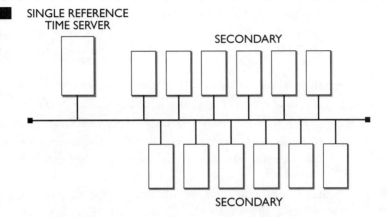

FIGURE 7.5-B

A single reference time server provides time to the other secondary time servers.

SINGLE REFERENCE
TIME SERVER

SECONDARY

SECONDARY

A single reference time server enables you to have all other servers remain as secondary time servers, which will adjust their times to the single reference time during each polling cycle. Like the reference server, a single reference time server can be connected to an external source to feed the network accurate time of day.

In addition, the single reference server's own clock can be used as the time source instead of an external source. Occasionally, it may be necessary to check the server's time against a reliable source because some of your applications may require accurate network time such as backup or archiving software programs.

Time Synchronization Design

TIME SYNCHRONIZATION CONFIGURATION OPTIONS

There are two basic time server configurations for your IntranetWare network: Single Reference (the default) or a Time Provider Group. All other configurations that may be used are variations of these two. As part of your NDS design, evaluate the time synchronization configurations and choose the one that best meets the needs of your company. Two important factors to consider are listed below:

▸ Is your network multisite connected by a WAN? If it is, then we recommend always using the second option of a time provider group. A time provider group gives your network greater fault tolerance in a wide area network configuration by distributing the time providers to multiple locations.

▸ If your site consists of 30 IntranetWare servers or fewer and is not connected by a WAN, the default option of single reference server will work extremely well. The LAN environment can easily contact a single reference server without crossing a WAN link. In addition, your servers can easily contact the single reference server without burdening the server.

Consider the configuration options discussed below in making your decision and use the SERVMAN utility to make the necessary changes. This utility is run from an IntranetWare server console by typing LOAD SERVMAN. From the Available Options menu select Server Parameters and then select the Time option as shown in Figure 7.6.

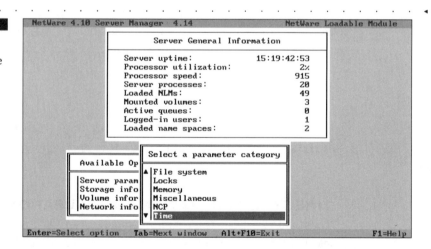

FIGURE 7.6

The main screen of the SERVMAN utility with the Time option selected

Default Option: Single Reference Time Server

When the first IntranetWare server is installed in the NDS tree it is automatically configured as a single reference server. All additional IntranetWare servers installed in the same tree are automatically configured as secondary time servers. The Novell installation utility assumes that your installation will initially consist of two levels of servers: A single reference at the first level and secondary servers at the second level provide you with a default installation.

The advantages of the default configuration are that it is easy to understand and requires absolutely no advanced planning. In addition, no configuration files are needed, and the possibility of errors during time synchronization is considerably minimized.

CONSULTING EXPERIENCE

Regardless of the size of your network, you can initially accept the single reference default until your installation grows beyond 30 servers or unless you immediately begin with IntranetWare on both sides of a WAN. Also, if you choose the single reference server option, do not use any other time provider, such as a primary or a reference. A single reference is the only time source required on the entire network under this configuration.

In the default configuration, select a central file server that can be easily contacted by the other IntranetWare servers in your network. Remember, the first IntranetWare server you install is automatically configured as the single reference server as shown in Figure 7.7. You can always designate another server as the single reference by using the SERVMAN utility. Figure 7.8 shows an example of a single reference time server configuration setup.

A potential drawback of the default configuration is that if the single reference time server should fail, the network has lost its only time provider. However, even if this happens for only a short period of time (a day or less), there is little problem with the timestamping of events. All IntranetWare servers should continue to maintain their time and continue to stamp NDS events. If your single reference is down for prolonged periods, we recommend that you designate a new server as the single reference to ensure that there is a source for time on your network. In order to designate a new server as the single reference, simply go to the server and make the change using SERVMAN.

FIGURE 7.7

Single reference time configuration with only one server providing time to the entire network. This configuration is suitable for a network that has fewer than 30 servers and is situated in one geographical location.

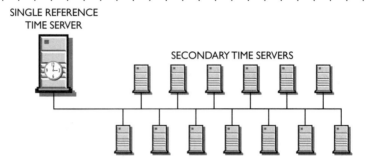

SINGLE REFERENCE
TIME SERVER

SECONDARY TIME SERVERS

FIGURE 7.8

Use the SERVMAN utility to designate another server as your single reference or to make other configuration changes.

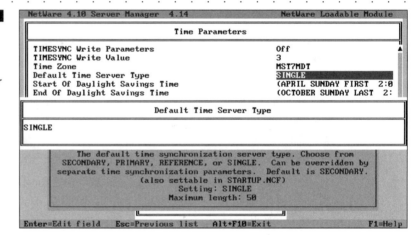

Custom Option: Time Provider Group

Other design option is the time provider group. The time provider group requires one reference time server and a minimum of two primary time servers that will participate in the synchronization process to coordinate the network time. These time source servers form a time provider group that in turn provides time to the rest of the IntranetWare servers.

The time provider group configuration works well for networks that have more than 30 IntranetWare servers or are situated in several locations in a wide area configuration. Figure 7.9 illustrates the placement of the time providers in the major hub sites of the ACME tree.

The placement of the time providers in the major hub sites of the ACME tree

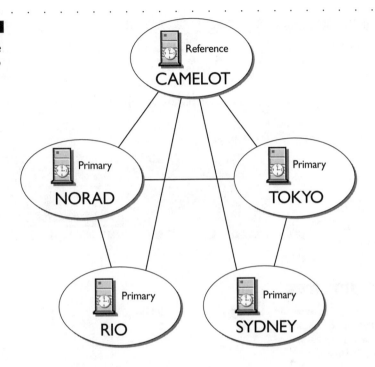

The time provider group configuration option requires simple configuration adjustments for a few servers you want to designate as participants in the time provider group. One server will be designated as the reference, and a recommended two to seven servers may be designated as primary time servers. Primary servers may be designated by using the SERVMAN utility's Time Parameters screen as shown in Figure 7.10.

The selection of your reference server should be based on a centralized location for your network infrastructure. For example, if your WAN is designed like the ACME WAN with a hub and spoke fashion, your reference server should be centrally placed at the hub location. The primary servers should be distributed across your wide area links to the other hub locations. If your network is a large WAN, place your primary servers in just a few strategic locations. The rest of the installed file servers will be secondary servers. Figure 7.11 shows you where the reference server and primary servers should be placed for network efficiency in the ACME tree.

*Using the SERVMAN
utility to designate a
primary server*

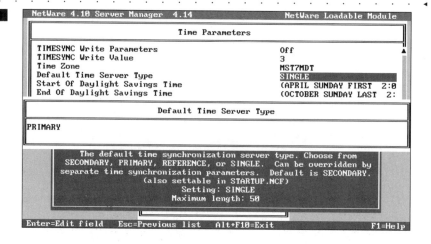

```
NetWare 4.10 Server Manager  4.14                    NetWare Loadable Module
┌────────────────────────────────────────────────────────────────────────┐
│                           Time Parameters                                │
│ TIMESYNC Write Parameters                    Off                         │
│ TIMESYNC Write Value                         3                           │
│ Time Zone                                    MST7MDT                      │
│ Default Time Server Type                     SINGLE                       │
│ Start Of Daylight Savings Time               (APRIL SUNDAY FIRST  2:0     │
│ End Of Daylight Savings Time                 (OCTOBER SUNDAY LAST  2:     │
└──────────────────────────────────────────────────────────────────────────┘
┌────────────────────────────────────────────────────────────────────────┐
│                        Default Time Server Type                          │
│ PRIMARY                                                                  │
└──────────────────────────────────────────────────────────────────────────┘
        The default time synchronization server type. Choose from
     SECONDARY, PRIMARY, REFERENCE, or SINGLE.  Can be overridden by
     separate time synchronization parameters.  Default is SECONDARY.
                      (also settable in STARTUP.NCF)
                           Setting: SINGLE
                         Maximum length: 50

 Enter=Edit field   Esc=Previous list   Alt+F10=Exit              F1=Help
```

*An example of time server
designations for a hub and
spoke infrastructure in
the ACME tree*

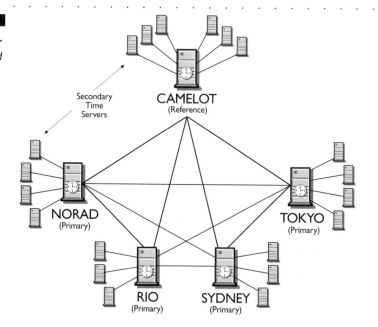

Secondary
Time
Servers

CAMELOT
(Reference)

NORAD
(Primary)

TOKYO
(Primary)

RIO
(Primary)

SYDNEY
(Primary)

It is highly recommended that you connect the reference server to an external time source to provide highly accurate time. Figure 7.12 shows an example of a time provider group in the ACME tree that is connected to an external time source. The ACME time provider group contains one reference server located in CAMELOT and four other primary time servers located in NORAD, RIO, TOKYO, and SYDNEY.

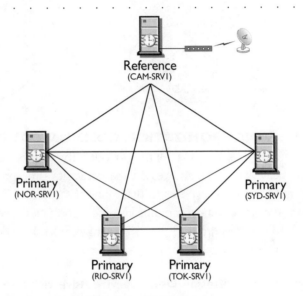

FIGURE 7.12

The ACME time provider group connected to an external time source for accurate time. This time provider group consists of one reference server and four primary time servers. You have redundancy with the five time servers and can balance the requests for time.

MULTIPLE TIME PROVIDER GROUPS

Some companies may need to use multiple time provider groups for redundancy in worldwide corporations. For example, we could create a time provider group at NORAD and also at CAMELOT so that time is distributed from each area rather than traversing a WAN. Multiple time provider groups require that your reference servers be connected to external clocks to converge their times. An example of multiple time provider groups is shown in Figure 7.13. Each reference is connected to an external source to provide accurate and automated time, thus ensuring that both groups are distributing the same (or very close to) time for the entire tree.

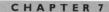

FIGURE 7.13

An example of multiple time provider groups in the ACME tree

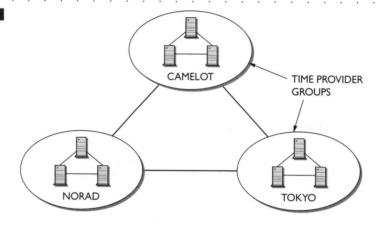

TIME SYNCHRONIZATION COMMUNICATION OPTIONS

Secondary time servers will periodically request time and will need to communicate with time sources on the network. Time providers also need to find other time providers in order to determine the correct UTC time.

IntranetWare servers communicate time information using one of two methods: Service Advertising Protocol (SAP) or configured lists. The following two sections discuss these two methods.

Time Synchronization Using Service Advertising Protocol

The SAP method is the default at installation and requires no intervention. As new IntranetWare servers are designated primary time providers, no custom configurations to the existing time servers or to new servers are required for time communication. Time providers such as a primary, reference, or single reference server advertise their presence on the network using SAP by default.

SAP can cause a small amount of additional traffic on your network. Also, because SAP is self-configuring, a new time server that is unintentionally configured as a wrong type in the same tree could disrupt your time synchronization.

Time synchronization SAP type is 0x026B. If you have decided to use SAP for your time communication you must not filter this packet type on any routers that connect your IntranetWare servers together.

TIP

Time Synchronization Using Configured Lists

The use of a configured list enables you to specify exactly which servers should be contacted for a time provider group and to make requests for time consumers as well. For all implementations using time provider groups, we recommend that you use a configured list as your communication option instead of SAP. The configured list option will keep time synchronization traffic to a minimum and also prohibit anyone from placing other time providers on your network that might cause problems with the network time. A server must obtain the configured list if it is to participate in network time for your tree. For the ACME tree we have chosen to use a time provider group along with a configured list that specifies the time servers in the time provider group. After the list is created, it is then distributed to all time servers in the group through the file called TIMESYNC.CFG.

The configured list is created by using the SERVMAN utility, selecting the Time option, and making the entries for each server name that you want to contact in your time provider group. The first step is to enable the configured list option as shown in Figure 7.14. Once set to ON you are able to begin creating your configured list.

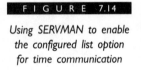

FIGURE 7.14

Using SERVMAN to enable the configured list option for time communication

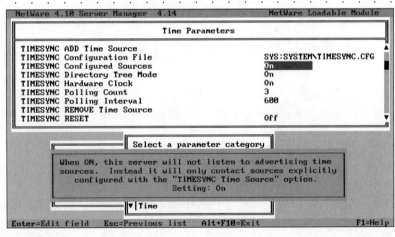

The configured list entries use the server names separated by spaces as shown in Figure 7.15 for the ACME tree. We have designated CAMELOT as their reference server location. All other major sites in our tree will contain one primary server to communicate with the reference server in CAMELOT.

F I G U R E   7.15

A configured list for the ACME time provider group. This list is stored on each file server in the time provider group.

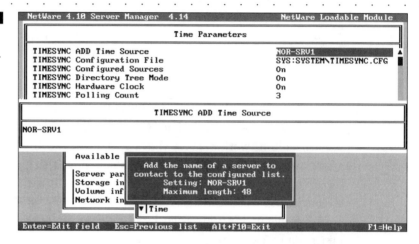

Configured lists give you complete control of the time synchronization hierarchy. The configured list also reduces the SAP traffic on your network because SAP broadcasts are not used. Instead, the configured list specifies the source server by name to contact.

A proposed time synchronization configuration is found in the example given below. In this example the corporate office is located in CAMELOT. The reference server in CAMELOT is linked to an external time source. This source server sets both the NetWare server clock and the hardware time-of-day clock. Primary servers are located in RIO, NORAD, SYDNEY, and TOKYO. These time sources will work together to determine the actual network time during each polling interval. The ACME tree is using the configured sources list so that all the servers can contact each other to determine the network time. In the example below, the TIMESYNC.CFG file is shown with its configured list.

TIMESYNC.CFG for reference server in CAMELOT

Configuration parameters for server CAM-SRV1

```
Configured Sources = ON
Directory Tree Mode = ON
Hardware Clock = ON
Polling Count = 3
Polling Interval = 10
Service Advertising = OFF
```

```
        Synchronization Radius = 2000
        Type = REFERENCE
```

Configured time source list server CAM-SRV1

```
        Time Source = RIO-SRV1
        Time Source = TOK-SRV1
        Time Source = SYD-SRV1
        Time Source = NOR-SRV1
        Time Source = CAM-SRV1
```

TIMESYNC.CFG for primary servers in RIO, TOKYO, NORAD, AND SYDNEY

Configuration parameters for server *TOK-SRV1*

```
        Configured Sources = ON
        Directory Tree Mode = ON
        Hardware Clock = ON
        Polling Count = 3
        Polling Interval = 10
        Service Advertising = OFF
        Synchronization Radius = 2000
        Type = PRIMARY
```

Configured time source list from server TOK-SRV1

```
        Time Source = CAM-SRV1
        Time Source = RIO-SRV1
        Time Source = SYD-SRV1
        Time Source = NOR-SRV1
        Time Source = TOK-SRV1
```

The secondary servers located in each geographical region would use the
following TIMESYNC.CFG file. The server xxxxx indicates any secondary server
located in the ACME tree.

TIMESYNC.CFG for secondary servers

Configuration parameters from server *xxxxx*

```
        Configured Sources = ON
        Directory Tree Mode = ON
```

```
Hardware Clock = ON
Polling Count = 3
Polling Interval = 10
Service Advertising = OFF
Synchronization Radius = 2000
Type = SECONDARY
```

Configured time source list from server *xxxxx*

```
Time Source = CAM-SRV1
Time Source = RIO-SRV1
Time Source = TOK-SRV1
Time Source = NOR-SRV1
Time Source = SYD-SRV1
```

In each geographical region, the time source list should be reordered to place the closest time provider first on the list. Next, place the lowest-cost (time and hops) providers and finally the rest of the providers. This will enable the secondary server to initially contact the closest available server to obtain the correct network time.

OTHER DESIGN CONSIDERATIONS

Configuring Secondary Servers to Follow Other Secondary Servers

In some cases it may be necessary for secondary servers to receive their time from other secondary servers. For large companies this situation may occur as you try to limit the number of primary servers spread across your WAN network as time providers. Therefore, if you use the configured list option, you can configure secondary servers to obtain their time from other secondary servers who are obtaining their time from a primary server elsewhere. As shown in Figure 7.16, the ACME tree has secondary servers that follow other secondary servers.

Time providers such as primary servers will not follow a secondary server. You can only configure a secondary server to follow another secondary server. For companies with many sites, you should consider placing a primary server at a hub location with your secondary servers contacting the hub. If your SPOKE or REMOTE locations have multiple servers, you may want to designate one secondary server contact the primary server for time on behalf of the other secondary servers. An example of this is shown in Figure 7.17.

F I G U R E   7.16

Secondary servers can be
configured to follow other
secondary servers. If you
use configured list.

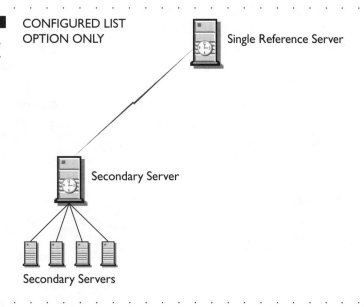

CONFIGURED LIST
OPTION ONLY

Single Reference Server

Secondary Server

Secondary Servers

F I G U R E   7.17

Hub and spoke
arrangement with primary
and secondary servers.
At the remote or spoke
locations, the secondary
servers contact other
secondary servers for
their time.

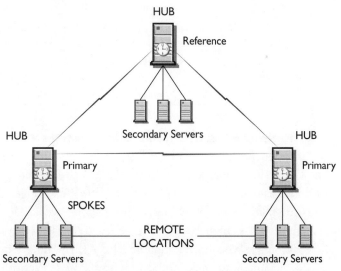

HUB

Reference

Secondary Servers

HUB

Primary

HUB

Primary

SPOKES

REMOTE
LOCATIONS

Secondary Servers

Secondary Servers

TIP

**The total allowable time radius for the entire system is ten seconds.
Therefore, keep the number of secondary servers following each to
a depth of only two to three servers. Any depth greater than two to
three servers may lead to time sychronization errors, which are
unacceptable for NDS.**

Having More Than One Reference Server

Some organizations may require more than one reference server because of their company's dispersed locations. For example, you may want to have a time provider group in two different countries, rather than having time traffic cross over expensive or extremely busy wide area connections. As shown in Figure 7.18, you can have multiple reference servers as long as they are each connected to an external source. The external source is needed so that these reference servers can maintain the same time and not drift.

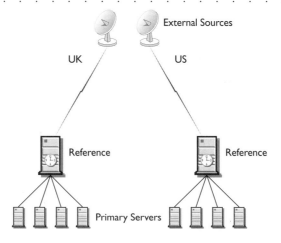

Time Synchronization Traffic Considerations

Although the amount of time traffic is generally small, it might be useful to know what kind of a network load is generated by time synchronization. The actual workload is controlled by the number of time exchanges during each polling loop. You can take steps to further minimize the workload if you have bandwidth constraints on your network. The actual traffic load is determined by how many time exchanges you have configured for each polling loop.

The default is to make three time exchanges, each of which involves an NCP send/receive pair totaling 332 bytes of data. Thus, the default three exchanges involve six packets totaling 996 bytes of data.

Therefore, you can calculate the amount of traffic for each server during a specific polling interval with the following equation:

```
NDS Traffic = (N - 1) * (Polling Count) * 332
```

(where N = the number of providers to contact)

For example, let's assume that a network has five time providers in its group (one reference and four primary servers) and is using the default intervals of three send/receive exchanges every ten minutes for each server. You can determine that the amount of traffic generated will be as follows:

```
(5 - 1) * (3) * (332) = 3984 bytes/10 minutes/per time
source server
```

Each time source server would, at its own ten-minute interval, generate 3984 bytes of traffic on your network. Obviously, the more primary servers you have, the more traffic will be generated on your network.

It is also possible, but not recommended, to change the polling interval to cut down on network traffic. The default polling interval is ten minutes. But as long as the server clock is not drifting and synchronization is maintained, that polling interval may be extended.

In situations where perhaps dozens of secondary servers would poll a single primary server across a slow LAN or WAN segment, it may be helpful to increase the polling period to even one or two hours. This would cut back on the network traffic and probably have little or no effect on synchronization, unless the server clocks drift by several seconds a day.

In fact, once a server has reached a stable state, the amount of network traffic attributed to time synchronization will probably be minuscule compared to the normal everyday traffic.

Check Time Sychronization Status

You can easily check the time synchronization status of all servers by using the DSREPAIR utility as shown in Figure 7.19. After typing LOAD DSREPAIR at the server's console, you can select Time Synchronization to check the status. Keep in mind that if you are running DSREPAIR on a server containing a copy of the [ROOT] partition, the Time Synchronization option will search all IntranetWare servers in the entire tree beginning at ([ROOT]) and searching downward. If you do not want this to happen, run DSREPAIR on a server that does not hold a copy of the [ROOT] partition.

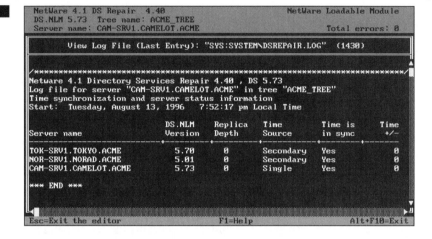

FIGURE 7.19

Using DSREPAIR to obtain a status of time synchronization

ADDING NEW TIME SERVERS

When adding a new server to an already synchronized network, time synchronization acts on two basic premises. First, it works from the notion that adding a server should not disrupt the network's time synchronization. Second, it assumes that if the new server's time doesn't agree with network time, the network time is more likely to be correct.

Therefore, the first act of time synchronization (for any server type) during boot up is to set the server time to the time reported by the first time provider contacted. This is true even for reference and single reference servers that do not normally adjust their clocks.

When you bring up a server, make sure that time synchronizes properly and, if necessary, reset the time on reference and single reference servers manually. It is always a good idea to check the time after bringing up a server just to make sure that all the time parameters are set correctly and that time is synchronized.

If you are currently using the default option of a single reference server and all other servers as secondary, you can continue reading this section to make the change to a time provider group. This configuration requires you to change the time type on the server you want to designate as a reference server by using the SERVMAN utility. An example of this is shown in Figure 7.20. Only one server will be designated as the reference server in our example.

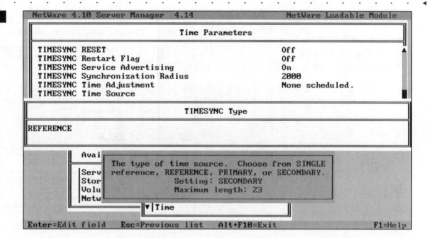

FIGURE 7.20

An example of a server being designated at the reference time server

The next step is to designate some server as a primary time server. Using the SERVMAN utility again you will change your selected server's type to primary. Repeat this procedure for all appropriate servers, however, for no more than seven servers. You can have more than seven primary servers, but keep in mind that the more primary servers, the greater the amount of traffic on your network during each polling interval for time.

Experience has shown that most companies can have very stable time by using only three or four primary servers in the entire network. Only a few servers need to work with the reference server to determine time for the entire network. Also, consider that there should be only one primary or time provider per hub location.

TIP

After you have made configuration changes for both the reference server and the primary servers, save the changes when prompted before exiting the SERVMAN utility. An example of how this screen appears is shown in Figure 7.21.

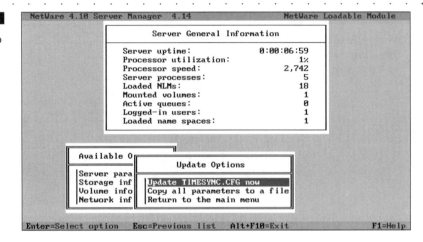

F I G U R E   7.21

Be sure to save changes to the TIMESYNC.CFG file before exiting the SERVMAN utility.

Time Synchronization Operations

This section discusses how you can configure the time on your IntranetWare servers and explains how to use the various SET parameters that are provided. In addition, you will learn the commands found in the SERVMAN utility for adjusting the time parameters. Most changes and configurations with time can be accomplished by using the SERVMAN utility, which is discussed in this section. The SET parameters will rarely need changing. However, some environments may require that you adjust some of them.

USING THE SET PARAMETERS FOR TIME SYNCHRONIZATION

IntranetWare includes a rich set of setable parameters governing time synchronization. The time synchronization parameters can be set from the server console using the SET commands or through the menu-driven SERVMAN utility. In addition, your current time synchronization SET parameters can be viewed from the server console by typing **SET** and then selecting option 9 as shown in Figure 7.22 and Figure 7.23. The setting for time synchronization can be stored in a special configuration file called TIMESYNC.CFG. This file is located in the SYS:SYSTEM subdirectory of your IntranetWare servers.

FIGURE 7.22

*To view SET parameters at the server console type **SET**.*

```
NOR-SRV1:set
Settable configuration parameter categories
    1. Communications
    2. Memory
    3. File caching
    4. Directory caching
    5. File system
    6. Locks
    7. Transaction tracking
    8. Disk
    9. Time
    10. NCP
    11. Miscellaneous
    12. Error Handling
    13. Directory Services
Which category do you want to view:
```

FIGURE 7.23

To view the current settings for time synchronization select option 9. This screen is only a partial view of the time SET parameters.

```
TIMESYNC ADD Time Source:  NOR-SRV1,TOK-SRV1
Maximum length:  47
    Description: Add the name of a server to contact to the configured list.

TIMESYNC Configuration File:  SYS:SYSTEM\TIMESYNC.CFG
Maximum length:  254
    Description: Sets a new path for operations involving the configuration
                 file.

TIMESYNC Configured Sources:  ON
    Description: When ON, this server will not listen to advertising time
                 sources.  Instead it will only contact sources explicitly
                 configured with the "TIMESYNC Time Source" option.

TIMESYNC Directory Tree Mode:  ON
    Description: Controls the use of SAP packets in conjuction with the
                 directory services tree structure.  The default, ON, causes
                 time synchronization to ignore SAP packets which do not
                 originate from within the tree to which this server belongs.
                 The default installation puts a SINGLE time source at the root
                 of every directory tree, which causes confusion since there
                 should only be one SINGLE time source on the entire network.
                 Setting this parameter to OFF allows this server to receive
                 SAP packets from any time source on the network.
<Press ESC to terminate or any other key to continue>
```

TIP

Do not place **TIMESYNC** parameters in the **AUTOEXEC.NCF** file because they will not work from that file. The only time synchronization parameters that can be placed in the **TIMESYNC.CFG** file are the parameters that start with the **TIMESYNC** label. Figure 7.24 illustrates an example of a **TIMESYNC.CFG** file.

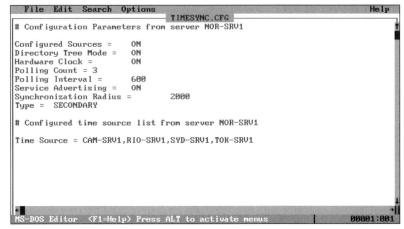

FIGURE 7.24

Sample TIMESYNC.CFG file

The easiest way to modify the time synchronization parameters is to use the SERVMAN utility. After you load SERVMAN from the server console select Server Parameters and then the Time option. The screen for the time synchronization parameters is shown in Figure 7.25.

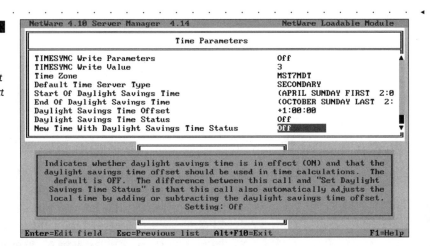

FIGURE 7.25

An example of the IntranetWare Server Manager (SERVMAN) that is displayed after you select the Time option from Server Parameters. The Time Parameters screen enables you to modify many aspects of time.

Each of the setable time synchronization parameters is discussed below as to its function and use.

TIMESYNC Add Time Source = <server name>

Default: Empty

This option enables you to add the name of a particular IntranetWare server or servers as potential time providers to your configured list. The server name that you enter here will be stored in the TIMESYNC.CFG configuration file. The TIMESYNC.CFG configuration file is updated if you choose the update TIMESYNC.CFG option after exiting the time parameter screen. Duplicate entries are not accepted in the time sources list and will be ignored.

You will use this option only if you are using a configured list and want to add a new server to the configured list as a time provider.

The name of the IntranetWare server is not the distinguished name. Instead, it is the least significant segment of its name. For example, an IntranetWare server in the ACME tree has a distinguished name of CN=NOR-SRV1.OU=NORAD.O=ACME. The name entered in this field is simply NOR-SRV1.

To add the servers NOR-SRV1, CAM-SRV1, and TOK-SRV1 to the list of time sources in the TIMESYNC.CFG files, enter the following:

```
SET TIMESYNC ADD TIME Source = NOR-SRV1
SET TIMESYNC ADD TIME Source = CAM-SRV1
SET TIMESYNC ADD TIME Source = TOK-SRV1
```

TIMESYNC Configuration File = <volume:subdirectory\file>

Default: SYS:SYSTEM\TIMESYNC.CFG

This parameter defines the path or location of the configuration file used by time synchronization. The TIMESYNC.CFG configuration file is the default name that stores all the settings for time on your IntranetWare server. There is little if any need to change the name of this file, and we recommend that you accept the default TIMESYNC.CFG. This file can easily be copied to multiple IntranetWare servers if needed.

If you want to store the TIMESYNC.CFG file in the SYS:SYSTEM\TIME subdirectory, you would issue the following command:

```
SET TIMESYNC CONFIGURATION FILE = SYS:SYSTEM\TIME
```

TIMESYNC Configured Sources = ON/OFF

Default: OFF

This parameter determines whether the IntranetWare server finds the time providers on the network using SAP or an existing configured list. A setting of OFF tells the server to listen to any time providers that are sending out the SAP. A setting of ON tells the server to ignore SAP and rely only on the configured lists set up in the TIMESYNC.CFG file. The server will only try to contact the time providers that are in its configured list. This parameter must be set to ON in order to support custom configured lists.

When using configured lists we recommend that each one of the secondary time servers have a primary or reference time server as the first member of its list. However, secondary time servers may also be entered in the configured lists. This option enables a secondary time server to get the time from other secondary time servers in the event that the primary and reference time provider does not respond.

If you want to view the list of servers that has been established as the time providers in the configured list on a particular server, you can type the following command from that server's console:

TIP

SET TIMESYNC TIME SOURCE =

Notice the equal sign is required with no following parameters.

TIMESYNC Directory Tree Mode = ON/OFF

Default: ON

This parameter controls the use of SAP in the NDS tree. A setting of ON, which is the default, tells the time server to ignore the SAP packets from servers that are not part of your NDS tree. A value of OFF enables the server to listen to all time SAP packets from any time provider on the network even if it is outside the same Directory Services tree.

When you leave this setting to ON, you maintain tighter control over the NDS tree of this server.

TIMESYNC Hardware Clock = ON/OFF

Default: ON

This parameter controls hardware clock synchronization to the software clock, which is maintained by IntranetWare servers. A value of ON, which is the default, has a different meaning depending on the type of time server that is being used. The value of ON for the single and reference time servers enables them to read their hardware clock at the beginning of each polling loop and to set the software clock accordingly. The capability of the single and reference time servers to read their hardware clock and reset the software clock provides the network with a basic external clock synchronization. In this case the hardware clock acts as an external time source. This is kind of a poor man's radio clock.

Set this parameter to OFF only if the single or reference time servers use an external time source, such as an atomic or radio clock.

The value of ON for the primary and secondary time servers means that the hardware clock is set to the time of the software clock after each polling process. This setting is useful because corrections made to the software clock during the polling process can be written to the hardware clock. Thus, the network time is reflected the next time the server is brought down and back up. Each time the server is booted it reads the hardware clock.

All primary and secondary servers in the same Directory tree should use the same setting for this parameter.

TIMESYNC Polling Count = <number (1 to 1,000)>

Default: 3

This parameter determines how many time packets to exchange during the polling process. Increasing the number of packets adds more traffic to the network. We recommend that you leave the default to 3, which works well in most cases. The only time you may want to change this value is when you have unreliable or erratic network communication links between the time servers.

The higher the value is set, the greater the amount of network traffic introduced. The lower the value, the less accurate the time information exchanged. Again, the default value of 3 is highly recommended.

TIMESYNC Polling Interval = <number (10 to 2,678,400)>

Default: 600 seconds (or 10 minutes)

This parameter determines the length of time between each polling process. In the case of the default, every 600 seconds (or 10 minutes) the server will poll the other time servers in the tree. After the initial installation of your IntranetWare servers, you may want to increase this value to reduce the total number of polling traffic on the network. Just remember that the time polling process does not generate an inordinate amount of traffic on your network. We recommend that you leave the default setting if you keep the total number of time providers under ten. We also recommend that all the time servers in the same NDS tree have the same setting for this parameter.

Decreasing this parameter creates an increase in network traffic but higher time synchronization accuracy. Increasing this interval is recommended when the time servers have to cross a WAN link to get time.

TIMESYNC Remove Time Source = <server name>

Default: Empty

This option enables you to specify a server or servers to be removed from the time source list. The server name entered in this field will be removed from the configuration file if you exit and choose YES to update TIMESYNC.CFG option after updating and exiting the time parameter screen. This field will return a blank screen after you have specified a value in this field. If you try to delete an entry from the time sources list, which does not exist, the request will be ignored.

This option is the reverse of the TIMESYNC Add Time Source. Like the Add Time Source the name of the IntranetWare server is not the distinguished name. Instead, it is the least significant segment of its name. For example, an IntranetWare server in the ACME tree has a distinguished name of CN=NOR-SRV1.OU=NORAD.O=ACME. The name entered in this field is simply NOR-SRV1.

This command is primarily used at the server console to remove a time provider that has gone down or become unavailable for any reason.

TIP

If you are trying to add or remove a time source permanently, using either the TIMESYNC Add Time Source and TIMESYNC Remove Time Server parameters can be difficult because they do not give you any feedback on whether the instructions were successful. An alternative to using these fields is to edit the configuration file directly using any text editor.

TIMESYNC Reset = ON/OFF

Default: OFF

This parameter resets all time parameters to the default values and clears the configured lists. A value of ON resets the time parameters and writes the configuration file after exiting from the SERVMAN screen. Be careful — any changes you have made previously to the TIMESYNC.CFG file will be lost. For example, all the configured server lists are cleared and set back to the internal defaults. If you set the parameter to ON and press Enter, the values are reset and the parameter automatically returns to the default OFF value.

You should never have to reset the time parameters on a production server. This option is valuable in restoring the parameters as you experiment with them in a lab situation.

TIMESYNC Restart Flag = ON/OFF

Default: OFF

This parameter controls restart time synchronization. You would use this feature to restart time synchronization after you have created or changed the configuration parameters in the file. After this command is issued from the file server console, the parameter automatically resets to OFF.

TIMESYNC Service Advertising = ON/OFF

Default: ON

This parameter controls the time servers that are time providers advertising through SAP. When ON, the single reference and primary time primary servers send out or advertise using SAP. Setting the value to OFF means that the time provider servers will not send out the SAP. You would want to set this parameter to OFF when you use configured lists. Turning the SAP off will reduce the traffic on the network.

TIMESYNC Synchronization Radius = <milliseconds (0 to 2,147,483,647)>

Default: 2,000 (or 2 seconds)

This parameter controls the maximum time a server's clock is allowed to vary from network time and still be considered synchronized. The default of 2,000 milliseconds works well for most installations. This time parameter can be adjusted or increased to enable a wider margin or error for time synchronization between servers. However, increasing this value reduces the collision resolution occurring in NDS. A lower value causes the server to maintain tighter time synchronization. Because the tighter synchronization radius may be difficult or impossible to achieve, the time servers lose time synchronization. We recommend that you never set the synchronization radius under the 2,000 millisecond value.

If you need to change this parameter you can do so through the SERVMAN utility as shown in Figure 7.26.

TIMESYNC Time Adjustment = [+ | −] hour:minutes:seconds [AT month/ day/year hour:minutes:seconds [AM | PM] | [CANCEL]]

Default: One hour from the current time or six polling intervals, whichever is longer.

This parameter enables time adjustments to be made to the network time. You should use this feature sparingly. The misuse of this parameter will affect the servers networkwide and could change the order of the NDS events. You should also use this parameter during the day, which will not be excessively disruptive to the network operation.

You can use the optional AT parameters to schedule the time adjustment to take place in the future. For example, the command for a time adjustment schedule in the future might look as follows:

```
SET TIMESYNC TIME ADJUSTMENT = +00:01:30 AT 4/6/99
11:00:00 PM
```

The command will adjust network time ahead one minute and thirty seconds on April 6, 1999, at 11:00 PM. Use the CANCEL command to remove a previously scheduled time adjustment from taking place. For example, in order to cancel the time adjustment of +00:01:30, enter the following:

```
SET TIMESYNC TIME ADJUSTMENT = +00:01:30 CANCEL
```

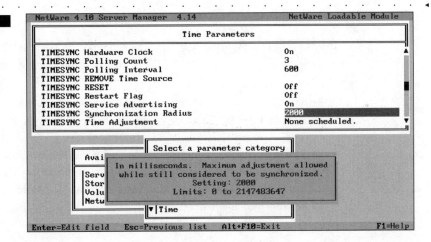

FIGURE 7.26

Changes to the synchronization radius can be made through the SERVMAN utility.

If you do not use the optional AM or PM parameters, then IntranetWare assumes a 24-hour (military time) clock. Use a plus sign (+) to indicate a time adjustment forward, and a minus sign (-) to indicate a time adjustment backward.

This command would not normally be used in a time server configuration that is receiving its time from an external source. We recommend that you use this option only when a significant one-time correction must be made to the network time. You should perform the time adjustment operation on either the reference or single reference time servers.

The TIMESYNC Time Adjustment parameter can modify the network time only on primary, reference, and single reference time providers because they can affect the network time. This parameter should not be used with a secondary time server.

TIP

TIMESYNC Time Source = <server name>

Default: None

This parameter is the same as the TIMESYNC Add Time Source parameter discussed above. You can specify a server to be added to the configuration list. So you may ask, why are there two parameters that perform the same function? This option makes more sense and is easier to enter at the server console command line. For example, you simply type:

```
SET TIMESYNC TIME SOURCE = <server name>
```

By entering this command at the server console you are adding the server to your configuration list. Use the TIMESYNC Remove Time Server parameter to remove the servers from the configured list.

To reduce the confusion, we recommend that you use this parameter only at the server console and use the TIMESYNC Add Time Source parameter in the SERVMAN utility.

TIP

You can display the current list of time servers that has been established in the configuration list by entering the TIMESYNC Time Source = command at the server console. Notice that there is no server name entered.

TIMESYNC Type = <time server type>

Default: Single (during the first installation of IntranetWare)

Secondary (during all subsequent installations)

This parameter sets the time server type for the IntranetWare server. The possible values are: SECONDARY, PRIMARY, REFERENCE, and SINGLE (for single reference). You can use this parameter to change the time server type for the IntranetWare server on the fly. This value is placed in the TIMESYNC.CFG configuration file and is used when TIMESYNC.NLM is initialized as the server is booted or when the restart flag is used.

TIMESYNC Write Parameters = ON/OFF

Default: OFF

This parameter writes all the current time synchronization parameters to the TIMESYNC.CFG configuration file. The value of ON will write the parameters; the value of OFF does not write the parameters. This SET parameter is a trigger and automatically resets to OFF.

TIMESYNC Write Value = <number>

Default: 3

This parameter controls which parameters are written to the TIMESYNC.CFG configuration file by the Write Parameter ON/OFF action. The possible values are:

1 • Write only the internal parameters.

2 • Write only the parameters for TIMESYNC Add Time Source.

3 • Write both internal and time source server parameters.

Default Time Server Type = <time server type>

Default: Secondary

This parameter is used when the server first initializes because it is placed in the AUTOEXEC.NCF file. The value of this parameter is overridden by the TIMESYNC type parameter found in the configuration file. The default server type is used if the TIMESYNC configuration file is not present or is invalid. We recommend that you set the default time server type to the same value as the TIMESYNC Type value given above. This will reduce confusion and the potential for problems if the configuration file is lost for some reason.

Time ZONE = <time zone string>

Default: <NO TIME ZONE>

This parameter specifies the time zone where the server is located. The value is a time zone string indicating the abbreviated time zone name, the offset from UTC, and the alternate abbreviated name for daylight saving time. This parameter causes UTC time to be recalculated from local time. To reduce confusion, we recommend that you set this parameter correctly for the actual physical server location.

The format for the time zone string is xxxN[yyy], where "xxx" is the time zone (MST = U.S. Mountain Standard Time or EST = U.S. Eastern Standard Time). The "N" is the number of hours offset from UTC (7 = U.S. Mountain or 5 = U.S East Coast). The "yyy," which is optional, indicates that daylight saving time is in effect (MDT = U.S. Mountain Daylight Saving Time or EDT = U.S. Eastern Daylight Saving Time). Thus, the time zone string for the U.S. Mountain Time Zone is:

```
MST7MDT
```

and the U.S. Eastern Time Zone is:

```
EST5EDT
```

Daylight Savings Time Status = ON/OFF

Default: OFF

This parameter indicates whether daylight saving time is in effect. Possible values are ON and OFF. If this parameter is set to ON, the DST (Daylight Standard Time) parameter should be used. The status of this parameter may be changed at any time. However, changing the status does not change the local time, but it does cause UTC to be recalculated.

Daylight Savings Time Offset = [+ | –]hour:minute:second

Default: +1:00:00

This parameter controls the offset applied to time calculations when daylight saving time is in effect. The offset, in seconds, is added to local time at the beginning of daylight saving time. A change causes UTC to be recalculated from local time.

Start of Daylight Savings Time = <Month [Day | Day of Week] [Condition] hour:minute:seconds>

Default: April Sunday First 2:00:00 AM

This parameter enables you to set up the local date and time or some simple rules for when the change from standard time to daylight saving time occurs. The following example sets the start of daylight saving time at 2:00 AM on the first Sunday of April (which is also the default):

```
SET START OF DAYLIGHT SAVINGS Time = (April Sunday First
2:00:00 AM)
```

End of Daylight Savings Time = <Month [Day | Day of Week] [Condition] hour:minute:seconds>

Default: October Sunday Last 2:00:00 AM

This parameter enables you to set up the local date and time or specify some simple rules for calculating when daylight saving time ends. The following example sets the end of daylight saving time at 2:00 AM on the last Sunday of October (which is also the default):

```
SET END OF DAYLIGHT SAVINGS Time = (October Sunday Last
2:00:00 AM)
```

The preferred method of setting the daylight saving time (DST) status is through the use of the SET Start of Daylight Savings Time and SET End of Daylight Savings Time commands placed in the AUTOEXEC.NCF file during system initialization. Note that there are two ways to indicate when DST should start or end:

▸ Specify an exact date when the change to daylight saving time occurs.

▸ Specify a rule for calculating the dates. The operating system recalculates the next change and automatically schedules it for the next year.

Both the start and the end date and time for daylight standard time (DST) must be set before either date is actually scheduled.

New Time with Daylight Savings Time Status = ON/OFF

Default: OFF

This parameter controls the adjustment of local time when DST is in effect. This command is similar to the TIMESYNC Daylight Savings Time Status parameter, but when this value is set to ON it adjusts the local time by adding or subtracting the DST time offset but does not change UTC for the server. This is accomplished by changing the daylight saving time status and adjusting the local time by the daylight saving time offset. This effectively leaves UTC unchanged. This is designed to correct a DST error. If a supervisor arrives and sees that DST did not change when it should have, this command will change it.

When changing daylight saving time information manually on a server, be aware that you may cause UTC time to be recalculated from local time. The SET New Time with Daylight Savings Time Status command is expressly intended to avoid the recalculation of UTC time and force local time to be recalculated instead. Use this command to change the daylight saving time status on a system that is otherwise correct and in time synchronization with the network.

TIP

Attempting to accomplish the same thing by changing local time and then changing the daylight saving time status will result in loss of time synchronization.

ADDITIONAL TIMESYNC SET COMMANDS

The following IntranetWare SET commands for time synchronization are not documented in Novell manuals. These SET commands can assist you in fine-tuning your environment even further. However, these parameters may or may not work in future versions of NetWare 4. We have documented them here so that you can have all of the options when working with time synchronization. We recommend that you do not adjust these parameters unless you are solving a specific problem and understand the use of each parameter.

TIMESYNC Immediate Synchronization = On/Off

Default: Off

This parameter triggers the time synchronization process, which simply means that it starts a polling process. After the value has been set to ON, it automatically resets to OFF, which is the default. This parameter is sometimes useful in creating screen output after the debug flag has been set, rather than waiting for the synchronization process to awaken normally.

Note that this SET parameter does not speed up synchronization in any way; it simply wakes up the synchronization process. Normally, the synchronization process will respond within two seconds. Occasionally there may be a delay of several seconds (ten seconds or fewer) because of normal network overhead while attempting to reach the target server.

TIMESYNC Short Interval = <number (10 to 600 seconds)>

Default: 10

This parameter determines the shortest interval between polling processes. This parameter is used when the server falls out of time synchronization. If the server falls out of time synchronization it immediately polls the network more frequently to establish time synchronization more quickly. The default interval is every ten seconds. You may want to increase this value for very expensive WAN links that you do not want to monopolize all the bandwidth just to support time synchronization when it has been lost.

TIMESYNC Maximum Offset = <number (10 to 16,777,215 seconds)>

Default: 600

This parameter specifies the maximum amount of adjustment that the server will try to gain between polling processes. The default is 600 seconds or 10 minutes. The greater the value, the faster the time server will adjust itself toward the network time.

TIMESYNC Correction Floor = <number (in milliseconds)>

Default: 1

This parameter sets the minimum value in milliseconds that the clock must differ before the correction is applied. Any adjustment must be larger than this value or the correction is ignored. This value must always be less than the synchronization radius. If it is not less than the synchronization radius, then time synchronization will not be possible.

This parameter is undocumented or hidden so that system administrators will not change it without knowing the consequences. We highly recommend that you leave the default setting of one millisecond to support NDS.

The only reason to change this parameter would be to eliminate the correction for the one-tick jitters that sometimes occur. This may be an issue if there are other applications that depend on time being synchronized and are extremely sensitive to larger amounts of error correction over a ten-minute period.

SET TIMESYNC Offset Ceiling = <number (0 to 315,532,800)>

Default: 10 years

A time provider whose clock is too far behind network time will not be able to participate in the voting process. This parameter sets the value that is used to determine if a server's clock is too far behind the network time. Again, if the time on a server is farther away from the network time than this value, it will be ignored and the time of the network will not be adjusted based on that server.

TIMESYNC DEBUG COMMANDS

IntranetWare enables you to monitor the status of time synchronization on a server using the time synchronization debug commands. These commands are useful for debugging, testing, and fine-tuning the synchronization configuration. However, note that as undocumented commands they may or may not work in future versions of NetWare 4.

When executed, the debug commands start a separate time synchronization screen on the file server console. After the debug screen is started, information about the time synchronization function is written to the console. This information may be helpful when trying to determine if the servers are contacting each other in the manner you expect for time synchronization. It is also educational to read the debug messages to see the way the system changes the times on each server to converge on the network time. To turn on the time synchronization debug screen and its information, type:

```
SET TIMESYNC DEBUG = 7     (turns on the debug screen)
SET TIMESYNC DEBUG = 0     (turns off the debug screen)
```

Figure 7.27 illustrates the time synchronization debug screen.

FIGURE 7.27

*Time synchronization
debug screen*

```
TIMESYNC: Polled server CAM-SRV1,RIO-SRV1,SYD-SRV1,TOK-SRV1
          Weight = 00, offset.h = 00000000  offset.l = 00000000

TIMESYNC: Polled server CAM-SRV1,RIO-SRV1,SYD-SRV1,TOK-SRV1
          Weight = 00, offset.h = 00000000  offset.l = 00000000

TIMESYNC: Polled server NOR-SRV1,TOK-SRV1
          Weight = 00, offset.h = 00000000  offset.l = 00000000

TIMESYNC: Polled server NOR-SRV1,TOK-SRV1
          Weight = 00, offset.h = 00000000  offset.l = 00000000

TIMESYNC: Polled server NOR-SRV1,TOK-SRV1
          Weight = 00, offset.h = 00000000  offset.l = 00000000

TIMESYNC: Polled server NOR-SRV1,TOK-SRV1
          Weight = 00, offset.h = 00000000  offset.l = 00000000
myPollDelay 135

TIMESYNC: Polled server NOR-SRV1,TOK-SRV1
          Weight = 00, offset.h = 00000000  offset.l = 00000000

TIMESYNC: Polled server NOR-SRV1,TOK-SRV1
          Weight = 00, offset.h = 00000000  offset.l = 00000000
```

TIP

You can set the debug flag to values other than 7, but the results are not very useful because each bit in the value controls a group of messages or disables output altogether. The debug information that appears on the screen is not particularly well formatted. Some portions are language enabled and may be translated.

The following messages are examples of the type of information provided by the debug screen.

```
TIMESYNC: Polled sever NOR-SRV1
Weight = 1, OFFSET.H = FFFFFFFF OFFSET.L = F1F06723
```

The most useful pieces of information are the name of the server (NOR-SRV1) and the weight (normally 0, 1, or 16). If time synchronization cannot actually exchange information with the other time server or if out-of-range data is detected, the weight will be zero. A weight of zero generally means that the server is not up or is not reachable across the network.

The values for OFFSET.H and OFFSET.L are the calculated deviation of the server's time from the target server's time. The values form a 64-bit signed number with an implied hexadecimal point separating the whole and fractional parts:

```
FFFFFFFF.F1F06723
```

This number means that this server is a fraction of a second ahead of NOR-SRV1. Another possibility that may occur is a weight of zero with nonzero offset values, indicating that the synchronization data is out of range (one server is more than ten years ahead of the other).

If this message does not appear at all, there are no time providers or sources in this server's list. Either the configured time source list is empty or no SAP time sources can be found, or both. Of course, if you have disabled the use of SAP, the only possible cause is that the configured time source list is empty. You can check the state of the list by typing:

```
SET TIMESYNC TIME SOURCE =
```

at the system console screen. Notice that the equal sign with no parameter following is required to return the list of time sources.

The next message is:

```
Uniform Adjustment Requested = -0.0E0F98DD
Server type = 2
```

This message shows the actual time adjustment that needs to be applied to the clock during the next polling interval. The message also shows the time server types, which are 2 = Secondary, 3 = Primary, 4 = Reference, and 5 = Single.

The adjustment value is hexadecimal, but the sign is displayed so that the magnitude of the adjustment is easier to understand. In this case, the value 0.0E0F98DD (one tick) is significant to time synchronization. This server is ahead of NOR-SRV1 by one tick. It is very common to see one tick or one-half tick errors that are caused by randomness between the two machines.

When the adjustment is +0.00000000, the servers are in exact synchronization, which really means that no error can be detected by the algorithm. It is also common to see this value stabilize at a very small negative value, such as − 0.00000094, because of a small round-off error in the synchronization algorithm when slowing the clock. The error of 0.00000094 is 34 nanoseconds, much smaller than the resolution of the clock and nothing to worry about.

The next message

```
Adjustment smaller than Correction Floor was ignored.
```

is mentioned because it is quite common. It means that the clock adjustment is so small that it is being ignored. Actually, the parameter that determines the cutoff point is called TIMESYNC Correction Floor and is set to one millisecond by default.

TROUBLESHOOTING TIME SYNCHRONIZATION

When time for a server fails to synchronize to the network, the most probable reason is that there are no reachable time providers. Check the configuration information to be sure it is correct. Make sure that the time providers are running and are synchronized themselves. Remember that a secondary server will not be synchronized until its time providers are synchronized. If necessary, turn on the debug option and verify that the server is actually contacting a time provider.

If the time on the file server has been set far ahead, time synchronization may take a long time. Remember that the server should not move time backwards. So, for example, it takes at least two hours of real time to lose two hours.

TIP

Setting time backwards on a server is not a good thing to do for most applications that require synchronized timestamps. If you set the time backwards on a server that is participating in NDS, the system will generate synthetic time to account for the local time being set backwards. You should always set the DOS time before booting the server, just to make sure that the hardware clock has the correct time. (For more information on synthetic time see the "Synthetic Time" section later in this chapter.)

Remember that time synchronization requires routing information to make contact with the time provider. Sometimes it takes a while for routing information to get to a server, especially when the server has just been booted. Even though time synchronization normally happens quickly, wait a minute or two before jumping to conclusions. Also, try executing the DISPLAY SERVERS console command to see if the target server is known to the router.

Booting Time Servers

A rare condition exists when the only two time provider on a network are booted for the first time. Since the first action of any server is to find a time provider and set its own clock, determining which server will first set its clock from the other server (the first server polled sets the time) can be problematic. Once servers have synchronized, and as long as one time provider remains active, other time providers can be shut down and rebooted. The booting server will set its time to the network time. Since one server remains in operation, that server is not attempting to set its clock, and the race condition does not exist.

Again, it is always a good idea to set the DOS time before booting a server to make sure that the hardware clock is correct and to minimize any possible time adjustment.

NDS Time Not Synchronized

NDS may report the following error message:

```
Time_Not_Synchronized Error -659 (FD6D)
```

Yet when users check the server's status with the TIME command, it reports that time is synchronized. What this error message actually means is that NDS has received a timestamp that is older than information already in the Directory. The server time has probably been set backwards because of a dead CMOS battery or because the time was incorrectly set when the server was booted.

This error message occurs mostly on small networks that use the default time synchronization configuration. Note that it is an NDS error, not a TIMESYNC.NLM error.

Correcting Local Time on a Server

Fortunately, once time information is correctly configured, there is little need to change it. When time synchronization is active, you need to be extremely cautious about changing local time information. If local time information is not configured correctly and time synchronization is active, UTC time will also be incorrect. Time synchronization will attempt to adjust local time to correspond to network time, which will, in turn, control UTC time. Time synchronization may, therefore, fight efforts to correct poorly configured local parameters.

To avoid this problem, you have to unload the TIMESYNC NLM, configure the local time information correctly, and then reload the NLM.

 The TIMESYNC NLM is automatically loaded when the NetWare server is booted.

TIP

As an alternative to unloading TIMESYNC, use the following command after correctly setting the server time and creating a TIMESYNC.CFG configuration file:

```
SET TIMESYNC RESTART/FLAG = On
```

Synthetic Time

When time synchronization is lost because the local time is set backwards, IntranetWare will continue to issue timestamps on the servers using synthetic time. When this situation occurs the synthetic time message will appear on your server console screen as shown in Figure 7.28, indicating that synthetic time is being used to create timestamps for the partitions on the server. Synthetic time is also issued when DS loads and time synchronization has not yet been established.

FIGURE 7.28

Synthetic time is created when the time on the Reference or Single Reference servers is set backwards. You will be notified with a server console message.

```
11-21-95  11:06:16 pm:      DS-4.89-12
           Synthetic Time is being issued on partition "ACME_TREE."

11-21-95  11:06:16 pm:      DS-4.89-12
           Synthetic Time is being issued on partition "OU=CAMELOT.O=ACME.ACME_TREE."

11-21-95  11:06:16 pm:      DS-4.89-12
           Synthetic Time is being issued on partition "OU=NORAD.O=ACME.ACME_TREE."

11-21-95  11:06:16 pm:      DS-4.89-12
           Synthetic Time is being issued on partition "OU=SYDNEY.O=ACME.ACME_TREE."

11-21-95  11:06:16 pm:      DS-4.89-12
           Synthetic Time is being issued on partition "OU=TOKYO.O=ACME.ACME_TREE."

11-21-95  11:06:16 pm:      DS-4.89-12
           Synthetic Time is being issued on partition
           "OU=OPS.OU=CAMELOT.O=ACME.ACME_TREE."

CAM-SRV1:
```

Synthetic time is the process of creating timestamps from the most recent timestamp in NDS. Synthetic time will take the most recent timestamp and modify just the event counter to create a new timestamp. This means that the time is not incremented, just the event counter. The event counter is a 2-byte value that will hold up to 65,535 events. Once the event counter rolls over, the number of seconds in the timestamp is incremented by one. Synthetic time will continue until the real time of day catches up with the synthetic timestamps being used.

Summary

IntranetWare includes several new, time-related features that form the basis for time synchronization. Time synchronization is the method by which all the IntranetWare servers maintain the same UTC time across the network. Although it is not directly part of NetWare Directory Services, time synchronization is used primarily by the Directory to maintain the order of events that occur. Because the computer hardware does not inherently maintain consistent time, time synchronization continually attempts to correct time variations.

Time servers are either time providers or time consumers. The time consumer is the secondary time server type, while the time providers are primary, reference, and single reference time servers. The time providers determine the official network time. Secondary time servers only attempt to stay synchronized with one other server.

The default configuration of a single reference for time synchronization is easy to understand and requires no advanced planning. The single reference default is a great place to start your installation. Depending on your needs you can keep the defaults or configure a time provider group as your needs change. A custom configuration or time provider group offers you complete control of the time synchronization hierarchy and enables you to build fault tolerance into the system. There is very little maintenance with time synchronization once it has been configured.

Next, decide which communication option works best in your environment. SAP is the default and adds very little additional traffic to your network as long as you keep the number of configured primary servers at no more than seven. You can also use a configured list in place of SAP.

There are many time synchronization parameters that you can set on an IntranetWare server. Altering these parameters can enhance the system performance for time on the network.

Once configured, time synchronization is stable and dependable. It is one of those features that almost never needs changing unless your network changes in size or location.

PART III

Operations and Maintenance of IntranetWare

CHAPTER 8

NDS Internals for
Server-Based Operations

"The first rule of intelligent tinkering is to save all the parts." Paul R. Ehrlich

Novell Directory Services' (NDS) main function is to provide a name service. The name service groups network resources together in a hierarchical structure called a tree. Each network resource can be represented in the NDS tree as a single NDS object. The information about all the objects or network resources can be distributed across the servers in the network. In NDS the object information and the rules to create and manage these objects are stored on the individual IntranetWare servers in special data files. The data files associated with Directory Services are created during the server installation.

This chapter will focus on all NDS concepts and the internal operations that take place on a single server. This chapter is a companion to Chapter 9. Using both of these chapters you will be able to better understand the "Black Box" called NDS.

First Server Installation

The best way to describe and examine the creation of NDS is to understand the installation procedure. We will discuss several basic concepts, including partitions, replicas, and bindery objects.

When you install the first IntranetWare server and NDS, the installation program prompts you to enter the name of the NDS tree, the server context, and the password for the ADMIN user, which is created by default.

The name of the NDS tree is important because it names the hierarchy in which each of the objects or network resources will reside. The name you choose for the tree must be a unique value on the network. For example, the name that we have selected for our sample tree is ACME_TREE.

TIP

Each tree is identified by a name, containing up to 32 ASCII characters. The tree name may contain only the capital letters "A-Z", digits "0-9", hyphen "-", and the underscore "_" character. The tree name must not start or end with an underscore or a space. The tree name cannot have more than one adjacent underscore character. This means that there cannot be back-to-back underscores in the NDS tree name. For example. "BAD__TREENAME" is illegal.

During the simple installation method for IntranetWare, the NDS tree name and the O=Organization container are named the same. In this case, the installation utility only prompts you for the password. This is the password for the ADMIN object.

The server context you choose is significant for several reasons. First, it forms the initial tree structure. Second, it becomes the parent or container object for the server object itself and all of its volumes. Third, it becomes the place in the tree where the bindery services context may be set for the server.

During the installation of the first server and NDS several events take place. These events are listed below:

▸ Creation of the NDS data files (Partition, Entry, Value, and Block files).

▸ Creation of the internal NDS partitions.

   ▸ System Partition

   ▸ Bindery Partition

   ▸ External Reference Partition

   ▸ Schema Partition

▸ Creation of the base schema.

▸ Creation of the system objects.

   ▸ Data storage for nonreplicating server data (Pseudo Server object)

   ▸ Data storage for the IntranetWare server's dynamic SAP type 4 server object

▸ Creation of the first user-created partition, called the [ROOT] partition.

▸ Creation of the [ROOT] object for the tree.

▸ Creation of an object for each container object in the server's name.

- ▸ Creation of the server object in the appropriate container.

- ▸ Creation of a volume object for each server volume, using the naming convention of file server name_volume name.

- ▸ Creation of the ADMIN user.

- ▸ Creation of the bindery SUPERVISOR account, which initially uses the ADMIN password. If the server is upgraded from the NetWare 3 bindery it uses the password of the Supervisor from the bindery.

- ▸ The ADMIN user is granted Supervisor object rights to the [ROOT] object.

- ▸ [PUBLIC] is given object Browse rights to the [ROOT] object.

- ▸ Upgrade of existing bindery objects to NDS (if the server is being upgraded from NetWare 3).

The installation of the first server creates a single partition, named [ROOT], as the topmost object in the tree. The master replica of the [ROOT] partition is stored on the server. Each of the objects created by the installation of the first server is in the master replica of the [ROOT] partition. Figure 8.1 illustrates a logical view of the NDS tree for ACME after the first server CAM-SRV1 is installed.

FIGURE 8.1

A logical view of the NDS tree for ACME after the first server CAM-SRV1 is installed

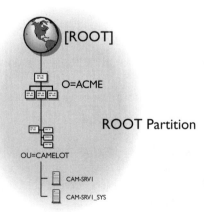

NDS PROGRAM FILE (DS.NLM)

The NDS program code is found in the DS.NLM file, which is placed in the SYS:SYSTEM directory during installation. This NLM file is loaded by the operating system during server bootup. The DS.NLM provides the Directory name services on the server. The most important thing to remember is the build number for the NLM. For example, IntranetWare ships with the build number DS 501.

The build number for DS.NLM can be found by running the NDIR.EXE program against the DS.NLM file. To find the build number for DS.NLM enter the following:

```
NDIR DS.NLM /ver
```

You can also find the build number for DS.NLM by using the MODULES console command and looking at the entry for the NLM. In order to use the MODULES command enter the following at the server console prompt and check the version of the DS.NLM that is loaded:

```
MODULES
```

One of the items shown by the MODULES command is the version of each module that is loaded at the server. See Figure 8.2.

```
IDEHD.CDM
   NetWare 3.12/4.x Fixed Disk Custom Device Module.
   Version 1.20    June 18, 1996
   Copyright 1992-96, Novell, Inc.  All rights reserved.
UNICODE.NLM
   NetWare Unicode Library NLM
   Version 4.10    July 8, 1996
   Copyright 1996 Novell, Inc.  All rights reserved.
DSLOADER.NLM
   NetWare 4.11 Directory Services Loader
   Version 1.48    July 15, 1996
   Copyright 1993-1996 Novell, Inc.  All rights reserved.  Patents pending.
TIMESYNC.NLM
   Netware Time Synchronization Services
   Version 4.15    July 8, 1996
   (C) Copyright 1991-96, Novell, Inc.  All rights reserved.
DIAG411.NLM
   Diagnostic/coredump utility for NW v4.11 (960708)
   Version 1.01    July 8, 1996
   Copyright 1996 Novell, Inc.  All rights reserved.
DS.NLM
   NetWare 4.11 Directory Services
   Version 5.73    July 29, 1996
   Copyright 1993-1996 Novell, Inc.  All rights reserved.  Patents Pending.
<Press ESC to terminate or any other key to continue>
```

Newer versions of the DS.NLM can be copied to the SYS:SYSTEM directory on your server system. You may want to save the older DS.NLM by renaming it.

In order to unload and reload the new DS.NLM from the SYS:SYSTEM directory without taking the server down, enter the following DSTRACE command:

```
SET DSTRACE = *
```

You can perform the reload of DS.NLM using the more conventional method by simply entering the following server console commands:

```
UNLOAD DS
```

and

```
LOAD DS
```

There is a new workstation utility called DUPGRADE that automatically copies the newer DS.NLM to each of your IntranetWare servers and performs the reload of the software. This utility is available from NetWire and the Novell Web Server.

Locating an IntranetWare Server

Novell Directory Services is a distributed name service by which a client can locate the network resources anywhere in the network. Once the client or workstation is attached to any IntranetWare server, then all the servers work together to locate the requested service.

The IntranetWare servers that contain NDS replicas advertise the tree using the Service Advertising Protocol (SAP). The SAP value contains two parts:

- Service Type — 0x0278 hex (or 632 decimal). The SAP type is used to advertise the tree.

- Service Name — The service name is 47 characters contained in two segments.

The first 32 characters of the Service Name are the NDS tree name. The tree is padded with the underscore characters to take up the entire 32 characters, if necessary.

The other 15 characters of the Service Name are made up from converting the server's network address. The server's network address contains the network address for the server, the internal IPX node number, and the NCP socket number in that order. The address is compressed to fit into the 15 bytes. The client connects to the server by reversing the compression and uses the address and socket numbers.

The workstation initially finds the first IntranetWare server by broadcasting or making a Service Request indicating the Service Type 0x0278. Any server receiving this request that has NDS replicas of the NDS tree will respond to the request.

By looking at the Service Name field, the workstation or client determines the NDS tree name supported by the server and uses that information in choosing a server to contact. If the workstation has a setting for the Preferred Tree in the NET.CFG, it looks for the name equal to that of the Preferred Tree. The workstation can then connect to the server at the address and socket number extracted from the Service Name field.

NOTE

The other Service Advertising Protocols (SAP) that you need to support IntranetWare are type 0x0004 and type 0x026B. A normal NCP Server or file server uses the SAP type 0x0004. This type is used for the SAP and RIP (Router Information Protocol) broadcasts between servers. The SAP type 0x026B is used by Time Synchronization. Time servers use SAP type 0x026B to communicate with the time providers.

WARNING

It is very important that you do not establish a Router Information Protocol filter between IntranetWare servers. Each IntranetWare server needs to be able to see every other IntranetWare server. This is especially true with IntranetWare servers that do not have any NDS replicas. Some people think that since an IntranetWare server does not have replicas that it can be filtered out. The server needs to be able to do a Service Request for type 0x0278 to find the NDS tree. In addition, the clients or workstations need type 0x0278 to boot up.

Novell Directory Services Data Files

The physical representation of the NDS tree and its objects relates to the actual NDS data files. The object and partition information are stored on the server in the data files under the SYS:_NETWARE directory, which is hidden by the operating system.

This directory is only visible using the RCONSOLE utility. After loading RCONSOLE and logging in to the appropriate server, press ALT + F1, which brings up the main menu, and then select the Scan Directory option. Figure 8.3 illustrates how to selectively scan the SYS:_NETWARE using RCONSOLE.

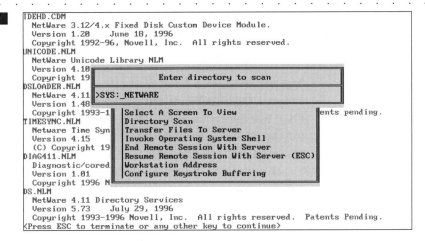

F I G U R E   8.3

Scanning the directory SYS:_NETWARE using RCONSOLE

```
IDEHD.CDM
   NetWare 3.12/4.x Fixed Disk Custom Device Module.
   Version 1.20    June 18, 1996
   Copyright 1992-96, Novell, Inc.  All rights reserved.
UNICODE.NLM
   NetWare Unicode Library NLM
   Version 4.10
   Copyright 19              Enter directory to scan
DSLOADER.NLM
   NetWare 4.11  >SYS:_NETWARE
   Version 1.48
   Copyright 1993-1    Select A Screen To View             ents pending.
TIMESYNC.NLM            Directory Scan
   Netware Time Syn     Transfer Files To Server
   Version 4.15         Invoke Operating System Shell
   (C) Copyright 19     End Remote Session With Server
DIAG411.NLM             Resume Remote Session With Server (ESC)
   Diagnostic/cored     Workstation Address
   Version 1.01         Configure Keystroke Buffering
   Copyright 1996 N
DS.NLM
   NetWare 4.11 Directory Services
   Version 5.73    July 29, 1996
   Copyright 1993-1996 Novell, Inc.  All rights reserved.  Patents Pending.
<Press ESC to terminate or any other key to continue>
```

Figure 8.4 illustrates a view of the contents of the directory SYS:_NETWARE using RCONSOLE.

There are four NDS files that have the .NDS file extension. There can be a number of stream files that are used to support login script files, print job configurations, and so on. The stream files use the 8.3 DOS file naming convention. However, they are distinguished from the others because the name consists of hexidecimal values only (0 to 9 and A to F). NDS uses the following files:

- PARTITIO.NDS

- ENTRY.NDS

▸ VALUE.NDS

▸ BLOCK.NDS

▸ Stream Files

FIGURE 8.4

*Viewing the contents of the
directory SYS:_NETWARE
using RCONSOLE*

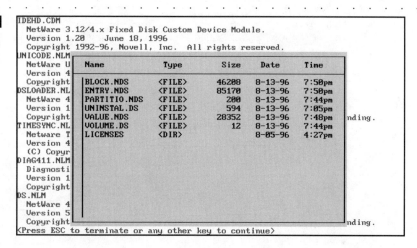

```
IDEHD.CDM
   NetWare 3.12/4.x Fixed Disk Custom Device Module.
   Version 1.20    June 18, 1996
   Copyright 1992-96, Novell, Inc.  All rights reserved.
UNICODE.NLM
   NetWare U   ┌──────────────────────────────────────────────────┐
   Version 4   │ Name          Type        Size    Date      Time   │
   Copyright   │                                                    │
DSLOADER.NL   │ BLOCK.NDS     <FILE>      46208   8-13-96   7:50pm │
   NetWare 4   │ ENTRY.NDS     <FILE>      85170   8-13-96   7:50pm │
   Version 1   │ PARTITIO.NDS  <FILE>        200   8-13-96   7:44pm │
   Copyright   │ UNINSTAL.DS   <FILE>        594   8-13-96   7:05pm │  nding.
TIMESYNC.NL   │ VALUE.NDS     <FILE>      28352   8-13-96   7:48pm │
   Netware T   │ VOLUME.DS     <FILE>         12   8-13-96   7:44pm │
   Version 4   │ LICENSES      <DIR>               8-05-96   4:27pm │
   (C) Copyr   │                                                    │
DIAG411.NLM   │                                                    │
   Diagnosti   │                                                    │
   Version 1   │                                                    │
   Copyright   │                                                    │
DS.NLM        │                                                    │
   NetWare 4   │                                                    │
   Version 5   │                                                    │
   Copyright   └──────────────────────────────────────────────────┘  nding.
<Press ESC to terminate or any other key to continue>
```

Each of the object, property, and partition information stored in NDS is held in these files. The files work together to provide the complete NDS tree information for each server. The relationship between each of the NDS data files is illustrated in Figure 8.4-A. This figure shows how the partition record points to the first object in the partition, which, in turn, points to specific property values.

The file name and its description or purpose are presented in the following sections.

THE PARTITION FILE (PARTITIO.NDS)

The partition file named PARTITIO.NDS contains a list of each of the partitions defined on the local server and within the local NDS database. The partition file holds a record for each partition. Each partition record points to the starting record within the ENTRY.NDS file for the specific objects.

F I G U R E   8.4-A

The relationship between
each of the NDS data files
is shown. Each partition
record points to the first
object in the partition,
which, in turn, points to the
specific property values.

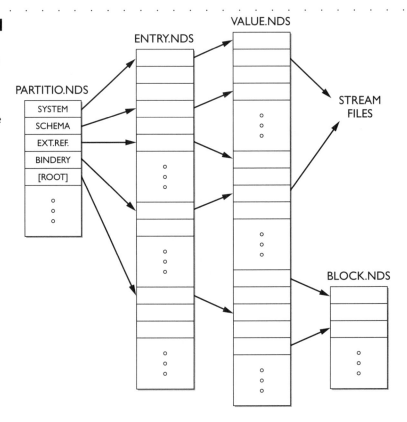

There are always at least four system partitions on each IntranetWare server.
These partitions are stored in the partition file — the System, Schema, External
Reference, and Bindery partitions.

System Partition

The first partition in the PARTITIO.NDS file is the system partition. The system
partition points or locates the Pseudo Server object as well as the NameBase version.
Data available from this partition is the server-specific information, such as the
name of the tree as well as the version of the database. Because the information in
this partition is server centric, it is not synchronized with any other IntranetWare
server.

Schema Partition

The second partition is the schema. The schema partition record is used to locate the top of the schema objects for NDS. The schema itself is the set of rules for the structure of the NDS tree and objects.

The initial installation of the server creates the base schema that ships with IntranetWare. The schema can be extended to include other custom objects and properties. In order to keep all copies of the schema on all servers throughout the tree the same, the information or objects in the schema partition are synchronized by NDS with the other IntranetWare servers.

To be more exact, this file contains the information to locate the Schema objects in the ENTRY.NDS file. There is nothing in this file specifically that is synchronized.

External Reference Partition

The third partition in the PARTITIO.NDS file is the external reference partition. This partition record is used as the partition for the external reference objects stored on the server. An external reference is created for an NDS object that is not stored locally but needs an object ID on the local server. The external reference holds the object ID for the object that is external to this server.

The information in this partition is server-centric and is not synchronized to the other IntranetWare servers. Again, to be more exact, this file contains just the information to locate the external reference objects in the ENTRY.NDS file.

The external reference partition can be used to locate the top of the NDS tree, which refers to the [ROOT] object. Note that this partition is present even if the local database contains a copy of the [ROOT] partition.

Bindery Partition

The fourth partition is the bindery partition. The bindery partition locates the bindery server SAP name and associated properties or attributes. The information in this partition is server centric and is not synchronized by NDS to the other IntranetWare servers.

The bindery partition also holds the dynamic bindery information, which contains the Service Advertising Protocol (SAP) and Routing Information Protocol (RIP) data received by the server during normal operation in the NDS tree.

The partition file contains a representation for every user-created partition on the server. These are the partitions that are created by the system administrators using the NetWare Administration utilities.

THE OBJECT FILE (ENTRY.NDS)

The ENTRY.NDS file contains the individual records of the NDS objects that are created to form the NDS tree. In addition to the NDS objects, this file contains the information for each of the schema, bindery, and external reference objects. The term "entry" is often used to refer to an NDS object. The object's name and its partition and its parent within the NDS tree are among several pieces of data recorded in an individual entry.

One of the objects is the Pseudo Server object, which stores the information about the specific server. This object is not synchronized to the other IntranetWare servers. The information held in the Pseudo Server object is as follows:

▸ The name of the NDS tree.

▸ The server object's public key, which is used for authentication.

▸ The server object's private key, which is used for authentication.

▸ The Synchronized Up To vector for the schema partition.

▸ The Remote ID list, which contains ID pairs consisting of a local ID and a remote ID. (See the "Object IDs for Servers in NDS" section later in this chapter.)

▸ The Monitored Connection, which cleans up connections that the client has terminated improperly.

THE PROPERTY OR ATTRIBUTE FILES (VALUE.NDS, BLOCK.NDS, AND STREAM FILES)

VALUE.NDS

The VALUE.NDS file contains the property or attribute records used by the objects contained within the ENTRY.NDS file. There is an entry in this file for every attribute value whether the attribute is single valued or multivalued. For example, some of the attributes for the user object in NDS are multi-value fields. If there are multiple values defined for the user, each additional value will have an entry in this file. The Access

Control List (ACL) attribute, for example, is multivalued and may have many entries or values. Each of the values will have an entry in this file. The VALUE.NDS file works in conjunction with both the BLOCK.NDS file and the stream files.

BLOCK.NDS

The BLOCK.NDS file contains records that are used by the record in the VALUE.NDS file. If the data entered into a value field of a property or attribute is large, it overflows into this file. For example, if an attribute value is large, the remaining information for that attribute is stored in the BLOCK.NDS file. Any given value record may have multiple records assigned in this file.

Stream Files

The stream files are individual files that exist in the SYS:_NETWARE directory. These files contain the value information for attributes that are free form and of variable length. For example, the login scripts, printer control files, and print job definitions attribute are stored in stream files.

THE NDS .TMP DATA FILES

There is a complete set of temporary NDS data files that are created when the DSREPAIR utility is executed. There are no .TMP files created for any of the Stream files. The temporary NDS data files are created by DSREPAIR when it is running and are used to perform all the changes against the partitions. At the end of the repair these temporary (.TMP) files become the permanent .NDS files, unless you choose not to accept the repairs that were made. The current NDS data files become .OLD files.

NOTE

DSREPAIR creates the .OLD set of NDS data files. These .OLD files will be overwritten by DSREPAIR only after 72 hours. This feature helps the Novell Technical Support organization react to customer problems that may be recently caused.

The .OLD files are stored on the server in the same place where the regular NDS data files are stored under the SYS:_NETWARE directory. These files are visible by using the RCONSOLE utility and selecting the Scan Directory option from the main menu. Figure 8.5 shows the .OLD files created by DSREPAIR.

FIGURE 8.5

Shows the .OLD
files created by the
DSREPAIR utility in the
SYS:_NETWARE directory

```
NOR-SRV1:

   Name           Type       Size      Date     Time

   BLOCK.NDS      <FILE>     400000    1-16-96   8:42pm
   BLOCK.OLD      <FILE>     400000    1-16-96   8:42pm
   ENTRY.NDS      <FILE>     975280    1-16-96   8:42pm
   ENTRY.OLD      <FILE>     975280    1-16-96   8:42pm
   MLS.000        <FILE>        320    1-15-96   6:21pm
   PARTITIO.NDS   <FILE>        400    1-16-96   8:42pm
   PARTITIO.OLD   <FILE>        400    1-16-96   8:42pm
   VALLICEN.DAT   <FILE>         72    1-16-96   6:21pm
   VALUE.NDS      <FILE>     384768    1-16-96   8:42pm
   VALUE.OLD      <FILE>     384768    1-16-96   8:42pm
```

Timestamps

Since the NDS hierarchy can be distributed or replicated across the servers in the network, the information in each of the replicas can change without the other replicas immediately knowing about it. This form of synchronization is known as being loosely consistent.

The sequence of events that occurs within NDS can become confused unless a mechanism is provided to ensure that the events are updated to each replica as they really happen. The term "event" is used to refer to a creation or modification to the NDS objects or properties.

The mechanism that ensures that the events are changed in sequence are the timestamps for each of the objects and properties. When an event occurs, NDS issues a new timestamp and associates the timestamp with the event. Synchronization between replicas of a partition uses the timestamps associated with every NDS object and property or attribute to indicate the time the modification was made. For example, if the same object (same property) is modified by two different administrators at approximately the same time, both updates may not take place because the last timestamp wins the update.

The purpose of the timestamp in NDS is to ensure that the information stored in NDS will converge across all IntranetWare servers over time.

There is a timestamp for each object when it is created or modified called the object creation timestamp and the last modification timestamp. There is also a timestamp issued for every change to a property value.

The timestamp value for the objects and properties is unique within an NDS partition because the timestamps are assigned by the replica where the objects exist. This provides an ordering of the events that occur across all the servers holding replicas of a partition. Figure 8.6 illustrates the timestamp structure, which has three parts or fields. Each of the fields for the timestamp value is described below.

FIGURE 8.6

The structure for a
timestamp attribute

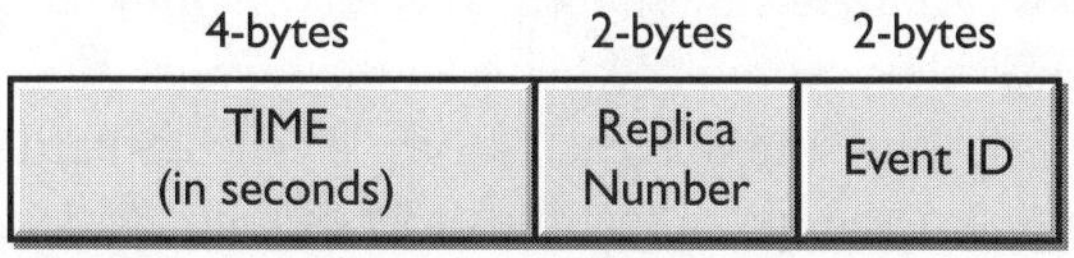

▶ Seconds — This is a 4-byte value that stores UTC time in whole seconds since midnight January 1, 1970. The whole seconds represent the actual time that the event (creation or modification) took place.

▶ Replica Number — This is a 2-byte field that stores the replica number where the event occurred and where the timestamp was issued. Every replica of a partition is assigned a unique number when it is created. The master replica is responsible for assigning a number to the new replica. The replica number ensures a unique timestamp within a partition.

▶ Event ID — This is a 2-byte field that stores the number of events that occurred during a second. Because computers are so fast, many events can occur within any one second. The event ID permits a timestamp to be issued for events that occur in one second. The event ID is a sequence number that starts at 0 and can increment to 64K. The event ID is reset every second.

The timestamp is a critical component in the replica synchronization process. When NDS updates a replica, it requests the timestamps from that replica to identify the data. The timestamp provides a unique value for the object and properties that identify the time and place of the event's origin. If the same object or property is updated on different replicas (or servers) at exactly the same second and event ID,

the replica number between the servers will be different. NDS will make the updates using the greater or latest timestamp. When compared, timestamps are treated as 32-bit, 16-bit, and 16-bit unsigned, with seconds as the most significant.

Whenever a client or workstation deletes an object or attribute from a replica on a server, the server does not immediately purge it from its local database. Instead, it issues a timestamp for the object or attribute and marks the object or attribute value as "not present" or deleted. After the replica synchronization process propagates the change to all other replicas, the Janitor process purges the object or attribute (see the "Obituaries" section later in this chapter).

To support accurate timestamps, the servers must maintain accurate time and that time must be synchronized between the servers. Time synchronization provides the mechanism to ensure that each server is synchronized to the network time. You want accurate timestamps so that the order of modification is accurate, which means that the last modification timestamp is accepted.

NDS Structures for Objects and Properties

The NDS tree hierarchy is composed of NDS objects and properties. The objects and properties are stored as records in the NDS data files. The pieces of the data stored for each object are shown in Figure 8.7. The description for each of the fields is shown below.

F I G U R E   8.7

The NDS object

Object Class	Object Name	Creation Timestamp	Last Modification Timestamp	Object ID	Parent ID	Flags

▸ Object Class — The object class is the base object class as defined in the schema for the object. An object is defined by a particular object type.

▸ Object Name — The object name is the relative distinguished name of the object.

▸ Creation Timestamp — The creation timestamp is issued to the object when it is created.

▸ Last Modification Timestamp — The last modification timestamp holds the timestamp of the last change received by this replica made to the object whether it was the object itself or its associated properties.

▸ Object ID — The object ID is a unique ID given to the object by the server where the replica is held.

▸ Parent ID — The object ID of the parent container object to this object.

▸ Flags — The flags are: present, not present, alias, partition root, created by reference, and so on.

NOTE **Sometimes the data contained in the object is called non-attribute object information because the information is stored with the object but not as attributes or properties.**

The property or attribute is shown in Figure 8.8. The description for each of the pieces of data defined for the attribute is given below.

The properties or attributes of the object

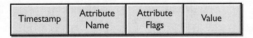

▸ Timestamp — The timestamp holds the timestamp of the creation time for the attribute.

▸ Attribute Name — The attribute name specifies the name of the attribute. The syntax or data type can be determined using the attribute name.

▸ Attribute Flags — The attribute flags control the states of the attribute.

▸ Value — The value is the actual information or data stored.

OBJECT'S UNIQUE NAME (TUNED NAME)

An object's tuned name is the distinguished name of the object plus the creation timestamp for each of the parent container objects. The tune name provides the

NDS system with an absolutely unique ID structure for each of the objects in NDS. To illustrate the concept of a tuned name, we will use the following example. A system administrator decides to rename the user SIRGALAHAD to user GALAHAD. He then decides to create a new user called SIRGALAHAD. In order to guarantee that Directory Services knows that these two are separate objects, the concept of a tuned name is introduced. The tuned name is really a global unique name for the object.

A tuned named for an object is the distinguished name of the object with a little extra information. Each segment of the distinguished name is made up of a combination of the relative distinguished name bound with its creation timestamp. Remember that a distinguished name includes each parent object all the way back to and including [ROOT]. This means that the tuned name includes not only each relative distinguished name but also the creation timestamp for each to build the tuned name of the object.

As an example, the tuned name for the user SIRGALAHAD.CHARITY. CAMELOT.ACME would be:

SIRGALAHAD (Creation Timestamp)
CHARITY (Creation Timestamp)
CAMELOT (Creation Timestamp)
ACME (Creation Timestamp)
[ROOT] (Creation Timestamp)

Including each creation timestamp for each object in the distinguished name removes any ambiguity about the object being identified. In the example, where SIRGALAHAD was created a second time under the same container, the first SIRGALAHAD differs from the second one created because of a difference in the creation timestamp.

The tuned name concept is used internally by NDS. You cannot see the tuned name for an object using the current NetWare Administration utilities.

Although objects have a unique object name or tuned name, you cannot have two objects with the same distinguished name. This would happen if two objects with the same relative distinguished name are in the same container. If two objects with the same name are synchronized into the same container but with different creation timestamps, NDS must rename one of the objects. The naming convention used by Directory Services to rename one of the objects is number_number. For example, a duplicate object is renamed to 1_2.

The rename problem has been noticed mostly in networks and servers that are migrating from NetWare 4.02 to IntranetWare. The reason is that NetWare 4.02 does not support tuned names and IntranetWare requires them. In order to cure the problems experienced with renamed objects, you must run DSREPAIR, option number 8 on the NetWare 4.02 server before upgrading. Make sure that the DSREPAIR utility you are running is the updated version for NetWare 4.02. This updated DSREPAIR utility is available on NetWire or the Novell Web Server.

OBJECT REFERENCE

The values of some attributes in the Directory are other NDS objects. To truly understand objects in NDS, you need to understand how the objects are referenced. When an NDS object stores another object as an attribute value it is said to have an object reference.

For example, a group object has a membership attribute, and the values of this attribute are NDS objects. A printer object has an attribute whose values are other objects. The Access Control List is an example of an attribute for an object that stores other object IDs. The rights assignments for the NDS system are held in the Access Control List.

An object can also have its own object as one of its own attribute values. For example, a user object receives the read/write attribute for its own login script and print job configuration. The object becomes a trustee of itself.

To describe object references we will use an example in the ACME tree. Consider Figure 8.9, where the user AEINSTEIN.LABS.NORAD.ACME is made security equivalent to the user KINGARTHUR.OPS.CAMELOT.ACME. The security equivalence attribute for AEINSTEIN has the value of the user to which he is security equivalent. In this case there is a value for KINGARTHUR.OPS.CAMELOT.ACME.

The object AEINSTEIN.LABS.NORAD.ACME is said to have an object reference to the object KINGARTHUR.OPS.CAMLEOT.ACME. Internally, NDS stores the security equivalent attribute value as an object ID for the user KINGARTHUR. The client sees the value of the attribute as the distinguished name of the object.

There are a number of properties or attributes defined in the schema that can contain object references. Some of these attributes are security equivalences, group membership, member, operator, and replica.

FIGURE 8.9

The user AEINSTEIN.LABS. NORAD.ACME is made security equivalent to the user KINGARTHUR.OPS. CAMELOT.ACME in the ACME tree.

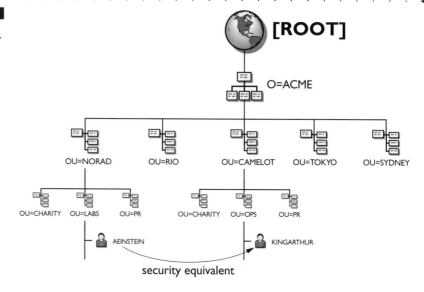

OBJECT ID

One of the most important fields contained in the object structure is the object ID. Most of the operations that can be performed on the NDS objects require that the requesting client have or obtain the object ID. The object ID is a 4-byte (32 bit) value that serves as a handle to the objects themselves.

Each object in a replica stored on an IntranetWare server has a corresponding object ID on that server. The object ID is assigned on a per-server basis, which means that it is not a global ID and is valid only on the server that assigned it. Since the object ID is server centric it is not replicated, except for the backlinks and replica pointer table.

Each server that stores a copy of the object will probably have a different object ID for the same NDS object. Figure 8.10 illustrates how each IntranetWare server has a different object ID for the user object stored in different replicas. In this example, KINGARTHUR in the ACME tree has different object IDs on servers CAM-SRV1 and OPS-SRV1.

F I G U R E   8.10

Servers CAM-SRV1 and OPS-SRV1 have a different object ID for the user KINGARTHUR, which is stored in different replicas of the same partition.

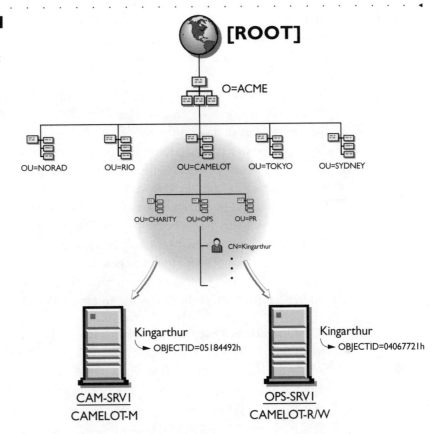

Obtaining the Object ID

The object ID is used in most of the internal operations performed by Directory Services. The client must first obtain the object ID for the object before it can execute the operation. There are several methods for the client to obtain the object ID.

The first method is known as name resolution where the client starts with the distinguished name of the object and makes the request to Directory Services to return the location and ID for the object. The name resolution method is used when logging in to the network, capturing to printers, mapping network drives, and using the NetWare utilities such as NWADMIN or NETADMIN to browse the tree. Each of the network resources is found using the name resolution process. The name resolution process is described in detail in Chapter 9.

The second method for obtaining the object ID is for the client to start with the current context and list the objects available in that container. Using the utilities provided, the client can then select any object and receive information that is of interest. This procedure is often called "yellow pages" or "white pages" in terms of the user interface and process.

This method of obtaining the object ID is used mainly within the NWADMIN, NAL, NETADMIN, or NWUSER utilities. The user navigates through the tree listing all the objects. Depending on the utility, you can set a filter to weed out unwanted object types. Filters are available by name patterns, NDS object classes, or modification timestamps. An example of how to navigate through the NDS tree is shown in Chapter 2 under the "Network Administration (NWADMIN.EXE)" section.

The third method for obtaining the object ID is for the client to execute a search. The search capabilities are the most powerful because you can select the objects by attribute values. The objects that match the value of the search criteria are returned. The search can be applied to the current container in the tree or it can extend to the entire subtree. An example of how to perform a search against the NDS tree is shown in Chapter 2 under the "Network Administration (NWADMIN.EXE)" section.

NDS Operations That Use the Object ID

Once the client has obtained a valid object ID, it operates on an object by sending requests to the NDS server where the object ID was obtained. Remember, the object ID is valid only on a per-server basis. The operating system also requires the object ID when performing operations. The file system, connection table, and other systems use this ID to identify the appropriate NDS object.

The most basic service provided is to read the detailed information about the object itself using the Read operation. The result of this operation is shown in NWADMIN when the Detail dialog box is opened for the object KINGARTHUR. See Figure 8.11.

Other operations are Add, Delete, Modify, Get Effective Rights, Compare, and a lot more. Each operation that can be performed against an NDS object is self-explanatory.

Object IDs for Servers in NDS

The object ID for the NetWare server objects is stored in pairs consisting of a local server ID and a remote server ID. The server ID pairs are used as a shortcut for the server-to-server authentication that supports NDS operations such as replica synchronization. An authenticating object ID for the server object is required and is used in the connection table of the server. Thus, a server stores an object ID for all the other IntranetWare servers that the local server has authenticated to.

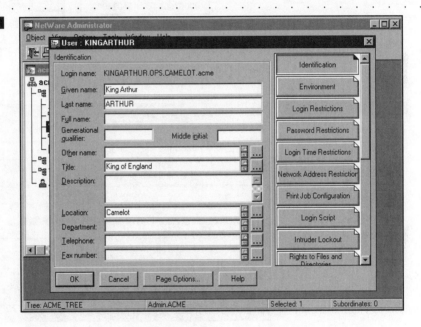

▶ The local server ID is the local ID held for the remote server.

▶ The remote server ID is the local server's ID on the specific remote server.

For example, the server ID pairs that are held by each of the servers CAM-SRV1 and NOR-SRV1 are shown in Figure 8.12.

The server ID pairs are also shown on a server basis in DSREPAIR under the Advanced Menu Option. Figure 8.13 illustrates the server ID pairs stored in NOR-SRV1.

FIGURE 8.12

The server ID pairs are held by each of the servers CAM-SRV1 and NOR-SRV1 in the ACME tree.

SERVER IDs

LOCAL ID	REMOTE ID
01023000	89007601

CAM-SRV1

LOCAL ID	REMOTE ID
89007601	01023000

NOR-SRV1

FIGURE 8.13

The server ID pairs are held by the server NOR-SRV1 as shown in the DSREPAIR utility.

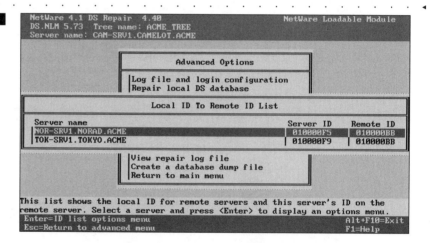

Object IDs Used as File System Trustees

In order to maintain backward compatibility, the operating system uses the object ID rather than the object name to assign trustees for file system rights. The trustees of the file system are not stored in NDS; instead the trustees are stored in the same place as they are in NetWare 3, which is in the Directory Entry Table (DET). The Directory Entry Table is part of the file system. Figure 8.14 illustrates how the assignments for the trustees of the file system rights are made using the object ID. In this example, the user KINGARTHUR is assigned Read and File Scan rights to the SYS:APPS directory on the server CAM-SRV1.

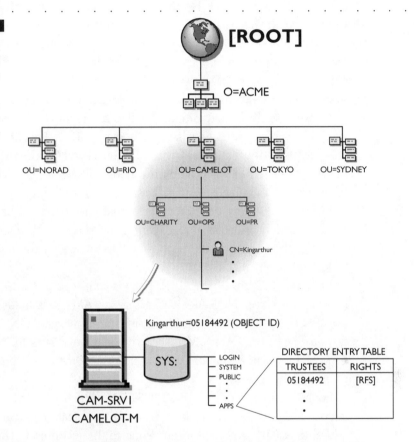

F I G U R E   8.14

The assignments for the trustees of the file system rights are made using the object ID. KINGARTHUR is assigned Read and File Scan rights to the SYS:APPS directory on the server CAM-SRVI.

External References and Backlinks

The object ID discussed in the previous section is valid on the server as long as the NDS object is stored in the replica on the server. Sometimes the server holds a temporary object ID for objects that are not stored locally. The temporary object ID is called an external reference. These external references work together with backlinks to provide the distribution of the Directory Service.

An external reference is created to reference an object that is not physically located on the local server. When an IntranetWare server needs to reference information about an NDS object that is not held in any local replicas, that server creates an external reference, which provides a local object ID for the real NDS object on the other servers.

In order for NDS to keep track of all the external references created, each object can have a multi-valued property called a backlink. The backlink points to the external reference with which it is associated. Each backlink value is periodically checked to verify that the associated external reference still exists. The backlink property of the object contains the name of the server that holds the external reference and the object ID that is assigned to the object on that server.

In order to understand how the external references and backlinks are used, you need to understand the object IDs on the server and when they are used. For example, the server needs the object IDs for use in the file system, connection table, and other systems.

In Figure 8.15, the object AEINSTEIN is contained in the NORAD partition, which is stored on server NOR-SRV1. The server CAM-SRV1 holds only a replica of the CAMELOT partition. Let's consider a situation in which AEINSTEIN maps a network drive to the server CAM-SRV1. The drive mapping forces the user to authenticate to CAM-SRV1 where a local object ID is needed by the connection table for assignment of file system rights.

Because the user object for AEINSTEIN, which mapped a drive to CAM-SRV1, is not physically stored on the server, it must create an external reference because a local object ID is needed to authenticate the real object. The real object is in the NORAD partition on the NOR-SRV1 server. The external reference created on the CAM-SRV1 server stores the object ID that is needed on the local server. In this case the object ID is 03 01 89 00 hex. Likewise, a backlink is created on the real object to track the external reference. Figure 8.16 illustrates the relationship of creating an external reference and backlink for the user object AEINSTEIN in the ACME tree.

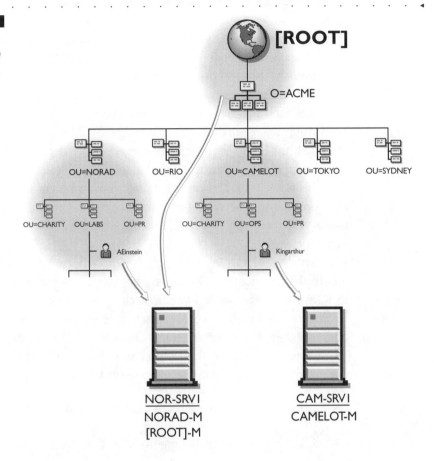

FIGURE 8.15

The NORAD partition is stored on NOR-SRV1, and the CAMELOT partition is stored on CAM-SRV1.

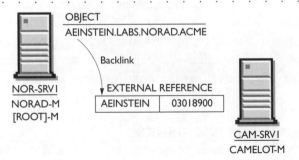

FIGURE 8.16

Example of an external reference and backlink for the user object AEINSTEIN

PURPOSE OF EXTERNAL REFERENCES

The purpose of the external reference is to be able to reference an object in Directory Services without requiring that object to be physically duplicated on the local server. The external reference architecture enables NDS to be distributed across the servers in the network while still being able to reference its objects. NDS can reference all the objects in Directory Services without having to store a complete replica of each partition on each IntranetWare server.

External references provide two major functions for NDS. First, they provide NDS with the capability to reference objects that are not local to the server. Second, they provide the complete NDS skeleton of the tree structure and maintain an object's lineage "up" the tree. The external references are stored on a per-server basis on each IntranetWare server in the external reference partition. Since the data in this partition is server centric, it is not synchronized to other IntranetWare servers in the network.

External references improve system performance by caching frequently accessed information. Currently, NDS caches only an object's public key. Since authentication requires the client's public key, it is cached on the external reference so it does not have to be read each time. The external references that are created for the server objects also store the server's status and DS revision or build number.

An external reference is an object stored in the ENTRY.NDS file as part of the external reference partition. The components for an external reference are given below:

▸ Object ID — A unique object ID issued by the local server for the real object

▸ Relative Distinguished Name — The real object's relative distinguished name

Whenever a server creates an external reference for an object in the NDS tree, it also creates external references for each of the parent containers, if needed. These are the parent containers that are in the distinguished name of the object all the way back to and including [ROOT]. An external reference for the parent container is needed only when it has not been previously created.

PURPOSE OF BACKLINKS

The backlink property of an object is used by the NDS system to enable easy maintenance of the external references of that object. When an object is renamed, moved, or deleted from the system, the backlinks facilitate the external references to that object to be modified to reflect the changes. This process provides data integrity for Directory Services. For example, when an object is renamed, moved, or deleted, the backlinks make it possible to change all external references to the object.

The format for the backlink property or attribute is defined below.

▸ Object ID — The object ID value that is issued for the external reference on the remote server. This value enables NDS to find the associated external reference or object ID on the remote server.

▸ Distinguished Name — The remote server object's distinguished name in the NDS tree. This value identifies the server holding the external reference.

CREATING EXTERNAL REFERENCES AND BACKLINKS

The external references are created for a number of reasons. For example, there are times when a server requires information about an object that is not stored locally. Having this information helps the local server maintain an object ID for an NDS object. NDS creates the object ID for each object. The external reference object supplies an object ID for the server where the real object is not stored. An example is a server that needs to grant file system rights to an object that is not local. The server requires the object ID to make the trustee assignment.

The corresponding property to the external reference is the backlink. A new value for the backlink property is written on the object each time an external reference is created. The backlink property value is used by Directory Services to keep track of where the external references of an object are located.

External references are created under several situations on an IntranetWare server. The situations requiring an external reference are listed below. For these situations, it is assumed that the object for which the external reference is created is not stored locally.

▸ Complete the distinguished names

▸ Authentication

▸ File system access control

▸ Attribute values that are NDS objects

▸ Replica removal

Complete the Distinguished Names

The name field for the object stores only the relative distinguished name of the object. Each object also requires the object ID for the parent objects. Therefore, external references are created on the server to complete the skeleton up the NDS tree for each of the objects that it holds in its partitions. There is one external reference created for each relative distinguished name in the complete name. This means that there are external references created for each of the parent container objects that are not physically stored on the server.

For example, the server CAM-SRV1 in the ACME tree holds only the CAMELOT partition, which defines each of the objects for that subtree. In order to complete the distinguished naming for the objects in the partition, the O=ACME and [ROOT] objects must have external references. The real objects for each external reference are stored in the [ROOT] partition on the server NOR-SRV1. Figure 8.17 illustrates this example.

For each replica a server holds, it must know the distinguished name of the partition, which is defined by the partition [ROOT] object. This means that external references will be created to complete each relative distinguished name of the partition all the way back to the [ROOT] object.

Likewise, an external reference object cannot exist without the server knowing about every object in its distinguished name. The external reference objects themselves are stored as relative distinguished names, not distinguished names. This is true for every NDS object, not just the external references. When a server creates an external reference, it will most likely create external references to complete the distinguished name of the object contained in the external reference. If an external reference for the parent containers of the object has been previously created, another reference is not needed.

For example, in Figure 8.18, server RIO-SRV1 does not hold any NDS replicas in the ACME tree. The user object KINGARTHUR.OPS.CAMELOT.ACME is created as an external reference on the server RIO-SRV1. The server would need to create additional external references for each of the objects in the distinguished name of KINGARTHUR, including the [ROOT] object. [ROOT] is implied in every object name.

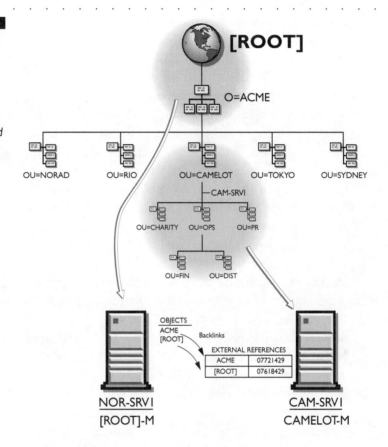

FIGURE 8.17

External references are created on server CAM-SRV1 for the O=ACME and [ROOT] objects. The external references are needed to complete the distinguished names of the objects in the partition CAMELOT.

[ROOT]

O=ACME

OU=NORAD   OU=RIO   OU=CAMELOT   OU=TOKYO   OU=SYDNEY

—CAM-SRV1

OU=CHARITY   OU=OPS   OU=PR

OU=FIN   OU=DIST

OBJECTS
ACME
[ROOT]   Backlinks

EXTERNAL REFERENCES

ACME	07721429
[ROOT]	07618429

NOR-SRV1   CAM-SRV1

[ROOT]-M   CAMELOT-M

FIGURE 8.18

Example of external reference created for the user KINGARTHUR on RIO-SRV1, as well as other external references created to complete the distinguished name for KINGARTHUR

EXTERNAL REFERENCES

KINGARTHUR	0615360E
OPS	02665801
CAMELOT	01008015
ACME	05225983
[ROOT]	18883608

RIO-SRV1

NO NDS REPLICAS

Authentication

NDS objects (typically users and NDS servers) can authenticate themselves to an IntranetWare server for access to specific network resources even though the objects are not stored locally on that server. The authentication mechanism needs to have an object ID defined for each NDS object that authenticates as well as an object ID for each security equivalence of the object.

The object ID is used in the server connection table to calculate the security privileges for the connection. One of the steps in the authentication process is the calculation of the object's security equivalencies. The results of the calculation are stored in the object's entry of the connection table of the server. All security equivalencies of the object that authenticate are included in the connection table. These security equivalencies are stored in the server's connection table as object IDs and not names.

For those objects that are not stored locally, an external reference is created that supplies an object ID to the connection table. This is true even for the other IntranetWare servers that attach and authenticate for purposes of synchronizing replicas.

An example of this situation is illustrated in Figure 8.19. (This is the same example that was illustrated in Figures 8.15 and 8.16.) The user object AEINSTEIN maps a network drive to the server CAM-SRV1. Since AEINSTEIN is not physically stored on the server, it must create an external reference for the real object. The real object is in the NORAD partition on the NOR-SRV1 server. The external reference created on the CAM-SRV1 server stores the object ID that is needed on the local server. Likewise, the real object stores a backlink property value to track the external reference.

The server CAM-SRV1 will create an external reference for each of the other objects in the distinguished name of AEINSTEIN. These objects are OU=LABS, OU=NORAD, O=ACME, and [ROOT] as shown in Figure 8.20. The objects O=ACME and [ROOT] should already exist on the server CAM-SRV1 as external references because they are needed to complete the distinguished name of the objects in the CAMELOT partition.

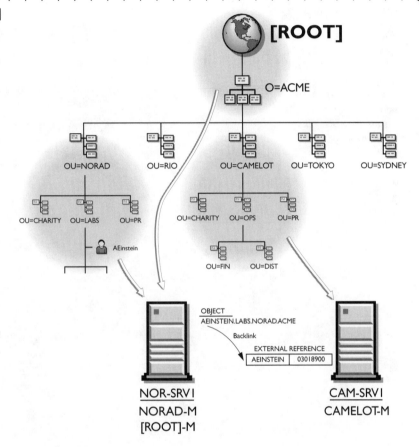

F I G U R E   8.19

*Example of an external
reference and backlink for
the user object AEINSTEIN
in the ACME tree*

File System Access Control

An external reference object can be created to supply an object ID for the file system rights assignments. The assignment of file system rights is maintained by IntranetWare using the object IDs. The object ID becomes the trustee for the files and directories rights assignments. The rights assignments for the file and directory system are stored in the Directory Entry Table. This control list stores the object ID for the user that has the rights.

*Example of an external
reference and backlink for
the objects OU=LABS,
OU=NORAD, O=ACME,
and [ROOT] which are
part of the distinguished
name for AEINSTEIN
in the ACME tree*

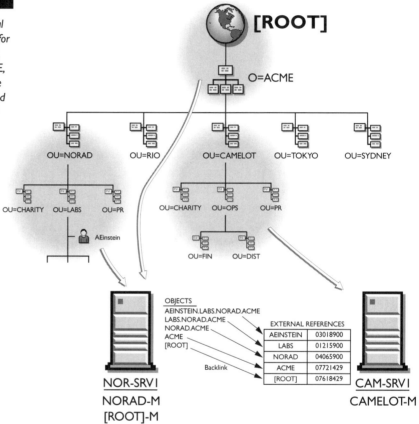

If the object does not exist on the server, an external reference is created, which supplies the file system's directory entry table with an object ID. For example, in Figure 8.21 a user KINGARTHUR can have file and directory rights to NOR-SRV1, even though the KINGARTHUR user object is not stored in a replica on the NOR-SRV1 server. In this example, KINGARTHUR is given Read and File Scan rights to the SYS:APPS directory on NOR-SRV1. The server requires an object ID for the user KINGARTHUR to place in the trustee list for the directory. An external reference is created for KINGARTHUR, but the real user object is stored on CAM-SRV1.

External references are also created for OU=OPS, which is the parent object in the distinguished name of the user. The OU=CAMELOT object already exists on the server NOR-SRV1 in a subordinate reference replica for the CAMELOT partition. The objects O=ACME and [ROOT] are not created as external references because they are real objects on the server NOR-SRV1 in the [ROOT] partition.

The user KINGARTHUR is granted Read and File Scan rights to the directory SYS:APPS on the server NOR-SRV1. An external reference is created for the user and its parents.

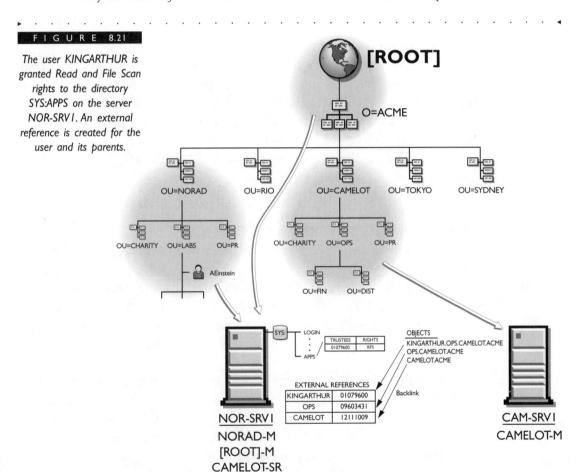

Attribute Values That Are NDS Objects

The values of some attributes are other NDS objects. These values are known as object references. For example, a group object has a membership attribute and the value of this attribute is an NDS object. A printer object has an attribute whose values are objects. The Access Control List (ACL) is an example of an attribute for an object that stores other object IDs.

All object references are stored in the Directory as object IDs. Thus, if an attribute references an object that is not stored locally, the server creates an external reference for that object. This means that external references are created on a server if the object is placed as the value of an attribute or property of another object.

Replica Removal

When you remove a replica of a partition from a server, the NDS system will create an external reference for each object in the partition. Although each of the objects in the removed replica changes into external references, NDS marks them with a zero modification timestamp. This means that the NDS system should check the external references at the next backlink interval to see if they are in use by the system. If the external references are not used, the system will clear them out as soon as possible.

MAINTAINING EXTERNAL REFERENCES

External references require updating when the real object is deleted, moved, renamed, or the security equivalence has changed. After successfully synchronizing all the replicas of a partition, Directory Services checks any object that has been renamed, moved, or deleted. The operation that deletes, moves, and renames an object adds obituary attribute values to that object. To maintain consistency between the external references and backlinks, there are backlink obituaries for every backlink attribute of the object.

At the end of a successful replica synchronization of a partition, a portion of the janitor process (known as the purger) processes the obituaries on the object in the partition. If NDS finds any backlink obituaries, it notifies the server that contains the object's external reference to update that external reference appropriately. The janitor process is discussed in more detail in Chapter 9.

Periodically, NDS checks the external references to see if the original object still exists. The NDS feature that checks the validity of the external references and backlinks is called the Backlink Process. The Backlink Process is discussed in more detail in Chapter 9.

DELETING EXTERNAL REFERENCES

On each server Directory Services deletes external references if they have not been accessed for a period of time. The types of external references that will be deleted after a period of time are the ones created for temporary use. For example, the external references created to support authentication should be removed by the NDS system after a period of time.

External references that are used as attribute values of an NDS object or external references that are used by the server are not deleted even if they are not accessed for a period of time. The period of time is determined by a SET parameter called External Reference Life Span.

The system administrator can use this Directory Services SET parameter to set the number of hours after which NDS deletes external references that have not been used. The Directory Services SET parameter that controls the life span for external references is set as follows:

```
SET NDS EXTERNAL REFERENCE LIFE SPAN = 192
```

The value of this SET parameter is set in hours. The default value of 192 (hours) or 8 days works well and we recommend that you leave it. The range for this SET parameter is 1 to 384 (in hours). The default is set to 8 days so that this operation does not occur exactly in one-week intervals.

When an external reference is accessed, it updates the modification timestamp to the current time. The process that removes the external references builds a list of unused external references by checking the modification timestamp of each external reference compared with the life span interval. Using the default value for this SET parameter, the process will remove the external reference after the eight days. The process that checks each server to see if the external references are still in use is called the Backlink Process or backlinker.

Each time the Backlink Process runs, the server checks each object ID associated with an external reference to make sure it is still in use. This means that the directory entry tables for the file system need to be scanned, which can be intensive. The janitor process then purges the deleted external references. For more information about the backlink and janitor processes, refer to Chapter 9.

When Directory Services removes an external reference, the server holding the external reference requests that the server holding the original object or real object delete the backlink attribute value associated with the external reference.

Obituaries

Directory Services uses a special attribute of an NDS object called an Obituary to track renames, moves, and deletions of both objects and external references. Since NDS is loosely consistent, each IntranetWare server needs a mechanism to keep track or record the instances of the NDS objects. The purpose for the obituaries is to maintain consistency in the instances of objects across all the different replicas of a partition until synchronization is completed.

The obituaries help maintain consistency because each server cannot receive all updates simultaneously. This means that the servers may not hold the same information at a given time. For this reason, each server holds on to the latest set of information until all the other servers holding replicas for a partition receive the updates. Directory Services uses obituaries to coordinate or keep track of instances of objects.

When an object is moved, renamed, or deleted in Directory Services, the system adds a new obituary attribute value to the object. There is one obituary for each move, rename, and delete operation. There is an obituary for each backlink attribute and one for each server in the replica pointer table (replica ring). See the "Obituary Types" section later in this chapter.

Since obituaries are attributes values of the NDS object, they are synchronized to the other servers using the same mechanism that all replica synchronization uses. This means that obituaries for the objects are synchronized across replicas of a partition.

For example, when an object is deleted, Directory Services marks the object as not present, which becomes not visible to the clients. However, the object is retained in the name service until the removal is propagated to the other servers. The attribute values are removed, and the proper obituaries are established to indicate that the object is no longer logically present. In this case the obituary is of type "Dead."

OBITUARY DATA

The obituary attribute for an NDS object can be a multi-valued attribute. The pieces of data for the obituary property or attribute are defined as a String. The obituary property or attribute is made up of the following pieces of data:

▶ Obituary Type — Indicates the operation that has taken place on the object.

▶ Obituary State — An obituary goes through several different states as it is processed. The Obituary State records the progress.

▶ Old Creation Timestamp — See creation time of the original object.

Obituary Types

The type of obituary determines the operation being performed. Directory Services classifies the obituary type internally into two categories: primary and secondary. Typically, when an object is changed, the primary obituary is the mechanism that conveys the change to servers holding replicas of the object. The primary obituaries are used for the types restored, dead, and moved.

Secondary obituaries convey the change to servers holding external references of the changed object. For any given primary obituary there can be several secondary obituaries.

The backlink obituary is the only secondary obituary currently in the system. It keeps external references synchronized with the real objects. All other obituaries are primary obituaries that keep track of changes made to the NDS object themselves.

The specific obituary types are defined below.

▶ 0 — Restored

▶ 1 — Dead

▶ 2 — Moved

▶ 3 — Inhibit Move

▶ 4 — Old Relative Distinguished Name

▶ 5 — New Relative Distinguished Name

▶ 6 — Backlink

- ▸ 7 — Tree Old Relative Distinguished Name

- ▸ 8 — Tree New Relative Distinguished Name

- ▸ 9 — Purge All

- ▸ 10 — Move Subtree

Obituary States

An obituary goes through several states. The sequence of states progresses as the servers process the operation.

The specific obituary states are listed below:

- ▸ 0 — Initial

- ▸ 1 — Notified

- ▸ 2 — OK to Purge

- ▸ 4 — Purgeable

Figure 8.22 shows how obituaries are used when an object is renamed. The servers CAM-SRV1 and OPS-SRV1 hold a replica of the CAMELOT partition. The user object SIRGALAHAD in the CAMLEOT partition is renamed to GALAHAD.

The rename operation for SIRGALAHAD to GALAHAD is started on the server CAM-SRV1, which establishes a New RDN obituary type for it. This obituary ensures that all servers can access the object using SIRGALAHAD, even if they have not been notified of the name change. The server then creates object GALAHAD and establishes an Old RDN obituary pointing back to the original object. Using this method, the object can be accessed either by the name SIRGALAHAD or GALAHAD while the rename is completed.

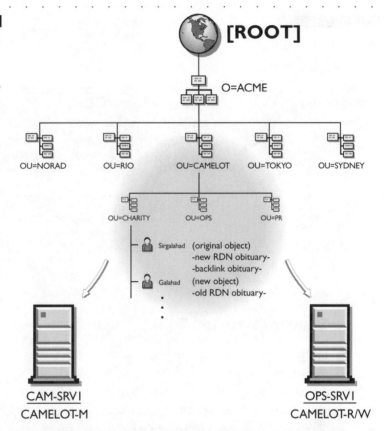

FIGURE 8.22

The user object
SIRGALAHAD in the
CAMELOT partition is
renamed to GALAHAD. The
appropriate obituaries are
established for each object.

[ROOT]

O=ACME

OU=NORAD   OU=RIO   OU=CAMELOT   OU=TOKYO   OU=SYDNEY

OU=CHARITY   OU=OPS   OU=PR

Sirgalahad (original object)
-new RDN obituary-
-backlink obituary-

Galahad (new object)
-old RDN obituary-

CAM-SRV1
CAMELOT-M

OPS-SRV1
CAMELOT-R/W

In order to complete the rename, each server holding a copy of the SIRGALAHAD object needs to be informed. In this case, the server OPS-SRV1 will receive the rename update via normal replica synchronization. After all replicas have been completely synchronized, the servers can delete the SIRGALAHAD object and remove the obituaries. The rename is completed as shown is Figure 8.23.

The process is a little more complicated than shown because the obituaries each go through all the state changes before the operation is completed. A more detailed discussion about the operation and how the obituaries function is included in Chapter 9.

The object SIRGALAHAD has completed the rename to GALAHAD, and the obituaries have been removed.

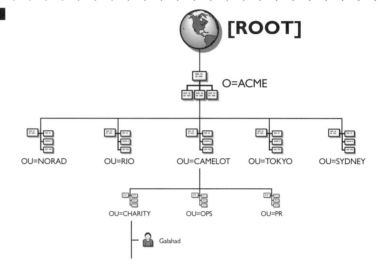

Server Partition Table

Each IntranetWare server maintains a list of the replicas that are physically stored in the server. This list is called the server partition table. You can think of the server partition table as the list of partitions that are stored on the server. The server partition table can be viewed using either NWADMIN under the NDS Manager, or in DSREPAIR under the Advanced Options menu and Replica and Partition Operations. Figure 8.24 shows the server partition table on the server NOR-SRV1 as shown from the NDS Manager utility. The server NOR-SRV1 holds a replica of the partitions NORAD and [ROOT].

The records for the server partition table are stored in the NDS data file called PARTITIO.NDS. The data included for the server partition table are shown below. This information is stored for each replica of a partition located on the server.

▸ Partition Name — The distinguished name of the top-most object in the partition, which is called the partition root object

▸ Replica Type — Master, read/write, read only, and subordinate reference

▸ Replica State — The current state of the replica

▸ Replica Timestamp — The next timestamp issued for the replica, including the timestamps that are issued for any modification on the replica

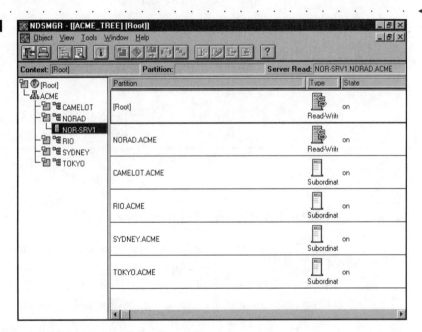

FIGURE   8.24

Server partition table on the server NOR-SRV1 as shown from the NDS Manager utility. The server NOR-SRV1 holds a replica of the partitions NORAD and [ROOT]. It also holds the subordinate reference for CAMELOT, RIO, SYDNEY, and TOKYO partitions.

REPLICA STATES

The replica state field contains the current state of the replica. This field is used as an attribute that is stored by each replica as defined in Table 8.1.

TABLE 8.1

The replica states definitions

STATE	VALUE	DESCRIPTION
RS_ON	0	On
RS_NEW_REPLICA	1	New replica
RS_DYING_REPLICA	2	Replica in the process of being removed
RS_LOCKED	3	Locked
RS_CTR_0	4	Change Replica Type, State 0
RS_CTR_1	5	Change Replica Type, State 1
RS_TRANSITION_ON	6	Transition On State
RS_SS_0	48	Split, State 0
RS_SS_1	49	Split, State 1
RS_JS_0	64	Join, State 0
RS_JS_1	65	Join, State 1
RS_JS_2	66	Join, State 2
RS_MS_0	80	Move Subtree, State 0

NDS Partition Structure

An NDS partition is created by selecting one NDS container object (usually an Organizational Unit) as the top of the partition boundary or root of the partition. The distinguished name of the top-most object becomes the name of the partition. This object is also referred to as the partition root object.

Do not confuse the partition root object with the [ROOT] object at the top of the NDS tree. The [ROOT] object is a special container object that defines the top of the NDS tree. The partition root object is just the top-most object in a particular partition.

NOTE

When a partition is created the NDS container object that is selected as the top of the partition has several new attributes added to support replica synchronization.

The partition root object is the container object with additional properties or attributes defined that reveal the details of the partition's status and replica placement. These attributes are also used by NDS to synchronize the information between replicas of the partition.

The attributes of the partition root object that define the partition and support the NDS functions are defined below:

- Replica Pointer Table — This multi-valued attribute stores the list of replicas for the partition.

- Synchronized Up To — This multi-valued attribute contains a timestamp for each replica in the replica pointer table. There should be a timestamp for every replica on which modifications have occured. Each timestamp indicates the value received from other replicas of the partition. It represents the time that the data is modified up to for that replica. This attribute is often referred to as the Synchronized Up To Vector.

- Partition Creation Timestamp — This attribute is known as the epoch. Although this attribute is in the timestamp syntax it does not hold a time value. Instead, it holds a counter that begins at 1 and increments for each new epoch. An epoch indicates when the repair timestamp is executed.

- Inherited Access Control List — This attribute contains access control information inherited from a parent partition. It is the summary of the access control lists to that point in the NDS tree.

- Partition Control — This attribute tracks the progress of partition operations like splitting, joining, adding, and deleting replicas.

- Replica Up To — This attribute contains a timestamp for each replica that is used to represent the purge time for replica. This is often called the Replica Up To Vector because there is a timestamp for each replica. This attribute is a forerunner to the next release of NetWare 4. This attribute is localized to a particular server, which means that it is not synchronized to the other servers.

▸ Partition Status — The status of the last synchronization effort. This value could show errors, if any. The Partition Status attribute is localized to the server and is not synchronized.

Each of these attributes is discussed in more detail in the following sections.

REPLICA POINTER TABLE

The replica pointer table stores or references all the servers having a replica of a given partition. The replica pointer table is often referred to as the Replica Ring or Replica List. Each of these names is equivalent. In this book we will refer to the attribute as the replica pointer table. The replica pointer table is an attribute of the partition root object. Each server with a replica of a particular partition will have the replica pointer table.

The replica pointer table attribute is extremely important to the internal function of NDS. The values in this attribute are used to perform the replica synchronization between IntranetWare servers. For example, when the local replica receives an update from the client, the replica can find the physical location of the other replicas by using the information in the replica pointer table attribute.

The replica pointer tables for each server should be identical. If the replica pointer tables are not identical, your NDS will not be able to complete the replica synchronization for the partition.

You can view the replica pointer table using either NWADMIN under the NDS Manager option or DSREPAIR. Figure 8.25 displays the replica pointer table for the [ROOT] partition as seen on NOR-SRV1 using the DSREPAIR utility under the Replica Ring option from the Replica and Partition Operations menu.

As mentioned earlier, the replica pointer table should be consistent across all servers that hold a copy of the partition. This means you should get the same results when viewing the replica ring using DSREPAIR, regardless of which server you execute it on.

FIGURE 8.25

The replica pointer table
for the [ROOT] partition as
seen on NOR-SRV1 using
the DSREPAIR utility

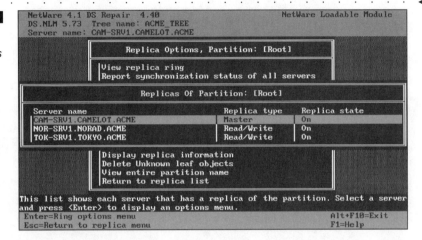

FIGURE 8.25

The replica pointer table
for the [ROOT] partition as
seen on NOR-SRV1 using
the DSREPAIR utility

Replica Pointer Table Structure

The replica pointer table attribute contains a list of the replicas for a partition. For each replica on the server, the replica pointer table has an attribute, which contains the server name, replica type, replica state, replica number, and internal IPX address for each server holding replicas of that partition. The replica pointer table attributes are as follows:

▸ Server Name — The server name is the distinguished name of the server where the replica is physically located.

▸ Replica Type — The replica type indicates the capabilities of the replica. The replica type will have one of the following values: 0=Master; 1=Read/ Write (Secondary); 2=Read Only; and 3=Subordinate Reference.

▸ Replica State — This value will typically be set to ON. During partition operations, a partition can go through several states. The states include On, New, Dying, Split, Join, and others. The complete list of replica states is provided in Table 8.1.

▸ Replica Number — The replica number is assigned when the replica is created. The replica number is assigned by the master replica for the partition. Each replica for a partition has a unique number.

▸ Partition Root Object ID — This is the object ID of the partition root object on the server. The partition root object ID identifies the root-most NDS object of the partition. This value is valid only on the server that stores the local replica of the partition.

▸ Number of Addresses — The network addresses for the server are held in this value. A server can be accessible over different protocols and will have different network addresses for each protocol. The number of addresses held in this value will depend on the number of protocols supported by the server. The IPX internal network number is always held in this value, which indicates the server's last known address. The address has three parts, including the address type (IPX, IP, and so on), address length, and address data.

The example of a replica pointer table in Figure 8.26 might help you understand how it looks. For this example, we will assume that the servers CAM-SRV1, NOR-SRV1, and TOK-SRV1 all hold replicas of the [ROOT] partition. It is also assumed that the servers NOR-SRV1, LABS-SRV1, and RD-SRV1 hold replicas of the NORAD

The replica pointer table for the [ROOT] partition on server CAM-SRV1 in the ACME tree

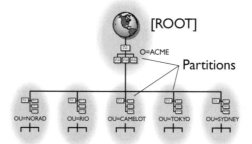

Replica Pointer Table on CAM-SRV1 for Partition [ROOT]

SERVER NAME	REPLICA TYPE	REPLICA STATE	REPLICA NUMBER	PARTITION ROOT OBJECT ID	ADDRESS
CAM-SRV1	READ/WRITE	ON	2	06001823	NET ADDRESS/ NODE/SOCKET
NOR-SRV1	MASTER	ON	1	50112030	NET/NODE/SOCKET
TOK-SRV1	READ/WRITE	ON	3	14830000	NET/NODE/SOCKET

partition. A logical representation for the replica pointer table for the [ROOT] partition on server CAM-SRV1 in the ACME tree is shown in the figure.

A logical representation for the replica pointer table for the NORAD partition on server NOR-SRV1 in the ACME tree is shown in Figure 8.27.

F I G U R E   8.27

Replica Pointer Table on NOR-SRV1 for Partition NORAD

The replica pointer table for the NORAD partition on server NOR-SRV1 in the ACME tree

SERVER NAME	REPLICA TYPE	REPLICA STATE	REPLICA NUMBER	PARTITION ROOT OBJECT ID	ADDRESS
NOR-SRV1	MASTER	ON	1	50112030	NET/NODE/SOCKET
LABS-SRV1	READ/WRITE	ON	3	81233010	NET/NODE/SOCKET
RD-SRV1	READ/WRITE	ON	2	61230010	NET/NODE/SOCKET
CAM-SRV1	SUBORDINATE REFERENCE	ON	5	06182300	NET/NODE/SOCKET
TOK-SRV1	SUBORDINATE REFERENCE	ON	4	14830000	NET/NODE/SOCKET

SYNCHRONIZED UP TO

The synchronized up to attribute is a multi-valued attribute that contains a timestamp for each replica in the replica pointer table plus one for each replica on which modifications have been made. The timestamp indicates the last update and point in time that the local replica has received from other replicas of the partition. This attribute is often referred to as the Synchronized Up To Vector.

The synchronized up to attribute is very important to the normal operation of NDS because using this list of timestamps the replicas of the partition know what information to synchronize between servers. Since the synchronized up to attribute contains the timestamp for updates received for this replica up to this time, other servers send updates only to this replica after that time. The synchronization process tests against it to determine if the other replicas on the other servers need updating. As mentioned earlier, this attribute is often referred to as the vector of timestamps for the server.

PARTITION CREATION TIMESTAMP

The partition creation timestamp is the attribute that determines the epoch for the partition. The epoch indicates what instance of the partition this is and which replica number is the master. The epoch value starts with one and increments each time the repair timestamp operation is executed. The repair timestamp operation essentially changes the instance of the partition.

During the replica synchronization process, epoch values are compared to ensure that obsolete information is not passed.

Normal partition and replica operations preserve this partition creation timestamp, although an administrator can change it indirectly by using DSREPAIR and executing the repair timestamp function. Refer to Chapter 10 before using the function to repair timestamps and declaring a new epoch.

The definitions of the partition creation timestamp attributes are given below. Although the data type or syntax of a timestamp is used, the parts of the timestamp are interpreted differently than the regular timestamp.

- Seconds — Holds the epoch counter, starting at one and incrementing sequentially.

- Replica Number — Holds the replica number for the local replica that assigns the epoch for the partition. This is the replica number that holds the master replica.

- Event ID — Not used.

INHERITED ACCESS CONTROL LIST

The inherited access control list attribute contains the access control information inherited from all the previous parent partitions. The attribute is a summary or cumulative effect of all the access control lists inherited from parent containers down to the object's context in the tree.

The access control list attribute helps the server calculate the rights of the objects more quickly because the security information is local. This means that when calculating rights the server does not have to go to other servers to find the security or rights information. A server should only have to make access control decisions using only local information.

NDS would be poorly designed if it forced the server to walk the tree and gather all the security or rights information for the users each time they accessed data. The inherited rights access control list attribute of the partition provides the capability of the server to look only at the local partition information to determine security rights all the way back to the [ROOT] object.

PARTITION CONTROL

The partition control attribute tracks the progress of partition operations. However, its primary job is to lock out further partition operations until the current one is completed. The partition operations are: split or create partition, join or merge partition, change replica type, move subtree, and repair timestamps. The add replica and delete replica operations are not tracked by the partition control attribute.

Typically, the partition will sequence through several states as the partition operation progresses. These states are the same used for the replica states. (See the "Server Partition Table" section earlier in this chapter.)

Because each replica of a partition can have only one state, there can be only one partition operation in progress at a time. The master replica of the partition controls the partition operations and acts like a traffic cop.

The partition operation in progress will use the partition control functions defined in Table 8.2.

TABLE 8.2	FUNCTION	VALUE	DESCRIPTION
The partition control function definitions	PC_IDLE	0	No operation in progress
	PC_SPLITTING	1	Splitting
	PC_SPLITTING_CHILD	2	Splitting child partition
	PC_JOINING_UP	3	Child of two joining partitions
	PC_JOINING_DOWN	4	Parent of two joining partitions
	PC_MOVE_SUBTREE_SRC	5	Source of the move subtree
	PC_MOVE_SUBTREE_DEST	6	Destination of the move subtree
	PC_LOCKED	7	Partition locked
	PC_REPAIRING_TIMESTAMPS	8	Timestamps being repaired
	PC_CHANGING_REPLICATYPE	9	Replicas changing types

PARTITION STATUS

The partition status attribute provides information about the success or failure of the last replica synchronization cycle. The attribute could contain Directory Services error codes, if necessary. For more information about the Directory Services error codes, refer to Appendix A.

Bindery Services

In previous versions of NetWare, information was not available from a distributed Directory. Instead, each server in the network stored a database that contained information such as the name, object ID, and password of every user or object that had access to the services provided by that server. The bindery also included information about all the services provided by the server and network.

Because the servers in the network did not share or communicate this information, the user or object's information was stored separately on every server to which it had rights. For example, if user BTHOMAS had rights to NetWare 3 servers called NCS, ENG1, and MKTG1, his information was stored on each of the three NetWare 3 servers. Each time BTHOMAS wanted to access services on a different server, he would have to establish a connection and log in to that server.

IntranetWare and Directory Services provide the network user with a single login to the entire network with access to additional network resources as needed. The user does not have to log in to each server to gain the resources on that server. Instead, Directory Services automatically authenticates the user to the server. The authentication process is completed seamlessly for the user.

However, in order for Directory Services to support backward compatibility for the bindery application and users, it provides the object information to these users through bindery services. These services are on a server-by-server basis. Bindery services enables the objects in a container to be accessed by both NDS clients and bindery-based servers and clients.

Unlike the NDS tree, which is hierarchical, objects in the bindery have no hierarchical relationship (a flat structure), and these objects are specific to one server. To provide access for bindery users and clients, NDS imitates a flat structure for leaf objects within one or more container objects.

SERVER BINDERY CONTEXT

The server bindery context is the name of the container object(s) where bindery services is set for the server. The server bindery context is also referred to as the bindery path. You can set the bindery context using a SET command at the console. In order to set the bindery context for the server NOR-SRV1 in the ACME tree, enter the following command at the server console prompt:

```
SET BINDERY CONTEXT = "OU=NORAD.O=ACME"
```

Bindery-based clients and servers can access the objects subordinate to the containers where the bindery context is set. Because IntranetWare now enables you to set multiple bindery contexts for the server, the handling of the invalid context error has changed. IntranetWare cannot fail the entire SET command because one of the containers specified may be valid.

In order to see or verify the effective bindery path for a server, you should enter the following command at the server console prompt:

```
CONFIG
```

When you can check the effective bindery path by using the CONFIG command you will see the distinguished names of each NDS container object listed on separate lines. Each container listed here is a valid bindery path. Objects created through bindery services are created as subordinate to the first effective (or valid) bindery path.

In previous versions of NetWare 4, you were limited to setting the bindery context at only one container object. With IntranetWare, you can set up to sixteen container objects as the bindery context.

Multiple Bindery Contexts

When multiple bindery contexts have been defined, a client searches for a bindery object by looking through the containers in the order they appear in the list.

Setting multiple bindery contexts can create one potential problem, which is known as eclipsing. In NDS, two objects can have the same relative distinguished name, but the objects must be in different containers. For example, in Figure 8.28, there are two user objects created in the ACME tree, with the relative distinguished name of JOHN. These objects exist in the OU=OPS and OU=PR containers. This example assumes that the server bindery context is set to both the OU=OPS and OU=PR containers in that order.

There are two user objects created in the ACME tree with the relative distinguished name of JOHN. These objects exist in the OU=OPS and OU=PR containers.

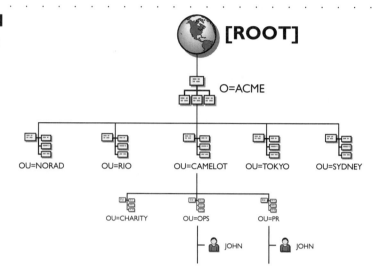

NDS distinguishes between the two objects because their distinguished names are different. However, the bindery client sees only the object's relative distinguished name. If a bindery client searches for the object JOHN, it finds an object in OU=OPS first and stops searching, whether or not that is the object the client is looking for. In this situation, the client is unable to access the object JOHN in the OU=PR container. This effect is called eclipsing and occurs only in bindery services and not in NDS.

You can solve this problem by making sure that no two objects in the NDS tree have the same relative distinguished name. A good naming standard is important and should be enforced.

Eclipsing also occurs when a dynamic bindery object has the same name as a static bindery object, although this situation is rare. In such cases, the dynamic object always eclipses the static object.

OBJECTS IN THE BINDERY

The bindery used in previous versions of NetWare enabled two categories of objects. These objects classes are:

▸ Static Bindery Objects

▶ Dynamic Bindery Objects

These object categories are specified by a flag on the object itself. The difference between the two categories (static and dynamic) refers to the longevity expected for each of the objects rather than a specific type of object.

Static Bindery Objects

The static bindery objects consist of the normal user, group, print queues, print server, and profiles objects defined in the bindery of NetWare 3. These objects are created permanently in the bindery until someone manually deletes them.

When migrated the static bindery objects are stored in NDS container objects specified in the bindery context of the IntranetWare server. If multiple containers are specified in the bindery context the objects are migrated or placed in the first valid container in the bindery path.

The NDS schema defines what attributes each object class has, thus regulating the makeup or creation of each object class. The NetWare 3 bindery is not hierarchical and does not need to distinguish objects by classes. Therefore, the bindery does not have formal schema definitions. However, the bindery does enable specific object types. These object types are used to identify the object within the bindery. For example, objects of type 1 are user objects and group objects are type 2.

Some of the well-known object types have direct counterparts in the NDS schema and can be converted or mutated during installation, migration, or creation. The mutation occurs for object types from the bindery to the appropriate NDS object class. For each bindery object type to be mutated, it must have all the mandatory attributes of the targeted NDS object class and cannot have the same name as another object in the container.

The bindery object types that are mutated by NDS are as follows:

▶ User

▶ Group

▶ Print Queue

▶ Print Server

▶ Profile

For example, a client using a bindery-based application wants to create a user object called JOE on an IntranetWare server in the NDS tree. The application makes a bindery API to create a user object. The request is made as follows:

```
CN=JOE+BinderyType = 1
```

The base object class is a bindery object type. The data are immediately converted to an NDS user object class, and the name then becomes:

```
CN=JOE
```

NOTE

Not all the NDS objects in the tree are available or visible to the bindery APIs. Bindery services applies only to leaf objects that are in the NetWare 3 bindery definitions, including the objects for user, group, print queue, print server, and profile. Also included is the bindery object base class CN=XXXX+BinderyType=643.

Dynamic Bindery Objects

The dynamic bindery objects are used for Service Advertising Protocol object names and information. This allows the advertising servers or services to have their objects added to the bindery as dynamic objects. For example, these objects are the file server and print server names that use SAP to become known on the network. In IntranetWare additional services use SAP to become known, such as the NDS tree and time synchronization.

If the bindery is closed and reopened, these objects and their properties are automatically deleted. Figure 8.29 illustrates how the information from the network would be directed logically to the appropriate section of the bindery according to the type of information.

The figure given above is a logical representation of the bindery services. In reality, the bindery does not have separate sections for the dynamic and static information. All bindery information is stored in the bindery files. The properties of the dynamic objects are mostly network addresses.

In order for IntranetWare to be completely compatible with previous versions of NetWare, the dynamic bindery objects need to be supported. Since the bindery no longer stores objects in IntranetWare, NDS must provide this functionality.

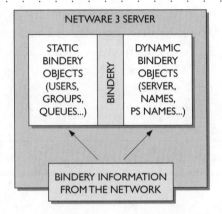

FIGURE 8.29

NetWare 3 bindery information from the network is directed to the appropriate section of the bindery according to the type of information.

The parent objects of dynamic bindery objects are not in the NDS hierarchy. They are not associated with a specific parent container in the tree. Instead, the dynamic bindery objects are stored in the NDS internal partition called the Bindery Partition. These objects can be accessed by a bindery client or server and are not dependent on whether the bindery context is set for the server.

Figure 8.30 illustrates logically how the information from the network would be directed to the appropriate section of NDS to provide the same function as the bindery.

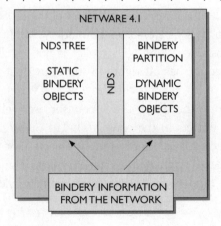

FIGURE 8.30

Information from the network is directed to the appropriate section of NDS to provide the same function as the bindery.

Again, the figure given above is a logical representation of NDS. In reality, the Directory does not have separate sections for the dynamic bindery object information. All the dynamic bindery objects are located physically adjacent to the other NDS objects in the NDS data files. See Figure 8.31 for an illustration of the object data file in NDS. The properties of the dynamic objects are mostly network addresses.

FIGURE 8.31

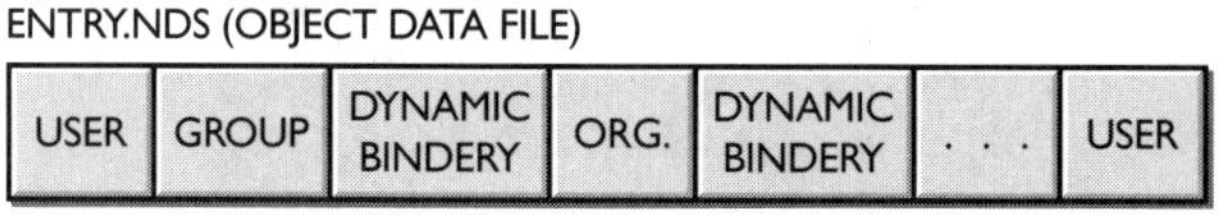

An example of the object data file in NDS. Notice that the dynamic bindery objects are stored adjacent to all the other NDS objects.

ENTRY.NDS (OBJECT DATA FILE)

USER	GROUP	DYNAMIC BINDERY	ORG.	DYNAMIC BINDERY	. . .	USER

BINDERY SUPERVISOR ACCOUNT

The bindery Supervisor account is created during the installation of the server. The Supervisor is a server-centric account created on every IntranetWare server. This account is created even when NDS replicas are installed on that server or when a Bindery Services context is set on the server. However, the Supervisor user is only accessible if a valid Bindery Context is set for the server. This is true with the exception of the Server Console Lock and Unlock operation, which can be performed using the Supervisor password.

The Supervisor account is not seen as an object of the NDS tree because it is server centric. The Supervisor user is stored in the Bindery Partition, which is one of the four partitions that exists even if an NDS replica is not installed on the server.

The Supervisor account has all rights to the individual server, which includes the objects and file system. This is the same as NetWare 3. If there is a Bindery Services context(s) set on the server, the Supervisor user will automatically have all rights to the bindery objects in the context(s). The Supervisor account has rights only to the NDS objects that are also bindery objects. For example, these objects are: users, groups, queues, print servers, and profiles. The profile object was first made available in the bindery by the NetWare Name Service (NNS) product.

Since the Supervisor user does not show up in the NDS tree, you cannot log in as Supervisor using an NDS connection. This means that the NWADMIN and NETADMIN utilities cannot be used by someone logged in as Supervisor. The Supervisor account can only access the objects using SYSCON.

CONSULTING EXPERIENCE

Although it is possible to use the administrative utilities such as NWADMIN to create an object in the Novell Directory Services tree called SUPERVISOR, the new user is not the same Supervisor user seen in the bindery. Any modifications made to the bindery Supervisor account are limited to bindery-based modifications. The individual logging in as the Supervisor user has to have a bindery connection to the server and use the bindery-based utilities.

The Supervisor account will always be assigned a password during creation. This was not the case in NetWare 4.01 because the individual installing the server was not required to have a password. The Supervisor user receives its password during creation under the following conditions:

▸ The server is a new IntranetWare server that is not migrated from NetWare 3. The Supervisor is assigned the password of the user, typically the ADMIN user, that logs in to the tree to perform the installation of the server.

▸ The server is being migrated from NetWare 3 to IntranetWare using the INSTALL.NLM program. The Supervisor account information remains the same as before the upgrade. If the Supervisor account in NetWare 3 does not have a password, the password of the user (usually ADMIN) that logged in to the tree to do the installation is assigned to the bindery Supervisor in IntranetWare.

▸ The server is being migrated from NetWare 3 to IntranetWare using the MIGRATE.EXE or Across-the-Wire Migration utility. When you migrate using the Across-the-Wire utility, the IntranetWare server is already installed and running. This means that the Supervisor account on the new IntranetWare server is already created and has a password. The password is created according to the first condition listed above. The Across-the-Wire Migration utility does not change the password to the password from the NetWare 3 server.

It is very important that you safeguard the password for the Supervisor. The password that the Supervisor is assigned is not completely synchronized with the user that installs the new IntranetWare server into the tree. If the ADMIN user ever changes its password, the password for the Supervisor account is not changed. The two accounts are completely separate after the initial installation.

NDS Internals for Multiple Server Operations

"Man is a slow, sloppy and brilliant thinker; the machine is fast, accurate and stupid." William M. Kelly

Novell Directory Services operates as a name service that can be split into partitions and distributed to any number of network servers. With NDS, information is not only distributed but also replicated to provide increased reliability and accessibility. These features provide Directory Services with the capacity to place the information close to the users for convenient access while enabling the job of the name service to be shared among the servers.

Since the information in the Directory can be distributed, the background processes that maintain the consistency of information are architected to support multiple servers. In order to support the operation between multiple servers, each server must be able to establish a connection and authenticate to the other IntranetWare servers in the tree.

The DS Client

We typically think of clients as the workstation software that logs the user in to the network and accesses the network services. However, each IntranetWare server uses the built-in NDS client software to attach and authenticate the server to the other IntranetWare servers. Thus, the servers become clients of the other servers in the NDS tree. The client software used to support server-to-server connections is called the Directory Services Client or DS Client.

Since NDS is distributed and replicated among any of the IntranetWare servers in the network, one server may need the NDS information stored by another server. This mechanism provides the interconnectivity needed to support all the NDS multiple server operations and processes. The DS Client is sometimes referred to as the Virtual Client. (This term is used mainly in DSTRACE.)

The IntranetWare servers use the same protocol as the workstation software to establish and authenticate to the other servers. The authentication process is initiated as a background authentication procedure.

CONSULTING EXPERIENCE

It is very important that you do not filter the Routing Information Protocol (RIP) from your IntranetWare network. If RIP is being filtered, the IntranetWare servers will not be able to find each other to synchronize. Directory Services stores the addresses for the other IntranetWare servers in its replica pointer table; however, it needs to find the route using RIP.

The connection made by the DS Client between IntranetWare servers is viewed in the MONITOR utility on the server. The connections made from server to server will authenticate using the distinguished name of the IntranetWare server object. These connections are marked with an "*" character to indicate that the connection is not a licensed connection but rather an authenticated Directory Services connection.

Figure 9.1 shows the DS Client connections made between servers on the MONITOR screen for the servers CAM-SRV1 and NOR-SRV1 in the ACME tree.

FIGURE 9.1

The DS Client connections made between servers on the MONITOR screen for the servers CAM-SRV1 and NOR-SRV1 in the ACME tree.

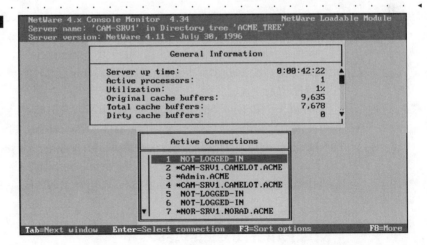

The messages related to the DS Client can be viewed on the Directory Services screen at the server console using the SET DSTRACE command VCLIENT (VC or Virtual Client). The command is entered as follows:

```
SET DSTRACE = +VCLIENT
```

The other IntranetWare servers not only occupy a lot of the Directory Services connections, but also the NOT LOGGED IN connections that may be shown on the MONITOR screen. Other IntranetWare servers perform the name resolution operation using the NOT LOGGED IN connection type and do not need to authenticate.

Name Resolution (Tree Walking) Operation

NDS's primary responsibility is to retrieve requested object or network resource information from the servers distributed across the network. NDS locates the object information using the operation or mechanism called name resolution. This operation walks the partitions of the NDS tree to locate objects or specific information requested by the user or client. Name resolution occurs when the client requests NDS object information from Directory Services and the IntranetWare servers. If the object information is not on the server to which the client is connected, the process will walk or navigate through the partitions on the other IntranetWare servers to find the correct information. The name resolution process is often called tree walking.

The name resolution operation starts with a distinguished name for an NDS object in the tree and attempts to obtain the object ID for the searched object on a specific server. The name resolution returns a list of addresses for servers that store the requested object information. Before we discuss the specific details associated with the name resolution operation, we need to quickly review the concepts of NDS partitions and replicas.

NDS PARTITION REVIEW

As mentioned previously, the NDS tree can be divided into pieces or subtrees called partitions and stored on the IntranetWare servers as NDS replicas. Partitioning provides distribution of the Directory Services information across the IntranetWare servers.

Each partition is named by the container object at the root of the subtree called the partition root object. The partition root objects have additional properties or attributes that are used to find the NDS information on other servers and keep it synchronized. These additional attributes are as follows:

▸ Replica Pointer Table — Stores the list of replicas for the partition

▸ Synchronized Up To — Contains a timestamp for each replica in the replica pointer table

▸ Partition Creation Timestamp — Determines the epoch for the partition

▸ Inherited Access Control List — Contains access control information inherited from the parent partitions

▸ Partition Control — Tracks the progress of partition operations like splitting, joining, change replica type, and move subtree operations

▸ Partition Status — Contains information regarding the last synchronization attempt

For more information about the partition root object, refer to Chapter 8.

SUBORDINATE REFERENCE REPLICA REVIEW

There are different types of replicas that can be stored on the IntranetWare servers. These replicas are the physical representation of the NDS tree. The replica type that helps the NDS tree stay physically connected is the subordinate reference replica. A subordinate reference replica is created by Directory Services on a server that holds a replica of the parent partition but not the child partitions.

The subordinate reference replica for a partition does not contain all of the objects in that partition. Instead, the subordinate reference contains only a copy of the partition root object (or the top-most object of the partition) including all its properties and attributes.

Since the subordinate reference replica holds a copy of the partition root object, it contains information such as the location of all the other replicas for the partition. An example of the contents of a subordinate reference replica for the partition CAMELOT, which is stored on server NOR-SRV1, is shown in Figure 9.2.

FIGURE 9.2

A subordinate reference replica for the partition CAMELOT, which is stored on server NOR-SRV1, contains the replica pointer table for the partition.

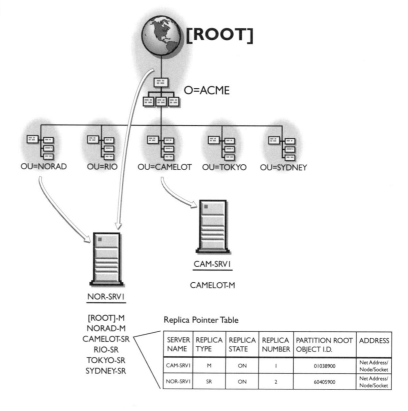

Replica Pointer Table

SERVER NAME	REPLICA TYPE	REPLICA STATE	REPLICA NUMBER	PARTITION ROOT OBJECT I.D.	ADDRESS
CAM-SRV1	M	ON	1	01038900	Net Address/Node/Socket
NOR-SRV1	SR	ON	2	60405900	Net Address/Node/Socket

The replica pointer table property contains a list of the replicas for a partition. The list holds the server name, replica type, replica state, replica number, object ID for the partition root object, and the addresses for each of the servers in the replica pointer table. Using this information, the subordinate reference replicas not only keep the NDS tree connected, but also can aid in the procedure to resolve a name.

NAME RESOLUTION METHODS

The purpose of the name resolution or tree walking mechanism is to eliminate the necessity of the user or client's awareness of the physical location of network resources. The term name resolution literally means resolving a name to an address; in this case, the address of the server where the requested object is stored.

In Figure 9.3 the client or workstation requests information about an NDS object. Because the client is currently authenticated to the server CAM-SRV1, that server will try to fulfill the request. Unable to fulfill the request, CAM-SRV1 walks the tree on behalf of the client. In this case, CAM-SRV1 contacts the server NOR-SRV1. The server NOR-SRV1 returns its lack of success. CAM-SRV1 contacts RIO-SRV1, which responds negatively. This process continues until the requested object information is located on SYD-SRV1. The physical location information is returned to the client. The client, in turn, connects directly to SYD-SRV1 to read the object information.

FIGURE 9.3

The workstation makes a request for information about an NDS object to the server CAM-SRV1. Then the server CAM-SRV1 will contact the other servers to find the object.

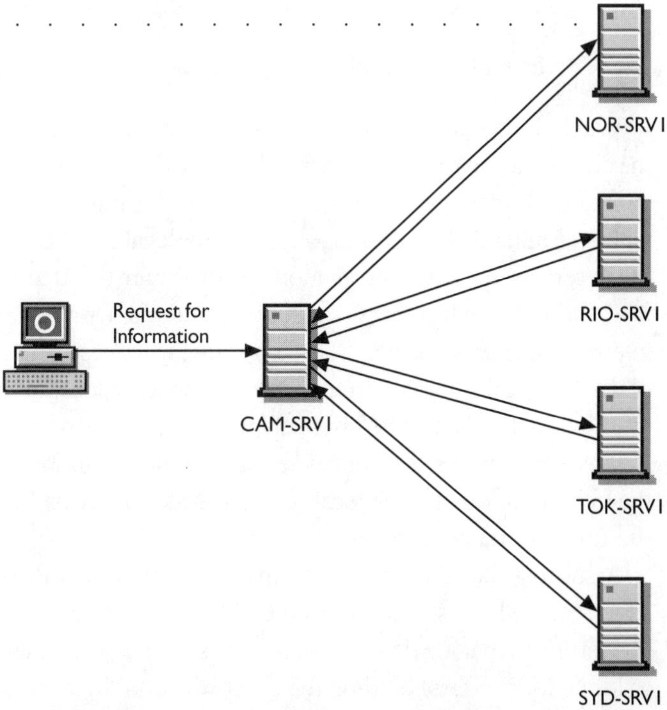

Request for Information

NOR-SRV1

RIO-SRV1

CAM-SRV1

TOK-SRV1

SYD-SRV1

The name resolution requests are made for only specific replica types. Even though the server may have the object information requested, it may not have the right type of replica to support the request made by the client. For example, the client wants to modify a certain object. If a read only replica responds it will not help. The replica type is an important part of the request for name resolution.

The name resolution operation is used to access resources and find object information during login and authentication. In other words, a client requesting information about an object is serviced by the server using the name resolution or tree walking process in the following ways:

- ▸ Object found on the local server

- ▸ Walk down the tree to locate the object

- ▸ Walk up the tree to locate the object

- ▸ Walk up and down the tree to locate the object

- ▸ Server without a replica

When the client makes the request for object information, the distinguished name of the object is always used. NDS uses the individual relative distinguished name (RDN) to compare against the values at each server. Using this method, Directory Services will determine if the information is on the local servers or whether it needs to go to other servers holding information up or down the tree.

If the current IntranetWare server contains a replica with the requested object information or target object, NDS completes the request by returning the physical location of the object information. In this case, the physical location of the object information is returned to the client. The physical location is the network address for the local server. If Directory Services determines that the name resolution operation will have to walk the tree (up or down), the local server acts as a proxy on behalf of the client to contact the other IntranetWare servers.

Assuming that the object information exists down the tree from the information stored on the local server, the server will read the replica pointer table (replica ring) for the partitions that are down the tree. The server can use subordinate references replicas to locate the server(s) holding the child partition. In a very interesting twist, the name resolution operation will use the attributes of the subordinate reference replicas to navigate up the tree to locate the servers that store replicas for the parent partition. We will discuss the details of each case in the following sections.

Object Found on the Local Server
When the client makes the request for object information, it passes the distinguished name to the server it is connected to. If the IntranetWare server

contains a replica with the requested object information or target object, NDS completes the request by passing the physical location of the object information back to the client. In this case, the physical location of the object information is the network address of the local server. The client then makes the read request for the specific object or property information.

For example, a workstation is connected to the server NOR-SRV1 in the ACME tree. The server NOR-SRV1 holds the master replicas of the NORAD and [ROOT] partitions as illustrated in Figure 9.4.

The workstation is connected to the server NOR-SRV1 in the ACME tree. The server holds a replica of the NORAD and [ROOT] partitions.

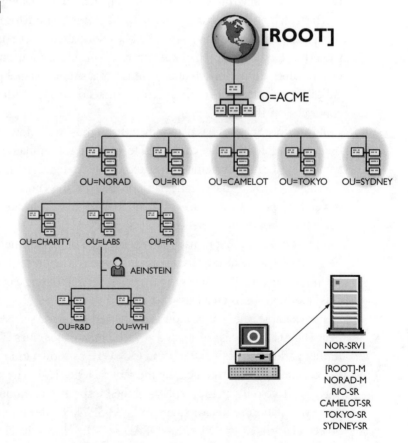

The workstation requests the location information about the user object AEINSTEIN.LABS.NORAD.ACME. The server NOR-SRV1 will check first to see if it has a copy of the requested object. Because NOR-SRV1 holds a replica (master replica) of the partition that contains the object information, it returns the physical location of the object information and the object ID back to the workstation. In this case, the physical location of the object information is the network address of NOR-SRV1. The workstation can then continue or complete the request (read, modify, and so on).

Walk Down the Tree to Locate the Object

If the object information is not found on the local server, Directory Services will determine that it needs to either walk down or up the tree based on the distinguished name of the object being requested. The direction that the Directory will search, either up or down, is determined using a partial match on the distinguished name.

The matching that occurs for the names is processed from the root-to-leaf (top-down). Any given name is matched object by object or parent by parent, checking each of the subordinate objects. The name is processed in this fashion until the object is found, or the names do not match and there is not a subordinate object for the parent. The subordinate reference replicas are then read (if going down) and the process continues on the next server.

If Directory Services has determined that it must walk down the tree, the server that the workstation originally connected to uses the subordinate reference replicas of the name being located. Remember, the subordinate references replicas are created on servers that have a copy of the parent partition but not the child partition. Therefore, each server that has a replica of a parent partition will know the location of each child partition using the subordinate reference replicas.

In this case, the subordinate reference replica of the partition is used to provide the best partial match to the distinguished name of the object requested. Using the DS Client, the server will connect to the nearest server holding a correct replica type of the child partition based on a least-cost route.

For example, the workstation is connected to the server NOR-SRV1 in the ACME tree. The ACME tree is partitioned at each of the major cities. The NORAD partition is further partitioned at OU=R&D and OU=WHI as shown in Figure 9.5. The partitions [ROOT] and NORAD are held by the server NOR-SRV1. The servers R&D-SRV1 and WHI-SRV1 hold the master replicas of their respective partitions as illustrated.

A workstation sends a request to NOR-SRV1 for the information about the user object LDAVINCI.R&D.LABS.NORAD.ACME. NDS will check it first to see if it has a copy of the requested object. Since NOR-SRV1 does not hold the object information, Directory Services must look on another server.

F I G U R E   9.5

The workstation is connected to the server NOR-SRV1 in the ACME tree. The server NOR-SRV1 holds replicas of the NORAD and [ROOT] partitions. The servers R&D-SRV1 and WHI-SRV1 hold the master replicas of their respective partitions.

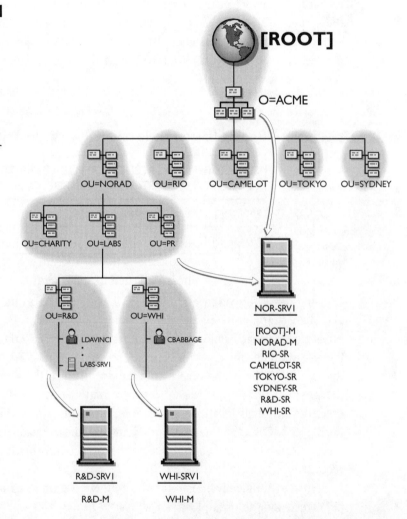

Directory Services compares each segment of the distinguished name of the object with the information stored on the server. By comparing and matching the names available on the server, the name resolution operation determines whether the object information is subordinate (down) the tree or up the tree.

Determining that the object information is down the tree, the server that the workstation originally connected to will walk the NDS tree as a proxy agent on behalf of the workstation. In this case, the NOR-SRV1 will perform the proxy for the workstation. In order to locate the servers that contain the lower-level partitions, the server NOR-SRV1 uses the subordinate reference replicas that will go down according to the name matched. In this case, the R&D subordinate reference replica is used. The server NOR-SRV1 will read the replica pointer table for the R&D subordinate reference replica as shown in Figure 9.6.

FIGURE 9.6

Replica Pointer Table on NOR-SRV1 for Partition R&D

The replica pointer table for the R&D partition. The replica pointer table is an attribute of a replica. In this case, the replica is the subordinate reference replica stored on the server NOR-SRV1.

SERVER NAME	REPLICA TYPE	REPLICA STATE	REPLICA NUMBER	PARTITION ROOT OBJECT I.D.	ADDRESS
R&D-SRV1	M	ON	1	06040000	Net Address/ Node/Socket
NOR-SRV1	SR	ON	2	14015016	Net Address/ Node/Socket

Using this information, the NOR-SRV1 will connect to the R&D-SRV1 using the DS Client software (server-to-server connection). Because the server R&D-SRV1 holds the requested object information for LDAVINCI.R&D.LABS.NORAD.ACME, the tree walking phase is completed. The server R&D-SRV1 verifies to NOR-SRV1 that it has a copy of the object information. In turn, the server NOR-SRV1 returns the physical location of the object information back to the workstation. In this case, the physical location of the object information is the network address of R&D-SRV1. Directory Services automatically authenticates the workstation to the server R&D-SRV1 to access or read the object information associated with the request.

Figure 9.7 logically illustrates the following name resolution steps that were performed for the example given above:

1 • The workstation makes a request to access specific object information. The server NOR-SRV1 receives the request.

2 • The object information is not stored on the NOR-SRV1 server. The server checks the R&D subordinate reference replica and reads the replica pointer table for the R&D partition.

3 • The server NOR-SRV1 makes a request for the object information to the server R&D-SRV1.

4 • The server R&D-SRV1 sends a list of the physical locations of the object plus the object IDs. In this case, it is the server address of R&D-SRV1.

5 • The list is returned to the workstation of the servers that contain the object location. In this case, the server R&D-SRV1 is the only server.

6 • Directory Services automatically connects the workstation to server R&D-SRV1 to provide access to the object information.

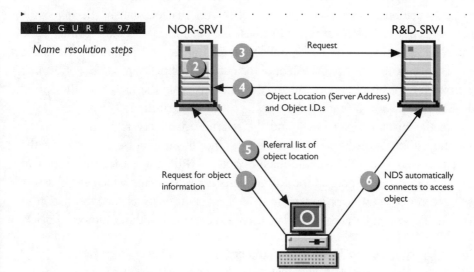

F I G U R E   9.7

Name resolution steps

Requested Object Information on Multiple Servers   Consider the same example given above in which the workstation is requesting object information for the user object LDAVINCI.R&D.LABS.NORAD.ACME. However, let's discuss what would happen if the server WHI-SRV1 also holds a read/write replica for the R&D partition. In this case, the replica pointer table for the partition R&D would appear as shown in Figure 9.8.

FIGURE 9.8
Replica Pointer Table for the Partition R&D

The replica pointer table for the partition R&D with the WHI-SRV1 added. The WHI-SRV1 has a read/write replica of the partition.

SERVER NAME	REPLICA TYPE	REPLICA STATE	REPLICA NUMBER	PARTITION ROOT OBJECT I.D.	ADDRESS
R&D-SRV1	M	ON	1	06040000	Net Address/ Node/Socket
NOR-SRV1	SR	ON	2	14015016	Net Address/ Node/Socket
WHI-SRV1	R/W	ON	3	83621020	Net Address/ Node/Socket

If there is more than one server holding a replica or copy of the partition that contains the information, Directory Services will take that into account. Once the object information is located and the list of servers that can satisfy the request is found, a referral list (list of server addresses) is built from the replica pointer table of the object's partition. The server builds the referral list and passes it back to the client. This client may be the DS Client of the current IntranetWare server performing the proxy for the workstation. Again, the referral list is the list of all the server addresses that have the requested replica type for the partition.

When the current server has found the referral list of servers by proxy for the workstation, it passes the list to the workstation. Once this referral list is received by the workstation, it makes a Router Information Protocol (RIP) request for each server in the referral list. The purpose of the RIP requests is to determine which server is the closest according to the least cost route. It is the responsibility of the workstation to determine the costing for each server based on a least cost algorithm (number of ticks).

Walk Up the Tree to Locate the Object

If Directory Services determines that it needs to walk up the tree, the servers use the replica pointer tables from the root-most partition stored on the server to find other IntranetWare servers in the tree. In the previous example (Walking Down the Tree), the subordinate references were used to locate object information lower in the tree. Well, the subordinate reference replicas stored in the replica pointer table of a server can also be used to walk up the tree to find an object.

Remember, the replica pointer table for a replica contains all the server names, server addresses, replica types, and so on for a particular partition. Using the information contained in a replica pointer table of a partition, Directory Services can determine not only where the child partitions are but also the names and addresses for the server that holds copies of the parent partition.

A subordinate reference replica is created by Directory Services on a server that holds a replica of the parent partition but not the child partitions. Thus, it can be reasoned that a server holding a replica of the child partition will have knowledge of the parent servers storing the subordinate references. To illustrate how the information in the replica pointer table can be used to walk up the tree, see Figure 9.9.

The server NOR-SRVI in the ACME tree holds replicas of the NORAD and [ROOT] partitions with subordinate reference replicas as needed. The servers R&D-SRVI and WHI-SRVI hold the master replicas of their respective partitions. The server WHI-SRVI holds a read/ write replica for the R&D partition.

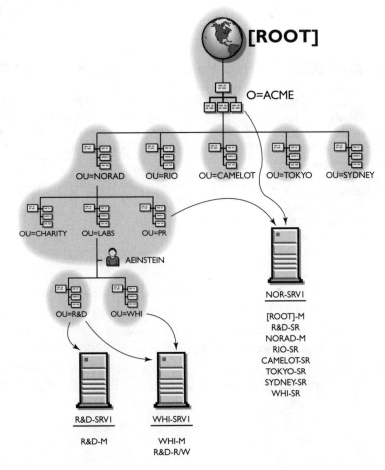

For this example, assume that a workstation is connected to the server R&D-SRV1. The workstation requests information about the user object ADMIN.ACME. NDS will check the server R&D-SRV1 first to see if it has a copy of the requested object. Because R&D-SRV1 does not hold the object information, Directory Services must look on another server.

Directory Services compares names and determines that the object information is up the tree. The server R&D-SRV1 will begin walking the NDS tree as a proxy agent on behalf of the workstation. In order to locate the servers that contain the upper-level information, the server will read the replica pointer table for the R&D partition as shown in Figure 9.10.

Replica Pointer Table for the Partition R&D

SERVER NAME	REPLICA TYPE	REPLICA STATE	REPLICA NUMBER	PARTITION ROOT OBJECT I.D.	ADDRESS
R&D-SRV1	M	ON	1	06040000	Net Address/Node/Socket
NOR-SRV1	SR	ON	2	14015016	Net Address/Node/Socket
WHI-SRV1	R/W	ON	3	83261020	Net Address/Node/Socket

The replica pointer is an attribute of the partition root object of a replica, which means that this information is available on every server that stores a replica of the partition. In this case, there are replicas on the servers R&D-SRV1 (master replica), WHI-SRV1 (read/write replica), and NOR-SRV1 (subordinate reference replica).

By reading the replica pointer table, the server R&D-SRV1 sorts the server addresses according to least cost and contacts one. Either one of these addresses could have the object information. If the server WHI-SRV1 is contacted, then it reads its root-most partition and returns the referral list. In this case, WHI-SRV1 is no closer than R&D-SRV1. Next, the server NOR-SRV1 is contacted. NOR-SRV1 is able to match the name and find the object. The location and object ID are returned in the referral list to R&D-SRV1. In turn, R&D-SRV1 sends the referral list to the client.

You may think that because the server NOR-SRV1 holds the subordinate reference replica, it would be given preference as the first server to contact. However, servers with subordinate reference replicas are not given preference over other servers in the replica pointer table of the server R&D.

No Subordinate Reference Replicas for a Partition It is possible for an IntranetWare server to have replicas for a partition, and the partition not to have any subordinate reference replica types. This would be the case if all servers that held parent partitions also held the child partitions.

In this situation the server information in the replica pointer table will guarantee a server with a parent partition. Remember, if the server with a parent partition does not hold the child partition then a subordinate reference replica is created.

To illustrate this issue, we will use the previous example but with a slight modification. We will change the replica type on the server NOR-SRV1 from a subordinate reference replica to a read/write replica for the R&D partition as shown in Figure 9.11.

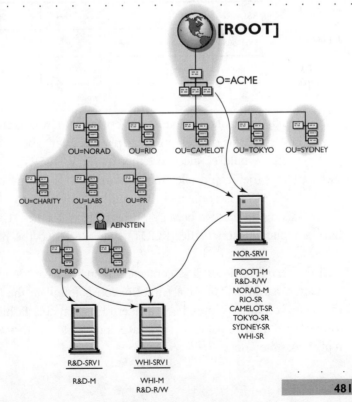

F I G U R E   9.11

The server NOR-SRV1 in the ACME tree holds replicas of the [ROOT], NORAD, and R&D partitions with subordinate reference replicas as needed. The servers R&D-SRV1 and WHI-SRV1 hold the master replicas of their respective partitions. In addition, the server WHI-SRV1 holds a read/write replica for the R&D partition.

The station that is connected to the server R&D-SRV1 requests information about the user object AEINSTEIN.LABS.NORAD.ACME. NDS will check the R&D-SRV1 server to see if it has a copy of the requested object. R&D-SRV1 does not hold the object information so NDS must find another server.

By comparing the names, Directory Services determines that the object information is up the tree. The server R&D-SRV1 will perform the tree walking as the proxy on behalf of the workstation. In order to locate the servers that contain the upper-level information, the server will read the replica pointer table for the R&D partition as shown in Figure 9.12.

FIGURE 9.12

Replica Pointer Table for the Partition R&D

The replica pointer table for the partition R&D. The replica pointer table is the same on every server that stored a replica of the R&D partition. In this case, there are replicas on the servers R&D-SRV1 (master replica), WHI-SRV1 (read/write replica), and NOR-SRV1 (read/write replica).

Notice that there are no subordinate references for this partition.

SERVER NAME	REPLICA TYPE	REPLICA STATE	REPLICA NUMBER	PARTITION ROOT OBJECT I.D.	ADDRESS
R&D-SRV1	M	ON	1	06040000	Net Address/Node/Socket
WHI-SRV1	R/W	ON	2	83261020	Net Address/Node/Socket
NOR-SRV1	R/W	ON	3	47819010	Net Address/Node/Socket

NDS reads the replica pointer table on the current server, which is R&D-SRV1. The closest server (least cost) in the replica pointer table is used.

R&D-SRV1 would connect to either server WHI-SRV1 or server NOR-SRV1 in the hope that they could offer more information about moving up the tree. If the server WHI-SRV1 is contacted, it would not be able to offer more information about walking up the tree because of the replicas it stores. The WHI-SRV1 does not have a replica closer to the [ROOT] than R&D, so the referral list returned is discarded by R&D-SRV1.

If the server NOR-SRV1 is contacted, then we have found the server that holds the parent partition. The object information is found in the NORAD partition, and the name resolution sends back a referral list. In this fashion, Directory Services can walk up the tree using the replica pointer table whether a subordinate reference replica exists or not.

Walk Up and Down the Tree to Locate the Object

When Directory Services needs to find information about an object that is located in the NDS tree in peer partitions, the name resolution operation will walk up the tree to the nearest common parent and then back down.

For example, a workstation is connected to the server R&D-SRV1 in the ACME tree. The ACME tree is partitioned at each of the major cities. The NORAD partition is further partitioned at OU=R&D and OU=WHI as shown in Figure 9.13. The partitions [ROOT] and NORAD are held by the server NOR-SRV1. The server CAM-SRV1 holds the master replica of the CAMELOT partition, while the servers R&D-SRV1 and WHI-SRV1 hold their respective partitions as illustrated.

The workstation is connected to the server R&D-SRV1 in the ACME tree. The server NOR-SRV1 holds replicas of the NORAD and [ROOT] partitions. The server CAM-SRV1 holds the CAMELOT partition, while the servers R&D-SRV1 and WHI-SRV1 hold their respective partitions.

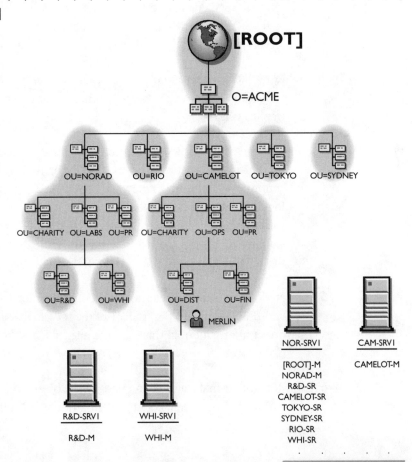

483

Figure 9.14 logically illustrates the name resolution steps that are performed to resolve the name MERLIN.DIST.OPS.CAMELOT.ACME starting from the server R&D-SRV1:

1 • A workstation makes a request for information about the user object MERLIN.DIST.OPS.CAMELOT.ACME. The server R&D-SRV1 receives the request. The server R&D-SRV1 will perform the proxy on behalf of the workstation.

2 • NDS will check R&D-SRV1 first to see if it has a copy of the requested object by comparing names. Because R&D-SRV1 does not hold the object information, Directory Services must look on another server. In order to locate the servers that possibly contain the proper partitions, the server R&D-SRV1 uses the replica pointer table of the root-most partition on the server; in this case, the R&D partition.

3 • R&D-SRV1 makes a proxy request for the object information to the server NOR-SRV1 because it is the only other server in the replica pointer table (replica ring).

4 • The server NOR-SRV1 will then determine (by comparing names) if the object information is found locally or if Directory Services needs to continue walking up or down the tree. The object information is not found locally on NOR-SRV1. And because the server NOR-SRV1 has a subordinate reference replica of the CAMELOT partition, it continues walking down the tree to find MERLIN.DIST.OPS.CAMELOT.ACME in the CAMELOT partition.

5 • NOR-SRV1 sends a referral list (replica pointer table of the partition CAMELOT) back to R&D-SRV1 of the servers that could possibly hold the object information. In this case, the referral list is the server address for CAM-SRV1.

6 • R&D-SRV1 make a proxy request for the object information to the server CAM-SRV1 because it contains the partition CAMELOT.

7 • The server CAM-SRV1 determines (by comparing names) if the object information is found locally or if Directory Services needs to continue walking up or down the tree. The object information for MERLIN.DIST.OPS.CAMELOT.ACME is found locally on CAM-SRV1 in the CAMELOT partition.

8 • CAM-SRV1 sends a referral list back to R&D-SRV1 of the servers that contain the object information. In this case, the list is the server address for CAM-SRV1.

9 • The referral list is returned to the workstation for the servers that contain the object information, which includes the object ID. In this case, the server CAM-SRV1 is the only server.

10 • The workstation contacts server CAM-SRV1 to provide access to the object information.

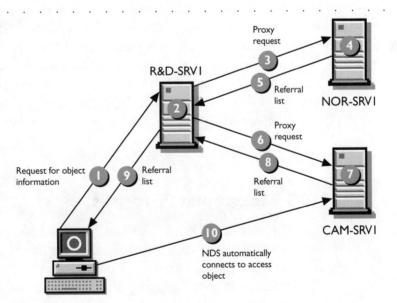

FIGURE 9.14

The name resolution steps that are performed to resolve the name MERLIN.DIST.OPS.CAMELOT. ACME starting from the server R&D-SRV1

The DS Client software provides the server-to-server connections for walking the trees. Because the server R&D-SRV1 did not hold the requested object information for MERLIN.DIST.OPS.CAMELOT.ACME, the tree walking was performed by Directory Services transparent to the user of the workstation.

Server Without an NDS Replica

If the workstation attaches to a server that has no NDS replicas, Directory Services must locate another IntranetWare server. When a server without NDS replicas receives a request for object information, the server sends a service request for SAP type 0x0278 to the network. The SAP type 0x0278 is the NDS tree SAP. Another IntranetWare server that is part of the NDS tree will respond.

IntranetWare servers without NDS replicas connect to the tree using SAP type 0x0278. The servers without NDS replicas will run the limber process, check external references, and provide authentication services just like a server with NDS replicas.

CACHING TO SUPPORT AUTHENTICATION

The total time required to authenticate between IntranetWare servers is reduced through caching important information. The reduction is a result of the IntranetWare servers remembering the object IDs of each of the servers they connected to during previous authentications. By storing the object ID for the other servers, the time required to authenticate to those servers in the future is reduced.

The specific information cached is the object ID of the server object on the other (remote) server. For example, if NOR-SRV1 authenticates to R&D-SRV1, then NOR-SRV1 stores the object ID for the R&D-SRV1 and vice-a-versa.

NDS Background Processes

The information for NDS is loosely consistent, meaning that after a modification is made on a replica and before synchronization, the data will be different from one replica to another. Several NDS background processes are implemented to ensure synchronization of Directory data over a period of time. Most notable among these NDS background processes is the replica synchronization process, which synchronizes the information between replicas of the NDS partitions.

The other NDS background processes run periodically and are responsible for a number of internal operations that keep the information on all servers in the Directory tree consistent. All of these background processes will execute automatically without user or administrator intervention. Many of these processes can be forced to execute immediately using the SET parameters for DSTRACE. There are other SET parameters for NDS that control the interval between execution for a few of the NDS background processes.

REPLICA SYNCHRONIZATION PROCESS

NDS is a loosely consistent database, meaning that changes or updates can occur at various replicas and that not all the replicas may have the exact information at the same time. However, since NDS is loosely synchronized, an update made at one replica propagates to other replicas of the partition over time. The replicas work together to exchange the information with each other to perform all updates. These changes are automatically sent to the other replicas of that partition by a background process called replica synchronization. The purpose of replica synchronization is to guarantee consistency of the information across all the replicas of a partition over a period of time.

The updates or modifications that affect the NDS data include adding, deleting, moving or renaming an object, as well as changing the properties or attributes of the object. The replica synchronization process passes only the data that has changed for each object or property between the replicas of the partition. By passing only the information that is updated, the total amount of information sent is reduced and network traffic for synchronization is kept to a minimum.

Replica synchronization is a background process that is event driven. Any modification to the NDS database activates the replica synchronization process. This means that replica synchronization is scheduled to run on a server after an object or property on that server has been updated. The process is scheduled according to the property or attribute being changed. Each property has a flag that determines if it is high convergence or not. The flag has the following settings:

- Fast Synchronization (high convergence)

- Slow Synchronization (not high convergence)

CHAPTER 9
. . . . . .
N O V E L L ' S
G U I D E   T O
I N T R A N E T W A R E
N E T W O R K S

Fast Synchronization

The fast synchronization is the normal synchronization, which is scheduled to occur ten seconds after a client update event occurs on the server. The changes or updates to NDS objects that are made by the client are scheduled using the fast synchronization. Synchronization scheduled for ten seconds after the first update is received enables several subsequent modifications, if any, to be processed at the same time.

Slow Synchronization

When a user logs in to the NDS tree, four properties or attributes of the user object are changed. These properties are:

▸ Network Address

▸ Last Login Time

▸ Current Login Time

▸ Revision Count

The slow synchronization is login-related synchronization scheduled to occur thirty minutes after the login event. The properties or attributes that are used when a user logs in to the network are scheduled for the slow synchronization.

The network address property added to the user objects when they log in indicates the physical workstation address from which the user is logging in. The last login time and current login time properties are modified to reflect the current status.

How Replica Synchronization Works

The replica synchronization process involves updating all the replicas for a specific partition with all the changes made to the partition since the last synchronization cycle. The process takes the replica pointer table (replica ring) and synchronizes each of the replicas one at a time with the most recent changes. The process must contact each server in the replica ring one at a time to complete a synchronization cycle for the partition.

The subordinate reference replicas are included in the synchronization process for a partition because they are found in the replica pointer table for a partition. This means that each of the replicas, including the subordinate reference replicas, is contacted during the synchronization cycle. The subordinate reference replica contains only the partition root object, and changes to that object are synchronized. The Synchronization Up To attribute of the partition root object changes frequently and is typically the only value synchronized for a subordinate reference replica.

After a server successfully sends all pending updates to a replica on another server, it proceeds to the next replica until all replicas have been updated. If the operation fails for any reason and is unable to update one or more replicas during the cycle, it reschedules the synchronization process to run at a later time.

Scheduling the Replica Synchronization Process

As mentioned in previous chapters, every object and property that exists in Directory Services has an associated timestamp. There is a creation timestamp and a last modification timestamp for the objects. The properties have a timestamp that indicates when it was last changed. The modification to a property or attribute value consists of deleting the old value and creating the new one. Thus, the timestamp associated with the property could be called a creation timestamp.

By way of review, each replica of a partition on a server maintains a property or attribute called the synchronized up to vector. The synchronized up to vector is a list of timestamps, one for each replica in the partition plus one for every modification. The synchronization process will examine the timestamp held in the synchronized up to attribute for each replica and determine if the information needs to be updated. The synchronized up to values for each replica of a partition can be viewed using either the NWADMIN or DSREPAIR utilities. Figure 9.15 shows the replica information for the CAMLEOT partition as shown in the NDS Manager of the NWADMIN utility.

Before starting the replica synchronization process and the first replica update, the server takes a snapshot of its own synchronized up to vector. The server saves the snapshot of these values in memory until all replicas have been contacted and successfully updated.

The replica information for the CAMELOT partition as shown in the NDS Manager utility

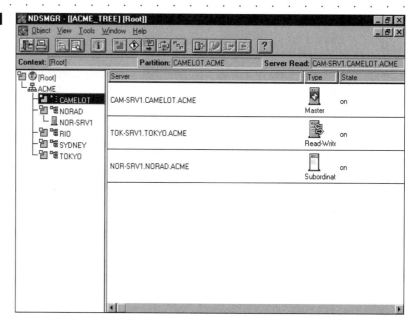

Performing the Replica Synchronization

The purpose of the replica synchronization process is to send any changes to the other servers that have a replica for a given partition. DSTRACE refers to this process as the skulker. Factors that determine whether synchronization is necessary are modifications or changes occurring with an associated timestamp. The synchronized up to vector from the other servers in the replica pointer table of a partition is compared with the local synchronized up to vector. If there are differences, the appropriate updates are made.

Directory Services examines the replica pointer table (replica ring) for the local partition to locate the replicas of the partition. The timestamps in the synchronized up to vector are compared to determine the need to synchronize changes. Figure 9.16 gives you a logical representation of the dialog that occurs each time the local server contacts one of the other servers in the replica pointer table.

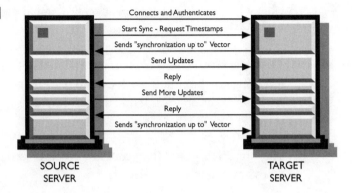

FIGURE 9.16

The dialog that occurs between servers during the replica synchronization process

SOURCE
SERVER

TARGET
SERVER

Connects and Authenticates
Start Sync - Request Timestamps
Sends "synchronization up to" Vector
Send Updates
Reply
Send More Updates
Reply
Sends "synchronization up to" Vector

The specific operations and steps that are performed during a replica synchronization process are listed below:

1 • The source (or local) server schedules its synchronization process after it receives a modification or event. If flagged as fast synchronization, the source server schedules synchronization at current time plus 10 seconds. Otherwise, the source server schedules synchronization at current time plus 30 minutes.

2 • The source server reads its synchronized up to vector.

3 • The source server reads the replica pointer table to determine which servers hold replicas of the partition being synchronized.

4 • The source server sets a flag that this partition is currently performing an outbound synchronization. This prevents the DSREPAIR utility from running multiple instances of synchronization for the same partition simultaneously.

5 • The source server connects and authenticates to a target server holding a replica to be synchronized. If the server cannot establish a connection, it displays a DS error –625 for the server and proceeds to the next replica.

6 • The source server requests the timestamp synchronized up to vector from the target server.

7 • The target server reads its own replica pointer table to determine whether the source server is in its replica ring. If not, the server returns a DS error –672 denying access.

8 • The target server checks if the specified replica is already processing incoming synchronization requests from another server. If yes, the server returns a DS error –692. If not, the server returns a start reply to the source server.

9 • The target server sends the requested synchronized up to vector of timestamps to the source server.

10 • The source server determines whether it needs to send updates by comparing its own synchronized up to values to that of the target server. If the timestamps for the source server are more recent than the target's, the synchronization will proceed. If the timestamps are not more recent, the source server completes the synchronization request with that server and begins synchronizing with the next replica in the ring. The source server then skips to Step 14.

11 • The source server sends the updates with the values to be changed for each object.

12 • The target server verifies that the objects sent from the source server should be updated. The target server compares the local timestamps for each of its objects with the one received from the source server.

13 • The target server updates the appropriate object and property information. The source and target servers repeat the update procedure until all updates are sent and received. The servers then send a reply indicating success or failure.

14 • The source server sends the target server an end synchronization message and includes the source server's own synchronized up to vector.

15 • The target server merges the timestamp values into its own synchronized up to vector using the higher values of the two vectors.

16 • The target server replies to the end synchronization request with a completion code indicating success or failure.

17 • The source server checks if all the replicas have been processed (All Processed=Yes).

    a • If the all the replicas have not been processed, then the source server either retries the synchronization for the replicas that were previously busy or reschedules the process for the partition if retries are exceeded.

    b • The source server creates the partition status attribute to indicate synchronization results.

    c • If all the replicas have been processed, the source server writes the synchronized up to vector that it began the process with to its replica up to vector for the partition.

18 • The replica synchronization process is completed.

By default the replica synchronization process is scheduled to execute only when changes are received to the object or properties in the NDS tree. However, using a DSTRACE command you can force the process to start (even if there are no changes to be propagated). To manually start the replica synchronization process enter the following DSTRACE command at the server console:

```
SET DSTRACE = *S
```

This setting checks to see if the partition has been marked as changed; if not, it won't do anything. The DSTRACE command or setting to force the replica synchronization process to exchange the timestamp (synchronization up to) is entered at the server console as follows:

```
SET DSTRACE = *H
```

See "The Replica Synchronization Heartbeat" section below.

The Replica Synchronization Heartbeat

NDS provides a trigger, or heartbeat, every thirty minutes to schedule replica synchronization. The heartbeat enables each IntranetWare server to contact all of the other IntranetWare servers that it has in its replica pointer tables. This is checked in case the server has become disconnected from the network. The heartbeat starts the replica synchronization process for each partition that it holds.

The network administrator can adjust the heartbeat time interval using the SET command called the NDS inactivity synchronization interval. The default value for this parameter is 30 minutes, but you can set this parameter by entering the following command at the server console:

```
SET NDS INACTIVITY SYNCHRONIZATION INTERVAL = 60
```

A SET DSTRACE command may be used to initiate the heartbeat synchronization immediately. This command is entered as follows:

```
SET DSTRACE = *H
```

The SET DSTRACE command, SET DSTRACE = !H [time in minutes] may be used to change the default time interval parameter. Although you can change the default time interval using this SET parameter, we do not recommend it.

INSPECTOR PROCESS

Directory Services uses the inspector process to verify that the object and property information in the NDS data files is valid. The inspector process specifically checks and verifies that the Directory Services information stored on the server is formed correctly. If there are anomalies in the information the inspector does not attempt to perform corrective action.

This process validates the object and property information, including the object name, class, timestamps, and references. It also checks to make sure that other objects reference the object correctly.

This process runs as needed with the flatcleaner process. The network administrator can manually activate the inspector using a DSTRACE SET command. To start the inspector process enter the following:

```
SET DSTRACE = +INSPECTOR
```
or
```
SET DSTRACE = +I
```

This process can be very expensive in terms of CPU utilization and should not be executed manually on a server during normal working hours.

LIMBER PROCESS

The limber process maintains tree and server connectivity. At specific times, each IntranetWare server in the NDS tree checks its distinguished name and addresses. The limber process will update or modify these values if necessary. The limber process checks the local server's entry to make sure that its distinguished name and address have not changed.

The limber process also ensures that if the relative distinguished name or internal IPX address is modified, the changes are replicated. The server name or IPX internal address can be changed in AUTOEXEC.NCF and then take effect when the server is restarted. The server name and IPX address are stored in the NDS server object created for the server.

If a server changes its name or address, the limber process is responsible for ensuring that the modifications are made to each replica pointer table in the partition. If the changes occur on the server with the master replica, the limber process changes its local address in the replica pointer table. If the changes occur on a server holding a nonmaster replica, the limber process tells the master replica. The limber process can initiate the backlink process, which does part of the checking for the limber process.

The limber process is initiated when each IntranetWare server boots up or Novell Directory Services is restarted. The process is also initiated every three hours by default. The limber process can be event-driven, meaning it is started when a server address is added, changed, or deleted. An address can be added for another protocol while the system is running.

The limber process verifies that the server has the correct tree name. If the tree name is changed, the limber process affects the change on the server. The tree name modification is performed by the server holding the master replica of the root partition. This server then sends the request to all the other servers in the tree. If the update request fails to reach a server, the limber process will eventually make sure that the change is received by the server after it becomes available.

The limber process can be started on a server manually by executing a SET DSTRACE command at the server console prompt. The command to schedule the limber process to start is as follows:

```
SET DSTRACE = *L
```

BACKLINK PROCESS

When creating an external reference, NDS also schedules the creation of a backlink attribute for the object. Thus, the corresponding attribute to an external reference object is the backlink. The purpose of the backlink is to keep track of external reference objects on other servers.

The backlink process checks the local external reference objects that are on the server. It also verifies the backlink attribute values that have been created for the objects contained on the server.

Directory Services periodically checks the external references to see if there is a reason for them to continue to exist. If an external reference is not needed, NDS will mark it to be removed.

The backlink process also enables maintenance of the external references by periodically verifying the information stored in the backlink attribute of the object. Each backlink attribute holds the remote server name and object ID of the associated external reference. By default, the backlink process checks consistency automatically every 780 minutes (13 hours). The default value can be changed for the backlink process by setting the SET parameter called NDS backlink interval, which is entered in minutes. In order to change the SET parameter at the server console enter:

```
SET NDS BACKLINK INTERVAL = 900
```

The range for this parameter is 2 to 10080 minutes. The backlink interval can also be changed using DSTRACE by entering the console command:

```
SET DSTRACE = !B [2-10080 minutes]
```

Using DSTRACE, the backlink process can be forced to execute immediately by setting the process flag. Enter the following DSTRACE server console command:

```
SET DSTRACE = *B
```

The backlink process will initiate sooner than the next regularly scheduled interval.

When an object is renamed, moved, or deleted, the backlinks make it possible for all the external references to that object to be changed. The backlink process has the responsibility to make the corresponding changes to the external references. Thus, the backlink process helps to maintain the integrity of external references by allowing them to be updated to reflect the changes made to the original objects.

JANITOR PROCESS

The janitor process's primary responsibility is to keep everything in the Directory Services clean. This process enables the Directory Services to efficiently reuse the storage or disk resources of the server. It accomplishes this task by performing several functions associated with the objects and properties in the NDS data files. The janitor process performs the following tasks:

▸ Purges the deleted objects and values from the NDS data files

▸ Schedules the flatcleaner

▸ Updates the Inherited Rights ACLs for the partitions

▸ Alerts for synthetic time

Purging the Deleted Objects and Properties

Before the object or property value is purged, the replica synchronization process makes sure that the object or value to be deleted is completely synchronized with all the other replicas of the partition. This ensures that each replica knows the object is going to be deleted before removing or purging it.

NDS reads the Replica Up To attribute of the partition and compares it against each object timestamp to determine which objects and property values need to be purged. A property value can be purged from an object if both of the following conditions are met:

▸ The property value is marked as deleted or not present

▸ The timestamp for the property is less recent than the purge time (the purge time is the same as the synchronized up to timestamp)

Once the janitor process has inspected all the property values for an object, it determines whether the entire object itself can be purged. The janitor process will purge any object that meets the following criteria:

▸ Object is marked as deleted or not present

▸ Object has no property values

NDS also checks if the partition root object (the top-most object in the partition) has been renamed. If the container object has been renamed, the janitor notifies all external references of the partition root object of the new name.

While scanning the partition, the janitor builds two lists:

▸ The release object ID list. This is a list of objects that have been marked as moved. For each object in the list, the master replica processes the obituaries for the move, which releases the move inhibit destination object.

▸ The notify external reference list. The server with the master replica builds a list of objects that have backlink obituaries to be processed. For each object in the list, the janitor uses this list to send synchronization messages to the associated external references. The messages specify the operation that must be performed on the external reference.

By default, the janitor process is scheduled every hour (60 minutes). The default value can be changed by setting the SET parameter called NDS janitor interval, which is entered in minutes. In order to change the SET parameter at the server console enter:

```
SET NDS JANITOR INTERVAL = 120
```

The range for this parameter is 1 to 10080 minutes. The janitor interval can also be changed using DSTRACE by entering the console command:

```
SET DSTRACE = !J [1-10080 minutes]
```

FLATCLEANER PROCESS

The flatcleaner process purges or removes the objects in Directory Services that are marked as deleted. The flatcleaner purges the expired dynamic bindery objects and external reference objects from the NDS data files. This process purges only the objects that have been marked as deleted or not present.

The flatcleaner process is scheduled by the janitor process. It is started after the flatcleaner interval has expired. By default the flatcleaner interval is one hour (60 minutes). The default value can be changed by setting the DSTRACE SET parameter at the server console as follows:

```
SET DSTRACE = !F (in minutes)
```

The flatcleaner can be forced to execute using a DSTRACE command at the server console as follows:

```
SET DSTRACE = *F
```

SCHEMA SYNCHRONIZATION PROCESS

The NDS schema can be modified or changed by creating new object classes or property definitions. The schema can be modified by client software. Typically, this would happen when new software applications are installed that require specific new kinds of objects or attributes. The user installing the software must have sufficient access rights before it can make the modifications.

NOTE

For example, Novell's GroupWise software product has an optional feature that extends the NDS schema. The feature is a snap-in option to the NWADMIN utility, which enables the administrator to create GroupWise accounts at the same time a user object is created in the NDS tree.

Schema changes are replicated or propagated among all the servers containing NDS replicas. The schema is replicated using a similiar synchronization process known as the replica synchronization process. Without this synchronization, the schema information on one server could become different from that on the other IntranetWare servers in the tree.

Using the schema synchronization process, which is event driven, schema modifications are scheduled ten seconds after the change. The updates to the schema are propagated automatically from one server to another in much the same way as other NDS updates. However, the schema synchronization differs in that partitions replicate according to the replica pointer table (replica ring), but schema synchronization occurs according to a trickle-down method. In this trickle-down method the schema synchronization or updates propagate in two directions:

- Across servers holding a replica of a given partition

- Downward in the partition tree

Propagation Across Replicas of a Partition

Like NDS objects, each schema object has a timestamp that indicates its last modification. The procedures for comparing and updating timestamps for the schema information between servers are the same as any other NDS objects.

To propagate the latest schema updated information among the replicas of a partition, a server uses the schema synchronization process with a few slight changes. IntranetWare servers without replicas can add themselves to the list of servers contacted. The specific operations and steps that are performed during a schema synchronization process for the replicas of a partition are listed below:

1 • The source server takes a snapshot of its own local synchronized up to attribute.

2 • The source server reads all the replica pointer tables (replica rings) in order to make a list of target servers to be sent the schema updates. The distribution list can include IntranetWare servers that do not have NDS replicas. The reference replica to the source server is stripped from the list, as well as all subordinate reference replicas.

3 • The source server will ping each target server in the distribution list to determine the tree depth of the root-most replica on the target server. If the replica depth is less than the source server's depth, the target server is skipped.

4 • A start synchronization request is then sent to the target server. The target server replies to the request by sending its synchronized up to vector.

5 • The source server compares the synchronized up to vectors to determine if the schema updates should be sent.

6 • The source server sends the updates to the schema.

7 • The source server sends the target server an end synchronization request containing its own synchronized up to vector.

8 • The target server merges the timestamps values into its own synchronized up to vector using the higher value of the two vectors.

9 • The schema synchronization is terminated for a partition after the source server has contacted and updated all the target servers.

Propagation Down to the Lower Partitions

In order to propagate the schema modifications down to lower partitions, the server where the modification is received starts the schema synchronization process with its partitions. Each time a target server receives a modification it will send the modification to lower partitions, if any. It will never send the modification to partitions that are higher. The procedures for the schema synchronization process are described above in the "Propagation Across Replicas of a Partition" section.

The trickle-down method of synchronizing the schema occurs when a target server receives the updated schema and builds its own list of servers to distribute the schema it just received. The target first checks to see if the partition(s) is lower than the original partition (partition where the modification is made). The procedures for updating the schema are performed across all replicas of a partition. In this way the schema updates are propagated downward to other partitions in the Directory tree and across all replicas of the partition.

CONTROLLING THE SCHEMA SYNCHRONIZATION

By default the schema synchronization process is scheduled to execute only when changes are made to the schema or after the expiration of the schema synchronization heartbeat. The default interval for the schema synchronization heartbeat is 4 hours (240 minutes). However, using a DSTRACE command you can force the process to start (even if there are no changes to be propagated). To manually start the schema synchronization process enter the following DSTRACE command at the server console:

```
SET DSTRACE = *SS
```

This flag starts the process, which will check to see if the schema on that server needs to be synchronized. This is the schema synchronization heartbeat.

You can disable schema synchronization altogether by entering the following DSTRACE command at the server console:

```
SET DSTRACE = !S   [0 = ON, Nonzero = OFF]
```

This flag both enables and disables the schema synchronization. The flag value of 0 will enable the schema synchronization. A nonzero value will disable the schema synchronization.

NDS Partition and Replica Operations

An administrator using the NWADMIN or NDS Manager utilities can make structural changes to the NDS tree. For example, the administrator can add and remove replicas, change replica types, create or merge partitions, or move subtrees.

The NDS is a multi-threaded system that enables the server to participate or perform multiple partition operations on different partitions on the server. A server can hold replicas of different partitions, and these replicas can be involved in their individual partition operations simultaneously on the server.

PARTITION AND REPLICA OPERATION CONTROL AND STATUS

All partition and replica operations are initiated by contacting the master replica for the partition. Since each partition can have only one operation in progress at a time, the master replica of the partition controls the operation. The master replica ensures that other partition operations are not started until the first operation is completed. The master replica is the traffic cop for partition operations.

The partition has certain attributes that are used to manage the partition operations. For example, some of the attributes used to help with the partition operation are replica pointer table, replica status, partition control, and partition status. As the operation proceeds through several states each server involved records the activity of these states in the partition control and status attributes.

Most partition operations are processed in several major passes. In the first pass, all affected servers are contacted with the details of the change. They report errors, if any. If any errors are detected in the first pass, this means the operation did not start and the message is returned to the utility. If there are no errors, the second pass contacts all the servers with replicas of the partition to finalize the modification.

The following sections summarize the operations that create and manage the NDS partitions and their replicas. The partition operations we will discuss include:

▸ Add Replica

▸ Remove Replica

▸ Change Replica Type

▸ Create (Split) Partition

▸ Merge (Join) Partition

▸ Move Subtree or Partition

Add Replica Operation

The add replica operation causes a new replica for a partition to be added to the partition's replica point table. The major events that occur during the add new replica operation are listed below:

1 • An administrator with the proper rights issues a request using the NWADMIN or NDS Manager utilities to add a new replica for the partition. Directory Services client automatically authenticates the workstation to the server holding the master replica of the partition.

2 • The administrator determines the replica type (read/write or read only) and selects the target server that will store the new replica.

3 • The server holding the master replica verifies the access rights of the user or administrator to the partition and destination server and checks that:

a • The target server object exists in the NDS tree

b • The replica type requested is read/write or read only

c • The partition is not involved in another partition operation

4 • The master replica server obtains the object ID for the partition root object on the target server.

5 • The master replica assigns the first unused replica number to the new replica.

6 • The master replica adds replica pointer table attribute values to the target server and sets the state for the new replica to RS_NEW_REPLICA. The master replica server adds the new replica created on the target server to its replica pointer table. This change to the replica pointer table will be synchronized out to the other replicas in the partition during the replica synchronization process already scheduled.

7 • The master replica schedules an immediate replica synchronization process to begin downloading the contents of the partition to the target server.

8 • The master replica server informs the client or workstation that the add new replica request was successful.

9 • The replica state begins with the replica in the RS_NEW_REPLICA state. During this replica state:

a • The target server accepts updates requests from only the master replica.

b • Clients cannot access the new replica; it is treated as not available.

10 • After all the information is sent to the new replica, the master replica server changes its replica state attribute from RS_NEW_REPLICA to RS_TRANSITION_ON. The replica state attribute will be propagated to the other replicas of the partition by the normal replica synchronization process.

11 • When the target server receives the replica state value of RS_TRANSITION_ON, it sends a request to the other replicas to obtain any updates more recent than those of the master replica.

12 • The target server synchronizes with all other replicas of the partition as needed.

13 • The target server then sends a request to the master replica server to change the replica state value to RS_ON.

14 • The master replica server receives the request and sets the replica state for the new replica to RS_ON. The replica state attribute will be propagated to the other replicas of the partition by the normal replica synchronization process.

15 • If needed, the master replica server sends a request to create the necessary reference replicas that are subordinate to the new replica. If the subordinate references replicas are created, the target server sends a request to the master of each child partition to update the replica pointer table to reflect the change.

16 • Each change will be propagated to the other replicas of each partition by the normal replica synchronization process.

17 • The add new replica operation is complete.

Remove Replica Operation

The remove replica operation deletes a replica from a specific server, which also removes it from the replica pointer table of the partition. The master replica cannot be removed. To remove a replica, a user must have managed rights at the partition root object and the server from which the replica is being removed. The major events that occur during the remove replica operation are listed below:

1 • An administrator with the proper rights issues a request using the NWADMIN or NDS Manager utilities to remove a replica from a server. Directory Services automatically authenticates the workstation to the server holding the master replica of the partition.

2 • The administrator selects the target server from which the replica is being removed.

3 • The master replica server verifies the access rights of the user or administrator to the partition and server and checks that:

    a • The master replica exists on that server

    b • The replica state is RS_ON

    c • The partition is not involved in another partition operation

4 • The master replica server changes the replica state to RS_DYING_REPLICA.

5 • The change to the replica state is propagated to the other replicas of the partition through the normal replica synchronization process.

6 • The target server knows that it has a replica whose state is RS_DYING_REPLICA. It checks to see if it holds the parent of the partition being removed.

7 • If the target server holds a parent:

    a • It sends a request to the server holding the master replica to update the replica pointer table to reflect the change. This request indicates that the replica being removed from the target server is changed to a subordinate reference replica.

    b • The target server sends the pending changes to at least one other replica not being removed and whose replica state is RS_ON.

c • The master replica server changes the replica type in the replica pointer table to subordinate reference for the target server replica.

d • The master replica server changes the replica state to RS_ON.

8 • If the target server does not hold the parent partition:

    a • The target server sends the pending changes to at least one other replica not being removed and whose replica state is RS_ON.

    b • The target server sends a request to the master replica server to remove the replica from the replica pointer table of the partition.

    c • The change to the replica pointer table will be propagated to the other replicas of the partition by the normal replica synchronization process.

9 • The target server converts its objects in the removed replica to external reference objects. It sends a request to create a backlink to a server holding the real object for each external reference created.

10 • All changes are propagated to the other replicas for the partition through the replica synchronization process.

11 • The remove replica operation is complete.

Change Replica Type Operation

The change replica type operation changes the type of any replica. The operation is started when an administrator decides to change the type of a replica on a specific server. The types of replicas that can be chosen are master, read/write, and read only. You cannot change a replica to a subordinate reference. The subordinate reference replicas are maintained by NDS.

The change replica type operation differs when the operation assigns a new master replica. This section discusses changing both nonmaster replica types (read/write and read only) and changing to a master replica. In order to change a replica to a master replica, the target server must hold a read/write or read only replica of the partition.

The major events that occur during the change replica type operation of a nonmaster replica are listed below:

1. • An administrator with the proper rights issues a request using the NWADMIN or NDS Manager utilities to change the replica type to either read/write or read only. Directory Services automatically authenticates the workstation to the server holding the master replica of the partition.

2. • The master replica server checks the access rights of the user or administrator to the partition.

3. • The master replica server changes the replica type in its copy of the replica pointer table.

4. • The change to the replica pointer table will be propagated to the other replicas of the partition by the normal replica synchronization process.

5. • The change replica type operation is complete.

The steps to change the Replica Type to a Master Replica are listed below:

1. • An administrator with the proper rights issues a request using the NWADMIN or NDS Manager utilities to change the replica type to the master replica. Directory Services automatically authenticates the workstation to the server holding the master replica of the partition. This server will be called the source server.

2. • The source server checks the access rights of the user or administrator to the partition.

3. • The source server identifies the target server in using the partition control attribute's distinguished name field.

4. • The source server sets the partition control attribute to PC_CHANGING_REPLICATYPE.

5 • The source sets the replica state of each replica in the replica pointer table to RS_CRT_0.

6 • The change to the partition control and replica pointer table attributes will be propagated to the other replicas of the partition using the normal replica synchronization process. This enables all the replicas in the partition to change the partition state to RS_CRT_0.

7 • The source server sends a request to the target server to set the replica to the new master. This routine tells the target server that it is now the master replica of the partition.

8 • The target server waits until its clock is ahead of the timestamps issued by the source (old master replica) server. It then issues new timestamps on the replica pointer table of this partition.

9 • The target server removes its name from the partition control attribute's distinguished name field.

10 • The target server is now the master replica and sets the partition state in the replica pointer table to RS_CRT_1.

11 • The target server changes its replica type in the replica pointer table to read/write (secondary) for the source server.

12 • The target server replies to the source indicating that the replica type has been changed to master successfully.

13 • The change to the replica pointer table on the target server will be propagated to the other replicas of the partition using the normal replica synchronization process.

14 • The source server changes its own replica type to read/write in the replica pointer table.

15 • The source server changes its replica state to RS_CRT_1.

16 • The changes made to the source server will be propagated to the other replicas of the partition using the normal replica synchronization process.

17 • The source server changes its replica state to RS_ON.

18 • The change will be propagated to the other replicas of the partition.

19 • The change replica type operation is complete.

Create (Split) Partition Operation

The create partition operation causes a partition (parent) to split and form a new child partition in the NDS tree. You can create any partition as long as it has a single container object as its partition root object. The major events that occur during the create partition operation are listed below:

1 • An administrator with the proper rights issues a request using the NWADMIN or PARTMGR utilities to create a new partition in the NDS tree. Directory Services automatically authenticates the workstation to the server holding the master replica of the partition.

2 • The master replica server identifies the NDS container object that will become the new partition root object where the partition is created.

3 • When the master replica server changes the master replica of the partition where the split will occur, the following events take place:

    a • The access rights of the user or administrator to the partitions and servers involved are checked.

    b • The replica state in each of the replica pointer tables is set to RS_SS_0.

    c • The partition control attribute is set with the distinguished name of the new partition root object and sets the current operation, which is a split partition.

4 • The changes made to the master replica will be propagated to the other replicas of the partition using the normal replica synchronization process.

5 • The master replica server sends a request to each server holding a replica of the partition to perform a split procedure. The subordinate references replicas are not included.

6 • The servers holding replicas of the partition process the split request by taking the partition attributes and values from the parent to the partition root object of the child partition.

7 • Each server returns a reply indicating success or failure to the split request.

8 • The master replica server performs the split procedure on its own replica list.

9 • The master replica server sets the replica state to RS_SS_1 (split state 1).

10 • The replica state (RS_SS_1) is propagated from the master replica to each of the other replicas of the partition.

11 • The master replica server advances the partition state and replica state to RS_ON for both the parent partition and new child partition.

12 • The changes made to the master replica will be propagated to the other replicas of the partition.

13 • The create or split partition operation is complete.

Merge (Join) Partition Operation

The merge partition operation causes a child partition to be joined back together with its parent partition. This operation requires that there is both a parent and child partition already existing in the NDS tree structure.

At the beginning of the merge operation, the replicas for each of the two partitions do not have to be stored on the same servers. However, the operation first proceeds by copying a replica of either the parent or child partition to all the servers involved. This ensures that each server will have the replicas for both the parent and child partition.

CONSULTING EXPERIENCE

It is highly recommended that before you execute a merge operation of a parent and child partition, you manually place replicas of each partition on the servers that will be involved. If the replicas do not exist, the merge operation will place them for you. However, the merge operation will complete faster if you manually place the replicas in advance.

The merge operation will make the replica pointer table the same for both the parent and child partitions, excluding the subordinate references from the parent's replica list. When NDS creates all the replicas of the new partition, it simply erases the partition boundary between the parent partition and the child partition.

The major events that occur during the merge partition operation are listed below:

1 • An administrator with the proper rights issues a request using the NWADMIN or NDS Manager utilities to merge a child partition with its parent. Directory Services automatically authenticates the workstation to the server holding the master replica of the child partition.

2 • The workstation sends the request to the server holding the child partition.

3 • The master replica of the child partition locates the parent partition's master replica.

4 • The master replica of the child partition verifies the access rights of the user or administrator to the partitions and servers involved and checks that:

   a • The request is valid.

   b • The child partition is not involved in another partition operation.

c • The software versions on the servers involved support the merge operation. This means that all servers involved must be running IntranetWare v4.63 or later.

5 • The master replica of child partition sends a request to the server holding the master replica of the parent partition to start the merge procedure.

6 • The master replica of the parent partition receives a request to start the merge operation and changes the master replica as follows:

> **a** • The replica state in the replica pointer tables and partition control attribute is set to RS_JS_0.
>
> **b** • The partition control attribute also receives the distinguished name of the child partition root object.
>
> **c** • The current operation is set to PC_JOINING_DOWN.

7 • The changes made to the master replica will be propagated to the other replicas of the parent partition using the normal replica synchronization process.

8 • The master replica of the parent partition replies to the server holding the master replica of the child partition the success or failure of the request to start the merge.

9 • The master replica of the child partition receives the reply and changes the master replica as follows:

> **a** • Replica state in the replica pointer tables and partition control attribute is set to RS_JS_0.
>
> **b** • Partition control attribute also receives the distinguished name of the parent partition root object.
>
> **c** • Current operation is set to PC_JOINING_UP.

10 •   The master replica of the child partition replies to the client or workstation that the merge operation client is successful or not.

11 •   The changes made to the master replica will be propagated to the other replicas of the parent partition using the normal replica synchronization process.

12 •   The master replica servers for both the parent and child partitions check the replica pointer table (replica ring) to determine which servers must add replicas. Both a replica of the parent and child partitions are required before the merge can take place.

13 •   The master replica server sends a request to other servers as follows:

    a •   Servers containing replicas of the child partition, but not the parent, receive new replicas of the parent with new replica numbers.

    b •   Servers containing replicas of the parent partition, but not the child, receive new replicas of the child partition with new replica numbers. Does not include the servers containing subordinate reference replicas.

14 •   The master replica of the child partition advances the replica state to RS_JS_1.

15 •   The master replica of the parent partition checks that the child partition state is PC_JOINING_UP.

    a •   If the state is not PC_JOINING_UP, it sets the partition and replica states to RS_ON. This stops the partition merge procedure.

    b •   If the state is PC_JOINING_UP, it sends a request to all servers holding replicas of the two partitions to perform a merge procedure.

16 • The nonmaster server receives the request and erases the boundary between the partitions by placing all objects from both partitions into one partition.

17 • The master replica of the parent partition then performs the merge procedure on itself.

18 • The master replica of the parent partition sets the replica state of the new merged partition to RS_ JS_2.

19 • The changes made to the master replica will be propagated to the other replicas of the parent partition.

20 • The master replica of the child partition then performs the merge procedure on itself.

21 • The master replica of the child partition sets the replica state of the new merged partition to RS_ JS_2.

22 • The changes made to the master replica will be propagated to the other replicas of the parent partition.

23 • The master replica of the child partition sets the replica state to RS_ON.

24 • The master replica of the parent partition sets the replica types as follows:

    a • The master replica of the parent becomes the master replica of the merged partition.

    b • The master replica of the child partition becomes read/write replica.

    c • All other replicas of the child partition become replicas of the new partition.

25 • The changes made to the master replicas will be propagated to the other replicas of the partition using the normal replica synchronization process.

26 • The merge or split partition operation is complete.

Move Subtree or Partition Operation

NetWare Directory Services allows you to move any subtree of the NDS tree as long as it is a partition. The subtree or partition being moved cannot have child partitions.

The move subtree operation moves a container with all its subordinate objects to another logical location in the NDS tree. The objects in the partition moved changed their distinguished name but the relative distinguished name remains the same. The servers that hold replicas for the partition being moved remain the same during the operation. This means that the move is logical (in the NDS tree) and not physical.

In the following example, the NDS tree has three partitions (NORAD, CAMELOT, and OPS), which are involved in moving the subtree. Figure 9.17 illustrates the OPS partition being moved from CAMELOT.ACME (source) to NORAD.ACME (destination).

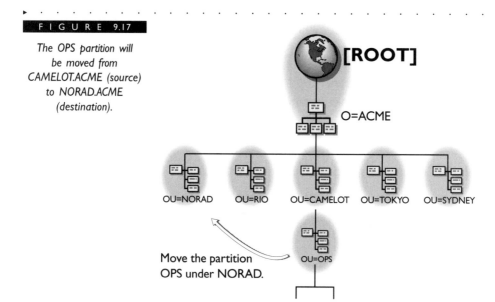

FIGURE 9.17

The OPS partition will be moved from CAMELOT.ACME (source) to NORAD.ACME (destination).

The major events that occur during the move subtree operation are listed below:

I • An administrator with the proper rights issues a request using the NWADMIN or NDS Manager utilities to move the subtree or partition

OPS from CAMELOT.ACME (source) to NORAD.ACME (destination). Directory Services automatically authenticates the workstation to the server holding the master replica of the OPS partition.

2 • The workstation sends the request to server holding the master of the NORAD partition. This is the destination partiton.

3 • The master replica server of NORAD creates the following control list of information:

   a • The access rights of the user or administrator to the partitions and servers involved

   b • The operation's expiration time, which is set to one hour

   c • The partition root object ID for NORAD (the destination)

   d • The distinguished name of the server holding the master replica of OPS

   e • The new relative distinguished name of the moved object

4 • If the expiration time passes before a moved object is received from the source server, the destination server purges its record of the move details and does not continue moving the partition.

5 • The master replica of NORAD checks its ACL attribute to see that the administrator or client has create rights and that the partition is idle.

6 • The client sends a message to finish the move to the master replica server of OPS.

7 • The master replica server of OPS checks that its software version and all the other servers holding replicas of the OPS partition are at least DS v4.63.

8 • If the source and destination partitions are the same partition, then a PartitionOverlab flag is set.

9 • At the request of the source server, the master replica of OPS sets the following:

    a • The replica state in the replica pointer table to RS_MS_0.

    b • The partition control function to PC_MOVE_SUBTREE_DEST.

    c • The partition control attribute also receives the distinguished name of the destination partition.

    d • Adds an OBT_TREE_OLD_RDN to the source object if its relative distinguished name is being changed. This obituary records the old name of the partition being moved.

10 • The master replica server of OPS sends the client a reply indicating success or failure.

11 • The changes made to the master replica will be propagated to the other replicas of the CAMELOT partition using the normal replica synchronization process.

12 • The master replica of NORAD sets the following:

    a • Sets the replica states in the replica pointer table to RS_MS_0.

    b • Partition operation to PC_MOVE_SUBTREE_SRC.

    c • Partition control attribute also receives the distinguished name of the source partition.

    d • Adds an OBT_TREE_OLD_RDN to the source object if its relative distinguished name is being changed. This obituary records the old name of the partition being moved.

13 • The changes made to the master replica will be propagated to the other replicas of the NORAD partition.

14 • The master replica of OPS builds a server notification list of servers that will participate in moving the subtree:

    a • Servers holding replicas of the CAMELOT partition

    b • Servers holding replicas of the NORAD partition

    c • Servers holding replicas of the OPS partition

    d • Servers holding external references to objects in the CAMELOT partition (as identified by backlinks)

15 • The master replica server for OPS records the server notification list as an OBT_MOVE_TREE obituary for each server in the list.

16 •. If the PartitionOverlap flag was set in Step 8, then the master replica server for OPS sends a partition lock request to the server holding the master replica of the NORAD partition. This prevents other partition operations on the partitions while the subtree is being moved.

17 • The master replica server for OPS sends a reply indicating success or failure. The client no longer participates in moving the subtree.

18 • The master replica server for OPS will drive the completion of the move subtree operation.

19 • The master replica server sends a request to every server in the server notification list to start the move subtee. This request is driven by the obituaries.

20 • Each server on the notification list changes its replicas according to the new NDS tree structure. The change to each server depends on the replicas it holds.

21 • The master replica server sends a request to each of the servers on the notification list to end the move operation.

22 • Servers on the list set their obituary flags to OBF_PURGEABLE and return a reply.

23 • The master replica sends a partition unlock request to the master replica of CAMELOT and also sends a partition unlock request to the server holding the master replica of NORAD if the PartitionOverlap flag was set.

24 • The master replica server receiving the unlock request sets the partition state to RS_ON.

25 • The master replica of OPS sets the replica states to RS_ON.

26 • The changes made to the master replicas will be propagated to the other replicas of the appropriate partition.

27 • The move subtree partition operation is complete.

CHAPTER 10

Troubleshooting Novell Directory Services

"What we anticipate seldom occurs; what we least expected generally happens."
Henrietta Temple

Chapters 8 and 9 should have given you a much better understanding of how the internal operations of IntranetWare work together to provide an enterprise network system. In fact, you should make sure to read Chapters 8 and 9 before reading this chapter because the material covered in this chapter uses terms explained in those chapters. This chapter also deals with partition and replica operations. For the details on these concepts, you can refer back to Chapters 6 and 9. Troubleshooting has been described as a combination of art, science, and luck. One reason troubleshooting tends not to be much fun is that administrators often do not know enough about the underlying technology to properly define network problems. Unfortunately, as networks grow larger and larger, they are also becoming more complex. Under NetWare 3, troubleshooting was usually confined to tracking down a server or two that was experiencing a problem. Typically, you could focus on a single server and identify problems quickly.

Troubleshooting IntranetWare can be easy. However, you are now dealing with a more complex multiserver environment in which servers communicate with one another. In addition, the technology is still new to many companies and may be unfamiliar to users and administrators. Novell continues to introduce improved repair utilities and procedures for maintaining your IntranetWare network. Make sure to keep informed about patches and announcements by checking Novell's NetWire and Web site regularly.

Novell is dedicated to providing the best operating system available in the industry. In fact, no other network operating system comes close to IntranetWare in terms of speed and scaleability. In addition, Novell is the only company currently with a Directory Services solution.

This chapter describes NDS primarily from the point of view of supportability. Based on information gathered, in part, by the staff on Novell's technical support teams, this chapter explains how to maintain and troubleshoot NDS. Experience has shown that, if NDS operations are properly verified before and after being initiated, NDS management can be virtually error free. This chapter covers three key topics:

▸ Understanding and using the IntranetWare repair tools

▸ Performing and verifying partition operations

▸ Troubleshooting *do's* and *don'ts*

Understanding and Using the Repair Tools

The following sections describe the IntranetWare repair tools: the DSREPAIR and the DSTRACE SET commands. These utilities are very important tools you will use during normal NDS maintenance and troubleshooting. By using a combination of DSREPAIR and DSTRACE you will be able to perform three basic NDS troubleshooting steps. These steps are:

▸ Identify the partition that is experiencing errors by using and understanding the DSTRACE set parameters and using the DSREPAIR utility.

▸ Identify the replica(s) in the partition that have errors. Identify these errors by using the DSTRACE SET commands and the DSREPAIR utility.

▸ Identify the error and take the appropriate action. Appendix A of this book lists the errors and recommended remedies.

DSREPAIR UTILITY

The DSREPAIR utility enables you to monitor Novell Directory Services, check for errors, and correct problems in the name service on an individual server basis. The utility runs as a NetWare Loadable Module (NLM) at the server console. The utility is menu driven and is written with the well-known C-worthy user interface. The following are the main functions of DSREPAIR:

▸ Correct or repair inconsistencies in the NDS name service

▸ Check NDS partition and replica information

▸ Initiate replica synchronization

CONSULTING EXPERIENCE

You should not run the Unattended Full Repair option in DSREPAIR on a regular basis or as a scheduled maintenance procedure. Running this option on a regular basis is not a proactive measure and will not guarantee against NDS problems. Instead, you should run this option in DSREPAIR only as needed to monitor and repair specific problems.

You can run the DSREPAIR utility on any IntranetWare server in the Directory tree. You can either load the utility while at the server console or access a server via the RCONSOLE utility and initiate and operate the DSREPAIR utility remotely. Figure 10.1 illustrates the DSREPAIR utility main menu.

FIGURE 10.1

The DSREPAIR utility
main menu

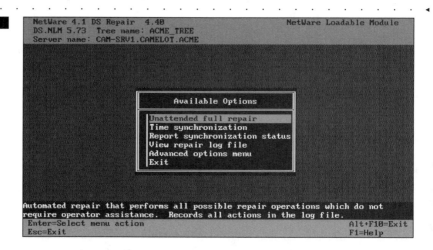

The DSREPAIR utility can provide the following options:

▸ Unattended Full Repair — This feature automatically performs repair operations on the local NDS name service without operator assistance.

▶ Time Synchronization — This option checks the time synchronization for all servers that are known to the local server. You must monitor and correct time synchronization problems before performing any repair operation. A replica of the [ROOT] partition must be on the local server running DSREPAIR for this feature to contact all servers in the tree.

▶ Replica Synchronization — This option lets you check the status of any partition on the server.

▶ View/Edit Repair Log File — This option lets you track all the operations of the DSREPAIR utility by consulting a log file stored on your server. The default log file is SYS:SYSTEM\DSREPAIR.LOG. You should always view the log file after running the utility.

▶ Advanced Options Menu — The advanced options on this menu give you greater flexibility to manually control the repair of your NDS tree.

Unattended Full Repair

The Unattended Full Repair option automatically performs all possible repair operations that do not require operator assistance. This option goes through five major repair procedures:

▶ It repairs the local NDS database, which locks the database during the repair operation so that no new database updates can occur until completed.

▶ It repairs any NCP server object's network address; the database is not locked during this operation.

▶ It verifies all remote NCP server object IDs; the database is not locked during this operation.

▶ It checks replica rings; the database is not locked during this operation.

▶ It authenticates every server in the ring and verifies information on the ring.

You can control which of the preceding items are checked or repaired by using the Repair Local DS Database option, which is described later in this chapter under the "Advanced Options Menu" section. Refer to the Repair Local DS Database selection screen for more information shown later in this chapter.

The log file records all the actions during the Unattended Full Repair operation. When the repair operations are completed, the log file is opened so you can see what repairs were made and check the current state of the database.

Time Synchronization

The Time Synchronization option contacts every server known to the local server and requests information about time synchronization, Directory Services, and server status. The information is written to the log file. When the operation has completed, the log file is opened so you can check the status of time synchronization plus other Directory Services information. Figure 10.2 shows the log file after the time synchronization operation has been run on the ACME tree.

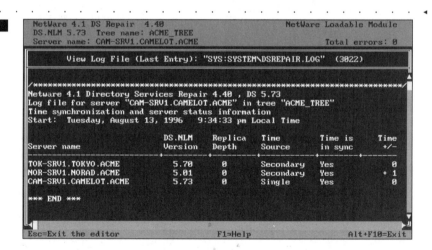

FIGURE 10.2

The log file after the time synchronization operation has been run on the ACME tree

```
NetWare 4.1 DS Repair  4.40                        NetWare Loadable Module
DS.NLM 5.73  Tree name: ACME_TREE
Server name: CAM-SRV1.CAMELOT.ACME                       Total errors: 0
┌────────────────────────────────────────────────────────────────────────┐
│        View Log File (Last Entry): "SYS:SYSTEM\DSREPAIR.LOG"   (3022)   │
├────────────────────────────────────────────────────────────────────────┤
│/********************************************************************/    │
│Netware 4.1 Directory Services Repair 4.40 , DS 5.73                      │
│Log file for server "CAM-SRV1.CAMELOT.ACME" in tree "ACME_TREE"           │
│Time synchronization and server status information                        │
│Start:  Tuesday, August 13, 1996   9:34:33 pm Local Time                  │
│                                                                          │
│                        DS.NLM   Replica   Time       Time is      Time   │
│Server name             Version  Depth     Source     in sync      +/-    │
│                        -------  -------   ------     -------      ----    │
│TOK-SRV1.TOKYO.ACME       5.70      0      Secondary    Yes          0     │
│NOR-SRV1.NORAD.ACME       5.01      0      Secondary    Yes        + 1     │
│CAM-SRV1.CAMELOT.ACME     5.73      0      Single       Yes          0     │
│                                                                          │
│*** END ***                                                               │
│                                                                          │
├────────────────────────────────────────────────────────────────────────┤
│Esc=Exit the editor              F1=Help                  Alt+F10=Exit    │
└────────────────────────────────────────────────────────────────────────┘
```

An explanation of each field in the log file is provided in Table 10.1.

	FIELD	CONTENT
	Server Name	The distinguished name of the server responding to the request.
	DS.NLM Version	The version of the DS.NLM running on the responding server. This information is valuable as a quick reference to see the versions of NDS running on the servers of your network.
	Replica Depth	The replica depth indicates how deep in the NDS tree moving away from [ROOT] the first replica is on the responding server. Each server knows which replica is highest in the NDS tree. This value is the number being reported. A positive number indicates how many objects there are from the [ROOT] to the highest replica. A value of -1 indicates that no replicas are stored on the server.
	Time Source	The time source is the type of time server the responding server is configured to be.
	Time is in Sync	This field indicates the time synchronization status of the responding time server. The possible values are Yes and No. The value displayed is the status of the synchronization flag for each server. This means that the server's time is within the time synchronization radius. Refer to Chapter 7 for more information on time synchronization.
	Time Delta	This field reports the time difference, if any, from the time synchronization radius for each server. The time synchronization radius is 2 seconds by default, so you will probably not see a server with more than a 2-second difference. If the value is larger, the Time is in Sync field is probably set to No. The maximum the field can report is up to 999 minutes and 59 seconds.

TABLE 10.1

Fields in the log file

Replica Synchronization

The Replica Synchronization option starts a replica synchronization process for all the partitions that have replicas on this server. This operation starts the synchronization process for all partitions and replicas. If you want to perform the same operation for individual partitions, you need to select the Replica and Partition Operations option from the Advanced Options menu.

The Replica Synchronization operation contacts each server in each of the replica lists stored on the server. A server does not attempt to synchronize to itself, so the status returned for a server's own replica is the value of "host."

The operation uses the log file to track the actions of the requests and displays any errors that occur. This operation is a quick and easy way to determine that the partitions and servers are communicating and synchronizing properly.

View/Edit Repair Log File

The View/Edit Repair Log File option lets you view the DSREPAIR log file, which contains the results of the previously performed operations. The default log file is stored in SYS:SYSTEM\DSREPAIR.LOG. When DSREPAIR performs an operation, the results are written to this log file. A record of each succeeding operation is appended to the log file, which increases in size with each repair operation. The size of the log file is displayed on the title line in parentheses after the name of the file.

Using the advanced options menu in DSREPAIR, you can turn the log file off, turn it on, change the name of the file, and delete the file.

Advanced Options Menu

The Advanced Options menu enables you to control the individual repair operations manually. You can also use it to monitor status and access diagnostic information about your Novell Directory Services tree. These options provide advanced repair operations that you should execute only if you understand the procedures and how they function. The Advanced Options menu provides the options shown in Figure 10.3, several of which are identical to the main menu options.

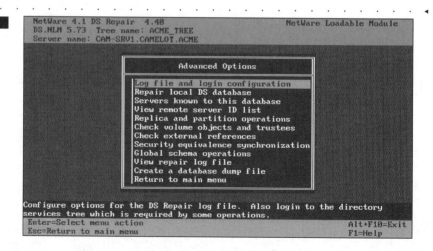

FIGURE 10.3

The Advanced Options menu in DSREPAIR

```
NetWare 4.1 DS Repair  4.40                         NetWare Loadable Module
DS.NLM 5.73  Tree name: ACME_TREE
Server name: CAM-SRV1.CAMELOT.ACME

                         Advanced Options
                 ┌─────────────────────────────────────┐
                 │ Log file and login configuration     │
                 │ Repair local DS database             │
                 │ Servers known to this database       │
                 │ View remote server ID list           │
                 │ Replica and partition operations     │
                 │ Check volume objects and trustees    │
                 │ Check external references            │
                 │ Security equivalence synchronization │
                 │ Global schema operations             │
                 │ View repair log file                 │
                 │ Create a database dump file          │
                 │ Return to main menu                  │
                 └─────────────────────────────────────┘

Configure options for the DS Repair log file.  Also login to the directory
services tree which is required by some operations.
 Enter=Select menu action                               Alt+F10=Exit
 Esc=Return to main menu                                 F1=Help
```

Log File and Login Configuration   This option lets you configure the log file and log in to the Directory tree. Configuring the log file enables you to manage where DSREPAIR writes the information it gathers. You can turn the log file off, delete it, and change the name of the file itself. The file can be stored on any volume or DOS drive.

The login function presents a login screen that lets you enter an administrator user name and password. Once you have logged in, the authentication information is maintained in server memory for all other repair operations that require an administrator to log in.

Repair Local DS Database   This option repairs the local NDS name service and performs the same function as the Unattended Full Repair option in the main menu. Figure 10.4 shows the Repair Local DS Database selection screen. You can select or deselect each item to turn it on or off for the unattended full repair.

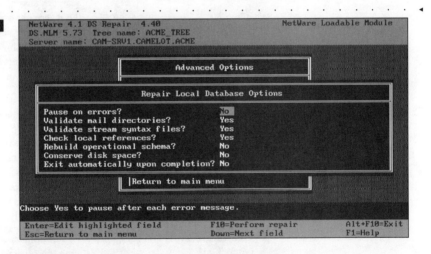

F I G U R E 10.4

The Repair Local DS
Database selection screen

During the repair operations, Novell Directory Services is temporarily locked, preventing clients from logging in. Several items are checked during the repair operation. For example, the Directory tree structure is checked to ensure that all records are linked to the [ROOT] object and that the object and property records are linked. The partition records are checked for validity and any errors are fixed. A check is made for invalid checksums and links between records and any errors are fixed.

The repair operation creates a set of temporary NDS files that are used to perform all the changes. The temporary files have the .TMP extension. At the end of the repair operation these temporary files become the permanent NDS files, unless you choose not to accept the repairs that were made.

Descriptions of the Repair Local DS Database options are listed in Table 10.2.

TABLE 10.2 The Repair Local DS Database options	OPTION NAME	DEFAULT	DESCRIPTION
	Pause on errors?	No	Turn on this option if you want DSREPAIR to stop on errors. After the repair is complete, you can view all actions it performed in the log file.
	Validate trustee IDs?	Yes	This option checks all the volumes in the NetWare file system for valid trustees after the repairs have been made and searches all mounted volumes for trustee IDs. It creates a report of the trustee IDs that don't have an object in NDS and then deletes the trustee assignment from the volume. This option is similar to a feature found in NetWare 3's BINDFIX utility.
	Validate mail directories?	Yes	This option checks the mail directories on volume SYS for users who no longer exist after the repairs have been made. Novell Directory Services does not require the user to have a mail directory. The mail directories are migrated from NetWare 3 to support bindery users in NetWare 4.11.
	Validate stream syntax files?	Yes	This option checks for valid stream files after the repair operation. Stream files contain data for a property whose data type syntax is stream, such as a login script. The files are associated with a specific user object or other object. If the user (or other object) no longer exists in NDS, the stream files associated with the user (or other object) are removed.

TABLE 10.2	OPTION NAME	DEFAULT	DESCRIPTION
The Repair Local DS Database options (continued)	Rebuild operational schema?	No	The operational schema is the set of rules that NDS uses to create objects and properties. The schema is required for base operations. If the schema becomes damaged or corrupted, you should rebuild it using this option. However, it is extremely unlikely that this situation will arise.
	Conserve disk space?	No	DSREPAIR creates temporary copies of the NDS files and operates on these files. You can choose to save or discard the changes after a repair has completed. If you save the changes by leaving this option set to No, the temporary files become the real NDS files and the current NDS files are assigned the .OLD extension. This ensures that DSREPAIR has an old set of files that Novell technical support can review in case of emergency. The drawback to saving at least one old copy of the NDS files is that it takes up a little more disk space. In most cases this will not be an issue because the NDS files don't take up a large amount of disk space.
	Exit automatically upon completion?	No	This option lets you look at the log file before saving the changes to the repaired NDS files. If you choose Yes, the utility automatically saves the changes and exits DSREPAIR.

Servers Found in this Directory Services Database This option displays all the servers that the local NDS knows about. Each server must contact all servers in the replica list during replica synchronization. The local server will only know about the servers it needs to contact. If the local server has a copy of the [ROOT] partition, the list of known servers most likely contains all the servers in the tree because of remote and local IDs.

Figure 10.5 shows the servers found in this Directory Services Database screen. This information shows servers from replica lists, servers from remote/local IDs, and NCP server objects in any partition.

FIGURE 10.5

The Servers found in this Directory Services Database screen in DSREPAIR

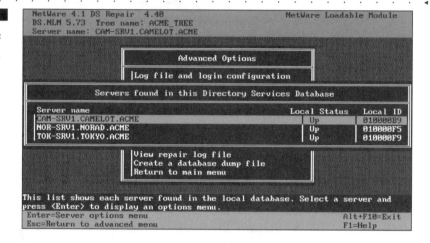

The Local Status field displays the state of the server as seen from the local server. If the value for a server is UP, the remote server is active. However, if the value is DOWN, the local server cannot communicate with the other server.

If you can select a server from the list, the Server Options menu shown in Figure 10.6 becomes available. This menu applies to the selected server.

FIGURE 10.6

The DSREPAIR Server Options menu

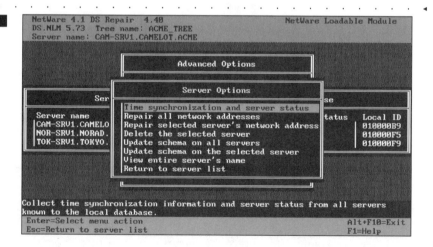

The Server Options menu provides the following options:

▸ Time Synchronization and Server Status — This option contacts every server known to the local server and requests information about time synchronization, Directory Services, and server status. This option is the same as the Time Synchronization option on the main menu.

▸ Repair All Network Addresses — This option checks every server object known to this server and searches for the server's name in the local SAP table. If the address is found in the SAP table, this address is compared with the value stored by the local server. If the two addresses do not match, the address in the SAP table is assumed to be correct and the other addresses are changed to match it. This operation is performed if you select the Unattended Full Repair option from the DSREPAIR main menu.

▸ Repair Selected Server's Network Address — This option repairs the highlighted server's network address in replica rings and server objects in the local database.

▸ Delete the Selected Server — This option enables you to delete the server that you selected from this list. This option should be used carefully, and you will want to delete the highlighted server only when you are having problems cleaning up a server that has been removed from the NDS tree structure.

▸ Update Schema on All Servers — This option verifies the NDS schema on all servers known to the local server. It updates the schema if needed. This option is the same as Global Schema Update in the Advanced Options menu, except that it only checks servers known to the local server. This option can be applied to servers running NetWare versions 4.02 and earlier.

▸ Update Schema on the Selected Server — This option verifies the schema and updates the base schema (if needed) on the selected server. This option is applicable to servers running NetWare versions 4.02 and earlier.

▸ View Entire Server's Name — This option allows you to view the server's distinguished name.

View Remote Server ID List   The View Remote Server ID List option displays the local and remote ID for all the servers that this server has authenticated to. Figure 10.7 shows the screen that is displayed when you select the View Remote Server ID List option.

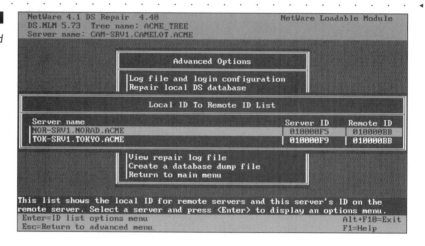

FIGURE 10.7

The screen that is displayed when you select the View Remote Server ID List option in DSREPAIR

If you select a server from the list displayed in the View Remote Server ID List, the Remote Server ID Options menu shown in Figure 10.8 is immediately displayed and becomes the active menu. This menu applies only to the server you selected in the previous menu.

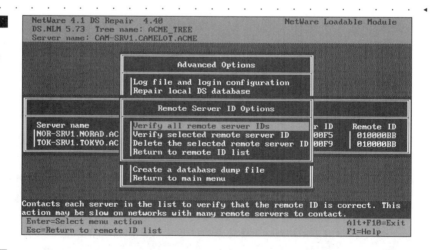

FIGURE 10.8

The DSREPAIR Remote Server ID Options menu

The Remote Server ID Options menu provides three additional options that you can perform for the selected server:

▸ Verify All Remote Server IDs — This option uses the remote server ID cache table on the selected server to locate other servers. It then contacts each server in the list to verify that its ID on that server is correct. This option checks all remote servers and repairs or deletes any IDs that are not correct. This operation is also performed by the Unattended Full Repair option in the main menu.

▸ Verify Selected Remote Server ID — This option is the same as the Verify All Remote Server IDs except that it checks only the selected server.

▸ Delete the Selected Remote Server ID — This option removes or deletes the selected server's ID from the local server table. Choose this option only if you are correcting a problem that is causing a bad remote server ID and that the Unattended Full Repair option cannot fix.

Replica and Partition Operations   You should become very familiar with the Replica and Partition Operations option on the Advanced Options menu. You will use this menu more than any other menu during the maintenance of NDS. When this option is selected, DSREPAIR displays a list of all the replicas stored on the server. This list applies only to the server on whichwhere you are running DSREPAIR. This is the Replicas Stored on this Servere list of replicas displayed is called the Replicas Stored on this Server menu shown in Figure 10.9. Each replica isThe replicas are shown in list format, with the replica type (master, read/write, read only, and subordinate reference) and replica state (ON, OFF, and so on).

From the Replicas Stored on this Server menu, you can select an individual replica or partition, which enables you to obtain more specific information and perform maintenance functions. After you select an individual replica or partition from the list, you'll see a larger Replica Options menu called Replica Option, Partition: <partition name>. Figure 10.10 shows this Replica Options menu. In the figure the name of the partition is CAMELOT.ACME. This menu includes an extensive list of specific options and operations that enable you to perform specific diagnostic and repair functions. These operations apply only to the partition selected.

F I G U R E 10.9

The Replicas Stored on this
Server menu in DSREPAIR

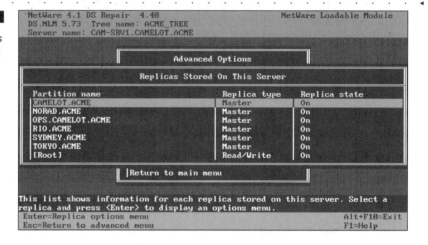

F I G U R E 10.10

The Replica Option
Partition menu in
DSREPAIR for the
CAMELOT.ACME partition

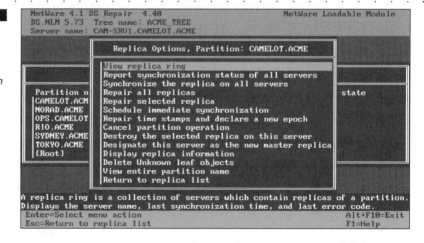

The Replica Options menu is the most heavily used menu in DSREPAIR because it enables you to monitor, diagnose, and repair specific problems with the replicas stored on a particular server. Several repair options in this menu require you to log in as a user who has rights to perform the operation. The utility makes you log in before running all of the important repair options as a final check that you are authorized to perform the operation.

The operations in this menu affect the entire partition and all of its replicas. This is one place that the DSREPAIR utility can start operations on the other servers through the use of a replica list.

If you want to affect only the replica that is stored on a specific server, select the View Replica Ring option, select a specific replica on any server, and then perform partition and replica operations on only that server.

The Replica Options menu supplies several additional options that you can execute for the partition and all of its replicas, as described below:

▶ View Replica Ring — This option provides another menu or list of all the servers that contain replicas for the selected partition. The menu that appears is called Replicas of Partition: <partition name>. A replica ring is equivalent to a replica list, which is a list of all the servers that hold replicas for a specific partition. The replica ring shows the replica type and replica state information for each server. You can choose a server or replica in this list and display the Replica of Partition: <partition name> menu, as shown in Figure 10.11, which provides more functionality on the selected server. This figure illustrates information for the CAMLEOT.ACME partition.

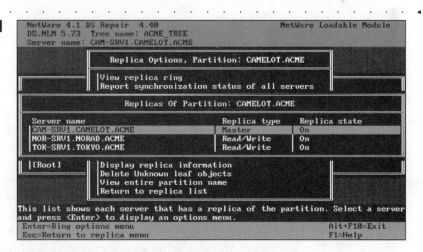

FIGURE 10.11

The Replicas for Partition: menu in DSREPAIR

Selecting the View Replica Ring option will display the Replicas for Partition: <partition name> menu, which supplies the following options. These options affect only the selected partition:

▸ Report Synchronization Status on the Selected Server — This option checks the synchronization status of every server that has a replica of the selected partition. If all the servers with a replica response are synchronizing, the partition is functioning properly.

▸ Synchronize the Replica on the Selected Server — This option determines the synchronization status of the selected partition on the selected server. If the selected server can synchronize with the other servers that hold a replica, the system is functioning properly. This option tells the selected server to start an immediate synchronization of the partition and report the results.

▸ Send all Objects to Every Replica in the Ring — This option sends all objects from the selected server in the replica ring to all the other servers that contain a replica of the partition. This operation cannot be executed from a subordinate reference replica. Note that this function can generate high network traffic.

▸ Receive All Objects from the Master to this Replica — This option sends all objects from the master replica to the replica on the selected server, which is marked as a new replica.

▸ Remove this Server from the Replica Ring — This option removes the selected server from the replica ring on the server where DSREPAIR is running. *Be extremely careful with this option!* If a server is either no longer in the tree or no longer contains a replica but still appears in the replica ring, you should first delete the server object (unless you have a single partition) with the NDS Manager utility. The server object being deleted will update the replica ring accordingly, and you should not have to run this option.

WARNING

You should execute the Remove this Server from the Replica Ring option only if Directory Services does not complete the removal of the server using the procedure explained above. This would mean that Directory Services is sufficiently damaged to prevent normal operation. You should be aware that misuse of this option can cause further damage to the Directory Services tree.

▸ View Entire Server Name — This option lets you view the distinguished name of the server.

▸ Synchronize All Servers in all Replicas — This option determines the synchronization status for every replica stored on the server on which DSREPAIR is running. It contacts each server in the replica ring and tells that server to start an immediate synchronization to every other server. This option is the same as the Replica Synchronization option in the main menu.

This operation should contact every server in the replica ring. If all replicas on every server are synchronizing properly, the tree is functioning properly. Servers do not synchronize to themselves, so the status for a server's own replica is shown as "host."

▸ Repair All Replicas — This option repairs all of the replicas displayed in the Replicas Stored on this Server menu. It checks and validates the information on each server that contains a replica, as well as the IDs of both the remote and local servers. This is the same information that is checked when you select the Unattended Full Repair option from the main menu. In other words, you can run an Unattended Full Repair or a Repair Local Database instead of choosing the Repair All Replicas option.

▸ Repair Selected Replica — This option is the same as the Repair All Replicas option, except that it repairs only the selected replica. Before choosing this option, you can run an Unattended Full Repair or Repair Local Database, both of which are equivalent to this operation.

▸ Schedule Immediate Synchronization — This option starts an immediate synchronization of all the replicas stored on this server. You can use this option to initiate synchronization activity if you want to view the Directory Services trace screen started by DSTRACE.

▸ Send All Objects to Every Replica in the Ring — This option sends all objects from this server to all the other servers that contain a replica of the selected partition. You cannot execute this option from a subordinate reference replica. You should also be aware that this function can generate high network traffic.

This option behaves the same as the View Replica Ring option, except that the selected server is the server on which you are running DSREPAIR.

▶ Receive All Objects from the Master to this Replica — This option sends all objects from the master replica to the replica on this server. The replica on this server is marked as a new replica. This option is the same as the View Replica Ring option, except that the selected server is this server.

▶ Repair Timestamps and Declare a New Epoch — This option always affects the master replica, even though the master replica may not be the local replica or the replica in this server where DSREPAIR is being run. This operation checks all the time value stamps in the master replica to see whether any of them are ahead of the current time. If they are, they are replaced with the current timestamp. After all the timestamps are consistent, a new epoch is declared.

An *epoch* is a number (the first one is 1, next one 2, and so on) selected as a point of reference for Directory Services. The epoch is also known as the *partition creation time*. An epoch is used to create a new timestamp, which controls the replica synchronization. When a new epoch is declared, it starts at the master replica, and the other replicas will not receive updates from a different epoch. The master replica sends out all objects until all replicas are fully synchronized with the new epoch. All objects on other replicas are tagged as unknown. The master then marks all replicas as new and resends all information.

Be careful with the Repair Timestamps and Declare a New Epoch option because it will lose changes made in a previous epoch. For example, changes to a read/write replica will be lost if they have not yet synchronized to all other copies, including the master. If a modification has not been synchronized to the master replica before a new epoch is declared, the change is lost.

Before using this option, make sure that all servers in the replica ring are communicating. You also should not perform this function during times of high server utilization.

▸ Cancel Partition Operation — This option attempts to cancel a partition operation that was started for the selected partition. This operation talks to the master replica, which is responsible for the partition operations. Some partition operations may not be canceled if they have progressed too far. Other partition operations — such as the Add Replica Partition operation — cannot be canceled.

▸ Designate this Server as the New Master Replica — This option designates the local replica of the selected partition as the new master. Each partition can have only one master replica, so the previous master replica is changed to a read/write replica.

This option is useful for designating a new master replica if the original one is lost. This situation may arise, for example, if the server holding the master replica has a hardware failure and will be down for a while or indefinitely.

▸ View Entire Replica Name — This option displays the distinguished name for the selected replica.

Security Equivalence Synchronization   The Security Equivalence Synchronization option allows synchronization of security equivalence properties throughout the global tree. This operation walks the Directory tree, checks each object for the Equivalent To Me property, and checks it with the corresponding Security Equals property on the referenced object.

You should never have to run this option if you are using the standard NetWare security and rights administration. The Equivalent To Me property is not used by default. Enabling this option can cause performance degradation on your server.

Global Schema Update   The Global Schema Update option checks that all servers in the NDS tree contain the correct schema up to the IntranetWare base schema. If an IntranetWare server does not contain the correct schema it will be updated.

After you select the Global Schema Update option, you are provided with the following methods for updating the schema:

▸ Update All Servers' Schema — This option updates the schema on all servers in the tree and is useful for updating previous versions of NetWare 4 (4.0, 4.01, 4.02, 4.1) to the current IntranetWare schema.

▸ Update the [ROOT] Server Only — This option updates the schema on the server that contains the master replica of the [ROOT] partition.

▸ Import Remote Schema — This option is used for equalizing the schema before merging two trees.

▸ View/Edit DSREPAIR Log File — The View/Edit DSREPAIR Log File option allows you to manage the log file created when you run the other DSREPAIR options. The default log file is SYS:SYSTEM\DSREPAIR.LOG. When DSREPAIR is loaded, the log file is opened. When repair operations are performed, the activity is appended to the log file. The size of the file is displayed within parentheses on the far right side of the title line. You can use this option to control the log file. For example, you can turn the log file off, turn it on again, change the file name, and change its location. You can place the log file on a NetWare volume or on a DOS drive.

Create a Database Dump File   The Create a Database Dump File option lets you copy the NDS files to disk in a compressed format to be used by Novell technical support. Creating a dump file can be useful for diagnostic and troubleshooting efforts. However, note that the dump file is not a backup that you can restore later.

When you select this option, you are asked to enter the path name for a dump file. The default is SYS:SYSTEM\DSREPAIR.DIB. The dump file can be written only to a NetWare volume and not to a DOS drive.

DSTRACE SET COMMANDS

DSTRACE refers to a group of SET commands available at the server console. DSTRACE is often referred to as a utility; however, it is really just a group of server SET commands. These SET commands are useful for monitoring how NDS is functioning. DSTRACE is primarily used to determine and track the health of NDS as it communicates with the other IntranetWare servers in the network.

You can use the DSTRACE SET commands to:

▸ Monitor the status of NDS synchronization processes

▸ View errors that occur during NDS synchronization

After you enable DSTRACE, you can see a Directory Services trace screen on the IntranetWare server console. You can display the Directory Services trace screen by entering the following command at the server prompt

```
SET DSTRACE = ON
```

and toggling (Alt + Esc) at the server console to the Directory Services screen.

Figure 10.12 illustrates the Directory Services trace screen, which enables you to view internal NDS processes and determine whether it is synchronizing completely with the other IntranetWare servers. You can also see whether errors are occurring in any of the processes.

F I G U R E 10.12

To start the Directory Services screen type **SET DSTRACE = ON** *at the server console.*

```
(96/01/16 20:43:10)
SYNC: Start sync of partition <[Root]> state:[0] type:[0]
 SYNC: Start outbound sync with (#=3, state=0, type=1) [010000CE]<TOK-SRV1.TOKYO
.ACME>
  SYNC: sending updates to server <CN=TOK-SRV1>
  SYNC: update to server <CN=TOK-SRV1> successfully completed
  SYNC: Start outbound sync with (#=1, state=0, type=1) [010000B8]<CAM-SRV1.CAMEL
OT.ACME>
  SYNC: sending updates to server <CN=CAM-SRV1>
  SYNC: update to server <CN=CAM-SRV1> successfully completed
SYNC: End sync of partition <[Root]> All processed = YES.

(96/01/16 20:43:11)
SYNC: Start sync of partition <CAMELOT.ACME> state:[0] type:[3]
 SYNC: Start outbound sync with (#=3, state=0, type=3) [010000CE]<TOK-SRV1.TOKYO
.ACME>
  SYNC: sending updates to server <CN=TOK-SRV1>
  SYNC: update to server <CN=TOK-SRV1> successfully completed
  SYNC: Start outbound sync with (#=1, state=0, type=0) [010000B8]<CAM-SRV1.CAMEL
OT.ACME>
  SYNC: sending updates to server <CN=CAM-SRV1>
  SYNC: update to server <CN=CAM-SRV1> successfully completed
SYNC: End sync of partition <CAMELOT.ACME> All processed = YES.
```

NOTE

DSTRACE was originally developed and used by the Novell Directory Services engineers to help develop Novell Directory Services. Novell technical support uses it to diagnose NDS errors and determine the health of the IntranetWare system. The DSTRACE set commands are now provided for all administrators.

In IntranetWare, the DSTRACE screen now displays the important information in color. Different colors highlight key events that occur during the synchronization process for the server. The trace screen displays synchronization information for every replica stored on that server.

CONSULTING EXPERIENCE

Always check the DSTRACE screen to see that NDS is communicating before performing any partition operation. Never start a new partition operation if there is an error communicating to the other servers or replicas of the same partition.

Look for the message "ALL PROCESSED = YES" for each partition on the server, especially the partition you are going to modify. This message indicates that all replicas in the partition are synchronized without error.

Saving DSTRACE Messages to a File

You can save the information scrolling across the DSTRACE screen to a file for later examination. The default name of this file is SYS:SYSTEM\DSTRACE.DBG. This file will grow to one megabyte and then will wrap and write additional text to the beginning of the file, overwriting the previous text.

To begin saving the screen messages to this file, enter

```
SET TTF = ON
```

at the server console prompt. To stop saving screen messages to the file, enter:

```
SET TTF = OFF
```

These commands are equivalent to NDS Trace to File = ON/OFF in the SERVMAN utility under the Novell Directory Services option.

You can change the name of the file being written to by entering

```
SET NDS TRACE FILE = <path\filename>
```

at the server prompt. You can also change the filename using the SERVMAN utility.

Using DSTRACE

The quickest way to become familiar with the DSTRACE screen is to use it and learn what all the messages mean. Here is a standard set of DSTRACE commands that you can try:

```
SET DSTRACE = ON

SET DSTRACE = <your preferred set of trace flags>

SET TTF = ON
```

(Begins saving screen messages to the file)

```
SET DSTRACE = *H <Toggle (Alt + Esc) to the Directory Services
screen and wait until it completes.>
```

(Forces a heartbeat process. Forces activity)

```
SET TTF = OFF
```

(Ends saving of messages and closes the file)

As mentioned in the SET DSTRACE=*H command, the heartbeat causes a server to exchange timestamps with every server in the ring of every partition stored on that server.

DSTRACE has three main parts:

▸ Basic functions

▸ Debug messages

▸ Background process

Basic Functions

The basic functions of DSTRACE are to view the status of the Directory Services trace screen in IntranetWare and initiate limited synchronization processes. To start the Directory Services trace screen, you enter the following command at the server prompt:

```
SET DSTRACE = ON
```

You can turn off or disable the Directory Services screen by entering the following command:

```
SET DSTRACE = OFF
```

These commands are equivalent to NDS Trace to Screen = ON/OFF in the SERVMAN utility under the NDS option.

To initiate the basic DSTRACE functions, you need to enter commands at the server prompt using the following syntax:

```
SET DSTRACE = <command option>
```

Table 10.3 lists the commands that you can enter using the preceding syntax.

Debugging Messages

When the DSTRACE screen is enabled, the information displayed is based on a default set of filters. If you want to view more or less information than the default, you can manipulate the filters using the debugging message flags. The debugging messages help you determine the status of NDS and verify that everything is working well.

T A B L E 10.3	COMMAND OPTION	DESCRIPTION
Basic DSTRACE commands	ON	Starts the NDS trace screen with basic trace messages.
	OFF	Disables the trace screen.
	ALL	Starts the NDS trace screen with all the trace messages.
	AGENT	Starts the NDS trace screen with the trace messages that are equivalent to the ON, BACKLINK, DSAGENT, JANITOR, RESNAME, and VCLIENT flags.
	DEBUG	Turns on a predefined set of trace messages typically used for debugging. The flags set are ON, BACKLINK, ERRORS, EMU, FRAGGER, INIT, INSPECTOR, JANITOR, LIMBER, MISC, PART, RECMAN, REPAIR, SCHEMA, SKULKER, STREAMS, and VCLIENT.
	NODEBUG	Leaves the trace screen enabled, but turns off all debugging messages previously set. It leaves the messages set to the ON command option.

Each NDS process has a set of debugging messages. To view the debugging messages on a particular process, use a plus sign (+) and the process name or option. To disable the display of a process, use a minus sign (–) and the process name or option. Here are some examples:

```
SET DSTRACE = +SYNC
```

(Enables the synchronization messages)

```
SET DSTRACE = -SYNC
```

(Disables the synchronization messages)

```
SET DSTRACE = +SCHEMA
```

(Enables the schema messages)

You can also combine the debugging message flags by using the Boolean operators & (which means AND) and | (which means OR). The syntax for controlling the debugging messages at the server console is as follows:

```
SET DSTRACE = +<trace flag> [<trace flag>]
```

or

```
SET DSTRACE = -<trace flag> [& <trace flag>]
```

Table 10.4 describes the trace flags for the debugging messages. You can enter abbreviations for each of the trace flags. These abbreviations or alternatives are listed within parentheses in the table.

T A B L E 10.4	TRACE FLAG	DESCRIPTION
Trace flags for the debugging messages	AUDIT	Messages and information related to auditing. In many cases, this will cause the server to pop into the debugger if auditing encounters an error.
	AUTHEN	Messages that are displayed while authenticating connections to the server.

(continued)

TABLE 10.4

Trace flags for the
debugging messages
(continued)

TRACE FLAG	DESCRIPTION
BACKLINK (BLINK)	Messages related to verification of backlinks and external references. The backlink process resolves external references to make sure there is a real object in NDS. For real NDS objects the backlink process makes sure that an external reference exists for each backlink attribute.
DSAGENT (DSA)	Messages relating to inbound client requests and what action is requested.
EMU	Messages relating to Bindery Services (emulation).
ERRET	Displays errors. Used only by the NDS engineers.
ERRORS (ERR, E)	Displays error messages to show what the error was and where it came from.
FRAGGER (FRAG)	Fragger debug messages. The fragger breaks up and rebuilds DS NCP packets — which can be up to 64K — into packets that can be transmitted on the network.
IN	Messages related to inbound synchronization traffic.
INIT	Messages that occur during the process of initializing or opening the local name service.
INIT	Messages that occur during the process of initializing or opening the local name service.
INSPECTOR (I)	Messages related to the inspector process, which verifies the DS name service and object integrity on the local server. The inspector is part of the janitor process. If errors are detected, it could mean that you need to run DSREPAIR. Be aware that messages reported by this process may not all be actual errors. For this reason, you need to understand what the messages mean.
JANITOR (J)	Messages related to the janitor process. The janitor controls the removal of deleted objects. It also finds the status and version of NCP servers and other miscellaneous record management.

T A B L E 10.4

*Trace flags for the
debugging messages
(continued)*

TRACE FLAG	DESCRIPTION
LIMBER	Messages related to the limber process, which verifies tree connectivity by maintaining the server name, address, and replicas. This involves verifying and fixing the server name and server address if it changes.
LOCKING (LOCKS)	Messages related to name service locking information.
MERGE	Not currently used.
MIN	Not currently used.
MISC	Miscellaneous information.
PART	Messages related to partitioning operations. This trace flag may be useful for tracking partition operations as they proceed.
RECMAN	Messages related to the name base transactions, such as rebuilding and verifying the internal hash table and iteration state handling.
REPAIR	Not currently used.
RESNAME (RN)	Messages related to resolve name requests (tree walking). Resolve name resolves the name maps and object names to an ID on a particular server.
SAP	Messages related to Service Advertising Protocol when the tree name is sent via SAP.
SCHEMA	Messages related to the schema being modified or synchronized across the network to the other servers.
SKULKER (SYNC, S)	Messages related to the synchronization process, which is responsible for synchronizing replicas on the servers with the other replicas on other servers. This is one of the most useful trace flags available.
STREAMS	Messages related to the stream attributes information.

(continued)

TABLE 10.4

Trace flags for the debugging messages (continued)

TRACE FLAG	DESCRIPTION
TIMEVECTOR (TV)	Messages related to the synchronization or exchange of the timestamps between replicas. These messages display local and remote Synchronized Up To vectors, which contain the timestamps for the replica.
VCLIENT (VC)	Messages related to the virtual client, which handles the outbound server connections needed to pass NDS information.

CONSULTING EXPERIENCE

As you use the debugging messages in DSTRACE, you will find that some of the trace flags are more useful than others. One of the favorite DSTRACE settings of Novell technical support is actually a shortcut:

```
SET DSTRACE = A81164B91
```

This setting turns on (by setting the appropriate bits) a group of debugging messages.

Background Process

In addition to the debugging messages, which help you check the status of NDS, there is a set of commands that forces the NDS background processes to run. To force the background process to run, you precede the command with an asterisk (*). An example would be:

```
SET DSTRACE = *H
```

You can also change the status, timing, and control for a few of the background processes. To change these values, you must precede the command with an exclamation point (!) and enter a new parameter or value. An example would be:

```
SET DSTRACE = !H 15
```

(parameter value in minutes)

Here is the syntax for each statement controlling the background processes of NDS:

```
SET DSTRACE = *<trace flag> [parameter]
```

or

```
SET DSTRACE = !<trace flag> [parameter]
```

Table 10.5 lists the trace flags for the background processes, any required parameters, and the process the trace flags will display.

T A B L E 10.5	TRACE FLAG	PARAMETERS	DESCRIPTION
Trace flags for the background processes	*.	None	Unloads and reloads DS.NLM from the SYS:SYSTEM directory. For a short period of time, both DS.NLM and DSOLD.NLM will be loaded.
			This command is extremely useful when you are updating a version of DS.NLM. You can perform this operation during normal business hours without disrupt-ing the users on that server.
	*B	None	Forces the backlink process to begin running. The backlink process can be traffic intensive, and you should probably wait until a slow time on the network before setting this command.
	!B	Time (in minutes)	Sets the backlink process interval used by NDS to check the backlink consistency. This command is the same as the NDS SET parameter NDS Backlink Interval, which is seen in the SERVMAN utility.
			The default is 1500 minutes (25 hours). The range for this parameter is 2 to 10080 minutes (168 hours).
	*D	Replica rootEntryID	Aborts the Send All Updates or *I. This command is used only when a Send All Updates or *I cannot complete (and is therefore endlessly trying to send the objects to all replicas). This situation usually occurs because one of the servers is inaccessible.

(continued)

*Trace flags for the
background processes
(continued)*

TRACE FLAG	PARAMETERS	DESCRIPTION
*F	None	Forces the flatcleaner process, which is part of the janitor process. The flatcleaner purges or removes the objects marked for deletion in the name service.
!F	Time (in minutes)	Sets the flatcleaner process interval, changing when the flatcleaner process automatically begins. The flatcleaner process purges or removes the deleted objects and attributes from the name service. The default interval for this process is 240 minutes (4 hours). The value entered must be greater than 2 minutes.
*G	None	Gives up on a server when there are too many requests being processed. The process gives up on the server and sets the server status to down.
*H	None	Forces the heartbeat process to start. This flag starts immediate communication to exchange timestamps with all servers in replica lists. This command is useful for starting the synchronization between servers so that you can observe the status.
!H	Time (in minutes)	Sets the heartbeat process interval. This parameter changes when the heartbeat process begins. The default interval for this process is 30 minutes.
*I	Replica rootEntryID	Forces the replica on the server where rootEntryID the command is issued to send a copy of all its objects to all other servers in the replica list. This command is the same as Send All Objects in DSREPAIR.
!I	Time (in minutes)	Sets the heartbeat base schema interval. This parameter changes the schema heartbeat interval. The default interval for this process is 30 minutes.

TABLE 10.5	TRACE FLAG	PARAMETERS	DESCRIPTION
Trace flags for the background processes (continued)	!J	Time (in minutes)	Sets the janitor process interval. This parameter changes when the janitor process executes. This command has the same function as the SET command NDS Janitor Interval in the SERVMAN utility. The default interval is 2 minutes, with the limits of 1 to 10080 minutes (168 hours).
	*L	None	Starts the Limber process. The Limber process checks the server name, server address, and tree connectivity of each replica.
	*M	Bytes	Sets the maximum size of the trace file in bytes, with a range of 10,000 to 10,000,000 bytes.
	*P	None	Displays the tunable parameters and their default settings.
	*R	None	Resets the TTF file, which is the SYS:SYSTEM\ DSTRACE.DBG file by default. This command is the same as the SET parameter NDS Trace File Length Set to Zero.
	*S	None	Schedules the Skulker process, which checks whether any of the replicas on the server need to be synchronized.
	*SS	None	Forces immediate schema synchronization.
	!T	Time (in minutes)	Sets the server UP threshold. This flag changes the server state threshold, which is the interval at which the server state is checked. The default interval is 30 minutes.
	*U	Optional ID of server	Forces the server state to UP. If object no server ID is specified, all servers in replica lists are set to UP. This command performs the same function as the SET parameter NDS Server Status.
	!V	A list	Lists any restricted versions of the DS. If there are no versions listed in the return, there are no restrictions.

(continued)

TRACE FLAG	PARAMETERS	DESCRIPTION
!W	Time (in ticks)	Changes the IPX Request in Process (RIP) delay. This is the length of time to wait after getting an IPX time-out before resending the packet. The default value is 15 ticks. The range is 1 through 2000 ticks.
!X	Number of retries	Changes the number of IPX retries for the DS (server-to-server) client. After the retry count has been exceeded, an NDS error -625 is displayed. The default is value 3. The range is 1 through 50.
!Y	Number	Factors the estimated trip delay. It is used in the equation: IPX Timeout = (T *Y) + Z. This is where T is equal to the ticks required to get to the destination server. The default is value 2. The range is 0 through 530.
!Z	Number	Adds additional delay for the IPX time-out. To increase the time-out, change this parameter first. It is used in the equation: IPX Timeout = (T *Y) + Z. This is where T is equal to the ticks required to get to the destination server. The default value is 4. The range is 0 through 500.

Performing and Verifying Partition Operations

Due to the loosely connected nature of NDS, any kind of partition operation change needs to be synchronized to other replicas of the partition. Because partition operations are performed by the master replica of that partition, master replicas should be used to verify any partition operation. The example of the NDS partition operations in this chapter uses the tree and partition information in Figure 10.13. The partitions are shown as circles. Figure 10.14 shows a view of the servers and their respective replicas. Some people prefer to view the different replicas of partitions stored on a particular server, while others prefer to view each partition and the servers on which they are stored.

. . . . ◄

F I G U R E 10.13

A partitioned view of the ACME tree

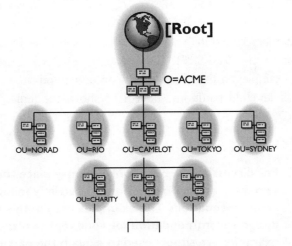

► . . . . ◄

F I G U R E 10.14

A grouping of ACME servers and their partitions

CAM–SRV1	CAM–SRV2	CAM–SRV3	CAM–SRV4	CAM–SRV5
[ROOT]–M	[ROOT]–RW	[ROOT]–RW	CAMELOT–RW	PR–RW
NORAD–M	CAMELOT–RW	CHARITY–RW	OPS–RW	
RIO–M	CHARITY–M			
CAMELOT–M	OPS–M			
TOKYO–M	PR–M			
SYDNEY–M				

Before starting any NDS partition operation, remember that there is a parent-child relationship between partitions. This entire section refers to the information in Figure 10.14. Notice in Figure 10.13 that the [ROOT] partition is a parent with five children — NORAD, RIO, CAMELOT, TOKYO, and SYDNEY. Notice that CAMELOT's parent partition is [ROOT]. The CAMELOT partition is also a parent partition with three child partitions: CHARITY, OPS, and PR. As shown in Figure 10.14, the tree includes the five servers CAM-SRV1, CAM-SRV2, CAM-SRV3, CAM-SRV4, CAM-SRV5. Most of the examples in this chapter will concentrate on the CAMELOT partition and its subordinate child partitions. Table 10.6 shows the replica assignments for [ROOT], NORAD, RIO, CAMELOT, TOKYO, SYDNEY, CHARITY, OPS, and PR.

NOTE

For discussion purposes only, we may place the replicas on the servers in a fashion that does not strictly follow our design recommendations. The examples used in this chapter do not imply a design recommendation for your replica placement; instead, these examples are simply used to explain the partition operations.

T A B L E 10.6	[ROOT]	NORAD	RIO	CAMELOT	TOKYO	SYDNEY	CHARITY	OPS	PR
Replica assignments for [ROOT], NORAD, RIO, CAMELOT, TOKYO, SYDNEY, CHARITY, OPS, and PR (M indicates a master replica and RW indicates a read/write replica.)	CAM-SRV1-M	CAM-SRV1-M	CAM-SRV1-M	CAM-SRV1-M	CAM-SRV1-M	CAM-SRV1-M	CAM-SRV1-M	CAM-SRV1-M	CAM-SRV2-M
	CAM-SRV2-RW			CAM-SRV2-RW			CAM-SRV3-RW	CAM-SRV4-RW	CAM-SRV5-RW
	CAM-SRV3-RW			CAM-SRV4-RW					

As mentioned previously, some people prefer to view the partitions and replica assignments by server. Using the same set of information that is shown in Table 10.6 and displaying or representing this information by server is illustrated in Table 10.7. Notice that each server is shown and then the partitions.

For each NDS partition, there is a replica list. In order to have a complete replica list for each partition, you have to consider the subordinate reference replicas (also known as subrefs) that are created automatically by NDS. When a server holds a copy of a partition such as read/write (RW), read only (RO), or master (M) of a parent partition, but does not hold the copy of the child partition, NDS automatically creates a subordinate reference, facilitating a link from the parent partition to the child partition. The link is necessary so that if the server holding the parent partition is queried about an object that exists on one of its child partitions, it knows which server to talk to. In other words, subordinate reference replicas are critical to the tree walking process, which is performed by the IntranetWare servers. Therefore, including the subordinate reference replicas, the replica list indicated above will actually appear as shown in Table 10.8.

T A B L E 10.7	CAM-SRV1	CAM-SRV2	CAM-SRV3	CAM-SRV4	CAM-SRV5
Partition and replica assignments shown for each of the servers CAM-SRV1, CAM-SRV2, CAM-SRV3, CAM-SRV4, and CAM-SRV5 (M indicates a master replica and RW indicates a read/write replica.)	[ROOT]-M	[ROOT]-RW	[ROOT]-RW	CAMELOT-RW	PR-RW
	NORAD-M	CAMELOT-RW	CHARITY-RW	OPS-RW	
	RIO-M	CHARITY-M			
	CAMELOT-M	OPS-M			
	TOKYO-M	PR-M			
	SYDNEY-M				

T A B L E 10.8	CAM-SRV1	CAM-SRV2	CAM-SRV3	CAM-SRV4	CAM-SRV5
Replica list for each server (M indicates a master replica, RW indicates a read/write replica, and SR indicates a subordinate reference replica.)	[ROOT]-M	[ROOT]-RW	[ROOT]-RW	CAMELOT-RW	PR-RW
	NORAD-M	NORAD-SR	NORAD-SR	CHARITY-SR	
	RIO-M	RIO-SR	RIO-SR	OPS-RW	
	CAMELOT-M	CAMELOT-RW	CAMELOT-RW	PR-SR	
	TOKYO-M	TOKYO-SR	TOKYO-SR		
	SYDNEY-M	SYDNEY-SR	SYDNEY-SR		
	CHARITY-SR	CHARITY-M	CHARITY-RW		
	OPS-SR	OPS-M			
	PR-SR	PR-M			

The following sections discuss the various partition operations that you can perform and explain how to properly verify their status and completion.

CONSULTING EXPERIENCE

We are often asked "Is there something that we can do on a daily basis as a proactive measure to tell whether NDS is performing smoothly?" As a network administrator, you can follow the steps below to ensure that your IntranetWare network is running smoothly. Take some time to learn and practice these steps. You should also follow these steps before you initiate any partition operations.

- ▶ Check time synchronization status of the servers using DSREPAIR.

- ▶ Check to make sure that the servers are communicating properly. Use the replica synchronization option in DSREPAIR.

- ▶ Check to make sure the replica synchronization process has completed for the partitions. You can use DSTRACE to do the checking.

- ▶ Check the replica state for each partition. Use DSREPAIR to check the replica states. If the state of the partitions is okay, then you can initiate the partition operation that you choose. Make sure to check the state of all the partitions involved in the operation.

- ▶ Always check the log file in DSREPAIR for errors that may show up in the replica synchronization status.

ADDING REPLICAS

The Add Replica operation adds a new replica to a partition's replica list and may be used fairly often by your administrators. Here are the steps involved in this operation:

I   • The master replica of the partition adds the server name as New Replica to the replica list.

2   • The master replica sends all the objects in the partition to the new replica. You have a NEW state until the master has successfully sent all changes to the new replica.

3 • The master replica sets the state in the replica ring to TRANSITION ON.

4 • All the other replicas begin synchronizing with the new replica.

5 • The master replica sets the replica state to ON.

At this point, let's add a read/write replica of the CAMELOT partition to the CAM-SRV3 server. You should follow these steps to successfully carry out the Add Replica operation.

Step One:

1 • Run DSREPAIR and choose the Report Synchronization Status option. The CAMELOT partition has both parent and child partitions. Therefore, the placement of a read/write replica of CAMELOT on CAM-SRV3 will cause the new replica to get involved in replica synchronization with servers that hold a replica of [ROOT] (the parent replica) and CHARITY, OPS, and PR (the child replicas). For this reason, you should check the synchronization status of the partition itself and of the child partitions. Use DSREPAIR to check the replica synchronization status.

2 • Load DSREPAIR.NLM on the servers holding the master of CAMELOT and CHARITY, OPS, and PR partitions. In this case, CAM-SRV1 and CAM-SRV2 would need to be checked. In order to check the status of the replica synchronization, you need to choose the Report Synchronization Status option. An example of this report is shown in Figure 10.15.

This first step verifies that there are no synchronization errors on the partition itself, its parent, and its children. Only after you know that there are no errors should you initiate the Add Replica option.

If there are any errors on DSREPAIR's Report Synchronization Status option, you need to find out what they are before continuing with the ADD REPLICA operation. For more information, refer to Appendix A for a listing of error codes and recommended actions.

FIGURE 10.15

*A view of the REPORT
SYNCHRONIZATION
STATUS option*

```
NetWare 4.1 DS Repair  4.40                        NetWare Loadable Module
DS.NLM 5.73  Tree name: ACME_TREE
Server name: CAM-SRV1.CAMELOT.ACME                      Total errors: 0

         View Log File (Last Entry): "SYS:SYSTEM\DSREPAIR.LOG"  (5953)

/******************************************************************************
Netware 4.1 Directory Services Repair 4.40 , DS 5.73
Log file for server "CAM-SRV1.CAMELOT.ACME" in tree "ACME_TREE"
Start:  Tuesday, August 13, 1996   9:39:38 pm Local Time
Retrieve replica status

Partition: [Root]
  Replica: TOK-SRV1.TOKYO.ACME            1996/08/13 21:27:06
  Replica: NOR-SRV1.NORAD.ACME            1996/08/13 21:27:06
  Replica: CAM-SRV1.CAMELOT.ACME          1996/08/13 21:27:06
All servers synchronized up to time:      1996/08/13 21:27:06

Partition: NORAD.ACME
  Replica: TOK-SRV1.TOKYO.ACME            1996/08/13 21:18:54
  Replica: NOR-SRV1.NORAD.ACME            1996/08/13 21:18:52
  Replica: CAM-SRV1.CAMELOT.ACME          1996/08/13 21:26:56

Esc=Exit the editor              F1=Help                      Alt+F10=Exit
```

NOTE

You can also use the Partition Status option in DSREPAIR to search for any errors. For example, you may see a –698 error indicating that the partition is busy synchronizing. This is normal unless the error continues indefinitely.

Step Two:

1 • Set the DSTRACE screen on the master replica to monitor the operation. In this case, the server holding the master replica is CAM-SRV1.

2 • Follow this step if the partition status shows an error or the status does not change. If there are no errors shown in the report from Step 1, it is time to SET DSTRACE on the server holding the master replica of the partition as follows:

SET DSTRACE = ON

(Turn on debug trace screen. Press Alt+Esc to see the trace debug screen.)

SET TTF = ON

(Open DSTRACE.DBG file)

SET DSTRACE = *R

(Reset DSTRACE.DBG to zero length)

SET DSTRACE = 1

(Turn off all the switches)

SET DSTRACE = +S

(Show detailed synchronization)

These steps capture the operations the master replica must take to finish the Add Replica operation. The text file that holds the trace information is in SYS:SYSTEM\DSTRACE.DBG file on the master.

Step Three:

▸ Issue the Add Replica operation using NDS Manager or the DOS program PARTMGR.EXE.

Figure 10.16 shows an example of adding a replica.

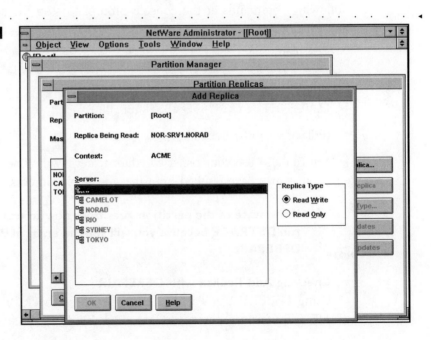

FIGURE 10.16

An example of the Add Replica function using NDS Manager

Step Four:

1 • Verify the partition operation from the back end.

2 • After issuing the call from the NDS Manager utility, you need to check the master server that controls the back end process. There are two ways to verify that the Add Replica operation has completed: You can use DSTRACE or you can use DSREPAIR and the Report Synchronization Status option. It is a good idea to use both methods to gather all possible information about the operation.

Checking Add Replica with DSTRACE

DSTRACE is a window to an IntranetWare server's NDS activity. It shows what the background processes are doing. We set DSTRACE to ON in Step 2 above to monitor the replica synchronization activity from the master while it is sending all the objects in the CAMELOT partition to CAM-SRV3. Now it is time to execute the following commands at the console prompt to stop the accumulation of trace information:

```
SET TTF = OFF
```

(Closes the DSTRACE.DBG file)

```
LOAD EDIT SYS:SYSTEM\DSTRACE.DBG
```

(Edit or view the trace file)

You can also use your preferred editor to review the trace file and look for any errors that may have resulted from the Add Replica process.

NOTE
If the state of the partition goes from new to transition, you needn't run DSTRACE because you will see the error in Partition Status of DSREPAIR.

Checking Add Replica with DSREPAIR

Using DSREPAIR or Partition Manager, first check the master partition of CAMELOT, which is stored on CAM-SRV1, by doing the following:

1 • Choose the replica partition operation.

2 • Choose the CAMELOT partition.

3 • View the replica ring.

DSREPAIR should confirm that CAM-SRV3 holds a read/write replica and the state of the replica should say ON. If the state says New Replica, the Add Replica operation has not finished. The states of partitions range from New Replica to Transition ON to ON. The Transition ON state means the master replica has finished sending all the objects and CAM-SRV3 is waiting for other read/write replicas to send any other updates that the master didn't have when the operation was performed.

After confirming that the master replica has sent the updates to CAM-SRV3 as a read/write and confirming a state of ON in the replica list, you can use the DSREPAIR Report Synchronization Status option on the servers holding the master of [ROOT], CAMELOT, CHARITY, OPS, and PR to make sure that all the servers are successfully talking to CAM-SRV3.

Table 10.9 shows the replica list for the partitions in our scenario. Notice that the new replica added for the CAMELOT partition is stored on CAM-SRV3.

T A B L E 10.9	CAM-SRV1	CAM-SRV2	CAM-SRV3	CAM-SRV4	CAM-SRV5
Replica list (M indicates a master replica, RW indicates a read/write replica, and SR indicates a subordinate reference replica.)	[ROOT]-M	[ROOT]-RW	[ROOT]-RW	CAMELOT-RW	PR-RW
	NORAD-M	NORAD-SR	NORAD-SR	CHARITY-SR	
	RIO-M	RIO-SR	RIO-SR	OPS-RW	
	CAMELOT-M	CAMELOT-RW	CAMELOT-RW	PR-SR	
	TOKYO-M	TOKYO-SR	TOKYO-SR		
	SYDNEY-M	SYDNEY-SR	SYDNEY-SR		
	CHARITY-SR	CHARITY-M	CHARITY-RW		
	OPS-SR	OPS-M	OPS-SR		
	PR-SR	PR-M	PR-SR		

DELETING REPLICAS

For a replica to be deleted successfully:

▸ Master(s) must remove the server from the replica list(s).

▸ The deleted replica server must destroy the replica.

After the replica has been destroyed, the IntranetWare server will turn all the objects on the deleted replica into external references.

The external references will be removed from that server if they haven't been used by the next time the backlinker process runs. For more information on the backlinker process, refer to Chapter 9.

NOTE

For the Delete Replica operation, we will remove a read/write replica of CAMELOT from the server CAM-SRV4. Follow these steps to delete the replica from the server CAM-SRV4.

Step One:

▸ Run the DSREPAIR Report Synchronization Status option. The CAMELOT partition has both parent and child partitions. Therefore, removing the replica of CAMELOT from CAM-SRV4 will also remove the subordinate reference replicas of CHARITY and PR from CAM-SRV4. Although the OPS partition is a child partition to CAMELOT, it is not affected because it is a full read/write replica. The CHARITY and PR replicas are removed from the server because they are subordinate reference replicas. Subordinate reference replicas are removed once the parent replica is removed from CAM-SRV4. Therefore, we should also check the synchronization status on the parent and children using DSREPAIR.

▸ Load DSREPAIR.NLM on the servers holding the CAMELOT, CHARITY, OPS, and PR partitions. You need to choose the Report Synchronization Status option.

The first step verifies that there are no synchronization errors on the partition itself and its children. You must make this determination before running the Delete Replica operation.

If the DSREPAIR's Report Synchronization Status option discovers any errors, you need to find out what the error is before continuing with the operation. For more information, refer to Appendix A for a listing of error codes and recommended actions.

Step Two:

▸ Set the DSTRACE screen on the master replica to monitor the operation.

If no errors are reported in Step 1, set DSTRACE on the server holding the master replica of the partition you intend to delete as follows:

SET DSTRACE = ON

(Turn on trace screen)

SET TTF = ON

(Open DSTRACE.DBG file)

SET DSTRACE = *R

(Reset DSTRACE.DBG)

SET DSTRACE = 1

(Turn off all the switches)

SET DSTRACE = +S

(Show detailed synchronization)

With this step you can capture the operation the master replica must take to finish the operation. The information is in the SYS:SYSTEM\DSTRACE.DBG file on the master.

Step Three:

▸ Issue the Delete Replica operation using NDS Manager or the DOS program PARTMGR.EXE.

Step Four:

▸ Verify the Delete Replica operation from the back end.

After issuing the call from the front end, you must check the master server that controls the back end before the operation is considered complete. There are two ways to verify the Delete Replica operation. You can use DSTRACE or you can use the DSREPAIR Report Synchronization Status option. It is a good idea to use both methods.

Checking Delete Replica with DSTRACE

DSTRACE is a window to a server's NDS activity. It shows what the background processes are doing. DSTRACE on the master shows us the process of removing CAM-SRV4 from the CAMELOT replica list. We can also capture DSTRACE on CAM-SRV2, which holds the master of CHARITY, OPS, and PR. Now you can issue the following commands at the console prompt:

```
SET TTF = OFF
```

(Close DSTRACE.DBG file)

```
LOAD EDIT SYS:SYSTEM\DSTRACE.DBG
```

You can also use your preferred editor to review the trace file and look for any errors that may have resulted from the process.

Checking Delete Replica with DSREPAIR

In this scenario, we first check the master of CAMELOT, which is stored on server CAM-SRV1, and then choose the Replica and Partition Operations option. We next choose the CAMELOT partition, and then choose View Replica Ring. This approach should confirm that CAM-SRV4 has been removed from the replica list of the master. If the state says Dying Replica, the Delete Replica operation has not yet finished.

After you confirm that the master replica of CAMELOT has CAM-SRV4 removed from the replica list, you can use DSREPAIR on CAM-SRV2 (the master of CHARITY, OPS, and PR) to make sure that CAM-SRV4 has been successfully removed from their replica lists. It is a good idea to check the Synchronization Report Status using DSREPAIR on CAMELOT, CHARITY, OPS, and PR.

The final step is to run DSREPAIR on CAM-SRV4 to verify that Delete Operation has finished. Run the DSREPAIR.NLM Advanced Options menu and then select Replica and Partition Operations option to verify that CAMELOT, CHARITY, and PR have been removed.

The replica list for the partition in our scenario is shown in Table 10.10.

T A B L E 10.10					
Replica list (M indicates a master replica, RW indicates a read/write replica, and SR indicates a subordinate reference replica.)	**CAM-SRV1**	**CAM-SRV2**	**CAM-SRV3**	**CAM-SRV4**	**CAM-SRV5**
	[ROOT]-M	[ROOT]-RW	[ROOT]-RW	OPS-RW	PR-RW
	NORAD-M	NORAD-SR	NORAD-SR		
	RIO-M	RIO-SR	RIO-SR		
	CAMELOT-M	CAMELOT-RW	CAMELOT-RW		
	TOKYO-M	TOKYO-SR	TOKYO-SR		
	SYDNEY-M	SYDNEY-SR	SYDNEY-SR		
	CHARITY-SR	CHARITY-M	CHARITY-RW		
	OPS-SR	OPS-M	OPS-SR		
	PR-SR	PR-M	PR-SR		

CHANGING REPLICA TYPES

Change Replica Type is another very important partition operation. The master replica is in charge of all the partition operations. If there are any synchronization errors at the time of the Change Replica Type operation, it can cause confusion between replicas and prevent the operation from completing. Therefore, no more partition operations are possible on that partition while it is in the change replica state.

To successfully change the read/write replica to a master the old master changes the replica type in two stages and synchronizes the changes to the other replicas, including the new master.

This example changes the master of CAMELOT from CAM-SRV1 to CAM-SRV2.

Step One:

1 • Run the DSREPAIR's Report Synchronization Status option. Change Replica Type is the only partition operation that requires a replica synchronization check of the partition itself. This operation affects only the CAMELOT partition in this example.

2 • Load DSREPAIR.NLM on the master of CAMELOT partition. Choose the Report Synchronization Status option.

The first step verifies that there are no synchronization errors on the CAMELOT partition before you issue a Change Replica Type operation.

If there are any errors on DSREPAIR's Report Synchronization Status, you need to find out what the error is before continuing with the operation. For more information, refer to Appendix A for a listing of error codes and recommended actions.

Step Two:

▶ Set the DSTRACE screen on the master replica to monitor the operation.

Once you have resolved any errors discovered in Step 1, you can set DSTRACE on the master of the partition as follows:

```
SET DSTRACE = ON
```

(Turn on trace screen)

```
SET TTF = ON
```

(Open DSTRACE.DBG file)

```
SET DSTRACE = *R
```

(Reset DSTRACE.DBG)

```
SET DSTRACE = 1
```

(Turn off all the switches)

```
SET DSTRACE = +S
```

(Show detailed synchronization)

This step captures the operation the master replica must take to finish the operation. The information is in the SYS:SYSTEM\DSTRACE.DBG file on the master.

Step Three:

▸ Issue the Change Replica Type operation using NDS Manager or PARTMGR.EXE.

Step Four:

▸ Verify the Change Replica Type operation from the back end.

There are two ways to verify the Change Replica operation: DSTRACE and the DSREPAIR Report Synchronization Status option. It is a good idea to use both methods.

Checking the Change Replica Type with DSTRACE

DSTRACE is a window to a server's NDS activity. It shows what the background processes are doing. DSTRACE on the master shows us the process of changing the master replica type from CAM-SRV1 to CAM-SRV2. Now it is time to execute the following commands at the console prompt:

```
SET TTF = OFF
```

(Close DSTRACE.DBG file)

```
LOAD EDIT SYS:SYSTEM\DSTRACE.DBG
```

You can also use your preferred editor to review the trace file and look for any errors that may have turned up as a result of the Change Replica Type operation.

Checking the Change Replica Type with DSREPAIR

First check the old master of CAMELOT, which is CAM-SRV1, and choose the Replica and Partition Operation options, choose the CAMELOT partition, and then select View Replica Ring option. It should confirm that CAM-SRV2 has been assigned as the new master replica. If the state says Changed Replica Type, the operation is not yet finished.

Next, check the new master CAM-SRV2, and then use the DSREPAIR's View Replica Ring option to verify the change.

After confirming that the master replica of CAMELOT has been changed to CHR-SRV1, use DSREPAIR on CAM-SRV2 to check Synchronization Report Status option for CAMELOT and make sure the change was successful.

The replica list for the partition in our scenario will now look like this:

CAMELOT
CAM-SRV1-RW
CAM-SRV2-M
CAM-SRV3-RW

CREATE (SPLIT) PARTITIONS

Partitions are created when any container in the NDS Manager utility is marked as a new partition. In other words, the container is already part of another partition and it gets split off as a new partition. This process establishes the new partition boundary. A new child partition gets created with respect to the parent. The servers that hold the copy of the parent partition will receive the copy of the new child partition with the same replica ring as the parent. It makes sense because the only servers that have the real copy of all the objects in the child partition will get a copy.

In a create partition operation:

▸ The master of the partition directs all the replicas in the list that a new partition is being created.

▸ The master of the parent becomes the master of the new child partition.

▸ Read/write copies of the parent will establish a new boundary for the read/write replica of the new child partition.

▸ Subordinate reference replicas of the parent are not involved in the operation.

The following example creates a new partition called OPS, which is a container below the CAMELOT partition.

Step One:

I • Run the DSREPAIR Report Synchronization Status option. As usual, you should check synchronization status before starting the operation. The CAMELOT partition needs to be checked. You don't need to check synchronization status on the sibling partitions to the new partition because the replicas of the sibling partitions won't get involved in the create operation.

2 • Load DSREPAIR.NLM on the server holding the master of CAMELOT partition. Choose the Report Synchronization Status option.

The first step verifies that there are no synchronization errors on the CAMELOT partition before you carry out the Create Partition operation.

If DSREPAIR's Report Synchronization Status should turn up any errors, you need to find out what they are before continuing with the operation. For more information, refer to Appendix A for a listing of error codes and recommended actions.

Step Two:

▸ Set the DSTRACE screen on the master replica to monitor the operation.

Once you've determined that there are no errors as discussed in Step 1, it is time to set DSTRACE on the master of the partition as follows:

SET DSTRACE = ON

(Turn on trace screen)

SET TTF = ON

(Open DSTRACE.DBG file)

SET DSTRACE = *R

(Reset DSTRACE.DBG)

SET DSTRACE = 1

(Turn off all the switches)

SET DSTRACE = +S

(Show detailed synchronization)

This step captures the operation the master replica must take in order to finish the operation. The information is in the SYS:SYSTEM\DSTRACE.DBG file on the master.

Step Three:

▸ Issue the Create Partition operation using NDS Manager or PARTMGR.EXE.

Step Four:

▸ Verify the Create Partition operation from the back end.

There are two ways to verify the Create Partition operation: DSTRACE and the DSREPAIR Report Synchronization Status option. It is a good idea to use both methods.

Checking the Create Partition with DSTRACE

DSTRACE shows what the background processes are doing. DSTRACE on the master shows us the process of creating the partition. Enter the following commands at the console prompt:

```
SET TTF = OFF
```

(Close DSTRACE.DBG file)

```
LOAD EDIT SYS:SYSTEM\DSTRACE.DBG
```

You can also use your preferred editor to review the trace file and look for any errors that may have resulted from the Create Partition process.

Checking the Create Partition with DSREPAIR

DSTRACE shows what happened during the process. In contrast, DSREPAIR shows the state of the replicas and how they are synchronizing. First, check the master of CAMELOT, which is stored on CAM-SRV1, and choose Replica Partition Operation to make sure that the OPS partition is listed. Then choose the CAMELOT partition and View Replica Ring option; it should confirm that all the replicas are ON. Carry out the same procedure on the OPS partition. If the state says Split State, the operation has not yet finished.

After you confirm that the OPS partition has been successfully created, you can run DSREPAIR on CAM-SRV1, which contains the master of both CAMELOT and OPS, and run the Report Synchronization Status on the two partitions to make sure synchronization is successful after the operation.

MERGE (JOIN) PARTITIONS

In the Merge Partition operation, the existing child partition will be merged with the parent partition. Because it is not possible to delete the partition, you must merge it with the parent. This process destroys the partition boundary and then removes all the partition properties. Thus, the container is simply an object in the tree that can hold other objects. Now you can delete the container object if it doesn't hold any objects.

By default, the Merge Operation option makes the replica ring the same for both the parent and child partitions, excluding the subrefs from the parent's replica ring. In other words, any server that holds the readable copy of the child or parent will get a read only copy of either one. This is probably the most time-consuming part of the process and will possibly create network traffic if the partitions are large. The Add Replica operation is the first part of the process. A read only replica of the child partition is added everywhere the parent is and a read only replica of the parent is added everywhere the child is.

In the Merge Partition operation:

► The master of the child partition finds the master of the parent partition to start the process.

► The master of the parent partition starts the first phase of the merge and the master of the child partition sets the states accordingly.

► The master of parent and child compare replica rings to determine which servers they must add replicas to.

► The partition boundary is deleted.

► The parent's master replica becomes the master of the new partition. The child's master and read/write replicas become read/write copies of the new partition.

The following example merges the CHARITY partition into the CAMELOT partition.

Step One:

1 • Run the DSREPAIR Report Synchronization Status option. As usual, you should check synchronization status before starting the operation. The CAMELOT and CHARITY partitions need to be checked.

2 • Load DSREPAIR.NLM on the master of the CHARITY and CAMELOT partitions. Choose the Report Synchronization Status option.

The first step verifies that there are no synchronization errors on the CAMELOT and CHARITY partitions before you perform the Merge Partition operation. If there are any errors on DSREPAIR's Report Synchronization Status option, you need to find out what the errors are before continuing with the operation. For more information, refer to Appendix A for a listing of error codes and recommended actions.

Step Two:

▸ Set the DSTRACE screen on the master replica to monitor the operation.

Once you have eliminated any errors found in Step 1, set DSTRACE on the master of both the CHARITY and CAMELOT partitions as follows:

SET DSTRACE = ON

(Turn on trace screen)

SET TTF = ON

(Open DSTRACE.DBG file)

SET DSTRACE = *R

(Reset DSTRACE.DBG)

SET DSTRACE = 1

(Turn off all the switches)

SET DSTRACE = +S

(Show detailed synchronization)

This step captures all the operations the master replicas must take to finish the operation. The information is in the SYS:SYSTEM\DSTRACE.DBG file on the master.

Step Three:

▸ Issue the Merge Partition operation using NDS Manager or the DOS program called PARTMGR.EXE.

Step Four:

▸ Verify the Merge Partition operation from the back end.

The replica list for the partition in our scenario is shown in Table 10.11.

T A B L E 10.11	CAM-SRV1	CAM-SRV2	CAM-SRV3	CAM-SRV4	CAM-SRV5
Replica list (M indicates a master replica, RW indicates a read/write replica, and SR indicates a subordinate reference replica.)	[ROOT]-M	[ROOT]-RW	[ROOT]-RW	CAMELOT-RW	PR-RW
	NORAD-M	NORAD-SR	NORAD-SR	OPS-RW	
	RIO-M	RIO-SR	RIO-SR	PR-SR	
	CAMELOT-M	CAMELOT-RW	CAMELOT-SW		
	TOKYO-M	TOKYO-SR	TOKYO-SR		
	SYDNEY-M	SYDNEY-SR	SYDNEY-SR		
	OPS-M	OPS-M			
	PR-SR	PR-M			

There are two ways of verifying the Merge Partition operation: DSTRACE and DSREPAIR's Report Synchronization Status option. It is a good idea to use both methods.

Checking the Merge Partition with DSTRACE

DSTRACE shows what the background processes are doing. DSTRACE on both master replicas shows us the process of merging the partitions. Enter the following commands at the console prompt:

```
SET TTF = OFF
```

(Close DSTRACE.DBG file)

```
LOAD EDIT SYS:SYSTEM\DSTRACE.DBG
```

You can also use your preferred editor to review the trace file and look for any errors that may have resulted from the Merge Partition process.

Checking the Merge Partition with DSREPAIR

DSTRACE shows what happened during the process. In contrast, DSREPAIR shows the state of the replicas and how they are synchronizing. First, check the master of CAMELOT, which is held on CAM-SRV1, and choose the Replica and Partition Operations option to make sure that the CHARITY partition is not listed. Then choose the CAMELOT partition and View Replica Ring option; it should confirm that all the replicas are ON. If the state says Join State, the operation has not yet finished.

After confirming that the CHARITY partition has been successfully merged, run DSREPAIR on CAM-SRV1, which holds the master of CAMELOT, and the Synchronization Report Status option to make sure synchronization is successful after the operation.

CHARITY should now be only an organizational unit inside the CAMELOT partition.

MOVING SUBTREES OR PARTITIONS

The Move Subtree operation moves a partition and all its child entries as a unit to another logical location in the tree. The replicas of the partition being moved are held on the same servers they were held on previously. In other words, NDS moves the subtree logically, not physically. However, the objects' full names in the partition will change.

A Move Subtree operation involves a destination server and a source server:

▸ The destination server is the server holding the master replica of the parent partition under which the child partition is moving. This server prepares for the operation and signals the source server.

▸ The source server is the server holding the master replica of the partition that is moving. This server forms a list of servers that will participate in moving the subtree.

▸ Large numbers of packets are exchanged between the source server and the destination server during a Move Subtree operation.

The following example moves the subtree CHARITY under the PR partition.
Step One:

1 • Run the DSREPAIR Report Synchronization Status option. As usual, you should check synchronization status before starting the operation. The PR, CAMELOT, and CHARITY partitions need to be checked.

2 • Load DSREPAIR.NLM on the servers holding the master of the CHARITY, CAMELOT, and PR partitions. In this case, the servers are CAM-SRV1 and CAM-SRV2. Choose the Report Synchronization Status option.

The first step verifies that there are no synchronization errors on the CAMELOT, CHARITY, and PR partitions before the Move Subtree operation.

If there are any errors on DSREPAIR report synchronization status, you need to find out what they are before continuing with the operation. For more information, refer to Appendix A for a listing of error codes and recommended actions.

Step Two:

▸ Set the DSTRACE screen on the master replica to monitor the operation.

Once you have resolved any errors that turned up in Step 1, set DSTRACE on the master of both the CHARITY and PR partitions as follows:

```
SET DSTRACE = ON
```

(Turn on trace screen)

```
SET TTF = ON
```

(Open DSTRACE.DBG file)

```
SET DSTRACE = *R
```

(Reset DSTRACE.DBG)

```
SET DSTRACE = 1
```

(Turn off all the switches)

```
SET DSTRACE = +S
```

(Show detailed synchronization)

This step captures all the operations the master replicas must take to finish the operation. The information is in the SYS:SYSTEM\DSTRACE.DBG file on the master.

Step Three:

- ▸ Issue the Move Subtree operation using NDS Manager or PARTMGR.EXE.

Step Four:

- ▸ Verify the Move Subtree operation from the back end.

    There are two ways of verifying the Move Subtree operation: DSTRACE and the DSREPAIR Report Synchronization Status option. It is a good idea to use both methods.

Checking the Move Subtree with DSTRACE

DSTRACE shows what the background processes are doing. DSTRACE on both master replicas shows how the process of merging the partitions finished. Enter the following commands at the console prompt:

```
SET TTF = OFF
```

(Close DSTRACE.DBG file)

```
LOAD EDIT SYS:SYSTEM\DSTRACE.DBG
```

You can also use your preferred editor to review the trace file and look for any errors that may have resulted from the Move Subtree process.

Checking the Move Subtree with DSREPAIR

DSTRACE shows what happened during the process. In contrast, DSREPAIR shows the state of the replicas and how they are synchronizing. First, check the Master of PR, which is stored on CAM-SRV2, and choose Replica and Partition

Operations. Make sure that the CHARITY partition's full name is under PR. Then choose CHARITY partition and the View Replica Ring option; it should confirm that all the replicas are ON. If the state says Move Subtree State, the operation has not finished. You should check the PR partition in the same way.

After confirming that CHARITY has been successfully moved, run DSREPAIR on CAM-SRV1, which holds the master of CAMELOT, and Synchronization Report Status option to make sure synchronization is successful after the operation. Follow the same procedure for CHARITY and PR. Remember that the replica ring for CHARITY will remain the same.

Troubleshooting *Do's* and *Don'ts*

This section describes some of the most common mistakes people make when installing and managing IntranetWare and Novell Directory Services.

DO NOT TEMPORARILY CHANGE THE INTERNAL IPX OR FILE SERVER NAME

If a server is brought up without running AUTOEXEC.NCF for any reason, the NetWare OS requires that you enter a server name and internal IPX number. In IntranetWare, the server name and internal IPX number must be the same as what is stored in the AUTOEXEC.NCF. Otherwise the IntranetWare server treats the change as permanent and synchronizes the change to all the other servers in your tree. Even if the server is not connected to the network, the change happens on its database and as soon as the server is connected to the network it sends the change. If this happens, let the system resolve the change first, and then change the name or internal IPX back to what it should be. Do not change the server name and internal IPX number back immediately because this can cause problems with NDS.

CHECK REPLICA RING SYNCHRONIZATION BEFORE DOING A PARTITION OPERATION

Always run the DSREPAIR Check Report Synchronization option before starting any partition operation. This action will ensure that there are no synchronization errors, and any change you make will be synchronized to other replicas.

DO NOT CHANGE READ/WRITE TO MASTER UNDER PARTITION ERROR CONDITIONS

If you change the master replica of a partition under error conditions, the operation can get stuck. This means that NDS has not properly or fully completed the process and NDS is in an inactive state. In this situation, no other partition operation is possible since the master replica controls all the partition operations. If you check the DSREPAIR option View Replica Ring, it should confirm that the replica states are Change Replica Type. If Change Replica Type doesn't resolve itself, you may have to call Novell technical support to resolve the issue.

CENTRALIZE THE PARTITION OPERATION ADMINISTRATION

Novell technical support has found that centralized management of all the partitions in the tree is critical to maintaining a healthy NDS tree. Managing NDS should be divided into:

▸ Partition management

▸ User and server management

Partition management is the only area that needs to be centralized. User and server management can be decentralized, as in a NetWare 3 environment. NDS is loosely connected, and it takes a while for changes to synchronize to other replicas. If the change happens to be partition information and there are multiple administrators performing multiple partition operations, the replicas may not synchronize properly. Centralizing partition operations eliminates many of the related problems.

DO NOT DESIGN A FLAT TREE

Flat tree design is inefficient and causes unnecessary overhead to the system. The reason is that a very wide and flat tree (meaning many peer organizational units) creates a large number of subordinate references if each container is partitioned. An inefficient tree design can compound NDS problems and actually decrease the performance of your network. For more information on designing an NDS tree, refer to Chapters 5 and 6.

USE INSTALL TO REMOVE OR DELETE A SERVER

Always use the INSTALL.NLM option Remove Directory Services when deleting a server object. This option removes a server from the tree properly. Even if the server has a copy of any replica, INSTALL removes the copy from the server for you. Never delete a server object unless the server has been removed from the tree with the Remove Directory Services option.

IF YOU SUSPECT ERRORS, VERIFY THE PARTITION OPERATION ON THE BACK END FROM THE MASTER REPLICA

After issuing the call from the front end to perform a partition operation, check the master partition on the server that is controlling the back end process before considering the operation completed. There are two ways to verify that the operation is completed: DSTRACE and the DSREPAIR Report Synchronization option. Verifying partition operations from the servers holding the master replicas will tell you whether the operation has finished or whether any errors have been generated as a result of the operation.

DO NOT DELETE SERVER OBJECTS

Never delete a server object from the PARTMGR.EXE utility unless the server has been properly removed and the server object still exists in the tree.

BE CAREFUL WITH DECLARE NEW EPOCH AND REBUILD REPLICA OPERATIONS

This option can be issued from the DSREPAIR utility. Use this option only if instructed to do so by Novell technical support. It destroys all replicas of that partition except the master replica. In other words, the master will be the only copy left. Unsynchronized changes from other replicas will be lost. The master replica will resend every object in the partition to all the other replicas. Always run the DSREPAIR option Repair Local Database to determine how many unknown objects the partition has. Also make sure there are no synchronization errors on that partition before issuing the call.

DO NOT COPY .NDS FILES FROM ONE SERVER TO ANOTHER

The .NDS files are located in the SYS:_NetWare directory and are specific to the server. Copying these files to another server will generate unexpected results and can cause serious problems for the tree.

USE NDS REPLICATION BEFORE A TAPE RESTORATION

Always rely on the replicas of a partition before using tape backup. This is why you should have at least three copies of any partition.

CONSIDER HOW THE PARTITION OPERATION WILL AFFECT THE TREE

Network administrators need to adjust to the new network-centric environment of IntranetWare, instead of thinking in terms of the server-centric world of NetWare 3. When you made a change in NetWare 3 it happened only on that server. However, when you make a change to an IntranetWare server, the change affects both the tree and the network. In the IntranetWare environment, you have to continually ask "How will the change affect the partitions of the tree?"

AVOID DUPLICATE SERVER NAMES, INTERNAL IPX NUMBERS, OR TREE NAMES

Duplicate server names, internal IPX numbers, and tree names can result in some irrational behaviors on the network, confusing all the clients and servers in the network.

DO NOT INSTALL THE SAME SERVER IN MORE THAN ONE TREE

Installing the same server name in multiple trees can create problems in replica synchronization. Normally, INSTALL.NLM will not let you do this, but if there are synchronization errors this situation is possible.

Basic NDS Troubleshooting Guidelines

▸ Identify the partition that is experiencing errors by using and understanding the DSTRACE set parameters and the DSREPAIR utility.

▸ Identify the replica(s) in the partition that have errors. Identify these errors by using the DSTRACE SET commands and the DSREPAIR utility.

▸ Identify the error and take the appropriate action. Appendix A of this book lists the errors and recommended remedies.

Tuning and Optimizing the IntranetWare Operating System

"Good is not good, where better is expected." Thomas Fuller

Tuning and optimizing the IntranetWare operating system is one of the responsibilities of the network administrator. Tuning and optimizing the IntranetWare operating system can seem difficult because modifications are not always immediately perceived by the users. However, the question most people ask is, "What do I change in order to tune the operating system?"

One of the first steps in the tuning and optimizing process requires you to understand the basic characteristics of your network, servers, and user community. You should measure the baseline performance of your system during both periods of peak and off-peak production. Having a baseline beforehand allows you to gauge the changes in performance and reliability during the tuning effort.

For most implementations of the IntranetWare operating system, the default settings for each of the internal parameters work very well. There are some server implementations that may make it necessary to modify some of the system settings to increase the capacity and performance of your system. These implementation may include heavy use of imaging or document retrieval types of software.

This chapter will provide you with a better understanding of the vital configurable IntranetWare system parameters. Becoming familiar with the internal system parameters will help you to make changes to increase capacity and performance without compromising the reliability of your server. This information will also help you prioritize the tuning options and reduce the trade-off between system performance and reliability.

Performance Versus Reliability

As most network administrators know, there is a kind of balancing act with tuning and optimizing the operating system for performance and providing maximum reliability. For example, there is a setting in IntranetWare that allows disk writes to the NetWare volumes to be verified. This parameter is called "read after write verification" and should always be enabled on IntranetWare volumes, which utilize disk hardware devices that do not perform the write verification inherently. Turning the parameter to ON will increase reliability of the data being written to disk, but will decrease the overall performance of the system. In this case, the reliability gained through verifying all writes to disk usually outweighs any side effects of slightly slower performance. IntranetWare turns the read after write verification parameter ON by default.

CONSULTING EXPERIENCE

For most systems with high-end (RAID 5) hardware and advanced disk drive technology, the parameter "read after write verification" is automatically enabled in the hardware. Most high-end disk drive manufacturers provide read after write verification within the hardware drive itself. The setting in NetWare is redundant and can be turned off to increase the performance.

Before you turn the "read after write verification" setting off for IntranetWare, make sure that the disk drive device is doing this process for you.

Surprisingly, for many users and administrators performance is not the single most important issue for their IntranetWare servers. When forced to prioritize the different functions of a network server, many users will rank reliability and security as the two most important, with performance coming in a close third. Of course, each of these areas is important and each needs attention when you are the network administrator. But it's important to understand that tuning for performance's sake should not be allowed to compromise reliability and security.

Since most of the server resources or subsystems are closely tied together, changing the parameters on one subsystem can affect the performance of other subsystems. The best place to start the process of tuning the IntranetWare operating system is with the defaults after installation. For the most part the system will tune itself and simplify your efforts.

IntranetWare Is Self-Tuning

One of the key traits of Novell's NetWare operating system is its capacity to self-tune to provide your users with the best possible performance. Autotuning is NetWare's capacity to automatically increase necessary resources for the NetWare operating system. It determines workload requirements and makes enough resources, such as memory, available to provide maximum efficiencies. The procedure used to self-tune is the capability to dynamically alter the internal system parameters and configuration in order to accommodate changing or increasing user demands.

Autotuning occurs when there are not enough service requests to handle all the incoming requests. Therefore, autotuning will request greater bandwidth by increasing some of the operating system parameters. Keep in mind that once the parameters are increased, they are never decreased automatically. For this reason there are maximums applied to all parameters, so that bandwidth allocation is very carefully controlled on the server and is not allowed to dominate all available resources. The method to restore these parameters to their original state is to restart the operating system or to change them manually with the SET command.

Using the SET Parameters

For most resources on the server, the SET parameters are available to adjust the values to help fine-tune a particular resource. These parameters cover a wide variety of internal systems all the way from communications to the file system. The SET parameters enable you to set minimum and maximum limits.

IntranetWare uses SET commands to manage the minimum and maximum values and wait times for its adjustable features. The minimum values define the number of resources that the operating system will allocate immediately upon startup. The maximum value is the upper limit for the resource allocation. A wait time is a specified length of time that the operating system must wait before allocating a new resource.

There are also wait times or conditions that prevent the operating system from reacting to peak loads by performing well only to one specific operation. The wait time limits parameters help smooth out the peak load demands for server resources.

The SET parameters can be controlled, adjusted, or viewed using either the server console SET commands or through the SERVMAN.NLM, which is a new server utility introduced in IntranetWare.

The server console SET command is issued at the server prompt as follows:

```
SET
```

The SET command responds with a listing of all the server resource categories or subsystems that can be controlled or configured with the individual SET parameters. Figure 11.1 illustrates the category list that can be configured using the SET commands at the server console.

F I G U R E   11.1

The server resource category list can be configured using the SET commands at the server console.

```
RIO-SRV1:set
Settable configuration parameter categories
    1. Communications
    2. Memory
    3. File caching
    4. Directory caching
    5. File system
    6. Locks
    7. Transaction tracking
    8. Disk
    9. Time
   10. NCP
   11. Miscellaneous
   12. Error Handling
   13. Directory Services
Which category do you want to view:
```

In order to view the current settings for each of the server resources categories or subsystems listed, simply select the corresponding number and scroll through the listings. Figure 11.2 shows the screen that is displayed for the Communications category or subsystem.

The syntax for viewing the setting for an individual SET parameter is to use the following command at the server console:

```
SET parameter_description
```

The syntax for changing the individual SET parameter is to use the following command at the server console:

```
SET parameter_description = new_value
```

F I G U R E   II.2

*Viewing the settings for the
Communications category
using the SET commands
at the server console*

```
Maximum Packet Receive Buffers:  100
   Limits: 50 to 4000
   Can be set in the startup ncf file
   Description: Maximum number of packet receive buffers that can be allocated
                by the server
Minimum Packet Receive Buffers:  50
   Limits: 10 to 2000
   Can only be set in the startup ncf file
   Description: Minimum number of packet receive buffers allocated by the
                server
Maximum Physical Receive Packet Size:  4202
   Limits: 618 to 24682
   Can only be set in the startup ncf file
   Description: Size of the largest packet that can be received by an MLID

<Press ESC to terminate or any other key to continue>
```

SERVMAN Utility

New to IntranetWare is the server based utility, SERVMAN, to help you easily
manage and configure each of the system SET parameters through a menu interface.
The SERVMAN utility enables you to view and set each parameter, as well as gather
at a glance the network performance statistics.

For example, the General Information screen visible at the top when the utility
is loaded, enables you to view processor utilization, server up time, processor speed,
server processes, number of NLMs loaded, mounted volumes, active queues, users
logged in, and name spaces loaded. Figure 11.3 shows the main screen, which
includes general information about the server performance.

F I G U R E   II.3

*The SERVMAN main
screen includes general
information about the
server performance.*

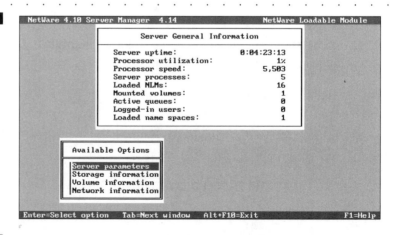

```
NetWare 4.10 Server Manager  4.14              NetWare Loadable Module
               ┌─────────────────────────────────────┐
               │     Server General Information       │
               │                                      │
               │  Server uptime:          0:04:23:13  │
               │  Processor utilization:          1%  │
               │  Processor speed:             5,503  │
               │  Server processes:                5  │
               │  Loaded NLMs:                    16  │
               │  Mounted volumes:                 1  │
               │  Active queues:                   0  │
               │  Logged-in users:                 0  │
               │  Loaded name spaces:              1  │
               └─────────────────────────────────────┘

          ┌─────────────────────────┐
          │    Available Options     │
          │ ┌─────────────────────┐ │
          │ │Server parameters    │ │
          │ │Storage information  │ │
          │ │Volume information   │ │
          │ │Network information  │ │
          │ └─────────────────────┘ │
          └─────────────────────────┘
 Enter=Select option   Tab=Next window   Alt+F10=Exit         F1=Help
```

The main menu in SERVMAN provides you with a menu driven interface to the system SET parameters available on the server. A list of categories (similar to the one displayed if you type "SET" at the server console) is displayed. At this point you can select a specific category or area to view and edit. Other options from the main menu are IPX/SPX configuration, storage information, volume information, and network information.

Most of the information from the options screens are available using other server-based utilities like MONITOR. However, the advantage of this utility is that the information plus the ability to change the settings are all included together.

Subsystems of the Operating System

From a performance standpoint, many of the system parameters are closely related and can be separated into specific subsystems of IntranetWare. Because of the association, we have categorized many of the most important SET parameters into the subsystems categories as follows:

▸ LAN Communication Subsystem

▸ Disk and File System

▸ Server Processes and CPU Utilization

▸ Memory

LAN COMMUNICATION SUBSYSTEM

The LAN communication SET parameters control the characteristics of the buffers used to send and receive data packets to and from the LAN. In order to tune and optimize the server for communications, there are several issues that you will need to address:

▸ Physical Packet Size

▸ Packet Receive Buffers

- ▸ Media Statistics

- ▸ Large Internet Packets

- ▸ Packet Burst

- ▸ NCP Requests

- ▸ NetWare Link State Protocol (NLSP)

Physical Packet Size

The physical size of the packet that is transmitted on the network is determined by the network topology or media access attached to the server. IntranetWare enables you to set or define the maximum physical packet size that the server will support using the SET command:

```
SET MAXIMUM PHYSICAL RECEIVE PACKET SIZE = n
```

The default physical packet size for Ethernet is 1514 bytes and the default for Token Ring is 4202 bytes. IntranetWare defaults the physical receive packet size to 4202 bytes to accommodate the larger size. This is true even if the network uses only Ethernet. When a workstation makes a connection to the server, the packet size for the session is negotiated. The value set for the session with the workstation is typically established as the largest packet the workstation can support.

Figure 11.4 shows the screen used in SERVMAN, called the Communications Parameters screen, which lets you set the maximum size of the buffers for incoming and outgoing packets. You should set this size to the largest packet size on your network.

You should always make sure the MAXIMUM PHYSICAL RECEIVE PACKET SIZE parameter is set large enough to support the protocols for the server. If the setting for the SET parameter MAXIMUM PHYSICAL RECEIVE PACKET SIZE is 1514 bytes, you should change it if you need to support Token Ring workstations as well.

To set the value for Token Ring, you need to enter the following at the server console or in SERVMAN:

```
SET MAXIMUM PHYSICAL RECEIVE PACKET SIZE = 4202
```

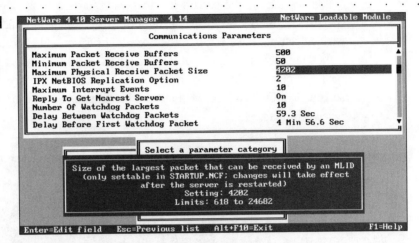

The Communications
Parameters screen used in
SERVMAN lets you set the
maximum size of the
buffers for incoming and
outgoing packets.

The parameter value ranges from 618 to 24682 (in bytes). If you want to have this value established each time the server is started, you will need to place it in the STARTUP.NCF. You cannot add this parameter to AUTOEXEC.NCF. The reason is that the server needs to know how large each packet receive buffer should be as the server is booting. The packet receive buffers are taken from memory and the size is not adjustable after the server is running.

Packet Receive Buffers

The server needs to keep a certain number of packet receive buffers free to service incoming requests from clients. Having additional packet receive buffers available will reduce the chance that the server will be overrun by incoming or outgoing requests which share these buffers. Each packet receive buffer is equal in size to the maximum physical receive packet size. In most cases, this is 1514 bytes for Ethernet segments and 4202 bytes for Token Ring.

A lack of packet receive buffers results in a "No ECB Available Count" error message, as shown in the Media Errors section in this chapter. When a client sends a packet to a server which has no available packet receive buffers, the server is forced to discard the packet. The client waits for the specified time-out period and will receive no reply from the server. It is then the client's responsibility to retry and resend the packet. If a buffer has become available in the meantime, the incoming packet is received and the client notices no network errors — just a slightly slower response time.

Meanwhile, at the server, IntranetWare starts a timer after the server discards the packet due to no available buffers. If no buffer is freed up after 0.1 seconds (default setting) have elapsed, the operating system will allocate a new packet receive buffer for incoming and outgoing packets. You can view the current number of packet receive buffers that the operating system has allocated by using the main screen of MONITOR.NLM. Figure 11.5 illustrates an example of current packet receive buffers.

F I G U R E   11.5

The current number of packet receive buffers that the operating system has allocated is viewed using the main screen of MONITOR.NLM.

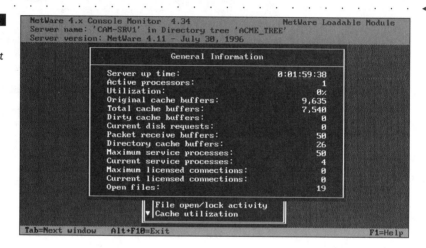

```
NetWare 4.x Console Monitor  4.34              NetWare Loadable Module
Server name: 'CAM-SRV1' in Directory tree 'ACME_TREE'
Server version: NetWare 4.11 - July 30, 1996

                          General Information

          Server up time:                      0:01:59:38
          Active processors:                            1
          Utilization:                                 0%
          Original cache buffers:                   9,635
          Total cache buffers:                      7,540
          Dirty cache buffers:                          0
          Current disk requests:                        0
          Packet receive buffers:                      50
          Directory cache buffers:                     26
          Maximum service processes:                   50
          Current service processes:                    4
          Maximum licensed connections:                 0
          Current licensed connections:                 0
          Open files:                                  19

                      File open/lock activity
                    ▼ Cache utilization

 Tab=Next window   Alt+F10=Exit                              F1=Help
```

As an administrator, you will want to pay special attention to the number of current packet receive buffers on your system, especially if your users are complaining of slow response time from the server. An occassional problem is that the server receives so many packets that it runs up to the maximum packet receive buffer count. If all buffers are full, the incoming packets will be dropped. This usually means that the workstations will have to resend any packets to the server multiple times, which slows response time for each user.

Setting the Packet Receive Buffer Values   Normally, NetWare dynamically allocates the packet receive buffers based on its needs. However, the operating system allows you to set both a minimum number of buffers that can be preallocated when the server boots and a maximum number or upper limit that prevents them from allocating too many resources during very high utilization.

You can adjust the settings for packet receive buffers by using the communication parameters SET commands described below:

```
SET MINIMUM PACKET RECEIVE BUFFERS = n
```

In this parameter n can be 10 to 2000 with the default being 50. This setting specifies the minimum number of buffers that will be immediately allocated by the operating system when it is booted. This parameter can only be permanently set in the STARTUP.NCF file.

```
SET MAXIMUM PACKET RECEIVE BUFFERS = n
```

In this parameter n can be 50 to 4000 with the default being 100. This parameter specifies the maximum number of packet receive buffers to be used by the IntranetWare operating system. Once the maximum is reached, no more packet receive buffers will be allocated even if more are needed. If all the allocated buffers are in use, the operating system will have no choice but to discard incoming packets. This parameter should be changed to meet the needs of your network environment. The parameter is set in the AUTOEXEC.NCF file.

It is extremely important to monitor the value of the current packet receive buffers to see if the value is close to the maximum value. If this is the case, you should increase the maximum to account for the increased workload performed by the server.

One of the most common errors people have when using these parameters is that the current packet receive buffers become equal to the maximum and the system can no longer dynamically tune itself.

```
SET NEW PACKET RECEIVE BUFFER WAIT TIME = n
```

In this parameter n can be 0.1 to 20 with the default being 0.1 seconds. This setting specifies the wait time necessary before allocating any new packet receive buffers. It is recommended that you not change this setting.

CONSULTING EXPERIENCE

We recommend that you have at least one packet receive buffer for each client that will be attached to your server. For example, a server supporting 500 users needs the possibility to allocate 500 packet receive buffers if necessary. In addition, you should account for 10 packet receive buffers for each LAN adapter installed in the file server.

Thus, we recommend that you use the following equation to calculate the proper value for the MAXIMUM PACKET RECEIVE BUFFERS:

Maximum = (1 * (# of connections)) + (10 * (# of LAN cards))

The proper setting for the MINIMUM PACKET RECEIVE BUFFERS parameter is the value currently in use at the file server. Using the MONITOR utility, you can compare the number configured versus the number currently in use. For example, the total number of packet receive buffers may peak at 350 after several days or weeks of continuous server operation. You can take advantage of the SET MINIMUM PACKET RECEIVE BUFFERS parameter to preallocate more than the default of 50 buffers the next time the server is rebooted. This will help overcome any sluggishness of the server after it is rebooted. Thus, we recommend that you use the following equation to calculate the proper value for the MINIMUM PACKET RECEIVE BUFFERS:

Minimum = Number of packet receive buffers in use currently

Media Statistics

The communication media statistics are reported by each LAN adapter installed in the server through the LAN driver. The statistics can be viewed using the MONITOR.NLM program at the server. This statistics can be useful in helping you diagnose specific problems with the physical network media and supporting software.

For example, a lack of packet receive buffers results in a "No ECB Available Count" error message, which is reported and viewed on the media statistics screen in MONITOR.. An example of the statistics screen for a LAN driver is seen in Figure 11.6.

F I G U R E   11.6

This figure illustrates the statistics reported by the individual LAN driver in the server, using MONITOR.NLM program.

```
NetWare 4.x Console Monitor   4.34                    NetWare Loadable Module
Server name: 'CAM-SRV1' in Directory tree 'ACME_TREE'
Server version: NetWare 4.11 - July 30, 1996

    XPSODI_1_USP [XPSODI port=320 mem=D2000 int=3 frame=ETHERNET_802.2]

    Version 1.5
    Node address: 0080C7A72C8B
    Protocols:
       IPX
          Network address:   AAAAA333

    Generic statistics
       Total packets sent:                            38,928
       Total packets received:                        26,730
       No ECB available count:                             0
       Send packet too big count:                          0
       Reserved:                              Not supported
       Receive packet overflow count:                      0
       Receive packet too big count:                       0
       Receive packet too small count:       Not supported
       Send packet miscellaneous errors:                   0
       Receive packet miscellaneous errors:                0

Esc=Previous list   Alt+F10=Exit                             F1=Help
```

As mentioned in the previous section, when a client sends a packet to a server which has no available packet receive buffers, the server is forced to discard the packet. Each time the server or LAN driver discards a packet, the "No ECB Available Count" is incremented.

Large Internet Packets (LIP)

One new feature in IntranetWare which has greatly increased the performance of the communications between the workstations and servers is the support for Large Internet Packets (LIP). The capability of the server to inherently support LIP solves a problem where the maximum physical packet size in previous versions was not always used during the negotiation from a server to a workstation.

During the process that connects the workstation to the server, a physical packet size is negotiated which is used for the duration of the session. The packet size selected is the largest physical packet size that both the workstation and server can support. For this reason, it is a good idea to set the MAXIMUM PHYSICAL PACKET SIZE parameter on the server according to the protocols of the workstations.

Prior to NetWare 4, when the workstation and server negotiated the physical packet size and the packet passed through a router device (such as a file server or hardware router) the packet size was always set to 512 bytes. At the time of the client login, the server looked at the transport control field in the IPX header of the packet. If it was incremented (meaning the packet had crossed at least one router), the server responded with a 512-byte packet size.

The reason for the reduced packet size is that a server cannot anticipate what packet size might be supported on the other side of a router. NetWare supports a mixture of Ethernet, Token Ring, and seldom used Arcnet, with their respective packet sizes. To accommodate the different topologies, the NetWare router decides to use the least common denominator, which — at the time the NetWare router software was developed — happened to be Arcnet at 512 bytes.

The Large Internet Packet support gives you a way to get around this 512-byte router packet size limitation. The LIP software allows the largest common physical packet size to be used when a workstation and server communicate through an intermediate router. With LIP, the packet size proposed by the client is accepted regardless of the information in the IPX header.

In order to enable Large Internet Packets type:

```
SET ALLOW LIP = ON
```

The default for this SET parameter in IntranetWare is already set to ON.

In order to enable the LIP features for the workstation or client, the user must have the VLMs (Virtual Loadable Modules) or NetWare 32-bit client. The older NETX code does not inherently support LIP without the addition of special client software.

Packet Burst

IntranetWare automatically supports packet burst which improves data delivery over latent links. Packet burst technology eliminates the ping-pong effect of the sent/return packets during communication. For example, using packet burst, the client sends a request to the server. The server responds to the client with multiple packets without requiring a "return receipt" for every packet. The server is content to have just one return receipt for the whole transmission. This means that the total transmission time is reduced and the "chattiness" of the NCP protocol is eliminated. This is particularly beneficial for communication across WANs where line speeds are often a bottleneck.

There is a SET command available which enables a separate packet burst statistics screen that can be used to see if specific workstations or clients are connected using packet burst. In order to start the packet burst statistics screen enter the following at the server console:

```
SET ENABLE PACKET BURST STATISTICS SCREEN = ON
```

NCP Requests

This section discusses the adjustments you can make to the NetWare Core Protocol (NCP) requests.

```
SET NCP PACKET SIGNATURE OPTION = n
```

where n is 0,1,2,3. The default setting is 1. The purpose of this setting is to enable Novell's packet signature security. Packet signature attaches a unique signature to each NCP packet that is transmitted between a NetWare client and a NetWare server. You use these parameters to enable or disable packet signature and to designate varying levels of security. This feature is only used where extremely high levels of security are required. Packet signature does impact performance because of the translation that must take place between receiving and sending entities on your network. The following are the settings for packet signature at the server. The packet signature for the client is set in the user's NET.CFG file.

Server settings:

▸ 0 — Do not do packet signature.

▸ 1 — Do packet signatures only if the client requires them.

▸ 2 — Do packet signatures if the client can, but don't require them if the client doesn't support them.

▸ 3 — Require packet signatures.

For most companies packet signature is not used. If you do have a client using packet signature, the default setting of 1 is sufficient to have that client use this feature.

```
SET ENABLE IPX CHECKSUMS = n
```

where n is 0,1,2. The default setting is 1. The purpose of this setting is to require a checksum calculation on packets. A checksum is calculated and placed in the packet being sent across the network. Once received the checksum can be recalculated to ensure that the same number of bits are received as were sent. This parameter

CHAPTER II
. . . . . .
N O V E L L ' S
G U I D E   T O
I N T R A N E T W A R E
N E T W O R K S

allows you to enable or disable IPX checksums. The values for the checksum have the following meanings:

▸ 0 — No checksums

▸ 1 — Checksums if enabled at the client

▸ 2 — Require checksumming

Most sites will not need to enable checksumming because this type of checking is done at the data link level of your network. However, some older bridges have been known to cause IPX packet corruption. So, in some unique circumstances you may want to enable this parameter. Keep in mind that you will experience performance degradation with this feature enabled. Additionally, this feature is only supported by Ethernet 802.2 frame type, not 802.3.

NetWare Link State Protocol (NLSP)

Novell's NetWare Link State Protocol (NSLP) provides a solution for routing RIP and SAP protocols across a wide area network. For network administrators who have a concern about routing such protocols in a WAN environment, NLSP offers a more efficient approach to routing these protocols across your WAN.

The basic concern with SAP and RIP is that it will broadcast its information every 60 seconds using a distance vector routing protocol. A distance vector protocol will try to rebuild all the information in the routing tables every time the servers communicate routing information. NLSP is architected using a link-state routing protocol to eliminate all the RIP and SAP broadcasts. NLSP only sends out changes to the routing information when a change occurs. Thus, link-state routing protocols are smarter, cause less network chatter, and are more efficient than distance vector protocols.

The network users find the network resources such as file and print services using both RIP and SAP. The servers on the network automatically discover all the services and route those services through SAP and RIP. This feature makes the network dynamic, flexible, and easy to access. The other network protocols such as IP, XNS, and AppleTalk also use SAP and RIP to propagate information. Therefore, it is difficult to entirely eliminate SAP and RIP because other protocols use it as well.

NLSP does not replace the SAP information and RIP information but only handles its propagation in a manner that is complete and efficient. With NLSP, the SAP and RIP information will no longer be broadcast every minute. Once the NLSP routers and servers have learned about all the routes and services available on the network, they will communicate with each other only when changes occur. When a server or link is added to a network, NLSP servers and routers communicate that change throughout the network. When a server or link disappears, that change is also communicated.

For backward compatibility, NLSP automatically detects the presence of routers and servers that require SAP and RIP broadcasts and will generate these periodic advertisements.

DISK AND FILE SYSTEM

IntranetWare optimizes the use of the server file system with several new improvements over previous versions of NetWare. These improvements enable IntranetWare to take full advantage of the available disk space and offer speed improvements as well as savings in server memory. The specific improvements that are addressed in this chapter are:

- ▸ Volume Block Size

- ▸ Suballocation

- ▸ File Compression

- ▸ Read Ahead

- ▸ Prioritization of Disk Requests

Volume Block Size

One of the new features in the IntranetWare operating system is the capability to support large volume block sizes. The large volume block size increases the performance of almost every associated subsystem, such as disk channel, file cache, directory cache, directory entry table, and file allocation table (FAT). This large volume block size does not waste disk capacity when storing lots of small files because of how the files are suballocated.

In the previous versions of NetWare (including the initial releases of NetWare 3), the volume block size or allocation unit was typically set at 4K. In NetWare 3 larger volume block sizes were possible, but they resulted in a lot of unused disk space at the end of files. For example, if the last part of a file took up 1K of a 16K block, the remaining 15K was wasted.

With the release of IntranetWare, the default volume block size is no longer 4K. The default volume block sizes calculated during volume creation are not based on performance criteria but on volume size to conserve server cache memory. The new defaults are listed in Table 11.1.

T A B L E 11.1	VOLUME SIZE	DEFAULT BLOCK SIZE
Default volume block sizes are based on volume size.	Less than 32MB	4K
	32 to 150MB	8K
	150 to 500MB	16K
	500 to 2000MB	32K
	2000MB and up	64K

CONSULTING EXPERIENCE

We recommend a 64K volume block size for all volumes regardless of size. The larger 64K volume block size allows IntranetWare to use the disk channel more efficiently by reading and writing more data at once. This results in faster access to mass storage devices and improved response times for network users.

Suballocation

One of the greatest cost benefits to migrating to IntranetWare is the use of volume block suballocation. Suballocation in IntranetWare subdivides the volume blocks, regardless of size, into smaller suballocation units of 512 bytes. This process ensures that you will never waste more than 511 bytes when saving any file. You now have the flexibility to set your IntranetWare volume block size to the recommended maximum of 64K without sacrificing valuable hard disk space. This ensures the disk space is more efficiently used.

As mentioned above, previous versions of NetWare worked with a 4K volume block size determined at the time of installation. The block size became the smallest unit of storage on the NetWare volume and server's hard drive. Generally, the larger the block size, the better the throughput between file server hard drive and file server's RAM or cache. But the large block sizes also had the most potential of wasting disk space or creating disk slack.

For example, if your volume block size is 16K (without suballocation) and you save a small file of 1K, the remaining 15K in the disk block is not used. The used space is referred to as "slack." Figure 11.7 shows that there is a problem with large block sizes without suballocation because it creates slack.

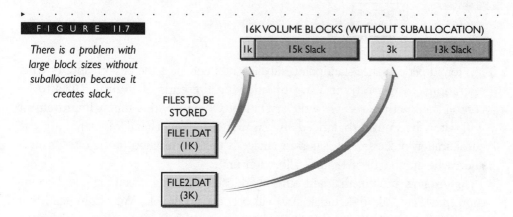

F I G U R E   11.7

There is a problem with large block sizes without suballocation because it creates slack.

16K VOLUME BLOCKS (WITHOUT SUBALLOCATION)

| 1k | 15k Slack |
| 3k | 13k Slack |

FILES TO BE STORED

FILE1.DAT (1K)

FILE2.DAT (3K)

Figure 11.8 shows the same example as above but with suballocation of the volume block which reduces the slack. You will notice that the volume block size is still 16K, but the volume block has been suballocated by the IntranetWare operating system into 512 byte blocks. FILE1.DAT (a 1K file) would ordinarily be allocated a full 16K but only takes the required 1K using two suballocated blocks. The other 15K is not wasted but can be used by other files. Another file, FILE2.DAT (3K file), is written to disk and starts in the middle of the volume block using six more suballocated blocks. There is no slack in this example.

Notice that new files can start in the middle of a volume block that has been suballocated. They do not have to start on the volume block boundary. This means that if you select the recommended 64K volume block size, then several files can be started and stored in the middle of the 64K block.

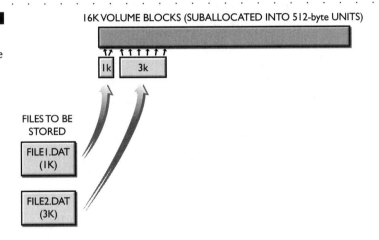

FIGURE 11.8

Large block size with suballocation of the volume block reduces the slack.

From a performance standpoint, suballocation enhances the performance of write operations within IntranetWare by allowing the ends of multiple files to be consolidated within a single write operation. Of course, this minor improvement will often be counterbalanced by the increased overhead of managing the suballocation process. The major advantage is the optimization of the disk channel and cache around the 64K disk allocation unit.

As imaging, multimedia, and other workloads involving streaming data become more prevalent, the 64K block size will become invaluable. We recommend that everyone use the 64K disk block size for greater efficiency, elimination of wasted space, and to take advantage of read-ahead.

File Compression

IntranetWare provides the capability to automatically compress any files on the server that have not been used for a period of time. This compression can result in space savings of up to 50 to 60 percent in some cases for a particular file. The file listing in the directory structure (FAT table) shows the file as if no change has occurred. When the user wants to retrieve the file, the operating system automatically decompresses the file. This file compression and decompression process is completely transparent to the user.

CONSULTING EXPERIENCE

The customers that we have visited have experienced significant benefits from migrating to IntranetWare and suballocation. A typical customer has seen a return of about 25 to 30 percent of hard disk space after migrating to IntranetWare. The savings do not include file compression.

This implies that their NetWare 3 servers had more than 25 to 30 percent slack, and that this slack was reduced by moving to IntranetWare. It is obvious that the suballocation feature alone is reason to migrate.

The slack can be estimated to equal the total number of files × (volume block size /2). The total savings in disk space from migrating from NetWare 3 to IntranetWare can be estimated using the following equation:

Savings = total number of files * ((old block size / 2) − (new block size / 2)).

Some example numbers follow:

1. Slack in NetWare 3: 50,000 files (4096 bytes / 2) = 102.4MB

2. Slack in IntranetWare: 50,000 files (512 bytes / 2) = 12.8MB

3. Savings for migrating to IntranetWare from NetWare 3 is:

$$50,000 ((4096 / 2) − (512 / 2)) = 89.6MB$$

The file compression feature in IntranetWare is completely optional and you can determine which servers can benefit from its use. You can choose which files, directories, or volumes to compress. The compression process runs as a background task, which means that it will usually not affect the performance of the file server. In order to enable file compression use the following SET parameter at the server console:

```
SET ENABLE FILE COMPRESSION = ON
```

You can decide the hours during the day when you want the file compression process to start and stop scanning for files that meet the compression criteria. The default start time is 0 which represents 12:00 PM. The possible range is 0 through 23 which represents each hour of the day. To set the hour in the day to start scanning type:

```
SET COMPRESSION DAILY CHECK STARTING HOUR = 0
```

To stop scanning type (default is 6 or 6:00 AM):

```
SET COMPRESSION DAILY CHECK STOP HOUR = 6
```

If the COMPRESSION DAILY CHECK STARTING HOUR parameter is the same as the COMPRESSION DAILY CHECK STOP HOUR then it starts each day at that time and runs as long as necessary to finish all files that meet the criteria.

You can also set a parameter at the server that specifies the period of time the file has not been accessed before the system compresses it. The default setting is seven days. The parameter to specify the period of time can be set at the server console by entering:

```
SET DAYS UNTOUCHED BEFORE COMPRESSION = 7
```

You can control the minimum space savings that must be accomplished before the compressed file is saved. If the operating system cannot gain a given amount of space from the compression of a file, it does not compress the file. The default for this parameter is 2 percent. The parameter to set the minimum space saving is entered at the server console as follows:

```
SET MINIMUM COMPRESSION PERCENTAGE GAIN = 2
```

Decompression is automatic when the user requests a compressed file. The algorithms provided are extremely fast and do not affect either the client or the server's performance. You can also control the decompression options when the compressed file is accessed by the users. The default setting is 1 but the range is 0 to 2. Enter the compression/decompression options as follows:

```
SET CONVERT COMPRESSION TO UNCOMPRESSED OPTION = 0
```

(0 — means that the operating system will always leave compressed)

```
SET CONVERT COMPRESSION TO UNCOMPRESSED OPTION = 1
```

(1 — means leave compressed if it has only been read once in the last seven days or DAYS UNTOUCHED parameter, see above)

```
SET CONVERT COMPRESSION TO UNCOMPRESSED OPTION = 2
```

(2 — means always decompress)

IntranetWare also enables you to control the percentage of disk space that must be present before the system attempts to decompress a file. The default is 10 percent. The parameter is entered at the server console as follows:

```
SET DECOMPRESS PERCENT DISK SPACE FREE TO ALLOW COMMIT = 10
```

Read Ahead

The read ahead feature in IntranetWare provides the requesting workstation faster response when reading files from the server. The operating system anticipates the read requests from the workstation and caches the next volume or disk block of a file.

For example, when the workstation makes a request for a file open, the operating system opens the file and assumes that the next request from the workstation is going be a read request. In anticipation of the read request, the read ahead feature caches (places into file cache) the first block of the file.

The result is that when the request from the workstation comes in for the first block, the server already has the block available in cache. The workstation request is serviced immediately instead of waiting for a hard disk access. As the workstation reads the information out of the block in cache, the operating system will fetch the next block of the file and place it in cache anticipating more read requests. When the workstation has read one-half of the current block in memory (or cache) the operating system determines that the next block is needed. Using this algorithm the operating system can calculate when the next blocks are needed and reads them from disk before the request is made.

This read ahead feature is a low-priority task that will not be executed when the server is busy handling other processes. The greatest impact of read ahead is when accessing optical media. A CD-ROM drive, for example, is not as fast as a hard drive.

Read ahead pulls the next block into cache so that it is ready when the workstation needs it.

Prioritization of Disk Requests

In previous versions of NetWare, there were situations when a server would start servicing heavy write requests and would seem to ignore other transactions involving read requests. For example, if a user would perform a large COPY to the file server, the other users would see poor performance for the duration of the COPY.

This condition resulted when a large number of cached writes (dirty cache buffers) hit a threshold where the server needed to switch writes from background to foreground in order to service all the requests. However, when the server switched priorities, it switched completely to foreground writes, leaving less consideration for the higher priority read requests.

IntranetWare includes a tiered prioritization of the disk elevator that reduces the possibility of ignored reads. It also supports lower priorities for read ahead requests. There are four bins, prioritized as follows:

▸ Critical events (such as file commits and TTS log file writes)

▸ Read requests

▸ Write requests

▸ Read ahead requests

Critical events are typically guaranteed events and are always processed with greater priority. Reads are almost always generated by client foreground tasks and make up the majority of work processed by any server. Most writes can occur in the background as a write-behind process. Read ahead requests are prioritized so as not to preclude the processing of any higher priority events.

Instead of using the normal first-in, first-out (FIFO) build sequence for the disk elevators, IntranetWare takes a percentage of requests from each priority bin. The higher the priority, the more requests are placed on the current elevator. In this way, none of the levels gets locked out due to an overabundance of requests in one of the levels.

NEW FILE SYSTEM ENHANCEMENT IN INTRANETWARE

With the advent of IntranetWare, there have been several enhancements made to the file system. These new features are listed below.

Volume Capacity Supports 16 Million Directory Entries

The IntranetWare file system has been enhanced to support 16 million directory entries per volume. The previous limit was 2 million entries per volume for NetWare 3 to NetWare 4.1. These additional directory entries will be used by the long name space, which is used on the server by default. For example, using just the DOS name space requires one directory entry per file. With the DOS and long name spaces loaded, two directory entries are required. The default for IntranetWare is DOS with the long name spaces.

The additional directory entries are needed by large customers who are simply running out of directory entries on very large volumes because of the current 2 million directory entry limit in NetWare 3 and NetWare 4.1.

Faster Volume Mounting

The volume mount code responsible for mounting NetWare volumes has been optimized to increase the speed of volume mounts. The result is that volumes can be mounted much faster, sometimes more than twice as fast as previous versions of NetWare. This enhancement is a great benefit to those administrators who have implemented large NetWare volumes because it reduces the total amount of time needed to bring the servers up.

Background Process for Purging Volume

A background process has been added to the file system to monitor volume space usage and to proactively purge deleted files. This process will help administrators avoid the problems caused by running out of space by freeing up valuable disk space.

New Client32 NetWare Core Protocols (NCPs)

New NetWare Core Protocols (NCPs) have been added to the IntranetWare server to enable the new Client32 software to operate more efficiently and deliver a higher level of performance. The result is that the file system responds more efficiently to the new NetWare Client32-bit NetWare client architecture by delivering a higher level of performance to the workstations.

Support for Long Filenames

With IntranetWare, LONG.NAM provides the extended name spaces available with the Windows 95, Windows NT, and OS/2 workstation platforms on a NetWare volume. LONG.NAM is a special type of NLM that enables non-DOS filenames on a NetWare volume. Because extended name spaces are used more often now, LONG.NAM is loaded as part of the default server configuration. In previous versions of NetWare 4, the OS/2 name space was provided by OS2.NAM. LONG.NAM replaces OS2.NAM.

SERVER PROCESSES AND CPU UTILIZATION

Service Processes

A service process is an execution thread that handles incoming service requests to the server. IntranetWare has the capability to allocate up to 100 service processes. Typically, your IntranetWare server will not use more than 40 service processes. In fact, most installations may never see this number rise above 10 because of how well NetWare handles multiple user connections. However, you can use the server set parameters to manage this function by typing:

```
SET MAXIMUM SERVICE PROCESSES = n
```

where n can be a value from 5 to 100. The default is 40. This setting allows for the maximum number of service processes available for the server

```
SET NEW SERVICE PROCESS WAIT TIME = n
```

where n can be 0.3 to 20 seconds. The default is 2.2 seconds. This setting specifies the wait time before the operating system can allocate any new service processes.

You can view the number of service processes in use by using the MONITOR.NLM utility and viewing the first screen as shown in Figure 11.9.

*Using the MONITOR.NLM
to view the number of
service processes in use on
an IntranetWare server*

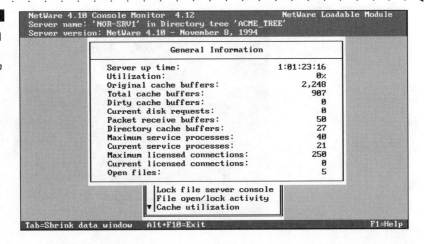

```
NetWare 4.10 Console Monitor   4.12              NetWare Loadable Module
Server name: 'NOR-SRU1' in Directory tree 'ACME_TREE'
Server version: NetWare 4.10 - November 8, 1994

                     ┌─────────────────────────────────────────┐
                     │            General Information           │
                     ├─────────────────────────────────────────┤
                     │  Server up time:              1:01:23:16 │
                     │  Utilization:                         0% │
                     │  Original cache buffers:           2,248 │
                     │  Total cache buffers:                907 │
                     │  Dirty cache buffers:                  0 │
                     │  Current disk requests:                0 │
                     │  Packet receive buffers:              50 │
                     │  Directory cache buffers:             27 │
                     │  Maximum service processes:           40 │
                     │  Current service processes:           21 │
                     │  Maximum licensed connections:       250 │
                     │  Current licensed connections:         0 │
                     │  Open files:                           5 │
                     └─────────────────────────────────────────┘
                          │Lock file server console │
                          │File open/lock activity   │
                        ▼ │Cache utilization         │
 Tab=Shrink data window    Alt+F10=Exit                        F1=Help
```

Changing these parameters is only necessary in a few circumstances. For example, if you are running 500 to 1000 users on a single server, you will want to increase this parameter. You might also consider increasing this value if you are using this service to store imaging or other graphics-intensive data. Do not increase this value to the maximum in one single adjustment. Instead, keep raising the number of service processes in small increments until your performance improves.

CPU Utilization

The CPU is usually the last place to look for a bottleneck on your server. Naturally, if you are trying to run 500 users on a 486/33 with IntranetWare you are going to have some performance issues. But most of your tuning should be with the server's subsystems and not the CPU itself.

For example, if you were to use a bus mastering NIC in your server, you would have very little CPU activity in terms of disk read and writes. Almost all activity is handled on the NIC card itself without the intervention of the CPU. You can easily check the performance of your server's CPU through the MONITOR.NLM's main screen. If you select Processor Utilization followed by the F3 key you will see a screen similar to the one shown in Figure 11.10.

FIGURE 11.10

The Processor Utilization
screen found in
MONITOR.NLM

```
NetWare 4.x Console Monitor 4.34              NetWare Loadable Module
Server name: 'CAM-SRV1' in Directory tree 'ACME_TREE'
Server version: NetWare 4.11 - July 30, 1996

    Process Name                     Time        Count       Load

    *STREAMS Q-Runner                   0           0       0.00%
    BWriter 0                           0           0       0.00%
    BWriter 1                           0           0       0.00%
    BWriter 2                           0           0       0.00%
    BWriter 3                           0           0       0.00%
    Console Command                     0           0       0.00%
    DSREPAIR                            0           0       0.00%
    Idle Loop                   2,923,428          55      98.56%
    IPXRTR I/O                        147           2       0.00%
    IPXRTR LSP Flood                  114           3       0.00%
    IPXRTR Timer                      639          54       0.02%
    MakeThread                          0           0       0.00%
    Media Manager                       0           0       0.00%
    MONITOR main                        0           0       0.00%
    NLS LSP Thread  1                   0           0       0.00%
    NLS LSP Thread  2                   0           0       0.00%
    Remirror                            0           0       0.00%

Esc=Previous list    Alt+F10=Exit                            F1=Help
```

Paging down the Processor Utilization screen displays the percentage of CPU utilization that each process on your server is using. The Idle Loop category shows the percentage of the CPU that is sitting idle. Look carefully at this statistic to see how busy your CPU actually is. If you are only using 20 to 30 percent of the CPU that means 70 to 80 percent is going unused and is sitting idle. The idle loop value is the inverse of the most accurate CPU percent utilization figure available from NetWare.

Not all processes are calculated when this screen is active. Novell Directory Services, for example, uses a process known as the work-to-do process. These types of processes are not monitored by the Process Utilization screen. These processes are not too significant in terms of CPU power and therefore are not registered on the MONITOR screens.

NOTE

Novell provides a custom utility called STAT.NLM that can record your server's long-running CPU percent utilization. STAT is available on NetWire in a self-extracting file called STAT.EXE. Use this utility to gain a better perspective on what your average utilization is for a server.

Keep in mind that when you make a determination to purchase new hardware, you want to spend money where it will have the greatest impact for performance on your systems. Sometimes your money may be better spent on the subsystems of the server rather than the CPU itself.

If your CPU appears to still have capacity, you should look at the following suggestions for other ways of improving performance on your current system:

▸ Avoid the use of ISA systems and upgrade to the EISA or MCA bus architectures to increase I/O channel capacity. Consider upgrading EISA or MCA systems to PCI to increase I/O channel capacity.

▸ Increase the server RAM for additional file cache.

▸ Upgrade the LAN channel to 32-bit intelligent bus master adapters.

▸ Segment the LAN across multiple LAN adapters.

▸ Upgrade the disk channel to SCSI-2.

In some cases you may have a server experiencing high utilization and actually see the CPU reach 100 percent utilization. In some cases this activity is normal and generally does not pose a problem for your server or users. If you notice utilization occurring for long periods of time there are some areas that you will want to look at to understand why this may be occurring.

NDS Design   Having an efficient tree design is essential to avoiding utilization problems. The size and number of partition replicas can cause utilization problems if they are not managed properly. DS needs to keep synchronization among all servers in its replica ring. The more replicas there are of any partition, the more traffic there will be on the wire. Novell recommends having three replicas of each partition in the tree. This provides Directory Services fault tolerance and allows for a recovery if a replica were to become corrupt.

For more information on designing your NDS tree refer to Chapters 5, 6, and 7.

NEW ABEND RECOVERY OPTIONS

With IntranetWare, the NetWare server has improved recovery options for handling abends (abnormal ends) in the operating system. In addition, the

IntranetWare operating system source code has been modified to reduce the total number of abends conditions. For example, software errors in previous versions of the operating system caused the system to abend. Some of these errors could have been corrected or ignored with no adverse effect. Other errors could have been changed to be conditional based upon whether the developer option in the operating system is set to OFF. This reduces the number of events that could potentially disrupt the IntranetWare operating system but allows them to be turned back on when the software engineers or developers are debugging a new NLM product.

You may now be wondering if abends are good or bad. The answer depends on your perspective. An abend stops the server processes before data is damaged or harmed. While this is a positive feature, an abend will disrupt or halt the entire service. This disruption in service is definitely an inconvenience. However, the abend information about the software or hardware problems helps the administrators troubleshoot the server. Thus, the abend information can decrease the troubleshooting time. One of the primary goals of the new abend recovery options is to improve the information or messages displayed on the server console. The abend recovery enhancements that are new to IntranetWare include the following features and capabilities:

- Additional abend information is displayed on the server console.

- When an abend occurs, the header "Additional Information:" is displayed on the server console followed by the probable cause of the abend. The information displayed will identify the specific NLM or hardware problem that caused the abend so the administrator can take immediate corrective action to prevent the problem from occurring again.

The new abend recovery options are:

- ABEND.LOG file

- SET AUTO RESTART AFTER ABEND parameter

- SET AUTO RESTART AFTER ABEND DELAY TIME parameter

ABEND.LOG File

When an abend occurs, information about the abend is automatically written to a text file called ABEND.LOG. The abend information is formatted and written to appear like a mini core dump. The ABEND.LOG file is initially created on the DOS partition of the server. However, the next time the SYS: volume is mounted, the information is appended to the ABEND.LOG file stored in the SYS:SYSTEM directory, and the ABEND.LOG on the DOS partition is removed. This method will provide a running history of all the abends that occur on a specific server and also provide detailed information about abends. This will help the administrators and support engineers identify and resolve server problems.

SET AUTO RESTART AFTER ABEND Parameter

There is a new SET parameter called AUTO RESTART AFTER ABEND that enables the IntranetWare server to automatically recover from an abend. According to the value selected, the server will recover in a variety of ways. The three values you can set are 0, 1, or 2. The default value for this parameter is 1.

If the parameter is set to 0, the server will not try to recover from the abend. However, the server will display the standard abend information to the system console screen and write it to the ABEND.LOG file. The server will also provide the option to the user to attempt to take the server down gracefully (as if the option had been turned ON). The administrator has the option to do a core dump or simply exit to DOS at that point.

If you set the parameter to 1 (which is the default), the server will attempt to recover from the abend. In order for the server to recover from the abend it must first check the state of the SET DEVELOPER OPTION parameter. If the DEVELOPER OPTION parameter is set to OFF (which is the default), then when the abend occurs the standard abend information will be displayed on the system console screen and logged to the ABEND.LOG file. Next, if the running process is a Page Fault, Protection Fault, Invalid Opcode, Divide Overflow Exception, or if the process can be restored to a stable state, the server will continue to run and service all requests. If the SET DEVELOPER OPTION parameter is set to ON, then the server is scheduled to be restarted after 2 minutes. When the server is scheduled to be restarted, a broadcast message is automatically sent to the system error log file and to all the users notifying them that the server will be going down in 2 minutes. The server is then automatically downed and automatically restarted. The server will then come up in a clean state, reloading all the drivers and NLMs previously loaded. The clients running the new client requesters with auto-reconnect will automatically reconnect to the server and continue accessing the same network files they had open before the abend occurred.

If you set the parameter to 2, the server attempts to recover from the abend while suspending the faulting process. If the SET DEVELOP OPTION parameter is off when the abend occurs the standard abend information will be displayed on the system console screen and logged to the ABEND.LOG. The running process, which is the faulting process, will be suspended (if possible). Next, the server is scheduled to go down after 2 minutes. A broadcast message is sent to the system error log file and to all the users notifying them that the server will be going down in 2 minutes. The server is then automatically downed and restarted and all the drivers and NLMs are reloaded. The clients running the new client requesters with auto-reconnect will automatically reconnect to the server and continue accessing the same network files they had open before the abend occurred. The faulting process continues to be suspended.

A value of 1 or 2 allows the IntranetWare servers to automatically recover from abends and come back online rather than sitting in a halted state waiting for administrator intervention. All the error messages, conditions, and necessary information are written to a file to help the system administrator debug the problem after it occurs. These settings also allow the server to go down in a graceful fashion, which prevents both client and server file system data from being lost. This greatly reduces the need to need to run VREPAIR after an abend.

SET AUTO RESTART AFTER ABEND DELAY TIME Parameter

This SET parameter allows the user to configure the amount of time (in minutes) the server will wait before going down and restarting automatically if the SET AUTO RESTART AFTER ABEND parameter is turned on (set to 1 or 2). Although the default for this parameter is 2 minutes it can be set anywhere between 2 and 60 minutes, in one-minute intervals. It can be changed at any time after the abend has occurred but before the server actually goes down.

When you enter the SECURE CONSOLE command at the server prompt, DOS is not removed from memory automatically. To remove DOS from memory, you have to explicitly use the REMOVE DOS command. This enables abend logging and the SET AUTO RESTART AFTER ABEND functionality when the console is secured.

MEMORY SUBSYSTEM

The total amount of server memory has the largest impact on the overall performance of the operating system than any other subsystem. The memory supports the file server cache, which provides both file and directory caching. The cache memory allocates space for the hash table, the File Allocation Table (FAT), the Turbo FAT, directory caching, and finally file caching.

The first step in understanding memory is to understand what is the appropriate memory size for your systems. A memory calculation worksheet has been provided to assist you with this effort.

Calculating Memory Requirements for your Server

Calculating server memory requirements can be done by first understanding what information is required and then applying the data to a formula that will give you an estimate of memory requirements. Here are some memory requirements that are always needed:

Core Operating System Requirements   The IntranetWare operating system requires an additional 3MB of memory than NetWare 3.12. This memory supports the additional core services added to IntranetWare.

File Compression   File compression requires a static 250K of memory when activated.

Block Suballocation   Block suballocation requires five bytes of memory for every file managed by the server. This is an insignificant amount of memory for many systems.

The Worksheet

The following worksheet requires you to make some preparations before getting started with the calculations. You'll need to know the following about your server:

Total Disk Capacity   This is the *total* number of megabytes attached to your server. Use 1024MB for each gigabyte.

Total Useable Disk Capacity   If your disk storage subsystem will be duplexed or mirrored, this is half the total disk capacity above. Otherwise, the two numbers are equal.

Total Number of Clients   This is the total number of end-users or connections that will be simultaneously using the server.

Volume Block Size   This is the block size used during the installation of your NetWare volumes. The accuracy of this variable is important because volumes with 4K blocks require 16 times the amount of memory required by volumes with 64K blocks.

Estimated Total Number of Files   This is your estimate of the total number of files that will reside on the server. A ballpark estimate will suffice because the directory tables only require 6 bytes per file. If you're using block suballocation, this requirement increases to 11 bytes per file.

Once you've got this information, use it to calculate the server variables on the worksheet. Then run through the worksheet's ten-line calculation to arrive at your server's total memory requirement.

If you're building a server with Name Spaces, CD-ROM, NetWare for Macintosh, or other specialized server applications, the worksheet will only give you a baseline memory requirement. Look up the following resources and add the necessary memory at the bottom of the worksheet for an accurate total.

Name Spaces   See "Name Spaces: Server Memory Requirements for Additional Name Spaces" in the Novell Application Notes, January 1995.

Server Applications   Memory calculations for NetWare for Macintosh, NetWare for SAA, OracleWare, and other NetWare server applications can be found in their documentation and on the Network Support Encyclopedia (NSEpro) CD-ROM.

STEP 1: Calculate the following variables:

VI.   Enter the *total* number of megabytes of disk connected to the server.
_____MB

(For example: enter 1 for each MB, enter 1024 for each GB)

V2.   Calculate the number of megabytes of *useable* disk space connected to the server. _____MB

(If you are mirroring or duplexing multiply V1 * 0.5, otherwise copy V1)

V3.   Enter the server's volume block size (4, 8, 16, 32, or 64). _____K

V4.   Calculate the number of disk blocks per MB (divide 1024 / V 3). _____Blocks/MB

V5.   Calculate the total number of disk blocks (Multiply V2 * V4). _____Blocks

V6.   Enter the maximum number of clients (end-users) attached to the server. _____Clients

(For example: enter 24 for 24 end users)

V7.   Enter the maximum number of files that will reside on the server. _____Files

STEP 2: Calculate your individual memory requirements:

▸   Line 1 — Enter the base memory requirement for the core OS.
    _____K

(Enter 5120 for IntranetWare)

▸   Line 2 — Calculate the memory requirement for the Media Manager (Multiply V 1 * 0.1). _____K

▸   Line 3 — If File Compression is enabled, enter 250; otherwise, enter 0.
    _____K

▸   Line 4 — Calculate the memory requirement for directory tables.
    _____K

(continued)

(continued)

(Multiply V7 * .006, or if suballocation is enabled multiply V7 * .011)

▸ Line 5 — Calculate the memory required to cache the FAT (Multiply Line V5 * .008). _____K

▸ Line 6 — Calculate the memory requirement for file cache using the following table. _____K

This calculation uses a 0.4MB file cache per client memory requirement. The decrease as the user community size increases is based on assumptions regarding increased repetitive use of shared data (temporal and spacial locality) within cache.

Less than 100 clients   V6 * 400

Between 100 and 250 clients 40,000 + ((V6 − 100) * 200)

Between 250 and 500 clients 70,000 + ((V6 − 250) * 100)

Between 500 and 1000 clients   95,000 + ((V6 − 500) * 50)

▸ Line 7 — Enter the total memory (K) required for support NLMs. _____K

2,000K total is recommended for BTRIEVE (700), CLIB (500), INSTALL (600), and PSERVER (200)

▸ Line 8 — Enter the total memory (K) required for other services. _____K

Other services include NetWare for Macintosh, NetWare for SAA, OracleWare, NetWare Management System, and so on

(continued)

STEP 3: Calculate your total memory requirement:

▸ Line 9 — Total Lines 1 through 8 for your total memory requirement (in K).
  _____K

▸ Line 10 — Divide Line 9 by 1024 for a result in MB. _____MB

Using this result, round up to the server's nearest memory configuration. NetWare will enhance server performance by using all leftover memory for additional file cache.

File Caching

IntranetWare uses the cache memory on the server to speed up the file access for the clients. The file cache provides a temporary data storage area (in RAM) for the files that are being read or written to the server.

The most dramatic file server performance increase can be seen when the appropriate number of file cache buffers are allocated. The objectives for the file cache buffers should be sufficient to keep the Cache Hit Ratio high. The greatest performance increase is achieved when the hit ratio is between 90 and 100 percent. As a rule of thumb, the 90 percent hit ratio is achievable (in a read-intensive environment) when the Cache Buffers are 75 to 80 percent of Total Server Work Memory. File cache buffers are assigned from the memory that is left after the operating system is booted and the core functions and NLMs are loaded.

The most important parameter to measure cache efficiency is the LRU Sitting Time statistic that is updated and displayed once per second in MONITOR.NLM. This statistic is found under the Cache Statistics menu as shown in Figure 11.11 and is calculated by taking the difference between the current time and the time stamp of the LRU cache block at the end of the cache list. The result is then updated every second and is displayed. The LRU Sitting Time measures the length of time it is taking for a Most Recently Used (MRU) cache buffer at the beginning of the list to work its way down to the end of the list, where it becomes the LRU cache buffer. This measurement is also known as the cache churn rate.

FIGURE II.II

A view of the LRU sitting
time statistic in the
MONITOR utility

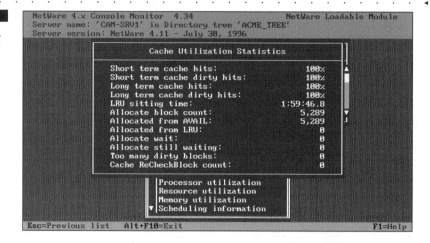

In environments with very large amounts of cache, the LRU Sitting Time will be up in the hours of time. A good rule of thumb is that your LRU sitting time should not go below 15 minutes. If your LRU value falls below 15 minutes it usually means that you do not have enough memory to create a large enough cache for your directories. Therefore, the sitting time is very short because of the churn rate of MRUs versus LRUs. It's time to take a look at adding more memory to your server if this value remains consistently below 15 minutes. Here are some other helpful ideas to tuning your cache:

1 • Estimate your server memory requirements. You can use the previous memory calculation worksheet to estimate your server memory requirements. You must first determine if your server has adequate memory from an overall standpoint.

2 • Observe the Cache Statistics parameter. You should monitor the LRU Sitting Time during peak workload periods and record that information. You should then monitor the LRU sitting time at other, slower, times of the day. Obtain an average for your LRU sitting time. Record your observations for at least one week or longer to obtain a pattern of activity on your server. Estimate a low watermark based on the information you have gained from your observations. This low watermark will help you to adjust cache if necessary.

3 • Tune the Cache parameter by increasing its size. A simple rule of thumb is if your LRU sitting time falls below 15 minutes, you should probably increase the cache size by adding more memory to your server. You'll need to add memory to increase the LRU Sitting Time during your peak workloads. The added memory increases the likelihood that repeatedly used data will still be cached when the next user request is received from a client.

On the other hand, if your LRU Sitting Time is several hours, you have more than adequate cache resources. In this case, it is not necessary to increase your memory and you can leave the memory in the server to support additional growth.

The point is not whether you actually add or remove memory from your server. This information is intended to improve your ability to interpret the LRU Sitting Time statistic and thereby provide you with a meaningful way to understand the efficiency and performance of NetWare's file cache.

Directory Caching

Directory caching is the ability of NetWare to read directory and cache directory entries for faster lookup. Rather than search the disk for directory entries, the server can hold the entries in memory. Disk access performance is greatly increased with this feature. Because some directories can be extremely large, the directory cache uses what is called the Least Recently Used (LRU) algorithm to store only the most recent directory cache blocks. By doing this, the operating system can more efficiently make use of memory. Each cache buffer is 4K and holds up to 32 directory entries. This parameter can be set as follows:

```
SET MAXIMUM DIRECTORY CACHE BUFFERS = n
```

where n is a number between 20 and 4000. The default is 500. This setting allows you to define what the maximum number of directory cache buffers are that IntranetWare can allocate. IntranetWare will only allocate extra buffers if necessary.

```
SET MINIMUM DIRECTORY CACHE BUFFERS = n
```

where n is a number between 10 and 2000. The default is 20. This setting defines the minimum number of directory cache buffers that can be allocated by the

IntranetWare operating system without waiting for the directory cache allocation wait time.

```
SET DIRECTORY CACHE ALLOCATION WAIT TIME = n
```

where n is a value between 0.5 and 120. The default is 2.2 seconds. This parameter specifies how long the IntranetWare operating system must wait before allocating one more directory cache buffer.

In very few circumstances do you need to adjust this parameter upward. Keep in mind that the minimum number of buffers is the number of directory cache buffers that can be set by the operating system using the wait time. If your server is functioning as a document server where many searches are being performed, you may want to increase this parameter.

Additional directory set parameters allow you to control cache functions listed here. They are also set parameters that are manipulated at your server console.

```
SET MAXIMUM CONCURRENT DIRECTORY CACHE WRITES = n
```

where n is from 5 to 10. The default setting is 10. This parameter allows you to control the number of cache writes through the disk channel. When you create a new directory addition, deletion, or other modification, a directory cache write is created. You can limit the number of cache writes through your disk channel if your disk subsystem is not extremely fast.

```
SET DIRECTORY CACHE BUFFER NONREFERENCED DELAY = n
```

where n can be 1 to 300 seconds. The default setting is 5.5 seconds. The purpose of this SET parameter is to specify the amount of time a cache buffer can remain unreferenced before it is removed. Novell does not recommend that you make any changes to this parameter as you can better control performance by setting the number of cache buffers.

```
SET DIRTY DIRECTORY CACHE DELAY TIME = n
```

where n can be 0 to 10 seconds. The default is 0.5 seconds. The purpose of this parameter is to reduce the likelihood of redundant cache writes. This setting causes NetWare to wait for the delay time specified before performing a directory request (write) to the directory cache. The reason for the wait is to see if there are any more requests to change the same block. If there are duplicate requests then the operating system only processes those requests once with a single write. This makes writing more efficient. Only very large directory cache (hundreds of thousands of entries) will realize any benefit by changing this parameter.

Obtain the Latest Patches

Make sure that you have the latest patches loaded for the IntranetWare operating system and Novell Directory Services. Each Novell patch contains a readme file that explains the problems being resolved and any special loading instructions. To find out about the latest patches you can search Novell's NetWire forum on Compuserve or their Web site at www.novell.com.

Administration of IntranetWare

Understanding and Managing Client Access

"Good counselors lack no clients." Shakespeare

IntranetWare Network Client Software

The network client provides an extension to each network user to access the corporate resources on the servers. The network client is tasked to communicate with the desktop operating system and the network operating system and serves as a liaison between the two. If a desktop application requires the use of network services, the client redirects the output to a server. If a server application needs to communicate with a client, it directs that communication to the network client in response to the client request.

Because of the variety of clients that may exist in your network, your responsibility as a LAN administrator will be to determine what type of client access is needed for a workstation to connect to IntranetWare, and to create the appropriate accessibility to meet those needs. Providing access to NDS will be accomplished through the different client software components available in conjunction with NetWare login scripts. The client software provides access to IntranetWare, and the login script creates the environment for the user.

The IntranetWare client software is designed to support connectivity to workstations including DOS/Windows, OS/2, Macintosh, NT, and UNIX operating systems. Through various connections discussed in this chapter, you can connect to a IntranetWare server and access files, applications, and Novell Directory Services.

As a network designer, you will probably have most of your users running on the same desktop operating system, with a few exceptions that use other systems across your departments. As you design for user access to the NDS tree and IntranetWare servers, you should first begin by designing access (login scripts and so on) for the majority of your user community that uses the same operating system. You can then create your access designs for the less commonly used workstations on your network. You may also have some mobile users that require special login scripts.

This chapter reviews the user login scripts for setting up user environments. We will review container, profile, and user login scripts and how they can be used to meet any user need. Figure 12.1 illustrates the different client access mechanisms and will serve as the basis of our discussion. As shown in the diagram, client access can be broken down into multiple categories. Each of these categories is discussed in this chapter.

Access

Type of Connection	Authenticated and Licensed	Not Authenticated Not Licensed	Authenticated
Workstation Software	NETX		VLM and 32-bit Client
Type of Service	Bindery		NDS
Login Scripts	User Script in Mail Directory	System Script NET$LOG.DAT	Container L.S. Profile L.S. User L.S.
Type of User	Network / Remote / Mobile		

Desktop support is key to IntranetWare. A server cannot serve the user community unless access is provided for the clients to communicate with NetWare servers across the entire network. This access requires speed and reliability for all users and must make good use of limited memory at each workstation. Once a connection is made, the login script can set up the user's environment. Chapter 18 provides a list of currently supported clients with their latest version of software.

WORKSTATION SOFTWARE

The newest client software is Novell's Client32 architecture, which provides network connections for both DOS/Windows and Windows 95 users. Currently, the most common workstation software used for connecting to IntranetWare is the NetWare DOS Requester, which supports both DOS and Windows clients. The DOS Requester is actually a group of virtual loadable modules that work together to provide client connectivity to a IntranetWare server. The great advantage of this type of software is that you can install only the VLM modules that are required for your user environment. You can create a standard configuration for the majority of your users.

An important difference between the older NetWare 3 NETX.EXE shell and the NetWare DOS Requester is how each client handles network requests. Because NETX.EXE is a shell, all calls from an application to the workstation operating system are intercepted by the shell and then directed to either the network or to DOS.

The NetWare DOS Requester, on the other hand, receives all calls from DOS through the DOS Redirector Interface known as Int2Fh. Therefore, any calls sent to this interrupt are always intended for the network. Each of these approaches has its advantages and disadvantages in terms of memory usage and performance.

A visual example of how the NETX.EXE shell works is found in Figure 12.2.

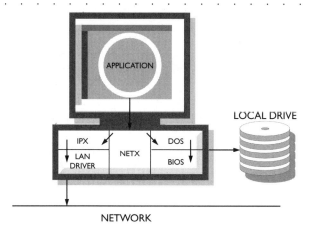

F I G U R E   12.2

A view of NETX.EXE routing operating system requests from an application

A visual example of how the NetWare DOS Requester receives the network requests from DOS is shown in Figure 12.3.

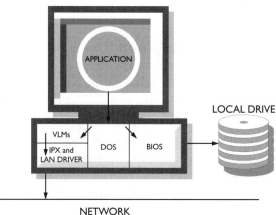

F I G U R E   12.3

A view of NetWare DOS Requester routing operating system requests from an application

TYPES OF SERVICE

Two types of connections exist for IntranetWare — the NDS connection and a bindery services connection. The basic difference between these two connections is that a bindery services connection is server centric. Server centric means that connections to multiple servers require a username and password at each server, and the login process is repeated at every server.

With the NDS connection, on the other hand, you can have a single login to multiple IntranetWare servers. A single login enables the user to enter their name and password once. Any additional drive mappings to other IntranetWare servers will be handled in the background by NDS. The great benefit of the NDS connection is that administrators need to manage only a single user account if they are operating completely on IntranetWare servers.

NDS Connections

An NDS connection requires the use of the VLM client or the NetWare 32-bit Client software for authentication to a IntranetWare server. An NDS connection provides a security mechanism known as RSA encryption between the client and server to provide background authentication for a single sign-on to multiple IntranetWare servers.

An NDS connection is said to be in one of three states:

▸ Connected but not logged in

▸ Authenticated

▸ Licensed/Authenticated

Connected but Not Logged In This state occurs when a user has attached to a IntranetWare server through either the NETX shell or the VLM client. An NDS connection that is not logged in can exist for either NetWare 3 or IntranetWare users to the first attached server. If a connection is made after walking the tree, the state can exist after the first attached server.

For example, when a connection is neither authenticated nor licensed, the users can navigate the NDS tree through the CX (Change conteXt) command. They have attached to a server, but have not yet authenticated.

Authenticated   Authentication is a process of proving identity to a server. In NetWare 3, this meant logging in. In IntranetWare, the authentication process happens as a "behind the scenes task" at the client.

This type of connection indicates that a IntranetWare server has established a user's identity after the user has entered a correct name and password. Authentication occurs for both NetWare 3 and IntranetWare users, but IntranetWare adds more security to this process.

Authentication is invisible to the user. During the login sequence, the user will enter a password when prompted, and the remaining process occurs behind the scenes. All sensitive data are never transmitted across the wire for security purposes. Authentication relies on encryption algorithms that are based on a public/private key system.

After successful authentication has taken place, a process known as background authentication may occur if the user's login script specifies connections to other servers. A connection to another IntranetWare server, for example, does not require the user to reenter his password. However, all connections are authenticated the same way; the process makes no distinction between the first and subsequent server logins.

Licensed   A connection is said to be licensed when a user has made a request of the server, such as mapping a drive or capturing to a printer. Each user will cause the user license to decrement by one after a connection has been licensed. Only an authenticated connection can be licensed.

A combination of these states determines what level a user currently has in a IntranetWare environment.

If users are licensed and authenticated, they can access NDS and file system information to the extent allowed by their rights.

Additive Licensing

Additive licensing increases the total number of licenses on any given IntranetWare server. This enhancement enables administrators to more closely match the number of licensed users to their company's needs. A company that currently has a 100-user license can add a 25-user license to the IntranetWare server to accommodate increased growth. IntranetWare supports 5, 10, 25, 50, 100, 250, 500, and 1000 user versions in any combination.

Bindery Services Connections

The NetWare client software provides compatibility to previous versions of NetWare through bindery services connections. This connection does not provide the capability of a single login to the network. For example, a client using the NETX.EXE shell or the LOGIN/B option with VLMs to log in to an IntranetWare server must enter a username and password for that server. Additional connections to other IntranetWare servers would require the user to enter another username and password.

Bindery services can be enabled on any IntranetWare server through the SET BINDERY CONTEXT command. The server can select one container or multiple containers in the NDS tree to set as the bindery context. All the leaf objects in the NDS container(s) that are also objects in the NetWare 3 bindery (for example, users, groups, queues, print servers, and profiles) are seen as the bindery.

Bindery services in IntranetWare allows you to select up to 16 containers as the server bindery context. Bindery services requires that the server store at least a read/write replica of the partitions where the bindery context is set.

LOGIN SCRIPTS

Network users will execute login scripts to access IntranetWare servers and other network resources. Traditionally, login scripts were used to establish the user's network environment. Login scripts for IntranetWare, however, are used to map network drives, map to applications, capture to printers and print queues, and set other important environment variables. Login scripts are the standard mechanism for user access and may require careful consideration.

When a user logs into the IntranetWare network or server, login scripts associated with the user are executed. There are two categories of login scripts available to the user of the IntranetWare network — NDS login scripts and bindery-based login scripts. NDS login scripts support the Directory connections, and bindery-based login scripts support the bindery services connections.

Our focus on login scripts in this chapter is to provide information on designing access to IntranetWare, not to encompass every login script variable and command. (Definitions and functions of all variables and commands are included at the end of this chapter.) Well-designed login scripts will help you create effective working environments for your users.

TIP

It is recommended that you execute the login scripts before launching Windows 3.1. If there are users who access Windows immediately after they boot their workstations, you need to have them log in to the network, which runs the login scripts before launching Windows 3.1. The exception to this tip is if you are running the new NetWare Client32 software that provides a Windows login utility. See Chapter 18 for more information on NetWare Client32.

Login scripts execute in a specific order as shown in the following sequence of login script execution for IntranetWare:

1 • User logs in to a server.

2 • User executes container script if available.

3 • User executes Profile if that user's Profile property is set.

4 • User executes User Script if available.

5 • If user login script is not available, then the user executes the default script.

Bindery-based Login Scripts

The bindery-based login scripts that you may place in IntranetWare are the same bindery login scripts found in NetWare 2 and NetWare 3. These login scripts can be copied onto the IntranetWare servers to provide bindery services scripts to your NETX.EXE clients. For example, a user attaching to a IntranetWare server with the NETX.EXE workstation software will have a bindery connection and look for the system and user login scripts on the server. The user script is in the SYS:MAIL directory, and the system login script would be placed in the SYS:PUBLIC directory as NET$LOG.DAT. Even if the user is using the VLM workstation software and selects the LOGIN/B option, that user will be attached to the server as a bindery connection.

The system login script is used for commands that affect all the bindery-based users on that server. Commands that might be placed in the system login script include the commands for displaying messages, mapping network drives and search drives, and setting environment variables. The system login script is the best place to manage the mapping and capture statements for all the bindery users that may still exist on your IntranetWare network.

After a user successfully attaches to the server with a bindery connection, the system login script will execute from SYS:PUBLIC\NET$LOG.DAT if it exists. If the user login script is present it will execute from the SYS:MAIL\USERID subdirectory. If the user login script does not exist then the default login script is executed. The default login script is hard coded into the LOGIN.EXE program.

Figure 12.4 shows the order of execution for bindery-based login scripts. If you are familiar with NetWare 3, notice that the bindery-based login scripts for IntranetWare are executed in the same order.

F I G U R E 12.4

The bindery-based login scripts in IntranetWare are executed in the same order as NetWare 3 login scripts.

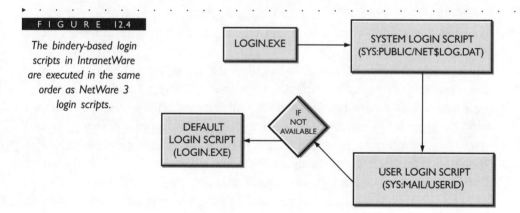

The individual user login scripts are stored in each user's mail subdirectories on the SYS volume of any server where a bindery account exists. For example, user GWASHINGTON (with object ID of 19000023) stores the bindery-based user login scripts in the SYS:MAIL\19000023 subdirectory.

The individual user login script customizes the user environment to the specific needs of the user. The same commands placed in the system login scripts can also be placed in the individual user login scripts. It is recommended that the user login scripts be used only in situations in which the system login script will not suffice.

The bindery-based login scripts are server centric, meaning that they are used only if a bindery user logs in to the server that is holding them. Because the login scripts are server-centric, there are not alot of design issues to consider. However, you should try to move all the users to the NDS login scripts as soon as possible so that you have fewer scripts to support.

You can make changes to both the system and user login scripts using the NetWare 3 SYSCON.EXE utility. You can also edit the NET$LOG.DAT file (or any script) directly with any text editing program. Although the bindery-based login scripts can be edited, any changes you make to the scripts are not automatically synchronized to the corresponding NDS login scripts. You can use Novell's NETSYNC utility to synchronize login scripts if you need to maintain consistency between NetWare 3 and IntranetWare. Refer to Chapter 2 for more information on NETSYNC.

NDS Login Scripts

The login scripts used in NDS are different than those used by bindery services. The NDS login scripts are a property of an object and are accessible only through an NDS connection. The only NDS objects that have the login script property are the container objects (O=Organization and OU=Organizational Unit), profile objects, and user objects.

Users who obtain an NDS connection to the network and run LOG.EXE will execute the container login script in which the users reside. The container script is roughly equivalent to the NetWare 3 system login script. After the container login script is executed, a profile login script can be executed if the user is associated with one. The user may also have a user script, which is executed after the container and profile scripts. If no user login script exists, the user will execute a default script. Again, the default login script is hard coded into the LOGIN.EXE program.

Figure 12.5 shows the order of execution for the NDS login scripts. Notice the profile login script, which falls between the container and user login scripts.

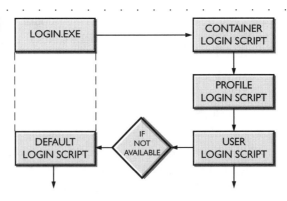

F I G U R E   12.5

The order of execution for the NDS login scripts in IntranetWare

In order to manage the NDS login scripts, you can use either the NWADMIN or NETADMIN utility that ships with IntranetWare. With these utilities, you can create and edit all the login scripts, except for the default login script. You can also add a profile login script for execution by selected users. An example of editing a login script is shown in Figure 12.6. In this example, the administrator is editing a container login script for the FAC container.

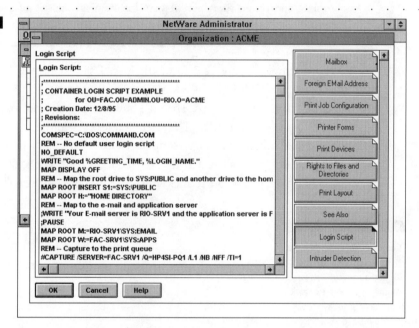

NDS Container Login Script   Typically, the NDS users needing the same network resources will be grouped together in the same NDS container. These users will probably need similar drive mappings and capture statements to establish access to the network resources with which the users are grouped. You can then use the container login script to provide users access to the NDS tree in this fashion.

After the LOGIN utility has authenticated a user to the IntranetWare network, the program checks the container login script in which the user resides. If the container login script exists it will then be executed. NDS will search only the immediate container (O or OU) in which the user is a member. If the container login script is not defined, the system will not automatically search higher in the tree for another container login script.

CONSULTING EXPERIENCE

It is highly recommended that you use the NDS container login script to replace the functionality of the NetWare 3 system login script. The container login script is stored as a property of the O=Organization object, the OU=Organizational Unit object and other container objects. Maintaining one set of login scripts allows for easier administration.

For example, Figure 12.7 shows the user JMadison in the ACME tree named under the container OU=FAC.OU=ADMIN.OU=RIO.O=ACME. The container OU=FAC does not have a login script. There is, however, a container login script defined higher in the tree at OU=ADMIN. The user JMadison is an occupant of OU=FAC and will not execute a container login script because there is not one currently in FAC. The user JMadison will not search up the tree for a container login script. In other words, no other container login scripts above the user JMadison will be executed.

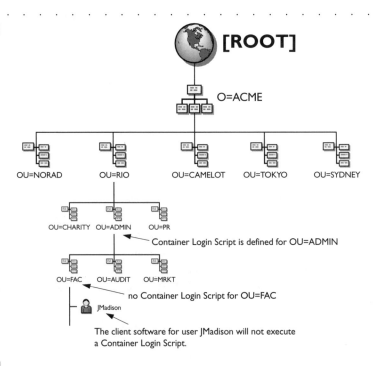

FIGURE 12.7

Container login scripts are executed only for the immediate occupants of a container. In this example, the user JMadison does not have a container login script in FAC.

The NDS container login script commands should establish the network environment of the users. These commands include the network drive mappings, printer and print queue captures, and other environment settings. The users in the container are best managed by using the NDS container login script.

The following is an example of a container login script that we have just added for the OU=FAC container in the RIO location of ACME tree.

```
;**********************************************************
; CONTAINER LOGIN SCRIPT EXAMPLE
; for OU=FAC.OU=ADMIN.OU=RIO.O=ACME
; Creation Date: 12/8/95
; Revisions:
;**********************************************************
COMSPEC=C:\DOS\COMMAND.COM
REM — No default user login script
NO_DEFAULT
WRITE "Good %GREETING_TIME, %LOGIN_NAME."
MAP DISPLAY OFF
REM — Map the root drive to SYS:PUBLIC and another drive to the
home directory
MAP ROOT INSERT S1:=SYS:\PUBLIC
MAP ROOT H:="HOME DIRECTORY"
REM — Map to the e-mail and application server
;WRITE "Your E-mail server is RIO-SRV1 and the application server
is FAC-SRV1"
;PAUSE
MAP ROOT M:=RIO-SRV1\SYS:EMAIL
MAP ROOT W:=FAC-SRV1\SYS:APPS
```

```
REM — Capture to the print queue

#CAPTURE /SERVER=FAC-SRV1 /Q=HP4SI-PQ1 /L1 /NB /NFF /TI=1
```

The previous script can be created in either the NWADMIN utility or the NETADMIN utility as shown in Figure 12.8.

FIGURE 12.8

Using the NWADMIN utility to create a script for the FAC container

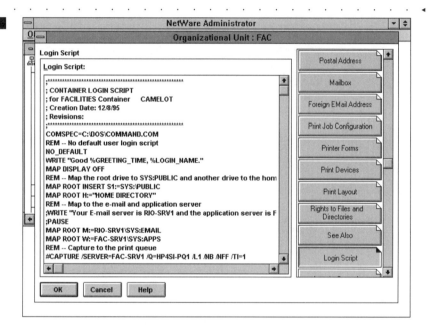

NDS Profile Login Script   If a user has a profile script assigned, it will be executed immediately after the container login script. The profile login script is optional and is used in special cases or for groups with special needs. The profile has the capability to include users that are in different containers in the tree. Its purpose is to assign additional environment settings that you may not want to assign to everyone in the profile. The scripts and the commands used in the profile login script are identical to the NDS container login scripts.

Because the profile login script is a special-purpose login script it can provide you with greater flexibility during the login process. Multiple users can be associated with the profile login script and they can reside in different containers in your tree. Figure 12.9 shows the creation of a profile login script through the NWADMIN utility. You can enable users to execute the profile script by assigning individual users to the script by making the assignment to the user object at creation. This method can be accomplished through the NWADMIN or NETADMIN utilities as shown in Figure 12.10.

F I G U R E   12.9

*Assigning an individual
user to execute a
profile login script*

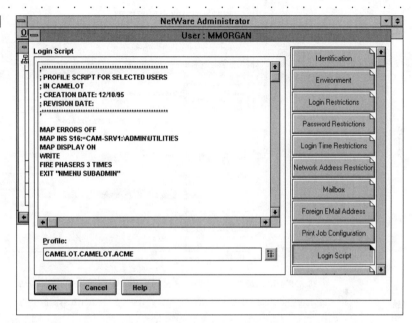

Typically, the profile login script is used:

► For an entire company (if the company and tree are small)

► To create a user environment based on location

► For a special group of users

The profile script is represented by the profile object, which can be placed anywhere in the Directory tree. Using the profile login script to span all the users in the entire company is recommended only for small networks. A small network consists of fewer than ten servers and is not widely distributed over wide area links. We recommend using the profile login script across small networks only because this method is expensive in terms of the NDS traffic that will be generated to manage this object.

FIGURE 12.10

*Creation of a profile login
script through NWADMIN*

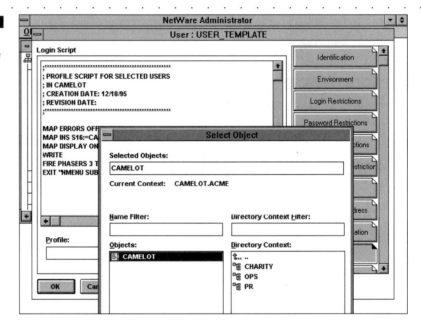

The profile login script is also used to create a user environment for a location. This method is similar to simply using a container script, except that you may want to create an environment for specific users within the container. Users that are organized around a particular site, building, or floor can have specific environment settings based on their particular needs. With the profile login script it is not necessary to create floor or building containers in your tree just to have a common login script.

For example, you have a specific set of users in a building and you want them to always map to the same e-mail and applications servers. You may also have users on one floor who want to capture to the same printers. You can accomplish these tasks using the profile login script. Using the profile login script in this fashion is considered to be a locational use of the script.

Figure 12.11 illustrates a profile login script being used as a locational login script that includes the containers in the ACME tree below the OU=ADMIN container in the RIO location. Specifically, the OU=FAC and OU=AUDIT are in the same building and need similar environment settings.

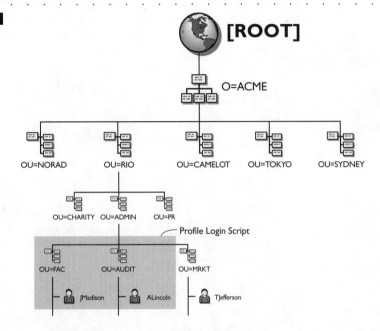

The users in both the OU=FAC and OU=AUDIT containers are using the same profile login script.

The profile login script can also serve as a special-purpose login script for a group of users. The group members can all be in the same NDS container or they can span across a number of OUs. If the profile login script makes assignments for users within a single OU, then the profile login script is similar to a group object with its sole purpose of executing a script.

A more powerful use of the profile login script is to span more than one NDS container. In Figure 12.12, you will see three users in a different NDS container. These users are members of a special group of administrators who need specialized access to resources in the NDS tree. When each user logs in to the network, he receives the additional drive mapping to perform various job functions. Users JMadison, ALincoln, and TJefferson are each associated with the same profile login script that gives them the extra drive mappings.

NDS User Login Script   The NDS user login scripts are stored as a property in each of the user objects. Like the bindery-based user login script, the NDS user login script customizes the user environment to the specific needs of that user. All the login script commands and variables can be used in the individual user login scripts. However, we strongly recommend that user login scripts be used only when the commands in the container system login script are not adequate.

FIGURE 12.12

The users JMadison, ALincoln, and TJefferson are each associated with the same profile login script.

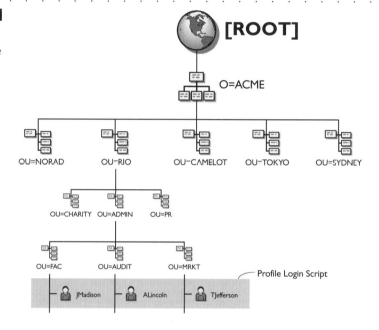

Most, if not all, scripting can be accomplished through container login scripts. For most large NetWare environments it is generally unfeasible to implement user scripts because of the difficulty in maintaining them. As a network administrator you don't need the extra work.

TIP

If you decide to let your users have personal login scripts, keep in mind that maintaining all the users' login scripts will be a difficult task.

The following is an example of a user login script for JMadison in the OU=FAC container in the RIO location of the ACME tree. These users support their own user login scripts and do not request the assistance of a network administrator.

```
MAP DISPLAY OFF

MAP ERROR OFF

MAP F:=FAC-SRV1\SYS:USERS\JMADISON
```

```
;***** EMAIL *****

SET EMAILUSER = "JMADISON"

MAP M:=RIO-SRV1\SYS:POSTOFF

;***** PRINTERS *****

#capture L=1 Q=HP4SI-PQ1 NB NFF TI=1

;***** WINDOWS *****

MAP ROOT W:=FAC-SRV1\SYS:APPS\WINDOWS

;***** BRIEF EDITOR FLAGS *****

MAP S16:=FAC-SRV1\SYS:APPS\BRIEF

SET BPACKAGES = "c:t;h:t,r"

SET BPATH ="z:\\apps\\brief\\macros"

SET BHELP = "z:\\apps\\brief\\help"

SET BBACKUP = "c:\\backup"

SET BFLAGS = "-i70 -u300 -l200 -Dega -k1 M"

SET BFILE = ""

SET BTMP = "c:\\tmp"

SET BCC = "\"cl /c %s.c\""

SET BCH = "\"cl -c -Tc %s.h\""

;***** WP *****

MAP S16:=FAC-SRV1\SYS:APPS\WP\6.1

SET WP = "/U=JM"

;***** Misc. *****

MAP S16:=FAC-SRV1\SYS:APPS\PROGRAMS\BIN

MAP
```

Default Login Script   The default login script is executed only when the user login script does not exist. The default login script is hard coded into the LOGIN.EXE program and tries to create enough drive mappings to the server so that the user can function properly. The purpose of the default login script is to back up the absence of a user login script. The default login script will execute even if you have a container or profile login script.

If you do not want to run the default script, then you need to place the NO_DEFAULT command in the container login script or in a profile script. The container login script can also have an EXIT command at the bottom of the script. The EXIT command prevents any other login script from running, including the default login script.

The following commands are executed as the default login script:

```
WRITE "Good %GREETING_TIME, %LOGIN_NAME."

MAP DISPLAY OFF

MAP ERRORS OFF

MAP *1:=%FILE_SERVER\SYS:

MAP *1:=%FILE_SERVER\SYS:%LOGIN_NAME

IF "%1" = "SUPERVISOR" || "%1" = "ADMIN" THEN MAP
*1:=%FILE_SERVER\SYS:SYSTEM

MAP INS S1:=%FILE_SERVER\SYS:PUBLIC

MAP INS

S2:=%FILE_SERVER\SYS:PUBLIC\%MACHINE\%OS\%OS_VERSION

MAP DISPLAY ON

MAP
```

MOBILE OR TRAVELING USERS

IntranetWare lets the user log in and access resources from anywhere in the network. This feature helps you to manage the mobile or traveling user more easily. In order to completely support traveling users and their specific computing requirements, you will need to consider the following questions:

▶ Does the user carry a laptop computer?

▶ Where is the user geographically located?

▶ Where is the user's home office?

As users move from one location to another, they access the network and its resources differently. Knowing how each user wants to access the network will help you set up the user environments. For example, some users just want dial-in access to the network from remote locations. These locations can range from their homes, hotel rooms, and even airplanes. Typically, this type of user dials into the network from a laptop or home computer.

Some users may travel from one office to another and need full access to all the local network resources of the office they are visiting. Although the users need full access to the local resources, they still want the data from their home directory and server. Essentially, the definition of a traveling user is broken into two types: remote users and mobile users.

CONSULTING EXPERIENCE

Your approach to designing access for IntranetWare should be to first design for the majority of the users and then design for the traveling users. In order to design the access properly, you need to know how many users in the network are traveling users. Then determine from the total number of traveling users how many are remote users and how many are true mobile users.

Remote Users

The remote users are the individuals who travel or carry a laptop computer and simply access the network resources through dial-in. The remote user who takes a laptop on the road is usually self-contained, meaning that the laptop computer is configured with all the necessary applications software. The user can continue to work when on the road and merely dials into the network to transfer e-mail messages, download files, or briefly access other resources.

Remote users require less design considerations for access because they will access the NDS tree only as needed for a connection to the network. Supporting remote users will not impact the design of the Directory tree or require you to create any special NDS objects. Users simply dial into specific predetermined access points in the network and use their normal NDS context or location. After the normal login to the network, the users can download files and access other necessary resources.

Some remote users dial in just to transfer their e-mail messages. Typically, a company may dedicate special phone lines for just the remote e-mail users. These lines may have their own security and access method and would not affect the Directory tree access.

If a remote user travels to another office and plugs his laptop computer into the network and wants access to all the local resources, he has really become a mobile user. The design considerations for the mobile users are addressed in the following section.

Mobile Users

The mobile users are individuals who travel from one office to another or from one computer to another. They expect full access to all the local network resources of the office they are visiting while maintaining the ability to access data from their home server. The mobile user may not carry a computer (laptop) with him, but expects to have a computer available at the other site. Some mobile users decide to carry laptop computers and plug them into the network when they arrive. Thus, the best definition of a mobile user is an individual who uses a computer on the network from a location that is away from his home office.

Whether the user travels thousands of miles or across the building, the issues are the same for moblile users. The user wants access to the network applications, such as word processing, spreadsheets, e-mail, and printing from the local servers, but also wants to retrieve the data from his home server. The user wants these capabilities to be as seamless as possible.

In order to support the needs of the mobile user, you need to answer the following questions:

▸ Where is the user geographically located?

▸ Where is the user's home office?

CONSULTING EXPERIENCE

Users who carry laptop computers to a new location are not considered mobile users if they do not need access to the local network resources. If the users are content to access their home resources across the network, then they are simply remote users. There are no special design considerations for remote users. Remember, IntranetWare enables the users to login from anywhere on the network. A user simply looks for a network connection and logs in to the server at his home office.

There are several mechanisms in IntranetWare to help you answer each of these questions. These mechanisms include the NDS name context, alias objects, configuration files, login scripts, login script variables, and environment variables.

NDS Name Context   The name context in NDS helps you determine where in the NDS tree the user belongs. The name context is important because NDS requires it for every user logging in to the network. The context can be set in the user's NET.CFG file or by typing the user's full name during login as well. While a mobile user's physical location may change, his context will remain constant.

If the mobile user has traveled without a laptop computer, he expects to use any available computer in the office he is visiting and log in to the network. The main issue with this scenario is how to determine the user's name context for login purposes. There are several ways to work around this problem. The mobile user can manually enter the context at the computer console before login, you can create alias objects that point to the user in his normal context, and the name context of the alias can be set in the workstation configuration file.

Manually Changing the NDS Name Context   The first option involves the mobile user manually entering his name context into the computer he is using. This option assumes that the user understands how to use the proper utilities and is familiar with their complete context in the NDS tree. The CX (Change conteXt) utility is used to set the user's context before login.

For example, the user JMadison in the ACME tree as shown in Figure 12.13 would need to set his name context by typing:

```
CX  .FAC.ADMIN.RIO.ACME
```

FIGURE 12.13

The name context for the user JMadison in the ACME tree

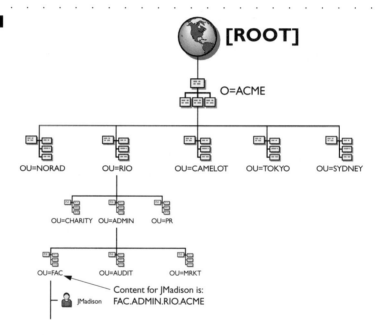

Notice the leading period in the CX command line. The leading period tells the utility that this is a distinguished name and to start at the [ROOT] object when setting the name context. This is a little easier than trying to figure out where your current context is set in the tree.

The CX utility is stored in the LOGIN subdirectory on the server. The user must have a connection to a server and be in the directory (typically the F: drive) or type the path before running this utility.

Using an Alias Object to Help Set the Name Context   The second option that could help set the name context is the use of alias objects. If you have a small number of mobile users you can create an alias object below the O=Organization for each mobile user. The alias would point to the user's primary object in the appropriate container.

The value of this strategy is that it creates a simple context for each of the mobile users. The users do not need to know where the context is or even how to set it. The users would simply enter the name of the alias object during the login process.

For example, an alias object has been created for the user JMadison in the ACME tree. Figure 12.14 shows that the alias object called JMADISON was created directly in the O=ACME container. The alias object points to the real object in the OU=FAC in the RIO location. When the user JMadison wants to log in to the network from any site, he uses the name of the alias object as follows:

```
LOGIN  .JMADISON.ACME
```

Notice the leading period in the LOGIN command line before the name of the alias object. The leading period instructs the utility to start at the [ROOT] object when looking for the alias object.

This method of using the alias object to support the mobile users works well if you have a small number of mobile users at your site. Setting up an alias object for each individual mobile user is feasible if the total number is small. This method may not work if your mobile user population is high. You will need to determine how many alias objects you can manage.

NOTE

You can also use third-party utilities that search the tree for a user object and set the appropriate context for your mobile user. You should consider these types of utilities when you have many mobile users.

Using the Configuration Files to Set the Name Context   The name context for the user can be set using the standard workstation configuration file called NET.CFG. The NET.CFG file is read during the loading of the workstation client. The following is an example of setting the name context for the user JMadison in the ACME tree. Within the NET.CFG file there is a section called the NetWare DOS Requester where the NAME CONTEXT = "OU.FAC.OU=ADMIN.OU=RIO.O=ACME". Users traveling to different locations with their own notebook or laptop will typically have the NET.CFG file set already. When they arrive on site and connect to the network, their name context is resolved from setting in the NET.CFG file on the laptop.

```
Link Support

    MemPool 6192

    Buffers 10 1580

    MAX STACKS 8

Link Driver NE2000

    INT 5

    PORT 300

    MEM D0000

    FRAME Ethernet_802.2

NetWare DOS Requester

    NAME CONTEXT = "OU=FAC.OU=ADMIN.OU=RIO.O=ACME"

    PREFERRED SERVER = FAC-SRV1
```

```
FIRST NETWORK DRIVE = F

NETWARE PROTOCOL = NDS,BIND

SHOW DOTS = ON

USE DEFAULTS = ON

PB BUFFERS = 10
```

You can use the PREFERRED SERVER variable in the NET.CFG file (in the NetWare DOS Requester section) to connect the mobile user to the server that has this user's bindery context. If you force the user to connect to the proper server using the PREFERRED SERVER variable, the user can log in using bindery services. This enables users running the older NETX.EXE workstation client to participate in mobile computing if needed. For example, in the previous NET.CFG file, the variable is set as PREFERRED SERVER = FAC-SRV1. This enables the user JMadison to log in and access the server using bindery services if he is still running NETX.EXE.

Login Scripts for Mobile Users

The two mechanisms for creating a mobile user login script are the login script variables and an environment variable that can be called NW_SITE.

The following is an example of a container login script for mobile users. In this example, we have defined a mobile script that will allow the user to easily log into the network from any of the five major sites shown in the ACME tree. The script demonstrates how a user is mapped to the local e-mail server and the local application server. This login script is used as a container login script and also requires the NW_SITE DOS environment variable to be set on the user's workstation in the CONFIG.SYS file.

```
;***********************************************************

; MOBILE CONTAINER LOGIN SCRIPT

; for OU=FAC.OU=ADMIN.OU=RIO.O=ACME

; Creation Date: 10/8/95

; Revisions:

;***********************************************************
```

```
REM Do not execute default script

NO_DEFAULT

Write "Good %GREETING_TIME, %LOGIN_NAME"

REM Map public drive to local server

MAP S16:=SYS:\PUBLIC

REM Map F drive to the user's home server

MAP F:="HOME_DIRECTORY"

REM Map NetWare Drives according to the NW_SITE variable


IF <NW_SITE> == "NORAD" THEN BEGIN

    MAP ROOT M:= NOR-SRV1\SYS:MAIL

    MAP ROOT W:= NOR-SRV1\SYS:APPS\WP

    MAP ROOT Q:= NOR-SRV1\SYS:APPS\QPRO

    END

IF <NW_SITE> == "RIO" THEN BEGIN

    MAP ROOT M:= RIO-SRV1\SYS:MAIL

    MAP ROOT W:= RIO-SRV1\SYS:APPS\WP

    MAP ROOT Q:= RIO-SRV1\SYS:APPS\QPRO

    END

IF <NW_SITE> == "CAMELOT" THEN BEGIN

    MAP ROOT M:= CAM-SRV1\SYS:MAIL

    MAP ROOT W:= CAM-SRV1\SYS:APPS\WP

    MAP ROOT Q:= CAM-SRV1\SYS:APPS\QPRO

    END
```

```
IF <NW_SITE> == "TOKYO" THEN BEGIN

    MAP ROOT M:= TOK-SRV1\SYS:MAIL

    MAP ROOT W:= TOK-SRV1\SYS:APPS\WP

    MAP ROOT Q:= TOK-SRV1\SYS:APPS\QPRO

    END

IF <NW_SITE> == "SYDNEY" THEN BEGIN

    MAP ROOT M:= SYD-SRV1\SYS:MAIL

    MAP ROOT W:= SYD-SRV1\SYS:APPS\WP

    MAP ROOT Q:= SYD-SRV1\SYS:APPS\QPRO

    END

EXIT
```

NOTE

In the previous script you can specify the actual NDS volume object names instead of the server names for mapping drives. The drives M and W in our example default to searching in the bindery, which relies on SAP because we do not specify the NDS volume object names in the login script.

NetWare Login Command Switches

Table 12.1 lists the NetWare general login command switches and their syntaxes.

TABLE 12.1			
NetWare Login Command Switches	**COMMAND**	**COMMAND SYNTAX**	**PURPOSE**
	General Login Commands	LOGIN [File Server\] username [options]	Log clients into NetWare server with a bindery or NDS connection.
	/NS (No Script option)	LOGIN /NS	Executes a login without a login script.
	/CLS (Clear option)	LOGIN /CLS	Clears screen before Screen execution of the login script.

(continued)

T A B L E   12.1

*NetWare Login
Command Switches
(continued)*

COMMAND	COMMAND SYNTAX	PURPOSE
/S (Script option)	LOGIN /S filename or LOGIN /S object name	Executes a login script contained in the text filename or NDS object name.
/B (Bindery option)	LOGIN /B	Logs into a server using bindery services.
/TR (Tree option)	LOGIN /TR treename	Specifies a certain NDS tree by its tree name for logging in.
/SWAP	LOGIN /SWAP	Swaps LOGIN.EXE into Extended RAM if you use external commands from inside the login script.
/? (help option)	LOGIN /?	Provides a help screen.

Login Script Commands

There are many login script commands that can be used in any of the login scripts. Table 12.2 lists each login script command and its function.

T A B L E   12.2

Login Script Commands

COMMANDS	FUNCTION
ATTACH	The ATTACH command allows you to attach workstation to other NetWare servers. The ATTACH command only provides a bindery services connection to the selected server. This command enables you to have login scripts that are compatible and coexist with previous versions of NetWare (specifically NetWare 2 and NetWare 3). This command no longer works on the command line for IntranetWare but is still provided in login scripts as a means of backward compatibility with NetWare 3 scripts that may be migrated into IntranetWare.
BREAK	The BREAK command has two settings, either ON or OFF. The ON setting enables you to execute your login scripts by pressing CTRL+C or CTRL+BREAK. The default setting is always OFF.
CLS	The CLS command clears the workstation screen or display. It is functionally similar to the CLS command that you can execute from DOS.

	COMMANDS	FUNCTION
TABLE 12.2 *Login Script Commands* *(continued)*	**COMSPEC**	The COMSPEC command specifies the subdirectory where DOS should load the command line processor called COMMAND.COM.
	CONTEXT	The CONTEXT command is a smaller version of the CX.EXE command line utility that enables you to set the workstation context in the NDS tree. An example of using the CONTEXT command is as follows: CONTEXT .R&D.NORAD.ACME
	# CHARACTER	The # character provides external program execution. For example, to execute the capture program from within a login script type the following: #CAPTURE L=1 Q=HP4SI NB NFF TI=1 You can enter a complete pathname/filename for the external program or make sure that the proper drive mapping and search drives have been set. The # character must be the first character on the line.
	DISPLAY	The DISPLAY command enables you to shows the contents of any file on the screen. The following syntax is used: DISPLAY [pathname]\filename The difference between this command and the DISPLAY command discussed later in this section is that this command shows all the characters in the file including control codes and ESC sequences.
	DOS BREAK	The DOS BREAK command has two settings, either ON or OFF. The ON setting enables you to terminate any DOS program that has been executed from the login script by pressing CTRL+C or CTRL+BREAK. The difference between this command and the BREAK command is that this command enables CTRL+BREAK checking for DOS. The BREAK command checks only CTRL+BREAK within the login script itself.
	DOS SET, TEMP SET, or SET	These commands can be used to establish the DOS environment variables for the workstation and user. The syntax is as follows: [OPTION] [DOS] SET name = "value"

(continued)

CHAPTER 12
. . . . .
N O V E L L ' S
G U I D E   T O
I N T R A N E T W A R E
N E T W O R K S

*Login Script Commands
(continued)*

COMMANDS	FUNCTION
DOS SET, TEMP SET, or SET	The [OPTION] parameter can be used or replaced with an optional keyword. The keywords are TEMP, TEMPORARY, LOCAL, which means that the variable is set only during the processing of the login script. The variable is not set in DOS.
DOS VERIFY	The DOS VERIFY command has two settings, either ON or OFF. The ON setting means that the data copied to the local drive is written without errors.
DRIVE	The DRIVE command specifies which network drive will be used as the default drive.
EXIT	The EXIT command tells the login script to terminate the processing of the login script and exit immediately. You can use the EXIT command in conjunction with the following program name: EXIT [filename] The login script passes control to the program specified. You should place the EXIT command statement as the last line in the individual login script. The EXIT command can be placed in system or container login scripts to guarantee that no individual user login scripts are executed.
FDISPLAY	The FDISPLAY command shows the contents of the specified text file on the screen. The following syntax is used: FDISPLAY [pathname]\filename Only the text or characters in the file are displayed. The control characters in the file are not shown.
FIRE PHASERS	The FIRE PHASERS command produces blasts that sound like you are firing a toy weapon. You can fire 1 to 9 phasers as dictated in the following syntax: FIRE PHASERS n TIMES (where n is the number of times) You typically use this command for special effects during the login process.

TABLE 12.2	COMMANDS	FUNCTION
Login Script Commands (continued)	**GOTO**	The GOTO command enables you to program the login script and jump or repeat specific locations in the login script. You can place labels in the login script to control the GOTO statements.
	IF ... THEN ... ELSE	The IF ... THEN ... ELSE command enables you to build conditional logic into the login scripts. This command lets you execute certain portions of the login scripts conditionally.
	INCLUDE	The INCLUDE command enables you to direct the login script to specific files that you have predefined. The following syntax is used:
		INCLUDE [pathname]\filename
		The contents of the file specified in the INCLUDE statement are the next lines processed in the script. After the file has been processed, control is returned to the statement immediately following the INCLUDE statement in your login script.
	LASTLOGINTIME	The LASTLOGINTIME command checks or displays the last date and time of login.
	MACHINE	The MACHINE command sets the hardware machine type. This variable receives its value from the LONG MACHINE TYPE variable in the NET.CFG. The default value is IBM_PC.
	MAP and MAP DISPLAY	The MAP command is equivalent to the MAP.EXE program. The command enables you to establish network drive mapping.
		The MAP DISPLAY command can be set to either ON or OFF. The ON setting shows all the drive mapping during the login process. The default is ON. The OFF setting will not show the drive mapping during the login procedure.

(continued)

Login Script Commands
(continued)

COMMANDS	FUNCTION
NO_DEFAULT	The NO_DEFAULT command disables the execution of the Default Login Script, which is part of the LOGIN.EXE program. Disabling the Default Login Script can be useful when you want to control all the drive mapping for the user. This includes the drive mapping to the SYS:PUBLIC subdirectory.
PAUSE or WAIT	The PAUSE command causes the login script to stop execution until a key is pressed. This command is useful so that long messages can be read without scrolling off the screen. This command can also be helpful when debugging the login script.
PCCOMPATIBLE	The PCCOMPATIBLE command indicates that the workstation hardware is compatible with an IBM PC. For some workstations, if you do not use this command, then some NetWare utilities such as NETADMIN and FILER will not work.
REMARK or REM	The REMARK command documents the lines or place comments in the login script file. The use of comments will always improve the readability and maintenance of the scripts. To place comments in the login scripts the following syntax is used: REM [text] or * text or ; text
WRITE	The WRITE command displays text messages to the workstation screen during the login process. The following syntax is used: WRITE [text] You can use the semicolon (;) to join text messages together.

Login Variables

IntranetWare has always had the capability to use login variables in login scripts to help you manage the login scripts and make them more efficient and flexible. Table 12.3 lists the login script variables and their definitions that can be used to enhance your login scripts. These variables can be used in the login script to help you:

▸ Build conditional statements

▸ Provide date and time functions

▸ Establish DOS environment and workstation settings

▸ Provide NDS properties to the user

Most of the variables can be displayed using the WRITE login script command preceding the variable. There are also some examples provided in the use of these variables. In Table 12.3, note that some of the variables have underscores in them and some do not.

Table 12.4 lists the date and time login variables.

T A B L E 12.3	VARIABLE	FUNCTION
Conditional Statement Login Script Variables	%ACCESS_SERVER	Displays or checks if the access server is functional (TRUE=functional, FALSE=not functional).
	%ERROR_LEVEL	Displays or checks the DOS error level. A value of 0 indicates that no DOS errors have occurred. For example, this variable can be used to check and see if a drive mapping was successful.
	%MEMBER OF "group"	Tests to see whether user is a member of the "group." Returns TRUE or FALSE.
	%NOT MEMBER OF "group"	Returns TRUE if the user is NOT a member of the "group."

*Date and Time Login
Script Variables*

VARIABLE	FUNCTION
%AM_PM	Displays time as day or night, using a.m. or p.m.
%DAY	Displays the current day value ranging from 01 to 31.
%DAY_OF_WEEK	Displays the written day of the week.
%GREETING_TIME	Displays time of day as morning, afternoon, or evening.
%HOUR	Displays time of day in hours ranging from 1 to 12.
%HOUR24	Displays the hour in 24-hour time ranging from 00 to 23.
%MINUTE	Displays the minutes ranging from 00 to 59.
%MONTH	Displays month (from 01 to 12).
%MONTH_NAME	Displays name of the month.
%NDAY_OF_WEEK	Displays number of week day.
%SECOND	Displays the seconds ranging from 00 to 59.
%SHORT_YEAR	Displays year in short format (92, 93, 94, 95, 96, 97, and so on).
%YEAR	Displays year in full format (1992, 1993, and so on).

Any DOS environment variable can be used in a login script if you place angle brackets (< and >) around the variable. A common example of a DOS variable used in login scripts is:

```
<COMSPEC>
```

In order to use a DOS environment variable with login script commands, you need to add a percent sign (%) in front of the variable. For example, to map a drive to the COMSPEC DOS environment variable type the following:

```
MAP S16:=%<COMSPEC>
```

The following list of DOS Environment and Workstation variables in Table 12.5 will help to set up the workstation for the specific network users. Some variables have more than one key word, which is shown in parentheses.

*DOS Environment and
Workstation Variables*

VARIABLE	FUNCTION
%LAST_NAME	Displays the user's last name (surname) in Novell Directory Services, or full login name in bindery-based NetWare. This value returns the same result as the SURNAME variable in the user properties.
%LOGIN_ALIAS_CONTEXT	Displays the context of the alias object user logged in with. This variable is valid only with NDS.
%LOGIN_CONTEXT	Displays the context for the user. Returns the context where user exists in the NDS tree. This variable works only with IntranetWare.
%LOGIN_NAME	Displays the user's login name. This returns the same result as the CN variable in the user property list, although CN is multivalued.
%MACHINE	Displays the machine type of a workstation (IBM_PC, and so on).
%NEW_MAIL	Displays the status of the variable.
%OS	Type of operating system on the workstation (MSDOS, OS2, and so on).
%OS_VERSION	Operating system version on the workstation (3.30, and so on).
%P_STATION (PHYSICAL_ STATION)	Workstation's node number shown as a 12-digit hexadecimal.
%PASSWORD_EXPIRES	Displays the number of days before the user password will expire.
%REQUESTER_VERSION (optional names: NETWARE_ REQUESTER, REQUESTER)	Displays the version of the VLM requester.
%REQUESTER_CONTEXT	Displays the context that is found in the workstation's NET.CFG file at the time of login.
%SHELL_TYPE (SHELL_VERSION)	Version of the workstation's DOS shell (1.02, and so on); supports NetWare 2 and 3 shells and NetWare 4 Requester for DOS.
%STATION (CONNECTION)	Displays the workstation address for that user.

IntranetWare extends the list of login variables, as shown in Table 12.6, through the use of the user properties found in Novell Directory Services. If the property includes a space, enclose the name in quotation marks or replace the spaces with an underscore.

TABLE 12.6

NDS User Properties Variables

VARIABLE	FUNCTION
%ACCOUNT_BALANCE	Displays account balance information if being used.
%ALLOW UNLIMITED CREDIT	Displays whether unlimited credit has been assigned for that user. The value returned is "Y" or "N".
%BACKLINK	Established for any user object in which there is an associated external reference on a different server.
%BINDERY PROPERTY	Used to emulate the bindery properties that are not represented by the other user properties.
%CN	Displays the login name of the user who logs in to the network.
%DESCRIPTION	Displays any value contained in the description property for the user.
%EMAIL ADDRESS	Displays the first value in the e-mail address property for the user.
%EQUIVALENT TO ME	Displays only the first value in the list.
%FACSIMILE TELEPHONE NUMBER	Displays the first number in the fax number property for the user.
%FULL NAME	Displays the user's full name value. This value is the property stored in NDS and the bindery if the server is bindery-based NetWare. Spaces are replaced with underscores.
%GROUP MEMBERSHIP	Displays the values of the membership attributes.
%HOME DIRECTORY	Displays the complete path for the home directory property set for the user who has logged in.

T A B L E   12.6

*NDS User
Properties Variables
(continued)*

VARIABLE	FUNCTION
%INITIALS	Displays the value of the user's middle initial property.
%LANGUAGE	Displays the current language being used by the user.
%L	Displays the first value of the location property for the user.
%LOCKED BY INTRUDER	Displays status of locked by intruder property. The value returned is "Y" for yes or "N" for no.
%LOGIN DISABLED	Displays account disable status. The value returned is "Y" for yes or "N" for no.
%LOGIN GRACE LIMIT	Displays the value of the login grace limit property.
%LOGIN GRACE REMAINING	Displays the number of remaining grace logins for the user.
%LOGIN INTRUDER ATTEMPTS	Displays the number of incorrect login attempts for the user.
%LOGIN MAXIMUM SIMULTANEOUS	Displays the value of the maximum simultaneous connections for the user.
%LOGIN TIME	Displays both the date and time of the login time for the user.
%MAILBOX ID	Displays the mailbox ID for the user.
%MAILBOX LOCATION	Displays the mailbox location for the user. MHS can, but does not have to, be installed in order to have a value for the mailbox location.
%MESSAGE SERVER	Displays the default server or message server name.
%MINIMUM ACCOUNT BALANCE	Displays the value of the minimum account balance or low balance limit.
%NETWORK ADDRESS	Displays the physical network address, node, and socket number for the workstation.
%OBJECT CLASS	Displays the base class for the user object.

(continued)

TABLE 12.6

*NDS User
Properties Variables
(continued)*

VARIABLE	FUNCTION
%OU	Shows the first value defined in the Department list for the user.
%PASSWORD ALLOW CHANGE	Shows the value of this user property "Y" or "N".
%PASSWORD EXPIRATION INTERVAL	Displays time in total seconds before the user password will expire.
%PASSWORD MINIMUM LENGTH	Displays the minimum password length setting for the user.
%PASSWORD REQUIRED	Displays the value of the password required. Displays or returns "Y" or "N".
%PASSWORD UNIQUE	Displays the property value of REQUIRED unique password required. Displays or returns "Y" or "N".
%PHYSICAL DELIVERY OFFICE NAME	Displays the value of the city property for the user.
%POSTAL OFFICE BOX	Displays the user's postal office box value if any.
%POSTAL CODE	Displays the value of the user's postal zip code, if any.
%POSTAL ADDRESS	Displays the value of the user's postal address property, if any.
%PROFILE	Displays the name of the profile object if the user is associated with a profile.
%REVISION	Displays the value of the revision property for the user. The revision increments each time the user is accessed.
%S	Displays the value of the state or province property for the user.
%SA	Displays the value of the street address for the user.
%SECURITY EQUALS	Displays security equivalence assignments made for that user. Only displays the first value in the list.

VARIABLE	FUNCTION
%SEE ALSO	Displays the first value in the see also property for the user.
%SERVER HOLDS	Displays the number of accounting charges pending while the server performs a chargeable action.
%SURNAME (LAST_NAME)	Displays the user's surname property value, if any. User's last name (surname) in NetWare Directory Services, or full login name in bindery-based NetWare.
%TELEPHONE NUMBER	Shows the user's phone entered in his phone number property. Only displays the first value in the list.
%TITLE	Displays the title for the user if one has been entered as a user property. Only shows the first value in the list.
%UID	Displays a unique user ID assigned to the user for use by UNIX clients.

CHAPTER 13

Managing NetWare Security

"Even in the common affairs of life, in love, friendship, and marriage, how little security have we when we trust our happiness in the hands of others!" William Hazlitt

As networks become increasingly more distributed the exposure of information has also increased. Therefore, it makes sense that in large networked environments, you'll have to pay more attention to security and take measures to ensure that your data is protected.

Securing your network actually encompasses many areas of security including physical access, login, NDS, and file system restrictions. Other areas that can be classified within the physical access category include natural disasters and hardware failures. Another area of security violations is caused unintentionally by users who have authorized access and simply make mistakes. Computer viruses also pose a threat to security and can be caused intentionally or unintentionally.

While each of these areas is important, the goal is to secure your important data from theft, eavesdropping, or destruction. Every organization may place greater emphasis on a particular aspect of security depending on the sensitivity of the data. Some organizations may attempt to enforce all available aspects of security, while other companies may only concentrate on a few areas. As a network administrator you must decide along with your other managers what is an acceptable level of security versus risk for your department or company's data. Any level of security you implement is more than what your users will want because of additional burdens placed on their ability to freely work on the network.

Some companies may be especially prone to disasters because of their geographical location and natural weather conditions. Other companies may be at a greater hardware risk because they are running their network in a factory or plant where the possibility of fire or other damage is greater.

This chapter discusses these topics including securing the physical access to hardware, understanding the authentication and login process, and applying NDS restrictions. NDS restrictions include security for objects and properties as well as for the file system. These various levels of security are represented in Figure 13.1.

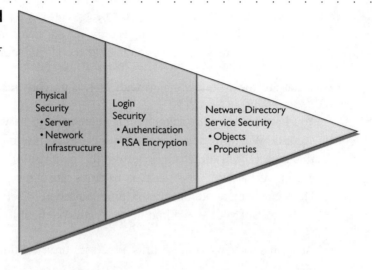

FIGURE 13.1

Security can be broken down into the categories of physical security, login security, and NDS security.

Physical
Security
• Server
• Network
  Infrastructure

Login
Security
• Authentication
• RSA Encryption

Netware Directory
Service Security
• Objects
• Properties

Designing a Security Model

One of the first steps to implementing security for your environment is to design what is commonly referred to as a security model. A security model is basically your own company's road map for implementing security. Consider the following questions when implementing your security plan:

▶ What security threats do you have at your company?

You must evaluate all aspects of threats including your building's age and entrance policies, the geographic location, the experience level of your users, the number of users, the age of your server hardware, and access points to your network from locations outside your company. Access points refer to gateways or other routing devices connected to the Internet or other wide-area links.

▶ What security do you currently have in place and what improvements can be made?

Most companies usually have some form of network security in place. If your network is growing or if you have recently connected to the Internet, you should consider increasing your security. If your company is in the process of relocating to a new building you should reevaluate your security measures.

▸ What are the costs associated with increasing your security?

You have to take into account what the costs will be when increasing your security. Will your added security measures require more staff to assist with this aspect? Will the changes require the purchase of newer, more expensive hardware such as tape backups and virus protection software? How much more administration time is needed to service each user? What is the cost of your downtime if your network should have a failure?

▸ Are you reviewing your security processes on a continual basis?

Each network administrator should perform a regular security check on the network to determine if new workstations or any other new devices have been added to the network. A review will also determine if any security policies need to be modified based on any other changes that may have occurred on the network.

Controlling Physical Access to Your Hardware

NETWORK HARDWARE SECURITY

One of the most basic aspects of providing a secure network is to physically secure your servers and workstations. If possible, your servers should be protected in a locked room such as a data center or wiring closet. Many large companies already place servers in their data centers. Smaller companies may not have this option, but there are other steps that can be taken to help safeguard your servers as explained at the end of this section.

Network administrators can secure their physical networks by encasing their network wiring in conduit to prohibit intrusion. Again, your company and administrators must determine if such an enormous expense is needed to secure your particular data. Most network administrators going to this length are probably considering installing a network that is C2 compliant. For more information on a trusted environment, you can refer to Novell's Application Notes April 1994 Special Edition "Building and Auditing a Trusted Environment with NetWare 4" and August 1994 "An Introduction to Novell's Open Security Architecture." At the time of this writing IntranetWare is now C2 compliant for IntranetWare servers and workstations running NetWare client software. For information on security and related topics you can also refer to the National Computer Security Center Document NCSC-TG-028, which is known as the "Orange Book."

IntranetWare introduces NetWare Enhanced Security, which is designed to meet the Controlled Access implementation (Class C2) requirements. Novell provides the following features to enable NetWare Enhanced Security:

▶ Novell's AUDITCON utility now provides C2 compliant auditing. The audit log files can now be represented and managed as Directory objects so that you can control access to the files through Directory rights assignments.

▶ An IntranetWare server can be configured as an Enhanced Security server by using the following SET parameter:

```
SET Enable SECURE.NCF
```

▶ This parameter enables a set of scripting commands on an IntranetWare server to be an Enhanced Security server.

For more information refer to Novell's IntranetWare Security Features User's Guide and NetWare Enhanced Security Administration. See also the discussion of AUDITCON in Chapter 2 and Novell's IntranetWare documentation Auditing the Network.

Network administrators may also want to consider enabling auditing on various activities for servers that are designated as highly secure. For more information on the auditing functions using the AUDITCON utility, see Chapter 2. There are also additional third-party products that monitor network activity as well.

You also should consider taking the following steps to secure your servers:

- Keep all servers in a data center or an air-conditioned locked room and limit access to these areas.

- Provide a tape backup for all servers on your network to back up files as well as NDS. Restore data to a test directory to periodically check that the restore procedure is working properly.

- Remove DOS from the file server by typing REMOVE DOS at the server console.

- Use an auditing tool such as Novell's AUDITCON or another third-party utility to track server events on highly sensitive servers.

- Lock the file server console using MONITOR.NLM and do not store the password in the AUTOEXEC.NCF file.

- Require passwords for print servers that need to log in to the IntranetWare servers.

- Periodically check containers that are under your responsibility for new objects. Investigate all new objects added to your containers.

- Carefully control the use of RCONSOLE and its password. You can encrypt the RCONSOLE password for your AUTOEXEC.NCF by following these steps:

a • At an IntranetWare console type **REMOTE ENCRYPT**.

b • You will then be prompted for an RCONSOLE password to be encrypted.

c • After entering the password, the file LDREMOTE.NCF will be created.

d • You can call this file in your AUTOEXEC.NCF or copy the contents out of the file into your AUTOEXEC.NCF.

CONTROLLING PHYSICAL ACCESS TO WORKSTATIONS

Workstations are more problematic to secure because some of your employees may use notebook computers that are transported away from the office each day. Also, very few companies ever go to the bother of physically securing workstations to desks or tables. Even if your users have stationary computers, there is always the possibility that unauthorized individuals will have access to your data.

You may also want to consider using a protocol analyzer such as Novell's LANalyzer, which provides a feature known as "new station" alarm to notify network administrators when a new node address has been discovered on your network. This application could be run on a nightly basis to search for any new hardware that may have been added to your network. It is usually quite easy for anyone to attach a notebook computer to your network infrastructure.

You can also limit access to your servers through Novell's station restriction and time restrictions procedures, which can be accomplished with the NWADMIN or NETADMIN utilities. These procedures limit a user to a particular workstation for logging in and also to specific times of the day.

You should consider taking the following steps to secure your workstations:

- ▶ Encourage users not to leave their workstations unattended while logged in to the network unless they are using password protected screen saver software.

- ▶ Always log out of the network before leaving your work location for the day.

- ▶ Keep office doors locked when not in use and workstations powered off if possible.

- ▶ Administrators especially should not leave their workstations unattended while logged in with supervisor rights to the tree, its containers, or servers.

- ▶ At a minimum you should have an asset tag for each piece of hardware on your network in case of theft or other damage.

- ▶ Use an antivirus product for your network that is loaded from the container login script.

- Carefully monitor the use of the ADMIN or any tree administrator user object. Change the password frequently.

- Require periodic changes in users' passwords. Do not allow them to use the same password twice.

- Have a company policy that no external diskettes are to be brought into the workplace unless they are scanned for viruses first.

- Dial in access should be closely monitored and employ automatic call back features built into remote dial software.

Understanding the Login and Authentication Process

After you have physically secured your servers, the IntranetWare login security is the next line of defense in network security. The authentication procedure verifies that any requests the server receives are from legitimate clients. The authentication process consists of the login and the authentication. IntranetWare uses its own authentication process that is compatible with NetWare 3 as well. The mechanism used to make the authentication process extremely secure is known as encryption and is discussed later in this section.

PASSWORD SECURITY AND VERIFICATION

The purpose in having a password is to prevent unauthorized access to your network resources. IntranetWare security must be reinforced by all network users and administrators practicing good password security. Any disclosure of passwords will allow a user to access that account to the extent of that user's rights. Therefore, you can take numerous precautions to secure your network, but the human factor is always the biggest threat to your security. You can take some steps to help minimize the threat of a password breach in your security:

- Without exception, require a user password for all users.

▸ Always require periodic changes of passwords for mobile users dialing into your network or users who work from home.

▸ Users should never post their passwords anywhere.

▸ Users should be encouraged to avoid easy passwords such as family member names, and so on.

Through the IntranetWare utilities you can do the following:

▸ Require a minimum password length of five to eight characters.

▸ Enforce periodic changes of passwords.

▸ Enforce unique passwords.

▸ Frequently change the password for your ADMIN or tree administrator user objects.

RSA ENCRYPTION/DECRYPTION

NDS uses encryption to secure authentication information that is being sent across the network from one server to other servers or from a workstation to a server for authentication purposes. IntranetWare uses the RSA encryption technology to provide public and private key encryption. The encryption process produces transmissions across the network that are unreadable except to the receiving entity.

The public and private key encryption is also known as asymmetrical cryptography because there is a mathematical relationship between the two keys. If data is encrypted with the object's public key, the receiving object will use its private key to decrypt the information. The public key can be read by any requesting object. The receiving object holds the private key but never discloses it. Figure 13.2 shows the relationship between the public and private keys during transmission of authentication data. Keep in mind that only the server objects keep their own private key. Users obtain their encrypted private key during the login process. This key is then decrypted, used to generate a signature, and then discarded.

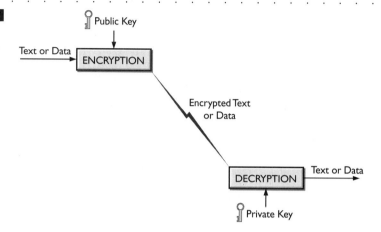

FIGURE 13.2

*The use of public and
private key encryption of
authentication data*

Directory Services uses encryption to ensure that authentication information is secure while it is being transmitted on the wire. There will always be a public key/private key pair for each encrypted transaction. To prevent intrusion during a transmission by capturing and replaying encrypted messages, the NetWare authentication process uses what is known as a nonce value. A nonce value is a random value that is generated for each encrypted transaction. The nonce value is associated only once with each encrypted message. Because the nonce is used only once, it will not do an intruder any good to capture an encrypted message and attempt to impersonate the sender.

Each transaction uses the network layer infrastructure to send and receive packets. This means that for authentication IPX and NCP requests are made between a client and a server, but for NDS authentication the data is encrypted before transmission on the wire. Keep in mind that the term "client" can mean a Directory Services server communicating with another server. As discussed previously in Chapter 12, there are varying degrees of authentication access. We list them here again briefly.

Connected but Not Logged In

This state is a client who has attached to an IntranetWare server either through the NETX shell or the VLM client. It could also be a DS server that does not use NETX or VLMs. A connected but not logged in state can exist for either NetWare 3 or IntranetWare users to the first attached server or, if a connection is made for tree walking, after the first attached server. This state is seen in the MONITOR utility as NOT LOGGED IN and does not take a licensed connection.

Authenticated

Authentication is a process of proving identity to a server. In NetWare 3, this meant logging in. In IntranetWare, it happens as a "behind the scenes task" at the client and is called authentication.

This type of connection indicates that an IntranetWare server has established a user's identity after the client has entered a correct name and password to obtain the encrypted private key. Authentication occurs for both NetWare 3 and IntranetWare users, with IntranetWare adding more security to this process. The authentication process includes creating a proof and a server verifying that proof. Proof is constructed with the client's public key, signature, and credential and is built at the time of login.

Licensed

A connection is said to be licensed when a client has made a request of the server such as mapping a drive or capturing to a printer. At that time the client requests the server to license the connection. This will cause the license count on the server to be decremented by one. Only an authenticated connection can be licensed.

A combination of these states determines what level a user currently has in an IntranetWare environment. For example, when a connection is neither authenticated nor licensed, users can navigate the NDS tree through the use of the CX (Change conteXt) program (presuming [PUBLIC] has the Browse right at the [ROOT] object of the tree) and the execution of the LOGIN.EXE utility as well. They have attached to a server, but have not yet authenticated.

If a user is licensed and authenticated, he can access NDS and file system information to the extent allowed by his rights.

The Change Connection State NCP call switches the connection between Not Licensed and Licensed.

NOTE

THE USER LOGIN

The first step to authenticating in an IntranetWare environment is the identification phase, also known as the login phase. When the client first logs in to an IntranetWare server he must establish his identity with the server and then proceed through the authentication phase. This is accomplished by the client broadcasting a Service Request, with the broadcast type 0x0278 if the *preferred tree* is set on, or the broadcast type 0x0004 if the *preferred server* is set. A server or router that receives this request will reply with a response. The client will examine the response and accept the first response with the correct tree/server being sought. This gets the client a connection to begin the tree walking (resolve name operation). NDS will then search the tree to find a writeable replica of the user's object. The following steps then occur during login and authentication phases:

Login Phase

1 • Once a writeable replica is found with the user object, the user is prompted for a name and password.

2 • After successfully proving knowledge of the password, the client receives the encrypted private key from the server.

3 • The private key of the client is used to generate a signature.

4 • The public key of the client is used to generate a credential.

5 • The signature and credential are used to build a proof that is used later in this sequence.

Authentication Phase

6 • The public key attribute of the server is read by the requesting client.

7 • The proof previously generated is encrypted with the server's public key and sent to the server.

8 • The server decrypts the proof with the server's private key.

9 • The proof is verified by the server through a mathematical computation of the client's public key and the client key stored on the server.

10 • If the proof is correct, then authentication is successful.

11 • The finished authentication request will then call Directory Services for the user's security equivalence vector.

12 • The login process is then passed back to Directory Services to execute the applicable login script and apply NDS access controls.

For more information on user login and authentication, refer to Novell's October 1994 Application Notes "Identification and Authentication in NetWare 4."

Keep in mind that the client's password is never transmitted across the wire. Therefore, it is not possible for someone to capture a password packet on the wire. In addition, the authentication data is valid only during the current login session. If a user terminates the session and then reconnects, the authentication process is repeated.

Another feature, known as Packet Signature, requires each packet to have a valid signature in order to be executed by the server. Packet signing makes it far more difficult for someone to forge NCP packets and send them on to the server for processing.

BACKGROUND AUTHENTICATION

During the initial login process a NetWare client will identify a hosting server. Although the login process in IntranetWare is performed only once, the authentication process may occur throughout the entire session in order to enable services from other servers.

Background authentication is the ongoing identification process that occurs after the initial login. If a connection needs to be made to other network services, authentication is done through the process of background authentication. Background authentication can occur because the IntranetWare servers can verify the proof provided by the client from the client's public key without additional user intervention. A server making a request of another server is also considered a client. Keep in mind that the proof is constructed at the client using the signature, credential, and public key.

When a user logs out of the network, the IntranetWare license manager is notified and makes the license available to any other validated user needing a license. The logout includes destroying the service connection to all but one server along with all bindings that were part of the user connection. The authentication data is also destroyed on the workstation at logout.

NDS Access Control

NDS security actually consists of two parts known as file system security and object security. Both aspects of IntranetWare security work together to provide a flexible and effective method for controlling access to your network. The file system security provides access control to files and directories. The object security provides access control to NDS objects and associated operations. You must determine to what extent you want to enable the many file system and NDS security features at your disposal. NetWare is well regarded for providing a high degree of network security, and much of the security administration happens by default as explained later in this chapter.

The first step to understanding NetWare security is to begin with the file system security. The file system security consists of the security that was introduced in previous versions of NetWare. Your familiarity with the security concepts in NetWare 3 will be a great help to you in understanding security in IntranetWare.

UNDERSTANDING FILE SYSTEM SECURITY

Very little has changed in file system security from NetWare 3. All the rules governing rights administration are the same in IntranetWare. As an administrator you don't have to learn any new concepts to manage your IntranetWare files. However, if you are new to NetWare you will want to read this section and refer to Novell's documentation on managing the file system. IntranetWare does introduce some additional file system attributes that can be useful for particular situations.

File system security basically consists of assigning trustee rights and file/directory attributes. The trustee rights assignments can be applied to any NDS object including containers, user objects, group objects, and organizational roles. Table 13.1 shows the file system rights available in IntranetWare.

	RIGHT	DEFINITION
TABLE 13.1 *File System Rights*	Access Control	Adds/modifies rights to files and directories
	Supervisor	Enables all file and directory assignments to be made and grants all rights listed in this table
	Read	Enables the trustee to open, read, and execute application files
	Write	Enables the trustee user to open, write to, and modify a file
	Create	Enables the trustee to create subdirectories and files
	Erase	Enables the trustee to delete directories and files
	Modify	Enables the trustee to modify, rename directories and files, and change file attributes
	File Scan	Enables the trustee to view file and directory names in the file system

File Attributes

IntranetWare file system security includes the capability to manage access at file and directory levels just as it did in previous versions of NetWare. Attributes control what actions can or cannot be taken on a file or directory. For certain files, such as application files on the network, you may want to make sure they are flagged as Read Only and Shareable so that no unintentional or intentional deletions occur.

Additional file and directory attributes have been added to the NetWare 4 file system to provide more functionality to IntranetWare. These new file system attributes are listed below in Table 13.2. For a complete list of all attributes associated with IntranetWare files and directories, refer to Novell's documentation.

For more information on administering file system security, refer to Novell's IntranetWare manual Supervising the Network.

TABLE 13.2

New file system attributes that have been added to NetWare 4

ATTRIBUTE	ABBREVIATION	DEFINITION
Compress	Co	Status attribute that indicates the file is compressed.
Can't Compress	Cc	Status attribute that indicates the file cannot be compressed because of limited space savings.
Don't Compress	Dc	Added to a directory, this attribute keeps all files within the directory from being compressed. This attribute can also be added to a specific file.
Immediate Compress	Ic	Added to directories or files, this attribute alerts the file system to compress a file as soon as the operating system can handle the action.
Migrated	M	This status attribute indicates that the file has been migrated.
Don't Migrate	Dm	Added to a directory, this attribute will not allow files within the directory to be migrated to secondary storage. This attribute can also be added to a specific file.

UNDERSTANDING OBJECT SECURITY

Your understanding of NetWare 3 file system security will assist you in mastering IntranetWare security because both use the same terminology and the same rules. The rules for file system security in both versions of NetWare are identical. IntranetWare extends security to the NDS environment by adding access controls to all objects and properties found in your tree.

As shown below in Figure 13.3, security features in the IntranetWare environment are similar to that of NetWare 3.

FIGURE 13.3

*Security features between
the two versions of
NetWare are similar.*

NETWARE 3	INTRANETWARE
BINDERY	NOVELL DIRECTORY SERVICES
FILE & DIRECTORY RIGHTS FILE ATTRIBUTES	FILE & DIRECTORY RIGHTS FILE ATTRIBUTES
SUPERVISOR OPERATOR OBJECT RIGHTS ONLY	OBJECT & PROPERTY RIGHTS
SUPERVISOR USER	ADMIN USER AND BINDERY SUPERVISOR
EVERYONE GROUP	O=ORGANIZATION
GUEST USER	[PUBLIC] TRUSTEE (NOT THE SAME AS GUEST)
INHERIT RIGHTS MASK (IRM)	INHERITED RIGHTS FILTER (IFR)
DIRECTORY ENTERY TABLE (DET)	DET, ACL (ACCESS CONTROL LIST)

The exceptions between NetWare 3 and IntranetWare are as follows:

▶ **Inherited Rights Filter (IRF)** terminology is used instead of Inherited Rights Mask (IRM). In IntranetWare, the term IRF describes the operation of filtering out rights for a particular object. IRFs are explained in detail below.

▶ **NetWare Object classes** have been expanded from four in NetWare 3 to 32 in IntranetWare.

▶ **The SUPERVISOR user** is used only for bindery requests in IntranetWare. Another NDS user object (typically called ADMIN) is granted Supervisor object rights at the [ROOT] of the tree. This user object is the functional equivalent of the Supervisor found in NetWare 3 and has default Supervisor rights over all NDS objects in the tree as well as the file system for any IntranetWare server installed. One other major difference to note is that you cannot filter Supervisor rights in the IntranetWare file system, which is just like NetWare 3. You can, however, filter Supervisor rights in the NetWare Directory Services tree.

- **Guest** is not automatically created in IntranetWare. The [PUBLIC] Trustee is similar to Guest by enabling users to see the NDS tree before logging in to a server. However, Guest is a real object and [PUBLIC] is not, so the similarities are few.

- **Group Everyone** is not automatically created in IntranetWare. However, an equivalent feature is available by using either the [ROOT] object or O=Organization object. For example, O=ACME includes every object in the NDS tree and rights can be assigned to O=ACME, which all users receive automatically.

- **Operators** for print queues found in NetWare 3 are now an attribute of the Queue object found in IntranetWare Directory Services.

- **Directory Entry Tables** are still used to store file system trustees in IntranetWare. In addition, IntranetWare uses the Access Control List (ACL) to store NDS trustee information.

Object Rights Defined

Object rights are simply rights granted to a particular object to access or manage another object. In NetWare 3 servers the Supervisor object has rights to manage all other bindery objects on the server. IntranetWare has expanded on this concept by allowing all NDS objects rights to other objects. As shown in Table 13.3, NDS objects can receive many different rights.

TABLE 13.3	NDS OBJECT	OBJECT LEVEL RIGHTS
An object can receive many different object level rights to manage other objects in the Directory.	Supervisor (S)	Grants full privileges to the trustee over an object and has complete access to all the object's property rights.
	Browse (B)	Enables a trustee to see an NDS object in the tree during a browse of the tree.
	Create (C)	Enables a trustee to create objects below this object (applies to container objects only).
	Delete (D)	Enables a trustee to delete an object. Subordinate objects must be deleted first if you are deleting a container.
	Rename (R)	Enables a trustee to rename an object.

An example of how object rights appear in the NWADMIN utility is shown in
Figure 13.4 below.

*An example of object rights
as they are displayed in
the NWADMIN utility*

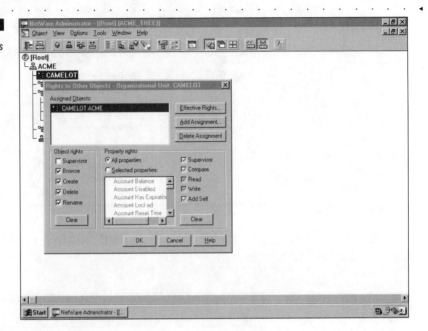

Property Rights Defined

Property rights enable a trustee to view or change the values of a particular
object's properties. You can have rights to certain properties (selected property
rights) or to all properties (all property rights) for a particular object. For example,
the Supervisor right over an NDS object also grants Supervisor privileges for all
properties in that object. All other rights assignments made at the object level are
not affected on the properties. In fact, Supervisor rights at the property level do not
grant Supervisor rights at the object level. Only the reverse is true. Table 13.4
shows a list of the available property rights in IntranetWare.

TABLE 13.4

*IntranetWare
property rights*

PROPERTY RIGHT	FUNCTION
Supervisor (S)	Grants all rights to the object's properties.
Compare (C)	Enables a test for a value match and returns a true or false. Compare is a subset of read. If you have read/writes you automatically have Compare rights at the property level.
Read (R)	Returns a value (contents) of a property. Read contains the Compare right.
Write (W)	Enables you to modify, add, change, and delete a property value.
Add/Remove Self (A)	Enables you to add or remove yourself as a value of a property. It is a subset of the write right. If you have write rights to a property you automatically have the Add/Remove Self right.

An example of how property rights are displayed in NWADMIN is shown in Figure 13.5 below.

FIGURE 13.5

*Property rights in the
NWADMIN utility*

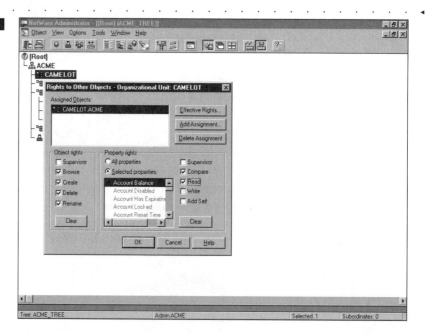

The Access Control List

The Access Control List (ACL) is a special property of every object. It can actually be considered the most important mechanism for determining NDS access. The Access Control List contains trustee assignments for an object and its properties. A user object, for example, with the write right to the ACL of another user object has what is known as managed rights over that user object. This means that an object with the write right of any object's ACL can make any rights assignments to that object.

Each object can have an ACL. The ACL is a property value and contains three entries: the trustee ID, the type of access (object or property), and the actual rights assignment. This concept is shown in Figure 13.6.

Every object may have an Access Control List as one of its properties.

ACCESS CONTROL LIST (ACL)

TRANSFER OBJECT ID	TYPE OF ACCESS (OBJECT OR PROPERTY)	RIGHTS ASSIGNMENT
07721429	OBJECT	[S]
07618424	OBJECT	[CR]
01099600	PROPERTY	{S }

NOTE

The ACL is extremely powerful, and its access should be closely controlled for every object on your network. Because the ACL is a property of an object, it can be modified by anyone who has write rights to the ACL property for the object. This means that someone with the write rights to the ACL can give rights assignments for that object.

By default, users do not receive write rights to their own ACL. In the NDS schema, some of the object classes specify a default ACL template. The default ACL template grants basic access control to newly created objects. If the object (for example, the organizational unit object) contains a default ACL template when created, it would have information in its ACL as shown in Table 13.5 below.

T A B L E 13.5	OBJECT NAME	DEFAULT RIGHTS	AFFECTED ATTRIBUTES (PROPERTIES)
Container object default ACL	[ROOT]	Read	Login script and print job configuration

When a container object is created, the [ROOT] object automatically obtains the Read property right to the container's login script and print job configuration. The user class is another example of an object that receives a default ACL during initial creation. Its default ACL would appear as shown in Table 13.6 below.

T A B L E 13.6	OBJECT NAME	DEFAULT RIGHTS	AFFECTED ATTRIBUTES (PROPERTIES)
User object default ACL	[PUBLIC]	Read	Message server
	[ROOT]	Browse	[Object rights]
	[ROOT]	Read	Group membership
	[ROOT]	Read	Network address
	[self]	Read	All attributes
	[self]	Read/Write	Login script
	[self]	Read/Write	Print job configuration

Therefore, as was mentioned earlier, access control is limited, and your default security is a closed-door approach. As a NetWare administrator, you must open up security doors (granting additional rights) only when necessary. Otherwise, the majority of your users receive by default sufficient access rights when they are created.

NOTE

As we have stated earlier, an object may or may not have an ACL. If an object already has the effective right, the ACL is not created. For example, all objects have the default ACL that specifies that the ADMIN (or appropriate object) has object Supervisor rights to the user object. If the ADMIN already has the Supervisor object right (and it does if it creates a user object), the default ACL is not created when the NDS user object is created.

Learning the Rules of NDS Security

The first step in understanding NDS security is to understand the rules that govern it. This section will outline the concepts and rules for each area of security. With the groundwork in place we will then focus on some specific examples and explain how security is implemented for each.

NDS security uses the same terminology as file system security. In fact, your familiarity with NetWare 3 file system security will provide you with a great foundation for understanding IntranetWare security. The following concepts will be discussed and are shown in Figure 13.7:

▸ Trustee Assignments

▸ Security Equivalence

▸ Inheritance

▸ Inherited Rights Filter

▸ Effective Rights

The NDS security pyramid serves as a visual basis for understanding the order and concepts of NDS security.

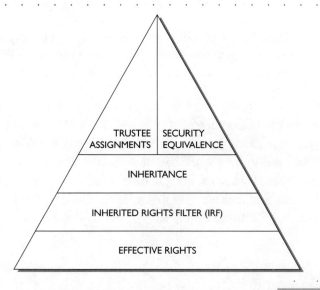

TRUSTEE ASSIGNMENTS

A trustee assignment indicates the rights granted to an object for a specific file, directory, object, or property. An object that has been granted rights to manage another object is said to be a trustee of that object. A trustee assignment is a direct, explicit assignment of rights to a particular object. Sometimes you will hear the term explicit trustee assignment, which means the same thing. A trustee assignment is listed first in our pyramid diagram because it is the first point at which rights assignments are made. It is the basis for all subsequent security assignments, such as security equivalence and inheritance. Security always begins with a trustee assignment. For example, the use of a group object requires you to grant the group a trustee assignment that the members of the group receive through security equivalence.

The installation of IntranetWare, as another example, causes some default trustee assignments (templates) to be made for user and server objects. As an administrator you will most likely make additional trustee assignments for groups, containers, and other administrators as explained in the following section.

Default Trustee Assignments for Users

During the installation of your first IntranetWare server the ADMIN user object (if you've named it that) receives an explicit assignment of object Supervisor at object [ROOT] as shown in Figure 13.8 This assignment is the first trustee assignment made by the IntranetWare installation software and initially is the only object in the tree with object Supervisor rights at [ROOT].

NOTE **The ADMIN object is just a user object like any other object, but it has been granted object Supervisor rights at [ROOT]. It can be renamed, deleted, and moved like any other user object. Be careful.**

Also, during installation of IntranetWare, [PUBLIC] receives an object trustee assignment of object Browse at object [ROOT]. With this right all users can browse the tree after attaching to a server before logging in. This enables users to use the CX command to browse the tree and discover object names once they have loaded the NetWare client software and have attached to an IntranetWare server. Figure 13.8 shows a graphic representation of the PUBLIC rights received at the time of installation of IntranetWare.

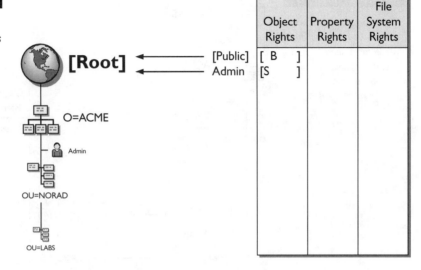

This diagram shows the default trustee assignments made at the installation of IntranetWare.

	Object Rights	Property Rights	File System Rights
[Public]	[B]		
Admin	[S]		

IntranetWare Server Default Trustee Assignments

The IntranetWare installation utility also makes trustee assignments at the file system level. The ADMIN object has object Supervisor rights to the tree. The server object is in the tree and therefore has rights to your servers. Because the ADMIN object has object Supervisor rights to the server object, the ADMIN object also receives Supervisor rights to the NetWare file system of that server. This is the only instance in IntranetWare security where object rights have an impact on file system rights. In fact, any object with write rights on a server's ACL has Supervisor rights on the file system of that server.

[PUBLIC] receives the Read property right to the server object's Messaging Server property right so that if the server is being used for the default login server, its property can be located. This assignment is in the template for the server object.

The container object that the new server is installed into receives Read and File Scan rights to the server's \PUBLIC directory. This default access enables all users in the container to execute any files stored on the server's \PUBLIC directory.

The container also receives Create rights to the server's \MAIL directory.

Figure 13.9 shows how these trustee assignments are made when a server object is first created.

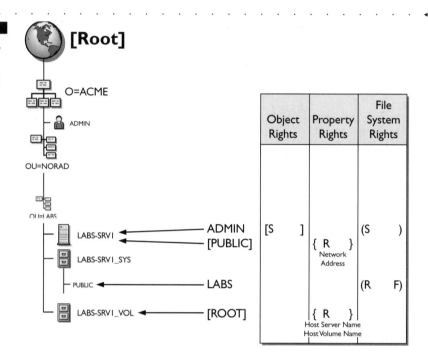

FIGURE 13.9

This example shows how
trustee assignments are
made for a server object
during installation of
IntranetWare.

[Root]

O=ACME

ADMIN

OU=NORAD

OU=LABS

LABS-SRV1   ← ADMIN
                 ← [PUBLIC]

LABS-SRV1_SYS

PUBLIC   ← LABS

LABS-SRV1_VOL ← [ROOT]

	Object Rights	Property Rights	File System Rights
	[S]	{ R } Network Address	(S)
			(R F)
		{ R } Host Server Name Host Volume Name	

Default Trustee Assignments for Users

When user objects are created they also receive some default trustee assignments (refer back to the section on ACLs and default ACLs). These assignments greatly reduce the amount of work required by a NetWare administrator to set up user accounts and provide for their access. The following access is automatically granted during creation of a user object.

For our purposes let's assume that a new user object has been created in the TOKYO container. The newly created user object receives the Read and Compare rights to All Properties by default. The All Properties is a category that is visible with either NWADMIN or NETADMIN by selecting Rights to Other Objects as shown in Figure 13.10. Having the Read right to All Properties allows the user to read the values of his or her own user properties. The Compare right is a subset of Read and enables the value of the property to be compared with another value.

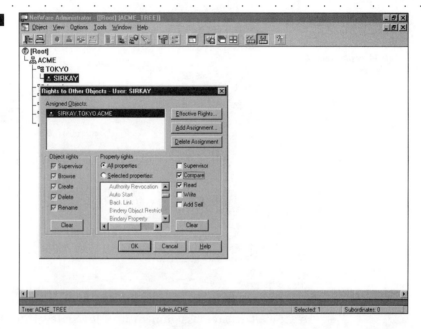

*The user object
SIRKAY.TOKYO.ACME
receives by default the
Read and Compare
rights to All Properties
for its own object.*

The user object is granted read and write rights to its own login script and print job configuration. These rights permit the users to change their own login script and print job configuration if they want. Figure 13.11 shows these rights assigned along with the others when a user object is created.

Understanding the Rules of Trustee Assignments

As was mentioned earlier, there are rules that govern the functionality of trustee assignments. Learning these rules can make it much easier for you to understand and use NetWare security.

> ▶ **Trustee assignments flow down the tree** — A trustee assignment for objects and All Property rights flows down the tree unless it is blocked by an Inherited Rights Filter (IRF). The IRF is explained later in this chapter. For example, if user SIRKAY were granted Supervisor rights to the TOKYO container, these rights would flow down to any subsequent containers and objects below TOKYO unless an object has an inherited rights filter.

FIGURE 13.11

Rights assignments are made when a user object is created.

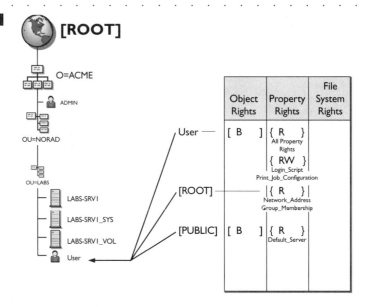

▸ **An explicit trustee assignment at a lower level in the tree replaces all previous trustee assignments** — As shown in Figure 13.12, user SIRKAY has been granted explicit Create and Rename rights beginning at object TOKYO. This trustee assignment flows down until it is blocked by an IRF or reassigned by another explicit assignment. In this example, we reassign the object the BROWSE right at the OU=CRIME. This explicit assignment will replace all other higher assignments at the OU=CRIME level in the tree.

▸ **Selected property rights override any assignment made in the All Properties category** — At the time of user creation, a user object receives the Read property right to all of its own properties. Any selective assignment of a property right using the Selected Properties category will override anything assigned through the All Properties category. For example, by default all users have the Read property right to all of their own user object properties. Notice also that a user also receives by default the read and write rights to his login script and print job configuration. The fact that the read write is given again in the selected properties assignment indicates that it has overridden the previous assignment made in the All Properties category.

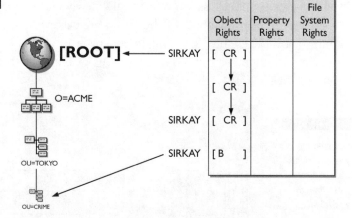

F I G U R E   13.12

An explicit rights assignment made at a lower level in the tree will replace any previous explicit assignment made to that object.

	Object Rights	Property Rights	File System Rights
SIRKAY	[CR]		
	[CR]		
SIRKAY	[CR]		
SIRKAY	[B]		

[ROOT]

O=ACME

OU=TOKYO

OU=CRIME

▸ **The Access Control List (ACL) property of every object stores trustee assignments to that object** — Each object can contain a property known as the ACL. A user by default does not have write rights to its own ACL or to that of any other object. Keep in mind that some objects may not have ACLs if they already have received the explicit right.

WARNING

Do not grant users the write rights to any ACL, including their own user object, because the write right to the ACL controls all access to that particular object.

For example, a user possessing the write right to a container ACL has the ability to make any changes to that object's ACL. The user could assign anyone Supervisor object rights to that container and could modify the object as well.

UNDERSTANDING SECURITY EQUIVALENCE

Security equivalence simply means that an object can be equivalent in rights to another object. The majority of rights assignments should be made by administrators through the use of security equivalence. It is quick and easy to use security equivalence because you can deal with a large number of users rather than a single user at a time. Time is always a factor for network administrators, and we recommend that you assign security equivalence to groups or containers as the best way to make rights assignments to large numbers of people.

To meet the needs of many users requiring the same rights to a directory or file, you can create a group, assign rights to the newly created group, and add members to the group. The members of the group are security equivalent in rights to the group object. Therefore, any assignment made to a group will be received by its members through security equivalence. An example of this process is shown in Figure 13.13.

FIGURE 13.13

An example of creating a group and granting rights to the group. The users receive rights through security equivalence.

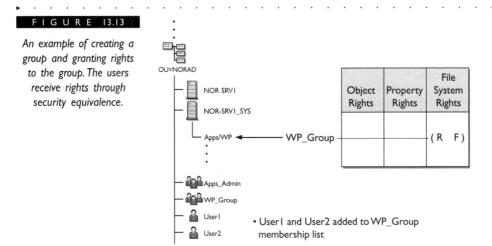

	Object Rights	Property Rights	File System Rights
Apps/WP ← WP_Group			(R F)

- User1 and User2 added to WP_Group membership list

In addition, a container functions much the same way as a group except that the group is used in your login scripts and a group can span multiple containers. If all users in a container access the same resources, it may not be necessary to use groups. However, if you want to further differentiate your environment setting within a container, the group object is an effective way to go.

Rules Governing Security Equivalence

Because the use of security equivalence will be so common on your network, it is very important to understand how IntranetWare security functions. You will save time as a network administrator if you understand the rules that govern security equivalence.

▸ **Security equivalent rights cannot be masked** — If you receive a security equivalence, this assignment cannot be masked by an IRF.

▶ Every object is security equivalent to all container objects that are part of its distinguished name. This security is known as implied security equivalence. For example, the user GUINEVERE.FIN.OPS.CAMELOT in the ACME tree is security equivalent to every object in its name. Therefore, if you were to grant the container FIN rights to a particular e-mail server, user GUINEVERE would receive those rights through security equivalence.

NOTE

You cannot single out users to not receive rights granted to a container by using an IRF. If you grant rights to a container, *all* users in or subordinate to that container will always receive those rights.

▶ Every object is security equivalent to [ROOT] — Once a user has successfully logged in to a server, that user is security equivalent to [ROOT].

▶ Every object is security equivalent to [PUBLIC] — [PUBLIC] with the default rights of Browse enables users to browse the tree before logging in to a server. Each user is security equivalent to [PUBLIC], and [PUBLIC] has been granted Browse rights at object [ROOT]. This assignment can be changed if you like.

▶ An object is security equivalent to all objects listed in its Security Equals property — An NDS object will keep a list (known as the Security Equals Property) of all objects that it equals in rights.

CONSULTING EXPERIENCE

Be very careful with assigning rights to the [PUBLIC] trustee because of the security equivalence with all users since they do not need to be authenticated to receive those rights. The assignment of file system rights is nonfunctional when using the [PUBLIC] trustee. This means that you cannot grant access to files before the user has successfully logged in to the server. Generally, the use of the [PUBLIC] trustee for granting rights should be avoided.

Keep in mind that when a user logs in to an IntranetWare server and authenticates to the Directory, Directory Services creates what is known as a security equivalence vector that is stored in the connection table on the server. The security equivalence vector contains a list of that object's security equivalencies and is created on every server that the client authenticates to.

INHERITANCE

Inheritance is the method by which rights to objects and files flow down to subordinate levels of the tree. As previously stated, explicit trustee assignments at a higher level in your tree will flow down. The rights you receive at lower levels without assignment are known as inherited rights. Inherited rights include only the object rights and the All Properties rights. Selected property rights are not inherited.

NOTE **Sometimes there is the tendency to confuse security equivalence and inheritance. Keep in mind that inheritance is simply the way that previously granted rights flow down the tree to subordinate levels.**

Earlier in our discussion we mentioned that explicit rights, such as the ADMIN user object possessing the Supervisor right at the [ROOT] object, flow down the tree. As shown in Figure 13.14, the Supervisor assignment continues to flow down the tree unless it is otherwise blocked or reassigned. Therefore, at each subsequent level in the tree the ADMIN object's rights are being received through inheritance.

Inherited rights also flow down independently of other rights assignments, such as those obtained through security equivalence. This means that the rights received through inheritance are not affected by actions you may take on other explicit rights assignments. The two operate under separate rules. Do not mix up your security rules. Figure 13.15 shows how explicit rights assignments flow down independently of security equivalence rights.

Understanding Inherited Rights Filters (IRFs)

The filter known as the Inherited Rights Filter (IRF) is used to block inheritance. The IRF can be applied to object rights, the All Properties category, and the Selected Properties category.

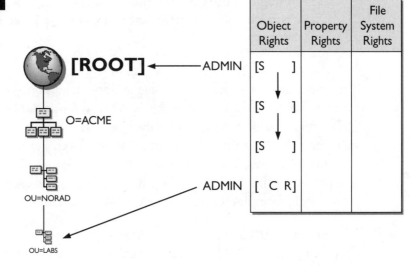

Inheritance of the Supervisor right at the second and third levels of the tree

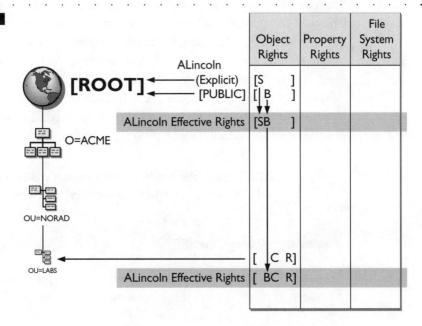

The explicit assignment of the Supervisor right flows down the tree independently of the Browse right, which was received because user ALincoln is security equivalent to the [PUBLIC] trustee.

NOTE

As mentioned earlier, you cannot place an IRF on rights received through security equivalence. You can apply the IRF only to object rights, the All Properties category, and the Selected Properties category.

The IRF enables the NetWare administrator to specify which rights can be inherited from an object. It is easier to understand the concept of the IRF if you compare it to a shell around an object. When you place an IRF on an object you are placing an imaginary shell around the object. The rights that are enabled in the IRF are the only rights that users will have to an object. For example, you could place an IRF of Browse on a server object in a container. One user must maintain Supervisor rights over the object, however. All other users can inherit only the Browse right because of the IRF that is placed around the server object.

Inherited ACLs

Each partition [ROOT] object contains a property known as the inherited Access Control List. For more information on the partition [ROOT] object, refer to Chapter 6. The inherited ACL property contains the summation of ACLs from parent containers. Unless an IRF is in effect all objects in the partition will receive the rights contained in the inherited ACL. NDS can then calculate rights for objects in its partition without having to walk the Directory tree. As changes to ACLs are made to the Directory tree, NDS will update the multivalued inherited ACL property.

The NDS janitor process has the responsibility to maintain the inherited ACLs by recalculating inheritance if any changes are made to the inherited ACLs. For more information on the janitor process, refer to Chapters 8 and 9.

NOTE

The ACL is both the trustee assignments made and the filters applied. The same attribute (property) name is used for both.

Rules that Govern the IRF

▸ The IRF cannot grant rights; it only revokes previously assigned rights. Keep in mind that the IRF is an imaginary shell wrapped around an object.

▶ **You can enable an IRF for every Object, Property, File, and Directory.**
In most cases you will not need to use that many IRFs because the user's
default rights are limited to begin with. As shown in the scenarios at the
end of the chapter, most IRFs are used to protect servers and to separate
file system and NDS administration.

▶ **The Supervisor Object/Property rights can be revoked by an IRF.**
An IRF can be applied to all objects, including the server object. Therefore,
you can limit a person's Supervisor access to an IntranetWare file server by
applying an IRF to the server object. Remember that a user possessing the
managed right (write right to the ACL) to a server object also has rights to
the file system volumes for that server as well.

▶ **The Supervisor File/Directory rights cannot be revoked by an IRF.**
This feature is identical to NetWare 3 Supervisor rights in that any user that
has Supervisor rights to a file system directly cannot have file system rights
masked on that file server.

UNDERSTANDING EFFECTIVE RIGHTS

The last step in the security pyramid is the calculation of effective rights. Effective
rights are what an object can actually do after all other security factors are calculated
against the object. The following sources are used in the calculation of effective
rights of one object to another:

▶ The object's ACL

▶ The object's explicit assignments

▶ All security equivalent access privileges

For example, we will discuss an object A with access to object B using security
equivalence calculated at the time of authentication. The rights would be calculated
as follows:

1 • The sum of explicit assignments would be calculated back to partition root. Object B would be calculated back to object B's partition root. Of course, an IRF would negate some assignments.

2 • Add in the inherited ACLs from partition root.

3 • Object A receives all explicit and inherited ACLs to which A is security equivalent.

UNDERSTANDING MANAGED RIGHTS

Managed rights (or management rights) is a term used to describe an object (ADMIN, for example) that has the write right to an object's ACL. Managed rights means that the trustee has all power over an object and can modify anything pertaining to that object. For some operations in NDS you must have managed rights to perform that operation. Below is a list of NDS operations and the managed rights that are required to perform them:

▸ All partition operations including Create, Merge, Add replica, and Move Subtree require the trustee to have write rights to the target partition server object. The Merge operation requires managed rights to the [ROOT] objects of both trees.

▸ A schema modification requires the trustee to have write rights to the ACL of the Directory's [ROOT] object.

▸ Any modifications to the following properties require write rights to that object's ACL:

  ▸ Security Equals

  ▸ Group Membership

  ▸ Profile Membership

▸ Backup requires managed rights on the object(s) being backed up.

▸ The Add/Remove replica operation requires the following:

  ▸ Managed rights on the partition root

  ▸ Managed rights on the target server

Implementing NDS Security

With an understanding of the basic concepts of security, we can now begin a discussion of how to use and implement NDS security for your network. Figure 13.16 is the basis for our security discussion. As stated earlier, the pyramid shown in this figure shows a very logical approach for understanding IntranetWare security. Each section of the pyramid will now be explained with examples on how you can implement security in your environment for the greatest benefit.

For our examples we will refer to the ACME tree to implement security procedures throughout the entire organization. The following scenarios will be discussed in terms of NetWare security. All scenarios make the assumption that you are an administrator with object Supervisor rights at the [ROOT] of your tree are assigned.

FIGURE 13.16

The NDS security pyramid shows graphically the order in which rights

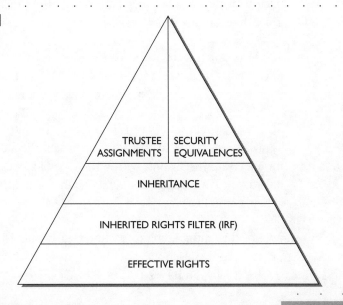

SECURITY REQUIRED TO INSTALL AN INTRANETWARE SERVER UNDER THE OU=NORAD CENTER

Security Concepts to Understand

▸ Trustee Assignments

▸ Security Equivalence

As a temporary administrator you are asked to install an IntranetWare server in the NORAD container into the ACME tree. There are currently no administrators in your location, and this server must be brought up immediately.

1 • Contact your main administrator to obtain Create rights for the NORAD container. Supervisor rights at your container are needed to install an IntranetWare server into your own container or to add a partition replica to partition root. This can be accomplished in several ways as described in the following steps.

2 • The first way is to simply have the administrator explicitly grant you Supervisor rights to the NORAD container. This method is difficult to track if many similar requests are made to the main NDS administrator. The administrator soon forgets who has been granted rights.

3 • The second and recommended way is to use NWADMIN or NETADMIN to create an organization role in the NORAD location and grant the role Supervisor rights to the NORAD container known as NORAD_ADMIN.

4 • The main administrator can then move you into the role temporarily as an administrator so that you can install the IntranetWare server. An IntranetWare installation with an add replica will NOT complete unless you have Supervisor rights to the container in which the server is being installed.

An example of this entire scenario is shown in Figure 13.17.
An example of an organizational role being created with NWADMIN is shown in Figures 13.18, 13.19, and 13.20.

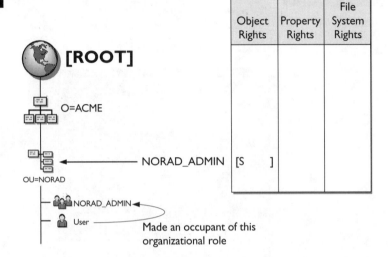

FIGURE 13.17

Rights necessary to install a server in the NORAD container

Object Rights	Property Rights	File System Rights
[S]		

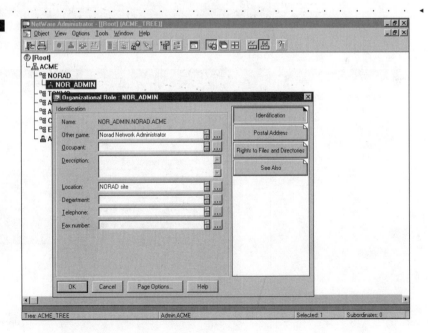

FIGURE 13.18

Creating an organizational role

FIGURE 13.19

Assigning the necessary rights

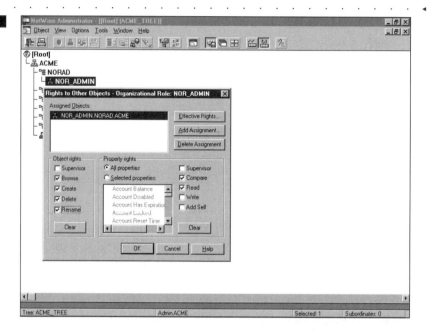

FIGURE 13.20

Moving a user into the role as an occupant

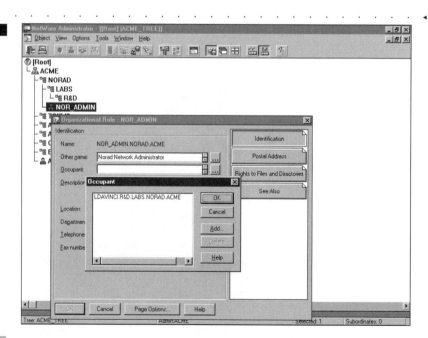

SECURITY REQUIRED TO INSTALL AN APPLICATION ON YOUR INTRANETWARE SERVER IN THE CAMELOT CONTAINER AND GRANT APPLICATION ACCESS TO YOUR USERS

Security Concepts to Understand

▶ File System Trustee Assignments

▶ Supervisor rights to a server object

You are a file system administrator in the LABS location responsible for installing all new applications on the location's file servers.

1 • You must have at a minimum the Create right to the APPS subdirectory on your IntranetWare, for example. In most cases you will use Supervisor trustee rights to perform these operations.

2 • If you have Supervisor object rights over the file server object, you will also have Supervisor rights over the file system.

3 • Install your application according to the directions.

4 • Make sure that all executable files related to this application are flagged as sharable read only. Most application installations automatically do this for you, but it doesn't hurt to check.

5 • Create any supporting objects that may be needed such as groups or directory maps. This requires Create rights at the container. You may also need file system rights as well.

6 • Consider using Novell's NetWare Application Manager to launch applications as NDS objects from a user's desktop. For more information on the NetWare Application Manager, refer to Chapter 2.

An example of this entire scenario is shown in Figure 13.21.

FIGURE 13.21

Using NWADMIN to assign rights necessary to install an application on an IntranetWare server in the LABS container

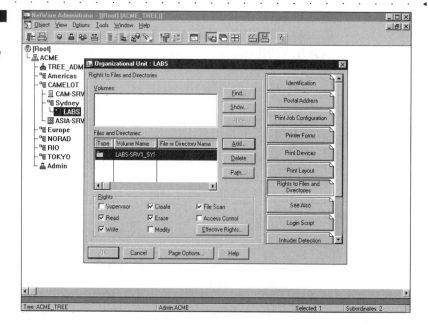

SECURITY PROCEDURES FOR GRANTING AN INDIVIDUAL RIGHTS TO MANAGE A HELP DESK CENTER AT THE CAMELOT LOCATION

Security Concepts to Understand

▶ Trustee Assignments

▶ Security Equivalence

Your responsibility is to assist in managing a help desk at the CAMELOT location.

1 • Using NWADMIN or NETADMIN, create a series of specialized organizational roles for your help desk administration such as user administrators, server administrators, and tree administrators. Although currently Directory Services does not enforce rights to a specific object class, you can create organizational roles that designate these type of administrators.

2 • Assign Create, Delete, and Rename rights to the user administrator's role.

3 • Assign Supervisor file system rights to the server administrator's role for each server in the container to be managed.

4 • Create an organizational role at the top of your tree with explicit Supervisor rights at [ROOT]. Move the top help desk administrators into the organizational role as occupants.

5 • Make IRF assignments where appropriate to limit administrator access to certain areas of your system.

Examples of this entire scenario are shown in Figures 13.22, 13.23, and 13.24.

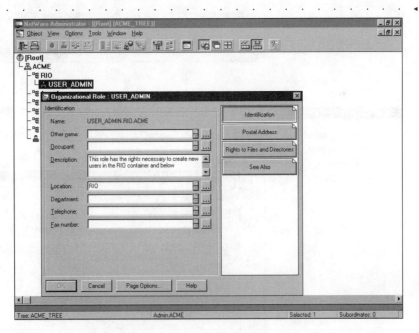

FIGURE 13.23

Creating an organizational role for the server administrator

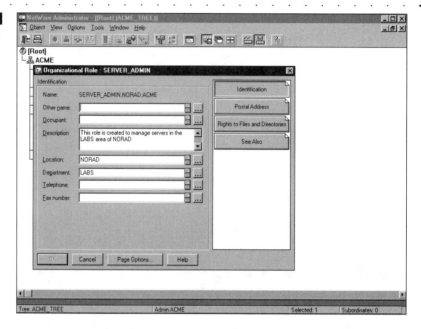

FIGURE 13.24

Creating an organizational role for the tree administrators

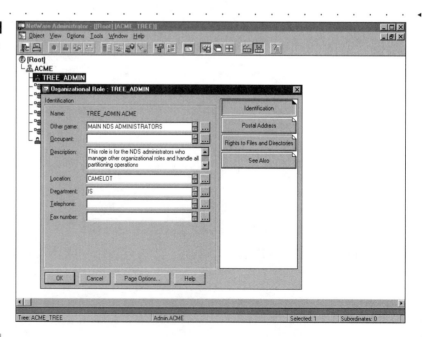

CREATION OF SUBADMINISTRATORS FOR EACH MAJOR LOCATION IN THE ACME TREE

Security Concepts to Understand

▸ Trustee Assignments

▸ Security Equivalence

▸ Inheritance

You have been given the assignment to create subadministrators for each major location in the ACME network and assign individuals to manage the network from that level down. You currently manage the network with only the ADMIN user object.

1 • Using NWADMIN or NETADMIN, create an organizational role object in the containers NORAD, RIO, TOKYO, CAMELOT, SYDNEY, and TOKYO.

2 • Using NWADMIN or NETADMIN, grant the newly created organizational role objects Supervisor rights to their respective containers.

3 • Choose an administrator or administrators to participate in the organizational role and add them as role occupants using NWADMIN or NETADMIN.

4 • Assign the ADMIN user explicit Supervisor rights to each of the organizational role objects.

5 • Using NWADMIN or NETADMIN, place an Inherited Rights Filter of Browse (and possibly Read) on each of the organizational roles to prohibit management of the role by the occupants.

6 • These new administrators will have the power to create additional objects, including subordinate containers, in their respective locations. The administrators have Supervisor rights at these lower levels in the tree through inheritance.

An example of this entire scenario is shown in Figure 13.25.

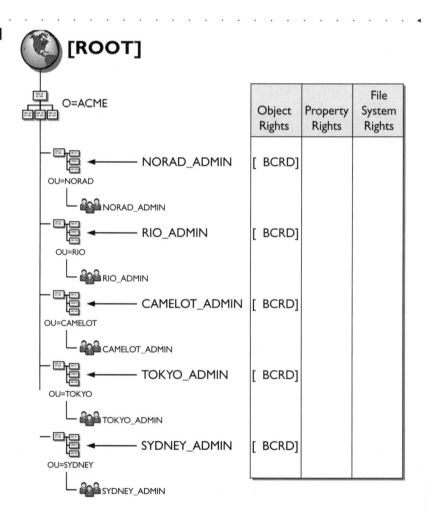

	Object Rights	Property Rights	File System Rights
NORAD_ADMIN	[BCRD]		
RIO_ADMIN	[BCRD]		
CAMELOT_ADMIN	[BCRD]		
TOKYO_ADMIN	[BCRD]		
SYDNEY_ADMIN	[BCRD]		

CREATING A FILE SYSTEM ADMINISTRATOR AND AN NDS ADMINISTRATOR IN THE OU=TOKYO LOCATION

Security Concepts to Understand

▸ Trustee Assignments

▸ Security Equivalence

▸ Inherited Rights Filter

Administration in the TOKYO container is being broken out into two responsibilities. One individual will handle only the file system administration, while the other administrator will handle NDS administration. Each must have separate rights.

1 • Using NWADMIN or NETADMIN, create two organizational roles. Name the first role NDS_ADMIN and the second role FILE_ADMIN.

2 • Using NWADMIN or NETADMIN, assign the NDS_ADMIN role Supervisor Rights to the TOKYO container.

3 • Using NWADMIN or NETADMIN, assign the FILE_ADMIN role Supervisor rights to the server objects TOK-SRV1 and TOK-SRV2.

4 • Using NWADMIN or NETADMIN, place an Inherited Rights Filter of Browse (and possibly Read) on the server objects TOK-SRV1 and TOK-SRV2.

An example of this entire scenario is shown in Figure 13.26.

*Separating NDS and file
system administration*

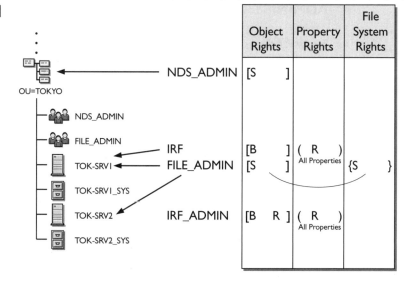

RIGHTS NECESSARY TO PERFORM PARTITIONING OPERATIONS AT DIFFERENT LEVELS IN THE NDS TREE

You have been made responsible for partitioning operations on the ACME network. You want to prohibit all partitioning operations except those performed by you and another administrator.

1 • Using NWADMIN or NETADMIN, grant the other administrators in their organizational roles all rights to their respective containers except the Supervisor object right. Grant Read and Create rights on the container ACL also. (Keep in mind that other administrators will not be able to install IntranetWare servers into the tree without the Supervisor right to the container if they are adding a replica. You can grant them the right temporarily to handle this situation or add the replica for them.)

2 • Create an organizational role for yourself and other tree administrators for partitioning operations called OR_PARTITIONS.

3 • If you have not already done so, grant the organizational role explicit object Supervisor rights to each container immediately subordinate to [ROOT].

An example of this entire scenario is shown in Figure 13.27.

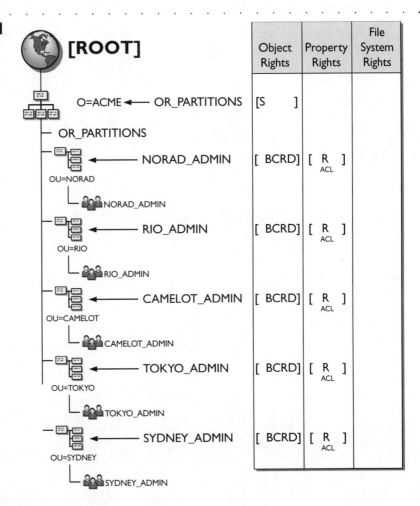

	Object Rights	Property Rights	File System Rights
O=ACME ◄— OR_PARTITIONS	[S]		
OR_PARTITIONS			
NORAD_ADMIN	[BCRD]	[R] ACL	
RIO_ADMIN	[BCRD]	[R] ACL	
CAMELOT_ADMIN	[BCRD]	[R] ACL	
TOKYO_ADMIN	[BCRD]	[R] ACL	
SYDNEY_ADMIN	[BCRD]	[R] ACL	

IntranetWare Print Services

"Learning hath gained most by those books by which the printers have lost."
Thomas Fuller

IntranetWare enables a printer to be shared by any or all network users. In order to print, an entire print job must be created and placed in a print queue on the server and then wait until a print server can process the job and send it to the network printer.

IntraNetWare Print Services uses the same basic concepts and architecture available in earlier versions of NetWare. In this chapter we will discuss these concepts and demonstrate how to design and implement IntranetWare Print Services in either a pure IntranetWare environment or mixed NetWare 3 and IntranetWare networks.

Differences Between NetWare 3 and IntranetWare

One of the major differences between the print services in NetWare 3 and IntranetWare is where the print objects are stored. In NetWare 3, the print objects are stored in the bindery, which is a server centric database. On the other hand, the print objects in IntranetWare are placed in Novell Directory Services, which can be replicated to multiple servers on the network. Table 14.1 outlines some of the major differences between NetWare 3 and IntranetWare.

TABLE 14.1	NETWARE 3	INTRANETWARE
Differences between NetWare 3 and IntranetWare	The print queue and print server are stored as objects in the bindery. The printers are attributes of the print server.	The print server, print queue, and printer objects are stored as NDS objects in the tree.
	The print server can support only 16 printers.	The print server can support up to 256 printers attached to one print server. This increase will help you reduce the number of print servers you have in your network and will also help you consolidate the print infrastructure.
	The print server's configuration information is stored in SYS:SYSTEM files.	The print server's configuration information is stored as an attribute of the NDS printer server object.

TABLE 14.1	NETWARE 3	INTRANETWARE
Differences between NetWare 3 and IntranetWare (continued)	Print queues and print servers must be manually set up using the PCONSOLE utility.	You are responsible for setting up the printing relationship. IntranetWare has the Quick Setup feature in the PCONSOLE utility. This feature is the quickest and simplest procedure for setting up any number of printers. The Quick Setup creates a print server, print queue, and printer, and it performs all of the necessary assignments automatically. The print server is created only if it does not already exist.
	Print layout page is not available.	The print layout page in NWADMIN provides a visual snapshot of the print layout relationship for a particular container object or print server. The print layout page for a print server graphically shows all printers attached to the print server, the queues serviced by those printers, and the print jobs in the queues.
	The PRINTCON information is stored as files in users' SYS:MAIL directories. Files are stored directly in users' SYS:MAIL\ID# directory.	The PRINTCON information is stored as attributes of the user object or the container object in NDS.
	Print job configurations are limited to 32.	IntranetWare supports an almost unlimited unlimited number of print job configurations.
	The PRINTDEF information is stored in SYS:PUBLIC files.	PRINTDEF information is stored as an attribute of the container object in NDS.
	Users are required to send all of their print jobs to a print queue.	Users can still send their print jobs to print queues or send their print jobs directly to a printer that is functioning as a queue server by simply specifying the printer name.
	There is no auto-reconnect capability.	IntranetWare has an auto-reconnect feature that reconnects the printers to print print servers after a connection has been lost.
	Dedicated PSERVER.EXE is supported.	PSERVER.EXE is no longer supported.

The NDS Print Objects

The print objects are the building blocks for the IntranetWare Print Services architecture. These print objects define the network's printing infrastructure. In IntranetWare, these objects are stored in NDS as three separate objects:

- Print Queue

- Print Server

- Printer

The IntranetWare Print Services infrastructure is created by the association or relationship you set up between these three objects. The print queue should be assigned to represent a specific network printer or group of printers. The printer, in turn, is assigned to a print server, and the print server is assigned to service specific print queues. With these structures, a user creates a print job that is stored in a print queue until a print server can service the print job and send it directly to a printer. The print server waits until the printer is ready to accept the print job before sending it. This relationship is shown in Figure 14.1.

FIGURE 14.1

Relationship between the print objects in the IntranetWare Print Services infrastructure

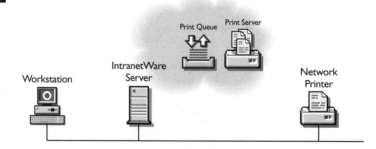

Users using IntranetWare Print Services redirect their print jobs to network printers or to printers attached to the network workstations. The user's data (or print job) is not sent directly from the workstation to the printer. Instead, the data is captured and redirected to a file in a print queue where it is stored waiting to be sent to the printer. The data is first sent to a print queue to avoid multiple print jobs contending for the same shared printer. Multiple print jobs from different network users may stack up in the print queue until the printer server is able to send them to the printer. The print server will service the print jobs in the order they are received unless otherwise stipulated by the network administrator or printer server operator.

PRINT QUEUE

The print queue is a key object or component in NetWare printing. When a network user sends a print job to a network printer, NetWare temporarily stores the print job as a file in a directory on the server called a print queue. The print jobs wait in the print queue until the print server is able to process them and then send them to the waiting printer. The print queue objects represent the directories where the print jobs are sent to be serviced.

CONSULTING EXPERIENCE

Placement of the print queues and printers in the NDS tree should be with the users who will use their print services. For example, place the print queues and printers in the same OUs as their users. If you have users in different OUs in the tree who want to use these print objects, you can either alias the print objects or place them at upper levels in the tree to support the greatest number of users.

The print queues store print jobs in subdirectories on server volumes that you specify when you create them. In NetWare 3, the print queue subdirectory was located in SYS:SYSTEM by default and could not be moved. In IntranetWare, the print queue subdirectory can be created on any server volume. The print queue will then be found in a default root subdirectory called QUEUES of that selected server volume. This subdirectory name can also be changed if you like.

> **CONSULTING EXPERIENCE**
>
> It is a good idea to take advantage of this new IntranetWare feature that enables you to create the print queues on server volumes other than SYS:SYSTEM. We recommend that you leave extra space on the SYS volume because NDS files are stored on the SYS:SYSTEM in a hidden directory. NDS will stop accepting changes if the SYS volume fills up.

You can create print queues using either PCONSOLE or NWADMIN utilities. When you define a print queue using these utilities, you give it a descriptive name. This name should follow your naming convention and identify the kind of printer the print queue is associated with, where the printer is located, or the type of print jobs that can be sent. For example, the print queue associated with a Hewlett-Packard Laser Jet 4si could be called HP4SI-PQ1.

> **CONSULTING EXPERIENCE**
>
> Although you can set up a print queue associated with multiple printers, we recommend that for simplicity and manageability you set up only one print queue for each printer on your network.

The print queue name is used by the users and should be as clear and convenient as possible. Internally, NetWare assigns a print queue a server centric ID number, which is an eight-digit hexadecimal number. For example, the print queue named HP4SI-PQ1 might have an ID with the value of 8034D4CF. You can view this ID number in the utilities. This number is important because it is used as the corresponding subdirectory name under the QUEUES directory.

The use of print queues provides an orderly method for multiple users to send print jobs to a single printer device. Queuing print jobs at the NetWare server ensures that the printer deals with only one print job at a time.

The print jobs are stored as files in the print queue subdirectory. Their file names always start with a "Q$" and include the last four digits of the print queue ID, plus a three-digit job number as the file extension. For example, the seventh print job in the print queue with the ID of 8034D4CF would have a file name of Q$D4CF.007.

When a user creates a print job and forwards it to the print queue, the print job passes through several states before being printed. These states are outlined in Table 14.2.

TABLE 14.2	STATE	DESCRIPTION
Different states that a print job passes through while in the print queue	Adding	The print job is being added to the print queue by the workstation.
	Ready	The print job is waiting to be serviced by the associated print server.
	Active	The print job is being sent to the appropriate printer.
	Removed	The print job is finished and is removed from the print queue.

PRINT SERVERS

Another key software component of NetWare printing is the print server, which binds the print queues to the network printers. A print server takes print jobs from the print queue and sends them to the assigned network printer. The printer server software program can be either loaded as a NetWare Loadable Module on a NetWare server or run as firmware in a network attached printer.

In IntranetWare the PSERVER.NLM supports up to 256 printers, which can help you consolidate or reduce the total number of print servers you have in the network. In order to start the print server on the server, type the following at the server console prompt:

```
LOAD PSERVER PrintServerName
```

Substitute the name of the specific print server for PrintServerName. You can place this command in the AUTOEXEC.NCF file if you want the print server to load automatically during the server bootup. Figure 14.2 displays the main screen for the print server software.

FIGURE 14.2

Main screen for the print server software running on the NetWare server

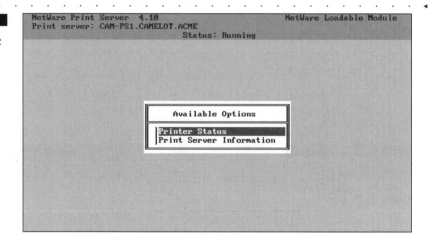

```
NetWare Print Server  4.10                        NetWare Loadable Module
Print server: CAM-PS1.CAMELOT.ACME
                              Status: Running




                        ┌──────────────────────────────┐
                        │      Available Options         │
                        ├──────────────────────────────┤
                        │ Printer Status                 │
                        │ Print Server Information       │
                        └──────────────────────────────┘
```

The print server software running at the network attached printer is often referred to as a queue server because the printer is set up to service the print queue directly. The queue server software logs in to the server where the print queue is stored and polls the print queue to see if it has any print jobs ready for the printer. In this configuration the printer device performs both functions of the print server and printer.

CONSULTING EXPERIENCE

For ease of administration and use, we recommend that you configure the network printers as queue servers. This configuration requires that you connect the printers directly to the network cable system.

PRINTERS

If you use the NLM-based print server, you will need to use the new NetWare NPRINTER printer program that enables the print server to send jobs to a network printer. This printer can either be physically attached to the back of the IntranetWare server, a DOS or OS/2 workstation, or directly to the network itself. Each printer requires the NPRINTER program in order to attach to the printer server and service print jobs.

There are several different versions of the NPRINTER printer program that can be loaded in several different situations. For instance, NPRINTER can be loaded as a terminate-and-stay resident (TSR) program, as a NetWare Loadable Module, or in the memory of the printer device itself. NPRINTER can be loaded in the following three ways according to the printer configuration:

▸ Workstations with printer devices connected should run NPRINTER.EXE as a TSR to support the network printer. The printer is cabled to the parallel or serial port of the workstation.

▸ Printer devices that are connected to an IntranetWare server use the NPRINTER.NLM. The printer is cabled to the parallel or serial port of the NetWare server.

▸ Printer devices connected directly to the network run the NPRINTER program from firmware or flash-memory.

With NPRINTER loaded on a workstation, the user of that workstation can run applications and function normally. The user can even access the printer device as a local printer in stand-alone fashion, as well as a network printer. However, the users are not encouraged to use the printer as a local printer because it might conflict with the network printing activities. Naturally, the type of workstation and CPU speed will affect the printing performance. For most large network sites this type of configuration is not used.

IntranetWare enables users to specify the printer object instead of a print queue when sending their print jobs. Users no longer have to know anything about print queues; they can simply send their print jobs to a printer by specifying the printer name. The network takes care of all print queue and print server activities. Sending a print job to a printer instead of a print queue is more intuitive to the user.

IntranetWare Print Utilities

In order for you to create and manage the IntraNetWare Print Services, there are several utilities that you should become familiar with. These utilities help you set up, control, and monitor the network printing. You may or may not use all of the utilities depending on the applications and how you configure the printing infrastructure for your network.

The most important utilities are the NWADMIN utility in Windows and the PCONSOLE utility in DOS. These are the utilities you will use to create the printing objects and establish their relationship. If you have experience with NetWare 3, PCONSOLE will already be somewhat familiar to you. However, PCONSOLE is bimodal, which means that it supports both bindery mode and NDS mode.

The IntranetWare print utilities and their functionality are described below.

NWADMIN (NETWARE ADMINISTRATOR)

This utility is a windows-based program that enables you to manage NDS objects, including the printing objects. You can browse, create, modify, and grant rights to the printing objects. This utility offers the graphical interface for managing objects.

PCONSOLE (PRINT CONSOLE)

This DOS utility enables the user or administrator to create printing objects and establish the proper assignments between objects. This is the only utility that has the Quick Setup option. The Quick Setup creates a print server, print queue, and printer and performs all of the necessary assignments automatically. The print server is created only if it does not already exist.

You can also use this utility to set up, view, and control the print service objects. You can set up the printers, print servers, and print queues. You can also view and manage the print jobs placed in the print queues.

PSC (PRINT SERVER COMMAND)

This utility controls print servers and printers from the command line. The PSC utility can be used as an alternative to PCONSOLE.

PRINTCON (PRINT JOB CONFIGURATION)

In order to automate and customize the printing setup for the users, you can create print job configurations files to specify the printer, banner page, form feeds, time-outs, and other options. The print configurations files can be stored for individual users or the container objects (such as Organizational Units). The print job configurations are also used with PCONSOLE, CAPTURE, and NPRINT.

PRINTDEF (PRINTER DEFINITION)

This utility provides printer definitions, which include special control codes to help format the specific users' print jobs. You need the printer definitions only if the application doesn't format the print job. NetWare provides you with 58 unique print drivers for the most common industry printers. The printer definitions can be placed at the NDS container (such as Organizational Units).

This utility also enables you to monitor, modify, and create printer forms to be specified in CAPTURE, NPRINT, or PCONSOLE.

CAPTURE

This utility runs as a TSR to intercept the output to a local printer port and redirect it to the appropriate network print queue. This program is used mainly with applications and situations that are not network aware.

ENDCAP (END CAPTURE)

This utility ends the capturing or intercepting of the local printer port, enabling you to use the local port to send print jobs to a local printer.

NPRINT (NETWORK PRINT)

This utility is used from the command line to submit text files or previously formatted printer-ready files to the network print queues. This program is similar to the DOS PRINT command line utility.

PSERVER (PRINT SERVER)

This utility runs at the server to support the printers connected to the workstations and server. The print server runs as an NLM called PSERVER.NLM. The print server can support up to 256 printers.

NPRINTER.EXE (NETWARE PRINTER)

This utility runs at a DOS workstation and connects the printer to the print server. With NPRINTER.EXE, the workstation printers wait to receive the print jobs passed to it. The workstation can run any application while printing takes place in the background. This program must be used in conjunction with the PSERVER program running at the server.

NPRINTER.NLM (NETWARE PRINTER)

The NetWare printer program can be loaded at the server as NPRINTER.NLM. This utility supports printers attached directly to the server and must be used in conjunction with the PSERVER program running at the server.

PSERVER.NLM (PRINT SERVER)

This utility loads and runs on an IntranetWare server that can act as a print server. The print server supports the remote and local printers running NPRINTER.

MIGPRINT (MIGRATE PRINTING)

This utility helps you migrate the print services from NetWare 3 to IntranetWare. This utility moves printers, print queues, print job configurations, and print servers into IntranetWare

PUPGRADE.NLM (PRINT UPGRADE)

This utility is run on an IntranetWare server to migrate PRINTCON and PRINTDEF files from NetWare 3 servers.

Print Services Configurations

You should plan your printing needs in advance to determine which users need what kind of printers. For example, some users need strictly laser printers, while others may need dot matrix printers, plotters, and color printers. The type of printer has a significant effect on overall printing speeds. Where performance is a necessity, choose printers with a high page-per-minute (PPM) rating.

There are five printer configurations or relationships you need to consider when planning the printing infrastructure for your network. These five configurations are:

▸ Non-network workstation printers

▸ Network workstation printers

▸ Network server printers

▸ Network-direct printers (remote printer mode)

▸ Network-direct printers (queue server mode)

NON-NETWORK WORKSTATION PRINTERS

A non-network workstation printer is connected to a workstation but is not set up as a network printer. This means that the workstation is not running the NPRINTER program, which shares the printer among all network users. Without the network software NPRINTER, the users of this workstation are the only ones that can print to the local printer. The users simply send the print jobs from the workstation to the stand-alone printer. Figure 14.3 illustrates this configuration.

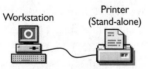

FIGURE 14.3

The printer is set up as a non-network workstation printer. This is a stand-alone printer configuration.

Workstation

Printer
(Stand-alone)

This configuration is simple for the user to set up and understand but is limited in a network environment. Since the printer is not shared by the other network users, the only person who can use the printer is the user sitting at the workstation.

You may want to consider setting up the printer in this fashion because the user requires a special purpose workstation/printer combination. For example, the user who is responsible for printing invoices or checks may have a dedicated printer with all the forms preloaded and therefore needs a separte printer that should not be used by everyone on the network.

NETWORK WORKSTATION PRINTERS (REMOTE PRINTER)

A printer that is connected to a workstation can be a network printer if the proper network software is loaded. The NetWare printer software NPRINTER.EXE needs to be loaded at the workstation while the PSERVER.NLM software needs to be running at the server to communicate with the printer. The PSERVER is configured with the setup for the printer at the workstation.

The workstation that has the printer attached always needs be powered on (but not necessarily logged in) and running the NPRINTER.EXE program. The NPRINTER.EXE program connects the workstation printer to the print server and waits to receive the print jobs passed to it. Figure 14.4 illustrates the network workstation printer or remote printer configuration.

F I G U R E   14.4

Network workstation printer, also called a remote printer

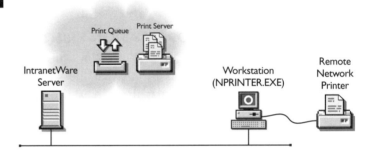

This configuration is also called a remote printer configuration because the printers are not attached physically to the server running the print server. Instead the printers are connected to the workstations in the network so that all the network users can print to them. You must start the NPRINTER.EXE for each remote printer you defined for the print server. Run NPRINTER.EXE on the workstation to which the remote printer is physically attached. If you have more than one remote printer attached to the same workstation, you need to run NPRINTER once for each printer.

The easiest way to execute the NPRINTER is by using the AUTOEXEC.BAT file for the PC. This way the NPRINTER software is running once the workstation is booted and even before a user logs in. The following is an example of loading the NPRINTER software using an AUTOEXEC.BAT file.

```
ECHO Off

PATH C:\DOS;C:\WINDOWS
```

```
PROMPT $P$G

LOADHIGH C:\NWCLIENT\LSL

LOADHIGH C:\NWCLIENT\NE2000

LOADHIGH C:\NWCLIENT\IPXODI

LOADHIGH C:\NWCLIENT\VLM

F:

NPRINTER PrintServer N

PAUSE

LOGIN . . .
```

Remember, the NPRINTER doesn't have to be logged in to run but it does need to be attached to the network, meaning that the NetWare shell or VLMs need to be loaded at the workstation. In order to execute the NPRINTER program before the user has logged in, you should copy it to the SYS:LOGIN directory of each server.

The remote printer configuration is a good option because the printing resources can be easily distributed around the network and placed close to the users that need them. One downside to this setup is that if the workstation is ever turned off or fails, the network printer becomes unavailable.

NETWORK SERVER PRINTERS

A printer that is connected directly to the server can be a network printer if you load the NPRINTER.NLM software on the server. The PSERVER.NLM software also needs to be loaded to communicate with the NPRINTER software and printer.

Using this configuration, the network users have the option to print to printers that are connected directly to the server. As with the network workstation printer, the users' print jobs are redirected to print queues that are serviced by the print server or PSERVER. Figure 14.5 illustrates the network server printer configuration.

F I G U R E   14.5

*Network server
printer configuration*

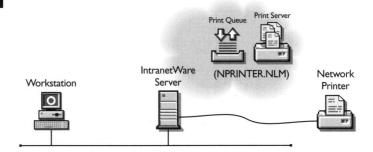

Since the printer is connected directly to the server, this configuration becomes less flexible in most large network environments. Typically, in large networks the servers are placed in the computer room and may not be close to the network users. The printer cable can only extend a limited distance, thus making access for the users difficult, if not impossible.

This configuration is very popular in networks or remote office networks in which the number of users is small. The server in this case can be situated close to the network users, and access to the printers is not limited. An important issue to remember when placing printers is that the users should not have to walk too far to pick up their print jobs. Printers should be placed in convenient locations.

Another issue with connecting printers directly to the server is that the printing load could slow the performance of the server. A printer connected to a server will demand CPU interrupts to process the print jobs. In a highly utilized environment, it is not wise to connect printers directly to the server.

NETWORK-DIRECT PRINTERS (REMOTE PRINTER MODE)

This printer is connected directly to the network using a special hardware device. These special hardware printing devices provide the connectivity to the network and are supplied by vendors such as Castelle, Compaq, Eagle Technologies, Hewlett-Packard, Intel, and Lexmark. Depending on the hardware, this device is either connected to the port of the printer and then to the network or is installed in a slot in the printer.

In the remote printer mode, the printer functions much like a network workstation running NPRINTER.EXE. The NPRINTER program resides in the firmware or flash-memory of the printer device. This configuration requires that the PSERVER.NLM be loaded on a NetWare server. The printer device then logs in to the IntranetWare server. It connects to the NetWare print server and polls print jobs. Figure 14.6 illustrates the network-direct printers running in remote printer mode.

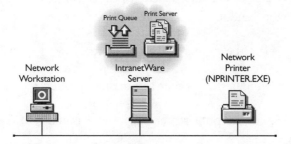

F I G U R E   14.6

Network-direct printer running in remote printer mode

Network Workstation

Print Queue   Print Server

IntranetWare Server

Network Printer (NPRINTER.EXE)

Using this configuration you can distribute the printers around the network and place them close to the network users who use them. The printers running in remote printer mode under IntranetWare run considerably faster than they did under NetWare 3. The increased speed and flexibility of IntranetWare makes remote printer mode a very effective way of providing network print services with these devices.

IntranetWare and NetWare 3 use the same NetWare SPX communication protocol between the print server and network-direct devices running in remote printer mode. This means that your existing NetWare 3 network-direct devices can attach and receive print jobs from a IntranetWare print server. Supporting a mixed NetWare 3 and IntranetWare printing environment will be discussed in more detail later in the chapter.

In general, setting up a network-direct print device in remote printer mode involves the following steps:

1 • Use the printer configuration utility supplied by the vendor to set up specific assignments.

2 • Start PCONSOLE or NWADMIN to create your print service objects.

3 • Create one or more print queues to be associated with the printer.

4 • Create a printer object for the printer. Configure the printer object as Other/Unknown and assign it to the print queue(s) previously created.

5 • Create the print server object to service the printer and assign the printer to the print server object. If you already have an existing print server, you can use it for this purpose. Simply assign to it the printer to be serviced.

6 • Run the network-attached printer configuration software supplied by the vendor.

7 • Select the printer to be configured.

8 • Configure the printer as a remote printer.

9 • Select the print server and printer number to represent this printer.

One possible inconvenience in this process is that some printer devices require the print server to be running in order to be configured. Typically, this is not a problem because the print server is running and servicing other printers. The new assignments made to the print server will take effect immediately, and there is no need to recycle (take down and bring back up) the print server.

Another possible inconvenience comes with some of the older varieties of network-direct devices. These devices need to be configured on the print server with a 16-printer limitation. (This 16-printer limitation was introduced in the NetWare 3 print servers.) You should reserve printer connections 0 to 15 for these printer devices. The remaining slots (16 to 255) can then be used for your other newer network printers.

NOTE

Some of the printer configuration utilities supplied by the vendors of the hardware can be operated only with explicit SUPERVISOR rights to the server; these utilities do not recognize a Supervisor equivalent. As a result, you will need to log in using the SUPERVISOR account in bindery mode rather than logging in as ADMIN or other administrative user under NDS.

NETWORK-DIRECT PRINTERS (QUEUE SERVER MODE)

This configuration is set up much like the network-direct printer described above in which the printer is connected directly to the network using a special hardware device. The difference with this configuration is that the printer in queue server mode acts like a special-purpose print server for the printer.

The queue server logs in to the IntranetWare server and services the associated print queue directly. The network-direct printers set up as queue servers are created and displayed in the NDS tree as print server objects.

In general, setting up a network-direct print device in queue server mode involves the following steps:

1 • Use the printer configuration utility supplied by the vendor to set up specific assignments.

2 • Start PCONSOLE or NWADMIN to create your print service objects.

3 • Create one or more print queues to be associated with the printer.

4 • Create a printer object for the network-direct printer. Configure the printer object as Other/Unknown and assign it to the print queue(s) previously created.

5 • Create the print server object to service the printer, and assign the printer to the print server object. This name must be unique on the network. There is a new print server object created for each network-direct printer set up in queue server mode.

6 • Run the network-attached printer configuration software supplied by the vendor.

7 • Select the printer to be configured.

8 • Configure the printer as a queue server.

9 • Type in the name of the print server.

10 • Select the file server where the print queues are located.

The network-direct printer setup in queue server mode is the most popular printing solution in the industry. In many cases, it offers a fast, effective, and low-cost method for printing. This configuration also offers a good distribution of the printers across the network because the printers are placed next to the network users. This configuration is also not dependent on any external software or hardware systems such as the PSERVER.NLM or a workstation. Figure 14.7 illustrates the network-direct printer running in queue server mode.

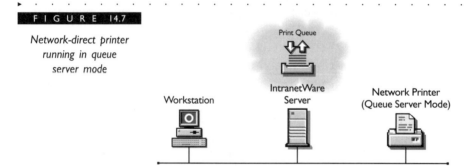

FIGURE 14.7

Network-direct printer running in queue server mode

Several issues need to be considered when you implement this configuration:

▸ One common drawback of this configuration is that the queue servers are required to log in to the network or server where the print queue resides. The queue server logs in using the normal user connection slots and will take one of the server's license connections, leaving you fewer connections for the network users. You should plan the distribution of the print queues accordingly. Of course, the PSERVER does the same thing as well.

▸ The print hardware devices that were purchased before the advent of IntranetWare are not NDS aware. This means the queue servers will log in to the IntranetWare servers using bindery services mode and cannot read the print server configuration files from NDS.

In order for the queue server to log in using bindery services it requires the NDS object definitions for the print queues to be in the server's bindery context. Any additional print queues serviced by the network-direct printers should also exist in the server's bindery context.

▸ NetWare 3 creates the group EVERYONE by default. Many of the network-direct print devices assume that this group exists for proper operation. For these devices running in IntranetWare, you may need to manually create a group called EVERYONE in the context where the print server is defined. This way the print server or queue server will be able to communicate with the network. Users do not have to be in the Group EVERYONE to print.

IntranetWare Printing Setup

In order to set up IntranetWare Print Services you should start by defining the print queues, print server, and printers using either PCONSOLE or NWADMIN. The following list outlines the steps necessary to install IntranetWare Print Services:

1 • Create network print queues on the file server by using PCONSOLE or NWADMIN.

2 • Assign queue operators and queue users to the printer queue through NWADMIN.

3 • Create a print server definition.

4 • Specify the file servers that have the print queues the print server will service.

5 • Create printers to be associated with the print server.

6 • Assign the print queues to the appropriate printers.

7 • You can optionally set up printing for additional file servers.

8 • Load PSERVER.NLM on the server.

9 • If a remote printer was assigned to the print server, run NPRINTER.EXE at the appropriate workstation or run NPRINTER.NLM at the server.

10 • Network printing should now be ready.

QUICK SETUP OPTION

The Quick Setup option is a quick way to create and set up each of the three print objects (print queue, printer, and print server) and automatically establish the appropriate relationships. This option is the simplest way to set up the IntranetWare Print Services, especially if you are starting without existing printing objects. Quick Setup is available only in PCONSOLE.

In order to run the Quick Setup option perform the following steps:

1 • Log in to the network as an ADMIN user with the Create object right to the specific NDS container.

2 • Load PCONSOLE and change to the appropriate context or use the CX command before executing PCONSOLE.

3 • Select the Quick Setup menu item.

4 • Enter the information required on the screen by selecting names for each of the printing objects.

5 • After saving the configuration, load the PSERVER.NLM software at a server console with the new print server object's name.

6 • Load the NPRINTER.EXE at the workstation with the printer or NPRINTER.NLM if the printer is attached directly to the server.

7 • Network printing should now be ready.

We recommend that you use the Quick Setup option in PCONSOLE if you are setting up the IntranetWare Print Services for the first time. Figure 14.8 shows the Quick Setup option screen in PCONSOLE.

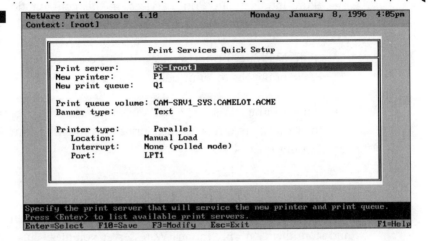

FIGURE 14.8

*The Quick Setup option
screen in PCONSOLE*

After a print queue is created, the user who created the queue is automatically assigned as a queue operator, and the users that exist in the same container in the NDS tree are assigned as print queue users. This is the default setup, and it works well for most networks.

If you want to delegate the responsibility for managing the print queues to other users, you can assign the other users to be queue operators through the PCONSOLE or NWADMIN utilities.

Only users designated as queue users can submit print jobs to the print queue. In larger networks, delegate responsibility to queue operators for a location or department and make only the members of the location or department queue users. The queue operators can then manage the print jobs for their area.

SETTING PRINT SERVICES ENVIRONMENTS

You are now able to set up a mixed IntranetWare and NetWare 3 printing infrastructure. The compatibility of the print services between the two NetWare versions is bi-directional. This means that IntranetWare can share printing services with NetWare 3. NetWare 3, in turn, can share the print services with IntranetWare. The benefit of this compatibility is that the users may capture to print queues whether they are on IntranetWare servers or NetWare 3 servers.

The best way to illustrate the capabilities of mixed print services is through the following examples:

▸ Pure IntraNetWare Print Services. In this configuration the network users send their print jobs to IntranetWare print queues.

▸ Pure NetWare 3 print services. In this configuration the network users send their print jobs to print queues stored on NetWare 3 servers.

▸ Mixed IntranetWare and NetWare 3 print services. In this configuration the network users can send their print jobs to either IntranetWare or NetWare 3 print queues.

Pure IntranetWare Print Services Implementation

You can choose to create all the print queues, printers, and print servers in NDS and store them on only IntranetWare server volumes. This configuration is known as a pure IntraNetWare Print Services implementation. IntranetWare users or users running the Virtual Loadable Modules (VLM) will access the print queue and read the configuration information from NDS.

Because NetWare 3 users or users running the older NETX workstation software will access the print queue and the configuration information from NDS through bindery services, you will be required to support bindery services at each IntranetWare server that has print queues. The NetWare 3 users will be able to use only the print queues in the server's bindery context. The NetWare 3 users must also to able to log in to the server using bindery services, which means that the user will have an account in the server's bindery context. You could implement a group or collective account that many users use just for printing services.

If the printers are using the NPRINTER program, the IntranetWare servers will need to load the appropriate PSERVER.NLM to support them.

If the printers are running the queue server mode, then the printer device is truly a print server and printer combination. Using the queue server mode the printer device logs in to the server in order to service the assigned print queue. Only some of the newest versions of the queue server software support an NDS authentication. The older versions require bindery services supported logins at each IntranetWare server that has print queues. The bindery services requirement forces you to place the print queue, print server, and printer NDS objects in the same container so that each can be resolved.

Figure 14.9 illustrates a pure IntranetWare printing infrastructure.

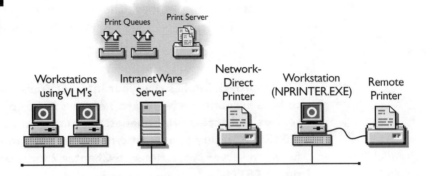

FIGURE 14.9

A pure IntranetWare Print
Services implementation

Pure NetWare 3 Print Services Implementation

If you are migrating from a NetWare 3 network environment, you may have a
temporary need to keep all the print services back on NetWare 3. This configuration
means that all the print queues and print server definitions are retained on the
NetWare 3 servers for the duration of the migration project. Figure 14.10 illustrates
a pure NetWare 3 print services implementation running with IntranetWare servers
and users.

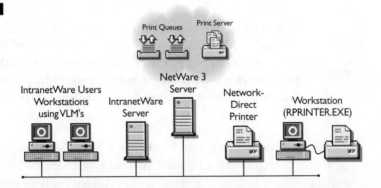

FIGURE 14.10

A pure NetWare 3
print services
implementation running
with IntranetWare users

Even with a pure NetWare 3 printing implementation, the IntranetWare users
are able to send print jobs to any of the print queues on a NetWare 3 server. The
user must first log in to every server with a print queue that the user wants to
access. You should also create an NDS print queue in the tree that points to the

NetWare 3 volume. The user can then select the print queue using either the NetWare 3 utilities or IntranetWare utilities. The NDS print queue object is a logical representation for the print queue that is physically located on the NetWare 3 server volume.

This approach implies that your IntranetWare users also need to have accounts on NetWare 3 servers if they plan to log in to servers and access print queues. You may want to consider Novell's NETSYNC utility to at least synchronize the same passwords between server types. Refer to Chapter 2 for more information on NETSYNC.

In order to create an NDS print queue object to represent a NetWare 3 queue, you can use the NWADMIN utility. On the Create Print Queue screen select the Print Queue Volume item, which will prompt you for the file server and volume where the print queue will be placed. You should enter the NetWare 3 server and volume name. Figure 14.11 illustrates the process of setting up an NDS print queue that is stored on the NetWare 3 server but that both NetWare 3 and IntranetWare users can share.

The print queue stored in the NetWare 3 server can be serviced by a print server running on either the IntranetWare or NetWare 3 operating systems. For more information on setting up a mixed print service environment, refer to the "Mixed IntranetWare and NetWare 3 Print Services Implementation" section below.

Mixed IntranetWare and NetWare 3 Print Services Implementation

If you are migrating from a NetWare 3 network environment, then the most common configuration is to have the print services defined on both the IntranetWare and the NetWare 3 servers. This configuration means that the print queues, print servers, and printers definitions are separated according to the version of the NetWare server. For example, the print services migrated to IntranetWare are those print services that the users need on that server. Likewise, the print services left on NetWare 3 are those needed by the users of that server. Figure 14.12 illustrates a mixed IntranetWare and NetWare 3 print services implementation.

FIGURE 14.11

*Creating an NDS print
queue in NWADMIN,
which is physically stored
on a NetWare 3 server*

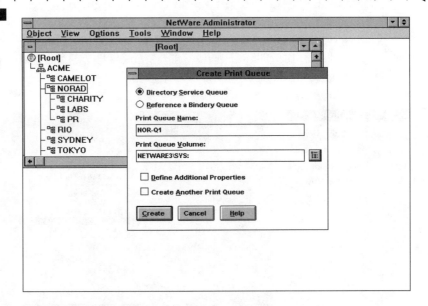

FIGURE 14.12

*A mixed IntranetWare and
NetWare 3 print services
implementation*

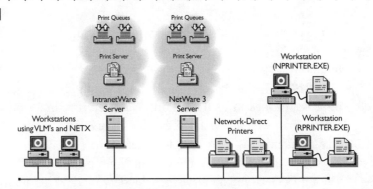

The print queues on either servers can be serviced by a print server running on the IntranetWare servers or NetWare 3 servers.

A printer device operating in queue server mode could also service any print queue on any servers in the network. Because all of the older network-direct print devices are not NDS aware, you must create the print server information in PCONSOLE in bindery mode. In order to switch to bindery mode in PCONSOLE, you should press F6 before creating the print server. Pressing this key enables the queue server to read the print server configuration files. In NetWare 3 the print server configuration files are stored in SYS:SYSTEM. In IntranetWare the print server configuration files are stored in NDS as properties of the printer server object.

Figure 14.13 illustrates the main menu of PCONSOLE where you can switch between bindery mode and Directory Services mode before the creation of a print server.

F I G U R E   14.13

Main menu of PCONSOLE
where you can switch
between bindery mode and
Directory Services mode

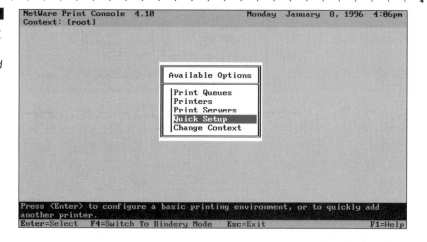

```
NetWare Print Console  4.10                    Monday  January  8, 1996  4:06pm
Context: [root]




                          ┌──────────────────────┐
                          │   Available Options   │
                          ├──────────────────────┤
                          │ Print Queues          │
                          │ Printers              │
                          │ Print Servers         │
                          │ Quick Setup           │
                          │ Change Context        │
                          └──────────────────────┘




Press <Enter> to configure a basic printing environment, or to quickly add
another printer.
Enter=Select   F4=Switch To Bindery Mode   Esc=Exit                    F1=Help
```

You should also use the bindery mode setting in PCONSOLE when setting up a NetWare 3 print server to service IntranetWare print queues. In order for the IntranetWare print queues to be serviced from a print server running on the NetWare 3 servers, the print server software must log in to the target server. The NetWare 3 print server logs in to the IntranetWare server using a print server object by the same name, which is defined on the IntranetWare server. The IntranetWare print server definition is used only for login purposes.

When you are creating the IntranetWare print server definition you must create it using PCONSOLE and switch to bindery mode. This approach enables the queue server to read the print server configuration files. The print queues that will be serviced also need to be created under bindery mode. If these objects are not created under bindery mode, the NetWare 3 print server will not be able to log in to the IntranetWare server and service the print queues.

This is important if you are migrating a NetWare 3 server to IntranetWare and using the Across-the-Wire Migration utility. If you want the print queues on the migrated IntranetWare server to be serviced by the original NetWare 3 print server, you must recreate each print server and print queue object. Running MIGPRINT to move the printing objects from NetWare 3 to IntranetWare will not save you the task of recreating each printing object.

MIGRATING THE PRINT SERVICES

When you are migrating from NetWare 3 to IntranetWare you should consider the effect the migration will have on the print services. Depending on the migration method you choose, the print services objects and print databases — PRINTCON and PRINTDEF — may not be moved. The two most popular migration options, the Across-the-Wire Migration utility and the In-Place Migration utility, are discussed below.

Using the Across-the-Wire Migration Utility

If you are migrating a NetWare 3 server using the Across-the-Wire Migration utility, all the print services objects, including print queues, print servers, and printers, are not migrated. The PRINTCON and PRINTDEF databases (these files are named after the DOS utility that administers them) are not migrated directly into NDS. Although the database files are physically copied during the migration of the volume data to their respective areas, they may not be useful. For example, the PRINTCON files are copied from the SYS:MAIL\USERID# directory from the source NetWare 3 server to SYS:MAIL\USERID# on the destination IntranetWare server. Instead, the PRINTCON information should be an NDS property of either the user or a container object (such as an Organizational Unit).

The PRINTDEF files are copied from the SYS:PUBLIC directory on the source server to the SYS:PUBLIC directory on the NetWare 4 server. This information should be stored as an NDS property of a container object, such as an Organizational Unit.

NOTE

The Across-the-Wire Migration utility provides a list of the type of information available for migration by this utility. One of the options is to migrate Print Queues and Print Servers. At first glance this option seems like the right choice to migrate the print services from NetWare 3 to IntranetWare. However, this option attempts to migrate only the LAN Server and LAN Manager print queues and print servers; it will not migrate the NetWare 3 printing services object from the bindery.

Once you have completed the migration of the server using the Across-the-Wire Migration utility, you can either recreate all the print services objects and databases in NDS or run the special MIGPRINT program, which moves the print objects and databases automatically into NDS. The MIGPRINT program is a DOS command line utility that comes on the IntranetWare CD-ROM. Figure 4.14 illustrates the main help screen for the MIGPRINT utility. MIGPRINT enables you to be selective about the specific print objects and information that you want to move.

Using the In-Place Migration Utility

If you use the In-Place Migration utility, which is the IntranetWare installation program, all the print services objects and the PRINTCON and PRINTDEF databases will be migrated directly into NDS. Each print queue, print server, and printer object will become an NDS object in the server's chosen context.

After migrating the databases during the In-Place migration, you will need to run the PUPGRADE.NLM to convert the databases from the NetWare 3 format to the IntranetWare format.

F I G U R E   14.14

*The MIGPRINT
main help screen*

```
MIGPRINT.EXE                                                    4.10.01

General Help

Purpose: To migrate print queues, print servers, and print job
         configurations from a bindery server to Directory Services.

Syntax: MIGPRINT /S=srcSrvr /D=dstSrvr [/VOL=queueVol] [/O=outputFile]


G:\NW410\MIGRATE>
```

NEW PRINT SERVICES FEATURES IN INTRANETWARE

The NetWare Administrator (NWADMIN) utility now includes a Print Services Quick Setup option under the Tools menu. This option provides functionality similar to the Quick Setup option in the PCONSOLE utility. The Print Services Quick

Setup option enables you to easily create and associate Print Server, Printer, and Print Queue objects in the NDS tree.

You can use the new graphical NPRINTER Manager (NPTWIN95.EXE) to enable network users to share a printer attached to a Windows 95 workstation. NPRINTER Manager (and its associated files) provides the same functionality that NPRINTER.EXE provides on a DOS or OS/2 workstation.

NetWare Distributed Print Services

NetWare Distributed Print Services (NDPS) is the next generation of print services. NDPS is designed to simplify access and administration of the network print services. NetWare Distributed Print Services (NDPS) is a distributed service that consists of client, server, and the connectivity software components to seamlessly connect the applications to the network printers.

NDPS gives users and administrators greater control over their printing. Features such as bidirectional feedback, print job status, automatic driver downloading, and event notification for printer status help simplify and streamline the usability and administration of the network printing. NDPS enables the user to get the characteristics for a selected printer before the print job is sent to ensure that the job will be printed correctly. NDPS can also let the user know whether a printer is available or busy, and it can even enable the user to copy or move print jobs between network printers as necessary.

NDPS uses a snap-in to NWADMIN to provide a single comprehensive management utility that enables and controls network printing for all major brands and models of printers. In the current print services, the initial setup currently requires creating print queues, printer objects, and print servers, and then establishing a relationship between them. NDPS eliminates the need to create and configure print queues, printers, and print server objects. In fact, NDPS doesn't require you to manage print queues at all. Instead, using NDPS a printer simply needs to be connected to the network to begin sending print jobs to it. The printer will indicate which driver it needs, and the driver will be automatically downloaded. This eliminates the administrator having to configure the users' workstations with drivers for specific printers and other devices.

The NetWare Distributed Print Services product is currently an add-on product that can be easily integrated into your existing IntranetWare networks. In the future, it will be included as the regular print services for the operating system. NDPS provides the following features and printing capabilities.

Simple Printer Access

When the client software is installed, a list of available printers (called a "short list") is immediately available. The printers are configured as NDS printers, which allow users to browse the NDS tree for new printers based on the printer's properties, such as location, type, and supported languages. Because NDPS allows bidirectional information to be passed between the client and printers, the users can match the print jobs with the printer's capabilities. The users can also query and receive the status of the individual printers. This enables the users to know whether a printer is available, get information about the status of the print jobs, and receive notification that the paper tray is empty.

Users also have the flexibility to indicate that a print job or document needs to be printed on a special paper type. The printer will then notify the user when the paper needs to be loaded or inserted and then print only that document on the special paper. For example, if the user specifies that a letter needs to be printed a single sheets of letterhead, the printer will prompt the user to insert the letterhead and then only that letter or document on the letterhead will be printed.

Easier Setup and Administration

The initial administrative setup and installation costs are reduced by having the new printers automatically register with NDPS. For example, using the current print services, when a new printer is added to the network, the printer immediately starts advertising its availability, which results in increased network traffic. This advertising continues as long as the printer is turned on. Using NDPS, when a new printer is added to the network, it registers with a single registration agent. The agent will then notify all the appropriate clients of the printer's availability and will advertise all the printers. This greatly reduces the overall network traffic caused by network printers.

Using NWADMIN the administrators have a centralized, simplified, and common interface to manage the print services. Because NPDS is closely integrated with Novell Directory Services, the administrator can create a printer object in the NDS tree and manage the printers even if they come from different vendors. Because the printer objects appear as NDS objects, they can take advantage of NDS security to control access to the printers and printer features for handling sensitive documents.

The NDPS printing can be set up to have multiple redundant physical printers represented by a single printer object in NDS. This feature allows print jobs to be shared or distributed among several printers without user intervention. Printer chaining will allow redundant backup printers to be accessed sequentially.

Any NDPS printer can be managed through a standard SNMP console using the standard printer Management Information Base (MIB).

NDPS Architecture

The components that comprise the NetWare Distributed Print Services architecture are independent of any single operating system. Thus, the architecture is designed to be portable to different environments. The major components of NDPS are the Virtual Printer, Print Client, Print Service Common Facilities, Communication Service, Print Device Subsystem, and Physical Printer.

Virtual Printer

The virtual printer (VP) performs all the tasks of the current print server, spooler, and print queue. These tasks are combined into a logical print management agent called the virtual printer. This logical print management agent maintains information about the specific physical printers, such as printer availability, status, and other property information in the NDS printer objects. The virtual printer accepts operations (queries, print jobs, and so on) from the print clients.

The virtual printer may reside in several places on the system. For example, the VP may be running on the NetWare server or in the physical printer device that is connected directly to the network. A virtual printer that has not been officially registered in NDS can advertise its presence and availability as a convenience printer. A convenience printer is a network printer that is available to anyone on the network but is not seen as an NDS object and thus does not take advantage of the ease of access and security.

Print Client

The print client is the agent for the service requester that resides on the workstation as part of the NetWare client software. The print client's responsibility is to send network print jobs from the workstation to the appropriate virtual printer on the network.

Print Service Common Facilities

The Print Service Common Facilities (PSCF) is an NLM loaded on the NetWare server that allows the virtual printer to accept and schedule print jobs sent from the client. The PSCF also receives information about the devices and resources it is managing. It validates security information and provides direct notification and feedback to the appropriate client or device. The PSCF is essentially the liaison between the virtual printers and the print clients.

The print clients communicate with the virtual printer using the NetWare Distributed Print Service Protocol (DPSP). The Novell implementation of a virtual printer supports the SNMP protocol, which enables the administrators to manage the virtual printer using ManageWise or any SNMP-based console.

Print Device Subsystem

The print device subsystem (PDS) is a driver that can be implemented and customized to control feedback and send it to the physical print device. Normally, the print device subsystem is develop by original equipment manufacturers (OEMs) and independent software vendors (ISVs) to take advantage of the functionality of each of the physical printer devices.

Physical Printer

The physical printer is the actual printer device that is attached to the network to service the print jobs sent by the users. In order for the physical printer to be involved with the NetWare Distributed Print Services, it must either have the virtual printer component embedded or be able to communicate to a NDPS server. With the second option the server will support the printer and make it a full NDPS printer.

Figure 14.15 illustrates how the NDPS components work together to provide a complete network printing solution. Notice that the virtual printer is embedded in the physical printer that is attached directly to the network. In this setup the client and printer will have full bidirectional communication and feedback capabilities.

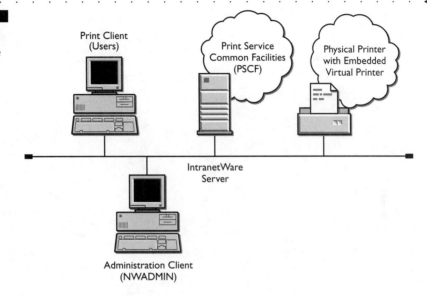

CHAPTER 15

Preparing for Migration to IntranetWare

"If you want things to stay as they are, things will have to change."
Giuseppe di Lampedusa

This chapter will help you prepare for and begin the process of migrating your current system to IntranetWare. There are several things you will want to do in order to prepare for the migration of your servers and workstations to IntranetWare. You will want to organize and educate the IntranetWare project team, create an implementation schedule, set up a testing lab, and do the pilot system.

In order to create a good implementation schedule and prepare for the design, implementation, and migration to IntranetWare, you need to organize and educate your IntranetWare project team.

Organize and Educate the IntranetWare Project Team

Your first objective is to organize the IntranetWare project team with one individual assigned as the project manager. The project manager should choose the members of the team, matching the network responsibilities needed with the individual's skills.

The project team will create the master schedule to manage all of the implementation tasks. In order to accomplish the individual tasks, the team members can be assembled into functional areas. Each individual presiding over a functional area would be responsible for seeing that task to completion. The following is a list of some suggested functional areas:

- Training

- NetWare Directory Services

- Servers

- Clients

- Printing

- Administration

PROJECT TEAM ASSIGNMENTS

The size of the IntranetWare project team will vary depending on the size of the corporation or the overall project. The smallest team consists of only one person performing all the tasks and functional assignments as compared with dozens of persons helping the project to succeed. Again, each team or functional area can include one individual or many people depending on the size or scope of the project. You must determine the scope of your project and how many people are needed to complete and maintain the installation of IntranetWare.

The primary responsibility of the entire project team is to determine the overall scope of the project, which includes a list of deliverables that the project team will create and accomplish for the company or steering committee. Depending on the demands of the project, the deliverables might also include a list of milestones, critical paths, success factors, risk analyses, and tracking mechanisms.

Following the assignments for the entire project team are the responsibilities and areas of focus for each of the individual teams and its members. We will discuss each individually.

TRAINING

This person or team is responsible for providing the other members of the project team, network administrator, and users with the proper IntranetWare training. This includes a lab environment for hands-on training, which is discussed later in this chapter.

There are several methods and sources of training available for your network personnel. The training includes formal Novell education, Novell-sponsored workshops or conferences, lab experience, white papers, Novell Application Notes, user groups, related books, and other available media.

Formal Education

Instructor-led courses are available through Novell Authorized Education Centers (NAECs) and Novell Education Academic Partners (NEAPs) worldwide. CBT products, videos, and self-study workbooks are available through NAECs and Novell resellers. For more information on Novell's education programs, or to find the NAEC or NEAP nearest you, in the United States and Canada call 1-800-233-EDUC. Outside the United States and Canada, call 1-801-429-5508, or contact your nearest Novell office.

Another quick 24-hour-per-day tool for information is the Novell Education FaxBack. Call 1-801-429-5363 for access to FaxBack. Ask for document 1448 for current courses.

Novell-Sponsored Workshops and Conferences

Novell develops and delivers various workshops throughout the year at the local sales offices. You should contact the local office account teams for the scheduled workshops in your area. Novell presents several BrainShare Conferences throughout the world. BrainShare is a conference for developers, consultants, and system integrators. Currently, there are BrainShare conferences held in the United States (March in Salt Lake City, Utah), Europe, Australia, Japan, China, South Africa, Russia, and China.

Lab Experience

There is no substitute for hands-on experience. You will provide skills that transfer to your system administrators in the lab environment. A test migration of the servers from a copy of a production server in the lab, for example, will give your personnel valuable experience as well as an understanding of migration issues before migration is attempted in a production environment.

Application Notes

Novell Application Notes (AppNotes) is published monthly by Novell. The material in the AppNotes is based on actual field experience and technical research performed by Novell personnel, covering topics in the following main areas:

- Network design and optimization strategies

- Network management tactics

- NetWare internals and theory of operations

- Novell product implementation guidelines

- Integration solutions for third-party products

- NetWare programming techniques

Current AppNotes is a good source of information for IntranetWare. The AppNote subscription rate for a one-year subscription (12 issues) is $95 in the United States and $135 outside the United States. To order AppNotes, call 1-800-377-4136 or 303-297-2725. Orders can also be faxed to 303-294-0930. Hardcopy subscribers are granted access to the electronic AppNote subscription area on NetWire.

Electronic-only subscriptions are available in the United States for $35 a year. Both hard-copy and electronic-only subscribers incur the cost of access time charges for downloading the AppNotes and Research Reports.

NetWare User International (NUI) Group

We also recommend that you join a NetWare User Group in order to share information and experiences with other IntranetWare users. They also periodically invite speakers from Novell to speak on topics of interest.

On-Line Services

Novell provides an On-Line forum through CompuServe called NetWire. This forum provides the customers with the latest Novell information, which includes fixes and patches, questions and answers, technical documentation, and support knowledge. NetWire is only available through CompuServe.

Novell's Web Site, WWW.NOVELL.COM, is also an excellent resource for updates, patches, and product information and can be accessed through the Internet.

NOVELL DIRECTORY SERVICES

This person or team is responsible for designing Novell Directory Services. The design includes the design of the NDS tree, NDS partitions and replicas, and the time synchronization. This team will work closely with other company personnel to establish the NDS naming standards as well. This team should have a good understanding of NDS objects and properties as well as an understanding of administration of the network. This team will also help manage and monitor the NDS system once it is moved into production.

SERVERS

This person or team is responsible for migrating the file servers from your current network operating system to IntranetWare. This group will work closely with or be a part of the NDS design group and will also assist in setting up the lab for testing and staging migrations. This includes the first pilot servers and all the additional servers added into the tree. This group will also be responsible for operational issues such as protocol support, backup and restore, and performance tuning of the IntranetWare servers.

If you are migrating from NetWare 2 or 3, the server team should spend some time cleaning up and preparing the NetWare 3 servers. This team can create guidelines for cleaning up the files in the file system as well as the NetWare 3 binderies. Cleaning up the files ensures that only files and objects you need are transferred during the migration process.

The server team may also want to consider upgrading the server hardware to newer and faster machines because IntranetWare requires more resources to load and operate than previous NetWare operating systems. The server team should work with your company's hardware vendor to procure the optimal hardware for IntranetWare.

The server team should also consider performing the following functions in preparation for the migration of each server:

▶ Apply the corporate NDS naming standard while the objects are still in the bindery.

NDS does not support different object types having the same name. By contrast, the binderies in previous versions of NetWare do support different object types with the same name. For example, in NetWare 3, a group object called HP4SI and a print queue called HP4SI have the same name because they are different object types. In IntranetWare you cannot have any leaf object with the same name in the same container. This conflict needs to be resolved before the migration of the server to IntranetWare. If there is a duplicate object name, the migration utilities will not migrate the second occurrence of the duplicate object name. There is a Novell utility called DUPBIND (found on NetWire), which displays the duplicate object names in the binderies so they can be changed before a migration begins.

▶ Clean up the binderies and delete users and other objects that are no longer in use.

Take this opportunity to remove security and access privileges that are no longer required. The SECURITY.EXE program in NetWare 3 will help you find and expose the detailed security information for each object in the bindery. Users who have left the company or who are no longer using that server should be removed.

▶ Make a complete backup of your servers before beginning a migration.

Some companies have individuals in an operations group that are responsible for backups. The server team should work with this group to ensure that a recent backup has been performed on any server that is about to be migrated.

▶ Run the BINDFIX utility in NetWare 3 to remove any objects that are corrupted in the bindery.

▶ If you are migrating multiple NetWare 2 or NetWare 3 servers into a single IntranetWare server, the server team should check for users with accounts on the multiple servers.

Migrating multiple servers and duplicate users will present you with several challenges during the migration to IntranetWare. First, the migrate utility prompts you to change the username on the second and subsequent servers. Second, the migrate utility will merge the user objects that have the same name into a single NDS object with cumulative rights. This may not be what you had intended.

▶ If each one of the multiple NetWare 2 or NetWare 3 servers is migrated into different containers in the NDS tree (OUs), the duplicate username will be migrated to each individual container that has the same relative distinguished name but a different context. In most cases you do not want to manage the same user twice in the tree.

▶ Delete old files and applications from the file system. This will free up disk space for other purposes. You will discover many old, unused, and duplicated applications that are wasting disk space.

▶ Ensure that your network uses the IntranetWare default Ethernet frame type of 802.2.

Although IntranetWare will support both the 802.3 raw and IEEE 802.2 frame types, 802.2 is the preferred standard and provides automatic check summing of packets to ensure greater communications reliability.

Always try to use the 802.2 frame type and begin phasing out the 802.3 raw frame type if it is in use at your site. Choosing just one frame type will eliminate additional network traffic.

TIP

The server team should understand how to install a new IntranetWare server from scratch and should have experience in the migration of your current servers to IntranetWare.

In order to perform a new installation of IntranetWare, run the INSTALL.EXE program from the NetWare 4.11 CD-ROM. The NetWare 4.11 CD-ROM can be mounted as a DOS device on the server machine, or mounted as a NetWare volume where the server is logged in as a client. The CD-ROM can also be completely copied to a server volume; this method is referred to as server to server installation.

Installing a new IntranetWare server on new hardware is simple and can be accomplished by referring to Chapter 16.

The server team needs to become familiar with the migration options available to them. In order to migrate an existing network server to IntranetWare, several utilities are offered. These include the In-Place (INSTALL.NLM), Across-the-Wire (MIGRATE.EXE and LM/NTS/LS), DS Migrate, and the NetWare File Migration utilities. The INSTALL.NLM offers support for migrating from NetWare 3 and previous versions of NetWare 4. The MIGRATE.EXE is a DOS-based utility that migrates NetWare 2 and NetWare 3. The LM/NTS/LS is a migration utility that enables you to migrate your LAN Manager, NT Server, and LAN Server operating systems to IntranetWare. For more information on this utility refer to Chapter 17.

Incorporated into the latest NWADMIN utility is a graphical migration utility called DS Migrate. DS Migrate enables you to upgrade a NetWare 2 or NetWare 3 server bindery by migrating modeled bindery information to an existing IntranetWare tree. DS Migrate migrates only bindery information. Data files are migrated using either the new graphical NetWare File Migration utility or the DOS menu-based MIGRATE utility.

The NetWare File Migration utility is a new utility for migrating files from NetWare 3 servers to IntranetWare servers. The NetWare File Migration utility is used in conjunction with the new DS Migrate utility after NetWare 3. Both the graphical DS Migrate and NetWare File Migration utilities are incorporated into the NetWare Administrator utility.

The In-Place migration method is the fastest method for migration because it does not move any data or files. This method is also recommended when you are upgrading an existing NetWare 3 server to IntranetWare on the existing hardware device.

The other migration methods are slower because the workstation has to move all the data across the network. It is recommended that you use the Across-the-Wire method and DSMIGRATE method when you want to migrate an existing network server from one machine to another. These methods enable you to replace or upgrade the server hardware.

CLIENTS

This person or team is responsible for migrating the workstations or clients to the latest client software for the preferred desktop operating system. If there are several different types of operating systems, then the team can be divided to support each desktop operating system. For example, DOS/Windows, Windows 95, OS/2, Macintosh, NT, and UNIX desktops can be supported by different people with the client team. This team would be responsible for optimizing, configuring, and updating or migrating the workstations.

If the user community is using primarily the NETX shell in DOS for connectivity to the network servers, then this team should upgrade these workstations as soon as possible to the newer 32-bit NetWare Client for DOS/Windows and Windows 95. These clients support connectivity to NetWare 2, NetWare 3, and IntranetWare.

CONSULTING EXPERIENCE

Consider moving the client team and other IS staff to the NetWare 32-bit Client first. This will enable your administrators to become familiar with the technology before they migrate the user community.

It is recommended that the client team migrate the workstations to the latest client software before the first migration of any servers to IntranetWare. For example, the NetWare Client32 can provide your workstation with more conventional memory. Once the server is migrated to IntranetWare, the user will have immediate support for single login and other services unique to the IntranetWare operating system.

The OS/2 Requester for NDS also provides many of the same benefits as the NetWare Client32, such as full backward compatibility.

The MAC client for IntranetWare also provides single login to any IntranetWare servers.

The client team should plan for about 10 minutes per workstation to complete the installation of the latest client software for the desktop operating system. The team should also combine all necessary changes into a single visit to each workstation. Some things to consider are the following:

▸ Determine and define the contents for each of the configuration files on the workstation. These configuration files include CONFIG.SYS, AUTOEXEC.BAT, NET.CFG, and STARTNET.BAT. You should define a standardized set of files across all workstations in the network.

▸ During the migration or installation of the new client software, the fastest installation method is to download from a server rather than using floppy disks. This method is possible only if you are migrating from NETX workstations.

▸ Consider upgrading other system software for the workstations. For example, you could take this opportunity to upgrade the workstations to the latest revision of Windows or to perform other upgrades.

▸ Schedule the migration of your workstations during a period that is long enough to migrate your selected set of users. You may need to schedule this process during a weekend. Obviously, the more people involved in the migration of workstations, the faster this process will go.

▸ The client team could also consider an automated strategy for upgrades from the server. For instance, when the user logs into an IntranetWare server, the automated program will download the required programs to the workstations. This implies that the workstations are standardized in their file structure.

APPLICATIONS

This person or team is responsible for performing compatibility testing for applications running on the servers and clients. There are several issues to consider during the compatibility testing. These issues include, but are not restricted to:

▸ Bindery-based software programs

▸ DS aware applications

▸ Connections greater than 250 users

▸ VLM and NetWare Client32 compatibility

This group is also responsible for migrating and implementing the applications into the IntranetWare production environment. Not all applications need to be tested for compatibility primarily because NetWare 4 has been around for a few years and also because mainstream applications are already known to be completely compatible. If your company has applications that were written by an internal staff, they should be tested for compatibility with IntranetWare.

PRINTING

This person or team is responsible for designing the printing strategies for IntranetWare. All the print software and hardware should be tested for compatibility, which includes connections greater than 250 users. The printing strategies could encompass printing in a mixed environment from both NetWare 3 and IntranetWare. This team should address the following issues for both a pure IntranetWare printing strategy and a mixed NetWare 3 and IntranetWare printing strategy:

▸ Setup for a pure IntranetWare printing strategy

  ▸ Quick Setup

  ▸ Default Print Queue for printers

  ▸ Workstations running VLMs

  ▸ Workstations running NETX

  ▸ Workstations running Client32 for Windows and Windows 95

▸ Support for a mixed IntranetWare and NetWare 3 printing strategy

    ▸ Queues on IntranetWare, with the Print Servers on NetWare 3

    ▸ Queues on NetWare 3, with the Print Servers on IntranetWare

    ▸ Queues and Print Servers on NetWare 3, with Client on IntranetWare, VLMs, and Client32 for Windows and Windows 95.

▸ Support for advanced printing capabilities, specifically distributed printing.

The print team should test all the possible printing configurations and help with the migration of the printing infrastructure to IntranetWare.

ADMINISTRATION

This person or group is responsible for assigning system administrators and users access to both the network and NDS. This includes login scripts, bindery services, mobile users, security, and the administration of NDS. This team will determine and establish the auditing requirements for the corporation.

Implementation Schedule

These are the possible team members for your IntranetWare design and installation. Some or all of these tasks may be performed by one person or by a team of people with specific assignments. After you have selected your project team you are now ready to define an implementation schedule.

You will want to create an implementation schedule to help you plan and track the migration of your servers to IntranetWare and NDS. The implementation schedule should provide detailed tasks that you will accomplish or perform during the installation or upgrade of your network servers. The implementation schedule should also include the time line and the individuals or team members assigned to complete the tasks. The schedule can also provide specific guidelines and recommendations necessary to properly perform the assigned tasks.

IDENTIFY IMPLEMENTATION OBJECTIVE AND TASKS

The objective for the NetWare 4 implementation schedule is to establish and perform the implementation tasks in the proper order. The individual tasks also need to provide a continual process for the migration to IntranetWare. This objective can be met only if all the network administrators work together using the same goals, schedules, and task lists.

The schedule helps you track the status of the project and can provide immediate feedback or reports to your staff and management. A well-planned implementation schedule will not only help you manage and track the status of the IntranetWare design and implementation project, but can be used to set the deadlines for each task. You should lay out a chart or schedule for each task that includes a description, guidelines, duration, start and end date, team or person assigned, and the percentage of the task completed. If possible, the schedule can also show the interdependencies of the tasks, measure team members' progress in completing tasks, review the work, and produce reports for management.

Creating an Implementation Schedule

The main responsibility of the project team as a whole is to create and lay out the implementation schedule to determine the overall scope of the project. This schedule should define what the end result of your migration will be.

The purpose for the implementation schedule is to provide the project team with a consistent set of tasks and objectives for the IntranetWare migration and roll out. The final goal of the project team is to establish an IntranetWare network that provides a single point of login for the users and simplifies network administration. You are also trying to enhance your network services by increasing the capacity of existing systems.

For example, in the ACME tree, we need to define an implementation schedule to accomplish the migration of 40 NetWare 3.12 servers. The schedule should outline each task, which includes the description, guidelines, duration, start and end dates, team or person assigned, and the percentage of the task completed. The implementation schedule presented in this section may be changed or customized to more closely meet the needs of your company. Table 15.1 outlines the ACME implementation schedule.

T A B L E 15.1

Proposed ACME
Implementation Schedule

TASK DESCRIPTION	DURATION	START DATE	END DATE	TEAM ASSIGNED	%COMPLETE
1. Project Scope	12w	1/1/97	2/1/97	Project Team	
1.1 Determine Roles and Responsibilities					
1.2 Determine Milestones					
1.3 Determine Critical Path					
1.4 Determine Success Factors					
1.5 Risk Analysis					
1.6 Establish Reporting and Tracking					
1.7 Documentation Procedures					
1.8 Test Strategies and Acceptance Testing					
2. Training	20w	1/1/97	6/1/97	Training	
2.1 Determine Training Needs					
2.2 Training Strategies					
2.3 Obtain Training					
2.4 Set Up the Lab					
3. NDS Design	6w	3/1/97	4/15/97	NDS Team	
3.1 NDS Naming Standard	2w	3/1/97	3/15/97	NDS Team	
3.11 Identify Existing Standards					
3.12 Create NDS Naming Documents					
3.13 Create File System Standard Structure					
3.14 Deliver Standards Documents					

TASK DESCRIPTION	DURATION	START DATE	END DATE	TEAM ASSIGNED	%COMPLETE
3.2 NDS Tree	5d	3/15/97	3/20/97	NDS Team	
3.21 Gather Corporate Documents					
3.22 Review WAN Maps					
3.23 Review Campus Maps					
3.24 Design Top of the Tree					
3.25 Review Organization					
3.26 Review Resource List					
3.27 Design Bottom of the Tree					
3.28 Place Network Resources in Containers					
3.29 Apply Design Considerations					
3.29.1 Administration					
3.29.2 Partitioning					
3.29.3 Login Scripts					
3.29.4 Bindery Services					
3.29.5 Test NDS Tree Design					
3.3 Design Partitions and Replicas	5d	3/21/97	3/26/97	NDS Team	
3.31 Review WAN Map					
3.32 Partition Top of the Tree					
3.33 Replica Strategy					
3.33.1 Replicate Locality					
3.33.2 Replicate for Fault Tolerance					
3.34 Partition Bottom as Needed					
3.35 Develop Partition and Replica Guidelines					

(continued)

TASK DESCRIPTION	DURATION	START DATE	END DATE	TEAM ASSIGNED	%COMPLETE
3.36 Test Partitions and Replica Strategy					
3.4 Design Time Synchronization	1d	3/27/97	3/28/97	NDS Team	
3.41 Evaluate TimeSync Options					
3.41.1 Single Reference (Default)					
3.41.2 Time Provider Group					
3.42 Choose Option Based on WAN					
3.43 Evaluate TimeSync Communications					
3.43.1 Service Advertising Protocol (SAP)					
3.43.2 Configured List					
3.44 Develop Time Synchronization Strategy					
3.45 Test Time Synchronization Strategy					
3.5 NDS Accessibility Plan	4d	3/30/97	4/4/97	NDS Team	
3.51 Analyze Existing Login Scripts					
3.52 Move System Login Script to Container Login Script					
3.53 Test Login Scripts					
3.53.1 Container Login Scripts					
3.53.2 Profile Login Scripts					
3.54 Establish Access with NetWare Application Launcher (NAL)					
3.55 Develop Mobile User Strategy					
3.56 Test Mobile User Access					
3.57 Deliver Accessibility Plan					
4. Security and Audit	10d	4/5/97	4/15/97	Administration	
4.1 Server Security					
4.11 Server Settings					

TASK DESCRIPTION	DURATION	START DATE	END DATE	TEAM ASSIGNED	%COMPLETE
4.2 NDS Security					
4.21 Object Security					
4.22 Property Security					
4.23 Develop NDS Security Strategy					
4.24 Test Security Strategy					
4.3 File System Security					
4.31 Develop File System Strategy					
4.32 Test File System Strategy					
4.4 Audit					
4.41 Define Audit Procedures					
4.42 Understand Audit Utilities					
4.43 Develop Audit Strategy					
4.44 Test Audit Strategy					
5. Client Migration	10w	3/1/97	5/15/97	Client Team	
5.1 Functional Testing for Each Desktop					
5.2 Evaluate Client Migration Options					
5.3 Determine Client Migration Strategy					
5.4 Test Client Migration Strategy					
6. Server Migration	20w	5/1/97	10/1/97	Server Team	
6.1 Evaluate In-Place Utility					
6.2 Evaluate Across-the-Wire Utility					
6.3 Evaluate DSMIGRATE Utility					
6.4 Determine Strategy for Server Migrations					

(continued)

TASK DESCRIPTION	DURATION	START DATE	END DATE	TEAM ASSIGNED	%COMPLETE
6.5 Perform Mock Migration in the Lab					
6.6 Test Server Migration Strategy					
6.7 Develop and Establish File System Standards					
6.8 Determine Cleanup Procedures					
6.9 Develop Backup and Restore Strategy					
7. Printing	5w	3/1/97	4/15/97	Print Team	
7.1 Identify Existing Printing Environment					
7.2 Evaluate Proposed Printing Layout					
7.3 Evaluate Direct Print Cards and Printers					
7.4 Determine Printing Migration Strategy					
7.5 Evaluate NetWare Distributed Print Services					
7.6 Test Printing Migration Strategy					
8. Applications	5w	3/1/97	4/15/97	Applications	
8.1 Identify All Server-based and Client-based Applications					
8.11 Identify and Create Application Objects in NDS					
8.2 For Internally Written Applications					
8.21 Install					
8.22 Test on a Desktop					
8.23 Test on Server					
8.24 Test Printing					
8.25 Document Compatibility					
8.3 Deliver Applications in Production Using NAL					
9. Server Pilot and Rollout	5w	4/1/97	5/10/97	Server and Administration	
9.1 Server Preparation					

TASK DESCRIPTION	DURATION	START DATE	END DATE	TEAM ASSIGNED	%COMPLETE
9.11 Perform Cleanup (Objects and Files)					
9.12 Apply Naming Standards on NetWare 3 servers					
9.13 Run BINDFIX					
9.14 Back up the Server					
9.2 Installation or Migration					
9.21 Upgrade Server to IntranetWare					
9.22 Test Server (production-like)					
9.23 Document Any Problems					
9.24 Modify Procedures Based on Results					
9.3 Acceptance Testing					
9.31 Provide Daily Support to User					
9.32 Validate Functionality of the Servers					

Setting Up a Testing Lab

Obtaining experience with a product such as IntranetWare can be assisted by creating a lab environment. The lab experience provides the opportunity to understand how IntranetWare operates at your particular site with your particular network characteristics. We recommend that a lab be utilized for any company or organization that can afford the additional resources or may already have a lab in place. For smaller sites without the resources of a lab you can obtain hands-on experience with IntranetWare through educational training or perhaps through your integrator.

The lab is a safe environment where you can make changes and view the impact of those changes on the NDS tree. You can test many of the features and functions of IntranetWare and become acquainted with the product. This section will first discuss the components of a lab. Next, it will cover the areas that you should test in your lab. Keep in mind that the lab experience can be short yet productive. After reading this section you should be able to define the areas of lab testing that fit your needs. You can create a checklist of these items to help you focus on a completion date for the lab process.

EVALUATING THE NEED FOR A LAB

The decision to have a lab is entirely dependent upon your circumstances. Although most small sites do not have the resources to install a lab, they can benefit by gaining some hands-on experience through their integrator or education center. For small sites that plan to use the default configurations, the lab is not as crucial but can provide you with valuable administrative experience. If your site is small and you do have a lab, we recommend a brief testing period in the lab to familiarize yourself with IntranetWare, especially from an administrative standpoint. Setting up a lab and installing IntranetWare will also instill confidence in your project team as they learn about the features and capabilities of IntranetWare. It will also give you time to work with the operating system, perform diagnostics, and test utilities and applications.

Implementation of an IntranetWare lab is recommended for any site that will install or migrate more than 30 IntranetWare servers. Many customers will move from the default settings of IntranetWare to configurable parameters at approximately this number of servers. Therefore, the lab gives you the opportunity to adjust and test various configuration parameters.

For larger sites with a Wide Area Network (WAN) in place, we recommend that you follow, where applicable, the lab procedures presented in this section. Network administrators of large sites should fully familiarize themselves with the functions and features of IntranetWare before beginning a full-scale migration to IntranetWare.

For the ACME site, lab testing is being handled at the NORAD facility in the LABS department. All new software and hardware is evaluated at this facility before being deployed onto the production network. Therefore, the new operating system being deployed in the ACME tree has gone through the lab process.

THE LAB SETUP

Many large organizations have a permanent lab for testing all new software and hardware that may be placed into production at their site. Others may be considering the creation of a temporary lab for this project. In either case, you will need to dedicate some hardware for use as IntranetWare servers and workstations for the duration of your lab project.

Your lab should consist of a minimum of four nodes — two IntranetWare servers and two workstations. The servers and adapter cards should be similar to the hardware that will be used in your network environment. If you are planning to upgrade your hardware, then use the new hardware in your lab environment. Each IntranetWare server should exceed the minimum recommendations provided by Novell. You want to duplicate your actual environment as closely as possible. In addition, you will want to duplicate your LAN topology where possible.

Figure 15.1 shows the ACME lab for testing IntranetWare for the entire ACME tree installation. This lab has four dedicated IntranetWare servers and three workstations to run the Novell and third-party utilities. In addition, because the ACME network is primarily a token ring, we have a token ring concentrator in the lab to connect the servers and workstations together. All file servers have a CD-ROM drive as well as sufficient disk and memory capacity. The lab ring also has a connection to the corporate backbone located in the labs division of NORAD.

Your lab can be smaller with three nodes. A three-node network would consist of two IntranetWare file servers and a single workstation. One of the servers must have a CD-ROM device for installing IntranetWare. Also, if possible, have a network connection to your backbone so that you can access any servers currently in operation on your network. A minimal configuration is shown in Figure 15.2.

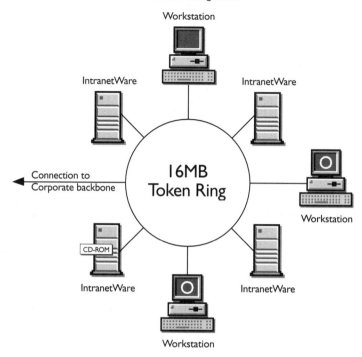

FIGURE 15.1

The ACME lab consists of four IntranetWare servers and three workstations.

ACME Lab Configuration

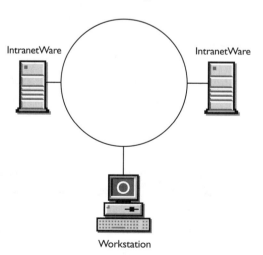

FIGURE 15.2

A minimal lab configuration would have two IntranetWare servers and a single workstation.

Minimal Lab Configuration

THE LAB PROCESS

The lab process simply provides order and direction to help you accomplish your objectives in the lab. Without such direction, a lab simply becomes a bunch of PCs that are not utilized, and the lab experience wears on until people lose interest in what they are trying to accomplish. With some specific objectives, you will be able to provide a thorough test of IntranetWare and obtain experience before beginning a large-scale migration.

Your network administrators can put into practice the information presented in this book such as NDS tree design, partitioning and replication strategies, and security procedures. The following areas can be evaluated in your lab and will be discussed here:

- ▶ Lab installation

- ▶ Hardware setup and required components

- ▶ Installation of IntranetWare Design

- ▶ NDS tree implementation

- ▶ Create partitions and replicas

- ▶ Time synchronization configuration

- ▶ Design and test container login scripts

- ▶ Design and test administration/security procedures

- ▶ Software testing

- ▶ Application testing

- ▶ Novell utility testing

- ▶ Third-party utilities

- ▶ Backup and restore procedures

- ▶ Implementation of the IntranetWare Pilot System

Lab Installation

For those sites that already have a lab in place, you can simply designate a group of servers for your test along with a few workstations. You will want to follow the IntranetWare installation procedures discussed in Chapter 16 as well as the procedures discussed in the "Install IntranetWare" section later in this chapter.

Companies creating a lab from scratch can follow the procedures outlined below.

Hardware and Required Components

Perhaps the most time-consuming aspect of installing IntranetWare is installing and connecting a CD-ROM drive. Your job will be made much simpler if you obtain the latest CD-ROM drivers from Novell and/or your third-party manufacturers. You'll save hours of frustration when mounting your CD-ROMs if you have the latest drivers running on your hardware.

For most hardware products, you can obtain their latest drivers by connecting to their bulletin boards. All drivers that are contained on the Novell NetWare 4.11 CD-ROM have been tested with IntranetWare.

Mounting a CD-ROM as a NetWare Volume   The following steps will help you install your CD-ROM as a NetWare volume:

1 • Access the following directory on the NetWare 4.11 CD: PRODUCTS\NW411\IBM\411DISKDRV.

2 • Download the appropriate .DSK files to your SYS:\SYSTEM directory. Then load ASPICD.DSK or CDNASPI.DSK or an appropriate driver depending on your hardware.

3 • From the server console type:

```
LOAD CDROM.NLM
```

(Your appropriate .DSK driver may require the setting ABOVE 16=y.)

4 • After loading the previous drivers, type the following at the console:

```
CD DEVICE LIST
```

(to list the CD loaded)

`CD VOLUME LIST`

(to list the volume name and number for CD currently loaded)

5 • You then issue a CD MOUNT <volume name> or CD Device # and the CD will mount as a NetWare volume.

With a NetWare volume mounted you can then map a drive to this volume and access the CD-ROM device.

Install IntranetWare

You can refer to Chapter 16 for detailed information on installation procedures. For the lab exercise you can install the IntranetWare operating system on each of your lab servers. Loading the software is not difficult, but you should familiarize yourself with the different installation options such as the Simple Install and Custom Install.

You should also practice removing NDS from the server. On occasion you may have to remove a server from the tree because of hardware repairs or shipment to another location, and you should follow the appropriate steps to remove a server from the tree.

Familiarize yourself with the INSTALL utility and its features. You may have to add new NLMs or additional licenses, and the INSTALL utility handles these procedures.

If you are migrating from NetWare 3 to IntranetWare and you have the hardware, you can perform a migration of a current NetWare 3 server to a lab IntranetWare server. This approach allows you to upgrade your hardware to a new platform for IntranetWare and does not endanger your current NetWare 3 server.

Create the NDS tree

The creation of your NDS tree in your lab should be based on the information discussed in the other chapters in this book. For modeling your lab tree you can use the DSMIGRATE Utility to simplify this process. In addition, refer back to Chapter 5 for information and design strategies.

The lab tree that you install either with the DSMIGRATE or with Novell's NWADMIN utility will eventually become your production tree. So, take the

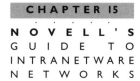
necessary time to define the appropriate levels and placement of resources. If you have a successful and functional lab tree, you do not need to re-create another tree unless you want to maintain separate trees for testing purposes.

Create Partitions and Replicas

The first partition created is the default [ROOT] partition. After your lab servers are up and running you can use the NWADMIN, or PARTMGR, or NDS Manager utilities to further partition each of your sites into separate partitions subordinate to [ROOT]. Use your lab to learn how to create replicas as well. Because the size of your lab may be somewhat limited, you still should learn how the partition utilities place replicas on servers. You can also learn how to identify the locations of the replicas by viewing them with the utilities.

Configure Time Synchronization

Your lab servers will initially have time synchronization set up with the defaults. Your first NetWare 4 server is installed as a Single Reference server. All other servers are Secondary.

Familiarize yourself with the TimeSync parameters through the various SET commands as well as the SERVMAN utility. You can change the default settings through the SERVMAN utility. For example, you can create a small-time provider group by changing your Single Reference server to a Reference server. Then change the other two or three lab servers to Primary servers. With a LANalyzer or other equipment you can view the packets sent and received for each time synchronization interval.

Use other commands such as SET TIMESYNC DEBUG=7 to enable the time synchronization screen on your IntranetWare server. This screen will show you the status of time synchronization and the adjustments being made if this server's time is not synchronized.

Design and Test Container Login Scripts

The lab is a great place to design and test your container login scripts. Populate one of your containers with actual user objects from your company. Test the container login script for errors and to verify that all necessary environment variables have been defined.

If you are planning to use Profile scripts as well, the lab is the perfect place to test the functionality of these scripts.

Application Testing in Your Lab

Not all applications need to be tested for IntranetWare compatibility. However, some applications, especially those written inside your corporation, may require some testing. The following points should be considered when you are testing applications:

▸ Is the application bindery based? Bindery-based applications require Bindery Services to be enabled on that server as well as a read/write replica of the defined context.

▸ Were these applications written for the NETX client of some other operating system? If so, they should be tested on a workstation with the new client software. Some basic and easy tests you can perform are listed below:

    ▸ Run the application to completion or proper termination.

    ▸ Print a document with the application.

    ▸ Using the application, do a file save of your work onto the IntranetWare server.

    ▸ Test your tape backup application support for IntranetWare and NDS.

    ▸ Keep your application testing procedure short and simple. You will never be able to test every feature and function of every product. Concentrate your efforts on the specialty applications that are not in the mainstream.

Administer network applications using NetWare Application Launcher (NAL). NAL enables you to represent applications as objects in the NetWare Directory. As Directory objects, you can manage Application objects the same way you manage other objects, using the NWADMIN utility. Using Application objects you can:

▸ Define an application's directory, icon, command line parameters, and other properties in one place

▸ Use trustee assignments to manage access to an application

▸ Define startup scripts that establish the appropriate network environment for the application (drive mappings, print captures, and so on) and cleanup scripts that restore the workstation's environment

Gain Experience with Your Utilities

The fact that you have installed a lab will automatically give you experience with Novell and NetWare and, most likely, third-party utilities. You will be exposed to the following utilities with a lab in place:

▸ NDS Manager

▸ NWADMIN (Partition Manager)

▸ PARTMGR (DOS based)

▸ SERVMAN.NLM

▸ INSTALL.NLM

▸ DSREPAIR.NLM

▸ DSTRACE (not really a utility, but a diagnostic tool)

▸ NWUSER

▸ DSMIGRATE

▸ MIGRATE.EXE

Review and work through each utility to gain experience and confidence with the operation of these tools.

Backup and Restore Procedures

Perform a full backup and restore of an IntranetWare server. This backup includes files as well as NDS tree information. Always have a clear understanding of backup procedures related to your specific backup product. The lab is the best place to gain experience in backup and recovery procedures. For more information on Backup and Restoration of NDS, refer to Chapter 19.

IntranetWare Pilot System

A pilot system is the first IntranetWare server placed into production on your network. A pilot system will be the baseline system you will use to test all the operational procedures that you have developed for the migration to IntranetWare. You can use either the In-Place or Across-the-Wire migration to perform the migration of users and data, depending on the previous network operating system from which you are migrating.

If you can use separate hardware for a migration, you can safely migrate a server without affecting the production server. Once you have successfully performed the migration, you can redirect the actual users or group of users to the new IntranetWare server. The server you choose to migrate as the pilot system should probably be a server that is used by the technical staff at your facility. This way the staff members will become familiar with the operation of the IntranetWare server in production.

Use the pilot system to optimize your workstation configurations including AUTOEXEC.BAT, CONFIG.SYS, NET.CFG, and any other files required for your installation.

The pilot system process for IntranetWare does not require an enormous amount of time. The purpose of the pilot system is to provide adequate experience for you and your staff with the IntranetWare server in your production environment. If you feel you have reached that point after only a couple of weeks, then the pilot system has most likely served its purpose.

Basics of Server Migration

"A permanent state of transition is man's most noble condition."
Juan Ramon Jimenez

This chapter explores the many methods for installing and migrating your servers to IntranetWare. Each method has its merits, and you can choose the method that most closely meets your needs and circumstances. There are many considerations when determining which migration method to use. These considerations are discussed here in each migration section. Some network migrations may require multiple methods depending on the circumstances of the migration. For example, some sites may decide to purchase new hardware for their migration to IntranetWare and use one migration utility for the entire process. Other companies may have multiple departments, each responsible for its own migration and each with its own budgetary constraints. They may choose to keep their existing hardware, and hence, a different migration process may be used. This chapter focuses on migrations from previous versions of NetWare. For information on migrations from other operating systems refer to Chapter 17.

IntranetWare provides you with four migration methods:

▸ In-place upgrade

▸ Across-the-wire migration

▸ Same server migration

▸ Upgrade existing NetWare 4 servers to IntranetWare

▸ DS MIGRATE

▸ File migration utility

For more information on migrating existing NetWare 4 servers to IntranetWare, refer to Novell's NetWire file called 4X241.EXE. Please see Novell's documentation and instructions found in this file for more information.

This chapter will also explore other migration alternatives such as Preferred Systems DS Standard product, or using Novell's NETSYNC and RCONSOLE to assist in migrations. While beyond the scope of this book, you may also want to consider using one of the many commercially available scripting languages for your migrations. Scripting languages have proven to be very useful in automating large scale migrations and server updates.

Spend some time analyzing and understanding the different migration options available to you. The advantages and disadvantages of each upgrade method are discussed here. For more information on actual installation steps and procedures for IntranetWare, see Chapter 2.

CONSULTING EXPERIENCE

Take some time to practice the migration options in your lab if you can. If you do not have the additional hardware to create a new server, make sure that you take all the necessary precautions to back up your current servers before beginning a migration. Our experience has shown that those who can practice migrations in a lab will have fewer problems during an actual migration to IntranetWare.

Basic Hardware Requirements

Novell's success over the years has been the capability of its products to operate on a large variety of hardware at either the server or workstation levels. As with the earlier products, IntranetWare and its associated client products operate well on a variety of hardware platforms. The speed of your server hardware, however, has become much more important when you are using IntranetWare servers to interoperate together on the network. Obviously, the faster your hardware, the better performance you will have with IntranetWare. Enhanced performance will not only increase the speed of access for your clients, it will improve the speed of NDS synchronization operations and the associated NDS background processes. So, look closely at your current hardware and understand that your most heavily utilized servers should be your fastest and most powerful. Below is a list of the minimum server hardware needed to operate IntranetWare. We also include a *recommended* list of hardware for IntranetWare.

MINIMUM CONFIGURATION

For 10 Users

▸ A PC with a 386 or 486 processor

▸ 8MB RAM

▸ 90MB hard disk space (SYS volume requires 75MB)

▸ 16-bit NIC card

▸ CD-ROM device installed on the server to be upgraded

▸ 3.5-inch floppy drive

▸ Any low-cost monitor with VGA card

RECOMMENDED CONFIGURATION FOR YOUR BUSIEST SERVERS

For 250 Users

▸ Intel Pentium class or compatible

▸ 32MB RAM (even more is better)

▸ 2GB hard disk minimum

▸ EISA or PCI bus-mastering NIC card

▸ 4X speed CD-ROM drive

▸ 3.5-inch floppy drive

▸ Any low-cost monitor with VGA card

Preparing for Your Migration

Regardless of the migration method you choose there are some basic preparations that need to be accomplished before you start your migration. These steps are listed and explained here.

PREPARE YOUR NETWARE SERVER FOR MIGRATION

NOTE

Refer to Chapters 15 and 19 for more information regarding the preparations listed below.

1 • Back up your NetWare server before beginning a migration. Always make sure that you have tested the restoration of a tape backup as well.

2 • Delete unneeded files and directories before beginning a migration. Your migration will be shortened if you have fewer files to migrate. Besides, this is a good time to perform that long overdue cleanup of your volumes.

3 • Run the SALVAGE utility to salvage or purge deleted files. Once a migration is performed you cannot salvage previously deleted files. So, if any deleted files need to be restored, you must do it before the migration.

4 • Ensure that no subdirectories exceed a depth of 25. The MIGRATE.EXE utility used in the across-the-wire migration process will copy subdirectories only to the 25th level.

5 • Prepare your bindery by deleting unnecessary objects. Keep in mind that duplicate user names migrated into the same container will have their trustee assignments combined into one user with the same name. For other duplicate objects, the first object migrated is accepted, while the second duplicate is discarded. Therefore, if you have a group and a print queue with the same name, the first is migrated and the second is discarded.

6 • Run the BINDFIX utility to clean up your bindery and discard entries for users that no longer exist on that server.

DESIGN YOUR NOVELL DIRECTORY SERVICES TREE

NOTE **Refer to Chapters 5, 6, and 7 for more information regarding the preparations listed below.**

1 • Implement your NDS naming standards.

2 • You should have an NDS tree design before starting your migration to IntranetWare. The design consists of three steps:

   a • Designing a Novell Directory Services tree

   b • Designing NDS partitions and replicas

   c • Designing time synchronization

NOTE **Before starting a migration, determine where you will install the new server in the Directory tree. Also, determine where you want to migrate the users, groups, and printing objects. These objects will migrate by default to the container specified as the destination IntranetWare server's bindery context.**

PERFORM THE MIGRATION AND POST MIGRATION ACTIVITIES

NOTE **Refer to Chapters 2, 12, and 14 for more information regarding the preparations listed below.**

1 • You can use the information explained below to help you make a decision on which migration option to use.

2 • Update your login scripts for your users and containers. For small sites you may have user login scripts that are migrated from NetWare 3 to IntranetWare. Verify that the scripts were migrated properly after the migration. In addition, you will most likely have to create container login scripts as well. You can cut and paste your old system login script into the container login script (usually requires modification) or you can create a new script within NDS.

3 • Distribute the migrated objects to their appropriate containers. The bindery objects are migrated into the same context as the server object. After a migration you may have to move some objects to other containers in your tree.

4 • Check any user restrictions that you may have set in NetWare 3 to make sure they are in effect in IntranetWare. There is no need to check all users; a few randomly chosen users will suffice to verify that things are okay.

5 • Verify that your print services are functioning properly. Verify that your users can print to the appropriate print queues and that all print services have migrated properly. Depending on the migration option you use, you will have to run some further print migration utilities.

6 • Verify that your users' applications work properly on IntranetWare. This should be a very simple test to see if the application can perform basic functions such as PRINT and SAVE. Further testing is not necessary for most commercially available applications.

In-Place Upgrade Migration Method

The in-place upgrade method is used primarily for migrating servers from NetWare 3 to IntranetWare using the same hardware. You can also use this method for upgrading from NetWare 2 to IntranetWare, as explained in the second half of this section.

For example, Figure 16.1 illustrates the process of upgrading a NetWare 3.12 server to IntranetWare on the same server hardware device.

FIGURE 16.1

*Upgrading a NetWare 3.12
server to IntranetWare
using the same server
hardware device*

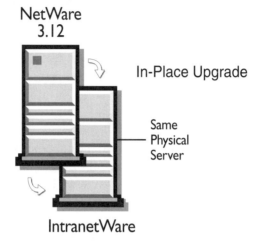

Since the file server hardware stays the same, the data volumes remain the same. Only new files are added to the SYS: volume in the system subdirectories and the DOS partition during the in-place migration process. The data files on the other volumes on the NetWare 3 server will not be moved or changed. The files that do get upgraded include LOGIN, SERVER.EXE, Lan drivers (*.LAN), Disk Drivers (*.DSK), and other NetWare Loadable Modules (*.NLM).

The IntranetWare INSTALL utility will install NDS onto a NetWare 3 server and then upgrade the bindery to NDS. This utility will attempt to migrate all objects found in the bindery to NDS.

The in-place migration method is the fastest migration method because it does not move the data files to another server. The other migration methods, such as across-the-wire and file copy, are slower because all the user data must be migrated across the LAN or WAN networks.

The NetWare 3.12 server is upgraded to IntranetWare by executing the In-Place Upgrade Migration utility known as the IntranetWare INSTALL.EXE program. The IntranetWare installation program can be started in DOS on the device being used as the server hardware by accessing the IntranetWare CD-ROM. The main menu for the installation program appears as shown in Figure 16.2. From the main menu you would select the NetWare Server Installation option.

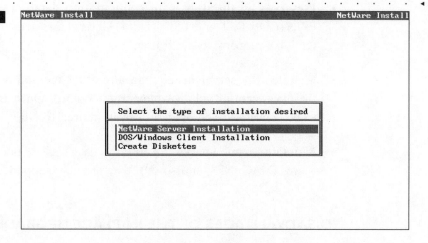

You then want to select the options IntranetWare and Upgrade NetWare v3 or v4.x to begin the in-place migration.

When making your decision on the type of migration method to use, keep in mind the following advantages and disadvantages of the in-place upgrade process.

ADVANTAGES OF THE IN-PLACE UPGRADE

▸ **Uses the same physical server hardware**, thus eliminating the cost of a new server hardware system just to perform the migration. Look carefully at your hardware at this point, however. That old 386 NetWare 3 server buried in your wiring closet somewhere may not pass muster with IntranetWare. You may still have to upgrade your hardware.

▸ **Preserves passwords.** Once on IntranetWare, your users will not need to enter a new password when they initially log in.

▸ **Migrates the existing bindery information with full NDS compatibility**, meaning that all the users, groups, and trustee assignments are migrated and preserved on IntranetWare. Users' login scripts will be placed directly into the corresponding NDS property for each user if they are present in the bindery.

▸ **Preserves all the user print configuration databases.** The
PRINTCON.DAT and PRINTDEF.DAT databases are written directly into
the NDS property for each user.

▸ **Migrates the server faster than any other method available.** The data in
the file system or volumes remain unmodified. Only the bindery files need
to be converted. The bindery files are moved to NDS.

▸ **Maintains name spaces.** Because the data files are not changing the name
spaces (MAC, NFS, and so on), they are fully supported.

DISADVANTAGES OF THE IN-PLACE UPGRADE

▸ **Does not allow the volume block size of the server to be changed.**
Whenever possible, we recommend that each IntranetWare server have
64K volume blocks, which provide for the greatest performance of disk
reads and writes. But, since the file system remains intact during the in-
place migration, you will have the original volume block size set for your
server (possibly 4K blocks).

NOTE

**If you use the In-Place Upgrade Migration utility you can still change
your volume block size after migration but only with some effort. In
order to change the volume block size follow these steps:**

1. Back up the data to tape.

2. Delete the NetWare volume.

3. Create the volume and specify the 64K block size.

4. Restore data from the tape.

5. Bring the IntranetWare server back up.

▸ **Does not allow suballocation for the file system to be turned on before
the migration begins.** Suballocation can easily be turned on after the
upgrade, but the suballocation will affect only the subsequent writing of
files to the disk. Therefore, any file that is rewritten to the disk will be
suballocated.

▸ May require a restoration from a tape backup if a failure occurs during the upgrade process.

NOTE **The in-place upgrade migration process is restartable if a failure should occur. There are, however, windows of vulnerability that may cause a failure and still require you to restore from tape.**

USING THE IN-PLACE UPGRADE FOR NETWARE 2 TO NETWARE 3

For servers running NetWare 2, you can use the In-Place Upgrade Migration utility called 2XUPGRDE.NLM to migrate from NetWare 2 to NetWare 3.12. Then use the IntranetWare installation program to finish upgrading to IntranetWare. The in-place upgrade NetWare Loadable Module (2XUPGRDE.NLM) reformats a server's NetWare 2.1x or NetWare 2.2 partition, without losing any data, and transforms it into a NetWare 3.12 file system partition.

NOTE **The in-place upgrade migration method upgrades only NetWare 2.1x or NetWare 2.2 servers to IntranetWare. For previous versions of NetWare, you will have to first upgrade to these versions before proceeding.**

The upgrade process actually occurs in several stages in which the NetWare 2 file system and bindery are upgraded to NetWare 3.12. The second stage is to install the new operating system.

WARNING **Many servers running any version of NetWare 2 will not have the horsepower to support IntranetWare. Carefully evaluate this situation as you may want to use only the in-place upgrade option to move to NetWare 3.12 so that you can migrate your data to a newer, more powerful server platform using the Across-the-Wire Migration utility.**

Keep in mind that user passwords are not retained when you upgrade to NetWare 3.12. As with the across-the-wire migration, you can have the utility generate random passwords. These random passwords are stored in a file called NEW.PWD in your SYS:SYSTEM directory.

In addition, all Value Added Processes (VAPs) and core printing services are not upgraded with this process.

Refer to the Novell documentation for step-by-step instructions for migrating from NetWare 2 to NetWare 3.

Across-the-Wire Migration Method

The across-the-wire migration method will migrate your data and bindery files from NetWare 2 or 3 to IntranetWare. The MIGRATE utility is run on a DOS workstation and facilitates the transfer of the files and bindery information from the NetWare 2 or 3 servers to the IntranetWare server. The workstation running the MIGRATE utility will read the administrative information and data files from the source server and write it to the IntranetWare server. The connecting workstation running the MIGRATE utility must have bindery Supervisor access on both servers (NetWare 2 or 3 and IntranetWare) before initiating the migration process. Figure 16.3 illustrates conceptually how the across-the-wire migration process is run on a DOS workstation between the servers being migrated.

Because the utility runs on the workstation and has the responsibility to move all the data, the faster the workstation's CPU, the faster the migration. We recommend that the workstation be a 486 66 MHz or better with at least 480K of free memory. The workstation needs at least a 16-bit LAN card, although a 32 bit will increase performance.

NOTE

Although a slower workstation with an 8-bit LAN card will perform an across-the-wire migration, it will increase the time needed to complete. We recommend that you find the fastest PC possible and place it on the same network segment as the server being migrated.

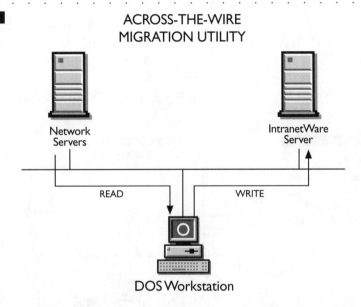

FIGURE 16.3

*The across-the-wire
migration process is run
on a DOS workstation
between the NetWare 3
and IntranetWare
servers being migrated.*

ACROSS-THE-WIRE
MIGRATION UTILITY

To start the migration process at the DOS workstation, you first need to connect and log in to both the source (NetWare 2 or 3) and destination (IntranetWare) servers as a supervisor or equivalent access rights. The MIGRATE.EXE utility is then executed and will bring up the main menu shown in Figure 16.4.

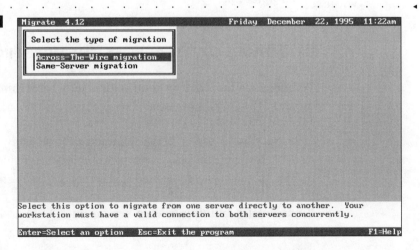

FIGURE 16.4

*Main menu for the Across-
the-Wire Migration utility
MIGRATE.EXE*

The Across-the-Wire Migration utility tracks and logs all of the actions of the migration's progress. The log file is written on the hard drive of the workstation running MIGRATE.EXE. The space required for the log file is approximately 1MB for every 1GB of data migrated. Figure 16.5 shows the log file created at the workstation during an across-the-wire process. Make sure that the workstation has the necessary capacity or the migration will not complete. The minimum is 5MB.

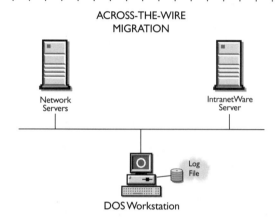

FIGURE 16.5

The log file that tracks the events and actions of the across-the-wire migration process is created and held on the DOS workstation.

ACROSS-THE-WIRE
MIGRATION

WARNING

Do not attempt to run the migration with less than the minimum disk space for the log file. The migration utility will not run to completion.

ADVANTAGES OF THE ACROSS-THE-WIRE MIGRATION

▸ **Migrates all the bindery information into NDS (bindery services mode).** The users, groups, and trustee assignments are maintained.

▸ **The NetWare 3 server being migrated is Read Only**, and the data files and bindery remain intact, thus preserving your original server if the migration cannot be completed because of any problems.

▸ **Consolidates multiple source servers into a single IntranetWare server.** The source servers can be migrated into a single, larger IntranetWare server.

▸ **Gives you the opportunity to replace or upgrade the server to newer, more powerful hardware.**

▸ **Selectively migrates the data files or bindery information.** You can select a volume from the source server to be moved to the new IntranetWare server as a new volume:directory combination.

▸ **Multiple DOS workstations can migrate the same server with different volumes at the same time**, meaning that you can have more than one workstation processing the information and migrating it.

▸ **You can change the volume block size on the new server volumes.** You can select the volume block size during the installation of the IntranetWare server to the recommended 64K.

NOTE

We recommend that you always select a volume block size of 64K. With the suballocation feature provided in IntranetWare, a block size of 64K will give you the best performance of file reads and writes without losing disk space.

▸ Enables file suballocation before the migration of the data files.

DISADVANTAGES OF THE ACROSS-THE-WIRE MIGRATION

▸ **Procedure is slower than the in-place upgrade method.** Because the DOS workstation is transferring all the data files across the network, the selected data being copied could disrupt other network traffic. For this reason, the across-the-wire migration process may need to be executed during off-peak hours.

▸ **Passwords are not preserved by the workstation doing the migration.** You have several options for handling passwords. You can migrate with the No Password option or you can have the utility generate random passwords for each user. See the "Using NETSYNC with Across-the-Wire Migrations" section later in this chapter.

▶ **DOS name spaces or files are the only name spaces supported.** The
MAC, NFS, and other name spaces are not supported through the DOS
workstation. You can do a file copy using a native desktop machine to move
the files with name spaces after the migration, thus preserving those files.

SERVER CONNECTIONS FOR ACROSS-THE-WIRE

The Across-the-Wire Migration utility is limited to a bindery services connection
from the DOS workstation for both the source and destination servers. You will be
required to establish the bindery connection before you initiate the MIGRATE.EXE
program. In order to establish the bindery connections, log in to the IntranetWare
server using only bindery services. This may require that you load the VLMs with
a /B option. For example, you would type:

```
VLM /B
```

After you are attached to the server, you need to log in as follows:

```
LOGIN <server name>/SUPERVISOR /B
```

This migration utility will not let you log in to the IntranetWare server if you are
previously logged in as an NDS client. You must log out of the NDS connection
and log back in with a bindery connection.

As the bindery is read from the source server, all the users, groups, and other
objects are placed in the NDS container where the IntranetWare server bindery
context is set. The server bindery context for the IntranetWare server should be set
before the migration is started. To set the server bindery context at the server console,
you would type:

```
SET BINDERY CONTEXT = <context>.
```

You can also set the context by using the SERVMAN.NLM utility.

MIGRATE SELECTED INFORMATION WITH ACROSS-THE-WIRE

The Across-the-Wire Migration utility enables you to perform selective migration between the servers. You can decide the type of migration information you want. You can decide whether to retain the user objects, trustee assignments, group memberships, print services, and others during a migration.

Figure 16.6 displays the information you can select to migrate during the migration process. The type of information you can migrate with a description is also shown in Table 16.1.

FIGURE 16.6

Across-the-wire migration screen used to select the information you want to migrate

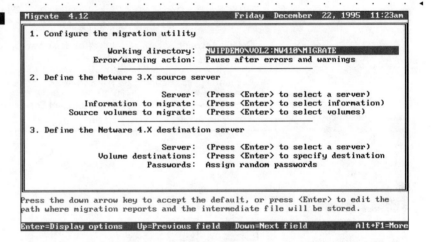

```
Migrate  4.12                          Friday  December  22, 1995  11:23am

 1. Configure the migration utility

            Working directory:  NWIPDEMO\VOL2:NW410\MIGRATE
            Error/warning action:  Pause after errors and warnings

 2. Define the Netware 3.X source server

                       Server:  (Press <Enter> to select a server)
          Information to migrate:  (Press <Enter> to select information)
       Source volumes to migrate:  (Press <Enter> to select volumes)

 3. Define the Netware 4.X destination server

                       Server:  (Press <Enter> to select a server)
            Volume destinations:  (Press <Enter> to specify destination
                    Passwords:  Assign random passwords


Press the down arrow key to accept the default, or press <Enter> to edit the
path where migration reports and the intermediate file will be stored.
Enter=Display options    Up=Previous field    Down=Next field    Alt+F1=More
```

CHANGING OR CONSOLIDATING SERVER HARDWARE

The across-the-wire migration process can be used to upgrade or replace server hardware, as well as consolidate multiple network servers into a single IntranetWare server. If new hardware is being installed, this utility is the best migration method to use. As mentioned above, this utility migrates data and bindery or bindery-like information from the current server or servers across the network to the new IntranetWare server via a DOS client workstation. It does not migrate a NetWare 4.0x server to IntranetWare. For information on how this process is accomplished, see Novell's documentation found on NetWire.

Figure 16.7 illustrates how multiple network servers can be consolidated into a single IntranetWare platform.

T A B L E   16.1

*The type of information
available for migration by
the Across-the-Wire
Migration utility*

TYPE OF INFORMATION	DESCRIPTION
All Information	(Default) Migrates all the information contained in the table
Data Files	Migrates all the data files and the NetWare attributes
Trustee Assignments	Migrates the file and directory rights associated with each object
Users	Migrates user accounts
User Restrictions	Migrates the user account restrictions
Groups	Migrates the group object and the membership lists
Default Account Restrictions	Migrates default account restrictions
Accounting Information	Migrates the accounting for each object
Print Queues And Print Servers	Migrates LAN Server and LAN Manager print queues only

F I G U R E   16.7

*The Across-the-Wire
Migration utility enables
you to migrate several
existing servers onto one
IntranetWare server.*

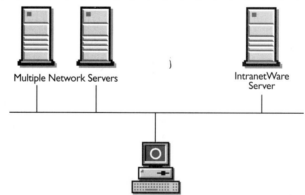

Multiple Network Servers

IntranetWare Server

DOS Workstation   MIGRATE.EXE

Same Server Migration Using **MIGRATE.EXE**

You can also use the MIGRATE.EXE utility to migrate other NetWare operating systems (for example, NetWare 2 and NetWare 3) even if you are not replacing the server hardware. You can choose the Same-Server option from the MIGRATE.EXE utility as shown in Figure 16.8. This method enables an upgrade without requiring a new server and migrates the bindery or bindery-like information from the source server to a DOS workstation for temporary storage during the migration.

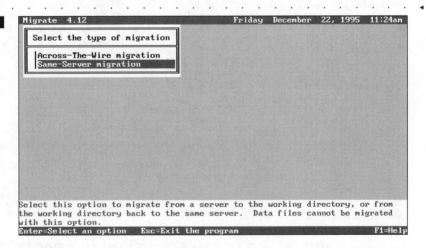

F I G U R E   16.8

*Same-Server migration
option on the main menu
with the Across-the-Wire
migration option*

The Same-Server migration option does not copy or migrate any data files. In order to keep the data files, you need to back them up using your tape backup utility before starting the migration. After you have rebuilt the physical hardware device (repartitioned the drive and selected the new block size) and loaded IntranetWare, you can restore the data files to the new IntranetWare server. After you have put the data files back down on the IntranetWare volumes, you can restore the bindery information associated with these files from the DOS workstation.

This option migrates your NetWare 2 or NetWare 3 binderies to a working directory on the DOS workstation. The utility will then stop and enable you to install IntranetWare on the server. You then can restore your files and directories from your tape backup. Once the IntranetWare installation is completed, you can continue the MIGRATE utility to restore the bindery information to NDS. An example of this migration concept is shown in Figure 16.9.

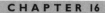

An example of the Same-Server migration option using MIGRATE.EXE

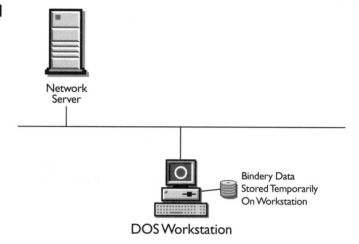

Network
Server

Bindery Data
Stored Temporarily
On Workstation

DOS Workstation

To ensure that trustee assignments are properly migrated, you must restore the data files from the backup copy of your NetWare 2 or NetWare 3 server before you migrate the bindery. Restoring the data files ensures that users and groups receive the proper rights to access files and directories when they are translated to NDS objects and placed in the tree.

MIGRATING LOGIN SCRIPTS WITH ACROSS-THE-WIRE

The system login script from NetWare 3 is not migrated during the across-the-wire migration. You will need the NET$LOG.DAT system login script if you still need to support workstations using the NETX shell or the VLM /B option after the migration. The NetWare client software looks for the system login script in the SYS:PUBLIC subdirectory as the file name NET$LOG.DAT.

You will need to manually move the file to the SYS:PUBLIC directory by copying between servers. The IntranetWare VLM clients or 32 bit clients will look for their container login scripts within NDS. This means that if you want to use your NetWare 3 login script you need to cut and paste the system login script into the container login scripts.

NOTE

You will most likely have to make slight modifications to the old system script once you place it into a container script. Server names, for example, will have changed, and possibly the drive mappings as well.

Container login scripts can also be created from scratch by using the NWADMIN or NETADMIN utilities and accessing the DETAILS section of the container object.

There have not been any significant changes in the login script commands bitbetween NetWare 3 and IntranetWare. (For a complete list of the login script commands, see Chapter 12.) All the old NetWare 3 statements still work the same way under IntranetWare. An exception is that the ATTACH command is no longer supported in IntranetWare as a command line utility. The ATTACH command still works in login scripts and is maintained for backward compatibility. There are, however, new variables and parameters available for use strictly with IntranetWare login scripts that you may want to add to a migrated NetWare 2 or NetWare 3 system login script.

User login script files are migrated from the source server to IntranetWare but remain as files in the SYS:MAIL\USERID subdirectory. The NETX user and bindery user will continue to access the login scripts from those areas. However, the user login scripts from NetWare 3 are not migrated as an NDS login script property for the user object. The across-the-wire migration process creates two UIMPORT control files in SYS:SYSTEM on the IntranetWare — UIMPORT.CTL and UIMPORT.DAT.

By using the UIMPORT utility and these files you can copy the login scripts for each user from his mail subdirectory into NDS and associate the script with the user's property. For more information on the UIMPORT utility, refer to Chapter 2.

MIGRATING PASSWORDS WITH ACROSS-THE-WIRE

During the migration process the passwords are not migrated. The MIGRATE utility enables you to assign random passwords for each user that are generated by the system and placed in a text file (NEW.PWD) in the SYS:SYSTEM subdirectory. Alternatively, the utility allows the option of having no passwords during the initial signon. Using this option, the users will be required to enter a password during their first login after the migration. Your network system will remain "open" until all users log in and enter their own passwords to secure their workstations.

The randomly generated passwords are stored in a file called NEW.PWD in the SYS:SYSTEM subdirectory on the IntranetWare server, and can be accessed only by the user object ADMIN or an equivalent. If you do decide to use random passwords, you can devise a way to distribute those passwords to your end users. One idea is to sort them with a word processor into alphabetical order and then have your help desk or administrator distribute the username and corresponding password to each user when he comes in for work.

Another option to consider for the migration of users and passwords is the Novell's NETSYNC utility. The NETSYNC process is explained in the following section and in Chapter 2.

MIGRATE PRINT SERVICES

The Across-the-Wire Migration utility does not migrate print queues and print servers for NetWare 3. It migrates only the print queues and print servers from the LAN Server and LAN Manager. In order to migrate the print services in NetWare 3, a separate utility known as MIGPRINT.EXE has been provided. When you set up the DOS workstation for migration by copying all of the files, the MIGPRINT.EXE is also copied. The MIGPRINT utility enables you to selectively migrate printers, print queues, print job configurations, and print servers from the source server to the IntranetWare server and NDS.

Unlike the MIGRATE.EXE utility, MIGPRINT.EXE requires an NDS connection from the DOS client to the IntranetWare server. It still needs a bindery connection to the source NetWare 3 server. The user using this utility must have sufficient access rights to the server bindery context where the print services are to be placed. Figure 16.10 illustrates the main menu or help screen for MIGPRINT.EXE.

The proper syntax or usage statement of MIGPRINT.EXE is as follows:

```
MIGPRINT /S=Source Server /D=Destination Server

    [/VOL=queueVol] [/O=outputFile]
```

IntranetWare no longer supports dedicated print servers outside of the file server. You will need to move these services back onto the file server or find third-party solutions.

F I G U R E   16.10

The MIGPRINT.EXE utility migrates the print services from NetWare 3 to IntranetWare.

```
MIGPRINT.EXE                                                  4.10.01

General Help

Purpose: To migrate print queues, print servers, and print job
         configurations from a bindery server to Directory Services.

Syntax: MIGPRINT /S=srcSrvr /D=dstSrvr [/VOL=queueVol] [/O=outputFile]


G:\NW410\MIGRATE>
```

USING NETSYNC WITH ACROSS-THE-WIRE MIGRATIONS

The NETSYNC utility can also be used to help ease the migration process from NetWare 3 to IntranetWare. NETSYNC is a management utility designed to expand the benefits of NDS to NetWare 3 file servers. With NETSYNC you have the ability to synchronize NetWare 3 users and groups with objects that are contained in a IntranetWare server's bindery context. This utility is useful if you want to maintain users and their passwords during a migration and when you are using the Across-the-Wire Migration utility. Some companies migrating to IntranetWare choose to use the across-the-wire process for migrating to IntranetWare because they are moving to new server platforms for the installation of IntranetWare. Some customers would also like to preserve their users passwords as well. NETSYNC will synchronize the bindery users and their passwords onto the IntranetWare Directory. Once the synchronization process is complete between the NetWare 3 and IntranetWare servers you will have the users and passwords on the IntranetWare hardware. You can then use the across-the-wire method to migrate your data and its corresponding trustee assignments.

You can use the following steps to assist you in this migration process:

1 • Load the NETSYNC3.NLM on the NetWare 3 server.

2 • Load the NETSYNC4.NLM on the IntranetWare server.

3 • Synchronize the bindery to the NDS bindery context.

4 • Use the MIGRATE.EXE utility to perform the across-the-wire migration of your data and trustee assignments. Do not specify any user objects to be migrated with this utility.

For more detailed information on using the NETSYNC NLMs, refer to Chapter 2.

Migration Using RCONSOLE Across Your LAN/WAN

You can also use the RCONSOLE utility to assist you with migrations of NetWare 3 and 4.0x servers to IntranetWare from a central location. The RCONSOLE utility can be used to connect to remote servers, copy over the necessary files, run the INSTALL utility remotely, and then restart the upgraded server. For more detailed information on this process, refer to Novell's May 1995 Application Notes article Upgrading to NetWare 4.1. A conceptual example of this process is illustrated in Figure 16.11.

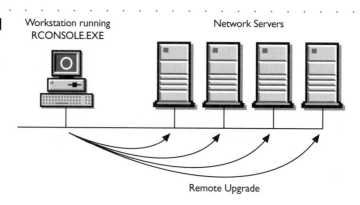

FIGURE 16.11

Using RCONSOLE to remotely upgrade NetWare servers to IntranetWare

Migration Using File Copy

Perhaps the simplest migration method you can use is copying the files and data from your current operating system to the IntranetWare file system. This is a very dynamic migration method because you can choose which files and subdirectories you want to move. You can move an entire volume, a group of subdirectories, or a single file.

In order to perform a file copy, your new IntranetWare server must be installed and running on the network along with the server you intend to migrate. You will need to choose a workstation and establish a concurrent connection to both servers using accounts with sufficient rights to read and write the data to and from the appropriate source and destination servers. Your workstation must have enough memory to support the concurrent login to both servers.

In a mixed operating system environment the workstation performing the migration will have to be loaded with two protocols to support both operating systems.

Both the source and destination servers must be visible to the workstation performing the copy. In Figure 16.12, a user logs into a NetWare 3.12 server called NetWare_312 and a IntranetWare server called NetWare_410. After connecting to both servers from a DOS workstation, the user maps a drive to the source server and the destination server. Then the user issues an XCOPY command with appropriate parameters and copies the data for volume VOL1 to the DATA volume on the destination server.

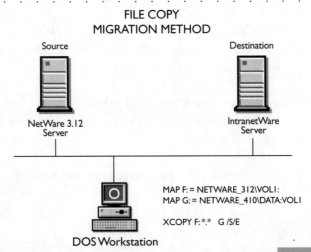

FIGURE 16.12

File copy for the volume VOL1 data from a NetWare 3.12 server to the IntranetWare server using a DOS XCOPY command

**FILE COPY
MIGRATION METHOD**

Source

Destination

NetWare 3.12
Server

IntranetWare
Server

MAP F: = NETWARE_312\VOL1:
MAP G: = NETWARE_410\DATA:VOL1

XCOPY F:*.* G /S/E

DOS Workstation

CHAPTER 16
. . . . .
N O V E L L ' S
G U I D E   T O
I N T R A N E T W A R E
N E T W O R K S

The drive mappings for the workstations are as follows:

```
MAP F:=SERVER_312\VOL1:
```

```
MAP  G:=SERVER_410\DATA:VOL1
```

The Copy command would appear as:

```
XCOPY F:*.* G: /S/E
```

to specify a copy of all files from the F drive to the G drive, including all subdirectories /S even if empty /E.

Although the file copy migration method is the simplest and quickest way to move information from one server to another, it may not be practical for those who require other information besides just the data. Other information would include trustee assignments, for example.

The file copy method is valuable for those who only need to move the data from the old server to the new one. In addition, for some migrations, the file copy method is currently the only option. For example, to migrate a network from DEC Pathworks to IntranetWare requires the use of the Copy command. There is currently no other mechanism. For accounts that do not wish to migrate trustee assignments but only data, this option is certainly viable. The advantages and disadvantages of the file copy migration method are listed in the following section.

FILE COPY ADVANTAGES

▸ Restricts the copy of the source server to Read Only on the data files. The copy procedure provides fault tolerance because the source server is only being read, not altered in any way.

▸ Selects volumes, directories, or files that you want to move. For example, the entire drive does not need to be immediately copied to the other server; you can do migrations in stages.

▸ Moves different kinds of name spaces. The file copy method supports MAC, NFS, and other name spaces if the native desktops connect to perform the copy of the data files.

▸ Supports file transfers between all popular network operating systems. For example, DEC Pathworks or LANtastic files can be copied.

▸ Moves data files anytime because the procedure is nondisruptive to the user. However, the increased network traffic may impact performance of the users.

▸ Many different utilities can be used to perform the file copy — COPY, XCOPY, NCOPY, File Manager in Windows, Norton Utilities, XTREE, and other third-party products.

FILE COPY DISADVANTAGES

▸ Does not move the bindery in NetWare 2 and NetWare 3. Thus, users, groups, and print services are not migrated to the new server.

▸ Does not maintain the existing file trustee assignments contained on the source server.

▸ Requires additional server hardware. Both the source and destination server need to be installed and running on the network. This method also requires availability of a workstation.

▸ Requires a concurrent connection to both the source and destination servers. Both servers need to be visible to the workstation unless you attach to only the source server to move the data files to a temporary storage device like a tape unit or the hard drive of the workstation. You can then move the files to the destination server in stages.

▸ Operation is slow because the file copy moves the data files across the network from one server to another.

TIP
If the servers are not visible or if you have problems communicating with the network, you should check to see if your workstation is set up with the same frame types as the NetWare servers. With the release of IntranetWare, Novell changed the default frame type from 802.3 to 802.2.

Before performing a file copy, take time to review the data structure on the source server. In particular, you should remove or clean outdated or unused files and programs from the system before starting the migration. This saves time and space when copying to the new server and prevents carrying around the old baggage. If the workstation cannot set up a concurrent connection to both the source and destination servers, you may want to move the file temporarily to the workstation. Then you can move the file to the destination server in stages. This method implies that there is a very large storage device at the workstation, such as a tape unit or additional hard drives. The workstation can move the data files in sets or stages according to the limitations of the workstation hardware. Follow the steps below to perform the workstation copy:

1 • Guarantee that the workstation has enough capacity to hold the selected data files. Add a tape unit or extra drive to increase the capacity.

2 • Copy the selected data files from the source server to the appropriate workstation device.

3 • Change connections to the new server or the destination server.

4 • Copy the data files over to the destination server.

5 • Continue this process in stages until all the data files are migrated.

Figure 16.13 illustrates how you can use a workstation to temporarily hold the data files from the source server.

If you are using the same hardware device as the source and destination servers, you will need to move the entire contents of the server to the workstation. Once the workstation holds all the information, you can down the source server and install the IntranetWare as the destination server. You can then copy the data file to the IntranetWare server.

The file copy migration method is valuable to companies that are performing file server data restructuring. If you need to change the layout of the server significantly or apply large changes in the naming of subdirectories, you may choose just to copy the files from server to server.

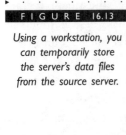

FIGURE 16.13

*Using a workstation, you
can temporarily store
the server's data files
from the source server.*

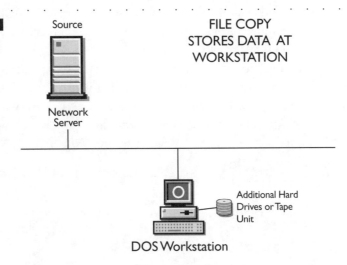

Source

FILE COPY
STORES DATA AT
WORKSTATION

Network
Server

Additional Hard
Drives or Tape
Unit

DOS Workstation

DS Standard as a Migration Tool

NOTE

**DSMIGRATE ships as a new migration tool under the new 32-bit
NWADMIN Tools menu. DSMIGRATE, from Preferred Systems, Inc.,
provides a subset of services offered in their full-scale product known
as DS Standard NDS Manager. These services provide some NDS
modeling assistance to help you design an NDS tree beforehand. For
migration purposes you can use DSMIGRATE to migrate a bindery
from NetWare 3.x to IntranetWare bindery objects only. For
migration of the file system you need to use the File Migration utility
provided in the NWADMIN Tools menu or another utility of your
choice.**

DS Standard from Preferred Systems, Inc., is a Windows-based tool that provides the capability to model, analyze, and manage NDS trees before you move into production with an NDS design. The design steps presented in previous chapters of this book can be placed into practice with the assistance of DS Standard. This tool can also minimize administration time once your network is in place.

DS standard will enable you to construct a tree and make adjustments before going "live" with your design. This product supports all the NDS objects found in IntranetWare and gives you the ability to create multiple tree designs and then compare your designs with those of your team members. Some of the other capabilities in DS Standard include applying your naming conventions, performing migrations, and backing up the NDS tree structure. We will discuss some of the features of DS Standard and how this product can be used as a migration tool.

The three steps to using DS Standard are:

1 • Discover your current network.

2 • Model/analyze/manage your network.

3 • Configure your network.

The *Discover* process searches your current network for available resources to populate the DS Standard database. If you are running a NetWare 3.12 network, the discover process will read the bindery information on your NetWare 3.12 server. If you are currently running on a IntranetWare network, the discover process will read the NDS database information. Keep in mind that the current version of DS Standard (2.0 as of this writing) does not discover any extensions made to the NDS database. See the DS Standard documentation for a list of supported NDS objects.

The *Modeling and Management* process is actually the design phase of your NDS tree. The creation of your tree can be based on information gathered from your current NetWare 3 or IntranetWare environments, or you can build a tree from scratch using only DS Standard. A tree built from scratch can be assisted with tree templates or previously discovered tree views from any NDS trees.

The *Configure* process will then take your NDS model and implement the changes into your network environment. The configure process works under the security of IntranetWare. Therefore, you must have rights at any level in the tree where you wish to configure objects and properties for a migration. The configure process actually writes the NDS database to your Directory tree. An example of the DS Standard migration concept is shown in Figure 16.14.

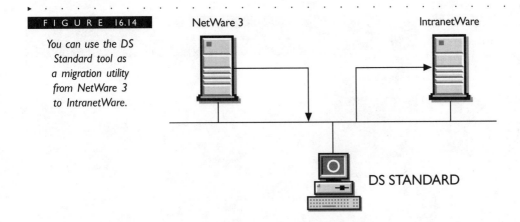

FIGURE 16.14

*You can use the DS
Standard tool as
a migration utility
from NetWare 3
to IntranetWare.*

NetWare 3

IntranetWare

DS STANDARD

USING DS STANDARD FOR THE ACME TREE

The DS Standard modeling process enables you to shape and define your NDS
tree before implementing it into your production environment. You can add, delete,
copy, rename, and merge objects during this phase. One of the design steps mentioned
in Chapter 5 optimizes your tree design by determining whether all the Organizational
Units or other objects you've defined are really necessary. During the modeling phase
you can delete any unnecessary objects or properties.

With DS Standard up and running you are presented with the main screen as
shown in Figure 16.15. You are now ready to define a project, which is a collection
of views.

You can assign views to a project or projects. To create a project you select the
New Project option from the File menu. You will be presented with a screen as
shown in Figure 16.16. Enter the information describing the name of your project
and continue. We will use the ACME name with the inclusion of our tree design
staff.

From the main screen we will also begin the basic design of our ACME tree by
creating a view of our tree. Select the New View option from the File menu as shown
in Figure 16.17

FIGURE 16.15

*DS Standard
main screen view*

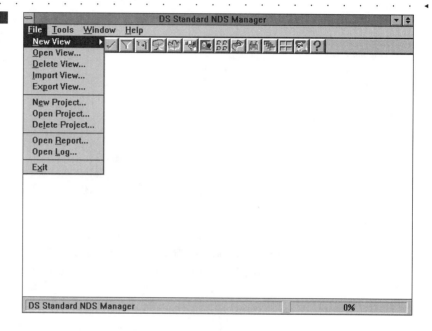

FIGURE 16.16

*Define a new project
through the New Project
option on the DS
Standard main screen.*

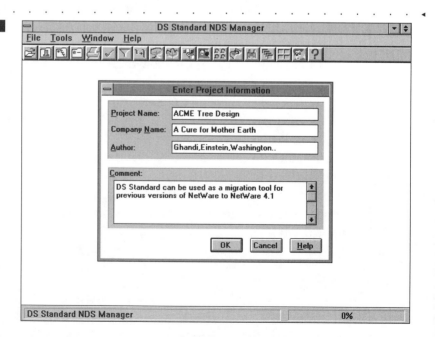

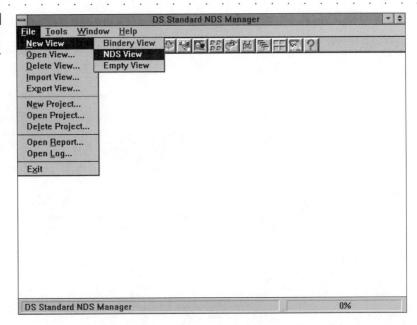

FIGURE 16.17

To create a tree from scratch select the New View option from the File menu.

The New View option enables you to choose a discover method such as Bindery View for bindery searches of NetWare 2, 3, or 4 (bindery services). An NDS View will build your tree based on information collected from a IntranetWare NDS server. The Empty View is the view we'll use to create our ACME design from scratch. Keep in mind that you can also select Empty View and use previous designs or NDS templates.

Selecting the Empty View option will ask for your tree name and author(s) as shown in Figure 16.18.

After you have entered this information you will be given an empty tree with only the [ROOT] object as shown in Figure 16.19. This is the new view you have just created. This view can be closed and viewed later. It can also be deleted, imported, or exported to another project as well. We are now ready to assign a project name to the view.

We now need to associate our view with the project we have created. Keep in mind that the previous two steps can be accomplished in either order. In other words, you can create multiple views first and then assign them to a project or you can create a project and assign it to multiple views.

F I G U R E   16.18

*Enter the empty New View
information as shown here.*

F I G U R E   16.19

*The newly created view is
now ready for your design.*

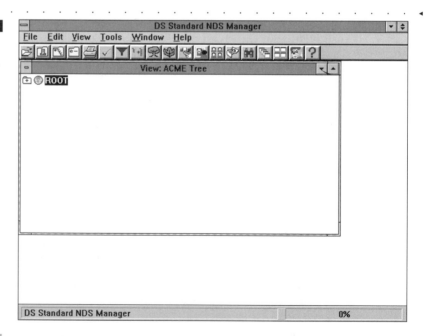

To add a view to a project simply select the Add View option under the Project menu as shown in Figure 16.20. You must have previously opened a project before you can add a view.

FIGURE 16.20

Adding a view to a project will bring up a list of available views.

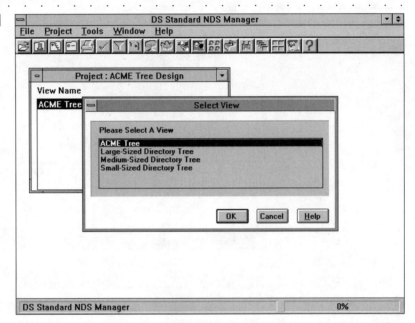

Select the appropriate view and continue. Notice in the previous figure that you could have selected some tree templates of varying sizes. These templates are designed to speed up the process of creating your tree. You can simply import these templates and then modify them to meet your needs. We are going to show you how to build the ACME tree here from scratch.

With your project named and a view created, you are now ready to add additional objects to the view. You begin by opening the ACME view (open view) and then selecting Add Object from the Edit menu. You can also copy objects or delete objects according to your needs. This selection will bring up the screen as shown in Figure 16.21. Notice that only the objects that can be created at this level are highlighted for you. These highlights follow the NDS schema structure containment rules. We will select the Organizational Unit object to begin our first layer of organizational units under [ROOT].

FIGURE 16.21

The Add Object selection screen gives you a choice of all available objects.

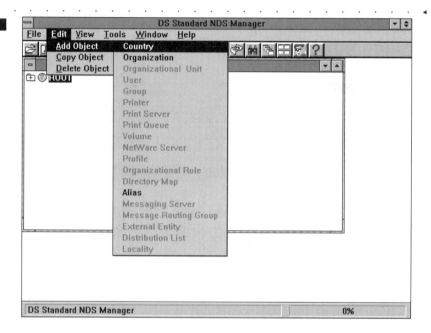

The organization object screen contains the property information as displayed in Novell's NWADMIN utility and enables you to define those properties. The Organization Identification screen is shown in Figure 16.22. We will, of course, give our organization the name of ACME.

Following the same procedure we will also create an Organizational Unit object for each location in the ACME tree subordinate to the Organization of ACME. We will then have the first two layers of our tree completed as shown in Figure 16.23. [ROOT] is not counted.

The tree then continues to take shape with the creation of all subordinate containers for ACME, such as department and workgroup containers as shown in Figure 16.24. Keep in mind that you can define each location as a separate view under the same project. A separate view enables you to focus on each particular location for your tree design if you prefer. This example simply shows a single view of the entire tree.

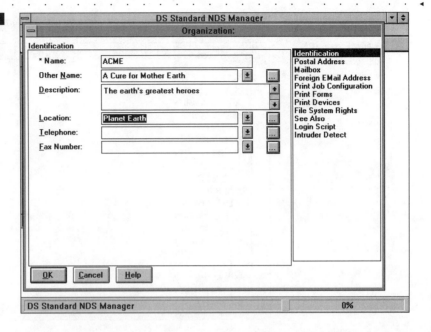

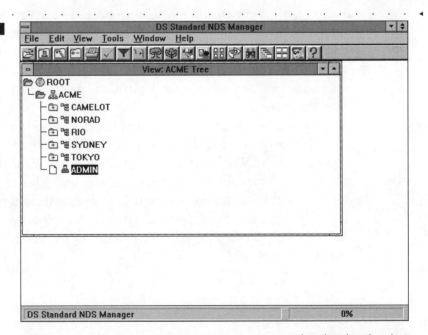

FIGURE 16.24

The ACME tree with
all subordinate
containers created

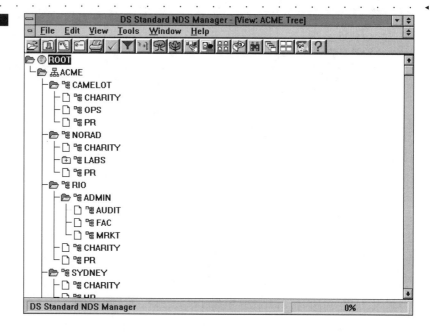

After you have your tree structure in place, you can place your resources into the appropriate locations in the tree. These resources would include servers, printers, and any other network devices that you may want to define in your NDS tree. You can use DS Standard to place these resources into the various departments. Again, a separate view of a location or department may be easier to view and maintain with this product.

Once you have completed your basic tree design, you can then access the View menu to run some basic checks on your network design for errors. For example, you can run the Verify Directory Tree option, which will check your NDS design for depth and number of objects per container and other useful information. This option will also check your tree for objects that contain unresolved references and enable you to make the appropriate changes through a feature known as Resolve References for Selected Objects. An example of the Resolve References feature is shown in Figure 16.25.

FIGURE 16.25

*Resolve References log file
showing no conflicts with
this particular container*

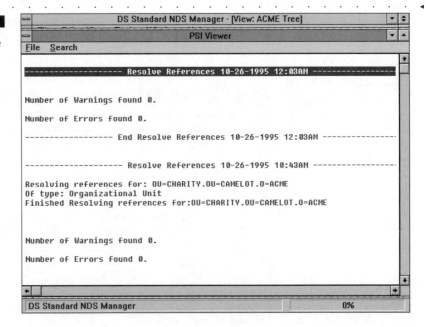

You also have the ability to create an object report on selected objects in your view. The object report will give you detailed information on an object's properties. You can create a report of multiple objects or a single object that can then be printed. A view of an object report is shown in Figure 16.26.

After you are satisfied that your NDS design is complete, you can now use the DS Standard Configure option to update your live NDS directory with object information created in the DS Standard database. Through this update process, new NDS objects can be added to your NDS database. You can also use the DS Standard Configure option to make changes to existing NDS objects as well. As a backup tool the Configure option can be used to selectively restore objects to your NDS tree.

The first phase of the Configure process is for DS Standard to run a consistency check on your current NDS tree if you have one installed. This check ensures that all changes can be successfully implemented in the tree such as the assignment of mandatory attributes and the assignment of various users to objects including operators of print queues or print servers. The Preconfigure Verify option will display a log file with NDS information. You can select this option by accessing Tools/ Options/Preconfigure Verify from the DS Standard log parameter screen as shown in Figure 16.27.

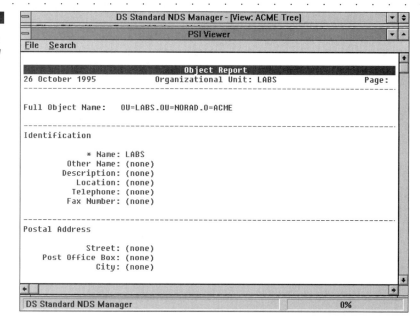

```
                    DS Standard NDS Manager - [View: ACME Tree]
                                    PSI Viewer
File   Search

                               Object Report
26 October 1995          Organizational Unit: LABS              Page:
------------------------------------------------------------------------

Full Object Name:    OU=LABS.OU=NORAD.O=ACME

------------------------------------------------------------------------

Identification

              * Name: LABS
         Other Name: (none)
        Description: (none)
           Location: (none)
          Telephone: (none)
         Fax Number: (none)

------------------------------------------------------------------------

Postal Address

             Street: (none)
    Post Office Box: (none)
               City: (none)

DS Standard NDS Manager                                        0%
```

You can then access the Verify screen to select the parameters settings that you would like checked according to your network design. Figure 16.28 shows an example of the Verify screen. Notice that the Verify Metrics option has default values placed in the categories. These default values can be modified to check for your particular values. For example, if you want to limit the number of levels in the tree to no more than five, you can simply change that parameter.

If you are satisfied with the metrics, you can then run the Verify Directory Tree under the View option to check your tree design. An example of this log file is shown in Figure 16.29.

You can also add, delete, search and replace objects during the Configure phase. These services are provided so that you can make changes and verify the accuracy of your tree before writing it to the NDS database. For more information on these operations, refer to the DS Standard documentation.

FIGURE 16.27

*Preconfigure Verify log
option as shown for
the ACME tree*

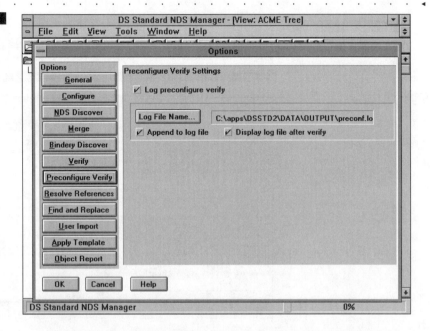

FIGURE 16.28

*The DS Standard Verify
option screen can
be configured to
suit your needs.*

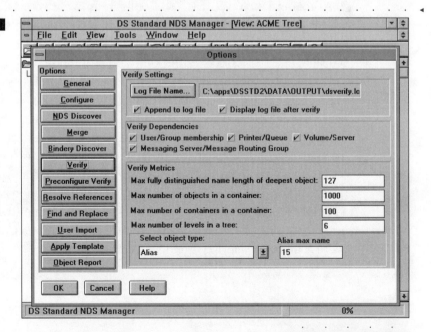

FIGURE 16.29

The Verify Directory Tree log screen also saved as a file

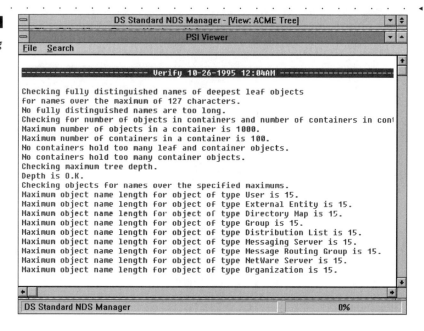

As the final step, you can use Configure to write your NDS tree or portions of the tree to the actual NDS database. For example, you can select all objects in the view or select only a certain container. If you have installed IntranetWare, you will probably select all objects in the view and write those objects into the NDS tree.

To initiate the Configure process you select Configure Selected Objects from the View menu. You will be prompted with a confirmation screen before proceeding with the configuration to NDS.

This process will cause the DS Standard objects to be added to your live network in the appropriate locations or will merge the DS Standard object into an existing NDS object. If you have read NetWare 3 bindery information during the discovery process, the configure step actually writes the bindery information to NDS. This process accomplishes the same task as an across-the-wire migration with MIGRATE.EXE. A benefit of using the DS Standard product is that you can manipulate the object information before moving it on to a IntranetWare server.

CHAPTER 17

Migrating Other Operating Systems to IntranetWare

"Change must be measured from a known base line." Evan Shute

Some of your network installations may be migrating from network operating systems other than NetWare. This chapter explores the options available for migrating to IntranetWare from LAN Manager, NT Server, LAN Server, DEC Pathworks, and Banyan.

As a network administrator, you need to decide which method of migration will work best for you. Depending on your needs, a migration can be as limited as doing a file copy to transfer the data from your current operating system to the IntranetWare server. Your migration may be more complex, such as migrating from NT Server to IntranetWare, including trustee assignments. You can use the following methods to migrate from other operating systems to IntranetWare:

- ▶ File copy

- ▶ Novell's migration utilities for other operating systems, including MIGRATE.EXE and the LM/NTS/LS migration utility

- ▶ Scripting solutions

The following sections detail the options for migrating other operating systems to IntranetWare and supply you with more information for devising your migration strategy. Table 17.1 identifies your options for migrating from other operating systems to IntranetWare.

T A B L E   17.1

*Options for migrating
other operating systems to
IntranetWare (fo = files only,
no trustee assignments)*

OPTION	NT SERVER	LAN SERVER	LAN MANAGER	OTHERS
File Copy	X fo	X fo	X fo	X fo
MIGRATE.EXE		X v1.x-1.3	X v2.0	PCLP v1.3
LM/NTS/LS	X. v3.5,3.51	X v2,3,4	X v2.0,2.2	
Scripting	X	X	X	X

File Copy

For some installations, file copy may be the easiest and fastest way to move data from your existing operating system to IntranetWare. If you need only your data and not the user objects or other trustee assignments, you may want to use a file copy. For some migrations, such as DEC Pathworks to IntranetWare, Novell does not provide a migration utility. You can use the file copy method or a scripting language, which entails more work in the design and scripting process. If you need to preserve a user's trustee assignments and so on, you can use one of Novell's migration utilities to accomplish this task.

To carry out the file copy method, you simply connect a workstation to the old and new server platforms and copy the data from one server to the other.

You must take the following steps in a file copy migration approach:

1 • Load a dual protocol stack on the workstation so that you can connect to both servers' operating systems simultaneously. This workstation needs to have sufficient memory for both protocols to be loaded.

CONSULTING EXPERIENCE

If the dual protocol option does not work for you, you can also look into doing a tape backup of the current operating system and a tape restore to IntranetWare, so that you can first preserve your data from the old operating system and then restore from tape onto the IntranetWare operating system. This option assumes a workstation backup solution that provides support for both networking platforms.

2 • Obtain a valid user account on both servers with Supervisor (or comparable) rights on both servers. You need these rights so that you can attach to both servers to do the copy.

3 • Load both protocol stacks on your workstation and log in to both servers.

4 • Map a drive on each server and select the directories you want to migrate to IntranetWare.

5 • Issue the copy command, either from DOS or from another utility, with the appropriate copy parameters (for example, use /s to include all subdirectories) to migrate from and to the two mapped drives.

Figures 17.1 and 17.2 show examples of these two copy approaches.

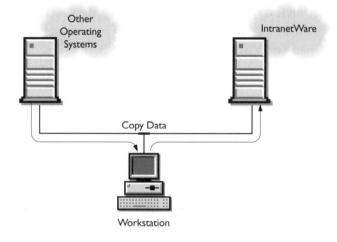

Using a workstation between two servers, you can copy the server's data from the old operating system to IntranetWare.

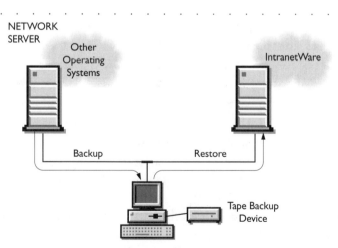

Using a tape backup, you can restore the data to the IntranetWare operating system.

Novell's Migration Utilities

Novell provides two utilities for migrating other operating systems to IntranetWare. These utilities are the MIGRATE.EXE utility (available in the red box) and a new utility offered by Novell Consulting known as the LM/NTS/LS Migration utility, or the Quiet Thunder utility. This utility is used to migrate LAN Manager, NT Server, and LAN Server operating systems to IntranetWare. You must use the LM/NTS/LS utility if you are planning to migrate any of the following versions:

▸ LAN Manager version 2.0 or 2.2

▸ LAN Server versions 2.x, 3.x, or 4.0

▸ NT Server versions 3.5 or 3.51

Both migration utilities work on the principle of across-the-wire migrations, meaning that you are moving data (users and their files, groups, trustee assignments, and so on) from one server to another server via a common workstation. The across-the-wire approach is nondestructive in that no information is deleted or destroyed on the source server. Information is simply read to the acting workstation and then written to the target server. Data files are not stored on the intermediate workstation.

These utilities can also perform the migration when a concurrent connection to the source and destination server cannot be made. Whenever possible, you should use the concurrent connection method because it provides the highest level of functionality and reliability.

Because the MIGRATE.EXE and LM/NTS/LS utilities both run as client programs, the migration will go more quickly if you choose a fast workstation (486 or better) with a 16- or 32-bit LAN card. Although a slower workstation with an 8-bit LAN card will work, it will increase the time it takes to complete the migration. The workstation is responsible for moving all the data from the source to the target server.

The Across-the-Wire Migration utility MIGRATE.EXE is included on the NetWare 4.11 CD-ROM. You can also obtain the utility from NetWire (CompuServe) free of charge. To obtain the most recent version of the utility from NetWire, download the file called MIGRATE.EXE from section 2 or 3 of NWOSFILES.

You can obtain the LM/NTS/LS migration utility by contacting Novell Consulting in Provo, Utah. At the time of this writing, the utility is available on a special CD-ROM known as the Migration Toolkit. This utility is also available on Novell's Web Site under the option Programs/Novell Consulting.

Figure 17.3 shows an example of the across-the-wire migration process.

FIGURE 17.3

The across-the-wire migration process

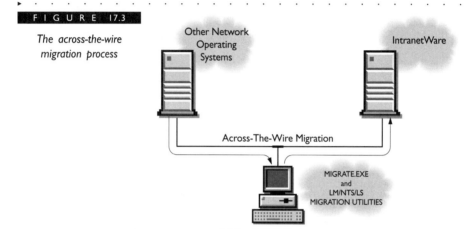

PREPARING FOR THE MIGRATION PROCESS

Once you have decided on an acceptable option for migration, you should begin the migration process by making the following basic preparations:

1 • Obtain training on IntranetWare.

2 • Design your NDS (Novell Directory Services) tree.

3 • Install the necessary hardware.

4 • Perform the migration.

Obtain Training on IntranetWare and Migration Utilities

Before beginning any migration, get some hands-on experience with IntranetWare in formal training or in a lab. Do not attempt to do a migration without first understanding exactly how the particular migration utility operates. Considering the importance of your data, the time you spend in a lab is well worth the investment.

You should also consider obtaining training from Novell Authorized Education Centers. Sites that are new to NetWare should obtain some formal training on IntranetWare or work closely with their integrator to fully understand the migration processes. For more information about Novell education, contact your local reseller or contact Novell directly.

In addition to understanding the IntranetWare operating system, you need to understand how the migration process works and how it interacts with a domain-based environment. The network paradigm used by LAN Server and LAN Manager is different than that of IntranetWare. Servers are grouped together in what is known as a domain. The Across-The-Wire Migration utility obtains domain information from the LAN Server or LAN Manager server designated as the domain controller. Only information that has been shared with the entire domain can be accessed; information (other than data files) specific to individual servers is not migrated.

To migrate from any of these LANs, you must be logged onto the domain as a user with administrative privileges. The types of information migrated from a domain include data files (including directory structures and data files) and DOS attributes for files and directories.

Files are copied from domain file servers one drive at a time. Once you select a drive on a domain server, all files on that drive are copied to the destination server.

Only DOS information is copied. If the drive contains files or directories that have OS/2 extended attributes, those attributes are not copied to the destination server.

Design Your NDS Tree

Be sure that you have your Novell Directory Services tree structure in place on at least one IntranetWare server before beginning the migration with MIGRATE.EXE and LM/NTS/LS. For more information regarding the design of your NDS tree, refer to Chapters 4, 5, 6, and 7 of this book.

Install the Necessary Hardware

Prepare Your Source Server(s) for Migration   Preparing your source server(s) for migration involves the following steps:

I   • Make sure that your current servers are properly backed up before beginning a migration of any kind. These migration utilities do not destroy any data found on the source server, so you have that as a backup. However, you should still have an additional backup for safety.

2 • Log out all users except your administrative user.

3 • Close all files before the migration. Neither of Novell's migration utilities will migrate open files.

4 • Delete any unnecessary files and directories on your servers before beginning the migration. You can obviously migrate a server faster if it contains fewer files.

5 • Delete all unused or unneeded user accounts, groups, and so on.

6 • Prepare your migration workstation. Refer to the sections on workstation requirements later in this chapter for more information.

Workstation Requirements for the MIGRATE.EXE Utility   These are the workstation requirements for using the MIGRATE.EXE utility:

▸ Minimum 486/66 workstation, 4MB of RAM

▸ Minimum 20MB free disk space

▸ Concurrent access to both the source and destination server by loading dual requesters, one for the source server and the other for IntranetWare

▸ High-performance NIC card to increase throughput

Perform the Migration

Because the across-the-wire migration approach will generate traffic on your network, you should perform your migrations during off-peak hours. Migrate one domain at a time into an NDS context and check for errors and other conditions to ensure that the migration was successful.

Both Novell migration utilities can generate an error report file. Use this file to determine whether your migration completed successfully and whether any objects or data were not migrated.

USING THE MIGRATE.EXE UTILITY

MIGRATE.EXE is Novell's utility for migrating servers using the across-the-wire method. You can use it to facilitate migrations for the following operating systems:

- LAN Manager versions 1.2 to 2.0

- LAN Server versions 1.2 and 1.3

If you're migrating from LAN Server, you must understand how the AMU names printer queues. LAN Server permits resource sharing through both netnames and aliases. With LAN Server, the AMU uses the alias rather than the netname. If you want to migrate from the LAN Server domain a printer queue that is shared via a netname, you should assign an alias to that printer queue before performing the migration. The alias name is used when creating the printer queue on the destination NetWare server.

Once the migration has been performed, review the results and make any necessary adjustments. The AMU keeps track of all operations performed on both the source and destination servers by writing them to a report file. Be sure to examine the contents of the report file and note any operations that could not be completed.

You can view report files by selecting the View Migration Reports option from the Select a Migration Action menu. These files are automatically assigned names that begin with the letters MIG and are followed by consecutive numbers, as in MIG000.RPT, MIG001.RPT, and so on.

IntranetWare Directory Services and Bindery Services

The AMU uses Bindery Services to access IntranetWare servers; it does not have direct access to Directory Services. The use of Bindery Services is the basis for several issues concerning migration.

First, if the destination server is an IntranetWare server running Directory Services, you must enable Bindery Services and set up the bindery context properly. All objects created by the AMU will be created in the bindery context that is in force when the migration takes place. If you change the bindery context for the server after the migration, the users created in the old context by the AMU will be able to log in through Directory Services but not through Bindery Services.

You can use this feature to your advantage if you want to migrate several servers to different locations in the Directory and you aren't worried about providing access to those locations through Bindery Services. Before migrating each server, change the bindery context of the destination server to the desired container in the Directory. Then, when the AMU is run, all objects migrated to the destination server will reside in that container. After migrating all the desired servers, change the bindery context back to the location in the Directory that you want Bindery Services clients to be able to access. You can change the bindery context at the IntranetWare server's console or via a remote console connection.

NOTE

For you to be able to change the bindery context for an IntranetWare server to a container in the Directory, a replica of the partition in which that container resides must reside on the server. In addition, the password for the Bindery Service's Supervisor user does not change when the bindery context is changed to a different container.

The second issue has to do with login scripts of migrated users. Because it does not have direct access to the Directory, the AMU cannot create a login script property in the Directory for those users that it creates, even though each login script is written to the user's mail directory on the destination file server. To help overcome this limitation, the AMU creates two files on the destination server — UIMPORT.CTL and UIMPORT.DAT — that can be used in conjunction with the UIMPORT utility to import the DOS login scripts into the Directory.

UIMPORT.CTL and UIMPORT.DAT are stored in the SYS:SYSTEM directory on the destination server but are only created if one or more of the migrated users has a nonempty DOS login script. To import the user login scripts from the file system to the Directory, follow these steps:

1 • Exit the AMU.

2 • Make sure that you have a Directory Services connection to the IntranetWare destination server and that you have rights to modify objects in the container where the AMU created the users. The easiest way to do this is to log in to the Directory as user ADMIN. Be sure that your context is set to the same container as the destination server's bindery context.

3 • Change to the SYS:SYSTEM directory on the destination server. You need to have Read and File Scan rights in this directory.

4 • Make sure that you have a search drive mapped to the SYS:PUBLIC directory on an IntranetWare server.

5 • Run the UIMPORT utility, providing the names of the control and data files as parameters. For example:

```
H:\SYSTEM> UIMPORT UIMPORT.CTL UIMPORT.DAT
```

The UIMPORT program creates the Directory Services login script property for each migrated user named in the UIMPORT.DAT file and copies the contents of the login script from the user's mail directory into that property.

The AMU's use of Bindery Services can also cause naming conflicts. In IntranetWare Directory Services, each name in a given context must be unique; two objects of different types cannot have the same name.

If you choose to migrate data files, you need to specify which domain drives to migrate, as well as a volume and optionally a directory on the destination server where you want each domain drive to be copied. Note that the AMU does not overwrite any existing files on the destination server. If it attempts to copy a file from the source server to the destination server, and a file with the same name already exists in the destination directory, a message is written to the report file stating that the file was not copied.

The following information is read from each user account:

▸ The user comment

▸ Whether the account is active

▸ Whether the user has administrative privileges

▸ Whether a password is required

▸ Whether the user is allowed to change his or her password

▸ The maximum password age

▸ The minimum password length

▸ Login time restrictions

▸ The account expiration date (if any)

If a user account has administrative privileges, this is translated into Supervisor-equivalence on the destination server.

Unlike LAN Server, LAN Manager permits usernames to contain spaces. While creating users on the destination NetWare server, the AMU converts spaces to underscores in each username.

The information read for each migrated group includes:

▸ The group comment

▸ Group members

Access control profiles include access permissions for both files and directories.

USING THE LM/NTS/LS MIGRATION UTILITY

Novell Consulting, a division of Novell, Inc., recently produced LM/NTS/LS (also called Quiet Thunder), a migration utility that enables you to quickly and easily migrate your LAN Manager, NT Server, and LAN Server operating systems to IntranetWare. This product is produced as the Migration Toolkit and is available on CD-ROM from Novell Consulting. LM/NTS/LS was produced as an addition to the regular MIGRATE.EXE utility provided by Novell.

The LM/NTS/LS utility provides migration support for the more recent versions of non-NetWare operating systems not currently supported by Novell's MIGRATE.EXE. Like the MIGRATE.EXE utility, LM/NTS/LS uses the across-the-wire method for migration and should be used for migrations in which you must preserve the old operating system's rights assignments and other access types of information.

NOTE **The Novell Consulting Migration Toolkit is offered "as is" and at the time of this writing is not yet a standard Novell product. Because the utilities in this Toolkit have not gone through standard Novell testing, Novell makes no warranties regarding the Toolkit or any situations arising from its use.**

Workstation Requirements for the LM/NTS/LS Utility

These are the workstation requirements for using the LM/NTS/LS utility:

▸ OS/2 Warp workstation

▸ Minimum 20MB free disk space

▸ Concurrent access to both the source and destination server by loading dual requesters, one for the source server and the other for IntranetWare

▸ High-performance NIC card to increase throughput

Server Requirements for the LM/NTS/LS Utility

The server requirements for using the LM/NTS/LS utility are a minimum of one IntranetWare server with the NDS tree installed. Install all the latest IntranetWare patches as recommended by Novell. For specific hardware recommendations, consult Chapters 2 and 16 of this book. The IntranetWare server will act as your destination server.

You should have a current source server of any of the following types and versions:

▸ LAN Manager version 2.0 or 2.2

▸ LAN Server version 2.x, 3.x, or 4.0

▸ NT Server version 3.5 or 3.51

For migration from older versions of these operating systems, you can use Novell's MIGRATE.EXE, as explained previously in this chapter.

Verify that your new hardware will be sufficient for the migration process. For example, if you plan to migrate several servers from a different operating system, make sure that you have sufficient disk capacity on the IntranetWare server to support all the migrated information.

Be sure to test any specially designed applications that will also reside on the IntranetWare system for compatibility with the operating system. While most applications will run on IntranetWare, it does not hurt to check this before migrating to the new IntranetWare platform.

The Migration Process

The migration process for the LM/NTS/LS migration utility includes the following options:

▸ Domain object migration

▸ File system migration

▸ Share emulation server support

▸ Client migration

These options are explained briefly in the sections that follow.

Domain Object Migration   Domain object migration is the first step in the migration process. It uses the LMIGRATE.EXE utility to migrate domain users and groups to an IntranetWare NDS context. There are several methods for accomplishing this task. One strategy is to create a one-to-one relationship between a domain on your source and destination servers. If you take this approach, each domain is migrated to a specific NDS context, thereby maintaining a functional tree structure.

The second approach is migrate multiple domains into a single NDS context. If you use this technique, you can consolidate the same user into one NDS container on IntranetWare. The domain information only needs to be migrated once. All objects during the migration are read from the Primary Domain Controller (PDC). Non-PDC file servers only need their data migrated to IntranetWare.

NOTE   **If your PDC has been lost or corrupted, you can also use a Backup Domain Controller to migrate your domain objects to IntranetWare.**

The LMIGRATE.EXE program will migrate the following NetWare NDS items from their respective LAN Manager, NT Server, or LAN Server objects when available:

▸ User Login Name (duplicate user information will be combined if in the same container)

▸ User Description

▸ Login Restrictions such as account expiration restrictions, password restrictions, and time restrictions

▸ Network address restrictions

▸ Home directories (requires the use of USER_TEMPLATE)

▸ Group Name

▸ Group Description

▸ Group Membership

▸ File system directory structure

▸ File data

▸ Extended Attributes

▸ Access Rights for files and directories

The following items are not migrated:

▸ User profiles

▸ Print Services

▸ Mail Services

▸ Passwords (you can generate randomized passwords, you can generate no passwords, or you can select the same password for all users)

File System Migration   The second step in the migration process uses the LMIGRATE.EXE utility to migrate all files, directories, and access rights from the source operating system to IntranetWare. This migration utility supports the migration of long names such as NTFS, HPFS, and Macintosh. You must load name space support on the NetWare server before starting your data migration.

Share Emulation Server   The share emulation server enables workstations running the LM/NTS/LS client software and workstations running NetWare client software to have concurrent access to shared files on a central NetWare server during the migration phase. The share emulation is only intended to ease the migration process and should not be used over extended periods of time.

Client Migration   The LM/NTS/LS migration utility also performs a migration of clients to the IntranetWare client software. You can run the upgrade utilities directly from the workstation. The utility verifies the workstation's configurations and attempts to install the NetWare client software. This process takes approximately 10 minutes per client.

Scripting Solutions

If neither a file copy nor one of the Novell utilities will work for your migration to IntranetWare, you can consider using a scripting language for migration. Although scripting languages are beyond the scope of this book, they can be a good alternative to the migration tools available.

Keep in mind that there is a trade-off between creating a migration script and simply re-creating the users or rights or whatever it is that you're trying to migrate. If you have a small number of users, it may be easier simply to re-create the users on the IntranetWare server. If you have a large number of users, scripting may be a good alternative.

MIGRATING FROM BANYAN VINES TO INTRANETWARE

To migrate from Banyan VINES to IntranetWare you can use Novell Consulting's BMIGRATE utility. This utility operates in the same manner as Novell's MIGRATE utility. However, unlike the MIGRATE utility, the BMIGRATE utility uses only the across-the-wire migration method.

When a workstation is logged in to both network systems, the BMIGRATE utility will read the data and trustee assignments from the VINES server, store them at the workstation, and then write the information to the IntranetWare server. The time necessary to complete the migration process will depend on the speed of your workstation and the amount of data you are trying to transfer.

NOTE

BMIGRATE is a special utility provided by Novell Consulting and is available from Novell's Web Site at WWW.NOVELL.COM in the directory Programs/Novell Consulting. Included with this migration utility is complete documentation for performing a migration from Banyan to IntranetWare.

The BMIGRATE utility lets you select specific information from the VINES StreetTalk directory and the VINES server's data files to create a customized destination server. BMIGRATE preserves the source server intact and only copies information onto the destination server. BMIGRATE also enables you to preserve your user environment (users and their rights assignments) as well as other user account information.

You should perform the following steps to migrate from Banyan to IntranetWare:

1 • Prepare prior to running the utility.

2 • Allow sufficient time to run BMIGRATE.

3 • Allow time to review the migration.

Preparing for a VINES Migration

Your system administrators should be trained in both VINES and NetWare network system administration, including Certified Novell Engineer (CNE) training, or have an equivalent background. Administrators should also have read and understood the respective publications for both network architectures. The Novell and Banyan product manuals are available from either company.

Other tasks for preparing for the migration include making full system backups and preparing your hardware for the installation of IntranetWare.

Hardware Requirements for Migrating from VINES Three computers will be needed to perform the upgrade using the BMIGRATE across-the-wire method:

▸ The Banyan VINES server, known as the *source* server

▸ A NetWare server running IntranetWare, known as the *destination* server

> ▸ A DOS workstation using the NetWare Client for DOS/Windows software, known as the *client workstation*

BMIGRATE Capabilities The BMIGRATE utility can migrate the following NDS objects and properties from their respective Banyan StreetTalk counterparts (where available):

- ▸ Aliases

- ▸ Directory and file rights

- ▸ User information

- ▸ User name

- ▸ Login restrictions

- ▸ Password restrictions (except grace logins)

- ▸ Login time restrictions

- ▸ Network address restrictions

- ▸ Group membership

- ▸ Group information

- ▸ Security equivalencies

Migrating Users from VINES to IntranetWare Users on the Banyan server are created as new users on the IntranetWare server. User login names and user account restrictions (such as account balance, expiration, password, and time restrictions) are migrated. Users with the same user names are merged on the IntranetWare server. User information such as login names, print job configurations, and login scripts are added together. However, user account restrictions are not merged; they remain unchanged.

Allow Sufficient Time for the Migration

Migration from a Banyan Directory-based network to an IntranetWare Directory-based network can take a lot of time. Migrating a large Banyan Directory tree can take a full day to complete. In some cases, you may find it more efficient to migrate a single group at a time. The BMIGRATE utility attempts to resolve all rights issues with the users and groups that it migrates. For example, if a user object is a member of a group that is not being migrated, and that user has rights to other users, groups, or files in a part of the tree you are migrating, those user's rights will not be migrated to the NDS tree.

Migrating Files from VINES to IntranetWare   BMIGRATE will migrate only Banyan DOS file systems. Banyan VINES network system shared files are not copied to the destination server. Any Banyan server file that has the same name as an IntranetWare server file is not migrated. If you attempt to migrate such a Banyan server file, an error message is displayed on the screen during the migration. This error is also written to a migration log to inform you that a file by the same name already exists on the IntranetWare server. You can choose to overwrite the file if the file on the IntranetWare server is older. In addition, if you want to keep the file, you can rename it and copy it to the IntranetWare server or you can manually copy it to the IntranetWare server after the migration is completed.

Migrating Directories from VINES to IntranetWare   If you attempt to migrate a directory that has the same name and path as a directory that already exists on the IntranetWare server, the files from both directories are merged under the destination directory name.

BMIGRATE does not migrate the following items to NDS from StreetTalk:

- ▸ User profiles

- ▸ Print services

- ▸ Mail services

- ▸ Name space files (Macintosh, UNIX, or OS/2)

- ▸ Informational attributes, such as mailing address, phone number, and fax number

- ▸ Nested groups (lists containing lists)

- ▸ Passwords

The BMIGRATE utility enables you to either assign randomly generated passwords for all migrated users or assign no initial passwords to users. Randomly generated passwords are stored in a file called NEW.PWD in SYS:SYSTEM on the IntranetWare destination server.

Review the Migration

The BMIGRATE utility is a variation of the MIGRATE.EXE utility, which is used to migrate earlier versions of NetWare 4 to IntranetWare. You can follow the same steps as you would when migrating using Novell's BMIGRATE utility. After you complete your first migration of a Banyan group to NDS you should pause and review the process for accuracy. Look at the error log generated by BMIGRATE and review the newly migrated objects on the IntranetWare server. Can the newly migrated users log in and print, and so on? Once you are confident that the migration was performed successfully, you can continue to migrate the rest of the Banyan information to IntranetWare.

Basics of Client Migration

"Progress is impossible without change; and those who cannot change their minds cannot change anything." George Bernard Shaw

This chapter explores the migration of your workstations from their current client software, if any, to an appropriate network client to enable your desktops to connect to IntranetWare. Novell's strategy has been to provide the services of NetWare to users on all desktop operating systems. Novell offers NetWare client software for all major desktop operating systems including DOS, Windows, OS/2, Macintosh, UNIX, Windows NT, and Windows 95.

This chapter will also briefly introduce all the Novell-supported clients. The primary focus, however, will be on migrating your workstations to the DOS/Windows Requester and to the client 32 installations since these will more than likely be your most common client.

Supported Desktop Operating Systems

NETWARE DOS/WINDOWS REQUESTER

IntranetWare can use the NetWare DOS Requester for workstations running the DOS/Windows operating system. This software replaces the older NetWare shell known as NETX.EXE. The NetWare DOS Requester is fully compatible with previous versions of NetWare 4, NetWare 3, NetWare 2, and Personal NetWare. The DOS/Windows client supports both NDS and bindery connections and is explained in detail in "The NetWare DOS Requester" section later in this chapter.

NETWARE CLIENT FOR OS/2

The NetWare Client for OS/2 supports a connection from an OS/2 workstation to a IntranetWare server. With this client software an OS/2 user can connect and log in to a IntranetWare server with full NDS capabilities, including file and print, management, and security. In addition, the NetWare Client for OS/2 enables you to run enhanced mode MS-Windows applications in a IntranetWare environment.

The NetWare Client for OS/2 supports connectivity to IntranetWare through IPX/SPX, NetBIOS, and Named Pipes.

In addition, the NetWare Client for OS/2 supports the following features:

- ▸ Graphical User Interface

- ▸ CID support

- ▸ DOS box/VLM load support

- ▸ NetWare Application Launcher support

NETWARE CLIENT FOR MAC/OS

The NetWare Client for Mac/OS is supported as an NDS connection to a IntranetWare server. The most current version is 5.1, and it enables MAC clients to communicate via IPX to IntranetWare. This client provides file and print services as well as Novell Directory Services.

NETWARE UNIX CLIENT

The NetWare for Unix Client (NUC) supports a bindery-based connection to a IntranetWare server. Users running UnixWare clients can access IntranetWare file and print services as well as attach to other servers on the network. Each IntranetWare server that supports UnixWare clients must load the NUC.NLM on the IntranetWare servers as well.

NETWARE CLIENT FOR WINDOWS NT

The NetWare Client for Windows NT 3.5 and 4.0 provides an NDS connection from a Windows NT workstation to a IntranetWare network. With these two products you can manage your IntranetWare network with an NT workstation running NT version 3.5 or 4.0 and Novell's NetWare Client for Windows NT.

You can access NetWare services and browse authorized NDS information including files and directories through mapping drives, configuring print queues, and attaching to other servers. The NetWare Client for Windows NT supports services over IPX or IP transport protocols. IP services are offered through NetWare IP over Microsoft's Windows NT TCP/IP protocol stack.

CHAPTER 18
. . . .
NOVELL'S
GUIDE TO
INTRANETWARE
NETWORKS

This client also provides synchronized login to the Microsoft Windows NT desktop and the IntranetWare network with a single username and password. The client also provides the following benefits:

▸ Autoreconnect service for client-side fault tolerance

▸ 32-bit ODI or NDIS drivers for a greater degree of protocol and more network adapter choices

▸ Windows NT long file names support through the NetWare server HPFS name space

▸ Win32 application and backward compatibility support for running 16-bit applications

▸ DOS box support for running many standard NetWare utilities, such as NETADMIN

NETWARE CLIENT32

NetWare Client32, Novell's client architecture, is based on the 32-bit architecture of desktop operating systems such as Windows 95. This client software provides complete connectivity to NetWare 2.2, NetWare 3, NetWare 4.1, and IntranetWare servers, and serves as a NetWare platform for both DOS/Windows 3.1 and Windows 95 operating systems. There are two 32-bit client offerings based on the same client architecture: NetWare Client32 for DOS/Windows 3.1 and NetWare Client32 for Windows 95. In addition, both clients provide the following features:

▸ Easy Installation and upgrades for NetWare clients

▸ Complete access to NDS

▸ Dynamic configuration capability

▸ NDS connections to multiple trees

For a detailed explanation on these clients, see the "NetWare Client32 Technology" section later in this chapter.

The NetWare DOS Requester

The architecture of the NetWare DOS Requester is based on VLM.EXE, which is a terminate-stay-resident (TSR) memory manager working in conjunction with other memory managers loaded on your system. The VLM.EXE will attempt to load other VLM modules into upper or extended memory, thus freeing up conventional memory for your applications.

After the VLM.EXE module is loaded, it then proceeds to load all the other VLM modules. VLM.EXE checks each module's overall size and its relationship to other modules loaded. Each module consists of a startup segment, global segment, and transient segment. Figure 18.1 illustrates how the VLM.EXE loads each segment of the other VLM modules. VLM.EXE coordinates the loading for all the VLM modules.

The VLM.EXE coordinates the loading of each of the other VLM modules. Each module consists of a startup, global, and transient segment.

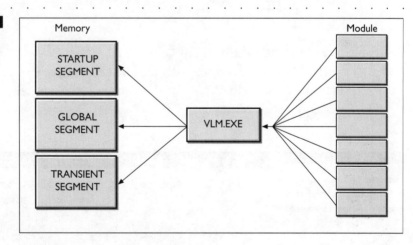

The startup segment for each VLM module is loaded first and is used to initialize the rest of the module. The startup segment remains until all the VLM modules are loaded, then is discarded.

Next, the global block is created, which stores the global segments (module ID numbers and other frequently accessed information) for each module. Segments of all loaded modules are stored together to create the DOS Requester Global Block.

All VLM modules include a transient segment that is used only for infrequently required services by the workstation. The VLM.EXE will record the size of each module's transient segment and create a transient block for the largest block needed.

When the VLM.EXE has completed a review of all modules, it will work with your memory manager (either XMS or EMS) to negotiate available memory in which to store the module's transient segments. When the VLM.EXE is executing at a workstation you will notice a series of dots across the screen as VLM.EXE reviews each module for size and memory requirements.

When the VLM.EXE is loaded at a DOS/Windows workstation it will attempt to load itself into upper memory if it is available, leaving a small footprint of approximately 5K in conventional memory. If you are not using a memory manager, the entire VLM.EXE program is loaded into conventional memory. After the VLM.EXE is loaded, it will then load each of the other VLM modules that you have not excluded in the client configuration file NET.CFG. Some VLMs are required and will always be loaded, while others are optional.

VLM MODULE LISTING

The VLM.EXE loads the individual VLM files that have the .VLM file extension. Table 18.1 shows the VLM modules, their capabilities, and whether the modules are required for operation.

TABLE 18.1	FILE	REQUIRED OR OPTIONAL	DESCRIPTION
Required and nonrequired VLM modules for NDS and a listing of their capabilities	AUTO.VLM	Optional	Automatically reconnects the shell to the server in case the connection goes down
	BIND.VLM	Optional	Supports bindery services requests and is required if you are making a bindery connection

FILE	REQUIRED OR OPTIONAL	DESCRIPTION
CONN.VLM	Required	Connection manager that manages connections between the VLMs and the servers
FIO.VLM	Required	File Input/Output manager that manages redirection of the files to and from the servers
GENERAL.VLM	Required	Provides general purpose services for the VLMs
IPXNCP.VLM	Required	Provides support for both the IPX and NCP protocol stacks
NDS.VLM	Required	Provides support for NDS calls
NETX.VLM	Optional	Provides compatibility with the older NETX.COM and modulates the NETX shell for backward compatibility
NMR.VLM	Optional	NetWare Management Responder that provides support for the network management software
NWP.VLM	Required	NetWare Protocol Multiplexer
PNW.VLM	Optional	Provides support for NetWare Lite
PRINT.VLM	Optional	Provides printing redirection to a network print queue and is required if client needs to print
REDIR.VLM	Required	Provides the DOS redirection
RSA.VLM	Optional	Used in part for auto-reconnect feature

(continued)

T A B L E   18.1

Required and nonrequired
VLM modules for NDS and
a listing of their capabilities
(continued)

FILE	REQUIRED OR OPTIONAL	DESCRIPTION
SECURITY.VLM	Optional	Provides packet level security for the workstation
TCPNCP.VLM	Optional	Provides support for the TCP/IP protocol stack and comes with NetWare/IP and LAN WorkPlace products
TRAN.VLM	Required	Provides transport services that guarantee packet delivery and provide additional reliability of network communications

By default, all the VLM modules are loaded automatically from the same directory where you execute VLM.EXE. You can control which VLMs are loaded by using a series of commands in the NET.CFG file. The list below illustrates how you can specify which VLMs are loaded and in which order. Notice that the USE DEFAULTS must first be set to OFF. This turns off the automatic loading feature. These commands must be under the NETWARE DOS REQUESTER heading in the NET.CFG file. The syntax for the command in the NET.CFG file is as follows:

```
VLM = <path>VLM_filename
```

LINK SUPPORT

MemPool 6192

Buffers 10 1580

MAX STACKS 8

LINK DRIVER NE2000

INT 5

PORT 320

MEM D0000

FRAME Ethernet_802.2

NETWARE DOS REQUESTER

NAME CONTEXT = "NORAD.ACME"

PREFERRED SERVER = NOR-SRV1

FIRST NETWORK DRIVE = F

NETWARE PROTOCOL = NDS BIND

USE DEFAULTS = OFF

VLM = CONN

VLM = IPXNCP

VLM = TRAN

VLM = NDS

VLM = NWP

VLM = FIO

VLM = GENERAL

VLM = REDIR

VLM Correct Load Order

VLM.EXE will load the following modules by default in the order shown below. Unless you specify otherwise, these modules will be loaded automatically during the startup of the VLM client software.

CHAPTER 18
. . . . . .
N O V E L L ' S
G U I D E   T O
I N T R A N E T W A R E
N E T W O R K S

1 • CONN

2 • IPXNCP

3 • TRAN

4 • SECURITY

5 • NDS

6 • BIND

7 • NWP

8 • FIO

9 • GENERAL

10 • REDIR

11 • PRINT

12 • NETX

13 • RSA

14 • AUTO

15 • NMR

VLM Load Options

You can load VLM.EXE with several different options. The load options control memory usage, preferred tree and server attachments, help screens, and messages that are displayed as the VLM is loaded. Table 18.2 gives you a general description of the options available to you during the loading of VLMs.

	OPTION	DESCRIPTION
TABLE 18.2 *VLM Load Options*	/?	Displays the help screen.
	/U	Unloads the VLM.EXE program and all the individual VLM modules. The unload option will fail if there is another memory-resident program that has been loaded after the VLM.EXE.
	/Mx	Specifies the memory type VLM.EXE should use. The memory types are as follows: C = conventional memory (CON) X = extended memory (XMS) E = expanded memory (EMS) VLM.EXE will automatically detect a memory manager and try to load it into extended memory. This option is useful in forcing the VLM.EXE to load in the specified memory type.
	/D	Displays a detailed VLM diagnostic screen. VLM /d "VLM memory type" (CON, XMS, EMS) shows the memory location of the transient swap block for the loaded VLMs.
	/C=[path] filename	Specifies a configuration file to be used when VLM.EXE is loaded. The default is the NET.CFG file in the current directory.
	/PS= servername	Attaches to a preferred server and forces the VLM.EXE to look for the server specified.
	/PT=	Attaches to a preferred tree and forces the VLM.EXE to look treename for the tree specified. This option is useful if you have multiple NDS trees implemented at your company, including any test trees that you might create.
	/Vn	Controls the level of messages displayed to the workstation screen. The range of value is 0 to 4 where: 0 = copyright and critical errors 1 = everything in 0 plus warnings 2 = everything in 0 and 1 plus module names 3 = everything in 0, 1, and 2 plus configuration settings 4 = everything in 0, 1, 2, and 3 plus diagnostic messages.

You can use the VLM /D option even after the VLM.EXE software has been loaded into the workstation memory. To use this option you simply type the following command at the DOS prompt:

```
VLM /D
```

The screen then displays the following message:

VLM.EXE — NetWare virtual loadable module manager v1.20 (941024)
(C) Copyright 1994 Novell, Inc. All Rights Reserved.
Patent pending.
The VLM.EXE file v1.20 is currently loaded
VLM transient switch count   : 1910
VLM call count   : 18857
VLM current ID   : 0040h
VLM memory type   : XMS
VLM modules loaded count   : 12
VLM block ID (0 if CON)   : A90Ah
VLM transient block   : 297Bh
VLM global seg (0 if CON)   : 20DBh
VLM async queue (h, t, s)   : 0000:0000, 1F9A:0030, 0
VLM busy queue (h, t, s)   : 0000:0000, 1F9A:003C, 0
VLM re-entrance level   : 1
VLM full map count   : 1908

Table 18.3 shows the diagnostic information that is displayed on the screen after you have entered the VLM /D option.

TABLE 18.3

Detailed diagnostic information is displayed on the screen after you enter the VLM /D option.

VLM DIAGNOSTIC INFORMATION				ADDRESS			MEMORY SIZES (DECIMAL)				
NAME	ID	FLAG	FUNC	MAPS	CALL	TSEG	GSEG	LOW	HIGH	TSIZE	GSIZE	SSIZE
VLM	0001	A000	0005	0000	12E5	1F9A	089F	FFFF	0000	5376	0	0
CONN	0010	B000	0011	0000	1BB8	20DB	21A6	FFFF	FFFF	3248	384	6704
IPXNCP	0021	B000	000B	0000	0039	21BE	22F5	FFFF	FFFF	4976	2912	2032

T A B L E   18.3

*Detailed diagnostic
information is displayed on
the screen after you enter
the VLM /D option.
(continued)*

| VLM DIAGNOSTIC INFORMATION | | | | | ADDRESS | | | MEMORY SIZES (DECIMAL) | | | | |
NAME	ID	FLAG	FUNC	MAPS	CALL	TSEG	GSEG	LOW	HIGH	TSIZE	GSIZE	SSIZE
TRAN	0020	E000	000B	0001	0703	21BE	22F5	FFFF	FFFF	311	182	2032
SECURITY	0061	A000	0005	000E	000D	297B	23AB	0000	0000	4192	0	3280
NDS	0032	A000	0010	0083	00CA	297B	23AB	1060	0000	6112	896	992
BIND	0031	A000	0010	0028	0010	297B	23E3	2840	0000	3008	448	720
NWP	0030	A000	0011	005D	00A5	297B	23FF	3400	0000	3040	1840	1248
FIO	0041	A000	000B	00F3	0618	297B	2472	3FE0	0000	7008	10224	496
GENERAL	0043	A000	000A	00B3	00BB	297B	26F1	5B40	0000	1760	720	1536
REDIR	0040	A000	0009	02D1	0874	297B	271E	6220	0000	10256	2688	1328
PRINT	0042	A000	000F	002A	0050	297B	27C6	8A30	0000	3952	2864	1520
NETX	0050	A000	0007	01BE	02A9	297B	2879	99A0	0000	10064	4112	2224
Total										62992	27088	
Maximum										10256	10224	6704

▸ The transient block of the VLM TSize in VLM /D is the portion that may be swapped in or out of XMS/EMS memory as shown in the previous diagram in the TSize column.

▸ The Total TSize memory is loaded in the memory type listed in: VLM Memory Type category under VLM /D.

▸ The Maximum listed under TSize in VLM /D is the worst-case swap from XMS/EMS to conventional memory. This becomes the transient swap block that will be located either in conventional or UMB memory.

- VLM shows 0 GSize memory; however, it takes about 4.8K of conventional memory (or 4.8K or UMB memory if loaded high, that is, LH VLM).

- VLM /D Address Low: FFFF means the VLM is loaded in conventional memory.

- The GSize listed under VLM /D is the Global Memory Requirements for each VLM. This GSize consists of: INT handler ESR (Event Scheduled Routines), buffers passed as pointers, and asynchronous events that MUST be loaded in conventional memory or in UMB memory at all times. The GSize cannot be located in XMS/EMS memory.

- The GSize memory must be allocated in one block. If insufficient UMBs are present to hold the entire GSize memory (GSize Total in VLM /D), then the total listed under GSize will be located in conventional memory.

- If you are using XMS/EMS memory, add 6K to 8.5K to the GSize Total for VLM memory management overhead.

- If you are using high memory (that is, HIMEM.SYS) or if an equivalent driver is not loaded, then subtract 2K to 4K from the GSize Total for VLM memory management that is not needed.

- If the user has loaded both HIMEM.SYS and EMM386.EXE but does not have the DOS=UMB parameter listed, then the VLMs will allocate their own UMB through the memory manager, rather than through DOS. The GSize Total in VLM /D will load into UMBs, but MSDOS MEM will not show any UMB usage since it is not in control of the UMB area. This makes it appear as if VLM is taking only 4.8K of conventional memory and no UMB memory. However, the GSize total is located in the UMB area.

Migrating Clients

One of the first steps in migrating your clients is to determine what type of clients you will need to migrate. For many customers a very prevalent client upgrade will be to Novell's DOS/Windows client (also referred to as the DOS Redirector client) or the Client 32 software. The next step is to determine which migration approach is most appropriate for your organization such as using diskettes, loading the client from a IntranetWare server, or using an automated approach.

LOADING THE CLIENTS FROM DISKETTES

If your site will be using any Novell Client you can create the necessary client installation diskettes from your IntranetWare CD-ROM INSTALL.EXE. Using installation diskettes is fairly slow and should be used only for small sites with a few workstations. In addition, if you specified during your server installation to load the client software on your server, you can create diskettes from the server.

NOTE

For larger sites that have more workstations, you should run the client installation from the IntranetWare server. This option requires that the installation utility be run from every workstation by your users, with the assistance of your network administrator, or from an automated process.

For very large sites that are running a previous version of NetWare, you can automate the process of installing the client on the workstations as explained later in this chapter.

Regardless of the size of your site, if you are moving from a non-NetWare operating system to IntranetWare, it may be necessary to visit each workstation to make the necessary changes. In order to load the DOS\Windows client, it is necessary to unload the previous operating system and then load the IntranetWare client in its place.

The migration process will take you approximately ten minutes per workstation if your are loading the client software from diskettes. However, if you need to perform any additional work on a workstation at the same time, the process may take longer. Also, the more standardized your workstations are before you begin, the faster the migration process will be.

If you are migrating a workstation from another operating system, you will need to remove or disable the other operating system from loading at startup. Once the other operating system has been disabled, you can run the client installation utility and begin your upgrade process.

You can create client installation diskettes from any IntranetWare CD-ROM by performing the following steps:

1 • At a workstation with an IntranetWare CD-ROM type **INSTALL** at the root. Select the Diskette Creation category and press Enter. Then you can select the type of client to load onto diskette. You will be presented with a screen as shown in Figure 18.2.

FIGURE 18.2

The CD-ROM INSTALL.EXE utility is used to create client installation diskettes.

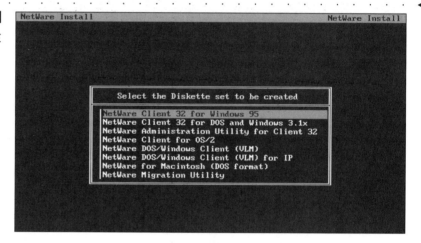

```
NetWare Install                                    NetWare Install




                    Select the Diskette set to be created

            NetWare Client 32 for Windows 95
            NetWare Client 32 for DOS and Windows 3.1x
            NetWare Administration Utility for Client 32
            NetWare Client for OS/2
            NetWare DOS/Windows Client (VLM)
            NetWare DOS/Windows Client (VLM) for IP
            NetWare for Macintosh (DOS format)
            NetWare Migration Utility
```

At the time of this writing, the INSTALL.EXE from the CD-ROM did not include an option to create diskettes for the NetWare Client for Windows NT or the Unix Client.

NOTE

2 • Select the client you wish to create on diskettes and press Enter.

3 • Have your diskettes available and select the target drive.

4 • At the DOS prompt, have your blank formatted diskettes ready. You'll need five to eight diskettes, depending on the type of client you select.

Another way to create your client diskettes is to use the MAKEDISK.BAT utility. This utility is found on your SYS:\PUBLIC\CLIENT directories. There is a MAKEDISK.BAT utility for both DOS/Windows clients and the OS/2 client. This option can create diskettes at a workstation rather than at the server, which may be more convenient for your administrators because they can create diskettes from any workstation that is logged in to the IntranetWare server.

SERVER INSTALLATION METHOD

The server installation method requires that you have a client running the NETX shell or an earlier version of the NetWare DOS Requester so that the workstation can access a IntranetWare server. The workstation simply logs in to the IntranetWare server and runs the installation utility from the following subdirectory:

```
F:\PUBLIC\CLIENT\DOSWIN\INSTALL.EXE
```

You will see the main installation screen appear as shown in Figure 18.3 You must specify information, such as adapter card and whether this client is being loaded on a Windows workstation. Once you enter the configuration information, the utility will begin the installation process.

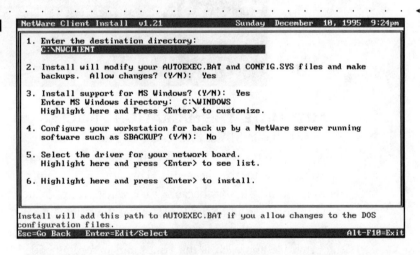

FIGURE 18.3

*Main Client
Installation screen*

```
NetWare Client Install  v1.21           Sunday  December  10, 1995  9:24pm
┌──────────────────────────────────────────────────────────────────────┐
│ 1. Enter the destination directory:                                    │
│    C:\NWCLIENT                                                          │
│                                                                        │
│ 2. Install will modify your AUTOEXEC.BAT and CONFIG.SYS files and make  │
│    backups.  Allow changes? (Y/N):  Yes                                │
│                                                                        │
│ 3. Install support for MS Windows? (Y/N):  Yes                         │
│    Enter MS Windows directory:  C:\WINDOWS                              │
│    Highlight here and Press <Enter> to customize.                      │
│                                                                        │
│ 4. Configure your workstation for back up by a NetWare server running  │
│    software such as SBACKUP? (Y/N):  No                                │
│                                                                        │
│ 5. Select the driver for your network board.                           │
│    Highlight here and press <Enter> to see list.                       │
│                                                                        │
│ 6. Highlight here and press <Enter> to install.                        │
│                                                                        │
└──────────────────────────────────────────────────────────────────────┘
Install will add this path to AUTOEXEC.BAT if you allow changes to the DOS
configuration files.
Esc=Go Back    Enter=Edit/Select                           Alt-F10=Exit
```

This option is faster than loading disks and can be accomplished by many of your users with little assistance. You will still need to answer the questions displayed on the installation parameter screen, but the utility will continue the installation process by itself. As mentioned earlier, the utility will pause on previously loaded duplicate files that have a newer date on the workstation.

CD-ROM CLIENT INSTALLATION METHOD

The CD-ROM client installation option is similar to the server option except that you are accessing the installation utility from the IntranetWare CD-ROM. This option is faster than installing from diskettes, but not as fast as installing from the server. You can quickly initiate the installation utility on the IntranetWare CD-ROM by typing **INSTALL** at the root of the CD. You can then select your particular option as shown in Figure 18.4.

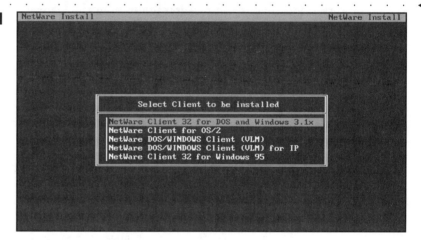

AUTOMATE THE MIGRATION PROCESS

Because the INSTALL.EXE is copying and modifying files, you can replace this utility with your own custom-designed batch files or script files to install the client software for your specific needs. This approach requires some work up front for network administrators because they will have to create batch or script files that perform some or all of the functions of the Client Installation utility.

For large installations with many workstations that are currently running NETX, the batch file approach is the fastest and is recommended because you can update clients from the IntranetWare server. The batch file approach is more difficult for sites not using NetWare because they are not connected to a IntranetWare server. Although script files are beyond the scope of this section, you can consider using a scripting language to assist you with migrations as well.

The automated process enables a container, profile, or system login script to query the workstation for the existence of the NetWare DOS Requester. If the current DOS requester is not found, the container login script can be directed to copy a set of newer client files onto that workstation.

One of the processes available from Novell for handling a client upgrade without administrator intervention is known as the Automated Client Update (ACU). The ACU automatically upgrades NetWare client software on your workstations by executing a series of instructions that have been placed by your network administrator in a container, profile, or system login script, and then upgrades clients during login. The process involves four separate utilities — NWDETECT.EXE, NWSTAMP.EXE, NWLOG.EXE, and REBOOT.COM — plus an enhanced version (version 1.22) of INSTALL.EXE.

Depending on the number of different NetWare client configurations in your internetwork, ACU may or may not be a practical way to efficiently upgrade your clients. For example, if your network workstations have the same configuration of 20 bindery-based (NETX) or NDS (VLM) workstations running DOS and MS Windows, and you need to upgrade all or a portion of them to the most recent VLMs, the ACU process would be a practical solution. However, if your network consists of 20 workstations, each with a different customized or nonstandard configuration (that is, multiple protocol stacks, different TSRs, or various memory configurations, and so on), the ACU option probably will not help much. This process is dependent on a group of standardized clients.

NOTE **As long as your network workstations are configured with the same standards, there is no limit to the number of workstations that can be upgraded using the ACU process.**

The ACU program is available on NetWire. The self-extracting file name is ACUVLM.EXE and includes the following files:

▶ NWDETECT.EXE — Begins the ACU process by looking for an Install Stamp in the NET.CFG file and detecting whether there is a difference between the stamp parameters within the login script and those currently within NET.CFG.

▶ NWSTAMP.EXE — Updates (or creates for the first time) the Install Stamp in the NET.CFG file. The Install Stamp is an entry in the individual workstation's NET.CFG file that displays four parameters. If any of these parameters are different from those defined by the network supervisor in the login script, the upgrade instructions within the login script may be invoked. Following the upgrade, the parameters are updated in the NET.CFG file. A sample Install Stamp in a NET.CFG file is shown below:

```
Install Stamp

    Name = Novell_Inc_vlm
    Major Version = 4
    Minor Version = 1
    Revision Version = 0
```

The four Install Stamp parameters are network supervisor-definable. The Name parameter can contain up to 63 alphanumeric characters, whereas the three Version parameters can contain 127 characters each. If you choose to use spaces, the entire name or version must be enclosed in double quotes (" ").

▶ NWLOG.EXE — Creates a log file of all upgraded nodes to a network supervisor-specified subdirectory. The log file lists the date, time, username, IPX external network number, and any network supervisor-defined text. Before individual workstation information can appear in the log file, all users must have Write and Create rights to the subdirectory where the log file will reside. A sample log entry for an upgraded NDS VLM client is shown below.

```
4-17-95 4:01:25 PM MMORGAN 010104A0:00001B021FDB
```

This log entry above indicates that user object MMORGAN was upgraded at the specified date and time. The IPX external network number and node number follow the username. A sample log entry for a bindery-based (NETX) client is shown below:

```
4-17-95 5:17:57 PM
```

```
Upgrade Successful for user "ALINCOLN"
```

The log entry above indicates that user ALINCOLN was upgraded at the specified date and time. The message on the second line is network supervisor-definable in the login script.

▶ INSTALL.CFG — Lists the client files that are copied to the workstation. INSTALL.CFG is a component of the DOS/MS Windows Client Installation utility. A copy of the INSTALL.CFG file is included with the ACU files. If you make changes to the INSTALL.CFG file, you should always make a backup of the original file. This can be very useful when you want to update only a few files (for example, some updated client files downloaded from NetWire) rather than an entire set of client files.

▶ REBOOT.COM — An executable file that automatically reboots the workstation.

Verify that the files you downloaded from NetWire are in the SYS:PUBLIC\ CLIENT\DOSWIN directory. You should have copied down the following:

▶ README.TXT

▶ NWDETECT.EXE

▶ NWDETECT.MSG

▶ NWSTAMP.EXE

▶ NWSTAMP.MSG

▶ NWLOG.EXE

▶ NWLOG.MSG

▶ INSTALL.EXE (version 1.22)

▶ INSTALL.CFG

▶ REBOOT.COM

You can follow the instructions found in the README.TXT file.

Using **INSTALL.EXE**

The Client Installation utility, also known as INSTALL.EXE, can be used for loading the NetWare DOS Requester on your workstations from either diskettes, your server, or the IntranetWare CD-ROM as previously discussed. The INSTALL utility handles the installation of the VLM files by automatically creating the C:\NWCLIENT directory on your workstation and loading other appropriate files such as the NET.CFG file. This utility will modify the workstation's CONFIG.SYS and AUTOEXEC.BAT files with the appropriate changes. For example, the CONFIG.SYS file will have the LASTDRIVE = Z entry to enable drive mappings, which start at Z and are assigned backwards from Z.

The Client Installation utility will also edit your AUTOEXEC.BAT file by adding one line at the top of this file to call the STARTNET.BAT file. When called, this file will automatically load your client software and attempt to connect you to a server. Refer back to Figure 18.4 for an example of the INSTALL screen where you can specify the previously discussed parameters. If you are installing the client in a language other than English, you must use the SET NWLANGUAGE= command to specify the appropriate language, such as SET NWLANGUAGE=SPANISH. This command directs the messages to appear in Spanish or any other chosen language. The default is English and this SET parameter will automatically be placed in your STARTNET.BAT file when English is the default.

CONSULTING EXPERIENCE

If the workstation you're migrating is currently running Windows 3.1, you must exit before beginning the client installation. Because some of the client files are copied into the Windows subdirectories, Windows 3.1 must be brought down beforehand. However, your workstation must have Windows loaded before you begin the installation.

Step 1 of the INSTALL utility will, by default, install the client software in the C:\NWCLIENT directory or in any other directory that you specify. There is really no reason to change this directory unless you want it nested in another subdirectory. For simplicity's sake, you should leave this directory as the default directory.

Step 2 modifies your AUTOEXEC.BAT and CONFIG.SYS files by adding PATH and CALL statements to automatically load the client at bootup. Your AUTOEXEC.BAT file will place a CALL statement at the top of the batch file and add the PATH statement to the NWCLIENT subdirectory. An example of this modification is shown in Figure 18.5.

FIGURE 18.5

Two entries are made to your AUTOEXEC.BAT file: A CALL command launches your STARTNET.BAT file @CALL C:\NWCLIENT\STARTNET.BAT, and a PATH command is added to your NWCLIENT directory PATH=C:\NWCLIENT.

```
@CALL C:\NWCLIENT\STARTNET
@REM   THE CHECK LINE BELOW PROVIDES ADDITIONAL SAFETY FOR STACKER DRIVES.
@REM   PLEASE DO NOT REMOVE IT.
@C:\STACKER\CHECK /WP
SET SOUND=C:\SB16
SET BLASTER=A220 I5 D1 H5 P330 T6
SET MIDI=SYNTH:1 MAP:E
C:\SB16\DIAGNOSE /S
C:\SB16\SB16SET /P /Q
REM ===== PC DOS 7.0 - Update  ===== C:\SBCD\DRV\MSCDEX.EXE /D:MSCD001 /M:8 /V
C:\DOS\MSCDEX.EXE /D:MSCD001 /M:8 /V
REM ===== PC DOS 7.0 - Update  ===== share
REM C:\DOS\share
C:\DOS\SHARE.EXE /l:500 /f:5100
LH /L:0;1,42384 /S C:\DOS\SMARTDRV.EXE
@ECHO OFF
PROMPT $p$g
REM ===== PC DOS 7.0 - Update  ===== PATH C:\WINDOWS;C:\DOS;C:\MOUSE
PATH C:\DOS;C:\WINDOWS;C:\MOUSE;C:\QLI
REM ===== PC DOS 7.0 - Update  ===== PATH C:\NWCLIENT\;%PATH%
PATH C:\DOS;C:\NWCLIENT\;%PATH%;C:\STACKER;
SET TEMP=C:\DOS
rem LH /L:1,63088 C:\DOS\VSAFE /4-
-- More --
```

Your CONFIG.SYS is modified to include the statement LASTDRIVE = Z so that drive mapping can work from Drive Z backwards.

Step 3 allows support for MS Windows, and the default is "yes." You can also customize the support for MS Windows, such as changing a country code for that workstation and using shared MS Windows directories from a network server. You will most likely accept the default "yes" to load the appropriate files required by the VLMs to work with Windows 3.

Step 4 enables you to configure your workstation for backup by a IntranetWare server running SMS compliant backup software. This configuration parameter asks you to specify a server name doing the backup along with a name for your workstation. You can also specify an optional password and the number of buffers available for file transfer. An example of this screen is shown in Figure 18.6.

FIGURE 18.6

Using the Client Installation utility to specify software to back up this workstation

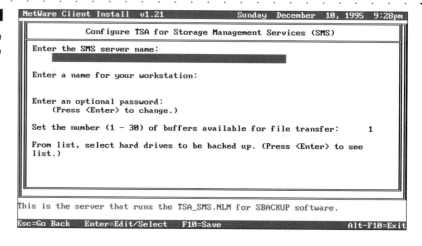

In Step 5 you select the appropriate driver for your particular network board. If you are already running the NETX client, the INSTALL utility will autodetect the driver and adapter you have currently running as shown in Figure 18.7. For new installations, the INSTALL utility will display a screen of available drivers or you can add a new driver to the list from your floppy drive.

FIGURE 18.7

The Client Installation utility will recognize a current NetWare driver loaded on your workstation.

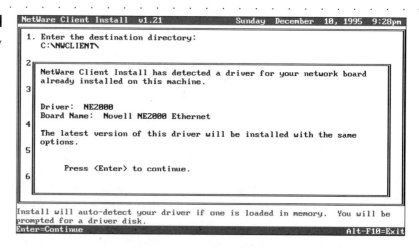

Step 6 initiates the installation of your client software. If you are running the INSTALL utility from a server or CD-ROM, it will run to completion unless you are installing from floppy disks. Other error conditions, such as trying to copy a corrupted file, will also prevent the INSTALL utility from completing. An example of the File copy status screen is shown in Figure 18.8.

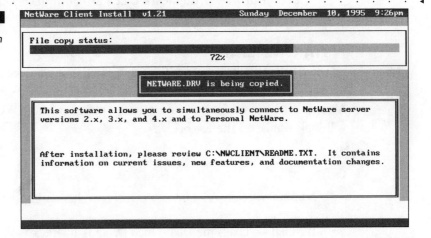

FIGURE 18.8

The File copy status screen informs you of the client installation's progress.

When you have successfully completed the client installation, you will see a screen as shown in Figure 18.9.

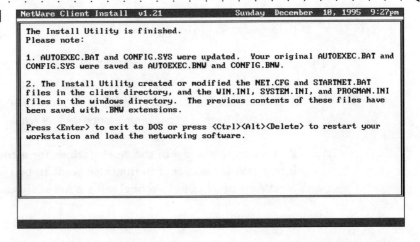

FIGURE 18.9

Upon successful completion of the client installation, this screen is displayed.

NOTE

Occasionally, the INSTALL utility may have DLL (Data Link Library) files that are older than the duplicate DLLs currently on your system. The INSTALL utility will prompt you to copy the older DLLs to the client. The Novell utility recommendation is to place the older DLLs from the INSTALL utility onto the workstation for compatibility reasons. You should follow this recommendation unless you know that your newer, duplicate DLLs are completely compatible.

STARTNET.BAT

The STARTNET.BAT is simply a batch file that automates the process of loading the necessary components of the client software during the startup of a workstation. After this file is created, it is automatically placed in the NWCLIENT directory and will look similar to the list below:

- ▸ **LSL** — Loads the Link Support Layer software

- ▸ **NE2000** — Network interface driver (or other appropriate NIC driver you use)

- ▸ **IPXODI** — Loads the ODI (Open Datalink Interface) software

- ▸ **VLM** — Loads the TSR VLM.EXE, which loads all selected VLM modules

- ▸ **F:** — Changes to the network drive letter F

- ▸ **LOGIN** — Logs in to the attached server

The client installation process is fairly automatic and requires only a single screen to be completed before the process begins. As mentioned previously, the INSTALL utility will pause if it encounters newer, duplicate DLL files that you may have previously updated from another source such as NetWire.

NOTE

Be sure to test a few of the workstations for a connection to the IntranetWare server. You may also want to briefly test some of the NetWare utilities before beginning a full-scale client migration.

Create a Common NET.CFG

The NET.CFG file contains various network parameters that are read during the loading of the network client software. This file can be compared with the boot parameters found in a workstation's CONFIG.SYS file, except the NET.CFG file provides parameters for the workstation to connect to a server. When you have loaded a workstation with the VLM client software, a default NET.CFG is placed in the C:\NWCLIENT directory. For many installations running a single protocol, the default NET.CFG file may suffice with the minimal settings. For other sites running multiple protocols and other complex workstation configurations, you may need to add or change some of the many parameters available. For a complete list of NET.CFG headings, refer to Appendix D.

The default NET.CFG contains the necessary startup information for that workstation to connect to the network. The following is an example of a basic NET.CFG text file.

```
NetWare DOS Requester

    FIRST NETWORK DRIVE = F
    NETWARE PROTOCOL = NDS BIND
    NAME CONTEXT = "OU=LABS.OU=NORAD.O=ACME"
    PREFERRED SERVER = NOR-SRV1

Link Driver PCMDMCS

    MEM D9000
    FRAME ETHERNET_802.2

Link Support

    Buffers 4 1500
    Mempool 4096
```

NetWare DOS Requester

The VLM configuration can be customized by placing commands in the NET.CFG file. The commands that affect the performance of the VLMs are placed under the heading NETWARE DOS REQUESTER. Other headings in the NET.CFG include Link Driver and Link Support, to name only a few. For a complete list of headings and their parameters, see Appendix D.

A standardized NET.CFG file is highly recommended for companies of all sizes because your time spent configuring each workstation will be reduced if you have a standard NET.CFG. The NET.CFG file is read at the time the VLM.EXE software is loaded at your workstation. The easiest way to define this file is to create a NET.CFG file that contains all the parameters you will need for your site. For more information on using the NCUPDATE utility to accelerate the updates of your existing client's NET.CFG file, see Chapter 2.

Use your lab environment to test your NET.CFG file. If you have standardized workstation hardware, you will have the same NIC card and driver. Standardized hardware simplifies the maintenance of this file, and you will not have to make exceptions for other drivers.

You can use the following steps to define your migration strategy:

1 • Determine your workstation types.

2 • Create installation diskettes for your workstations (regardless of the migration method you choose). See Novell Documentation for Macintosh and Unix workstations.

3 • Choose a migration method:

   ‣ Using diskettes

   ‣ From an IntranetWare server

   ‣ Automated

4 • Load the workstation software according to your chosen migration method and consider taking the following additional steps:

   ‣ Loading a standard NET.CFG file that you have created

   ‣ Upgrading your DOS version if necessary

   ‣ Taking inventory of the PC hardware

5 • Reboot the workstation and log in as an NDS user to verify that the workstation is completely operational.

NETWARE CLIENT32 TECHNOLOGY

NetWare Client32 is Novell's latest high-performance client technology for both MS Windows 3 and Windows 95 operating systems. Although separate products by name, Windows 3 and Windows 95 are based on Novell's 32-bit client technology. Each product has the same characteristics, including:

▸ Full 32-bit NLM execution environments

▸ Lower memory requirements

▸ NetWare caching algorithms for superior performance

▸ Improved installation and upgrade features

▸ Complete access to Novell Directory Services including the ability to browse and connect to multiple trees

It is also important to understand how Novell's client technologies have evolved over the years. First, a little about the Shell/Requester technology. The NetWare shell is also a DOS redirector that intercepts calls made to interrupts 21h, 24h, and 17h to handle DOS functions, error handling, and printing to local parallel ports. The shell technology enables users and applications to make requests that are first reviewed by the DOS requester and then forwarded to the network or on to DOS for processing. In addition, the shell builds tables for tracking information about network resources.

In an effort to increase performance and provide a modular approach for NetWare clients, Novell introduced the DOS Requester (VLM) technology. The DOS Requester enables DOS itself to handle the user and application requests. For network requests DOS uses the DOS Requester Interface (Int2Fh). Among the VLM modules is the REDIR.VLM module that communicates on behalf of the NetWare client to Int2Fh.

In its current generation of client technology Novell has attempted through the Client32 Requester to combine the strengths of both the NetWare shell and DOS Requester technologies. The Client32 maintains a set of internal tables similar to the older NetWare shell that provides speedy access to network resources. The network services are provided through internal modules that are similar to the VLM modules. The Client32 also uses the NetWare I/O Subsystem (NIOS) and an

XMS memory manager to load the client manager into extended memory. In fact, the Client32 loads only a 4K NIOS footprint into UMBs or into conventional memory.

Therefore, you receive the same functionality as you do with the VLM technology, but you get even more functionality. Some highlights of this new technology are listed below:

- 4K memory footprint

- Long filename support for MS Windows 95

- Dynamic configurable client settings

- Automatic reconnection capabilities including drive mappings, printers, files, and file locks

- Login script capability from a Windows 3.1x interface as well as from a DOS prompt.

- Better WAN support for packet burst

- Large internet packet support for NDS NCPs

- Full backward compatibility for the NetWare shell and NetWare DOS Requester

- NetWare Application Manager support

The Client32 technology requires the following minimum hardware for your workstation:

- 386 PC compatible or higher

- 4MB memory or higher

- 3MB free disk space

- VGA card or better

▸ MS DOS or PC DOS 3.1 or higher

▸ MS Windows 3.1, Windows for Workgroups 3.11, or Windows 95

▸ Multiple tree support

MIGRATING TO THE CLIENT32 FOR DOS/WINDOWS

The latest Client32 comes with software that helps you upgrade from other NetWare clients. You can run Setup from a login script using the Automatic Client Upgrade (ACU) utility, and you can also use the Network Application Manager to upgrade NDS clients.

As with other Novell client software there are several ways to install the NetWare Client32 for DOS and Windows 3.1x, and so you will need to determine which installation method works best for you before you run the Setup program.

If you want to upgrade a few existing clients, installing Client32 from the network is usually the easiest and fastest method. You can edit the INSTALL.CFG file so users do not need to supply information for the client during an installation. In addition, if you need to install Client32 on only a few workstations or if the computers are not yet connected to a network, you can install Client32 from a local drive.

Installing Client32 from a Local Drive

If you need to install Client32 on only one or two computers or if the computers are not yet connected to a network, you can install Client32 from a local drive. You can simply run Setup off an IntranetWare CD-ROM. If the workstation has an internet connection, you can download the Client32 software from Novell's NetWire or from Novell's web site WWW.NOVELL.COM. After copying the files to a workstation or network subdirectory you can then execute the appropriate SETUP (DOS or Windows) to migrate a client.

You can also download a diskette installation, although this method is much slower. The diskette installation creates eight (8) diskette images that are used to install Client32 from diskette or to first copy to a network subdirectory for faster installation.

Installing Client32 from the Network

Installing from the network is the most efficient way to upgrade multiple existing clients. It also enables you to minimize the amount of user input that the SETUP requires.

If you have already installed client files on an IntranetWare server, you can map a drive to the SYS:PUBLIC\CLIENT\DOSWIN directory and run INSTALL.EXE or SETUP.EXE from the workstation you want to upgrade. This process must be done by either the network administrator or by knowledgeable users. You can also run the install directly from the CD-ROM in the PRODUCTS\DOSWIN32\IBM_1 directory. You can copy the contents of the ENGLISH directory to a network directory or mount the CD-ROM as a volume of a NetWare server to run Client32 Setup from the network. To set up a Network Install Directory from the CD-ROM, follow the steps outlined below:

1 • Copy the ENGLISH directory to a directory on the network.

2 • Edit the INSTALL.CFG file as needed for your environment.

3 • Grant the users who need to install Client32 Read rights to the network install directory.

4 • Run SETUP.EXE or INSTALL.EXE from the root of the network install directory.

To set up a networked CD-ROM, follow these steps:

1 • Mount the Client32 CD-ROM as a volume on a NetWare server.

2 • Grant Read rights at the root directory of the CD-ROM to users who need to install Client32.

3 • Run SETUP.EXE or INSTALL.EXE from the root directory of the CD-ROM.

In addition, there are three methods for running Client32 SETUP from the network:

▶ Automatic Client Upgrade (ACU) — DOS-based SETUP only

▶ NetWare Application Manager (NAM) — Windows-based SETUP only

▶ Workstation-Initiated Install — DOS- or Windows-based SETUP

Setting Up Automatic Client Upgrade (ACU)   The Automatic Client Upgrade utility requires some initial time to set up, but it can greatly speed your migration to the Client32 software. As an administrator you will need to edit the system, container, or personal login script for the users you want to upgrade. Because the login script executes in DOS, only the DOS-based Setup program (INSTALL.EXE) can be used to automatically upgrade clients. The Windows-based Setup program (SETUP.EXE) will not run from a login script.

As discussed previously in this chapter the ACU consists of four programs that run from a login script. Three of these programs ensure that computers run Client32 Setup only when an update is required and the fourth program reboots client computers from a login script after an upgrade.

You can refer to ACU.TXT file in the \ADMIN1 directory of the Client32 software for more detailed information about ACU and how to set this up for your client migration.

Running Setup from NetWare Application Manager   The NetWare Application Manager (NAM) is an add-on utility to the NetWare Administrator (NWADMIN) that allows network administrators to create NDS objects for applications that are represented at the desktop. For more information on using NAM refer to Chapter 20.

Workstation-Initiated Setup from the Network   After you create a network install directory, network users can run the DOS-based or Windows-based Setup program from the network. A network administrator or an end user can perform the following steps to load the software:

1 • Log in to the IntranetWare network.

2 • Map a drive to the network installation directory.

3 • Run Client32 Setup from Windows 3.1x or DOS.

NOTE: A network supervisor can influence the amount of user input for the DOS-based Setup by editing the INSTALL.CFG file on the install directory.

As you run the Setup programs keep in mind that the Client32 software can be installed from DOS or from Windows 3.1x. Both Setup programs support the same installation options and both programs can run from network or local drives, with the following restrictions:

- If you want to install Client32 using Automatic Client Upgrade (ACU), you must run the DOS-based installation because the Windows Setup program cannot run from a login script.

- If you want to install Client32 using NetWare Application Manager (NAM), you must run the Windows-based installation.

- If you are using a networked version of Windows 3.1x, you must run the DOS installation.

Editing the NET.CFG File

Changes to the Client32 for DOS/Windows configurations are made using the NET.CFG file. The NET.CFG is an ASCII text file that maintains configuration information for Client32 modules. Several Client32 modules access information in this file when they load to establish starting values and environment variables.

For more information on NET.CFG parameters refer to Appendix D of this book.

MIGRATING TO THE CLIENT32 FOR WINDOWS 95

The Client32 for Windows 95 is a 32-bit protected mode NetWare client that runs on Windows 95 and provides connectivity to NetWare 2.2, 3.1x, and 4.x servers. Four methods of installing the NetWare Client32 for Windows 95 are:

- Install using the server-based Windows 95 Install (MSBATCH Setup)

- Install the Client32 on an existing Windows 95 workstation

- Install the Client32 using a custom Windows 95 setup

- Install using the Automatic Client Upgrade

Install the Client32 Using a Server-Based Windows 95 Install (MSBATCH Setup)

If you need to install Windows 95 and Client32 on multiple workstations consider installing Client32 using a server-based Windows 95 install. The MSBATCH Setup requires some preparation, but it can greatly simplify the installation of the Client32 on each workstation. User interaction for the Client32 portion of the installation can be completely eliminated. User interaction for the Windows 95 portion can be kept to a minimum. This procedure is based on a script contained in the MSBATCH.INF file. Network administrators can use a customized version of MSBATCH.INF to automate the installation and configuration of Windows 95 and Novell's Client32 at the same time from a NetWare server. Keep in mind the following limitations of this installation method:

▸ This procedure is designed for first-time installations of Windows 95 and Client32. It does not work properly on a machine running NetWare Client32 for DOS/Windows that you are going to upgrade to Windows 95.

▸ MSBATCH supports only NDIS drivers — it does not support Novell's ODI drivers. It will install and configure Client32 to use an NDIS driver. The MSBATCH process will fail if you have a 32-bit ODI driver installed on the workstation. Make sure you have a 16-bit (real-mode) LAN driver installed before you run MSBATCH.

The workstation preparation involves using some Windows 95 utility programs. These programs are available only on the Windows 95 CD-ROM, not on the Windows 95 diskettes. At the time of this writing, the programs are also available from Microsoft on the Internet. The programs prepare the Windows 95 and Client32 files on a file server, so that Windows 95 and Client32 can be installed at the same time. During the installation, the files are copied from the server to the workstation.

The following are the procedures for the server-based Windows 95 installation method in the order they should be performed.

Step 1: Run the server-based setup (NETSETUP.EXE)

1 • Log in to the NetWare server and map a network drive to the volume from which you want users to install Windows 95 and Client32.

2 • Run NETSETUP.EXE under Windows 95. (NETSETUP.EXE is in the ADMIN\NETTOOLS\NETSETUP folder of the Windows 95 CD-ROM.)

3 • Set the server install path to the MSBATCH Setup install folder (F:\WIN95, for example).

4 • Choose Set Path.

5 • Enter the path.

6 • Choose OK.

7 • Install the Windows 95 source files to the server install path.

8 • Choose Install.

9 • Choose Local hard drive.

10 • Enter the path that has the Windows 95 cabinet (*.CAB) files as the path from which to install (F:\WIN95CAB, for example).

11 • Choose OK.

12 • Respond to the Create Default prompt. (Choose either option.)

13 • Follow the instructions for responding when any other prompts are displayed.

Step 2: Place all the Client32 files into a new directory

▸ Copy the files from the PRODUCTS\WIN95\IBM_1 folder of the IntranetWare CD-ROM or from the Client32 diskettes.

NOTE

Do not copy the files from the PRODUCTS\ADM32\IBM_I\ BATCH95\NLS\ENGLISH folder of the IntranetWare CD-ROM or from the BATCH95\NLS\ENGLISH folder of the Admin2 diskette to the folder at this point.

Step 3: Remove all the .INF files from the new directory

▸ In the directory into which you put all the files for NetWare Client32 for Windows 95, move or rename all the files with an extension of .INF.

Step 4: Copy the .INF files from the BATCH95 Directory

1 • Copy the .INF files from the PRODUCTS\ADM32\IBM_1\BATCH95\NLS\ENGLISH folder of the IntranetWare CD-ROM or from the BATCH95\NLS\ENGLISH folder of the Admin2 diskette. Copy them to the folder where you put all the files for Client32.

Always copy the following files: NWCLIENT.INF, NWTRANS.INF, and NWLAYOUT.INF.

For NetWare/IPTM support, copy the NWIP.INF file.

For SNMP support, copy the NWSERV.INF file.

2 • If you want the Client32 help integrated with the Windows 95 system help, edit the NWCLIENT.INF file and remove the semicolon (;) in front of the line that has OEM.CNT.

Step 5: Create an MSBATCH.INF file

1 • Run BATCH.EXE.

2 • Fill in the Setup Information if desired.

3 • Remove network options.

4 • Choose network options.

5 • Uncheck any protocols, services, clients, or other options that are checked.

6 • Check IPX/SPXTM compatible protocol, which is listed under Available Protocols.

7 • Choose OK.

8 • Change the Installation Options.

9 • Choose Installation Options.

10 • Set as many of the installation options as you want. The more options you set at this time, the fewer interactions are required when installing Windows 95 and Client32 from the server.

11 • Choose OK.

12 • Select Optional Components.

13 • Choose Done.

14 • Save with a unique filename (such as C32BATCH.INF) in the MSBATCH Setup install folder (for example, F:\WIN95).

15 • Replace the existing MSBATCH.INF file with the file you just created.

16 • Remove the Read-only attribute from the existing MSBATCH.INF file.

17 • Rename the existing MSBATCH.INF file.

18 • Rename the file you just created to MSBATCH.INF.

Step 6: Run the INF Installer (INFINST.EXE)

1 • Log in to the NetWare server and map a network drive to the MSBATCH Setup install folder (NETSETUP.EXE).

2 • Run the INF Installer (INFINST.EXE).

3 • Choose Set Path.

4 • Enter the Server path. Specify the MSBATCH Setup install folder (F:\WIN95, for example).

5 • Choose Install INF.

6 • Choose NWCLIENT.INF.

The NWCLIENT.INF file must be in the folder where you put all the Client32 files. You should already have copied it there from the PRODUCTS\ADM32\IBM_1\BATCH95\NLS\ENGLISH folder on the IntranetWare CD-ROM or from the BATCH95\NLS\ENGLISH folder on the Admin2 diskette.

7 • Choose OK.

Do not keep the existing NETWARE.DRV file even if it is newer than the NETWARE.DRV file that is shipped with Client32. Choose No in response to the Version Conflict message.

IMPORTANT: Do not skip files. If the INF Installer cannot find a file, specify the path where you think the file is. For example, try the directory where you put all the Client32 files.

8 • Respond to any messages that are displayed as the INF Installer runs.

9 • Choose Exit when finished.

Step 7: Check the MSBATCH.INF file
There is a sample MSBATCH.INF file that includes the settings needed to install Client32. It also shows which Client32 settings can be configured directly in the MSBATCH.INF file and what their valid values are. The sample MSBATCH.INF file is in the PRODUCTS\ADM32\IBM_1\BATCH95\NLS\ENGLISH folder of the IntranetWare CD-ROM and in the BATCH95\NLS\ENGLISH folder of the Admin2 diskette.

1 • Compare the keys shown in the sample MSBATCH.INF file with the ones generated by the INF Installer.

2 • If any of the highlighted lines differ, click the highlighted line in the help file, read the note explaining the significance of the statement, and adjust your MSBATCH.INF file if necessary.

For more information about MSBATCH.INF parameters, see the Microsoft Windows 95 Resource Kit.

Step 8: Copy the NETDEF.INF file

▸ Copy the NETDEF.INF file from the BATCH95 directory to the MSBATCH Setup install folder on the NetWare server and to its INF and SUWIN subdirectories.

Step 9: Run the Windows 95 Setup program

1 • Log in to the NetWare server and map a network drive to the volume that has the Windows 95 and Client32 files.

2 • Run SETUP.EXE with MSBATCH.INF as the first parameter (SETUP F:\WIN95\MSBATCH.INF, for example).

Install the Client32 on an Existing Windows 95 Workstation

IMPORTANT: If you are upgrading from the NetWare DOS Requester (VLM) client or if you don't have any network client software installed, you need to have the Windows 95 CD-ROM or diskettes or the Windows 95 .CAB files. To install Client32 on a Windows 95 workstation that already exists, follow these steps:

1 • Run the Client32 installation program (SETUP.EXE).

2 • If you are prompted to select a network adapter, select one that matches your hardware.

3 • If you don't need to customize your installation, choose Reboot.

4 • If you want optional features or need to configure your workstation, choose Customize.

NOTE

You can put the Client32 files on a NetWare server, map a drive to that directory, and run SETUP.EXE from the mapped drive.

Install the Client32 Using a Custom Windows 95 Setup

1 • Run the Windows 95 installation program (SETUP.EXE).

2 • Select Custom when the Windows 95 Setup Wizard displays the Setup Options.

3 • If you have a NetWare client installed, remove it.

4 • Add NetWare Client32 for Windows 95.

5 • From the Network control panel, choose Add.

6 • Choose Client.

7 • Choose Add.

8 • Choose Have Disk.

9 • Specify the path for the NetWare Client32 for Windows 95 files.

10 • Choose OK.

11 • Configure NetWare Client32 for Windows 95.

12 • Choose Novell NetWare Client32.

13 • Choose Properties.

14 • Make sure the information for Preferred server, Preferred tree, Name context, and First network drive is correct.

15 • Make any other configurations.

Install the Client32 Using the Automatic Client Upgrade

To use the Automatic Client Upgrade, the network supervisor first places the NetWare Client32 for Windows 95 installation files and the Windows 95 installation .CAB files in a directory where they can be read during client login. Then, the network supervisor must add an instruction to the login script to run the Automatic Client Upgrade from that directory. With this instruction in place, the client login runs as usual if there is no need to upgrade. If the client version on the workstation is not current with the version on the server, however, ACU upgrades the client software and restarts the computer.

The administrator can set options in the NWSETUP.INI file so that ACU shows the user a dialog box stating that there are more recent files. In this case, the user can choose to continue or cancel the upgrade. By default, the user sees the NetWare Client32 Installation messages during the upgrade, and the computer restarts after the upgrade completes.

To give the user the option to continue or cancel the upgrade, set DisplayFirst-Screen=YES in the [AcuOptions] section of the NWSETUP.INI file in the ACU install folder. In this case, the user sees a dialog box before the upgrade begins and can choose to continue or cancel the upgrade. If the user chooses cancel, each time the user logs in with the older client, the option to upgrade is presented.

To let the user choose whether to restart the computer, set DisplayLastScreen=YES in the [AcuOptions] section of the NWSETUP.INI file in the ACU install folder. In this case, the user sees a dialog box after the upgrade completes and can choose to restart the computer. The upgraded Client32 files are not used until after the user restarts the computer.

Creating an ACU Install Folder   In order for the Automatic Client Upgrade to work, the client needs access to a directory where all the installation files are stored. To make this happen, the network supervisor needs to do the following:

1 • Create a directory for the Automatic Client Upgrade.

2 • Copy all NetWare Client32 for Windows 95 installation files to the ACU install folder.

3 • Copy all Windows 95 installation files that have a .CAB extension to the ACU install folder.

4 • Make sure that all clients scheduled for automatic upgrade have Read and File Scan rights to the ACU install folder.

Modifying the Login Script   Depending upon which login script is modified, the network supervisor can allow the following different clients to upgrade:

▸ If the user login script is modified, only that user will automatically upgrade.

▸ If the container login script is modified, all clients in that container will automatically upgrade.

▸ If the profile login script is modified, all clients using that login script will automatically upgrade.

In order for the Automatic Client Upgrade to work, the network administrator needs to do the following:

1 • Make sure that all clients accessing the Automatic Client Upgrade have Read and File Scan rights to the Automatic Client Upgrade install directory.

2 • Add the following to the login script (where, after the volume name, all directories are separated by a backslash [\ ]):

```
#\\servername\volume\..\setup.exe /acu
```

Using the Microsoft Client   When using the Microsoft Client for NetWare Networks that ships with Windows 95, SETUP must be run from the user's bindery login script (located in the SYS:MAIL directory) in order for the Automatic Client Upgrade to work.

When using ACU with the Microsoft Client for NetWare Networks Service for Novell Directory Services, SETUP must be placed in the login script that corresponds to the type of login (bindery or NDS).

Forcing an Upgrade   In some cases, a network supervisor might update one or more files without upgrading the entire client. For example, if Novell releases a new version of LOGINW95.EXE with additional functionality, the network supervisor might decide that all clients need to use this file. Because this isn't a new version of the Novell NetWare client, there isn't a client revision number for ACU to check, and the client will not be automatically upgraded. In this case, the network supervisor can force the clients to upgrade, using ACU, so that all clients use the newer file.

In the [ClientVersion] section of NWSETUP.INI (located in the directory where the NetWare Client32 for Windows 95 installation files are stored), there are four numbers separated by dots (for example, 0.0.3.0). The final number in this series, the level number, is what upgrades the client. To force the upgrade, the level number must be made higher than it is when NWSETUP.INI is first opened. For example, if the number is 0, make it a 1. With this done, when ACU compares the level numbers upon client login, it finds the discrepancy and upgrades the client to the system's newer files.

Installing Additional Protocols and Features   The following protocols and features can also be installed:

▸ Client32 optionally supports Novell SNMP Agent, Host Resources MIB, NetWare/IP, and NMR. You can install these options from the Network control panel after installing Client32.

▸ Simple Network Management Protocol (SNMP) is a cross-protocol language that allows computer management across diverse network platforms. If the management console supports Management Information Base (MIB) files, you might also want to load Host MIB support on the client. Host MIB support enables the management console to poll SNMP clients for inventory information.

▸ NetWare/IP is a protocol that sends and receives IPX packets in IP format. NetWare/IP enables networked applications that use only IPX to communicate over TCP/IP networks. It also provides a way for separate IPX networks to communicate across IP-based internetwork connections.

▸ Network Management Responder (NMR) is an application service that returns general workstation configuration information beyond what is normally available.

NEW CLIENT32 CONFIGURATION METHODS

Client32 is configured using property sheets or system policies. It can also be configured during installation using an ADMIN.CFG file. Except for 16-bit ODITM LAN drivers and for preserving existing settings during installation, Client32 is not configured using a NET.CFG file.

Property Sheets and System Policies

Property sheets allow you to change Client32 settings at a workstation using a graphical interface that includes help for each of the settings. System policies allow you to configure the Client32 settings for all the Windows 95 workstations on your network. They also allow you to do this remotely so you don't have to go to each workstation. In fact, you should be able to do all the work at your own desk. Some settings can be configured only by using system policies; other settings cannot be configured by using system policies.

Using Property Sheets to Change Client32 Settings   Property sheets provide a graphical way to change Client32 settings at a workstation. The changes apply only to the workstation where they are made. Some changes take effect immediately. Others require you to restart the workstation, in which case a message instructs you to restart the computer.

The changes are made by displaying the Network control panel, choosing an installed component, choosing Properties, choosing the appropriate tab, and then changing the setting.

Using System Policies to Change Client32 Settings   Client32 provides a custom policy template (the CLIENT32.ADM file) for use with the Windows 95 System Policy Editor (POLEDIT.EXE). You can use the System Policy Editor and the Client32 template to create a policy file (CONFIG.POL) that specifies the values for global Client32 settings.

After ensuring that the settings in the policy file work correctly, you can put the policy file in the SYS:\PUBLIC directory of every preferred server. The Client32 settings are read from the policy file and then stored in the registry each time a user logs in to the network.

The policy file that is used is the one in the SYS:\PUBLIC directory of the preferred server. If no preferred server is specified, the policy file in the SYS:\PUBLIC directory of the server with the first connection is used.

The ADMIN.CFG File

The ADMIN.CFG file allows you to configure the Client32 settings during installation. By installing from a NetWare server, you can configure multiple workstations using the same ADMIN.CFG file. The ADMIN.CFG file uses the same syntax as a NET.CFG file. However, you should be familiar with the settings that are supported by Client32. Some parameters from previous NetWare clients are no longer supported, some parameters have changed, and, of course, there are some new parameters.

Registry Configuration Settings

The Client32 configuration settings are stored in the system registry (not in the NET.CFG file). You should not edit the system registry directly. Use property sheets or system policies instead.

Dynamic Settings

Client32 dynamically adjusts as many settings as it can. Therefore, some configuration settings that were used in previous NetWare clients are no longer needed and are ignored if specified.

CHAPTER 19

Backing Up and Restoring Novell Directory Services

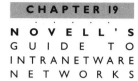
"Put all thine eggs in one basket and — watch that basket." Mark Twain

Because Novell Directory Services is a global and distributed name service, it requires a specialized approach to backup and restore processes. Not only must you back up your files and directories, but you should have a backup of your NDS tree for all situations that may occur, including catastrophes. In most cases you may simply need to restore a few objects or a subtree. Because IntranetWare is not server centric, as was NetWare 3, NDS information may be stored on multiple servers. Therefore, you must have a backup solution that can read this specialized NDS information across multiple servers and store it properly. The backup solutions for IntranetWare must be able to "see" the entire NDS tree by communicating with the other servers. A restore solution must also have the same capability.

This chapter refers frequently to NDS objects and partitions. For more information on these topics, see Chapters 3 and 6 of this book.

This chapter describes how to back up and restore NDS using an approved backup system and explains what steps you should take to institute a comprehensive backup plan in your company. The text will also cover how to devise a backup procedure through the use of replication, your first line of defense against NDS data loss. First, you'll learn about the components of the IntranetWare backup architecture.

This chapter will not try to discuss specific implementation of backup/restore products.

NOTE

Understanding the Basics

Before backing up and restoring NDS information, you should understand the basic components and architecture of NDS backup solutions. The process of backing up and, especially, restoring NDS information is complex and you should always first rely on your replicas for NDS fault tolerance. For more information on providing fault tolerance with replica placement, refer to Chapter 6.

The NDS name service actually exists as a set of files stored on one or many IntranetWare servers. These NDS files are stored on the SYS volume as hidden files for your network's protection. These are files that you definitely don't want deleted, accidentally or otherwise. When you do a Storage Management Services (SMS) backup of NDS, you are backing up the NDS file information. You do not back up information regarding the partition boundaries of the NDS tree. Instead, you back up every server that contains a portion of the NDS name space. You basically have an image of your entire NDS tree that appears as a single partition on a tape backup.

Consequently, during a restore of NDS, the image partition is split into its appropriate partitions as they exist on your actual tree. Some backup solutions also let you restore subtrees or individual objects. Novell's TSANDS.NLM, which ships with IntranetWare, supports this capability, as discussed later in this chapter. If there is no partition information on your tree because of a total loss of NDS, the entire image is restored to a single ([ROOT]) partition.

During a restore you will often see unknown objects, or objects that are lacking a mandatory attribute. When you use the NWADMIN utility, unknown objects appear with a "?" icon. During a restore, any number of your objects will have pointers to attributes of other objects that do not yet appear in your tree. For example, one user object may have been granted rights to another user object. Because the process restores only one object at a time, you may see a whole series of unknown objects until the restore is completed and these discrepancies are resolved.

STORAGE MANAGEMENT SERVICES (SMS)

Novell's Storage Management Services is an open architecture for interfacing storage management engines with Novell Directory Services. Third-party developers can develop backup solutions with their own functions and features written to the SMS standard interface. This platform provides a consistent architecture for storing, accessing, and managing data on many different client platforms, including NetWare servers, DOS/Windows clients, and Macintosh clients. Although the file systems may be different, SMS provides a consistent view of this data.

The SMS architecture was developed with the assistance of third-party developers and many backup products now comply with the SMS standard. In fact, you should not purchase any IntranetWare backup product that is not SMS compliant.

The SMS architecture actually consists of these three components:

- ▸ Storage Management Engine (SME)

- ▸ Target Service Agent (TSA)

- ▸ Storage Management Data Requester (SMDR)

These components are discussed in the following sections.

Storage Management Engine (SME)

One of the key components of the SMS architecture is the Storage Management Engine (SME). The SME is software that communicates with network clients through a common interface. The software provides cross-platform support and is easily modified to add new features or support. Novell's SBACKUP utility is an SME. Most third-party developers provide functions and features to support IntranetWare backups by including an SME with their product. The most common use of the SME is a backup and restore application.

The SME operates on an IntranetWare server as a NetWare Loadable Module (NLM). The SME manages all user requests and interaction between the Target Service Agents, discussed next, and the device driver for your tape backup system.

Target Service Agent (TSA)

The Target Service Agent (TSA) is software that can scan, read, and write data found on a target file system. A target can be any item on the network that needs backing up; in most cases this means a file server or group of file servers and NDS. Targets can also be SQL database engines or print servers.

A TSA must understand the file structure for the particular platform that it is accessing. Therefore, the TSA is specifically written for each type of platform that you need to back up. The TSA understands all the unique features of the platform you are backing up, such as name spaces, file and directory attributes, and security rights. The TSA can also present the data to the SME in a common format. For this reason, the SME can interact with many different types of TSAs, as shown in Figure 19.1.

Because the SMS components are very modular in nature, they make it easy to support many operating systems. A vendor releasing a new version of an operating system only needs to provide a TSA to support that operating system. That way all vendors selling an SMS-compliant backup solution can support the new operating system. Novell, for example, currently provides TSAs for the following operating systems:

- NetWare 3.11 and 3.12

- NetWare 4.01, 4.02, 4.1 and IntranetWare

- Novell Directory Services

- NetWare SQL

- DOS/MS Windows Clients

- OS/2 Clients

- Macintosh Clients

- UnixWare Clients

FIGURE 19.1

*Each TSA can talk to its
operating system platform.
The TSA then presents this
information to the SME in
a common format.*

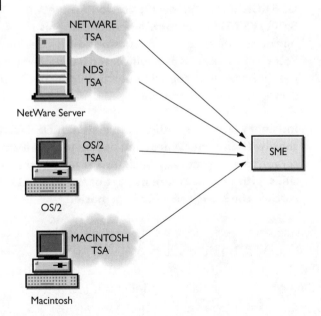

SMS TSAs are loaded as NLMs on the host or target server. You can also load them as memory-resident modules on your client workstations. For backing up your file systems, Novell provides the TSA400 and TSA410 modules.

The latest version of the TSA410.NLM supports IntranetWare and is backward compatible with NetWare 4.1. A new feature of the TSA410.NLM is the capability to back up server specific information. Server Specific Info is a new resource that the IntranetWare system Target Service Agent (TSA410.NLM) provides. This resource is provided in the Storage Management Engine's (SME) Resource list. The SYS volume and other volumes are major resources that can be selected from most backup utilities and backed up.

Select Server Specific Info packages critical data for recovery purposes. SERV-DATA.NDS, DSMISC.LOG, STARTUP.NCF, AUTOEXEC.NCF, and VOLSINFO.TXT are all backed up by selecting Server Specific Info. There are two ways to back up server specific information. The first way is to select a full file system backup on your NetWare Server. The second way is to select the Server Specific Information option from the resource list for a file system backup.

NOTE

If you are running NetWare 4.1 and would like to automatically back up this server specific information you must load the DSBACKER.NLM (specific version for NetWare 4.1) in your SYS:\SYSTEM directory. When loaded, this NLM automatically backs up the server specific information to the previously mentioned files. You then can perform a full server backup, which will include these files in its backup. You will need the DSMAINT utility to restore the server specific information.

IntranetWare uses a different version of DSBACKER.NLM (which ships with IntranetWare) and can be loaded from the IntranetWare server to automatically back up Server Specific Info. DSMAINT now ships with IntranetWare as part of the INSTALL.NLM and is used to restore the server specific information.

When the server specific information is restored, it places the files in the SYS:\SYSTEM\SOURCE_SERVER_NAME directory on the target server (by default). The SOURCE_SERVER_NAME directory that gets created uses the 8.3 naming convention. If your backed-up server name is SMS410_S1 and you restore the Server Specific Info to server S2, the source server name in the path above will be SMS410_S1. The new directory on S2 will be SYS:SYSTEM\SMS410_S1. All the Server Specific Info files will be put into this directory (SERVDATA.NDS, DSMISC.LOG, AUTOEXEC.NCF, STARTUP.NCF, and VOLSINFO.TXT). The following is a description of the server specific files that are backed up.

SERVDATA.NDS contains server specific NDS information. This file is used by INSTALL to recover from an unplanned SYS volume failure. The restore procedures show how to use this file to recover from a SYS volume failure in a multi-server environment with existing replicas on other servers that will be used to provide a complete recovery.

DSMISC.LOG a text file that contains the replica list and replica types that the backed-up server held at the time of backup. This file is used in the restore procedures to provide helpful information needed to prepare NDS for recovery of the failed server. It also provides a list of the other servers that were in the failed server's replica ring. A sample DSMISC.LOG is shown below:

```
Wednesday, August 28, 1996   2:30:21 pm

Backing up server-specific NDS data

Successfully read addresses of the local server object.

Current partition/replica list

Partition OU=NORAD.O=ACME, current replica list:

    CN=SMS410_S5.O=ACME, type read/write

    CN=SMS410_S4.O=ACME, type read/write

    CN=SMS410_S3.O=ACME, type master

Partition OU=LABS.OU=RIO.O=ACME, current replica list:

    CN=SMS410_S5.O=ACME, type read/write

    CN=SMS410_S4.O=ACME, type read/write

    CN=SMS410_S3.O=ACME, type master

Partition OU=CHARITY.OU=NORAD.O=ACME, current replica list:

    CN=SMS410_S5.O=ACME, type read/write

    CN=SMS410_S4.O=ACME, type read/write

    CN=SMS410_S3.O=ACME, type master
```

```
Partition OU=PR.O=ACME, current replica list:

    CN=SMS410_S5.O=ACME, type subordinate reference

    CN=SMS410_S4.O=ACME, type read/write

    CN=SMS410_S3.O=ACME, type master

Partition [Root], current replica list:

    CN=SMS410_S5.O=ACME, type read/write

    CN=SMS410_S4.O=ACME, type read/write

    CN=SMS410_S3.O=ACME, type master
```

AUTOEXEC.NCF   the NetWare server executable batch file located in the NetWare partition of the server's disk. This file is used to load modules and set the NetWare operating system configuration.

STARTUP.NCF   the NetWare server boot file that loads the NetWare server's disk driver and name spaces and various SET parameters.

VOLSINFO.TXT   a text file that contains needed information about the volumes on the server at the time of backup, including name spaces, compression, and migration information. This file can be used during restore procedures to provide helpful information in preparing volumes correctly for a restore. A sample VOLSINFO.TXT is given below:

```
SMS410_s123456789

Current File System Information by Volume

Wednesday, August 28, 1996 2:15:25 pm

SYS:

  Supported Name Spaces:

    DOS

    MACINTOSH

    NFS

    LONG
```

```
Extended File Formats:

    Compression is enabled.

VOL1:

    Supported Name Spaces:

        DOS

        MACINTOSH

    Extended File Formats:

        Compression is enabled.

VOL2:

    Supported Name Spaces:

        DOS
```

A special TSA known as TSANDS.NLM supports the backup and restoration of Novell Directory Services, including objects and trustee assignments. The backup includes NDS partitions and other crucial information. TSANDS can walk the entire NDS tree to access the appropriate NDS files for backup. Novell's SBACKUP utility and the other third-party SMS-based backup solutions use this TSA.

This current version of the TSANDS.NLM has the following Enhancements:

Extended Schema Backup

Extensions to the NDS base Schema are now included in the backup and restore function set of TSANDS.NLM. Backup and restore of the NDS Schema will be handled by TSANDS.NLM as a complete data set. A new target service resource SCHEMA is now exported by TSANDS.NLM. The backup of the Schema resource consists of the packaging of all attributes followed by all class definitions from the working Schema. A restore of the Schema data set will consist of the addition of all attributes from the backup, which are not part of the current work Schema. After the additions of the backup attribute set have been restored, the class definitions will be restored by updating the current classes with missing attributes from the backup or by the addition of a complete class when none is present.

Selecting the Full Directory Backup option includes the Schema Resource in its backup by default. If the backup application allows selection of resources, the

Schema resource can be selected and backed up separately. The Schema resource can be handled the same way for restores.

Error Handling

TSANDS.NLM now has the capability to log objects to an error log when an object cannot be backed up for whatever reason. For example, you are backing up a big tree with thousands of objects and by chance one or more of the replicas are off line so no referrals can be found, or an object is corrupt and cannot be read properly. The object name or container name will be logged to the backup error log file. The TSANDS.NLM will then continue to get the next object and continue the backup if possible. This allows TSANDS.NLM to discover and back up all the objects that are resolvable in the tree. After the backup is complete you can view the error log file and see what objects or container objects have not been backed up.

Resource Configuration Option

The following options ("How to scan what you are backing up:" and the TSANDS.CFG configuration file) have been added to improve the scaling of the TSANDS.NLM. These options allow administrators to back up subsections of NDS trees by assigning rights to backup users. Supervisor rights are required to back up NDS objects. It is the tree administrator's responsibility to assign Supervisor rights to the backup administrators. Backup administrators should be assigned supervisory rights to the subsection of the NDS tree that they will be responsible for backing up. Suppose you have five containers NORAD, RIO, CAMELOT, TOKYO, and SYDNEY that need to be backed up. You can create five backup administrators — BAdmin1, BAdmin2, BAdmin3, BAdmin4, BAdmin5 — and give each backup administrator Supervisor rights to his respective container.

In Novell's SBACKUP utility select "How to scan what you are backing up:" then select "Exclude objects for which user has no rights" and answer YES. This allows the backup administrator to back up only the objects for which he has been given Supervisor rights. If BAdmin1 has been given Supervisor rights to Container NORAD, then he can only back up objects in the container NORAD and below as long as his Supervisor rights are not filtered at a subordinate level to NORAD.

Since BAdmin1 has not been given Supervisor rights to organization ACME he cannot start the backup from ACME context. The TSANDS.CFG file can be created to help identify the starting context for each backup administrator. The TSANDS.CFG resides in SYS:SYSTEM\TSA\ directory. The content is shown below.

```
.OU=NORAD.O=ACME

.OU=RIO.O=ACME

.OU=CAMELOT.ACME

.OU=TOKYO.ACME

.OU=SYDNEY.ACME
```

You will need to create this .CFG file and enter the starting context for each backup administrator that you have in your tree. The starting context will show up in your backup utility as a selection item that each backup administrator can select as his or her starting context and initiate the backup from that point. This eliminates walking down a deep tree to select the correct starting context each time a backup needs to be performed. This also provides a starting context if browse rights are removed from each backup administrator and he cannot see below the [ROOT] object to start walking the tree down to the assigned container starting context. The backup administrator that possesses the Supervisor right to ACME does not need an entry in the TSANDS.CFG because that starting context is visible from the selection resource list.

In addition, the Supervisor rights are assigned by a tree administrator and can be assigned or filtered either at partition boundaries or at a container level. Depending on how you design and administer your tree backup procedure, these new options can help in effectively and efficiently improving your backup and restore of your NDS tree.

Storage Management Data Requester (SMDR)

The Storage Management Data Requester (SMDR) is the link between a vendor's backup application engine (SME) and the SMS TSAs. Its job is to locate and provide instructions to the TSAs on your network. The SMDR also provides the link to the storage device interface. For example, during a backup sequence, the SME receives from the TSAs data processed into the correct format. This information is communicated through the storage device interface to the backup device.

Figure 19.2 shows all of the components of the SMS architecture.

FIGURE 19.2

The SMS architecture consists of multiple components, including the Storage Management Engine (SME), the Target Service Agent (TSA), and the Storage Management Data Requester (SMDR).

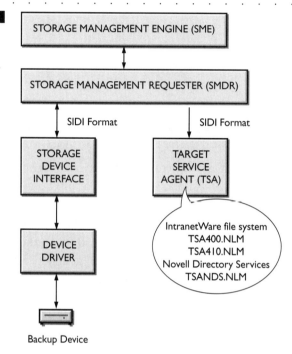

STORAGE MANAGEMENT ENGINE (SME)

STORAGE MANAGEMENT REQUESTER (SMDR)

SIDI Format   SIDI Format

STORAGE DEVICE INTERFACE

TARGET SERVICE AGENT (TSA)

DEVICE DRIVER

IntranetWare file system
TSA400.NLM
TSA410.NLM
Novell Directory Services
TSANDS.NLM

Backup Device

For data restoration, the SME talks to the device driver to tell it which data to restore from tape. After receiving the data, the SME passes it back to the TSA, which writes the data to the target. Again, the target could be a NetWare server, a SQL database, a print server, and so on.

Backing Up Novell Directory Services

An NDS replica is your first mechanism for fault tolerance of NDS because of the time sensitive nature of NDS. The replica can maintain the most recent event information about its objects and properties. You can use replicas to restore or rebuild information from a replica of the same partition that has been damaged. In contrast, a tape backup is like a snapshot in time and will become out of date, unlike the actual replica.

Nonetheless, you should have a tape backup of NDS for increased fault tolerance of your IntranetWare network. In some cases, such as single-server environments, tape backup provides fault tolerance for NDS. In addition, a tape backup protects data and NDS information in the event of a catastrophe such as a fire or flood. Novell highly recommends that you always have a tape backup of NDS and maintain this copy by performing regular backups.

A replica is a copy of a partition. Having multiple copies of replicas increases fault tolerance for your system. As discussed in Chapter 6, there is a point at which too many replicas can result in a performance decrease. Typically, three replicas are sufficient for fault tolerance. This would include a Master Replica and two Read/Write replicas. Figure 19.3 shows an example of the replication process.

F I G U R E   19.3

Using replication as a means of avoiding NDS data loss

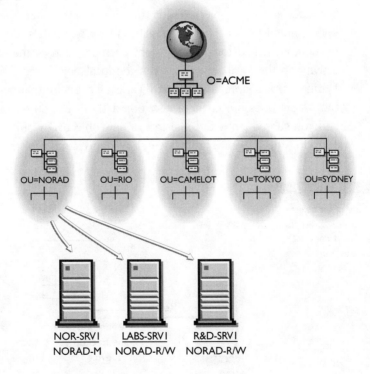

OBJECT IDS AND THE BACKUP PROCESS

An object ID is generated for each IntranetWare object created in your tree. In NetWare 3 the same process occurs and the object IDs plus all the file system data are placed on tape during the backup process. Instead of storing object IDs on tape, SMS-compatible backup products store an object's distinguished name in typeful format. Each object has a distinguished name that serves as the object's unique identifier. For example, the user object LDAVINCI.R&D.LABS.NORAD.ACME is backed up in its typeful format:

```
CN=.LDAVINCI.OU=R&D.OU=LABS.OU=NORAD.O=ACME
```

For more information on distinguished names, refer to Chapter 4.

IntranetWare objects only have one distinguished name that is unique across the entire tree. However, when a replica of a partition is placed on a server, NDS generates a unique object ID for the same object. Therefore, each NDS object has one distinguished name with possibly many object IDs, depending on the number of replicas created for that partition. Each server uses the object IDs to coordinate activity on the local server between the local object and, for example, file services. During a tape restore, if an object ID already exists for that object, the server receiving the restore does not create a new object ID. If the object on the tree were deleted and you subsequently did a restore, a new object ID would be created on the server receiving the restore. Figure 19.4 shows an example of this process.

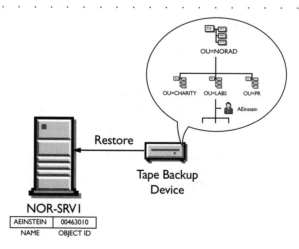

FIGURE 19.4

A restore of an object creates a new object ID if the object does not currently exist on the tree.

As in NetWare 3, trustee assignments for the file system are backed up along with the file system. The SMA TSA uses the object's distinguished name to back up the trustee rights from the file system in order to preserve an object's trustee assignments during restoration. For example, suppose a user object is deleted from the tree and subsequently re-created. If you then restored the user's files from tape, the TSA could match the file system assignments to the user because of the distinguished name. This also assumes that when you re-created the user you used the same name that was in use before.

WARNING **The preceding paragraph explains why you *must* restore your objects to NDS *before* you can restore file system information. The file system restore attempts to match the file assignments to the user object's distinguished names. If they are not on the server first, the files will not be assigned back to the users.**

Choose a backup approach that fits your needs. Whenever possible, you should have a centralized approach to the backup of your NDS tree. Ideally, a single administrator will have rights to all servers in the tree in order to perform backup functions. However, this may not always be possible because of the size of some corporate networks and the geographic nature of the network. In large environments you may want to designate a site administrator who is responsible for backups in his or her portion of the tree. Keep in mind that each administrator must have Supervisor rights to the servers for which he or she needs to perform backups. If several people are responsible for backups, it takes more coordination and organization to ensure that each location backs up their portion of the NDS tree consistently. Figure 19.5 illustrates an example of centralized backup approach.

You can follow these guidelines when backing up your tree:

▸ Perform backups regularly — once a week, for example. The number of backups you perform depends on how many changes are made to your tree. (Examples of changes are adding new users, moving subtrees, and so on.) If your tree does not change much, backups can be performed weekly. If it changes a great deal, backups should be more frequent.

▸ Create a company policy stating how often NDS backups should be performed. You may simply want to have your administrators perform the NDS backup each time they do a full server backup.

FIGURE 19.5

You should use a centralized backup approach for NDS whenever possible.

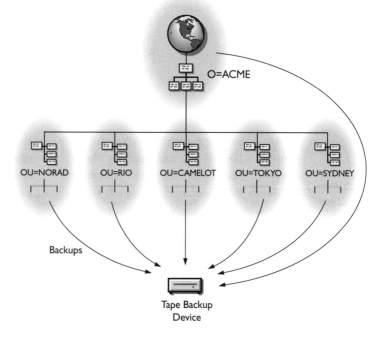

O=ACME

OU=NORAD   OU=RIO   OU=CAMELOT   OU=TOKYO   OU=SYDNEY

Backups

Tape Backup
Device

▸ Load the TSANDS.NLM on one IntranetWare server in your tree. Choose the server containing a replica of the largest partition in your tree. For more complex networks, the TSANDS.NLM can be loaded on more than one server.

▸ Keep a written record of your partitions and replicas. If you need to do a total restoration of NDS, you may need to know where to create your partitions and replicas. You can also use DSREPAIR to log partition and replica information to a file.

▸ Create an alternate administrative type user if you decide to reduce your ADMIN user rights. Typically, when you install the first IntranetWare server, you call the first user ADMIN, and this user has Supervisor rights at the [ROOT] of your tree. If you subsequently reduce the rights of the ADMIN (or equivalent) user and perform a tape backup on that object, the object will be backed up with the reduced rights. Subsequently, when you restore the ADMIN (or equivalent) object, it will be restored with the reduced rights, which will not allow you to complete your restore.

Follow these steps to actually back up your NDS tree:

1 • Load TSANDS.NLM on the server containing the largest replica of a partition. You can base this on a rough estimate of the number of user objects and so on in the partition.

2 • Load TSA410.NLM on *all* servers that will also require a file system backup. This will also allow "Server Specific Info" to be backed up.

3 • Load the appropriate drivers on the server on which you will run your tape backup software. Refer to your vendor documentation for the specifics about which drivers to install.

4 • Load your backup software.

5 • Log in to the appropriate NDS server as the backup user. This user must have Supervisor object rights to the server you log into. This is for the NDS backup portion.

6 • Initiate the NDS backup procedure based on your particular software's instructions.

7 • Back up the file system according to your vendor instructions.

8 • Repeat this process if necessary or automate the process to back up multiple servers after hours.

Restoring Novell Directory Services

As mentioned, before doing a tape backup restore of Novell Directory Services you should attempt to restore NDS information through replicas and repair operations. For more information on these processes, refer to Chapter 10. If you have to restore

NDS information, an active replica is faster and more up to date than a tape backup. Remember, two or three replicas are adequate for fault tolerance. Your particular circumstances may require more or fewer replicas.

Take the following precautionary measures before you begin your restoration:

1 • Make sure that your current tree is functioning properly in terms of replica synchronization. Use NDS Manager or DSTRACE to verify that all partitions are error free. Doing a restore when you still have replica synchronization errors will only compound your problems.

2 • *Always* restore NDS information first, and then restore file system data and trustees. Failure to do so may result in the loss of trustee assignments for your user objects.

PERFORMING A PARTIAL NDS RESTORE

IntranetWare provides SMS TSAs that enable you to selectively restore objects and groups of objects from your tape backup. This is known as a *partial restore*.

You need to determine whether a partial restore is the fastest solution to your particular problem. For example, if you are trying to restore a single object, it might be quicker to simply re-create the object using NWADMIN than to perform a partial restore. Remember, you must understand how the restore process works in terms of object IDs and dependent objects to successfully carry out a partial restore.

Object IDs

If you are restoring an object that no longer exists in your NDS tree, a new object ID is created when you restore the object. Any (old) object ID associated with the file system trustees, such as directories for user mail, is affected in this situation. The new object ID will not match the old file system ID assignments. If an object already exists in the tree and you do a restore, you will copy the object's properties from tape backup over the existing object's properties. This may or may not be what you intended to do.

Dependent Objects

Dependent objects are dependent upon other objects to exist in your tree. A print queue object, for example, maintains directory and host server properties to determine where the queue is stored and on what server. Without this information, the print queue object cannot function. Therefore, if you restore any dependent objects, they will not be functional in your tree without the other supporting objects.

You may restore some dependent objects, including Directory Map objects, print queue objects, and any schema extension objects you have created. Once restored, these types of objects are nonfunctional. The best way to resolve this problem is to restore the supporting objects for the dependent object, delete the previously restored dependent object, and re-create it with NWADMIN. Once you re-create the object it will make use of the supporting objects.

Unknown Objects

Restoring the NDS may create unknown objects. If a restored object is dependent on other objects in the tree that do not currently exist, the object will be designated as unknown. NDS creates an unknown object until the real object is restored. If the actual object is restored during the restore, the unknown category is replaced by the actual object name.

You will always see unknown objects during a restore until all the resources — such as servers, volumes, users, and so on — are in place in your tree. Most objects should be cleaned up once the restore is completed. If not, you can delete the unknown objects and re-create the actual objects, or you can attempt to selectively restore the actual objects and overwrite the unknown objects. Again, you have to determine whether it's easier to restore the objects or to re-create them with NWADMIN.

Bindery Objects and Applications

As mentioned, new object IDs are created for restored objects that do not exist in the tree. Bindery-based applications such as printing, e-mail, and others will probably not function because they use object IDs to communicate. If the bindery application has one list of object IDs and you restore the objects with new IDs, these applications will not function properly. In most cases, you will need to reinstall and reconfigure these applications after you restore the tree.

The login scripts of bindery-based user objects are stored in their mail subdirectories if the scripts were created with a utility such as SYSCON. These subdirectories are based on an object ID. Therefore, when you restore the user objects with a new object ID, the mail subdirectories are not automatically renamed.

A Novell utility called RENMDIRS.NLM changes the mail directory name (old object ID) to that of the new object ID created after a restore. This utility is available on NetWire or the NSD section of Novell's Web Site.

Print Services

After restoring NDS, you have to restore print services objects from your tape backup if you are using queue server mode printing. You also have to run any setup software from your third-party print package to reconfigure your printing environment. Because your queue ID has changed during the restore, you have to re-create the queue to allow for a reassignment of the queue ID to the new print server object ID. You will most likely need to reset your printers after reconfiguration as well.

For remote printing mode, your printing should be fully functional after a tape restore of NDS.

PERFORMING A FULL NDS RESTORE

You would need to perform a full NDS tree restore if all servers in the tree suffered a catastrophic failure. In large, geographically dispersed networks this situation is all but impossible. Some smaller companies in a single building or a few buildings in the same location are more likely to experience this situation.

Follow these steps to carry out a full NDS restore:

1 • Reinstall IntranetWare on your file servers to regain a [ROOT] partition of your network on the first server. Be sure to specify the exact tree structure organization (Organization and Organizational Unit objects) that was present in your first tree. Now is not the time to make changes to your tree.

2 • Reinstall additional IntranetWare servers as you had them before the failure. Any servers that you cannot install before the restore may cause some errors due to dependent objects that do not restore properly. This may require you to go back with NWADMIN and re-create objects.

NOTE

Be sure to re-create the ADMIN or equivalent user with the same name, same container, and same password that was used to create the original backup. If you made and backed up extensions to the schema, you need to make those extensions again. Extensions to the default schema are not backed up but the objects created with these extensions are. Therefore, you must extend the schema on your tree before restoring your objects. Failure to do so will result in an incomplete restoration.

3 • If you have reinstalled more than one IntranetWare server, you should remove the default replicas of [ROOT] before beginning the restoration. Having a single copy of the [ROOT] partition will simplify the restore process. This process assumes that you have a server holding [ROOT] with enough disk space to restore the entire NDS tree.

4 • Install your tape backup drivers and bring up your backup software. Restore the entire NDS backup to your server. The NDS tree will be placed in your [ROOT] partition.

5 • Restore the file information to each IntranetWare server in your tree. When performing a restore, be sure to set your backup software to delete any existing trustees before restoring the data. This purges any existing trustees before the tape backup and its trustee assignments are restored to the server.

6 • Re-create your partition boundaries using your written record of the partition boundaries. Alternatively, you can designate and place replicas of your partitions where they are needed.

7 • Run DSREPAIR on each server to verify the accuracy of your database.

SERVER/SYS VOLUME FAILURE

It's common to have a single server fail in your NDS tree. Often this occurs because of a SYS volume failure. Such a failure is serious because your SYS volume contains all or portions of the NetWare Directory and can affect other servers in your tree that participate in the same partition as the failed server.

If your SYS volume fails on a single-server network, the situation is similar to a total tree failure of many servers. The restore procedure is basically the same as a full NDS restoration, with the addition of a few steps:

1 • Replace or resolve the problem that caused your SYS volume to fail. This usually means replacing the hard drive unit itself.

2 • Reinstall IntranetWare on your file servers to regain a [ROOT] partition of your network on the first server. Be sure to specify the exact tree structure organization (Organization and Organizational Unit objects) that was present in your first tree. Now is not the time to make changes to your tree. Specify 64K for your volume block size. Have INSTALL mount all volumes during the installation process. Make sure that you install all the patches and updates to the operating system and utilities as well.

NOTE

Again, be sure to re-create the ADMIN or equivalent user with the same name, same container, and same password that was used to create the original backup. If you made and backed up extensions to the schema, you need to make those extensions again. Failure to do so will result in an incomplete restoration.

3 • Run DSREPAIR on any volumes other than SYS on the server to purge invalid trustees contained on those volumes. Run the option UNATTENDED FULL REPAIR to purge any invalid trustee information.

4 • Install your tape backup drivers and bring up your backup software. Load TSANDS and TSA410.

5 • Restore the entire NDS backup to your server. The NDS tree will be placed in your [ROOT] partition.

6 • Restore the file system information to your IntranetWare SYS volume from your tape backup. You need to choose an option for restoring without session files.

7 • Restore any trustee assignments (without data streams) for any other volumes that existed before the failure.

NOTE

If you restore data on volume SYS, you will no longer have trustee assignments for the other volumes because you ran DSREPAIR in step 3. You can restore only the directory without data streams on these volumes. Because the data files already exist, you only need the directory structure to obtain the trustee assignments. Consult the instructions for your third-party backup program for details on how to accomplish this task.

8 • Run DSREPAIR on each server to verify the accuracy of your NDS database.

When there is a multiserver environment in a partition, it's also extremely common to have a single server fail for whatever reason, including the failure of the SYS volume. This does not mean, however, that you have lost all your replicas of that partition. This situation requires a slightly different approach:

1 • Remove this server from the NDS by using the NDS Manager utility. Start by deleting the failed server's Server object and volume objects from the tree. If your failed server holds a master replica, you must run DSREPAIR or NDS Manager to designate another active replica in the partition as the master. Verify through NDS Manager or DSREPAIR that the server has been removed from the replica list and that your tree is functioning properly. If the server is not returning for use in your tree, this is all you need to do. If your server is returning to the tree, continue reading the following steps.

WARNING

Only follow these procedures if your server has failed and is completely inoperable. If you have a functioning IntranetWare server that you want to remove from the tree, instead load INSTALL and use the option Remove Directory Services from that server.

2 • Once you have repaired the failed server hardware, you can reinstall IntranetWare on that server. Make sure that your install includes all the latest patches and versions of the operating system and utilities that you were using before the failure.

3 • Restore the replica(s) that were present on the server before the failure. Allow the synchronization process to place the objects on the server. You do not need to use your SMS tape backup to restore NDS information. Verify through DSREPAIR and Partition Manager that the replicas are synchronizing properly on the restored server hardware.

4 • Use your SMS backup to restore the data and trustee assignments for the SYS volume that was lost during the server failure.

5 • Restore any other volumes besides SYS that were not affected by the failure. Again, you can only restore the trustee assignments without the data streams for those volumes.

NOTE

Be sure to delete existing trustees before restoring. This option will purge existing trustees before restoring the backed up trustee assignments from the backup. You can simply restore the directory structure without data streams on these volumes. Because the data files already exist, you only need the directory structure to get the trustee assignments back. Follow your backup vendor's guidelines to accomplish this task.

Devising a Disaster Recovery Plan

You should have a disaster recovery plan to protect your system and your data in case of an emergency. Your disaster recovery plan can include redundant hardware along with proper replication and tape backup.

For some sites requiring a high degree of redundancy, you should consider using SFTIII on IntranetWare for maximum fault tolerance of your server hardware. You can take other steps such as disk mirroring or disk duplexing, which also provide you with varying degrees of safety.

Always maintain at least two to three replicas of your partitions as your strongest backup defense of NDS. Some sites create one or two NDS servers that contain all replicas of all partitions for backup purposes. If you use an NDS server for replica storage, consider these recommendations:

▸ Have a centralized NDS server across the fastest WAN link possible.

▸ Use only fast hardware (Pentium-class machines) for your NDS replica server.

▸ If you have more than 100 replicas, distribute the replicas on two servers for the greatest performance.

▸ The synchronization process on these servers should complete in 30 minutes or less. If the server cannot complete a synchronization cycle (synchronizing all replicas on the server) in this amount of time, place some of the replicas on a second replica server.

▸ Make sure that you have a regular tape backup of your entire NDS tree, as discussed in this chapter.

CHAPTER 20

The NetWare Application Manager

Before the NetWare Application Manager (NAM) was available an administrator could install applications in one of two ways: as a standalone on each user's hard drive or as a networked application. Both installation options required an administrator to do considerable work at the workstation.

The NetWare Application Manager works with NDS to simplify management of network applications by allowing administrators to centrally control users' Windows desktops. NAM lets administrators use their workstations to install new network applications or upgrade existing applications. These applications dynamically appear on users' Windows desktops.

The NetWare Application Manager also enables an administrator to easily manage applications on the network by defining applications as NDS objects. As an administrator, you now have the ability to define NDS application objects and assign security to these objects for any number of users that are part of the NDS tree. NAM allows administrators to assign network applications by user, group, and container, or any combination of the three.

The NetWare Application Manager consists of two components that are easy to install and configure. First, NAM provides a Dynamic Link Library (DLL) that snaps into Novell's NWADMIN utility and allows an administrator to define a user's access to NDS application objects. Five application objects are created:

- Application object

- DOS application object

- Windows 3.x application object

- Windows 95 application object

- NT application object

The second component is the NetWare Application Launcher (NAL), which allows users to see and access the NDS application objects that have been defined by the administrator. The NetWare Application Launcher presents the applications to the user's desktop.

NAL can be run from a login script if the NetWare GUI login utility is being used, or it can be placed in the Windows startup group. NAL delivers a set of network applications to users that an administrator has previously assigned to them. Users simply double-click on the application they wish to execute. The Application Launcher will create appropriate drive mappings and paths.

Installing the NetWare Application Manager

The NetWare Application Manager is now part of the NetWare Client32 for DOS/Windows and the NetWare Client32 for Windows 95. You can use NAM with the VLM clients as well.

At the time of this writing Novell was completing NAM for Windows NT, due out shortly.

NOTE

NAM also requires at least one IntranetWare server because NAM and NAL use Novell Directory Services to deliver networked applications.

To install the NetWare Application Manager and create application objects, follow the steps below.

1 • The NetWare Application Manager files are located in the C32W95\ADMIN\NAM directory or in the \NAM directory on the ADMIN diskette. If you are installing a client from the NetWare Client32 CD-ROM you will also find the NAM files in the ADMIN\NAM directory. You can also copy these files to the SYS:PUBLIC directory of your server for easier access.

2 • Copy the application program files or create an image of applications installation disks on a network file server.

Applications can be stored on your NetWare 3.x servers, but at least one IntranetWare server is required to have access to NDS and the NWADMIN utility, which is required to run the NetWare Application Manager.

NOTE

3 • Create an NDS application object through the NWADMIN utility as explained later in this chapter.

4 • Associate the application object with a user, group, or container.

5 • Assign the necessary file system rights to the user, group, or container to access the previously defined applications.

Using the NetWare Application Manager

Once the NetWare Application Manager is installed it is part of the NWADMIN utility. You simply highlight a container in which you want to create an application object and then select the CREATE option to create a new object as shown in Figure 20.1.

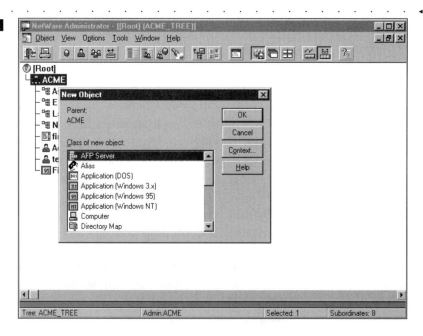

For example, you may want to create a Windows 95 application object as shown in Figure 20.2. You must assign an application object name and an executable path to specify the directory in which the application is located. You can type the directory path or you can click the Browse button to the right of the Path box. Clicking this box will let you search the NDS tree to locate the application you are trying to represent. You can also create application objects for DOS, Windows 3.1x, and Windows NT.

FIGURE 20.2

You can create a Windows 95 application object by assigning the object a name and an executable path.

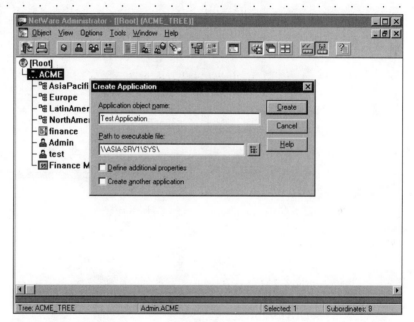

DEFINE PROPERTIES OF AN APPLICATION OBJECT

Clicking on the Define Additional Properties box will bring up the object's properties that you can further define if necessary for your environment. An example of the main properties screen is shown in Figure 20.3. You can also bring up this screen by double-clicking on the object in NWADMIN just as you do with any other object.

*The main properties screen
of the application object*

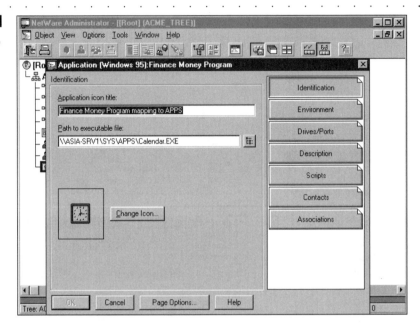

The following properties are shown in the previous figure and will be briefly discussed:

- ▸ Identification (shown as the first screen)

- ▸ Environment

- ▸ Drives/Port

- ▸ Description

- ▸ Scripts

- ▸ Contracts

- ▸ Associations

Identification

The Identification screen allows you to change either the icon or title of the application object. If other icons are available to choose from this will be an option for you.

Environment

The Environment screen allows you to enter command line parameters required by the application, such as working directories to store shared files.

Notice that the Clean Up Network Resources box is automatically checked. This option instructs NAM to set up all drive mappings, command line parameters, and printer ports when an application is launched. When the application is terminated, NAM will remove the mapped drives a printer port captures that are associated with the application being run.

Drives/Port

The Drives/Port screen allows you to specify additional drive mappings that may be needed for the application being executed. You can select an actual drive letter to be mapped or you can instruct NAM to use the next available drive letter. You can also select printer ports for capturing and overriding workstation printer settings such as Notify and Form Feed. An example of creating a drive mapping for an application is shown in Figure 20.4. When this particular application is executed, Drive M will be mapped for this application.

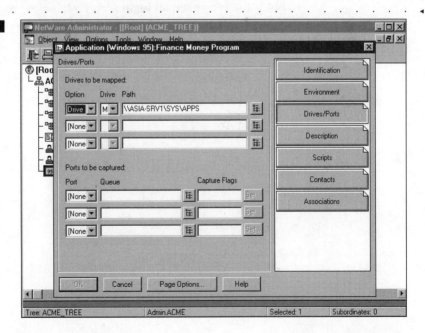

If the resource (a connection, drive mapping, or capture) has been previously assigned, NAL will map over that assignment and not clean up after exiting the application. Cleanup will also not occur if the application object has the Cleanup Resources flag unchecked.

NOTE

Description

Administrators can use the Description screen if they want to write a description of the application for other users. The description may include information on how to run the application, troubleshoot the application, or derive the greatest benefit from it.

Scripts

The Scripts screen allows the administrator to specify many of the login script commands and have them execute before or after the application runs. You can use most of the login script commands found in a regular IntranetWare container or user login script.

Not all login script commands work with the current shipping version of NAL 1.0. However, all login script variables work. The following commands do not emulate IntranetWare login script commands:

NOTE

- ▶ ATTACH (unless used to background authenticate)

- ▶ CLS

- ▶ DISPLAY

- ▶ FDISPLAY

- ▶ FIRE

- ▶ INCLUDE

- ▶ LASTLOGINTIME

- ▶ MACHINE=

- ▶ PAUSE

▸ WRITE

▸ EXIT filename

▸ NO_DEFAULT

▸ NOSWAP

▸ PCOMPATIBLE

▸ SCRIPT_SERVER

▸ SET_TIME

▸ SWAP

Contacts

The Contacts screen allows you to list administrators who can be contacted in case the application cannot be run.

Associations

The Associations screen is where you make rights assignments and specify whether a user, group, profile, or container has access to the application object.

Clicking OK after filling in the information on these screens will save the information to NDS for that object. The setup of each application object is very simple and easy to implement. Once you have created an object, the last step is to assign the appropriate rights access to either the user, group, profile, or container.

ASSIGNING RIGHTS TO ACCESS APPLICATIONS

As previously mentioned users, groups, profiles, or containers can be included in the associations list as shown in Figure 20.5.

After you've added individual users, groups, profiles, or containers to the associations list, you must grant them sufficient rights to access the application. The easiest way to grant rights is to use a group or container object. To assign rights to a container use the NWADMIN utility. Double-click on the container and then click the Rights to Files and Directories button. Then click the Show button and select the server volumes that appear in the container where your group of users resides.

The Associations screen allows you to add users, groups, profiles, or containers to the access list.

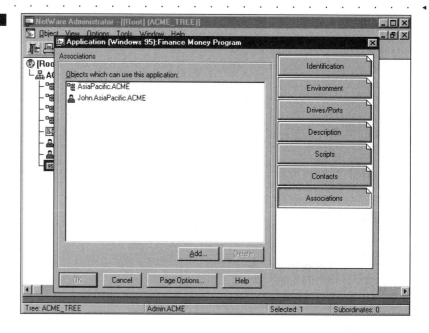

After selecting a server volume you can then select individual files and directories and assign the container rights to those files or directories. Keep in mind that individual users receive the rights granted to a group or container through security equivalence. Therefore, any member of the group or container to which you have granted rights will receive them automatically.

Using the NetWare Application Launcher

The NetWare Application Launcher is the user component of the NetWare Application Manager. As an administrator you must make available the appropriate executable file depending on the operating system being run at the desktop. Windows 3.x users will run NAL31.EXE and Windows 95 users will run NALW95.EXE.

For users running Windows 3.1x you can click the Group object in which you want to store NAL and select FILE, NEW. You can then search for the NAL31.EXE (usually stored in the SYS:\PUBLIC directory) and add it to the command line. Click YES to save NAL to the group.

Windows 95 users will use the NALW95.EXE, which can be added to the Windows 95 startup. In addition to any Windows 95 applications that are being delivered by NAL, the user will also see any Windows 3.1x-delivered applications.

You can also have NAL run as part of the startup folder to automatically deliver the NDS applications that you have previously defined. The NAL-delivered applications are refreshed every 60 minutes. As an end user you will see either the NAL icon or the execution of NAL.EXE, which will then show you the NDS-delivered applications.

USING NAM FOR SOFTWARE DISTRIBUTION

Another administrative feature of the NetWare Application Manger is the capability to assist in software distribution to the desktop. NAM version 1.0 can be used to perform the following administrative functions:

▸ Install stand-alone workstation applications from the network

▸ Install workstation portion of network applications

▸ Upgrade existing workstation-based applications

▸ Upgrade NetWare client software

▸ Upgrade Windows 3.x to Windows 95

For more information on these processes refer to Novell's NetWare Application Manager documentation.

Installing and Using the NetWare Web Server

Reading the Documentation

▸ To read the Web Server documentation, install a browser (such as Netscape Navigator, which is included with the Web Server) on a workstation and read the HTML formatted documentation from the CD-ROM.

Installing the Web Server

▸ To specify an IP address for the server and to bind TCP/IP to the network board, use INETCFG.NLM.

▸ To install the Web Server on the IntranetWare server, use INSTALL.NLM, select Product Options, and choose Install NetWare Web Server.

Configuring the Web Server

▸ To add a name service to your network, either create a hosts file on your server, or configure your server as a Domain Name Service (DNS) server or as a client of a DNS server.

▸ To configure the Web Server, use the NetWare Web Manager utility.

The NetWare Web Server 2.5 is an easy-to-install, high-performance World Wide Web (WWW) server that comes with IntranetWare. Installation and configuration is so easy that, if you already have TCP/IP configured on your server, you can view the sample NetWare Web Server home page in approximately 15 minutes. If you know how to create your own HyperText Markup Language (HTML) files, you can be viewing your own home page just a few minutes later.

This chapter introduces the NetWare Web Server 2.5 and explains how you can transform your NetWare Web Server into your own custom Internet or intranet Web site.

NOTE

Creating web pages (usually called "authoring") and administering a NetWare Web Server require different skills and are often performed by different people. This chapter focuses on NetWare Web Server administration, but it is undeniable that you can be a much better administrator if you also learn at least some of the basics of web page authoring. Your first indication of this will come when web page authors start linking pages to files all over the server and requesting write permissions. To learn more about web page authoring, consider taking Novell Education Course 654, Web Authoring and Publishing.

What is the NetWare Web Server?

A WWW server, such as the NetWare Web Server, is a file server that serves or publishes files in HyperText Markup Language (HTML) format. You read these HTML files from workstations by using client applications called *browsers*. HTML files are text files with special tags (usually enclosed in less-than and greater-than symbols, < >) that tell the browser how to format the file on screen. The main differences between HTML files and standard word processing files are that:

▶ HTML files do not contain proprietary custom symbols or formatting characters. All formatting is specified with special combinations of ASCII text characters. For example, to indicate that text should be printed in bold, you might use the following command:

▶ HTML files can include text or graphic *links*, which users can click on to move to another location in the same file or to another file on any web server in the world.

Many people get confused by the terms HTML and HTTP, and they are overwhelmed when WWW and Internet are also thrown into the same sentence. A WWW web server publishes files in HTML format. A web server communicates with browsers using the HyperText Transfer Protocol (HTTP), which runs over TCP/IP. The Internet is a global network of computers that provides many services, one of which is the WWW.

The NetWare Web Server provides the following features:

- Easy installation and configuration

- A Windows-based administration utility

- NDS Access control for Internet/intranet users and systems

- File security through NDS

- Internet/intranet access logging

- Browser access to NDS trees

- Support for dynamic web pages

- NetBasic for creating Internet scripts

- Netscape Navigator (single-user license in IntranetWare, or multi-user license — up to your allowed NetWare user limit — in IntranetWare)

Dynamic web page support allows web page authors to add commands to HTML files that enhance the pages in ways that are not possible with HTML tags. For example, web page authors can add commands that automatically insert variables such as the date or time into a page as it is sent to a browser. Other commands allow web page authors to display animations or perform calculations on data entered by a browser user. The NetWare Web Server supports dynamic web pages with the following features:

- Server Side Include (SSI) commands

- Local Common Gateway Interface (L-CGI)

- Remote Common Gateway Interface (R-CGI)

- BASIC script interpreters

- PERL script interpreters

- Support for Java applets

- Support for JavaScript

Installing the NetWare Web Server

Installing the Web Server consists of configuring the network to support TCP/IP and then running INSTALL.NLM to install the Web Server product.

To set up a NetWare Web Server site, you need the following hardware and software:

▶ A NetWare 4.11 (or IntranetWare) server with a CD-ROM drive.

▶ At least 2.5MB of hard disk space for the NetWare Web Server software plus additional disk space for your new HTML files.

▶ A client workstation running Windows 3.1x, Windows 95, or Windows NT. The workstation must have a 386 processor, 4MB of RAM, and 2.5MB of hard disk space available for the Netscape Navigator browser installation. (You can use a different browser if you prefer.)

▶ Although you can use Windows word processing tools to create and edit HTML documents, you may want to add HTML authoring software, which would require additional disk space and memory. An HTML authoring tool is not included with the NetWare Web Server.

LOCATING THE WEB SERVER DOCUMENTATION

The Web Server documentation is in HTML format on the IntranetWare Operating System CD-ROM. To read or print this documentation, you must use a web browser such as Netscape Navigator (included with the NetWare Web Server) on a workstation.

If you don't have a browser installed yet, complete the steps in the following checklist to install the Netscape Navigator browser on a Windows 3.1x workstation.

1 • Insert the *NetWare 4.11 Operating System* CD-ROM into a Windows 3.1x workstation's CD-ROM drive.

2 • From the workstation's Program Manager, choose Run from the File menu. Click Browse, and locate the SETUP.EXE file for the Web Server in the following directory: PRODUCTS\WEBSERV\BROWSER\N16E201. Select OK to begin the setup process.

To install the Netscape Navigator on a Windows 95 workstation, complete the steps in the following checklist.

1 • Insert the *NetWare 4.11 Operating System* CD-ROM into a Windows 3.1x workstation's CD-ROM drive.

2 • From Windows 95, click Start. Then choose Run and locate the SETUP.EXE file for the Web Server in the following directory: PRODUCTS\WEBSERV\BROWSER\N32E201. Select OK to begin the setup process.

After you've installed the viewer, launch it. From the Navigator's File menu, select Open File and select the drive and directory that contains the Web Server documentation (such as the CD-ROM drive or a directory if you've copied the documentation files to the server or the client). Then double-click on the file you want to open.

CONFIGURING TCP/IP

To prepare for NetWare Web Server installation, install IntranetWare on the server and establish IPX and TCP/IP communications between the two. (TCP/IP software is provided with IntranetWare.) Use INETCFG.NLM to specify an IP address for the server and to bind TCP/IP to the network board. Then load the PING NLM on the server and use it to verify TCP/IP communications with the client.

BRINGING UP THE NETWARE WEB SERVER

NetWare Web Server installation is easier than most NetWare installations because the critical configuration is completed when you configure TCP/IP. Simply load INSTALL.NLM on the server, choose Product Options, and then choose Install NetWare Web Server. Follow the instructions that appear on the screen.

When the NetWare Web Server installation is complete, press Alt-Esc at the server console to switch between the following active services:

▸ Novell HTTP Server 2.5, which is the NetWare Web Server NLM

▸ Novell Basic language interpreter, for dynamic Web page support

▶ Novell Perl language interpreter, for dynamic Web page support

You have now created a web site. Any network browser can now view the default home page if the user knows the TCP/IP address of your server.

To view the web site you have just created, start the browser on your client workstation, select Open Location from the file menu, and enter the following Universal Resource Locator (URL):

```
http://server_ip_address
```

After you enter this command with your server IP address, you should see the following web page shown in Figure 21.1.

F I G U R E 21.1

A Sample Web Page

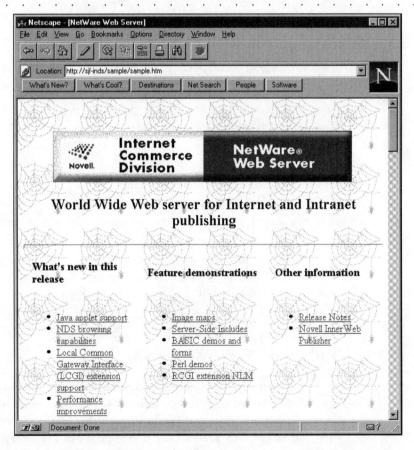

The default web site contains a number of sample pages and links. Browse through these pages to get an idea of what can be published on a NetWare Web Server. To see the HTML commands used to create any page, display the page and then select Document Source from the View menu.

Exploring Your Web Site

You are now a web site manager and, depending on your TCP/IP network connections, your site is available to your organization and possibly the world. Let's take a closer look at what you have.

When you look at the default directory structure of the NetWare Web Server, you'll notice the INDEX.HTM file. This is the default HTML file that web browsers see when they access your site using your IP address. We'll talk about changing the defaults and using names instead of IP addresses later. For now, what you need to know is that this is the entry point for your web site. To create your own home page, start by editing this file or by replacing it with your own INDEX.HTM file.

By default, the INDEX.HTM file is in the SYS:\WEB\DOCS directory, which is the document root directory of your web site. There are at least three root directories on your NetWare Web Server. The one you are most familiar with is the SYS: root directory, which is the NetWare volume root directory.

The NetWare Web Server has two root directories of its own: the server root directory and the document root directory. The server root directory contains all the configuration and control files associated with your web site; these are the files that you don't want your web site visitors to see. The server root directory on any NetWare Web Server is SYS:\WEB and cannot be changed.

The document root directory is the default path to all the files you want to publish. To protect your server configuration files from undesired access, the document root directory should be a subdirectory of the server root directory, or it should be placed on another volume.

NOTE

When browsers access your site, they are restricted to files and directories that are contained in the document root directory — with one exception. You can configure the NetWare Web Server to allow browsers to access user home pages in the users' home directories.

The document root directory can be changed to another directory or another volume, but it should be changed only after careful planning. Many links in the web pages will use relative references that define the path from the document root directory to another file. Carelessly moving the document root can make all your internal web site links invalid, rendering your web site useless.

NOTE

A NetWare Web Server is a live web site; users can connect to it at any time. To avoid user access errors, always edit published web pages offline in your home directory or on another computer. Otherwise your word processor or web authoring tool may lock the file and prevent other users from accessing it. Also, test all links that you create in your Web pages. It's less embarrassing to find the mistakes yourself.

Configuring Name Services

Your web server is up, but your customers (both internal and external) have to remember your server's IP address to access it. Simplify your customers' access by creating a name service.

Name services use a table of IP addresses and names to establish names that can be used in place of IP addresses. Each IP address can be associated with one or more names or aliases.

There are two common ways to add a name service to your network. The easiest is to create a hosts file on your server. The second is to configure your server as a Domain Name Service (DNS) server or as a client of a DNS server. The hosts file approach provides name services only on your network or subnet. DNS provides name services over an entire network or the Internet.

CREATING AND USING A HOST'S FILE

To create a table of IP addresses and host names for your network or subnet, use a text editor to create a file named HOSTS.TXT in the SYS:ETC directory. Create a name table similar to Table 21.1.

T A B L E 21.1	#IP ADDRESS	ALIASES	COMMENTS
Sample Name Table	ip_address	alias1 alias2#	NetWare Web Server
	ip_address	alias3#	jim's pc
	ip_address	alias4#	carol's pc

The # character indicates that all text to the right of it is a comment and is to be ignored. Each line starts with the IP address of a host, followed by one or more spaces. The second item on each line is the name you want to assign to the host. You can add several names, but be sure to separate each name with one or more spaces.

USING DOMAIN NAME SERVICES

Domain name service (DNS) is an internet protocol that allows administrators to associate internet addresses with names that people can remember. A DNS server stores the names and their corresponding IP addresses and responds to clients that need names services. DNS is provided with NetWare/IP and FTP Services for IntranetWare. You can use these products to add DNS to your network, or you can use an existing DNS server.

To configure your NetWare Web Server to use the name services of a DNS server, use a text editor to create a file named RESOLV.CFG in the directory SYS:ETC. Enter the following text in this file:

```
domain domain_name

nameserver  IP_address
```

The domain_name variable is the name of the domain in which your server is installed. The IP_address variable is the IP address of the DNS server. You should be able to get this information from the administrator of the DNS server.

NOTE

To use the services of a DNS server, you must create the RESOLV.TXT file. Installing the DNS server on the same server as your NetWare Web Server does not remove this requirement.

Configuration Tools for Your Web Site

Although the NetWare Web Server does not require configuration, there are a number of configuration changes you may want to make. We describe the following changes in this chapter:

▶ Controlling access to your web site

▶ Supporting dynamic web pages

▶ Supporting long filenames

▶ Moving the document root directory

▶ Controlling directory indexing

▶ Checking site status

▶ Adjusting the web server processing power

Most of the configuration changes you will want to make can be performed using the NetWare Web Manager utility. Some configuration changes must be entered manually into the configuration files.

USING THE NETWARE WEB MANAGER UTILITY

The NetWare Web Manager utility (WEBMGR.EXE) is installed in the SYS:\PUBLIC directory when the NetWare Web Server is installed. Because this is a Windows-based utility, you may want to create a program icon to launch this for you.

To start the NetWare Web Manager utility and select a NetWare Web Server to manage, complete the steps in the following checklist.

I • From your client computer, map a drive to the SYS volume on your NetWare Web Server.

2 • Start the WEBMGR.EXE program in SYS:\PUBLIC using the Windows RUN command or a program icon that you have created.

3 • If the Web Server's IP address or domain name appears in the bottom section of the File menu, select the Web Server. If the NetWare Web Server does not appear in the File menu, choose Select Server from the File menu, select the web server root directory, SYS:\WEB, and then click OK.

After you select the NetWare Web Server, the NetWare Web Server dialog box appears. This is the only dialog box that you can use to change the NetWare Web Server configuration.

4 • If the Full Server Name text box does not contain an IP address or a domain name for your server, you must enter it; this information is required. (Domain names are discussed later in this chapter.)

5 • Enter the e-mail address of the administrator for this server.

6 • After you complete your configuration changes, click OK to save the changes.

7 • If you have made changes to the Web Server configuration, the NetWare Web Manager utility will prompt you to restart the server. To activate the changes, click Save & Restart, and then enter the password for the NetWare Web Server.

NOTE

To restart the server using the NetWare Manager utility, you must know the password for the utility and your client must be configured for TCP/IP communications. If these conditions are not met, the utility saves your changes, but does not restart the server.

TIP

To restart the Web Server at the system console prompt, enter the following commands:

```
Unload HTTP

Load HTTP
```

EDITING THE NETWARE WEB SERVER CONFIGURATION FILES MANUALLY

The NetWare Web Server configuration settings are saved in the default configuration files shown in Table 21.2.

TABLE 21.2	CONFIGURATION FILE	DESCRIPTION
Default Configuration Files	SYS:\WEB\CONFIG\ HTTPD.CFG	This is the principal NetWare Web Server configuration file. This file cannot be moved. It specifies the server name, the Web Server TCP/IP port, the administrator e-mail address, the administrator password, log file options, the location of the other configuration files, and the maximum number of threads to be allocated to the Web Server.
	SYS:\WEB\CONFIG\ SRM.CFG	This file specifies the resources available to the NetWare Web Server. It defines the locations of the document root directory, any script directories, and any image map directories. The default index filename (Index.htm) is also defined here, as are the indexing options and other resource-related features. The location of this file is specified in HTTPD.CFG by the following directive: ResourceConfig config/srm.cfg
	SYS:\WEB\CONFIG\ ACCESS.CFG	This is the global web access configuration file, which controls access and indexing options to the directories within your server root. This is also where SSI commands are enabled for a directory. The location of this file is specified in HTTPD.CFG by the following directive: AccessConfig config/access.cfg
	path\ACCESS.WWW	This is the local web access configuration file, which controls access to the files within the directory in which it is located. The name of this file is specified in SRM.CFG by the following directive: AccessFileName access.www

(continued)

TABLE 21.2

Default Configuration Files
(continued)

CONFIGURATION FILE	DESCRIPTION
SYS:\WEB\CONFIG\ MIME.TYP	This is the MIME type configuration file. Each line in this file specifies a Multipurpose Internet Mail Extension (MIME) type and one or more file extensions to be associated with that type. When the browser requests a file, the server refers to the MIME.TYP file to determine if a MIME type has been configured for that extension. If a MIME type is specified, that MIME type is sent to the browser to identify the type of file the server is forwarding. The location of this file is specified in HTTPD.CFG by the following directive: TypesConfig config/mime.typ

Many, but not all, of your configuration changes can be made with the NetWare Web Manager utility, which saves changes to these files. To edit any of these files manually, open a text editor program, make the changes, and save the file. To better understand how the NetWare Web Server uses these files, you may want to view them before and after you make changes with the NetWare Web Manager utility.

Controlling Access to Your Web Site

After you install the NetWare Web Server, everyone that has IP access to your network has the ability to read all the files in your web site. Since you created the web directory structure, you may be the only one who can make changes to web pages. Most web server administrators will need to make some changes to the Web Server access rights. These changes fall into two categories: Web Access Rights and NetWare File System Rights.

CHANGING WEB ACCESS RIGHTS

You can use the NetWare Web Manager utility to limit access to the site or to specific directories (and their subdirectories). You can limit access by restricting the following types of entities:

▸ Select NDS users

▸ All valid NDS users

▸ NDS user groups

▸ Hostnames

▸ IP addresses

▸ IP networks

▸ Domain names

You can also limit access to your site using filters provided in IntranetWare or NetWare Multiprotocol Router.

TIP

Although the NetWare Web Server offers a variety of access control methods, they are not without their cost. Using any of these methods restricts access to only those users that are explicitly defined to the Web Server, which means you have to define and administer all the users and systems that can access your Web Server.

To administer access to NDS user groups, you must edit the ACCESS.CFG file manually. For instructions on this procedure, refer to the NetWare Web Server readme file. The README.TXT file is in the server root directory (SYS:WEB) and on the CD-ROM under the directory WEBSERV\DISK1.

NOTE

To restrict access to your Web Server, complete the steps in the following checklist.

1 • Start the NetWare Web Server Manager program and select your NetWare Web Server, as described earlier in this chapter.

2 • Choose the User Access page (to restrict access by users) or the System Access page (to restrict access based on IP addresses, host names, or domain names) on the dialog box that appears.

3 • Select the directory to which you want the restrictions to apply.

NOTE

Remember, you are disabling directory access to everyone who is not specified on this page. If your access list is going to be too large, you might want to reorganize your site so that you can create a smaller access list.

4 • Set the restrictions you want.

   a. If you're restricting access to specific NDS users, mark either the All Valid Users checkbox (to enable access to all valid NDS users) or select a user from the list that appears and click Add to Authorized Users List checkbox (to enable access for a specific user). If you do not enter a context for your users, each user will have to enter a fully distinguished name, starting with a period. To specify the NDS context of the users, enter a context in the NDS Context text box. If you need to support users in multiple contexts, enter the context that is common to all the users. The users will then need to enter their user names relative to this context.

   b. If you're restricting by system access, specify the IP address, full host name, or full domain name to which you want to give directory access. Then select a user from the list that appears and click Add to Authorized Systems List.

5 • Click OK to save your changes.

6 • If you have made changes to the Web Server configuration, the NetWare Web Manager utility will prompt you to restart the server. To activate the changes, click Save & Restart, and then enter the password for the NetWare Web Server.

NETWARE RIGHTS ISSUES

NetWare rights control who can view the web pages, who can edit and author web pages, and who can change the NetWare Web Server configuration.

Unless you have changed web access rights with the NetWare Web Manager, user Public (in the root container) should have read and file scan access rights to the site root directory and all subdirectories that contain pages, images, or page components that you want the public to view. When planning NetWare access rights for web page authors, remember that the authors will need write, create, and modify access to all directories that contain the files they are publishing.

Table 21.3 lists the default directories to which customers and web authors need rights.

T A B L E 21.3	DIRECTORY	GUIDELINES
Directories That Customers and Web Authors Use	Document Root Directory	Default location: Sys:\WEB\DOCS
	Server Side Include directory	Default location: Sys:\WEB\DOCS\SSI
	Images/Graphics	Default location: Sys:WEB\DOCS\IMAGES

Table 21.4 lists the directories that control NetWare Web Server configuration or enable program access to the server volumes. These directories should not be available to the public.

T A B L E 21.4	DIRECTORY	GUIDELINES
Directories That the Administrator Uses	\Config	Default location: SYS:\WEB\CONFIG Restrict rights to NetWare Web Server administrators. The files in this folder control NetWare Web Server operation and web access rights.
	\Maps	Default location: SYS:\WEB\MAPS Restrict rights to the web authors that create image maps. The files in this folder control how user mouse-clicks on a web page graphic are interpreted. Most user mouse-clicks will activate a link to another web page.
	Scripts directories	Default scripts directories: SYS:\WEB\SCRIPTS, SYS:\WEB\SCRIPTS\PERL Restrict rights to the people responsible for creating and maintaining scripts. Scripts enable the dynamic web pages described later and can write data to your server's hard disk.

Supporting Dynamic Web Pages

When creating dynamic web pages, the first feature you will need to address is the Server Side Include (SSI) command set. Next, you'll need to administer the Common Gateway Interface Scripts.

ADMINISTERING SSI COMMAND USAGE

Server Side Include commands allow web authors to insert variables into their otherwise static web pages. Using a server side include command, the author can dynamically insert text from another file or display the current date and time. The SSI commands supported by the NetWare Web Server are described in the default web pages (INDEX.HTM) provided with the NetWare Web Server. This section describes what you need to know to support the web page authors.

Three rules govern the use of SSI commands in web pages:

▸ Any file that contains SSI commands must use the .SSI extension.

▸ An SSI file cannot include text from another SSI file.

▸ Before any SSI processing occurs, the NetWare Web Server administrator must enable SSI processing for the directory in which the SSI command is stored. (The SYS:WEB\DOCS\SSI directory is enabled when the NetWare Web Server is installed.)

SSI processing is not enabled for all directories because it requires additional processing power from the server and reduces response times for web page viewers. This extra processing time is not excessive, but it is best to enable SSI processing only in those directories where it will be used.

To enable SSI command processing for a directory, complete the steps in the following checklist.

1 • Start the NetWare Web Server Manager program and select your NetWare Web Server as described earlier in this chapter.

2 • Choose the Directories page in the dialog box that appears.

3 • If the directory for which you want to enable SSI commands appears in the Existing Directories box, select it.

4 • If the directory you want does not appear in the Existing Directories box, use the Browse button to locate the directory, click Add, and then select your directory in the Existing Directories box.

5 • After you have selected the directory, check the Enable Includes checkbox and click Change. (You must click Change. If you click OK instead of Change, it will not change the directory setting.)

6 • Click OK to save your changes.

7 • If you have made changes to the Web Server configuration, the NetWare Web Manager utility will prompt you to restart the server. To activate the changes, click Save & Restart, and then enter the password for the NetWare Web Server.

SUPPORTING CGI SCRIPTS

The Common Gateway Interface (CGI) is the feature that allows the NetWare Web Server to modify web pages before they are sent to a browser. First, the NetWare Web Server scans an HTML file for SSI commands or commands that reference other programs called scripts. If any SSI commands or scripts are located, the NetWare Web Server processes them, inserts the results in the HTML file, and sends it to the web browser.

Because CGI scripts can write data to your server's hard drives, you should administer their use carefully. Store the script files in directories that the web page users cannot access, and limit create, write, and modify rights to the script programmers. Table 21.5 lists the default directories that store script files.

SCRIPT TYPE	DEFAULT DIRECTORY/NOTES
BASIC RCGI scripts	SYS:WEB\SCRIPTS These are BASIC computer programs. Remote CGI (RCGI) scripts are written to be platform independent so they can be easily adapted to other computer operating systems. This directory is defined in the SRM.CFG file with the following directive: RemoteScriptAlias /scripts/ localhost:8001/scripts
Perl RCGI scripts	SYS:WEB\SCRIPTS\PERL These are Perl computer programs. This directory is defined in the SRM.CFG file with the following directive: RemoteScriptAlias /perl/ localhost:8002/sys:Web/ scripts/perl
LCGI NLM	SYS:WEB\CGI-BIN Local CGI (LCGI) scripts are written to take advantage of a specific computer operating system — in this case, IntranetWare. This directory is defined in the SRM.CFG file with the following directive: RemoteScriptAlias /cgiproc/ localhost:8003/sys:Web/ samples/cgiapp

Moving the Web Server's Document Root Directory

The default location for the document root directory is on the SYS volume under the server root (SYS:\WEB\DOCS). As your web site grows, you may want to move the document root to another volume to avoid filling up the SYS volume.

To move the document root to another volume or directory, complete the steps in the following checklist.

I • Copy the document root directory and all of its subdirectories to the new location.

Be sure to copy the complete directory structure (using the /s option with NCOPY or XCOPY) so that relative links in the web pages are not invalidated.

CHAPTER 21
. . . . .
INSTALLING
AND USING
THE NETWARE
WEB SERVER

2 • Start the NetWare Web Server Manager program and select your NetWare Web Server as described earlier in this chapter.

3 • Change the Server Root Directory parameter on the Server page to specify the path to the web server document root directory.

4 • Click OK to save your changes.

5 • If you have made changes to the Web Server configuration, the NetWare Web Manager utility will prompt you to restart the server. To activate the changes, click Save & Restart, then enter the password for the NetWare Web Server.

6 • Test your web site links to be sure that the directory move did not invalidate any links.

All relative links within the document root should work in the new location, as should all explicit references to other web sites.

NOTE

You can still view your old document root pages in your browser by entering the domain name and path to the index file in the old root. For example: file:///SYS:/ path_to_index_file/index_file. This may be useful while you are troubleshooting links that aren't working.

7 • When you are satisfied that the web site is working correctly with the new document root, delete the former document root.

Controlling Directory Indexing

Directory indexing is a feature that creates an index for a browser when the default directory is missing. If a browser user enters a URL for a file, the browser receives that file. If a browser enters a URL for a directory, one of the following occurs:

▶ If the default index file (INDEX.HTM) is present, that file is displayed. (The default name is defined in the SRM.CFG file with the DirectoryIndex directive.)

▸ If the default index file is missing and directory indexing is disabled, no files are found.

▸ If the default index file is missing and directory indexing is enabled, the server builds an index page that appears at the browser. This page lists all the files in the directory, along with links that can display or download the files.

You can use the NetWare Web Manager utility to manage directory indexing on a directory-by-directory basis. This utility stores your configuration in the ACCESS.CFG file. Table 21.6 lists the index options.

TABLE 21.6 *Index Options*	INDEX OPTION	FUNCTION
	Fancy indexing	For each file in a directory, fancy indexing displays the filename listed by conventional indexing and adds an icon, the last modified date, the file size, and a file description.
	Icons are links	When fancy indexing is enabled, this option defines the file icons as links so that the browser user can select the file by clicking on the icon.
	Scan titles	When fancy indexing is enabled, the Scan titles option causes the server to scan all HTML documents and include the HTML document title in the index as a file description.
		If this option is disabled, the file description is blank.

To set the directory indexing options for a directory, complete the steps in the following checklist.

1 • Start the NetWare Web Server Manager program and select your NetWare Web Server as described earlier in this chapter.

2 • Choose the Directories page in the dialog box that appears.

3 • If the directory for which you want to set indexing options appears in the Existing Directories box, select it.

4 • If the directory you want does not appear in the Existing Directories box, use the Browse button to locate the directory, click Add, and then select your directory in the Existing Directories box.

5 • After you have selected the directory, check the Enable Indexing check box.

6 • If you want to enable any of the indexing options, check the corresponding check boxes.

7 • Click Change, and then click OK to save your changes.

8 • If you have made changes to the Web Server configuration, the NetWare Web Manager utility will prompt you to restart the server. To activate the changes, click Save & Restart, and then enter the password for the NetWare Web Server.

Checking Site Status

You can check your site status using the tools listed in Table 21.7.

TABLE 21.7	TOOL	PURPOSE
Tools for Checking Site Status	NetWare Web Server console	The Web Server console displays the server and document roots, server statistics, and server status messages, which are recorded in the Web Server error log.
	Access log	The access log specifies the IP address or domain name of all users who access your server. It also lists the files that have been accessed.
		The default configuration of the server records IP addresses in the access log. If you set up the server as a DNS client as described earlier in this chapter, the access log records domain names whenever they are available.
	Error log	The error log records the errors and messages that appear on the Web Server console.
	Debug log	The debug log records information that you can use to troubleshoot problems with the Web Server.

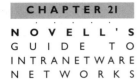
VIEWING THE NETWARE WEB SERVER CONSOLE

The NetWare Web Server console (see Figure 21.2) is available whenever the Web Server is active, which is whenever the HTTP NLM is loaded. Just press Alt-Esc until the Novell HTTP Server console appears.

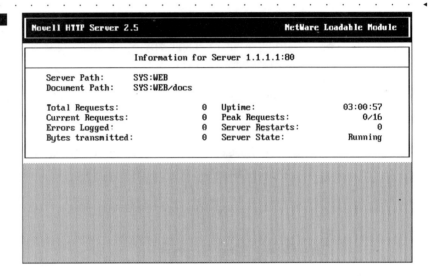

```
Novell HTTP Server 2.5                              NetWare Loadable Module

                        Information for Server 1.1.1.1:80

        Server Path:        SYS:WEB
        Document Path:      SYS:WEB/docs

        Total Requests:          0   Uptime:              03:00:57
        Current Requests:        0   Peak Requests:            0/16
        Errors Logged:           0   Server Restarts:             0
        Bytes transmitted:       0   Server State:          Running
```

Note the Peak Requests statistic on the Web Server console. This number, 0/16 in this example, lists the maximum number of server threads used (0) and the maximum number of server threads available (16). If the number of server threads used starts to approach the maximum number available, you can configure the NetWare Web Server to use more threads. If you are low on memory and the Web Server is not using many of the allocated threads, you can save memory by reducing the number of allocated threads. These procedures are provided later in this chapter.

VIEWING AND ADMINISTERING LOG FILES

You can use the NetWare Web Manager utility to view and administer log files. To view and administer any log file, complete the steps in the following checklist.

1 • Start the NetWare Web Server Manager program and select your NetWare Web Server as described earlier in this chapter.

2 • Select the appropriate Open command from the Log menu.

3 • Choose the Logs page in the dialog box that appears.

4 • Set the log options using the information in Table 21.8.

5 • Click OK to save your changes.

6 • If you have made changes to the Web Server configuration, the NetWare Web Manager utility will prompt you to restart the server. To activate the changes, click Save & Restart, and then enter the password for the NetWare Web Server.

TABLE 21.8	LOG OPTION	DESCRIPTION AND USAGE
Log Options	Log file handling	This option determines whether there are one or more log files. If you select the Do not roll logs option, the NetWare Web Server creates one of each type of log file. When the log file is full, the oldest entries are deleted. If you select the Roll logs as needed option, the Web Server will archive all the log file data when the log gets full, creating an empty log file in which to store new data.
	Server debug log options	This option enables or disables the logging of server debug messages.
	Maximum log size	This option defines the maximum size of each log file. Notice that the NetWare Web Manager utility calculates the maximum amount of disk space used by the log files and the old logs. This appears on the Logs page.
	Maximum number of old logs	This option specifies how many old log files will be created. If you already have filled all the old logs and then you fill the current log, the data in the oldest log file is lost.
	Default button	The default button returns all log options to the default options supplied with the NetWare Web Server

Adjusting the Web Server Processing Power

As mentioned earlier, the Web Server console displays the maximum number of threads used by the NetWare Web Server. To provide more performance capacity (at the expense of server memory), you can increase the number of threads available to the Web Server. To reduce the memory required by the Web Server (and decrease the performance capacity of the Web Server), you can decrease the number of threads available.

To adjust the maximum number of threads used by the Web Server, edit the MaxThreads directive in the HTTPD.CFG file. The valid entries are 1 through 255, but entries above 40 may decrease the server performance.

Getting More Information

This chapter has introduced the concepts and administration tasks that will help you establish your web site using the NetWare Web Server. For more information on the NetWare Web Server, refer to one of the following resources:

▶ The default web pages (INDEX.HTM) provided with the NetWare Web Server

▶ The *Dynamic Web Page Programmer's Guide*, which describes how to use BASIC and Perl CGI scripts to create dynamic web pages. You can view this guide with your browser by specifying the following URL (replace x with the drive letter of the IntranetWare CD-ROM: File:///x:/PRODUCTS/WEBSERV/DISK1/WEB/DOCS/ONLINE/WPGUIDE/INDEX.HTM

▶ The Novell web site, at www.novell.com, for updated information about the NetWare Web Server

CHAPTER 22

Installing the Novell Internet Access Server and FTP Services

Installing and Managing Novell Internet Access Server Components

▶ To install the Novell Internet Access Server components on the server, use INSTALL.NLM, select Product Options, and choose Install a Product Not Listed. Then specify the path to the *Novell Internet Access Server* 4 CD-ROM.

▶ To configure the IPX/IP gateway on the server, use INETCFG.NLM.

▶ To install the client support for the IPX/IP gateway on workstations, install NetWare Client32 and choose Additional Options (on Windows 3.1x) or Customize (on Windows 95).

▶ To work with the IPX/IP gateway object in NDS and to configure access rights, add the IPX/IP gateway snap-in utility to the NetWare Administrator utility by editing the NWADMN3X.INI file.

Installing and Managing FTP Services for IntranetWare

▶ To install FTP Services for IntranetWare, use INSTALL.NLM, select Product Options, and choose Install a Product Not Listed. Then specify the path to the *FTP Services for IntranetWare* CD-ROM.

▶ To configure FTP Services for IntranetWare and to create an Anonymous FTP user account, use UNICON.NLM.

Just when we were beginning to get comfortable with the Internet technology, the intranet technology appeared. From a technical standpoint, the intranet is simply a web server that is confined to a private internal network and publishes files to a private audience such as the employees of a corporation. A true WWW server is connected to the Internet and publishes files to the world.

The reason that intranet technology is so popular is that people can use their WWW browsers to view the private information. The intranet server publishes shared information in HTML files that can be created with almost any word processor or text editor and can be viewed with Internet browsers on almost every operating system.

IntranetWare is Novell's comprehensive platform for a modern, full-service intranet. It starts with NetWare 4.11, then adds the following intranet and Internet features:

- IPX/IP Gateway. This gateway enables administrators to allow IPX-based workstations to access TCP/IP-based resources, such as FTP and the World Wide Web, without having to install or configure TCP/IP on those workstations. The gateway also lets you implement access control — you can limit users by TCP port number, IP address or the target host, and the time of day.

- MultiProtocol Router 3.1. This feature provides WAN (Wide Area Network) connectivity, routing multiple protocols over leased lines, frame relay, or ISDN lines. This capability allows you to connect network users to an Internet Service Provider (ISP).

- Netscape Navigator. This is the web browser that lets you locate and read information stored on the Internet or intranet.

- FTP Services for IntranetWare. FTP services let you configure FTP access for your intranet.

In your IntranetWare package, you'll find the following CD-ROMs:

- The *NetWare 4.11* Operating System CD-ROM, which contains the regular NetWare 4.11 product software and the NetWare Web Server. The NetWare Web Server also contains the Netscape Navigator web browser (and a single-user license for the browser).

- The *NetWare 4.11* Online Documentation CD-ROM, which contains the DynaText documentation for NetWare 4.11.

▸ The *Novell Internet Access Server* 4 CD-ROM, which contains most of the
IntranetWare features: the IPX/IP gateway, MultiProtocol Router 3.1 for
WAN connectivity, and the Netscape Navigator web browser (multi-user
license). This CD-ROM also contains HTML-formatted documentation for
the IPX/IP gateway.

▸ The *FTP Services for IntranetWare* CD-ROM, which contains the FTP
services and configuration utilities.

**To read the HTML-formatted documentation for the Novell Internet
Access Server product, use a web browser from a workstation.**

NOTE

For instructions on installing the Netscape Navigator browser that comes with
the NetWare Web Server on the *NetWare 4.11 Operating System* CD-ROM, see
Chapter 14. For instructions on installing the browser from the *Novell Internet
Access Server* CD-ROM, see the *Internet Access Server 4 Quick Reference Guide*, which
comes with your IntranetWare kit. The two browsers are identical, and they are
placed on both CD-ROMs primarily for convenience.

**If you have IntranetWare, you are allowed to use as many copies of
the web browser as your IntranetWare user license permits. In
other words, if you bought a 50-user version of IntranetWare, you
can let 50 users use the browser. If you have NetWare 4.11 alone,
you have only a single-user license to the browser.**

NOTE

Installing the Novell Internet Access Server Software

Before installing the Novell Internet Access Server software, which will provide
the software necessary to run the routing, wan connectivity, and IPX/IP gateway, you
must first install a NetWare 4.11 server as usual. Then you can install the Novell
Internet Access Server software. During the installation, the Netscape Navigator
browser will be copied to the SYS:NETSCAPE so that you can later install it on
workstations.

To install Novell Internet Access Server components on the NetWare 4.11 server, complete the following steps.

1 • Insert the *Novell Internet Access Server 4* CD-ROM in a drive on the server and mount the CD-ROM as a NetWare volume.

2 • At the server console, load INSTALL.NLM.

3 • From the Installation Options menu, choose Product Options, then choose Install a Product Not Listed.

4 • To specify a path to the installation software, press <F3> and type

```
NIAS4:\NIAS\INSTALL
```

5 • Choose Install Product. The Install To Servers list displays the local server name. The value in the title reflects the number of servers to be installed. If you want to install Novell Internet Access Server software on a remote server, press Insert to add the server to the list. If an expected server is not displayed, ensure that the latest version of RSPAWN.NLM is loaded on that server. To remove a server from the Install To Servers list, select the server, press Delete, and select Yes at the prompt.

6 • From the Install To Servers menu, press Enter and select Yes to begin the installation. Servers are installed in alphabetical order. If you are installing to a remote server, you will be prompted to log in as an administrator. Enter the administrator's full login name and password.

7 • When the prompt "Install previously created configuration files?" appears, select No.

8 • When prompted for the Novell Internet Access Server license diskette, insert the NetWare 4.11/IntranetWare license diskette in the specified drive and press Enter. Once the login, license, and configuration file information for each server are provided, the installation begins copying files to the destinations.

9 • When the installation is completed, you can read the installation log file if you desire. Choose Display Log File. When you're finished reviewing the log, press Esc to return to the Installation Options menu.

10 • To verify that the Novell Internet Access Server software installed correctly, choose Product Options from the Installation Options menu, then select Configure/View/Remove Installed Products. The Currently Installed Products list appears, showing entries for the NetWare MultiProtocol Router 3.1 software, WAN Extensions 3.1, and Novell Internet Access Server 4. Press Esc to return to the Installation Options menu.

11 • From the Installation Options menu, select NCF Files Options, then choose the Edit STARTUP.NCF file. Modify the STARTUP.NCF file for each installed server to include the following line at the end of the file if you are using the IntranetWare server to make a WAN connection:

```
SET MINIMUM PACKET RECEIVE BUFFERS=400

SET MAXIMUM PACKET RECEIVE BUFFERS=1000
```

The value of the second parameter can be increased as needed.

12 • To exit the installation screen, press Esc and then select Yes to save the changes.

13 • Bring down and restart the server to make sure all the correct NLMs are loaded. At the server's console, type:

```
DOWN

RESTART SERVER
```

In addition to updating server NLM files stored in SYS:\SYSTEM, the installation process installs the client files in the SYS:\PUBLIC\CLIENT\WIN95 and SYS:\PUBLIC\CLIENT\WIN31 directories. The Netscape Navigator files are installed in the SYS:\NETSCAPE\32 and SYS:\NETSCAPE\16 directories.

The IPX/IP Gateway

The IPX/IP gateway is an important part of the Novell Internet Access Server components of IntranetWare. With this gateway, IPX-based clients can access the Internet and other IP-based resources without having to install TCP/IP on the workstations themselves. The IPX/IP gateway gets installed on the server as part of the Novell Internet Access Server installation. To take advantage of the gateway, you must install IPX/IP Gateway support on each workstation. Client gateway support is included as an option in the NetWare Client32 installation.

Not having to use TCP/IP on each workstation is a benefit in many cases because there are significant management tasks associated with maintaining TCP/IP workstations. With TCP/IP, you have to manually keep track of and configure many items for each individual workstation, such as the unique IP address, subnet mask, IP addresses of the default router and the domain name servers, and the domain name.

An IPX/IP gateway removes much of the individual management hassles that occur with maintaining TCP/IP workstations by letting you retain IPX on those workstations.

When the IPX/IP gateway is installed on the IntranetWare server, the server runs IPX to communicate with the IPX workstations on the network and TCP/IP so that it can communicate with the Internet. From the viewpoint of a remote host on the Internet, all traffic through the gateway seems to originate from the IP address assigned to the gateway server. Because the IPX/IP gateway uses only a single IP address, regardless of the number of users it supports, the private network is safe from outside interference. Using the Novell IPX/IP Gateway alleviates the difficulties of administering a TCP/IP environment by providing ease of management and centralized control over Internet access.

By using Novell's IPX/IP gateway, you can run only IPX on the network workstations. Compared to IP, IPX is simple to manage. It assigns user connections dynamically, eliminating the need for a registered address to be configured at each desktop. Since IPX addresses are assigned dynamically, workstation IPX address conflicts do not occur. Users can move transparently between IPX networks, and traveling IPX users can roam between multiple networks within an enterprise.

The Novell IPX/IP Gateway allows you to limit access to Internet services by the type of traffic (for example, web browsing or FTP) and by remote host. Either type of restriction can be limited to specific times during the day to reduce "rush hour" traffic on an Internet connection.

CONFIGURING THE IPX/IP GATEWAY

After you've installed Novell Internet Access Server on the server, you can configure the IPX/IP gateway. To do this, complete the following steps.

1 • At the server console, load INETCFG.NLM. If you are asked if you want to transfer your LAN driver, protocol, and remote access commands, choose Yes. What this really means is that you will move the LOAD and BIND commands from the AUTOEXEC.NCF file to INETCFG's startup files.

2 • From the main menu, select Protocols, then choose TCP/IP, then choose IPX/IP Gateway Configuration.

3 • Specify "enabled" in the Enabled for the IPX/IP Gateway field so that the gateway will become operational.

4 • If you want to record when clients access a service over the gateway, enable the Client Logging field. The log is stored in a field called GW_AUDIT.LOG in the SYS volume.

5 • In the Console Messages field, specify the type of messages you want to display on the gateway logging screen and the gateway status log file (GW_INFO.LOG in the SYS volume). You can choose "Informational, warning, and errors" (the default), "Warnings and errors only," or "Errors only."

6 • To enforce access restrictions (which you set using the NetWare Administrator utility), enable the Access Control field.

7 • In the Domain Name field, specify the name of the domain in which the gateway is installed. Your Internet Service Provider may provide you with this name.

8 • In the Name Server fields, specify the IP addresses of any active domain name servers. Your Internet Service Provider may provide these addresses.

9 • Press Esc twice, then log in as user Admin when prompted.

10 • If you want to configure the gateway to use leased lines, frame relay, or ISDN lines, complete the following steps (see the documentation that came with Novell Internet Access Server for more specific details about parameters):

a. Choose Boards from the INETCFG.NLM main menu. Then specify the appropriate WAN driver and configure any necessary parameters.

b. Choose Network Interfaces from the INETCFG.NLM main menu. Then configure the appropriate WAN interfaces.

c. Choose WAN Call Directory from INETCFG's main menu and press Ins to configure a new WAN call destination, then configure any necessary parameters.

d. Choose Bindings from INETCFG's main menu, press Ins, and bind TCP/IP to the appropriate board or driver.

11 • Exit INETCFG.NLM and save the changes you made.

12 • Reboot the server to make the changes take effect.

After you've enabled and configured the gateway, a gateway server NDS object appears in the NDS tree in the same context as the server on which it is installed. The gateway object's name is the same as the server's name, with -GW added to the end of the name. This gateway object assists gateway clients in locating active IPX/ IP gateway servers.

ADDING IPX/IP GATEWAY TOOLS TO THE NETWARE ADMINISTRATOR UTILITY

To work with the IPX/IP gateway object, you'll need to add the gateway's snap-in utility to the NetWare Administrator utility. This will allow NetWare Administrator to recognize the new gateway object and the new access control property that was added to certain objects. (This property is explained later in this chapter.)

The IPX/IP gateway snap-in utility works only with the 16-bit version of NetWare Administrator (which runs on Windows 3.1x).

To add the IPX/IP gateway support to the NetWare Administrator utility on a Windows 3.1 workstation, complete the following steps.

1 • If you haven't yet opened the NetWare Administrator utility, open it and close it.

2 • From the Windows File Manager on your workstation, double-click on the NWADMN3X.INI file (located in the WINDOWS directory) to open it for editing.

3 • Under the heading [Snapin Object DLLs WIN3X], add the following line:

```
IPXGW3X=IPXGW3X.DLL
```

4 • Save and close the file. Now the NetWare Administrator utility will recognize the IPX/IP gateway object.

CONTROLLING ACCESS TO THE IPX/IP GATEWAY

After the IPX/IP Gateway server is fully installed and configured, you can use the NetWare Administrator utility to give the IPX/IP gateway server access control information for the various objects in the NDS tree. Then you can use NetWare Administrator to set restrictions for users, groups, or containers.

To give the gateway server access control information, use the NetWare Administrator utility to make the following changes to the NDS tree:

▸ Make the Public object a trustee of the Gateway object, with browse object rights and read and compare property rights (for all properties).

▸ Make the Public object a trustee of the File Server Object that is running the IPX/IP Gateway, with browse object rights and read and compare property rights for the Network Address property only (under selected properties).

▸ Make the Gateway object a trustee in the Root object, with browse object rights and read and compare property rights (for all properties).

You control user access through the IPX/IP Gateway by using the NetWare Administrator utility. As the point of connection between a NetWare network and a TCP/IP network, an IPX/IP gateway is in an ideal position to enforce restrictions on traffic between the two networks.

These access restrictions can be stored in two properties that are added to the User, Group, Organization, or Organizational Unit objects when the gateway is enabled:

▸ The first property, service restrictions, tells the gateway object which applications may be used by the object and which are restricted. These restrictions are based on the port number.

▸ The second property, host restrictions, tells the gateway which remote hosts are restricted from the object. These restrictions are based on the IP address.

Storing access restrictions in the NDS objects provides a single database of restrictions that all gateway servers share. You do not need to configure access control separately on each gateway. Restrictions are active on all gateways regardless of whether they are applied to an entire organization or created individually for each user.

To place access restrictions on a User, Group, Organization, or Organizational Unit object, use the NetWare Administrator utility and select the object in question. Then choose Details under the Object menu and open the IPX/IP Gateway Service Restrictions page. On this page, you can enter restrictions for this object.

To restrict access to a specific Internet site, place a host restriction on the IP address of that site. To prevent certain types of traffic from being forwarded by the server, create a service restriction for the appropriate port number. For example, you might restrict web browser access to certain hours during the day, but allow

FTP or TELNET access during those same hours. You could also place the remote host "www.games.com" off-limits. To prevent news readers from operating across the gateway, you might place a restriction on traffic to port number 119 (News) at any site.

INSTALLING THE IPX/IP GATEWAY CLIENT

The IPX/IP gateway support is installed as an option in the NetWare Client32 workstation software. The following instructions explain how to install this support on Windows 3.1x workstations and Windows 95 workstations.

The Windows 3.1x Client

To configure the IPX/IP gateway support on a Windows 3.1x workstation, you install NetWare Client32 as explained in Chapter 4. During the installation process when the Additional Options screen appears, complete the following steps.

1 • Select the NetWare IPX/IP Gateway check box, then select Next to continue.

2 • When the Configuration menu for these options appears, enter the appropriate information and select Next to continue.

3 • When you've finished, choose OK to restart your computer. When the workstation comes back up, the Novell IPX/IP Gateway Switcher icon appears in the NetWare Tools program group. The gateway switcher program switches the client from gateway operation to native TCP/IP operation (if TCP/IP is available on the client).

4 • Double-click the Gateway Switcher icon, then click Enable Gateway to enable the gateway. You can also enter the name of a preferred gateway server if you have more than one gateway installed in the network. If a preferred gateway server is configured, the gateway task will attempt to locate that gateway server through NDS and connect to it. If the preferred gateway server is not available, the gateway client will search for other gateway servers, first in the user's NDS context, then in the bindery of the attached server, then finally it will query for a SAP broadcast of any gateway server.

There is no linkage between the preferred file server and the preferred gateway server. A user may be attached to file server A while using a gateway server that resides on file server B.

NOTE

The Windows 95 Client

To configure the IPX/IP gateway support on a Windows 95 workstation, you install NetWare Client32 as explained in Chapter 4. When the installation is finished, complete the following steps.

1 • Click on Customize to customize the client.

2 • Choose Add.

3 • In the Type of Network Component You Want to Install box, double-click on Protocol.

4 • In the Manufacturers box, choose Novell, then double-click on Novell NetWare IPX/IP Gateway.

5 • Choose OK to exit the Network configuration screen.

6 • If you receive a prompt to select a preferred gateway server, click Yes, enter the name of your preferred IPX/IP Gateway server, and select OK. If a preferred gateway server is configured, the gateway task will attempt to locate that gateway server through NDS and connect to it. If the preferred gateway server is not available, the gateway client will search for other gateway servers, first in the user's NDS context, then in the bindery of the attached server, then finally it will query for a SAP broadcast of any gateway server.

7 • If you asked for additional files, type the location of those files in the Copy Files From box. If you are asked for Client32 files, type in the path to the directory from which you ran SETUP.EXE.

8 • Click Yes to restart the computer. The IPX/IP Gateway Switcher program runs automatically during the first restart after installation. This switcher program switches the client from gateway operation to native TCP/IP operation (if TCP/IP is available on the client).

9 • To enable the gateway, click the Enable IPX/IP Gateway button, then click OK.

FTP Services for IntranetWare

In addition to the Novell Internet Access Server components, IntranetWare also includes FTP Services. This feature, which is a subset of the NetWare UNIX Print Services 2.11 product, allows NetWare clients to use FTP to work with files on the Internet or intranet.

INSTALLING FTP SERVICES

To install FTP Services for IntranetWare on your server, complete the following steps.

1 • Mount the FTP Services CD-ROM as a volume on the NetWare 4.11 server.

2 • Load INSTALL.NLM on the server.

3 • Choose Product Options, then choose Install a Product Not Listed.

4 • Press F3, then type in the following path to the FTP Services files on the CD-ROM:

```
NWUXPS:\NWUXPS
```

5 • If you are asked to specify a host name, either press Enter to accept the default name displayed or enter the correct host name.

6 • Accept the default boot drive (or specify the correct drive from which the server boots).

7 • To install the online documentation for FTP Services, choose Yes. This documentation is separate from the regular NetWare online documentation and describes how to install and use FTP Services.

8 • If you have already installed the NetWare 4.11 DynaText viewer, choose No when asked if you want to install a new one.

Note: If you receive the message "hosts.db does not exist," ignore it.

9 • When prompted for a user name, enter the ADMIN name and password.

10 • Choose the name service option you want to use on this server and answer any prompts necessary for the name service you choose. If you choose to use a local name service, the database that holds the name service information will be stored on this server and will be the master database. You can use the UNICON.NLM utility to work with the master database on a local server. If you choose to use a remote name service, that database will reside on another server. You can use UNICON.NLM only to view the database information but not modify it. You can choose one of the following options:

▸ Local DNS and Local NIS. This option stores both master databases on this server.

▸ Remote DNS and Remote NIS. This option uses the master databases stored on another server.

▸ Remote DNS and Local NIS. This option stores the master NIS database on this server and the DNS database on another server.

▸ No DNS and Remote NIS. This option stores the master NIS database on another server and does not provide DNS service at all.

11 • Follow any prompts necessary to initialize the name service and the product.

12 • To start FTP Services, press Ins and choose FTP Server. FTP Services will start running and will appear in the Running Services menu.

13 • To exit the installation program, press Esc as many times as necessary.

14 • Restart the server to make the new settings take effect, by typing:

```
DOWN

RESTART SERVER

CONFIGURING FTP SERVICES
```

With FTP Services, users can use FTP to access and transfer files from the intranet or Internet. If you desire, you can create an Anonymous FTP account for users to use. With an Anonymous account, any user can access the FTP service by typing in any password. (Any password will work; the FTP service doesn't actually authenticate the password.)

To configure an Anonymous FTP account, complete the following steps.

1 • At the server console, load UNICON.NLM.

2 • When prompted, enter the ADMIN user name and password.

3 • Choose Manage Services, then choose FTP Server, then choose Set Parameters.

4 • Choose Default Name Space and enter NFS. This will install the NFS name space on the server, which will allow the server to store UNIX files.

5 • Change the Anonymous User Access field to Yes so that the Anonymous account will be enabled.

6 • Choose Anonymous User's Home Directory and change the path from the volume SYS (displayed as /sys) to a directory you prefer to use as the login directory for Anonymous FTP users.

7 • When finished, press Esc to exit the installation program and save the changes you've made.

8 • Return to the main menu by pressing Esc twice, then choose Perform File Operations, then choose View/Set File Permissions.

9 • Enter the path to the Anonymous user's home directory (specified in Step 6) and press F9 to see the permissions (the UNIX equivalent of trustee rights) that have been set for this directory. If the permissions are not correct, modify them on this screen. The permissions should be:

```
[U = rwx] [G = ---] [o = ---]
```

10 • Press Esc multiple times to exit UNICON and save the changes you've made.

11 • Even though you specified the NFS name space in Step 4, you still need to add it to the volume. (You only need to add the name space to the volume once. To see if you've already added NFS name space to a volume, type **VOLUMES** at the server console — the display will show which name spaces are supported on each volume.) If you need to add the name space, type the following command, replacing volume with the name of the volume:

```
ADD NAME SPACE NFS TO volume
```

PART V

Appendixes

NDS Error Codes and Definitions

The following appendix provides a list of the NDS error codes and, where appropriate, any action that should be taken to resolve each error condition. You can use this appendix as a reference when troubleshooting NDS or other operating system problems on your IntranetWare servers. For more information on troubleshooting NDS and related problems, refer to Chapter 10 in conjunction with this appendix.

Novell Directory Services Error Codes

NO_SUCH_ENTRY – 601 0xFFFFFDA7 FDA7

Explanation: This error on an IntranetWare server during DSTRACE usually means that an entry is missing from the entry record table on the source server.

Client Action: Check the context specified for the object name entered. If the command line input was the object name, check the workstation's context. Make sure that it points to the correct level of the Directory for the object name specified. If the input includes the object's full or partial context, make sure that the leading and trailing dots are specified appropriately and that the types are correct. This error is common if you are trying to delete bindery type objects through NWADMIN or the 4.02 version of NETADMIN. Use the 4.01 version of NETADMIN to delete bindery type objects from a 4.0x server. This error should not occur in IntranetWare.

Server Action: Do a SET DSTRACE=+SYNC on both the source and the target server (and any other servers in the replica list) to see which object is returning the –601 error and what errors the target server is getting in return. If the object is not a server object, try deleting it. If the object with the error is a server object, see if DSTRACE returns any other errors besides –601 and attempt to resolve them. If there are no additional errors, do a Send All Objects from the server reporting the error (the source server), or Receive All Objects from the target server using DSREPAIR. (This method will help only if the source server is the master.) Send All Objects causes a lot of network traffic!

NO_SUCH_VALUE – 602 0xFFFFFDA6 FDA6

Explanation: The requested property value could not be found. If this error is encountered during the login or authentication process, it usually means that either the user's or the server's public keys could not be located. If this is the case, regenerate the user's key pair by changing the password with utilities.

An occurrence of this error during the synchronization process between servers means that a value of an object being synchronized is missing from the target server. This error may be a temporary condition that exists because of the loosely consistent nature of Directory Services.

Server Action: What error are you seeing on the target server? You may see one of the following without an error code:

▶ **Error unable to communicate** — Look in DSTRACE for the object with the problem (SET DSTRACE=+SYNC). The problem is either the public key or the remote ID. Run DSREPAIR to verify remote server IDs. If errors appear there, run this same option once more to verify remote server IDs. If you get a –602 or –603 in DSREPAIR when verifying remote server IDs, call your Novell Authorized Service Center for support. Be aware, however, that a public key cannot be repaired unless there is at least one server in the tree authenticating without problems to the target server. The server authenticating OK to the target server must also have a real copy of the target server object, so it must have a replica (other than a subordinate reference) of the partition holding the target server object. If this is only a 2-server tree, the target server will need to be removed from the tree and reinstalled.

▶ **Error sending updates** — Look in DSTRACE for the object with the problem (SET DSTRACE=+SYNC) and try deleting the object.

NO_SUCH_ATTRIBUTE   –603   0xFFFFFDA5 FDA5

Explanation: The requested property could not be found. In the Directory, if a property does not contain a value, then the property does not exist for the specific object.

Client Action: Ensure that the property being requested is a valid DS property (check spelling and syntax). Use NLIST.EXE to determine if the property exists for the specified object. For example, NLIST user=username /d will show all of the properties and their values for the specified user name. (To see all of the properties associated which the object requires supervisor rights to the object in question. Browse rights are given by default.) We have seen this error occur when users try to edit properties that are grayed out in the utilities (properties that are not supported in the current DS schema). This error can also occur when there are schema synchronization problems in a mixed tree (4.0x and IntranetWare servers in the same tree).

Server Action: This error is basically the same as a –602 error except that you get a –602 on a multivalued property and a –603 on a single-valued property. What error are you seeing on the target server? You may see one of the following without an error code:

▸ **Error unable to communicate** — Look in DSTRACE for the object with the problem (SET DSTRACE=+SYNC). This problem is either the public key or the remote ID. Run DSREPAIR to verify remote server IDs. If errors appear there, run this same option once more to verify remote server IDs. If you get a –602 or –603 in DSREPAIR when verifying remote server IDs, call your Novell Authorized Service Center for support. Be aware, however, that a public key cannot be repaired unless there is at least one server in the tree authenticating without problems to the target server. The server authenticating OK to the target server must also have a real copy of the target server object, so it must have a replica (other than a subordinate reference) of the partition holding the target server object. If this tree is only a 2-server tree, the target server will need to be removed from the tree and reinstalled.

▸ **Error sending updates** — Look in DSTRACE for the object with the problem (SET DSTRACE=+SYNC) and try deleting the object. If there is currently a mixed environment in the tree or if there were ever IntranetWare servers in a now completely 4.0x tree, this could be a schema problem. Run the Global Schema Update option in DSREPAIR on an IntranetWare server. If there are no longer any IntranetWare servers in the tree, or if the Global Schema Update does not fix the problem, bring the server down with the master replica of the partition return-ing the error and then bring the server back up. Upon startup, the server will force a schema update. The schema problem should now be resolved.

NO_SUCH_CLASS   – 604 0xFFFFFDA4 FDA4

Explanation: An object class that does not exist in the Directory is being referenced by a utility. An object class in NDS is similar to the object type in the bindery. For example, object type 1 in the bindery is a user object and in the Directory the object class is USER. The class indicates the kind of object to be created.

Action: NetWare 4 utilities access only Novell's base schema, which must be present for the Directory to operate. Determine what utility is being used to create the object.

This utility is attempting to use an object class that is currently not defined in NDS. The NetWare 4.0 utilities only display valid object classes. IntranetWare allows the schema to be extended, so this error in IntranetWare may point to schema synchronization problems.

NO_SUCH_PARTITION   – 605   0xFFFFFDA3 FDA3

Explanation: A partition with the specified name does not exist.

Action: Ensure that the partition name requested is valid and is a valid object name.

ENTRY_ALREADY_EXISTS   – 606   0xFFFFFDA2 FDA2

Explanation: An attempt was made to add an object at the same level as a preexisting object of the same name but not necessarily the same class.

Action: Specify a different name for the object being added or rename the existing object.

NOT_EFFECTIVE_CLASS   – 607   0xFFFFFDA1 FDA1

Explanation: This error indicates that the class being used to create the specified object is a non-effective class and cannot be used when creating an object. There are two types of object classes in the Directory — effective and non-effective. All effective classes can be used to create objects. (The class being used to create the specified object is referred to as the "base class" of the object.) User would be one example of an effective class. Non-effective classes are used as super classes to define information associated with various effective classes.

Action: The standard Novell utilities that ship with NetWare 4 only allow effective classes to be used when creating objects. Find out what utility is being used to create the object. This may mean that your non-Novell utility is not following the rules of the specified object.

ILLEGAL_ATTRIBUTE   – 608   0xFFFFFDA0 FDA0

Explanation: An attempt was made to add a property that is illegal to an object. The NDS schema determines which properties can be inherited by an object class. (Refer to the Directory Services Schema documentation in Chapter 3.) This error can also occur in mixed trees (4.0x and IntranetWare servers in the same tree) or in upgraded trees (4.0x servers have been upgraded to IntranetWare) when a server does not have the correct schema.

Client Action: You cannot add the specified property to the specified object.

Server Action: Do a SET DSTRACE=+SYNC and then SET DSTRACE=*H to see the object causing the error. If the object is not a server object, try deleting it. In the case of a schema problem, run Global Schema Update in DSREPAIR from an IntranetWare server. If there are no longer any IntranetWare servers in the tree or if Global Schema Update does not correct the problem, bring the server down containing the master replica of the partition showing errors and then bring the server back up. Upon startup, the server will force a schema update, which usually corrects these schema problems. If the problem persists, call your Novell Authorized Service Center for support.

MISSING_MANDATORY   **– 609   0xFFFFFD9F   FD9F**

Explanation: This error indicates that one or more of the mandatory properties for the object being created are missing. Each object class in the Directory has a set of mandatory properties (properties that must contain a value before the object can be created). For example, a USER object in the Directory is required to have a Common Name (CN) and a Surname. Without these properties the object will not be created. A property exists only if there is a value supplied for the given property. This error can also occur in mixed trees (4.0x and IntranetWare servers in the same tree) when a server does not have the correct schema.

Client Action: Input the required information when creating the object.

Server Action: Do a SET DSTRACE=+SYNC and then SET DSTRACE=*H to see the object causing the error. If the object is not a server object, try deleting it. In the case of a schema problem, run Global Schema Update in DSREPAIR from an IntranetWare server. If there are no longer any IntranetWare servers in the tree or if Global Schema Update does not correct the problem, bring the server down with the master replica of the partition showing errors and then bring the server back up. Upon startup, the server will force a schema update, which usually corrects these schema problems. If the problem persists, call your Novell Authorized Service Center for support.

ILLEGAL_DS_NAME   **– 610   0xFFFFFD9E   FD9E**

Explanation: Illegal Directory Names are those that are too long (more than 255 characters) or ones that contain illegal character combinations. The '\' character may be followed only by a '.' or '=' or '+' or '\'.

ILLEGAL_CONTAINMENT   **– 611   0xFFFFFD9D   FD9D**

Explanation: The containment rules of the Directory specify where an object class may appear in relation to other objects in the Directory tree. For example, the object class Country can only be created at the top of the Directory, and the object Class User can only be created under Organizations and Organizational Units. The Schema enforces the containment rules for NDS.

Action: Go to the appropriate container to create the object.

CANT_HAVE_MULTIPLE_VALUES   **–612   0xFFFFFD9C   FD9C**

Explanation: This error indicates that the specified property is single valued. All properties are either single or multivalued. For example, the Group Membership property is multivalued. A user can be a member of multiple groups. The Group Membership property exists once and contains multiple group names (values).

Action: For this property (information category in the utility), only one value (piece of information) can be supplied.

SYNTAX_VIOLATION   – 613   0xFFFFFD9B   FD9B

Explanation: An attribute value being added to an object is incorrect. This error is most often encountered if that value is the name of another object that does not exist. This error is also seen during the installation or upgrade to IntranetWare.

Client Action: For most cases, verify that the object name being added as a value is correct.

Server Action: If a new IntranetWare server being installed hangs while copying over the Directory Services objects, check the DSTRACE screen of the server with the master replica of the partition where the new IntranetWare server is being installed. If the master is giving errors, run DSREPAIR on the master. If problems persist, do a SET DSTRACE=+SYNC to find the object returning the error and check the description field (and any other field that accepts a string) for any unusual ASCII characters. Correct the corruption or delete the object, and the replica should complete copying to the new server.

We have also seen this error occur when a bindery-type object (usually created by a third-party party program) becomes corrupt. If the –613 errors are on these objects, delete all objects created by the program and then reinstall the program.

DUPLICATE_VALUE   – 614   0xFFFFFD9A   FD9A

Explanation: An attempt was made to add a duplicate value to the specified property.
Action: Enter a different value.

ATTRIBUTE_ALREADY_EXISTS – 615   0xFFFFFD99   FD99

Explanation: An attempt was made to add a property that already exists.

Action: If the attribute is multivalued just add the specified value to the existing property. If the property is single valued, you will need to delete the property in order to create it again with the new value.

MAXIMUM_ENTRIES_EXIST   – 616   0xFFFFFD98   FD98

Explanation: This error indicates that the maximum number of entries (objects) exists in the Directory tree. The maximum number of objects that can be created in the Directory is FFFFFF (3 bits of FF), which equal 16,777,220 decimal. Some of these entries are used by the Directory itself.

Action: For the current version of the Directory, you have reached the maximum number of objects that can be created. You will need to delete objects that are no longer needed.

DATABASE_FORMAT	– 617	0xFFFFFD97	FD97
INCONSISTENT_DATABASE	– 618	0xFFFFFD96	FD96

Explanation: This error indicates that an error has been encountered in the database itself. Usually this error means that the number of entries in a container does not match the number stored in the container's entry. When this error occurs during synchronization, the target server has a corrupted database.

Action: Run DSREPAIR only *once*.

 By running DSREPAIR a second time, the original .OLD database files will be overwritten after 72 hours, and it will not be possible to restore their former Directory Information Base (DIB).

WARNING

If the error persists after running DSREPAIR the first time, consult your Novell Authorized Service Center.

INVALID_COMPARISON	– 619	0xFFFFFD95	FD95

Explanation: An attempt was made to either compare two properties that are not comparable or to use an invalid compare syntax.

Action: Check the syntax and verify that the properties are comparable.

COMPARISON_FAILED	– 620	0xFFFFFD94	FD94
TRANSACTIONS_DISABLED	– 621	0xFFFFFD93	FD93

Explanation: This error indicates that Transaction Tracking (TTS) has been disabled for the server on which the Directory operation is taking place. When TTS is disabled, NDS operations, which require modifying the database on that server, are disabled as well.

Action: At the console prompt of the file server type **ENABLE TTS**. If TTS was disabled because the SYS volume is full, log in to the file server, delete unnecessary files from the SYS volume, and type **ENABLE TTS** at the file server. If you are unable to log in to the file server, try running VREPAIR on volume SYS and selecting Purge Deleted Files from the VREPAIR menu. If there still is not enough space, put another drive into the server and span the SYS volume across both drives to give SYS more space.

INVALID_TRANSPORT	– 622	0xFFFFFD92	FD92
SYNTAX_INVALID_IN_NAME	– 623	0xFFFFFD91	FD91
REPLICA_ALREADY_EXISTS	– 624	0xFFFFFD90	FD90

Explanation: This error indicates that a replica of the specified partition already exists on the server.

Action: Select a different server.

TRANSPORT_FAILURE   **– 625 0xFFFFFD8F FD8F**

Explanation: This error occurs when either a client and a server or two servers cannot communicate with each other across the network.

Action: Check for SAP filtering of the DS SAP types of 26B and 278. Check cabling, the LAN card, and the LAN driver. Make sure they can RCONSOLE to the target server. Does typing **DISPLAY SERVERS** on the source server show the target server? Are other servers also showing this –625 error to the same target server? Can workstations attach and log in to the target server from the same segment as the source server? Type **RESET ROUTERS** and then type **SET DSTRACE=*U** at the source server to flag all servers as UP and retry communicating with them. This error is *almost always* a LAN communication issue. Occasionally a change of the server's name, a move of the server object, or a change to the internal IPX number can also cause this error to occur. Run DSREPAIR with the option to Repair Network Addresses on the Source Server to check the internal IPX number of the target server. The change may not complete successfully. This error can also occur when trying to communicate with servers that have locked databases (that is, with DSREPAIR).

ALL_REFERRALS_FAILED   **– 626 0xFFFFFD8E FD8E**

Explanation: The object could not be found. It is still possible that the object does exist but that a server could not communicate with the server holding a copy of the object. The target server tried to walk the tree by contacting all other servers in the replica ring and was unable to do so. This error commonly occurs when partition management is requested and the requested operation cannot take place because a key server is inaccessible. Invalid creation timestamps can also return this error.

Server Action: Run DSREPAIR with the options to Repair Network Addresses and verify remote server IDs. Check the replica rings to verify that there is one master replica for the partition in question. Check the replica states and make sure they are all ON. Resolve whatever problems you find in the DSREPAIR.LOG file. Look in DISPLAY SERVERS to see if the tree name is present. If not, check the issues with –625 errors (including SAP filtering). If creation timestamps are invalid, running the IntranetWare DSREPAIR with the option to Check External References under Advanced Options (only available in newer DSREPAIRs) should repair this problem.

CANT_REMOVE_NAMING_VALUE **– 627 0xFFFFFD8D FD8D**

Explanation: This error indicates that an attempt was made to delete the naming property, but the naming value cannot be removed.

Action: Rename the object, then delete the property.

OBJECT_CLASS_VIOLATION   –628   0xFFFFFD8C   FD8C

Explanation: An object class violation has occurred.

Server Action: This error can occur when the source server's objects are unknown, but are fine on the target server. Isolate the bad replica by either locking the databases with DSREPAIR and then running NETADMIN or NWADMIN to view the objects or by using DSVIEW (available on NetWire). Then delete the bad replica and add it back again through Partition Manager (verifying first that the master is a good copy).

A schema synchronization problem can also generate this error. Run the Global Schema Update option in DSREPAIR on an IntranetWare server. If there are no longer any IntranetWare servers in the tree, or if the Global Schema Update does not fix the problem, bring the server down with the master replica of the partition returning the error and then bring the server back up. Upon startup, the server will force a schema update, which usually corrects a schema problem.

ENTRY_IS_NOT_LEAF   –629   0xFFFFFD8B   FD8B

Explanation: This error indicates that the object being deleted or modified is not a leaf object. A container object that does not contain any objects is considered a leaf object and therefore can be deleted. If you attempt to delete a container object that does contain objects of any class the following error message is returned: "The utility can't delete <object class>=<object name> because it is not a leaf object." A container object that is a partition root cannot be deleted.

Action: Delete all objects under the container object that are being deleted or modified. If the object is a partition root, merge the partition with the parent partition and then delete the object.

DIFFERENT_TREE   –630   0xFFFFFD8A   FD8A
ILLEGAL_REPLICA_TYPE   –631   0xFFFFFD89   FD89

Explanation: This error indicates that a request was made of a replica, but the replica was the wrong type and therefore the request could not complete.

Server Action: This is usually seen at the file server console when attempting to set the bindery context. The bindery context requires a writable replica (either a read/write or a master) in order to be set. Verify that the server has a writable replica of the partition containing the container to which you are attempting to set the bindery context.

SYSTEM_FAILURE   –632   0xFFFFFD88   FD88

Explanation: This error indicates that unexpected results have occurred. For example, the client requested that the Directory return a network address attribute and the Directory actually returned a public key attribute. This condition may be temporary. While the client usually returns errors in the −301 to −399 range, the client as well as the server returns this error during the authentication process. A server may return a −632 during synchronization because authentication could not complete due to an error in the public key — the key is the right key, but it is corrupt (not the right format). This error can also be returned in DSTRACE when the server is unable to open the local database. However, −632 is just a general error, which means that the process being attempted failed because the server(s) being contacted was busy, down, or the source server could not authenticate to it.

Symptom: After upgrading a server, the DS is unable to open the database. SET DSTRACE=ON and then SET DSTRACE=+MISC. Then dismount and remount the SYS volume. Check the DSTRACE screen and confirm that a −632 error is returned when DS tries to open the database. If so, the database is corrupted. DS will need to be removed from the server and reinstalled (either from another replica in the tree or, if a single-server environment, from backup).

Server Action: Run DSREPAIR with the option to verify remote server IDs on every server in the replica list. Then go back and run DSREPAIR a second time with the option to verify remote server IDs on every server in the replica list. If the remote server ID check returns a −632 after running it the second time, call your Novell Authorized Service Center. Otherwise, try to resolve the process that failed.

INVALID_ENTRY_FOR_ROOT   −633   0xFFFFFD87   FD87

Explanation: An attempt was made to either restore or move an object that is flagged as a partition root but whose base class is not a container, or to perform a split at an object whose base class is not a container.

NO_REFERRALS   −634   0xFFFFFD86   FD86

Explanation: This means that the target server does not have a copy of what the source server is requesting. In other words, the source server has no objects that match the request and no referrals to search for the object.

Action: This is not a serious error, just a response.

REMOTE_FAILURE   −635   0xFFFFFD85   FD85

Explanation: In order to complete some operations, a server will need to contact another server. If this is not possible (because of a link being down, for example), this error will be returned.

Action: The target server does not have the correct information about the source server. This error is often caused by a problem with local to remote IDs or the server object. Run DSREPAIR with the option to verify remote server IDs on every server in the replica list. Then go back and run DSREPAIR a second time with the option to verify remote server IDs on all servers in the replica list. Resolve any errors found after the second run of DSREPAIR.

UNREACHABLE_SERVER	–636	0XFFFFFD84	FD84
PREVIOUS_MOVE_IN_PROGRESS	–637	0XFFFFFD83	FD83

Explanation: Once an object has been moved from one context in the Directory to another, the Directory will not allow that object to be moved again until all replicas of that object have been updated. The length of time for a move to complete will vary depending on the size of the replica, the number of replicas, and condition of the communication links between all the servers holding the replicas. This error can be caused by a moved object that lost the original object (the primary obituary) or by a broken partition.

Action: Leave the object in its current context until it can be moved again. This may require that the object be left in its new context for several minutes. If the object still cannot be moved, load the IntranetWare DSREPAIR with –m (LOAD DSREPAIR –M) and then run Repair Local Database. (For 4.0x DSREPAIR, type **LOAD DSREPAIR –A,** Select Options, and toggle A until it reads "Find obituaries for move and move-inhibit.") View the DSREPAIR.LOG file, which will display objects that have move obituaries. Verify that the problem objects and all their attributes have been successfully moved to the new location by running NWADMIN or NETADMIN and viewing the objects. If the objects have been moved, load the IntranetWare DSREPAIR with –MR (load the 4.0x DSREPAIR with –A, Select Options, then toggle A until it reads "Purge obituaries for move and move-inhibit"), which will delete the move obituaries for those problem objects. Use SET DSTRACE=+J and SET DSTRACE=*F to verify that the purger ran successfully.

NO_CHARACTER_MAPPING	–638	0xFFFFFD82	FD82
INCOMPLETE_AUTHENTICATION	–639	0xFFFFFD81	FD81
INVALID_CERTIFICATE	–640	0xFFFFFD80	FD80
INVALID_REQUEST	–641	0xFFFFFD7F	FD7F

Explanation: The server did not understand the request. For example, a client workstation could have sent an incorrect verb.

Server Action: This error can be caused by a nonsynchronized schema. Run the IntranetWare DSREPAIR and do a Global Schema Update. This error can also be a response error, so check for errors on the target server and resolve any that you may find there first.

INVALID_ITERATION   −642   0xFFFFFD7E   FD7E

Explanation: A client workstation sent an invalid iteration handle.

SCHEMA_IS_NONREMOVABLE −643   0xFFFFFD7D   FD7D

Explanation: An attempt was made to delete an NDS structure or configuration.

SCHEMA_IS_IN_USE   −644   0xFFFFFD7C   FD7C

Explanation: An attempt was made to delete an NDS configuration or structure (such as a container object) that still contains an object using that structure.

Action: First delete the object or property, then delete the structure.

CLASS_ALREADY_EXISTS   −645   0xFFFFFD7B   FD7B

Explanation: This error indicates that the object class being created already exists as a class in the schema of the Directory. (See also ERR_NO_SUCH_CLASS −604 0xFFFFFDA4.)

Action: This error should occur only in a utility that updates the schema of the Directory. Determine the utility that is causing the error.

BAD_NAMING_ATTRIBUTES   −646   0xFFFFFD7A   FD7A

NOT_ROOT_PARTITION   −647   0xFFFFFD79   FD79

Explanation: An attempt was made to execute a function that is required on the root partition. Either the client did not pass on the root partition name or the client attempted to perform the function somewhere other than the root partition.

INSUFFICIENT_STACK   −648   0xFFFFFD78   FD78

INSUFFICIENT_BUFFER   −649   0xFFFFFD77   FD77

Explanation: The server ran out of memory. The operating system will self-correct this error.

Action: Be patient. See Novell's manual Supervising the Network under the category "Resolving Server Memory Problems."

AMBIGUOUS_CONTAINMENT −650   0xFFFFFD76   FD76

AMBIGUOUS_NAMING   −651   0xFFFFFD75   FD75

DUPLICATE_MANDATORY   −652   0xFFFFFD74   FD74

DUPLICATE_OPTIONAL   −653   0xFFFFFD73   FD73

PARTITION_BUSY   −654   0xFFFFFD72   FD72

Explanation: Another partition operation is currently taking place. For example, if a request has previously been issued to split a partition, a second request for a split (even at another point in the same partition) will result in this error.

Server Action: This is a normal error immediately after a partition operation has been initiated. If this error does not go away, in the 310 build of the DS this error can indicate that the target server does not think that the source server has a copy of that partition. Confirm this through DSREPAIR.LOG or by watching DSTRACE. Try running PTEST (4.0x) or Cancel Partition Operation (IntranetWare) to abort the partition operation on the source server. You can also remove the source server from the tree or call your Novell Authorized Service Center for support.

MULTIPLE_REPLICAS   –655   0xFFFFFD71   FD71

Explanation: This error is an internal error that appears as a result of a programming discrepancy, not a system inconsistency.

CRUCIAL_REPLICA   –656   0xFFFFFD70   FD70

Explanation: An attempt was made to perform one of the following illegal operations on a master replica: remove it, change its replica type (the correct way to change a replica type is to change the replica type of another server's replica to the master, which will indirectly force the master to become a read/write), or request that it receive all updates from the master. This error can also be caused by trying to add a replica to the server where the master of that replica already exists.

SCHEMA_SYNC_IN_PROGRESS   –657   0xFFFFFD6F   FD6F

Explanation: The function could not be completed because Directory synchronization is in progress.

Action: Wait a while and try again.

SKULK_IN_PROGRESS   –658   0xFFFFFD6E   FD6E

Explanation: The function could not be completed because replica synchronization is in progress.

Action: Wait a while and try again.

TIME_NOT_SYNCHRONIZED   –659   0xFFFFFD6D   FD6D

Explanation: NDS uses timestamps to determine the order of events that take place in the Directory. Time Synchronization services have been implemented to maintain a consistent time across the network. Modification operations require the issuance of a timestamp. If a replica on a server has issued a timestamp and the time on that server is set back, in 4.0x no further modification operations may take place until the time on the server moves past the last modification time on the partition. This applies only to operations that modify, not to those that just read information. In other words, users will be able to log in to the Directory, but no objects can be edited through the utilities. In IntranetWare, the Directory will issue synthetic timestamps on objects, enabling those objects to be modified, yet still not allow illegal timestamps. The server console will display a synthetic time error when the server time is behind the NDS time.

Action: Check DSTRACE for other errors first and resolve any you find. Then run Repair Timestamps (found in the IntranetWare DSREPAIR), which will reset the timestamps to the current server time. The 4.0x equivalent of Repair Timestamps is Rebuild Replicas and is performed from the Partition Manager. This action will delete the objects from all replicas except the Master and then recopy all objects from the Master copy to all other replicas. BEWARE! If the Master copy was corrupt in any way, the other replicas will also be corrupt when a Repair Timestamps or Rebuild Replicas action is performed. Repair Timestamps or Rebuild Replicas can also cause considerable traffic on the network. You may have to perform this action on a partition by partition basis.

RECORD_IN_USE	−660	0xFFFFFD6C	FD6C
DS_VOLUME_NOT_MOUNTED	−661	0xFFFFFD6B	FD6B
DS_VOLUME_IO_FAILURE	−662	0xFFFFFD6A	FD6A
DS_LOCKED	−663	0xFFFFFD69	FD69

Explanation: The Directory database is locked on the server. This error will be seen in DSTRACE when the source server is trying to synchronize with the target server, which has a locked database. There will be no activity in the TRACE screen on the server with the locked database. The server with the problem will often get an error when it tries to open the Directory while mounting the SYS volume. We have seen this error occur when DSREPAIR is loaded on the server, when DSDUMP has the Directory locked, when the hard drive on the server is going bad, and when a new 4.02 server installation does not complete properly.

Action: Try running DSREPAIR on the server

WARNING

Run DSREPAIR. If DSREPAIR is run more than once, keep in mind that the .OLD database files will be overwritten after 72 hours.

If DSREPAIR doesn't fix the problem, try bringing the server down and bringing it back up again. If running DSREPAIR and bringing the server down do not fix this error, the server may need to be removed from the tree.

If this is a new server with no replicas on it, remove DS from the server. If you don't want to remove DS from the server, escalate the call. When the DS is locked, the normal removal of DS on a 4.02 server may not complete properly. You may need to load install with the –dsremove switch (LOAD INSTALL -DSREMOVE) and then try to remove DS through install. This will most likely return an error about being unable to remove DS but will perform the removal anyway. Try loading install with the –dsremove switch again and try the removal a second time. DSI should report that DS was already removed from the server.

 Don't use –DSREMOVE unless the normal removal process won't work! The –dsremove switch will ignore errors and warnings and may not perform all the steps necessary to do a clean removal.

WARNING

OLD_EPOCH   –664   0xFFFFFD68   FD68

Explanation: This is an NDS timestamp error.

NEW_EPOCH   –665   0xFFFFFD67   FD67

Explanation: This is an NDS timestamp error.

INCOMPATIBLE_DS_VERSION   –666   0xFFFFFD66   FD66

Explanation: This error occurs when performing operations that require the same schema, but there are servers involved in the operation with dissimilar schema.

Symptom: Partition Manager returns this error when a partition operation is requested and the server with the Master replica is an IntranetWare server, but there are other 4.0 servers on the replica list (including servers holding subordinate reference replicas). DSREPAIR for IntranetWare may also return this error during a remote to local ID check.

Server Action: Most partition operations involving an IntranetWare server as the server holding the Master will not be able to complete to 4.0x servers. The 4.0x servers on the replica list must be upgraded to IntranetWare before the partition operation can be completed. If the Master replica were on a 4.02 server, you would not have this particular problem. If this error is seen in DSREPAIR during a remote to local ID check, do a SET DSTRACE=!V on the IntranetWare server. This check will reset the list of restricted versions (DS versions that are restricted from synchronization) to the default, which is DS 290 and above.

PARTITION_ROOT   –667   0xFFFFFD65   FD65

Explanation: This error indicates that the object being manipulated is the root of a Directory Services partition. This error would most commonly occur when you attempt to delete a container object that is a partition root.

Action: Using the partition management tools, merge this partition into the parent partition.

ENTRY_NOT_CONTAINER   −668   0xFFFFFD64   FD64

Explanation: An illegal function was attempted on a leaf object.

FAILED_AUTHENTICATION   −669   0xFFFFFD63   FD63

Explanation: An invalid password was sent. Authentication failed. This error is seen in DSTRACE when one server tries to synchronize with another server. The most likely problems are either the remote ID or the public key.

Server Action: Try running DSREPAIR with the option to verify remote server IDs on the source server and all other servers on the replica list. If there are errors in the DSREPAIR.LOG file, run DSREPAIR with the option to verify remote server IDs once more on every server in the replica list. This should resolve the problem with incorrect remote IDs. The other scenario is when the source server is either using or looking at the wrong public key (the key is the right format, but is for the wrong object). If the problem is the public key, then:

> ▸ If the source server has a REAL copy of the target server object (a Master, R/W, or R/O replica of the partition containing the target server object), check to see if the other servers on that replica list (for the partition containing the target server object) are able to authenticate to the target server. If another server can authenticate, do a Send All Objects from the good server, or a Receive All Objects on the target server (but only if the server with the "good" copy has the Master).

Also, remember that Send All Objects generates a lot of traffic. If no servers can authenticate to the target server, remove DS from the target server and reinstall it back into the tree or call your Novell Authorized Service Center for support.

If the source server has a subordinate reference replica or no replica of the partition containing the target server object, the external reference to that object will need to be re-backlinked. Call your Novell Authorized Service Center for support.

INVALID_CONTEXT	–670	0xFFFFFD62	FD62
NO_SUCH_PARENT	–671	0xFFFFFD61	FD61
NO_ACCESS	–672	0xFFFFFD60	FD60

Explanation: The client does not have sufficient results to complete the requested operation. This error in DSTRACE means that the target server's replica list doesn't match the source server's replica list.

Server Action: Compare the replica ring information for all the servers on the replica list (available though Display Replica Information). If you confirm that the target server doesn't have the source server on its replica list, then either remove DS from the target server or call your Novell Authorized Service Center for support.

REPLICA_NOT_ON	–673	0xFFFFFD5F	FD5F

Explanation: The replica is in the process of being created on a server. Until all the object information has been received on that server, the replica is "off" (not available for use by Directory clients).

Server Action: Wait. If the replica is stuck, look for the error that is preventing the replica from turning "on" and address that problem.

INVALID_NAME_SERVICE	–674	0xFFFFFD5E	FD5E
INVALID_TASK	–675	0xFFFFFD5D	FD5D
INVALID_CONN_HANDLE	–676	0xFFFFFD5C	FD5C
INVALID_IDENTITY	–677	0xFFFFFD5B	FD5B
DUPLICATE_ACL	–678	0xFFFFFD5A	FD5A
PARTITION_ALREADY_EXISTS	–679	0xFFFFFD59	FD59
TRANSPORT_MODIFIED	–680	0xFFFFFD58	FD58
ALIAS_OF_AN_ALIAS	–681	0xFFFFFD57	FD57
AUDITING_FAILED	–682	0xFFFFFD56	FD56
INVALID_API_VERSION	–683	0xFFFFFD55	FD55
SECURE_NCP_VIOLATION	–684	0xFFFFFD54	FD54
MOVE_IN_PROGRESS	–685	0xFFFFFD53	FD53
NOT_LEAF_PARTITION	–686	0xFFFFFD52	FD52
CANNOT_ABORT	–687	0xFFFFFD51	FD51
CACHE_OVERFLOW	–688	0xFFFFFD50	FD50
INVALID_SUBORDINATE_COUNT	–689	0xFFFFFD4F	FD4F
INVALID_RDN	–690	0xFFFFFD4E	FD4E
MOD_TIME_NOT_CURRENT	–691	0xFFFFFD4D	FD4D
INCORRECT_BASE_CLASS	–692	0xFFFFFD4C	FD4C

MISSING_REFERENCE   −693   0xFFFFFD4B   FD4B

Explanation: A required reference is missing from the object. This error is frequently seen in the IntranetWare utilities if you are trying to delete an object with a zero creation timestamp.

Server Action: Run the latest version of the IntranetWare DSREPAIR on the server. This will give objects with missing creation timestamps a valid timestamp. If the object continues to give a −693 error during deletion, there is still a server in that partition's replica list with a zero creation timestamp for that object. Run the latest DSREPAIR on each server on that partition's replica list.

LOST_ENTRY   −694   0xFFFFFD4A   FD4A
AGENT_ALREADY_REGISTERED   −695   0xFFFFFD49   FD49
DS_LOADER_BUSY   −696   0xFFFFFD48   FD48
DS_CANNOT_RELOAD   −697   0xFFFFFD47   FD47
REPLICA_IN_SKULK   −698   0xFFFFFD46   FD46

Explanation: The replica is busy skulking, and no other replica processes will be done until the skulk has completed.

Server Action: Usually this error occurs as a normal part of a partition operation and will resolve itself. If this error does not go away, check for other errors that may be preventing the partition operation from completing. Remember that the master replica is controlling all partition operations.

FATAL   −699   0xFFFFFD45   FD45

Explanation: An unrecoverable error has occurred and the operation cannot be completed. This error can be caused by a variety of problems.

Server Action: Go to the target server and look for a response TRACE error. (Turn off the DSTRACE filters by using a setting like FFFF6FF7 or 8164B19 in 4.0x or an 8164B91 in IntranetWare.) Sometimes you will see an error without an error code (such as "skulk lost entry"), which can also be important. Resolve the error on the target server. Treat a "skulk lost entry" error the same as a −601 error.

Error −709 (Hex: FFFFFD3B)

Explanation: Invalid response. A DS client makes an invalid request and receives an invalid response.

Error −715 (Hex: FFFFFD35)

Explanation: A checksum error has occurred.

Error −716 (Hex: FFFFFD34)

Explanation: An error was received because checksumming is not supported.

Other Error Codes

−1	FFFFFFFF	"DSERR_INSUFFICIENT_SPACE"
−19	FFFFFF89	"DSERR_BUFFER_TOO_SMALL"
−120	FFFFFF88	"DSERR_VOLUME_FLAG_NOT_SET"
−121	FFFFFF87	"DSERR_NO_ITEMS_FOUND"
−122	FFFFFF86	"DSERR_CONN_ALREADY_TEMPORARY"
−123	FFFFFF85	"DSERR_CONN_ALREADY_LOGGED_IN"
−124	FFFFFF84	"DSERR_CONN_NOT_AUTHENTICATED"
−125	FFFFFF83	"DSERR_CONN_NOT_LOGGED_IN"
−126	FFFFFF82	"DSERR_NCP_BOUNDARY_CHECK_FAILED"
−127	FFFFFF81	"DSERR_LOCK_WAITING"
−128	FFFFFF80	"DSERR_LOCK_FAIL"
−129	FFFFFF7F	"DSERR_OUT_OF_HANDLES"
−130	FFFFFF7E	"DSERR_NO_OPEN_PRIVILEGE"
−131	FFFFFF7D	"DSERR_HARD_IO_ERROR"
−132	FFFFFF7C	"DSERR_NO_CREATE_PRIVILEGE"
−133	FFFFFF7B	"DSERR_NO_CREATE_DELETE_PRIV"
−134	FFFFFF7A	"DSERR_R_O_CREATE_FILE"
−135	FFFFFF79	"DSERR_CREATE_FILE_INVALID_NAME"
−136	FFFFFF78	"DSERR_INVALID_FILE_HANDLE"
−137	FFFFFF77	"DSERR_NO_SEARCH_PRIVILEGE"
−138	FFFFFF76	"DSERR_NO_DELETE_PRIVILEGE"
−139	FFFFFF75	"DSERR_NO_RENAME_PRIVILEGE"
−140	FFFFFF74	"DSERR_NO_SET_PRIVILEGE"
−141	FFFFFF73	"DSERR_SOME_FILES_IN_USE"
−142	FFFFFF72	"DSERR_ALL_FILES_IN_USE"
−143	FFFFFF71	"DSERR_SOME_READ_ONLY"
−144	FFFFFF70	"DSERR_ALL_READ_ONLY"
−145	FFFFFF6F	"DSERR_SOME_NAMES_EXIST"
−146	FFFFFF6E	"DSERR_ALL_NAMES_EXIST"
−147	FFFFFF6D	"DSERR_NO_READ_PRIVILEGE"
−148	FFFFFF6C	"DSERR_NO_WRITE_PRIVILEGE"
−149	FFFFFF6B	"DSERR_FILE_DETACHED"

–150	FFFFFF6A	"DSERR_NO_ALLOC_SPACE"
–150	FFFFFF6A	"DSERR_TARGET_NOT_A_SUBDIR"
–150	FFFFFF6A	"ERR_INSUFFICIENT_MEMORY"
–151	FFFFFF69	"DSERR_NO_SPOOL_SPACE"
–152	FFFFFF68	"DSERR_INVALID_VOLUME"
–153	FFFFFF67	"DSERR_DIRECTORY_FULL"
–154	FFFFFF66	"DSERR_RENAME_ACROSS_VOLUME"
–155	FFFFFF65	"DSERR_BAD_DIR_HANDLE"
–156	FFFFFF64	"DSERR_INVALID_PATH"
–156	FFFFFF64	"DSERR_NO_SUCH_EXTENSION"
–157	FFFFFF63	"DSERR_NO_DIR_HANDLES"
–158	FFFFFF62	"DSERR_BAD_FILE_NAME"
–159	FFFFFF61	"DSERR_DIRECTORY_ACTIVE"
–160	FFFFFF60	"DSERR_DIRECTORY_NOT_EMPTY"
–161	FFFFFF5F	"DSERR_DIRECTORY_IO_ERROR"
–162	FFFFFF5E	"DSERR_IO_LOCKED"
–163	FFFFFF5D	"DSERR_TRANSACTION_RESTARTED"
–164	FFFFFF5C	"DSERR_RENAME_DIR_INVALID"
–165	FFFFFF5B	"DSERR_INVALID_OPENCREATE_MODE"
–166	FFFFFF5A	"DSERR_ALREADY_IN_USE"
–167	FFFFFF59	"DSERR_INVALID_RESOURCE_TAG"
–168	FFFFFF58	"DSERR_ACCESS_DENIED"
–190	FFFFFF42	"DSERR_INVALID_DATA_STREAM"
–191	FFFFFF41	"DSERR_INVALID_NAME_SPACE"
–192	FFFFFF40	"DSERR_NO_ACCOUNTING_PRIVILEGES"
–193	FFFFFF3F	"DSERR_NO_ACCOUNT_BALANCE"
–194	FFFFFF3E	"DSERR_CREDIT_LIMIT_EXCEEDED"
–195	FFFFFF3D	"DSERR_TOO_MANY_HOLDS"
–196	FFFFFF3C	"DSERR_ACCOUNTING_DISABLED"
–197	FFFFFF3B	"DSERR_LOGIN_LOCKOUT"
–198	FFFFFF3A	"DSERR_NO_CONSOLE_RIGHTS"

–208	FFFFFF30	"DSERR_Q_IO_FAILURE"
–209	FFFFFF2F	"DSERR_NO_QUEUE"
–210	FFFFFF2E	"DSERR_NO_Q_SERVER"
–211	FFFFFF2D	"DSERR_NO_Q_RIGHTS"
–212	FFFFFF2C	"DSERR_Q_FULL"
–213	FFFFFF2B	"DSERR_NO_Q_JOB"
–214	FFFFFF2A	"DSERR_NO_Q_JOB_RIGHTS"
–214	FFFFFF2A	"DSERR_UNENCRYPTED_NOT_ALLOWED"
–215	FFFFFF29	"DSERR_Q_IN_SERVICE"
–215	FFFFFF29	"DSERR_DUPLICATE_PASSWORD"
–216	FFFFFF28	"DSERR_Q_NOT_ACTIVE"
–216	FFFFFF28	"DSERR_PASSWORD_TOO_SHORT"
–217	FFFFFF27	"DSERR_Q_STN_NOT_SERVER"
–217	FFFFFF27	"DSERR_MAXIMUM_LOGINS_EXCEEDED"
–218	FFFFFF26	"DSERR_Q_HALTED"
–218	FFFFFF26	"DSERR_BAD_LOGIN_TIME"
–219	FFFFFF25	"DSERR_Q_MAX_SERVERS"
–219	FFFFFF25	"DSERR_NODE_ADDRESS_VIOLATION"
–220	FFFFFF24	"DSERR_LOG_ACCOUNT_EXPIRED"
–222	FFFFFF22	"DSERR_BAD_PASSWORD"
–223	FFFFFF21	"DSERR_PASSWORD_EXPIRED"
–224	FFFFFF20	"DSERR_NO_LOGIN_CONN_AVAILABLE"
–232	FFFFFF18	"DSERR_WRITE_TO_GROUP_PROPERTY"
–233	FFFFFF17	"DSERR_MEMBER_ALREADY_EXISTS"
–234	FFFFFF16	"DSERR_NO_SUCH_MEMBER"
–235	FFFFFF15	"DSERR_PROPERTY_NOT_GROUP"
–236	FFFFFF14	"DSERR_NO_SUCH_VALUE_SET"
–237	FFFFFF13	"DSERR_PROPERTY_ALREADY_EXISTS"
–238	FFFFFF12	"DSERR_OBJECT_ALREADY_EXISTS"
–239	FFFFFF11	"DSERR_ILLEGAL_NAME"
–240	FFFFFF10	"DSERR_ILLEGAL_WILDCARD"
–241	FFFFFF0F	"DSERR_BINDERY_SECURITY"
–242	FFFFFF0E	"DSERR_NO_OBJECT_READ_RIGHTS"
–243	FFFFFF0D	"DSERR_NO_OBJECT_RENAME_RIGHTS"
–244	FFFFFF0C	"DSERR_NO_OBJECT_DELETE_RIGHTS"

−245	FFFFFF0B	"DSERR_NO_OBJECT_CREATE_RIGHTS"
−246	FFFFFF0A	"DSERR_NO_PROPERTY_DELETE_RIGHTS"
−247	FFFFFF09	"DSERR_NO_PROPERTY_CREATE_RIGHTS"
−248	FFFFFF08	"DSERR_NO_PROPERTY_WRITE_RIGHTS"
−249	FFFFFF07	"DSERR_NO_PROPERTY_READ_RIGHTS"
−250	FFFFFF06	"DSERR_TEMP_REMAP"
−251	FFFFFF05	"DSERR_UNKNOWN_REQUEST"
−251	FFFFFF05	"DSERR_NO_SUCH_PROPERTY"
−251	FFFFFF05	"ERR_REQUEST_UNKNOWN"
−252	FFFFFF04	"DSERR_MESSAGE_QUEUE_FULL"
−252	FFFFFF04	"DSERR_TARGET_ALREADY_HAS_MSG"
−252	FFFFFF04	"DSERR_NO_SUCH_OBJECT"
−253	FFFFFF03	"DSERR_BAD_STATION_NUMBER"
−254	FFFFFF02	"DSERR_BINDERY_LOCKED"
−254	FFFFFF02	"DSERR_DIR_LOCKED"
−254	FFFFFF02	"DSERR_SPOOL_DELETE"
−254	FFFFFF02	"DSERR_TRUSTEE_NOT_FOUND"
−255	FFFFFF01	"DSERR_HARD_FAILURE"
−255	FFFFFF01	"DSERR_FILE_NAME"
−255	FFFFFF01	"DSERR_FILE_EXISTS"
−255	FFFFFF01	"DSERR_CLOSE_FCB"
−255	FFFFFF01	"DSERR_IO_BOUND"
−255	FFFFFF01	"DSERR_NO_SPOOL_FILE"
−255	FFFFFF01	"DSERR_BAD_SPOOL_PRINTER"
−255	FFFFFF01	"DSERR_BAD_PARAMETER"
−255	FFFFFF01	"DSERR_NO_FILES_FOUND"
−255	FFFFFF01	"DSERR_NO_TRUSTEE_CHANGE_PRIV"
−255	FFFFFF01	"DSERR_TARGET_NOT_LOGGED_IN"
−255	FFFFFF01	"DSERR_TARGET_NOT_ACCEPTING_MSGS"
−255	FFFFFF01	"DSERR_MUST_FORCE_DOWN"
−255	FFFFFF01	"ERR_OF_SOME_SORT"
−301	FFFFFED3	"ERR_NOT_ENOUGH_MEMORY"
−302	FFFFFED2	"ERR_BAD_KEY"
−303	FFFFFED1	"ERR_BAD_CONTEXT"
−304	FFFFFED0	"ERR_BUFFER_FULL"

−305	FFFFFECF	"ERR_LIST_EMPTY"
−306	FFFFFECE	"ERR_BAD_SYNTAX"
−307	FFFFFECD	"ERR_BUFFER_EMPTY"
−308	FFFFFECC	"ERR_BAD_VERB"
−309	FFFFFECB	"ERR_EXPECTED_IDENTIFIER"
−310	FFFFFECA	"ERR_EXPECTED_EQUALS"
−311	FFFFFEC9	"ERR_ATTR_TYPE_EXPECTED"
−312	FFFFFEC8	"ERR_ATTR_TYPE_NOT_EXPECTED"
−313	FFFFFEC7	"ERR_FILTER_TREE_EMPTY"
−314	FFFFFEC6	"ERR_INVALID_OBJECT_NAME"
−315	FFFFFEC5	"ERR_EXPECTED_RDN_DELIMITER"
−316	FFFFFEC4	"ERR_TOO_MANY_TOKENS"
−317	FFFFFEC3	"ERR_INCONSISTENT_MULTIAVA"
−318	FFFFFEC2	"ERR_COUNTRY_NAME_TOO_LONG"
−319	FFFFFEC1	"ERR_SYSTEM_ERROR"
−320	FFFFFEC0	"ERR_CANT_ADD_ROOT"
−321	FFFFFEBF	"ERR_UNABLE_TO_ATTACH"
−322	FFFFFEBE	"ERR_INVALID_HANDLE"
−323	FFFFFEBD	"ERR_BUFFER_ZERO_LENGTH"
−324	FFFFFEBC	"ERR_INVALID_REPLICA_TYPE"
−325	FFFFFEBB	"ERR_INVALID_ATTR_SYNTAX"
−326	FFFFFEBA	"ERR_INVALID_FILTER_SYNTAX"
−328	FFFFFEB8	"ERR_CONTEXT_CREATION"
−329	FFFFFEB7	"ERR_INVALID_UNION_TAG"
−330	FFFFFEB6	"ERR_INVALID_SERVER_RESPONSE"
−331	FFFFFEB5	"ERR_NULL_POINTER"
−332	FFFFFEB4	"ERR_NO_SERVER_FOUND"
−333	FFFFFEB3	"ERR_NO_CONNECTION"
−334	FFFFFEB2	"ERR_RDN_TOO_LONG"
−335	FFFFFEB1	"ERR_DUPLICATE_TYPE"
−336	FFFFFEB0	"ERR_DATA_STORE_FAILURE"
−337	FFFFFEAF	"ERR_NOT_LOGGED_IN"
−338	FFFFFEAE	"ERR_INVALID_PASSWORD_CHARS"
−339	FFFFFEAD	"ERR_FAILED_SERVER_AUTHENT"
−340	FFFFFEAC	"ERR_TRANSPORT"

–341	FFFFFEAB	"ERR_NO_SUCH_SYNTAX"
–342	FFFFFEAA	"ERR_INVALID_DS_NAME"
–343	FFFFFEA9	"ERR_ATTR_NAME_TOO_LONG"
–344	FFFFFEA8	"ERR_INVALID_TDS"
–345	FFFFFEA7	"ERR_INVALID_DS_VERSION"
–346	FFFFFEA6	"ERR_UNICODE_TRANSLATION"
–347	FFFFFEA5	"ERR_SCHEMA_NAME_TOO_LONG"
–348	FFFFFEA4	"ERR_UNICODE_FILE_NOT_FOUND"
–349	FFFFFEA3	"ERR_UNICODE_ALREADY_LOADED"
–350	FFFFFEA2	"ERR_NOT_CONTEXT_OWNER"
–351	FFFFFEA1	"ERR_ATTEMPT_TO_AUTHENTICATE_0"
–352	FFFFFEA0	"ERR_NO_WRITABLE_REPLICAS"
–353	FFFFFE9F	"ERR_DN_TOO_LONG"
–354	FFFFFE9E	"ERR_RENAME_NOT_ALLOWED"

IntranetWare Server Console Commands

Server console commands and utilities enable you to change server parameters, monitor the load on the server, and control its allocation of resources. This appendix lists and describes each of the server console commands for IntranetWare. The online help screen will list each of the commands for your use. You can access the help screen at the server prompt by typing:

HELP

The SFT III server console commands are not included in this appendix. If you need information about these commands you should refer to the documentation that comes with the IntranetWare SFT III product.

You can enter the server console commands only at the server prompt or command line. These commands can also be used in the AUTOEXEC.NCF file but not in the STARTUP.NCF file. A few commands are available only in the AUTOEXEC.NCF file and will not function at the server prompt. For example, the commands FILE SERVER NAME and IPX INTERNAL NET are available only in the AUTOEXEC.NCF file.

The server console commands can also be placed in NetWare command files other than the AUTOEXEC.NCF file. The NetWare command files have .NCF file extensions and are used to group the server console commands together to perform specific tasks. The command files should be stored in the SYS:SYSTEM directory. You can execute a command file by typing the command file name (without the .NCF extension) at the server prompt.

Server Console Commands

The following section presents each IntranetWare server console command, gives its syntax, and provides examples.

ABORT REMIRROR

This command stops the remirroring of a NetWare file system partition. By default NetWare will automatically begin remirroring a mirrored partition that is out of synchronization. The partition can fall out of synchronization if one-half of the mirror is disabled or damaged. The remirror process will start automatically after the pair is back up and running. The syntax for this command is:

```
ABORT REMIRROR partition_number
```

You can selectively stop the remirroring process for any of the NetWare partitions.
Example: abort remirror 3
Also See: REMIRROR PARTITION

ADD NAME SPACE

This command enables you to add and support non-DOS files, such as Macintosh, NFS (UNIX), OS/2 HPFS, and FTAM on the NetWare volume. The command is executed only once for each name space on each NetWare volume. The syntax for this command is:

```
ADD NAME SPACE name [TO [volume_name]]
```

The name parameter can be replaced with one of the following:

▸ Macintosh — used for Apple Macintosh files

▸ NFS — used for UNIX files

▸ OS/2 — used for IBM OS/2 HPFS files

▸ FTAM — used for OSI files

The name space support module (file with .NAM file extension) must be loaded on the server before you can execute this command. For example, to support the Macintosh files the MAC.NAM name space module must be loaded first.

Once a volume is configured for name space support, the appropriate name space NLMs must be loaded prior to mounting the volume. Therefore, you must copy the .NAM name space file to the DOS partition of the server and include the statement to load the file in the STARTUP.NCF file. Once a volume is set to store a non-DOS file system, the setting cannot be reversed unless the volume is deleted.

To display the name space support currently loaded on the server, you can enter the ADD NAME SPACE command without the other parameters. A list of all the loaded name spaces is displayed.

Example: add name space mac to sys

Also See: VOLUMES

ALIAS

This command creates an alias command that is used in place of an original command. For example you can type **ALIAS V VOLUME**. Typing V is now equivalent to typing the whole command VOLUME at the server prompt.

After you type ALIASES, a list of current aliases will be displayed on the server. The following is an example of an alias displayed on the server:

```
1. V alias for <VOLUME>
```

BIND

This command assigns or connects a specific communication protocol to a LAN driver loaded on the server. A communication protocol must be linked to the network board or it will not be able to send and receive packets to and from the network. The syntax to connect a protocol to the network board is:

```
BIND protocol [TO] board_name [protocol_parameter . . .]
```

or

```
BIND protocol [TO] LAN_driver [driver parameters . . .]

   [protocol_parameter . . .]
```

NetWare supports multiple communication protocol stacks in the server. The LAN driver and protocol stack modules must be loaded before this command can be used. The BIND command can be used to connect multiple protocol stacks to a single LAN adapter, or a single protocol can use multiple LAN adapters.

Example: bind ipx to ne3200 slot=3 frame=ethernet_802.2 net=12345678

Also See: UNBIND

BINDERY

This command adds or removes a bindery context to or from the list of all bindery contexts for this server.

Example: bindery add context = OU=Department OU=Division O=Corporation

Example: bindery delete context = OU=Department OU=Division O=Corporation

BROADCAST

This command enables you to send a message to all the users that are currently logged in or attached to the server. You can also broadcast to a list of users or connection numbers. The syntax for the broadcast message is as follows:

```
BROADCAST "message" [[TO] user_name | connection_number]

    [[and | ,] username | connection_number . . .]
```

Example: broadcast "Please log out of the server. Server going down in 5 minutes" or "Hello to supervisor 5 10 11 23."

Also See: SEND

CLEAR STATION

This command clears the connection for a specific connection number. After this command is issued against the user, the workstation will no longer be attached to the server and all the allocated resources at the server are removed. The syntax for this command is:

```
CLEAR STATION station_number
```

You can use the MONITOR program to determine connection numbers or match the connection number with the user.

Example: clear station 5

CLS

This command clears the console screen.

Example: cls

Also See: OFF

CONFIG

This command displays the current status of the following information:

▸ File server name

▸ Internal network number for the server

▸ NDS tree name

▸ Hardware settings on all the network boards installed

▸ Network address for each network board

▸ LAN drivers loaded

▸ Communication protocol bound to the network board

▸ Frame type assigned to the protocol

▸ Board name assigned

▸ Effective Bindery Services context

Example: config

DISABLE LOGIN

This command prevents additional clients from logging in to the server but does not log out the clients that are already logged in. This command applies to all clients of the server whether they are users trying to connect to the server or another IntranetWare server authenticating to support replica synchronization for NDS.

Example: disable login

Also See: ENABLE LOGIN

DISABLE TTS

This command manually turns off the Transaction Tracking System (TTS) feature. During normal operation there is no reason for you to ever turn TTS off. NDS depends on TTS, and you should not disable it. TTS will automatically become disabled when the TTS backout volume is full or when the server memory is insufficient.

The DISABLE TTS command is primarily a tool for application developers who need to test transactional applications with TTS disabled.

After you have manually disabled TTS you should enable TTS using the ENABLE TTS command or reboot the server.

Example: disable tts
Also See: ENABLE TTS

DISMOUNT

This command causes the selected volume to be dismounted. If you have open files on that volume, the server prints a warning on the server console screen and prompts you for confirmation before it dismounts the volume. The syntax for this command is:

```
DISMOUNT volume_name
```

You can use DISMOUNT to make a volume unavailable to your users. This allows you to do maintenance on the volume while the server is up.

If you have a volume that is not used very often, such as a CD-ROM, you can dismount it until you need to use it again. Mounted volumes take up memory.

If the volume being dismounted is the SYS: volume, which contains the NDS files, then the NDS is closed for that server. All requests that require NDS will be directed to another server in the network, which has another copy of the same NDS partition information.

Example: dismount sys
Also See: MOUNT

DISPLAY NETWORKS

This command displays the server's list of all the network numbers that the internal router is aware of. The list shows the IPX network number (which includes the internal network number of the server), the number of hops (networks that must be crossed) to reach the network, and the estimated time in ticks for a packet to reach the network. A tick is $1/18$th of a second. The total number of networks is displayed at the end of the list.

Example: display networks

Also See: DISPLAY SERVERS

DISPLAY SERVERS

This command displays the list of all the devices that send out a Service Advertising Protocol that the internal router is aware of. This command shows all servers regardless of type; for example, print servers, queue servers, and others are displayed.

The list shows the advertising name (typically a server) and the number of hops (networks that must be crossed) to reach the server. The total number of servers is displayed at the bottom of the list.

Example: display servers

Also See: DISPLAY NETWORKS

DOWN

This command brings the server down. The server going down means that all the connections are cleared, all volumes will be dismounted, and IPX packet routing is suspended. If there are files in use by a workstation when the DOWN command is issued, the server will display a warning on the console screen and ask for confirmation before it goes down.

You should always type the DOWN command before turning the power to the server off. The DOWN command ensures data integrity by writing all cache buffers to disk, closing all files, and updating the appropriate directory and file allocation table.

Example: down

Also See: EXIT, and RESTART SERVER

ECHO OFF

This command tells the server not to echo or display the commands in the NetWare Command File to the screen when they are executed. This command is only valid for use in the .NCF files. ECHO OFF is the default.

Example: echo on
Also See: ECHO OFF

ECHO ON

This command tells the server to echo the commands in the NetWare Command File to the screen as they are executed. This command is only valid for use in the .NCF files. The default is not to echo.

Example: echo off
Also See: ECHO ON

ENABLE LOGIN

This command allows clients to connect and log in to the server. This command is the default when the server is booted. You should use this command only if you have disabled login using the DISABLE LOGIN command. This command does not affect the users that are already connected.

The ENABLE LOGIN command enables the supervisor account from being locked out by the intruder detection.

Example: enable login
Also See: DISABLE LOGIN

ENABLE TTS

This command manually turns on the Transaction Tracking System feature of IntranetWare. During normal operation TTS is always enabled.

When volume SYS is mounted, TTS is automatically enabled if there is enough disk space and memory to allow transaction tracking. NDS depends on TTS, and you should always leave it enabled. If a problem occurs that disables TTS automatically, you must fix the problem before you can enable TTS.

The server will automatically disable TTS if one of the following occurs:

▸ Volume SYS becomes full

▸ Insufficient memory to operate TTS

Example: enable tts
Also See: DISABLE TTS

EXIT

After the server has been taken down, the EXIT command leaves the server program and returns to DOS. This allows you to access the DOS files or rerun the SERVER.EXE program.

The DOWN command must always be issued before the EXIT command. If the REMOVE DOS command was issued, the server will perform a reboot.

After you bring down the server, it is still connected to the network and receiving packets. You can still execute console commands that deal with packets such as TRACK ON and TRACK OFF.

Example: exit
Also See: DOWN, and RESTART SERVER

FILE SERVER NAME

This command sets the server name when the server boots up. The file server name is used to identify the server on the network. The file server name is distributed throughout the network using the SAP. The name chosen should be a unique value on the network because it does have the SAP. The syntax for this command is:

```
FILE SERVER NAME server_name
```

The clients find the server by knowing the name of the server. The file server name for IntranetWare is also widely used in NDS.

This command is available only in the AUTOEXEC.NCF file and cannot be used at the server prompt.

Example: file server name CAM-SRV1

HELP

This command displays the help screen at the file server console. The help screen lists all the server console commands with examples of how to use them. You can specify an individual command with HELP. The HELP ALL command will list all the server console commands in alphabetical order and pause in between each command.

Example: help, help bind, or help all

IPX INTERNAL NET

This command sets the internal network number that the router uses to identify all services/clients that reside in the same machine as the router. For IntranetWare, the internal network number is very important and is used in NDS. The syntax for this command is:

```
IPX INTERNAL NET network_address
```

The internal IPX network number chosen should be a unique number on the network. This command is available only in the AUTOEXEC.NCF file.

Example: ipx internal net 370DC321

LANGUAGE

This command sets the server console to use the language specified. The server console command and server utilities or NLM programs will use the appropriate language message files. The syntax for this command has several options:

- ▸ Language — displays current NLM language

- ▸ Language list — displays list of available languages

- ▸ Language name|number — sets language by name or number

- ▸ Language add number name — adds a new language name and number

- ▸ Language rename number new_name — renames the language specified

Example: language spanish

LIST DEVICES

This command displays all the physical device information for the server.

LOAD

This command executes a NetWare Loadable Module file and links it to the operating system. The file executed is named with one of the following extensions: .NLM (server utilities), .DSK (disk driver), and .LAN (LAN driver). The LOAD command searches the SYS:SYSTEM directory by default for the files. The SYS volume must be mounted. The syntax for the LOAD command is:

```
LOAD [path] load_module [parameter . . .]
```

You can also specify a complete path name for the file to be loaded or set up additional paths to search for the file by using the SEARCH command.

Example: load monitor

Also See: UNLOAD, SEARCH

MAGAZINE INSERTED

This command acknowledges the insertion of the specified media magazine in response to the "Insert Magazine" console alert.

Example: magazine inserted

MAGAZINE NOT INSERTED

This command acknowledges that the insertion of the specified media magazine was not performed.

Example: magazine not inserted

MAGAZINE NOT REMOVED

This command acknowledges that the removal of the magazine was not performed.

Example: magazine not removed

MAGAZINE REMOVED

This command acknowledges the removal of a magazine from the specified device in response to the "Remove Magazine" console alert.

Example: remove magazine

MEDIA INSERTED

This command acknowledges the insertion of the specified media in response to the "Insert Media" console alert.

Example: media inserted

MEDIA NOT INSERTED

This command acknowledges that the insertion of the specified media was not performed.

Example: media not inserted

MEDIA NOT REMOVED

This command acknowledges that the removal of the media was not performed.

Example: media not removed

MEDIA REMOVED

This command acknowledges the removal of the media from the specified device in response to the "Remove Magazine" console alert.

Example: remove media

MEMORY MAP

This command displays a map of server RAM.

Example: memory map

MEMORY

This command displays the total memory installed that the NetWare operating system can address.

Example: memory
Also See: REGISTER MEMORY

MIRROR STATUS

This command displays all mirrored logical disk partitions and the status of each.

Example: mirror status

MODULES

This command displays names and descriptions for all the NetWare Loadable Modules currently loaded on the server.

Examples: modules

MOUNT

This command causes the specified volume to be mounted as a NetWare volume. The syntax for the MOUNT command is:

```
MOUNT volume_name or MOUNT ALL
```

Example: mount sys, MOUNT ALL

NAME

This command displays the server's name. The NAME command is still supported in IntranetWare but is not very useful because the server prompt includes the server name.

Example: name
Also See: FILE SERVER NAME

OFF

This command clears the server console screen and is equivalent to the CLS command.

Example: off

Also See: CLS

PAUSE

This command causes the screen and processing to stop and waits for a key to be pressed while in a NetWare Control File (NCF).

Example: pause

PROTOCOL

This command displays the protocol identification numbers registered with the server. These numbers are based on the server's communication protocol and media type. The PROTOCOL command can also be used to register new protocol ID and numbers with the server. The proper syntax for this command is:

```
PROTOCOL or PROTOCOL REGISTER protocol_name frame id_number
```

If you load a communication protocol module and try to bind it, you may get an error message stating that the module is not loaded. The error message probably means that the communication protocol or the media type contained in the driver is not registered with NetWare. In this case, you should use the PROTOCOL REGISTER to register the new protocol.

Example: protocol register ip ethernet_ii 800

REGISTER MEMORY

For some hardware systems, IntranetWare does not recognize more than 16MB of RAM. In these situations, you must use the REGISTER MEMORY command at the console. This command uses the following syntax:

```
REGISTER MEMORY memory_start memory_length
```

You can replace the memory_start with a value in hexadecimal with a memory address beyond 16MB. In most cases, this is the value 0x1000000 (which equates to 16MB). The memory_length is the value of the memory installed that is beyond 16MB. This number must be an even paragraph boundary that is divisible by 0×10. For example, to add 4MB of memory above 16MB (for a total of 20MB RAM), you need to enter the following command:

```
REGISTER MEMORY 1000000 1250000
```

This command can be added to the AUTOEXEC.NCF file for automatic registration of memory when the server is booted. For EISA-based machines, memory above 16MB is registered automatically.

Also See: MEMORY

REM OR ; OR

Each of these commands is used to specify a comment line or a remark in the AUTOEXEC.NCF, or NCF.

Example: This line will load the LAN driver for the NE3200 network board

REMIRROR PARTITION

This command starts the remirroring of a logical disk partition. Partition remirroring typically consumes upwards of 70 percent of the CPU's time, so you might want to delay the remirroring process until activity on the server is reduced. The syntax for this command is:

```
REMIRROR PARTITION partition_number
```

Example: remirror partition 4

REMOVE DOS

After the server is running, the memory being used by DOS can be released and given to the server cache memory. Once this command is issued and the server is brought down, the EXIT command will not be able to return to DOS. You must power off the machine to reboot.

By removing DOS from the server's memory, you are providing an additional 1MB of memory for the server cache memory. However, since DOS is no longer residing in memory of the server, the files located on the DOS drives are no longer accessible. This can be implemented as a security step because the NLMs cannot be loaded from the DOS drivers.

You can also use the REMOVE DOS command to enable warm booting of the server using the EXIT command.

Example: remove dos
Also See: EXIT

RESET ROUTER

This command clears the information stored in the internal router tables of the server. The RESET ROUTER command erases all known servers and networks. The router will automatically rebuild the tables as SAP and RIP advertising information is received.

This command is useful when you want to debug communication problems you may have in the network or the server itself. By resetting the router, you can tell whether the server is receiving the routing information.

For example, if several servers or bridges on your network go down, any packets sent to or through their routers will be lost. If you reset routers in the server that are still up, the router sends a request to the nearest server to verify any other networks or routes it knows about. From this information, the router builds a new, accurate router table.

Example: reset router

RESTART SERVER

This command reloads the SERVER.EXE software after the DOWN command has been issued. This command is valid only if the server has not been exited. The following options are available with the RESTART SERVER command:

▶   -ns — Do not use the STARTUP.NCF file.

▸ -na — Do not use the AUTOEXEC.NCF file.

▸ -d — Break into the internal debugger.

Example: restart server

SCAN FOR NEW DEVICES

This command checks for storage devices and hardware that have been added since the server was last booted. This command causes the operating system to look for and add new devices on the system.

Example: scan for new devices

SEARCH

This command dictates where the server should automatically search for the NetWare Loadable Module (.NLM) files and the NetWare Command File (.NCF). The directory that the server searches by default is SYS:SYSTEM. You can use this command to add additional search paths and to display the current setting for the search paths on the server. The proper syntax for the SEARCH command is:

```
SEARCH [ADD [number]] path
```

or

```
SEARCH DEL [number]
```

Example: search add 4 c:\nwserver\nlms or search del 1

SECURE CONSOLE

This command enables you to restrict access to the server console by:

▸ Restricting the loading of NLMs from every place but the current search path

▸ Preventing keyboard entry into the internal NetWare Debugger

▸ Preventing anyone except the console operator from changing the data and time

▸ Removing DOS from the server

Example: secure console

SEND

This command enables you to send a message to all users logged in or attached to the server or a list of users or connection numbers. The syntax for the SEND command is:

```
SEND "message" [[TO] user_name | connection_number] [[and |,]

    username | connection_number . . .]
```

Example: send "Please delete some files" to jack and jill

SET

This command displays and changes the server's configuration information. Many configuration parameters can be adjusted by using this command. Typing the SET command without a configuration parameter name displays a small menu of configuration parameters. The display shows the configuration parameter name, its current setting, the limits that it can be set to, and a description of what the configuration parameter controls. The syntax for this command is:

```
SET [parameter_name] [=parameter_value]
```

The SET command can be used in the STARTUP.NCF and AUTOEXEC.NCF files. The following three configuration parameters can be set in the STARTUP.NCF (they cannot be set from the server console command line):

▸ Minimum Packet Receive Buffers

▸ Maximum Physical Receive Packet Size

▸ Cache Buffer Size

Example: set bindery context = OU=NORAD.O=ACME

SET TIME

This command sets the server date and time and accepts a variety of formats in setting the date and time. You can set just the date, the time, or both. The syntax for the SET TIME command is:

```
SET TIME [month/day/year] [hour:minute:second]
```

This command assumes that if the time is specified, a colon will separate the hours and minutes. If "am" or "pm" is not specified, the server will assume the time has been entered during working hours. Working hours are 7:00 to 12:00 AM and 1:00 to 6:00 PM.

The month can be entered as a number or name. If the month is entered as a number, the command assumes that the month precedes the day or year number.

Example: set time April 6 1999 3:45:00 pm

Also See: TIME, and SET

SET TIME ZONE

This command sets the server time zone using the specific time zone strings in IntranetWare. The SET TIME ZONE command is also used to display the current setting of the time zone on the server. The syntax for this command is:

```
SET TIME ZONE zone [hour[daylight]]
```

Example: set time zone MST7MDT

SPEED

This command displays the CPU speed rating for the server hardware. The speed is a processor relative value in which a 386-based machine has a slower rating than a 486-based machine. The pentium class of machines is faster or has a higher speed rating for the processor.

Example: speed

SPOOL

This command allows you to create, change, or display spooler mappings. These mappings are needed to set up default print queues for NPRINT and CAPTURE. They also support applications that make calls to printer numbers rather than to queues. The syntax for the SPOOL command is:

```
SPOOL
```

or

```
SPOOL number [TO] [QUEUE] queue_name
```

Example: spool 1 to queue hp4si

TIME

This command displays the current server date, time, and time synchronization status.
Example: time
Also See: SET TIME

TRACK OFF

This command closes the Router Tracking Screen on the server that views the activity on the server caused by sending and receiving advertising packets from the Service Advertising Protocol and Routing Information Protocol.
Example: track off
Also See: TRACK ON

TRACK ON

This command starts the Router Tracking Screen and makes it active on the server console. The screen displays the activity caused by sending and receiving advertising packets from the Service Advertising Protocol and Routing Information Protocol.
Example: track on
Also See: TRACK OFF

UNBIND

This command disconnects the specified communication protocol stack from a LAN adapter. The LAN adapter is specified by the LAN driver name if the driver is only servicing one adapter. If the LAN driver is servicing more than one adapter the optional parameters indicate the hardware settings of the adapter to be unbound. If either the LAN driver or the protocol stack are unloaded using the command, the protocol stack will automatically be unbound from the LAN adapter. The syntax for the UNBIND command is:

```
UNBIND protocol [FROM] LAN_driver [driver parameters . . .]
```

or

```
UNBIND protocol [FROM] board_name
```

Example: unbind ipx from ne3200 slot=3 frame=ethernet_802.2
Also See: BIND

UNLOAD

This command removes or unlinks the NetWare Loadable Module from the operating system. The NLM, which was previously loaded, is removed from the server memory. You can use the UNLOAD command to upgrade or change any of the NLMs loaded on the server.
Example: unload pserver
Also See: LOAD

VERSION

This command displays the server's version information and copyright notice.
Example: version

VOLUME

This command displays a list of all the volumes currently mounted on the server.
Example: volume
Also See: MOUNT

IntranetWare Debugger Commands

The IntranetWare operating system includes an internal assembly language debug utility. This debugger enables you to execute the commands listed in this appendix. You can use the debugger to help determine the cause of a server abend or to simply become more familiar with the internal structure of IntranetWare.

When the debugger is entered, it will display the following: a screen with a "#" as the prompt; default information, including the location in code at which the server abended or was manually interrupted; and the cause of the abend or trap. The general registers and flags are also presented.

Invoking the IntranetWare Debugger

Four methods are available to invoke the debugger: two from the server console, one from a program, and one from hardware.

FROM THE SERVER CONSOLE

1 • Press Alt + LeftShift + RightShift + Esc simultaneously at the server keyboard. You can supply this key combination either while the server is running or after an abend. This will not work if the server is hung in a tight infinite loop (some infinite loops are not too tight), has interrupts disabled, or if the server console has been locked.

2 • If the server abends or GPIs, you can type **386debug** to invoke the debugger. The characters you type are not echoed to the screen, but the "#" prompt will immediately appear. Remember the "#" prompt indicates that you are in the debugger.

FROM AN NLM PROGRAM

▸ If the NLM program supplies an INT 3 in the desired code segment, the program will invoke the debugger. If the programmer is using C and the CLIB interface, he or she can call a Breakpoint() function.

WITH HARDWARE OR MANUALLY

▸ You can break into a server by using an NMI board. After the server has abended, you can use steps 1 or 2 given above to enter the debugger. This method seems abrupt but may be required if the software program being debugged is in a tight infinite loop with interrupts disabled.

Debugger Commands

Once you have entered the debugger, there is a great deal of information you can display. The debugger commands and their functions are listed in the following tables.

<table>
<tr><td>TABLE APPC-1
Debugger Commands</td><td>COMMAND</td><td>FUNCTION</td></tr>
<tr><td></td><td>Q</td><td>Quits the debugger and returns to DOS.</td></tr>
<tr><td></td><td>G</td><td>Continues server execution (go) from the current position.</td></tr>
<tr><td></td><td>G [address(es)]</td><td>Begins execution at the current position and then sets a temporary breakpoint at the address or several temporary breakpoints at the addresses.</td></tr>
<tr><td></td><td>P</td><td>Proceeds with the next instruction. Using this command you can trace or single-step each of the following instructions. One limitation is that this command will not single-step through loops in the code or trace into a subroutine call. You can repeat this command by simply pressing Enter at the prompt.</td></tr>
<tr><td></td><td>T or S</td><td>Enables you to trace or single-step through the program code, through loops, and into subroutine calls.</td></tr>
<tr><td></td><td>U address</td><td>Enables you to unassemble instructions from a specific address, which can be done for count instructions. You can repeat this command by simply pressing Enter at the prompt.</td></tr>
<tr><td></td><td>V</td><td>Enables you to switch over and view the server console screens. You will be able to step through the screens sequentially.</td></tr>
</table>

(continued)

Debugger Commands
(continued)

COMMAND	FUNCTION
? address	Displays the closest symbols to the address if symbolic information has been loaded. By default, this command is the EIP register.
N symbol name address	Enables you to assign a symbol name to a specific address.
N -symbolname	Removes the specific symbol name.
N—	Removes all defined symbols.
Z expression	Evaluates the expression. This command is useful as a calculator in the debugger. Zd will evaluate the expression in decimal.

Help Commands

COMMAND	FUNCTION
H	Displays help for general commands.
.H	Displays help for the "." commands.
HB	Displays help for breakpoints.
HE	Displays help for expressions.
H3	Displays help for SFT III commands.

Dot "." Commands

COMMAND	FUNCTION
.a	Displays the abend or break reason.
.c	Does a diagnostic memory dump to diskette or disk.
.d	Displays page directory map for current debugger domain.
.d	Displays page entry map for current debugger domain.
.f	Toggles ON/OF the developer option flag.
.g	Displays the GDT.
.h	Displays help for the "." commands.
.I	Displays the IDT.
.I2	Displays the IDT for Processor 2. This command defaults to the math coprocessor on a single processor system.

COMMAND	FUNCTION
.l offset[offset]	Displays the linear address given to page map offsets.
.la[linear address][<cr3>]	Finds all aliases of a linear address.
.lp[physical address][<cr3>]	Finds all linear mappings of a physical address.
.lx address	Displays page offsets and values used for translation.
.m	Displays loaded module names and addresses.
.p	Displays all process names and addresses.
.p address	Displays address as a process control block.
.r	Displays the running process control block.
.s	Displays all screen names and addresses.
.?	Displays the server state.
.s address	Displays address as a screen structure. If address is not specified, this command display all screen names and addresses.
.t address	Displays address as a TSS structure.
.ts [segnum]	Displays GDT [segnum] as a TSS structure.
.v	Displays server version.

COMMAND	FUNCTION
C address	Interactively changes the contents of memory location.
C address = number(s)	Changes the memory contents beginning at the address to the specified number(s). Number is a hexadecimal value.
C address = "text string"	Changes the memory contents starting at the address to the text string value.

(continued)

COMMAND	FUNCTION
D address [count]	Dumps the contents of memory, starting at the address, for [count] number of bytes. The address and count are in hexadecimal values. Count is an optional value and if it is not supplied, one page (100h bytes) will be displayed. This command can be repeated continually by pressing Enter after each contents dump.
M address [L length] bytepattern(s)	Searches memory for a bytepattern match, starting at the location address and continuing until [L length] is reached. If a match is found, 128 bytes (starting with the pattern) are displayed. This command can be repeated by pressing Enter at the # prompt.

Registers

The following tables list the IntranetWare debugger commands used on the microprocessor's internal registers. These registers are both the general and flag registers.

COMMAND	FUNCTION
R	Displays the EAX, EBX, ECX, EDX, ESI, EDI, ESP, EBP, EIP, and flag registers.
Name of Register = value	Enables you to change a specific register to a new value. This command affects the EAX, EBX, ECX, EDX, ESI, EDI, ESP, EBP, EFL, and EIP registers.
Name of F flag = value	Enables you to change a specific flag register to a new value. The value has to be 0 or 1 since these are the only values the flag register can hold. This command affects the CF, AF, ZF, SF, IF, TF, PF, DF, and OF flag registers.

TABLE APPC-6

Input/Output Commands

COMMAND	FUNCTION
I[B,W,D] port	Inputs a (B)yte, (W)ord, or (D)ouble word from a port. Default is byte O[B,W,D] port = value. Outputs a (B)yte, (W)ord, or (D)ouble word value to a port.

TABLE APPC-7

Breakpoints Commands

COMMAND	FUNCTION
B	Displays all breakpoints that are currently set.
B = address	Sets an execution breakpoint at address. The break will occur if EIP = address is changed and condition evaluates to TRUE.
BC number	Clears the breakpoint specified by number.
BCA	Clears all breakpoints.
BI = address	Sets an IO read/write breakpoint at address. This breakpoint will occur when the specified IO port addres is accessed with either a read or a write.
BR = address{condition}	Sets a read/write breakpoint at the address specified when the indicated condition is true.
BW = address{condition}	Sets a write breakpoint at the address specified when the indicated condition is true.

Debug Expressions

In the following table all the numbers in the debug expressions are entered and shown in hex format. In addition to the numbers, the following registers, flags, and operators can be used in the debug expressions:

Registers: EAX, EBX, ECX, EDX, ESI, EDI, ESP, EBP, EIP

Flags: FLCF, FLAF, FLZF, FLSF, FLIF, FLTF, FLPF, FLDF, FLOF

SYMBOL	DESCRIPTION	PRECEDENCE
I		e
( )	(Expression) Causes the expression to be evaluated at a higher level	0
[ ]	[Size Expression] Causes the expression to be evaluated at a higher precedence and then uses the value of the expression as a memory address	0
{ }	{Size Expression} Causes the expression to be evaluated at a higher precedence and then uses the value of the expression as a port address	0
!	Logical Not	I
-	2's Complement	I
~	I's Complement	I
*	Multiply	2
/	Divide	2
%	Mod	2
+	Addition	3
-	Subtraction	3
>>	Bit Shift Right	4
<<	Bit Shift Left	4
>	Greater Than	5
<	Less Than	5
>=	Greater Than or Equal to	5
<=	Less Than or Equal to	5
==	Equal to	6
!=	Not Equal to	6
&	Bitwise AND	7

SYMBOL	DESCRIPTION	PRECEDENCE
^	Bitwise XOR	8
|	Bitwise OR	9
&&	Logical AND	10
||	Logical OR	11

CONDITIONAL EVALUATION

expression1 ? expression2, expression3

If expression1 is true, then the result is the value of expression2. Otherwise, if expression1 is not true then the result is the value of expression3.

NetWare Client Parameters

This appendix provides information on settable parameters for NetWare Client software. For more information on the Novell client software, refer to Chapters 12 and 18.

DOS Requester Parameters

AUTO RECONNECT = ON, OFF

Default: ON

This option reconnects the workstation to the server if the network connection is lost. The benefit of having this parameter set to ON is that small interruptions of network service will not be noticed by the user. AUTO.VLM must be loaded to support this feature.

AUTO LARGE TABLE

Default: OFF, 34 bytes

This option allocates a connection table of 178 bytes per connection for bindery reconnects. Use this parameter only if the length of your user names and passwords is more than 16 characters.

AUTO RETRY

Default: ON

This option reconnects a workstation to a NetWare server and attempts to reconnect a workstation's environment before the connection loss.

AVERAGE NAME LENGTH = number (2 to 48)

Default: 48

This option calculates the size of the server connection table enabled on the workstation. The size of the connection table is determined by the value in this option and the CONNECTIONS option. If you have standard server names that are shorter than 48 characters you can use a smaller value, which will return more conventional memory to the workstation.

BIND RECONNECT

Default: OFF

This option automatically rebuilds the bindery connections after a reconnect, including drive mappings and printer connections.

BROADCAST RETRIES

Default: 3

This option sets the number of broadcast requests by the NetWare DOS Requester. The range is 1 to 255.

BROADCAST SEND DELAY

Default: 0

This option sets the number of ticks delay between NetWare DOS Requester functions. The range is 0 to 255.

BROADCAST TIMEOUT

Default: 2

This option sets the number of ticks between broadcast retries of the NetWare DOS Requester. The range is 1 to 255.

CACHE BUFFERS = number (0 to 64)

Default: 5

This option sets the number of cache buffers the requester uses for caching files that are written to the server. More buffers increase the speed of processing sequential files. Lower values return memory to the workstation.

CACHE BUFFER SIZE = number (512 to 4096 bytes)

Default: 512 bytes

This option sets the size of each cache buffer. You should adjust the size of the cache buffer to match the size of the maximum packet supported by the workstation.

CACHES WRITES = ON, OFF

Default: ON

This option establishes the rules for file writes. The setting of ON forces the cache to be written to disk.

CHECKSUM = number (0 to 3)

Default: 1

This option enables checksum for NCP packets. Checksums are ordinarily enabled at lower layers in the packet transmissions. Setting a value here guarantees greater reliability but decreases performance The possible values are:

▶ 0 = No checksums (disabled).

▶ 1 = Enabled but not preferred. This means that NCP checksums are enabled but if the server is very busy and runs out of time, the checksum is not performed.

▸ 2 = Enabled and preferred.

▸ 3 = Required.

CONNECTIONS = number (2 to 50)
Default: 8

This option represents the maximum number of server connections that the VLM software will support. The larger the value the more conventional memory is used.

DOS NAME = xxxxx (five character limit)
Default: MSDOS

This option sets the name of your DOS version. The requester software tries to automatically recognize the name of your version of DOS.

EXCLUDE VLM
Default:Off

This option turns off the default loading of the VLM modules. The EXCLUDE VLM command is placed after the NetWare Protocol section in the NET.CFG file.

FIRST NETWORK DRIVE = x
Default: First drive available

This option sets the drive letter the user is assigned to initially access the server. If you have a machine with one floppy drive (A:) and one hard drive with two partitions (C: and D:), the first drive while be E:. You will typically want to set this value to F: by typing the following:

```
FIRST NETWORK DRIVE = F
```

HANDLE NET ERRORS = ON/OFF
Default: ON

This option sets how the requester handles any network errors. If the option is set to OFF, the requester will return the actual error code to the application program and take no further action. Some applications may crash because they cannot handle the returned error code.

LARGE INTERNET PACKETS = ON/OFF
Default: ON

This option tells the workstation to handle the largest packet between the workstation and server (4202 bytes for token ring and 1514 bytes for ethernet). Older versions of NetWare forced the largest packet size to 576 bytes, regardless of topology, if the packet crossed a router between the workstation and server. The smaller packet size increased the number of packets for each communication.

LOAD CONN TABLE LOW

Default: OFF

This option causes the CONN Table (CONN.VLM) to load into upper memory if set to OFF. Setting this parameter to ON is not recommended for the current release of IntranetWare because it will get loaded in conventional memory instead of upper memory.

LOAD LOW CONN = ON/OFF

Default: ON

This option causes the CONN.VLM (connection manager) to load in conventional memory. If this parameter is set to OFF, the module is loaded in upper memory, which saves memory but impacts the performance of the requester.

LOAD LOW FIO = ON/OFF

Default: OFF

This option provides additional tuning in favor of performance over memory usage. By loading FIO low, additional conventional memory is used by a return of better performance for the requester.

LOAD LOW IPXNCP

Default: ON

IPXNCP.VLM is loaded by default into conventional memory. This module can be loaded into upper memory but with a trade-off in performance.

LOAD LOW REDIR = ON/OFF

Default: OFF

This option provides improvement for small I/O performance. If this parameter is set to ON, the module is loaded into conventional memory, which takes more space in exchange for the increased performance.

LOAD LOW NETX = ON/OFF

Default: OFF

This option provides additional tuning in favor of performance over size. Setting the value to ON loads the NETX.VLM module low, which takes additional conventional memory but improves performance.

LOCAL PRINTERS = n (0 to 7)

Default: Determined by the workstation BIOS

This option informs the requester how many printers are available locally on the workstation. A value of 0 indicates no printers supported.

LONG MACHINE TYPE = typename (six characters or fewer)
Default: IBM_PC
This option enables you to change the value of the %MACHINE login script variable.

MAX TASKS = n (20 to 128)
Default: 31
This option defines the maximum number of tasks that can be simultaneously active at the workstation.

MESSAGE LEVEL = n (0 to 4)
Default: 1
This option adjusts the amount of information displayed when a module is loaded. Each value is cumulative upon the other levels. The values are:

▸   0 = Copyright message and critical errors

▸   1 = Warning messages

▸   2 = VLM program load information

▸   3 = Configuration information

▸   4 = Diagnostic information

MESSAGE TIMEOUT = n (0 to 10,000 ticks)
Default: 0
This option controls the amount of time the requester will wait before clearing broadcast messages. The range of values is 0 to 10,000 ticks (approximately 6 hours). If the value is set to 0, the requester will wait indefinitely until the user presses Ctrl+Enter.

MINIMUM TIME TO NET
This option sets a value in milliseconds (1000 = 1 second) of time to net for a workstation connection. This option would primarily be set in situations where you have a slow WAN link or a server not running Packet Burst.

NAME CONTEXT = xxx
Default: [ROOT]

This option enables you to enter the desired default NDS context for a user. The value of the context must be a distinguished name for the NDS container object where the context is being set.

NETWARE PROTOCOL

Default: load order default is NDS, BIND, PNW

This option designates the protocol priority for login and load order. You can change the load order for bindery users, for example, by placing the BIND protocol first in the load order.

NETWORK PRINTERS = n (0 to 9)

Default: 3

This option sets the number of printer ports the requester can capture to. If the value is set to 0, the PRINT.VLM will not load, which means that you do not want to send any print jobs to the network.

PB BUFFERS = n (0 to 10)

Default: 3

This option sets the number of buffers used by the Packet Burst Protocol. Setting this value to 0 disables Packet Burst on the workstation. Larger numbers of buffers increase performance but take more memory.

PBURST READ WINDOWS SIZE

Default: 10

This option enables you to set the read buffer size in the range of 2 to 64 bytes.

PBURST WRITE WINDOWS SIZE

Default: 16

This option enables you to set the write buffer size from 2 to 64 bytes.

PREFERRED SERVER = xxx

Default: None

This option enables you to force the requester to attach to a specific server on the network.

PREFERRED TREE = xxx

Default: None

This option enables you to force the requester to attach to a specific NDS tree on the network.

PREFERRED WORKGROUP

This option enables you to specify a preferred workgroup for Personal NetWare as your first connection.

PRINT BUFFER SIZE = n (0 to 255 bytes)

Default: 64 bytes

This option determines the size of the print buffer for 1-byte print requests. Increasing this value may improve print performance in a few cases.

PRINT HEADER = n (0 to 255 bytes)

Default: 64 bytes

This option sets the size of the initialization string for the printer that is sent before each print job.

PRINT TAIL = n (0 to 255 bytes)

Default: 16 bytes

This option sets the size of the reset string for the printer sent after each print job.

READ ONLY COMPATIBILITY = ON/OFF

Default: OFF

This option specifies if a file marked Read Only attribute can be opened for read/write. This is not a new parameter. In previous versions of NetWare the default was set to ON. However, the setting of ON caused problems with some applications, so the default has been set to OFF.

RESPONDER

Default: ON

This option controls the communication of a workstation using Personal NetWare. Turning this parameter to OFF causes the workstation to ignore broadcasts and other communications.

SEARCH MODE = mode (1 to 7)

Default: 1

This option specifies the search mode for the requester. This option can be used to extend DOS search capabilities for a data file on the network The search modes are:

- ▸ 1 = Search if the path is not specified for data file.

- ▸ 2 = Never search.

- ▸ 3 = Search and read a file but do not modify it.

- ▸ 4 = Reserved.

- ▸ 5 = Always search.

▶ 6 = Reserved.

▶ 7 = Always search if the request is only to read a file.

SET STATION TIME = ON/OFF
Default: ON
This option synchronizes the requester or workstation's time to the server's time
if the value is set to ON.

SHOW DOTS = ON/OFF
Default: ON
This option enables the requester to emulate DOS specific APIs. This parameter
provides complete compatibility with DOS and NetWare sharing files.

SHORT MACHINE TYPE = xxx (four characters or fewer)
Default: IBM
This option sets the %SMACHINE login variable to the specified value.

SIGNATURE LEVEL = n (0 to 3)
Default: 1
This option sets the level of security for the workstation. The security is for the
packet. Each packet can have a unique signature as it is sent from the workstation.
This is called packet signing and it prevents insertion of packets into the network
from an unauthorized source. The values are as follows:

▶ 0 = Disabled (no packet signing)

▶ 1 = Enabled but not preferred

▶ 2 = Preferred

▶ 3 = Required

TRUE COMMIT = ON/OFF
Default:OFF
This option causes NCP to control the commit requests issued from DOS if set
to ON. The ON setting improves data integrity but decreases server performance.

USE DEFAULT = ON/OFF
Default: ON

This option enables you to automatically load the VLM module. If the value is set to OFF, you must specify the individual modules you want loaded. Remember, some VLM modules are required.

VLM = xxx (filename.VLM)

Default: None

This option enables you to load a specific VLM module using the file name. You can include the path as well as the name of the file.

IP Addresses

Use the following parameters and values to specify your client workstation's IP address, the subnetwork mask, and the default network router address.

IP_ADDRESS IP_ADDRESS [NETWORK_NAME]

Default: None

This parameter specifies the IP address for your client workstation. The syntax is ip_address ip_address [network_name]. Replace the ip_address with the correct address in dotted notation. If this parameter is missing or is 0.0.0.0, the protocol stack uses BOOTP or Reverse ARP to determine the IP address. Replace network_name with a descriptive name for this network connection. The network name is used with the BIND, IP_ROUTER, and IP_NETMASK parameters to distinguish between the values for each network connection. The network name is required only if you are configuring multiple ODI LAN drivers for TCP/IP.

Example: To set the IP address for your client workstation and distinguish your connection to the network, you could place the following lines in your NET.CFG file: protocol tcpip   bind ne2000 2 finance-net   ip_address 129.47.30.6 finance-net   ip_router 144.52.6.6   ip_netmask 255.255.0.0

IP_NETMASK NET_MASK_ADDRESS [NETWORK_NAME]

Default: None

This parameter specifies the default subnetwork mask if subnetworks are used. The syntax is ip_netmask net_mask_address [network_name]. Replace the net_mask_address with the correct subnetwork mask address in dotted notation. If this parameter is missing or is 0.0.0.0, the protocol stack uses BOOTP or Reverse ARP to determine the IP address. Replace network_name with a descriptive name for this network connection. The network_name is used with the BIND, IP_ADDRESS, and IP_ROUTER parameters to distinguish between the values for each network connection. The network name is required only if you are configuring multiple ODI LAN drivers for TCP/IP.

Example: To set the IP netmask for your client workstation and distinguish your connection to the network, you could place the following lines in your NET.CFG file: protocol tcpip   bind ne2000 2 finance-net   ip_address 129.47.6.84   ip_router 144.52.6.6   ip_netmask 255.255.0.0 finance-net

IP_ROUTER IP_ADDRESS [NETWORK_NAME]

Default: None

This parameter specifies the default router address for all packets being sent to remote networks. All other gateways are dynamically discovered using the ICMP redirect mechanism. The syntax is ip_router ip_address [network_name]. Replace the ip_address with the correct address in dotted notation. If this parameter is missing or is 0.0.0.0, the protocol stack uses BOOTP or Reverse ARP to determine the IP address. Replace network_name with a descriptive name for this network connection. The network name is used with the BIND, IP_ADDRESS, and IP_NETMASK parameters to distinguish between the values for each network connection. The network name is required only if you are configuring multiple ODI LAN drivers for TCP/IP.

Example: To set the IP address for your client workstation and distinguish your connection to the network, you could place the following lines in your NET.CFG file: protocol tcpip   bind ne2000 2 finance-net   ip_address 129.47.6.84   ip_router 144.52.6.6 finance-net   ip_netmask 255.255.0.0 finance-net

Link Driver

The link driver options control your network interface card. Some examples of hardware settings include the Base Memory address and the I/O Port address.

Typically, you will use the LINK DRIVER section in the NET.CFG if your workstation NIC is using settings other than the defaults for that particular card.

ACCM

This option specifies the use of the asynchronous control character map for the PPP protocol.

ACCOMP[YES/NO]

This option instructs the PPP protocol to compress the address and control field of the PPP header.

ALTERNATE

This option specifies an alternate adapter for LANSUP, TOKEN, and PCN2.

AUTHEN PAP

This option allows authentication to be enabled for the PPP protocol. Password Authentication Protocol (PAP) identifies the local workstation to the remote peer host with a username and password.

BAUD

This option specifies a baud rate for PPP. Your options are 300, 1200, 2400, 4800, 9600, 14400, 19200, and 38400.

DMA

This option specifies the DMA channel number that can be used to configure up to two DMA channels if your adapter card supports two channels. You specify the channel numbers to be configured such as the following:

            LAN DRIVER 3C509
                DMA 2

FRAME

This option specifies alternate MAC layer encapsulation. Ethernet NICs can have IEEE 802.3 with 802.2 or ETHERNET_II encapsulation. If a frame is not specified, the default is IEEE 802.2, 802.3 for Ethernet NICs. Some other protocols may require different MAC layer encapsulation for proper operation. Refer to your NIC documentation or consult the manufacturer for specifications. Some examples of frame types are listed below:

▸ ETHERNET_802.2

▸ ETHERNET_802.3

▸ ETHERNET_II

▸ ETHERNET_SNAP

▸ TOKEN-RING_SNAP

INT[#1 | #2] NUMBER

This option specifies up to two interrupt line numbers if your NIC supports two configurable interrupt lines. If the first number is omitted, such as #1, it is configured along with the second number as shown in the following example:

        LAN DRIVER Interrupts
            INT #2 5
            INT 11
            ;The #1 can be omitted for INT 11

LINK STATIONS

This option is used in conjunction with the LANSUP driver from IBM to specify the number of link stations.

MAX FRAME SIZE

This option specifies the maximum frame size for Token-Ring. Depending on your NIC the default values are 2168 bytes and 4216 bytes. The value of the specified frame size must be a multiple of 8 as in the following example:

        LAN DRIVER
            MAX FRAME SIZE 2168

MEM [#1/#2] ADDRESS

This option specifies up to two memory address ranges if your NIC supports multiple ranges. For example:

        LAN DRIVER
            MEM #2 D8000
            MEM C0000

NODE ADDRESS

This option assigns a new MAC address for a NIC overriding any previous address that may be set for the NIC. Some NICs, such as IEEE 802.3, IEEE 802.4, IEEE 802.5, and FDDI, have local addressing capabilities whereby you can specify a local address. (This means lots of extra work to change all workstations, but it is sometimes necessary if you have two conflicting NICs.) For example:

        LAN DRIVER
            NODE ADDRESS D1002

PORT[#1| #2] hexStartAddr[hexNumberPorts]

This option specifies up to two I/O Port addresses if your NIC supports them. The hexStartAddr indicates the start address of the I/O port. hexNumberPorts refers to the number of ports as in the following example:

        LAN DRIVER With2Ports
            PORT #1 320
            PORT #2 380

PROTOCOL

This option registers new protocols to be used with your ODI driver. For example:

        LINK DRIVER XPSODI
            PROTOCOL E0 IPX ETHERNET_802.2
            FRAME ETHERNET_802.2

SAPS

This option specifies the Service Access Points for your LANSUP driver. The SAPS parameter uses the IBM LAN Support Program.

SLOT NUMBER

This option associates your NIC driver with a slot by disabling the default slot scan in Micro Channel or EISA machines. In cases in which you have multiple adapters in the same machine you can use this parameter to disable a default slot number on one of the cards. For example:

        LAN DRIVER Card1
            SLOT 1
        LAN DRIVER Card2
            SLOT 2

IPXODI PARAMETERS

IPXODI has some specialized parameters that are used with both IPX and SPX protocols.

BIND

This option causes the protocol to bind with any boards specified. For example:

```
BIND=NE2000
```

CONFIG OPTION

This option is used with WSGEN and DCONFIG to override the network driver configuration option.

INT64[ON|OFF]

This option provides compatibility with previous versions of NetWare, and its default is ON. This parameter configures IPX to use interrupt h64.

NT7A[ON|OFF]

This option provides compatibility with NetWare 2.0a, and its default is ON. This parameter configures IPX to use software interrupt h7A.

IPATCH=a

This option fixes bugs in IPX.COM. A memory location in IPX.COM can be "patched" with a specific value using the IPATCH parameter.

IPX PACKET SIZE LIMIT

Some drivers support the capability to change the maximum packet size set by the driver. The values range from 576 to 6500 bytes.

IPX RETRY COUNT

This option specifies the number of times a workstation will resend a packet. The retry default is 20.

IPX SOCKETS

This option specifies the number of sockets that may be opened by a workstation. The socket default is 20.

MINIMUM SPC RETRIES

This option specifies the number of retries for SPX before canceling a session, and specifies the number of transmissions with no acknowledgments before canceling a session. In some WAN situations that use SPX you may want to adjust this parameter. The default is 20, with a range of 0 to 255.

SPX ABORT TIMEOUT

This option specifies the number of ticks for SPX to wait without a response from a remote node before terminating the connection. The default is 540 ticks, where every 18 ticks is approximately 1 second.

SPX CONNECTIONS

This option specifies the number of SPX concurrent connections for a workstation. The connection default is 15.

SPX VERIFY TIMEOUT

This option specifies the number of SPX ticks to wait before sending a packet to a remote side to verify a connection. The verify timeout default is 54 ticks.

▶ .   .   .   .   ◀

Link Support for NETBIOS

The NETBIOS parameters provide support for applications using NETBIOS in a IntranetWare environment. The following parameters are used to support NETBIOS under LINK SUPPORT.

NETBIOS ABORT TIMEOUT

This option specifies the wait time in ticks for a response before terminating a session. Some large internetworks may need to adjust this parameter outward to compensate for slower link speeds. The default is 540 ticks.

NETBIOS BROADCAST COUNT

This option specifies the number of NETBIOS broadcasts to query a claim for the name used by a NETBIOS application. The range is 2 to 65535.

NETBIOS COMMANDS

This option specifies the number of NETBIOS commands to be buffered in the NETBIOS driver. The range is 4 to 250, with the default set at 12.

NETBIOS BROADCAST DELAY

This option specifies how long NETBIOS will wait between a query or claim broadcast. The range is 18 to 65535. The default is 36 if NETBIOS INTERNET=ON, or 18 if NETBIOS INTERNET=OFF.

NETBIOS INTERNET[ON|OFF]

This option sets the transmission of name claim packets to and from workstations on the internetwork or on the local network segment only. The default is ON.

NETBIOS LISTEN TIMEOUT

This option adjusts the amount of time in ticks that NETBIOS will wait before requesting a keep-alive packet from the other side. The default is 108 ticks.

NETBIOS RECEIVE BUFFERS

This option configures the number of IPX receive buffers that are used by NETBIOS. The default is 6, and the range is 4 to 20.

NETBIOS RETRY COUNT

This option specifies the number of NETBIOS transmits requested for a connection. The default is 20 if NETBIOS INTERNET=ON, and 10 if NETBIOS INTERNET=OFF.

NETBIOS RETRY DELAY

This option sets the number of ticks for NETBIOS to wait while establishing a connection or resending a data packet. The default is 10, and the range is 10 to 65535 ticks.

NETBIOS SEND BUFFERS

This option sets the number of IPX send buffers that will be used by NETBIOS. The default is 6, and the range is 4 to 250.

NETBIOS SESSION

This option enables you to specify how many concurrent NETBIOS sessions will be supported by the NETBIOS driver. The default is 32, and the range is 4 to 250.

NETBIOS VERIFY TIMEOUT

This option specifies the interval in which NETBIOS will send out a keep-alive packet to preserve a session. The default is 54 ticks and the range is 4 to 65535.

Protocol IDs for IPX

ETHERNET_802.2	EO
ETHERNET_802.3	0
ETHERNET_II	8137
ETHERNET_SNAP	8137
TOKEN-RING	E0
TOKEN-RING_SNAP	8137
IBM-PCN2_SNAP	8137
IBM-PCN2_802.2	E0
NOVELL_RX-NET	FA
IP 800	
ARP 806	
RARP 8035	

SAMPLE NET.CFG FILE

The following sample NET.CFG file uses some of the parameters listed above and may be used as a basis for the creation of your own standardized NET.CFG files:

```
NetWare DOS Requester
      FIRST NETWORK DRIVE = F
      NETWARE PROTOCOL = NDS BIND
```

> PB Buffers = 10
>
>> Name Context = "ou=blue.ou=crime.ou=tokyo.o=acme"
>
> Preferred Server=tok-srv1
>
> IPX SOCKETS = 60

Link Driver PCMDMCS

> MEM D9000
>
> FRAME ETHERNET_802.2
>
> NODE ADDRESS 4997777

Link Driver XPSODI

> Protocol IPX E0 ETHERNET_802.2
>
> Frame ETHERNET_802.2
>
> Frame Ethernet_II
>
> MEM DC000
>
> INT 7

Link driver NE2000

> INT 5
>
> Port 360

Protocol TCPIP

> PATH LANG_CFG   C:\apps\lanwp\LANG
>
> PATH SCRIPT   C:\apps\lanwp\SCRIPT
>
> PATH PROFILE   C:\apps\lanwp\PROFILE
>
> PATH LWP_CFG   C:\apps\lanwp\HSTACC
>
> PATH TCP_CFG   C:\apps\lanwp\TCP
>
> ip_router   xxx.xx.xx.xxx
>
> ip_address   xxx.xx.xx.xx
>
> ip_netmask   255.255.255.0

Link Support

> Buffers 4 1500
>
> MemPool 4096

Protocol IPX

> IPX SOCKETS 40

Index

(continued)

partition(s)
  basic description of, 279–350
  for bottom layers, 299–300
  cancelling, 341, 541
  control, 455
  creating, 292–302, 782
  design of, 292–302
  Directory Services tree and, 270–272
  DSREPAIR and, 525–542
  error conditions, 580
  managing, 74–75, 322–349
  merging, 74, 99, 503, 329–332, 511–516, 573–576
  moving, 332–334, 503, 516–520, 576–579
  name resolution and, 468–486
  NetWare security and, 718–719
  operations, 325–342, 502–520, 554–581
  parent/child, 283–285, 290, 321–322, 325, 329–332, 556–557, 570–572, 574–576
  PARTMGR and, 99–100
  pyramid shape for, 301–302
  replication design and, 310–322
  rules for, 286–288, 321–322
  server-based operations and, 407–408, 412, 413–415, 446, 449–454
  size, 299, 321–322
  splitting, 327–329, 503, 510–511, 570–572
  status, 456
  structure of, 448–456
  subordinate reference replicas and, 481–482
  tables, 446–448
  for top layers, 297–298
  total number of replicas per, 344–345
  transparent, 286
  views, 83–86
Partition Continuity Grid, 91
Partition Continuity option, 18, 83, 87
Partition Control attribute, 449, 469
Partition Creation timestamp, 449, 453–454, 469
Partition Creation Timestamp attribute, 449, 469
Partition object, 139
Partition Operations option, 535–542
Partition Overlap flag, 520
Partition Root Object ID attribute, 452
Partition Status attribute, 450, 469
PARTMGR utility, 59, 99–100, 323–324, 510, 782, 784

PARTMGR.EXE, 99–100, 323–324, 561, 565, 581
password(s), 13–14, 35–37, 120, 158
  auditing and, 36–37
  changing, 36, 678, 679
  installation and, 64
  length of, 668, 679, 840
  migrating other operating systems and, 839–840, 843, 846, 848
  NetWare Web server and, 944
  server migration and, 795, 801, 807–809
  unique, 668, 679
  verification of, 678–684
%PASSWORD ALLOWED CHANGE variable, 668
%PASSWORD EXPIRATION INTERVAL variable, 668
%PASSWORD_EXPIRES variable, 665
%PASSWORD MINIMUM LENGTH variable, 668
%PASSWORD UNIQUE variable, 668
patches, 625
Path attribute, 150
PAUSE command, 662, 928
Pause on errors? option, 530
PC_CHANGING_REPLICATYPE function, 455
PCCOMPATIBLE command, 662
PC_IDLE function, 455
PCI systems, 613, 790
PC_JOINING_DOWN function, 455
PC_JOINING_UP function, 455
PC_LOCKED function, 455
PC_MOVE_SUBTREE_DEST function, 455
PC_MOVE_SUBTREE_SRC function, 455
PCOMPATIBLE command, 929
PCONSOLE, 27–28, 71, 118, 723, 726, 730–731, 737, 739, 741–743, 747–748, 750
PC_REPAIRING_TIMESTAMPS function, 455
PC_SPLITTING_CHILD function, 455
PC_SPLITTING function, 455
PDC (Primary Domain Controller), 842
PDS (Print Device Subsystem), 753–755
Pentium processors, 271, 294, 322, 344, 790, 919. See also processors
percent sign (%), 664
performance
  vs. reliability, 586–587
  replicas and, 303
period (.), 202–204, 209
PERL, 47, 936, 939, 958

Person object, 139, 178
physical packet size, 591–593
%PHYSICAL DELIVERY OFFICE NAME variable, 668
Physical Printer, 753–755
Pilot System, 779, 785
PING utility, 55
Plato, 280
plug-in architecture, 47
plus sign (+), 78, 81, 142, 210, 547
PNW.VLM, 855
POLEDIT.EXE, 893
Polling Count parameter, 372–374
Polling Interval parameter, 372–374
Post Office Box property, 214
Postal Address attribute, 150
Postal Address field, 102, 103
%POSTAL ADDRESS variable, 668
%POSTAL CODE variable, 668
%POSTAL OFFICE BOX variable, 668
PPM (page-per-minute) ratings, 733
PPP (Point-to-Point Protocol), 38
Preconfigure Verify option, 825
PREFERRED SERVER variable, 655
Preferred Systems, 45, 185, 788, 815
PRINTCON.DAT, 796
PRINTCON utility, 723, 730–731, 749, 750, 796
PRINTDEF.DAT, 796
PRINTDEF utility, 723, 731, 749, 750, 796
printer(s), 29, 733–741. See also print services
  Directory Services tree and, 232–237, 258–264
  network-direct (queue server mode), 733, 739–741
  network-direct (remote printer mode), 733, 736–738
  network server, 733, 735–736
  network workstation, 733, 734–735
  non-network workstation, 733
Printer object, 29, 71, 94, 186, 208, 212–213, 218, 219, 724, 728–729, 739
Print Job Configuration property, 214
Print Layout Page feature, 71–72
Print Queue object, 29, 71, 94, 131, 186, 208, 212–213, 218–219, 459, 724–727, 749
Print Server object, 29, 71, 94, 134, 139, 169, 186, 219, 724, 727–728, 749
Print Server property, 135
print service(s), 11, 27–29, 66, 71–73, 721–755. See also printers

V

(continued)

IDG BOOKS WORLDWIDE LICENSE AGREEMENT

Important — read carefully before opening the software packet(s). This is a legal agreement between you (either an individual or an entity) and IDG Books Worldwide, Inc. (IDG). By opening the accompanying sealed packet containing the software disk(s), you acknowledge that you have read and accept the following IDG License Agreement. If you do not agree and do not want to be bound by the terms of this Agreement, promptly return the book and the unopened software packet(s) to the place you obtained them for a full refund.

1. **License.** This License Agreement (Agreement) permits you to use one copy of the enclosed Software program(s) on a single computer. The Software is in "use" on a computer when it is loaded into temporary memory (i.e., RAM) or installed into permanent memory (e.g., hard disk, CD-ROM, or other storage device) of that computer.

2. **Copyright.** The entire contents of the disk(s) and the compilation of the Software are copyrighted and protected by both United States copyright laws and international treaty provisions. You may only (a) make one copy of the Software for backup or archival purposes, or (b) transfer the Software to a single hard disk, provided that you keep the original for backup or archival purposes. The individual programs on the disk(s) are copyrighted by the authors of each program respectively. Each program has its own use permissions and limitations. To use each program, you must follow the individual requirements and restrictions detailed for each in the Appendix of this Book. Do not use a program if you do not want to follow its Licensing Agreement. None of the material on the disk(s) or listed in this Book may ever be distributed, in original or modified form, for commercial purposes.

3. **Other Restrictions.** You may not rent or lease the Software. You may transfer the Software and user documentation on a permanent basis provided you retain no copies and the recipient agrees to the terms of this Agreement. You may not reverse engineer, decompile, or disassemble the Software except to the extent that the foregoing restriction is expressly prohibited by applicable law. If the Software is an update or has been updated, any transfer must include the most recent update and all prior versions.

4. **Limited Warranty.** IDG warrants that the Software and disk(s) are free from defects in materials and workmanship for a period of sixty (60) days from the date of purchase of this Book. If IDG receives notification within the warranty

period of defects in material or workmanship, IDG will replace the defective disk(s). IDG's entire liability and your exclusive remedy shall be limited to replacement of the Software, which is returned to IDG with a copy of your receipt. This Limited Warranty is void if failure of the Software has resulted from accident, abuse, or misapplication. Any replacement Software will be warranted for the remainder of the original warranty period or thirty (30) days, whichever is longer.

5. **No Other Warranties**. To the maximum extent permitted by applicable law, IDG and the author disclaim all other warranties, express or implied, including but not limited to implied warranties of merchantability and fitness for a particular purpose, with respect to the Software, the programs, the source code contained therein and/or the techniques described in this Book. This limited warranty gives you specific legal rights. You may have others which vary from state/jurisdiction to state/jurisdiction.

6. **No Liability For Consequential Damages**. To the extent permitted by applicable law, in no event shall IDG or the author be liable for any damages whatsoever (including without limitation, damages for loss of business profits, business interruption, loss of business information, or any other pecuniary loss) arising out of the use of or inability to use the Book or the Software, even if IDG has been advised of the possibility of such damages. Because some states/jurisdictions do not allow the exclusion or limitation of liability for consequential or incidental damages, the above limitation may not apply to you.

7. **U.S. Government Restricted Rights**. Use, duplication, or disclosure of the Software by the U.S. Government is subject to restrictions stated in paragraph (c) (1) (ii) of the Rights in Technical Data and Computer Software clause of DFARS 252.227-7013, and in subparagraphs (a) through (d) of the Commercial Computer — Restricted Rights clause at FAR 52.227-19, and in similar clauses in the NASA FAR supplement, when applicable.

WE WROTE THE BOOK ON NETWORKING

Novell Press® and IDG Books Worldwide

Novell's GroupWise™ 5 User's Handbook

by Shawn B. Rogers and Richard H. McTague

Learn to use the ultimate electronic organizer with this authoritative guide to GroupWise™ 5. Authors Rogers and McTague provide more than 100 GroupWise Power Tips, revealing sophisticated shortcuts and tricks as well as how to exploit every feature of this powerful desktop control center.

300 pp
$24.99 USA/$34.99 Canada
0-7645-4509-4

Novell's GroupWise™ 4 Administrator's Guide

by Shawn B. Rogers

Discover practical solutions for setting up, maintaining, and troubleshooting GroupWise 4 as well as how to support remote users and connect to the Internet. The bonus CD-ROM includes a two-user version of GroupWise 4 and the GroupWare Software Developer's Kit.

606 pp plus CD-ROM
$39.99 USA/$54.99 Canada
1-56884-732-7

Novell's GroupWise™ 4 User's Guide

by Shawn B. Rogers and Richard H. McTague

Cover GroupWise 4 thoroughly, from the basics to advanced features such as proxies, rules, and calendaring with this concise guide. The expert authors also examine the GroupWise client interface and include hundreds of valuable tips and tricks from GroupWise 4 gurus around the world.

194 pp
$19.99 USA/$27.99 Canada
0-7645-4502-7

Novell's The Web at Work: *Publishing Within and Beyond the Corporation*

by Peter Jerram

Learn to make sound content and technology choices so you can efficiently and effectively implement corporate World Wide Web strategies. You'll sort out options, define issues, and consider real-life case studies in this invaluable book.

400 pp
$29.99 USA/$42.99 Canada
0-7645-4519-1

Novell's Guide to Internet Access Solutions

by Roger L. Spicer, Laura A. Chappell, and Colin E. Dixon

A nuts-and-bolts guide to building, maintaining, and troubleshooting an Internet connection. You'll learn client and server solutions as well as how to implement and troubleshoot each. A value-added CD-ROM provides exclusive Novell-delivered Web connectivity products of interest to any NetWare® network administrator.

400 pp plus CD-ROM
$39.99 USA
$54.99 Canada
0-7645-4515-9

 SMART BOOKS™
from the Novell Experts

Novell's CNE® Study Guide for Core Technologies

by David James. Clarke, IV

The ideal preparation guide for the two non-NetWare specific exams required for CNE® certification: Service and Support (801) and Networking Technologies (200). This study guide contains real-world case studies, sample test questions and other valuable information. You'll also receive the exclusive Novell NetWire Starter Kit, the ClarkTests v.2 and MICROHOUSE I/O Card Encyclopedia demo.

932 pp plus CD-ROM
$74.99 USA
$104.99 Canada
0-7645-4501-9

Novell's CNA℠ Study Guide for IntranetWare™

by David James Clarke, IV and Kelley J.P. Lindberg

A must for system managers studying for their CNA℠ credential. Organized and easy-to-read, this resource covers all CNA course material including NetWare 2.2 and NetWare 3.1x with real-world scenarios, sample tests and a live on-line NetWare lab. The accompanying Novell Advantage CD contains Novell exclusive software.

700 pp plus CD-ROM
$69.99 USA
$96.99 Canada
0-7645-4513-2

Novell's CNE® Study Guide for IntranetWare™

by David James Clarke, IV

Learn all aspects of Novell's IntranetWare CNE program as well as NDS design and implementation. Covers certification courses 520, 525, 526, 532 and 804. Includes a free Novell Support Connection CD plus hundreds of CNE test questions.

1600 pp plus CD-ROM
$89.99 USA
$124.99 Canada
0-7645-4512-4

Novell's Four Principles of NDS™ Design

by Jeffrey F. Hughes and Blair W. Thomas

Take full advantage of the powerful new features of the NetWare 4 operating system with this clearly illustrated reference guide zeroing in on four essential Novell Directory Services (NDS) design principles: physical infrastructure, organizational structure, optimal partition size and minimum replicas placements, and time synchronization.

343 pp
$39.99 USA
$54.99 Canada
0-7645-4522-1

SMART BOOKS™
from the Novell Experts

SMART BOOKS™ FROM THE NOVELL® EXPERTS

Complete your networking library with these titles from Novell Press®

Novell's GroupWise™ 4 Administrator's Guide

by Shawn B. Rogers
606 pp plus CD-ROM
$39.99 USA/$54.99 Canada
1-56884-732-7

Novell's CNE® Study Guide for NetWare® 4.1

by David James Clarke, IV
1543 pp plus CD-ROM
$89.99 USA/$124.99 Canada
1-56884-734-3

Novell's NetWare® 4.1 Administrator's Handbook

by Kelley J. P. Lindberg
481 pp plus disk
$29.99 USA/$42.99 Canada
1-56884-737-8

Novell's Guide to NetWare® 4.1 Networks

by Jeffrey F. Hughes and Blair W. Thomas
942 pp plus CD-ROM
$59.99 USA/$84.99 Canada
1-56884-736-X

Novell's Guide to Integrating NetWare® & TCP/IP

by Drew Heywood
556 pp plus CD-ROM
$44.99 USA/$62.99 Canada
1-56884-818-8

Novell's CNE® Study Guide for Core Technologies

by David James Clarke, IV
932 pp plus CD-ROM
$74.99 USA/$104.99 Canada
0-7645-4501-9

Novell's CNA℠ Study Guide for NetWare® 4.1

by David James Clarke, IV and Kelley J.P. Lindberg
812 pp plus CD-ROM
$54.99 USA/$76.99 Canada
0-7645-4500-0

Novell's GroupWise™ 4 User's Guide

by Shawn B. Rogers and Richard H. McTague
250 pp plus CD-ROM
$19.99 USA/$27.99 Canada
0-7645-4502-7

Novell's Four Principles of NDS™ Design

by Jeffrey F. Hughes and Blair W. Thomas
343 pp
$39.99 USA/$54.99 Canada
0-7645-4522-1

Novell's IntranetWare™ Administrator's Handbook

by Kelley J. P. Lindberg
475 pp plus disk
$39.99 USA/$54.99 Canada
0-7645-4517-5

Novell's GroupWise™ 5 User's Handbook

by Shawn B. Rogers and Richard H. McTague
300 pp
$24.99 USA/$34.99 Canada
0-7645-4509-4

Novell's Guide to Internet Access Solutions

by Roger L. Spicer, Laura A. Chappell, and Colin F. Dixon
400 pp plus CD-ROM
$39.99 USA/$54.99 Canada
0-7645-4515-9

Novell's Guide to NetWare® Printing

by J.D. Marymee and Sandy Stevens
512 pp plus disk
$44.99 USA/$69.99 Canada
0-7645-4514-0

Novell's Guide to IntranetWare™ Networks

by Jeffrey F. Hughes and Blair W. Thomas
1200 pp plus CD-ROM
$59.99 USA/$84.99 Canada
0-7645-4516-7

Novell's CNE® Study Guide for IntranetWare™

by David James Clarke, IV
1600 pp plus CD-ROM
$89.99 USA/$124.99 Canada
0-7645-4512-4

Novell's CNA℠ Study Guide for IntranetWare™

by David James Clarke, IV and Kelley J.P. Lindberg
700 pp plus CD-ROM
$69.99 USA/$96.99 Canada
0-7645-4513-2

Novell's The Web at Work: *Publishing Within and Beyond the Corporation*

by Peter Jerram
400 pp
$29.99 USA/$42.99 Canada
0-7645-4519-1

Nothing compares to Novell Press -

- Written by the leading networking experts.
- Reviewed by Novell's own technical and information professionals.
- Published with the authorization and collaboration of Novell, Inc.
- Based on released software - never on beta.

IDG BOOKS WORLDWIDE REGISTRATION CARD

Visit our Web site at http://www.idgbooks.com

ISBN Number: 0-7645-4516-7

Title of this book: Novell's Guide to IntranetWare™ Networks

My overall rating of this book: ❑ Very good [1] ❑ Good [2] ❑ Satisfactory [3] ❑ Fair [4] ❑ Poor [5]

How I first heard about this book:

❑ Found in bookstore; name: [6]

❑ Advertisement: [8]

❑ Word of mouth; heard about book from friend, co-worker, etc.: [10]

❑ Book review: [7]

❑ Catalog: [9]

❑ Other: [11]

What I liked most about this book:

What I would change, add, delete, etc., in future editions of this book:

Other comments:

Number of computer books I purchase in a year: ❑ 1 [12] ❑ 2-5 [13] ❑ 6-10 [14] ❑ More than 10 [15]

I would characterize my computer skills as: ❑ Beginner [16] ❑ Intermediate [17] ❑ Advanced [18] ❑ Professional [19]

I use ❑ DOS [20] ❑ Windows [21] ❑ OS/2 [22] ❑ UNIX [23] ❑ Macintosh [24] ❑ Other: [25]

(please specify)

I would be interested in new books on the following subjects:

(please check all that apply, and use the spaces provided to identify specific software)

❑ Word processing: [26]

❑ Data bases: [28]

❑ File Utilities: [30]

❑ Networking: [32]

❑ Other: [34]

❑ Spreadsheets: [27]

❑ Desktop publishing: [29]

❑ Money management: [31]

❑ Programming languages: [33]

I use a PC at (please check all that apply): ❑ home [35] ❑ work [36] ❑ school [37] ❑ other: [38]

The disks I prefer to use are ❑ 5.25 [39] ❑ 3.5 [40] ❑ other: [41]

I have a CD ROM: ❑ yes [42] ❑ no [43]

I plan to buy or upgrade computer hardware this year: ❑ yes [44] ❑ no [45]

I plan to buy or upgrade computer software this year: ❑ yes [46] ❑ no [47]

Name: Business title: [48]   Type of Business: [49]

Address (❑ home [50] ❑ work [51]/Company name:)

Street/Suite#

City [52]/State [53]/Zip code [54]:   Country [55]

❑ **I liked this book!** You may quote me by name in future IDG Books Worldwide promotional materials.

My daytime phone number is

IDG BOOKS WORLDWIDE

THE WORLD OF COMPUTER KNOWLEDGE®